POPULATION
MALTHUS
His Life and Times

PATRICIA JAMES

ROUTLEDGE & KEGAN PAUL

London, Boston and Henley

First published in 1979
by Routledge & Kegan Paul Ltd

39 Store Street, London WC1E 7DD,

Broadway House, Newtown Road,
Henley-on-Thames, Oxon RG9 1EN and

9 Park Street,
Boston, Mass. 02108, USA

Set in APS 5 Janson, 10½ on 12
and printed in Great Britain by
Unwin Brothers Limited
The Gresham Press, Old Woking, Surrey
A member of the Staples Printing Group

British Library Cataloguing in Publication Data
James, Patricia
Population Malthus.
1. Malthus, Thomas Robert 2. Economists -
England - Biography
I. Title
330'.092'4   HB863   79-40584

ISBN 0 7100 0266 1

To
the memory of
ROBERT MALTHUS
M.A., A.M.I.Mech.E.

1881-1972

'Biography, though dealing too much in pane-gyric, is always more or less entertaining and instructive, often affording at the same time historical facts and traits of character, that are by no means without their importance, though they may have escaped the general historian.'

William Smyth
Professor of Modern History
Cambridge, 1817

CONTENTS

PLATES

(between pages 240 and 241)

1 (a) Claverton Manor and Church, 'from the south', in 1790, from an ink and wash sketch by Samuel Hieronymous Grimm.
Reproduced by permission of the British Library, from Add. MS 15546 f. 201.

  (b) Okewood Chapel in 1849; from M. J. Starling's engraving of a sketch by Thomas Allom (1804-72); reproduced in Vol. IV of E. W. Brayley's *History of Surrey*, ed. E. Walford (1878); by courtesy of the Bodleian Library, Oxford.

2   The Rev. T. R. Malthus, from an engraving by John Linnell (1792-1882) of his own oil painting; photograph supplied by the National Portrait Gallery, London.

3   Harriet Malthus, oil painting by John Linnell. Private collection; photograph supplied by the National Portrait Gallery, London.

4 (a) Edward Daniel Clarke, engraved by Richard Golding (1785-1865) from the portrait by John Opie (1761-1807); reproduced in Vol. I of Clarke's *Travels* (1810); by courtesy of the Bodleian Library, Oxford.

  (b) William Smyth, from a drawing by Joseph Slater, lithographed by Isaac Slater. Photographed by the John Freeman Group by courtesy of the Trustees of the British Museum.

  (c) William Otter, Bishop of Chichester, from the posthumous engraving by John Linnell of his own oil portrait. Photographed by the John Freeman Group by courtesy of the Trustees of the British Museum.

5 (a) Charles Grant, from a drawing by an unknown artist, reproduced in *The Life of Charles Grant* by Henry Morris (1904); by courtesy of the Bodleian Library, Oxford.

  (b) David Ricardo, engraved by William Holl (1771-1838) from an earlier engraving by James Hodgetts (d. 1830) after the portrait painted in 1820 by Thomas Phillips (1770-1845). By courtesy of the National Portrait Gallery, London.

(*c*) John Murray II, from the portrait by Henry William Pickersgill (1782-1875), reproduced in Vol. II of *A Publisher and His Friends* by Samuel Smiles (1891); by courtesy of the Bodleian Library, Oxford.

6 (*a*) The East India College, Terrace Front, from a hand-coloured lithograph by T. Picken. Photographed by Timothy Hills.

(*b*) The East India House in 1817, from a water-colour drawing by Thomas Hosmer Shepherd (*c*. 1780-1840), engraved by J. C. Stadler. Photographed by the John Freeman Group by courtesy of the Guildhall Library, City of London.

7 (*a*) *The Squire's Kitchen*, from a water-colour drawing by Thomas Rowlandson (1756-1827); reproduced by courtesy of the Metropolitan Museum of Art, New York, Harris Brisbane Dick Fund, 1941.

(*b*) *The Country Cobbler*, from a water-colour drawing by Thomas Rowlandson, in the Albert H. Wiggin Collection; photographed by Stein-Mason Studio, Inc., by courtesy of the Boston Public Library, Print Department.

8 (*a*) Francis Horner, from the oil portrait by Sir Henry Raeburn (1756-1820); by courtesy of the National Portrait Gallery, London.

(*b*) Francis Jeffrey; engraving by Robert Charles Bell (1806-72) of the portrait by Colvin Smith (1795-1875); reproduced in Vol. I of Henry Cockburn's *Life of Lord Jeffrey* (1852); by courtesy of the Bodleian Library, Oxford.

(*c*) William Empson; engraving by W. Walker of the oil painting by John Linnell. Photographed by the John Freeman Group by courtesy of the Trustees of the British Museum.

(*d*) William Bray, from an engraving by John Linnell of his own oil portrait; photographed by the John Freeman Group by courtesy of the Trustees of the British Museum.

ACKNOWLEDGMENTS

Only somebody who has undertaken similar historical research - for one cannot avoid being a nuisance wherever one goes - will understand my deep gratitude to all who have helped in the making of this book. A young archivist has accused me of over-reacting in my appreciation of people like her 'who were, after all, only doing their job'. I firmly reply that the world would be a wonderful place if everybody were as efficient and considerate, as patient and hospitable, as the academics, archivists, clergy, lawyers, librarians and owners of manuscripts who made possible this first biography of Population Malthus.

My greatest debt is to Malthus's own family, the descendants of his siblings and those of his wife, beginning with the Robert Malthus to whose memory this work is dedicated. But I must record that we should never have met had it not been for the enterprise of an almost blind nonagenarian, Dr G. F. McCleary (1867-1962). His interest in his subject prompted him to make in 1960 what was for him a formidable excursion from London to the Isle of Wight, to visit the last surviving member of the Malthus family in England. From this one tea-party there sprang a friendship which was to result in the publication of Malthus's *Travel Diaries* in 1966, and now the present, long-overdue biography. It is appropriate that Malthus should owe the first full-length account of his life to a man whose interest in demography arose from his work as a pioneer in the movement for maternity and child welfare.

To the kindness of the descendants of Malthus's sister Mrs Bray - the late Miss Helen Lloyd and the Misses Clarice and Rachel Warren - I owe more than I can express; I am indebted to them for much documentary evidence, but even more for their cheerful support and encouragement over the years and years when my investigations seemed to be making little headway. I must also thank Messrs Warrens, the firm which succeeded Warren and Bray, for permission to use the letter-books and bill-books of Malthus's famous family solicitor, William Bray.

My debt to the principal descendant of Malthus's brother-in-law George Eckersall, Mr Noel Vicars-Harris, and to the descendants of two of his sisters-in-law, the late Mr George Nixon-Eckersall and Mr Anthony Boynton Wood, will soon become apparent to the reader. But I should also like to express my gratitude for their families' hospitality to a complete stranger, and the generosity with which they trusted me with their heirlooms. The same applies to Mrs Joan Linnell Burton; she allowed me to pore over the journals and correspondence of John Linnell, who painted the only known portrait of Malthus.

Equally helpful and hospitable were the clergymen of parishes with which Malthus was connected: I should like to thank especially the Rev. R. F. W. Coates of Ashley in Hampshire, and Mrs Coates; the Rev. Dennis Harvey of Claverton, and Mrs Harvey; the Rev. Michael Hewlitt of Poughill in Devonshire, and Mrs Hewlitt; the Rev. F. M. Massey of Walesby, and Mrs Massey.

For manuscripts in private ownership I am extremely grateful to Miss Jane Catchpole for Colonel Malthus's album of family notes; to Mrs Christina Colvin for letters from Maria Edgeworth and her step-siblings; to Lord Congleton for letters from Malthus to Henry Parnell; to Good-speed's Book Shop, Inc., of Boston, Mass., for a letter to Linnell from Malthus; to Lord Lyell for letters attached to Francis Horner's copy of the quarto on *Population*, and to his mother for enabling me to see it in London; to Mr D. W. H. Neilson for Malthus's correspondence with Robert Wilmot-Horton.

For manuscripts in corporate ownership I must thank the Académie Royale de Belgique; the Master of Haileybury; the Master and Council of Jesus College, Cambridge; the Provost and Fellows of King's College, Cambridge; Messrs John Murray (Publishers) Ltd; the Master and Fellows of Trinity College, Cambridge; and Messrs Josiah Wedgwood & Sons, Ltd. I also thank the Royal Society, the Royal Society of Literature, and the Royal Statistical Society, for letting me use material from their manuscript archives.

I am very grateful to Miss Geraldine Beck for her skilled help in the early stages of the work; to Mr Alan Bell for the Scottish connection, as well as for notes on Sydney Smith; to Messrs Colnaghi and the Leger Galleries for their assistance in tracing portraits; to Dr T. K. Derry and Mr Warren Derry for their encyclopaedic knowledge of Malthus's period; to Professor F. W. Fetter for much specialised guidance; to Dr Ian Fraser for his work on the Mackintosh papers at Keele; to Professor William Grampp for help with Malthus and the Combination Laws; to Mr A. E. Melville, formerly Senior History Master at Haileybury and now Headmaster of the Perse School, and Mrs Melville, for my physical acquaintance with the East India College; to Miss Heather Morrison, now Mrs Hemelryk, who took charge of me in the Goldsmiths' Library; to Miss Winifred Myers for information about autograph letters; to Mrs Celia Pearson Smith for what can only be described as a typing marathon; to Professor William Petersen, who volunteered to read the proofs; to Lord Robbins and Sir Austin Robinson for valuable introductions; to Miss Valerie Saunders, who acted as research assistant in the heavy task of checking Malthus's 1,155 pupils; to Mr Paul Sturges, without whose constant aid over many months I should never have found the important manuscript letters now in the United States; to Mrs Connie Ward of the Chipping Norton Branch of the Oxfordshire County Libraries, my unfailingly omniscient link both with them and with the magnificent service of the British Library Lending Division at Boston Spa; to Sir Robert Mackworth-Young and his staff at Windsor, whose references enabled me to find my way through the archives of the Royal Household in the Public Record Office; to Professor G. W. Zinke for information about a letter from Malthus to Dumont.

With regard to all those archivists and librarians who must remain anonymous for reasons of space as well as professional etiquette, I can only make a list of the relevant institutions, with my cordial thanks for the many pleasant memories which it arouses: the Avon County Library, the Baker Library of the Graduate School of Business Administration at Harvard University, the Berkshire Record Office, the Bodleian Library, the British Library and the British Museum, the British Newspaper Library, the British Library of Political and Economic Science, the Columbia University Libraries, the Reference Department of the Library of Congress, the City of Derby Central Library, the Goldsmiths' Library of the University of London, Guildford Muniment Room, the Hertfordshire County Record Office, the Historical Manuscripts Commission, the Houghton Library at Harvard, the Library of the University of Illinois at Urbana-Champaign, the India Office Library and Records (Foreign and Commonwealth Office), Keele University Library, the Lincoln Record Office, the London Library, the Marshall Library at Cambridge, the National Library of Scotland, the New College Library of the University of Edinburgh, Nuffield College Library, the Oxfordshire County Libraries, the Public Record Office, the Reference Library at Reading, Sir John Soane's Museum, the D. M. S. Watson Library of University College, London, and Dr Williams's Library.

Last but by no means least I must record my sincere gratitude to the British Academy, without whose assistance this work could never have been undertaken.

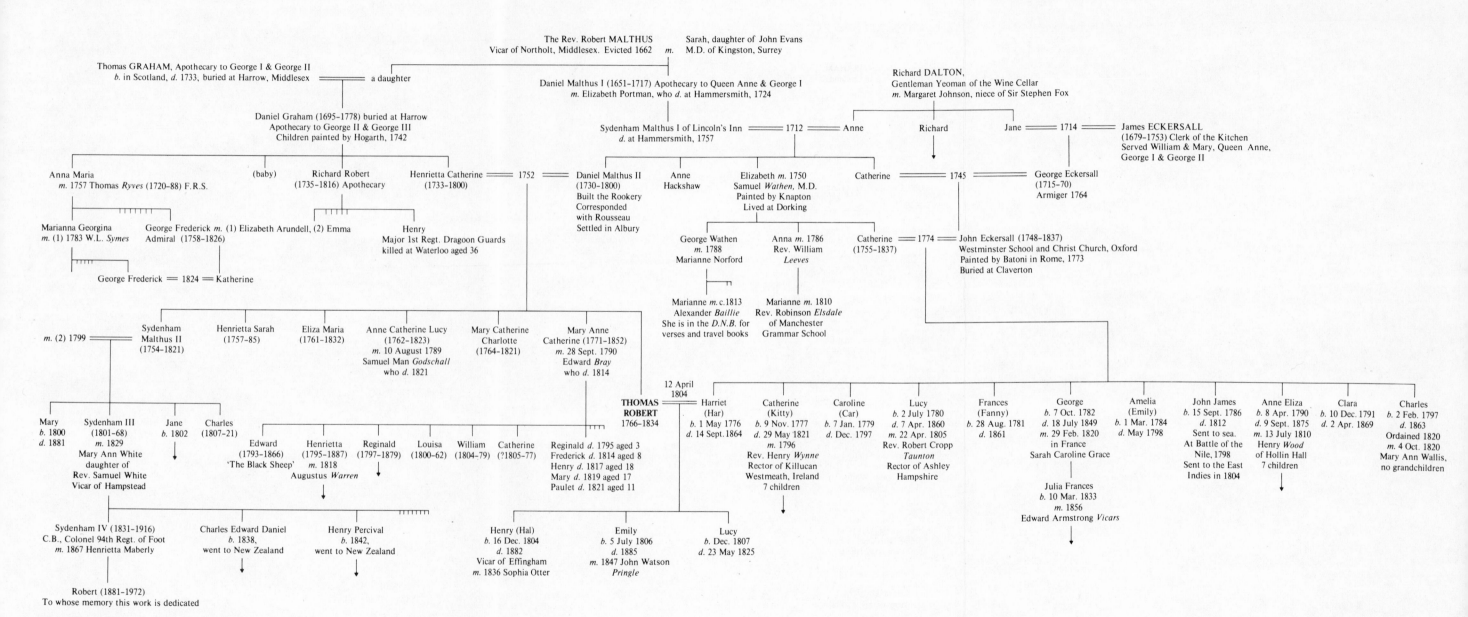

The Rev. Robert MALTHUS
Vicar of Northolt, Middlesex. Evicted 1662   *m.*   Sarah, daughter of John Evans
M.D. of Kingston, Surrey

Thomas GRAHAM, Apothecary to George I & George II
b. in Scotland, *d.* 1733, buried at Harrow, Middlesex ═══ a daughter

Daniel Malthus I (1651–1717) Apothecary to Queen Anne & George I
m. Elizabeth Portman, who *d.* at Hammersmith, 1724

Richard DALTON,
Gentleman Yeoman of the Wine Cellar
m. Margaret Johnson, niece of Sir Stephen Fox

Daniel Graham (1695–1778) buried at Harrow
Apothecary to George II & George III
Children painted by Hogarth, 1742

Sydenham Malthus I of Lincoln's Inn ═══ 1712 ═══ Anne   Richard   Jane ═══ 1714 ═══ James ECKERSALL
d. at Hammersmith, 1757   (1679–1753) Clerk of the Kitchen
                                                                                          Served William & Mary, Queen Anne,
                                                                                          George I & George II

Anna Maria   (baby)   Richard Robert   Henrietta Catherine ═══ 1752 ═══ Daniel Malthus II   Anne   Elizabeth *m.* 1750   Catherine ═══ 1745 ═══ George Eckersall
m. 1757 Thomas *Ryves* (1720–88) F.R.S.   (1735–1816) Apothecary   (1733–1800)   (1730–1800)   Hackshaw   Samuel *Wathen*, M.D.   (1715–70)
                                                                                                 Built the Rookery   Painted by Knapton   Armiger 1764
                                                                                                 Corresponded   Lived at Dorking
                                                                                                 with Rousseau
                                                                                                 Settled in Albury

Marianna Georgina   George Frederick *m.* (1) Elizabeth Arundell, (2) Emma   Henry   George Wathen   Anna *m.* 1786   Catherine ═══ 1774 ═══ John Eckersall (1748–1837)
m. (1) 1783 W.L. *Symes*   Admiral (1758–1826)   Major 1st Regt. Dragoon Guards   *m.* 1788   Rev. William   (1755–1837)   Westminster School and Christ Church, Oxford
                                                                             killed at Waterloo aged 36 Marianne Norford *Leeves*   Painted by Batoni in Rome, 1773
                                                                                                                                                                Buried at Claverton
George Frederick ═══ 1824 ═══ Katherine

                                                                                                         Marianne *m.* c.1813   Marianne *m.* 1810
                                                                                                         Alexander *Baillie*   Rev. Robinson *Elsdale*
                                                                                                         She is in the *D.N.B.* for of Manchester
                                                                                                         verses and travel books Grammar School

m. (2) 1799 ═══ Sydenham   Henrietta Sarah   Eliza Maria   Anne Catherine Lucy   Mary Catherine   Mary Anne
                 Malthus II   (1757–85)   (1761–1832)   (1762–1823)   Charlotte   Catherine (1771–1852)
                 (1754–1821)   *m.* 10 August 1789   (1764–1821)   *m.* 28 Sept. 1790
                                                                Samuel Man *Godschall*   Edward *Bray*
                                                                who *d.* 1821   who *d.* 1814

                                                                                       12 April
                                                                                       1804
Mary   Sydenham III   Jane   Charles   THOMAS ═══ Harriet   Catherine   Caroline   Lucy   Frances   George   Amelia   John James   Anne Eliza   Clara   Charles
b. 1800 (1801–68)   *b.* 1802 (1807–21)   ROBERT   (Har)   (Kitty)   (Car)   *b.* 2 July 1780 (Fanny)   *b.* 7 Oct. 1782 (Emily)   *b.* 15 Sept. 1786 *b.* 8 Apr. 1790 *b.* 10 Dec. 1791 *b.* 2 Feb. 1797
d. 1881 *m.* 1829   1766–1834 *b.* 1 May 1776 *b.* 9 Nov. 1777 *b.* 7 Jan. 1779 *d.* 7 Apr. 1860 *b.* 28 Aug. 1781 *d.* 18 July 1849 *b.* 1 Mar. 1784 *d.* 1812   *d.* 9 Sept. 1875 *d.* 1863
          Mary Ann White   *d.* 14 Sept. 1864 *d.* 29 May 1821 *d.* Dec. 1797   *d.* Dec. 1797   *d.* 1861   *m.* 29 Feb. 1820 *d.* May 1798   Sent to sea.   Henry *Wood*   Ordained 1820
          daughter of   *m.* 1796   in France   At Battle of the   of Hollin Hall   *m.* 4 Oct. 1820
          Rev. Samuel White   Edward   Henrietta Reginald Louisa   William   Catherine   Reginald *d.* 1795 aged 3 Rev. Henry *Wynne*   Rev. Robert Cropp   Sarah Caroline Grace   Nile, 1798   7 children   Mary Ann Wallis,
          Vicar of Hampstead   (1793–1866) (1795–1887)(1797–1879)(1800–62) (1804–79) (?1805–77) Frederick *d.* 1814 aged 8 Rector of Killucan   *Taunton*   Sent to the East   no grandchildren
                                                                                        'The Black Sheep' *m.* 1818   Henry *d.* 1817 aged 18 Westmeath, Ireland   Rector of Ashley   Julia Frances   Indies in 1804
                                                                                                   Augustus *Warren*   Mary *d.* 1819 aged 17   7 children   Hampshire   *b.* 10 Mar. 1833
                                                                                                                                         Paulet *d.* 1821 aged 11   *m.* 1856
Sydenham IV (1831–1916)   Charles Edward Daniel   Henry Percival   Henry (Hal)   Emily   Lucy   Edward Armstrong *Vicars*
C.B., Colonel 94th Regt. of Foot   *b.* 1838,   *b.* 1842,   *b.* 16 Dec. 1804 *b.* 5 July 1806 *b.* Dec. 1807
m. 1867 Henrietta Maberly   went to New Zealand   went to New Zealand   *d.* 1885   *d.* 1885   *d.* 23 May 1825
                                                                                        Vicar of Effingham *m.* 1847 John Watson
                                                                                        m. 1836 Sophia Otter *Pringle*

Robert (1881–1972)
To whose memory this work is dedicated

Prologue

Thomas Robert Malthus, always known as Robert or Bob, was born on 13 February 1766 and died on 29 December 1834.[1] Millions of words have been published, in many languages, about the Malthusian Theory of Population: nobody has ever written a full-length biography of the man. His date of birth is given incorrectly in the *Dictionary of National Biography*; in the introduction to a classic reprint of the *Essay on Population* he was alleged to have had eleven daughters,[2] whereas in fact he had but three children altogether – and so on. This book, based on fifteen years' intermittent research, is an attempt to set the record straight and to give some account of a man whom the author, at least, has found as interesting and lovable as his friends described him.

To begin at the beginning: I was told that 'with such an outlandish name, Malthus could not possibly have been an Englishman.' He was. I do not propose to trace the family history back to the time of Edward the Confessor, but I believe it could be done. The name is sometimes said to be derived from Malt-house, and I have come upon eighteen versions of the spelling of it. For our purpose, we need go no further back in time than the sixteenth century, and no further afield than the town of Reading. Here Malthuses (in all their variants of orthography) are scattered throughout the archives of the County of Berkshire and the Borough of Reading itself, where the name is familiar and correctly pronounced, and the Mayor and Corporation, with the boys of the Reading Blue Coat School, annually attend the Malthus Service in the church of St Laurence.

Reading, at the confluence of two navigable rivers, grew to prosperity through the manufacture of woollen cloth, said to have been established in the reign of Edward I. At the time of the Civil War, which ruined the trade, it was an attractive and flourishing town of some 7,000 inhabitants, 'comfortably maintained' as sorters, carders, spinners, weavers, dyers, and the like.[3] Throughout the sixteenth and early seventeenth centuries we come across innumerable Malthuses in every kind of record: they are listed as drapers, clothiers and mercers; they are churchwardens, chief constables of Charlton Hundred, and Mayors of Reading over and over again.[4]

Like other merchants of the time they invested in land, and the archives abound in deeds relating to their holdings in Binfield and Shinfield, Warfield and Swallowfield, Woolhampton, Whitley, Farnham and Old Windsor. Sometimes they were styled 'yeoman', at other times 'gentleman'; Richard

1

Malthus, who made his will in 1577, when he was 'sick in body, hole in mind', was a member of the Middle Temple. It is interesting to see that there was no distinction, at this period, between what a later generation sharply differentiated as Trade and the Professions. A seventeenth-century uncle left '£20 to Thomas, son of my brother Robert Malthouse to be paid him when apprenticed or sent to the University'; Thomas in fact went to Oxford, to Corpus Christi College, and became vicar of Alfriston in Sussex, while a little later his cousins William and John were apprenticed to a goldsmith.[5]

That the Malthuses were men of public spirit as well as substance, is shown by the offices they held, their gifts of plate to churches, and the many charitable bequests in their wills. Like other merchants, as the wool trade of Berkshire declined, they went off to London to seek their fortune, but their hearts must have remained in Reading.

The most conspicuous of these London benefactors of their home town was William Malthus; his will, made in November 1700, provided for the sale of his ships, as well as other property, in order to buy land for charitable endowments.[6] A childless man, he rather pathetically required that the ten 'Malthus Boys', whose places he provided at the Reading Blue Coat School, should wear coats of a distinctive green, with WM on their buttons – which they did, poor children, for nearly a century.[7] He also left money for the endowment of a charity at Blewbury which retained its character for nearly two centuries; it provided for the supply of medicines to the poor, and an establishment for twenty children, ten of each sex, with a resident master and mistress, who were to care for them and educate them until they were of an age to be apprenticed.[8] The administration of these endowments has changed with the years, and in 1956 part of the Malthus Foundation investments were realised for the modernisation of the Blue Coat School;[9] but the 'Malthus Sermon', for which William bequeathed two guineas annually, is still preached each year in July, before a large congregation, which the present writer has had the pleasure of joining.[10]

The first direct ancestor of whom we must take note was the Rev. Robert Malthus, who was evicted from his vicarage of Northolt in Middlesex in 1662; his parishioners had a number of grievances, including the fact that he had 'not only a low voice, but a very great impediment in his utterance',[11] which might have been due to a hare-lip and cleft palate. Population Malthus was born with this defect, and it should be appreciated at the outset that he was a badly handicapped child.

A hare-lip is of little importance nowadays and is usually dealt with in the first months of infancy, but at that period it was a serious disability. The lip was sutured, but no operation could be performed on the palate itself. Moustaches were completely out of fashion, so that there was nothing to conceal the immediately obvious disfigurement of the lop-sided upper lip and distorted nostril. Malthus must always have talked like someone with a very bad cold. Eating would have been difficult, although it is possible that he wore a silver plate to make an artificial roof to his mouth.[12]

I was surprised to find so little evidence of Malthus's deformity. The affliction was considered a disadvantage when, as an undergraduate, he discussed entering the church; 'a retired living in the country' was the utmost of his wishes;[13] we shall never know whether, or how unhappily, he sighed for the glories of the law and politics. Apart from this instance, the matter is not mentioned in family papers. In letters or memoirs published in the nineteenth century I have discovered only three references to Malthus's defective speech. One comes from the protégée of Horace Walpole's old age, who was later prominent in society for many years - Mary Berry (1763-1852); of a London dinner-party in 1811 she wrote: 'I sat by Malthus, and had a good deal of conversation with him - interesting, when one gets over his painful manner of speaking from wanting a palate to his mouth, and having had a hair-lip [sic] - not, however, at all unpleasant in appearance.'[14]

Another literary lady, Harriet Martineau (1802-76), whose hearing was peculiar, was astonished to find in 1832 that 'of all people in the world', she could follow Malthus quite easily without her ear-trumpet: 'Malthus, whose speech was hopelessly imperfect, from defect in the palate. I dreaded meeting him ... When I considered my own deafness, and his inability to pronounce half the consonants in the alphabet, and his hare-lip which must prevent my offering him my tube, I feared we should make a terrible business of it. I was delightfully wrong. His first sentence, - slow and gentle, with the vowels sonorous, whatever might become of the consonants, - set me at ease completely ... It really gratified him that I heard him better than anybody else.'[15]

As far as I know the only man to comment on Malthus's way of speaking was Sir Henry Holland (1788-1873). In his *Recollections of Past Life* he describes Malthus's 'tremulous stammering voice, seemingly little fitted for the utterance of any doctrine which could be deemed dangerous to social welfare'.[16] This is unexpected from a Physician in Ordinary to the Queen, but then Dr Holland was famous, almost to his discredit, for suavity and discretion.

In this connection it is important to remember that Victorian editors had no scruples over bowdlerising their texts. They excised or altered (without saying so) anything that might give offence, and this is perfectly illustrated in the case of Maria Edgeworth (1767-1849). In collections of her letters published about a hundred years ago, there is no mention whatever of Malthus's disability; Christina Colvin's fine edition shows that, much as Miss Edgeworth loved Malthus, 'his uncouth mouth and horrid voice' jarred her and her step-sisters whenever they met him. In 1822 Maria wished 'that hair lip [sic] were away and that he could speak more like a human creature - for if I were a child and had heard of his being an Ogre I should

3

run away if he were to come near me and begin to speak.'[17]

Since we admire people who overcome their handicaps, such editorial suppression is hard to condone. I am told that this reticence might have been due to a superstition - once widely held - that a hare-lip was a punishment for more than ordinary sin. Whatever the truth of this, I think his misfortune must have affected Malthus's career. There is, for instance, only the one portrait of him, painted a year before his death, in which Linnell handles the twist of the lip with great tact and skill; it is probable that there would have been a number of earlier portraits, were it not for this disfigurement, for Robert Malthus was otherwise an exceptionally handsome man.

CHAPTER I

Background

1 Family Tree

The seventeenth-century Rev. Robert Malthus married the daughter of John Evans, MD, and it was possibly through this connection that his son Daniel became an apothecary in London under the internationally famous Dr Thomas Sydenham (1624-89). Daniel Malthus (1651-1717) was made a freeman of the Society of Apothecaries when he was twenty-seven; he set up his shop, with the sign of the Pestle and Mortar, in a tall house on the north side of Pall Mall, next door to Dr Sydenham's (both houses were later demolished to make way for Waterloo Place). Dr Sydenham had a great regard for Daniel Malthus, and appointed him a trustee for his children.[1] Mary Beale's painting of Dr Sydenham is in the National Portrait Gallery, but her chalk drawings of Mr and Mrs Daniel Malthus cannot be traced.[2]

There is no doubt that Apothecary Daniel was the founder of the fortunes of this branch of the family, for sometime after 1691 (a special Act of Parliament was necessary) he purchased the Manor of Hadstock in Essex from 'the Trustees of James, late Earl of Suffolk' for over £5,500.[3] Meanwhile, his sister had married another successful apothecary, Thomas Graham. Having served a seven-year apprenticeship in Scotland, Thomas Graham was admitted as a 'foreign brother' of the Society of Apothecaries on 14 September 1698. He had a son whom he christened Daniel, and in due course Daniel Graham was apprenticed for eight years to his Uncle Malthus, starting on 6 December 1709.

By that time 'Daniel Malthus, Esq.,' was 'Apothecary to our Royall Person', Queen Anne having signed a Warrant to this effect on 22 November 1704, although he had been 'sworn' on 22 July.[4] By virtue of this appointment he 'came on to the Court of Assistants of the Apothecaries, was immediately elected Master but excused himself because of business and paid a fine of £50'. His salary from the Queen was £115, but he also received £205. 5s. for 'Physick for our Person in lieu of bills', making £320. 5s. per annum, paid quarterly. Daniel Malthus served his mistress well and was with her throughout the four days of her agonising death.[5] With his fellow-apothecary James Chase he prepared the anointing oil for George I's coronation, for which they received the customary fee of £206. When he retired in 1716 his brother-in-law Thomas Graham took over his shop, as well as his court appointment, since his son (Sydenham Malthus I) preferred law to physic.

But Daniel Malthus I had done far more than make his family comfortably well-to-do; he had established contact with two other families connected with the Royal Household – the Daltons and the Eckersalls, with whom Malthuses and Grahams were to marry and intermarry for just over a hundred years; finally in 1804 our Robert Malthus (whose mother was a Graham) married his cousin Harriet Eckersall, after he had obtained a living in Lincolnshire from his kinsman Henry Dalton.

A glance at the family tree will explain relationships which it would be tedious to describe, but it is, I think, worth while to spend a little more time over the records of the departments of the Lord Chamberlain and the Lord Steward. The Daltons in whom we are interested served Charles II: a Richard the Elder as Sergeant of the Wine Cellar, a Richard the Younger first as Page of the Cellar and then in a series of offices, including those of Keeper of the Ice and Snow and Yeoman of the Mouth (the duty of the latter was 'to fill and taste His Majesty's wine at the sideboard'). They must have been concerned with such things as the issue of 'Gascoigne Wine, For the Communions, For Healings, For Making of Jellies' and 'Canarie, For the Chaplaines upon Sermon Dayes, For Washing the King's Feet'.[6]

After the accession of William of Orange, as might be expected, the account books of the Royal Household are no longer decorated with gilt flourishes, and the total annual expenses fall sharply, but a bottle of sherry was apparently set aside weekly for the washing of the King's feet.[7] It is difficult to follow this line of Daltons, who were all called Richard, but we know from James Eckersall's diary that they were comfortably established near Leatherhead, Surrey, in 1741, at a manor house called Thorncroft.[8]

It was during William III's reign, in 1692, that James Eckersall entered the Royal Household at the age of thirteen, on the recommendation of the Countess of Derby, who had connections with Bury in Lancashire, where the Eckersalls lived, and was Groom of the Stole to Queen Mary. This remarkable man James Eckersall is still a family legend. His note-books are now distributed among the descendants of his only grandson, and I have been kindly allowed to see them in Yorkshire, Gloucestershire and Somerset by owners quite unknown to each other. It seems more than likely that Malthus looked at these diaries, and they are worth perusal for the light which they throw on the world in which his parents grew up and from which his own world evolved.

James Eckersall did not become Chief Clerk of the Kitchen until 1742, when his predecessor died at the age of ninety, but he had been doing the work of the office for the previous thirty years. His establishment was about 150 strong. Among the highest paid were the Clerk of the Spicery and the Table Laundress; among the lowest those who worked in the Larder (six of them), Scald House, and 'Scullery including Pankeeper'. On occasion he hired temporary turnspits. Four men worked in the woodyard, for the kitchens needed great quantities of logs and charcoal, with faggots for quick fires for pastry; coal was only used for warming a few rooms.[9] As one would expect, his account books are full of such items as French Beans and Green Pease, Sparragrass and Collyflowers, most expensively welcomed in April. When Jonathan Swift and some friends dined with 'James, I know not his other name', in February 1711, he inhabited 'a snug little house in St. James's, and we had the queen's wine, and such very fine victuals that I could not eat it'.[10]

But Eckersall had other interests. He is among the friends of Alexander Pope who are mentioned in John Gay's poem; they are all supposed to be assembled to welcome him on his return from Greece - that is, after he had finished his translation of the *Iliad* in 1720.[11] In February 1720 Pope wrote two letters to James Eckersall about lottery orders and speculation generally: 'I also hear there is considerably to be got by subscribing to ye new African Stock, Pray let us do something or other, which you judge the fairest Prospect, I am equal as to what Stock, so you but like it. Let but Fortune favor us, & ye world will sure to admire our Prudence. If we fail, let's e'en keep the mishap to ourselves. But 'tis Ignominious (in this Age of Hope and Golden Mountains) not to Venture.'[12]

However much other people suffered from the breaking of the speculative South Sea Bubble in 1720, James Eckersall prospered. His dealings with the Royal Africa Company may have come as a shock to Population Malthus, an ardent anti-slavery man, if he read these little books. Eckersall jotted down in his diary that the RA Company had made a contract with Messrs Thomas to supply them with 400 negroes in January 1740 and 200 more in May. He then mentions the ships the *Success* and the *Expedition*, both of 85 tons, each with twelve men and a boy, and a sloop, the *Catherine*, with four men and a boy, which was 'freighted with Provisions'. The two larger vessels each carried a cargo valued at £2,500, and 'All for Cape Coast Sign'd their Sailing Orders the 27th Sept' 1739.'[13]

Before we are too hard on James Eckersall, we must remind ourselves that he lived more than two hundred years ago. The very 'almanacks' in which he wrote, elaborately bound and full of official information, contain surprising advice for those whom we think of as educated people in a civilised country. In July, 'Get Rue, Wormwood, and Gall, to strew your Floors, to destroy Fleas.' In November, 'Kill Swine in or near the Full of the Moon, and the Flesh will prove the better in the Boiling.'[14] In this same year (1730) Cousin John Eckersall, who was Secretary to Queen Caroline, was keeping the accounts of the royal nursery, which included over £40 worth of lace for the nine-year-old Duke of Cumberland. We can also learn that he paid four shillings for 'A hundred of Clarified Quills'.[15] It is very remote from us, but not from Malthus, who used a quill pen all his life,

7

and took lace as a favourite example of the luxuries purchased by the rich, men and women, in contrast to the bare necessities consumed by the poor.

In his old age, James Eckersall attempted little doggerel verses, perhaps as toasts, and in 1748 he wrote:

> I wish my Friends Ease Health and Peace
> And that their Fortunes may Increase
> To Enable them to do Much Good
> To Friends and Those Allied in Blood.[16]

Again, we shall not understand the past if we judge dead men's actions in the light of present knowledge and present attitudes. We shall not be able to imagine Malthus's world until we realise that posts at court, public offices, college fellowships and church livings, were all then regarded as forms of property, of which it was stupid and undutiful not to make the fullest use for the enrichment of one's family.

To continue with this particular family history: Daniel Malthus resigned his post as Royal Apothecary two years after George I's accession. By that time his son Sydenham (named after the famous doctor) had married Anne Dalton, and James Eckersall had married (as his second wife) Anne's sister Jane. We can see from Eckersall's accounts that Daniel Malthus attended Mrs Eckersall when her only child, George, was born on 9 October 1715.[17] Of poor Jane her husband was to write that she was loved by him, 'Esteemed by her Superiours, and Admired by all her Acquaintance. Her Constitution was tender but of a chearfull disposition when her Infirmities were Supportable, she Miscarryed Eleven Times and Dyed much Lamented by all that knew her the 6 day of August 1729.'[18]

Eckersall goes on with his family history in the same notebook: George 'was 8 years at Westminster School and at 16 went to Queens College at Oxford a commoner for 3 years and a half, Then had Chambers in Lincolns Inn and was called to the Bar; in June 1745 he married Miss Catherine Malthus Daughter of Sydenham Malthus Esq.'.

This Sydenham Malthus was also a member of Lincoln's Inn; he was one of the six Clerks in Chancery, a director of the South Sea Company in 1741, and made money enough to buy land as an investment in Hertfordshire and near Cambridge. But both Sydenham and George seem shadowy intermediate figures between their fathers who established their fortunes and their sons who spent them, for both Daniel Malthus II and John Eckersall were what would now be called 'characters'. One became the economist's father, and the other was his first cousin and also his father-in-law.

Unfortunately, little is known of the youth of Daniel Malthus II, who was born in 1730. He entered the Queen's College at Oxford in 1747, but left without taking a degree; in 1749 he too was admitted to Lincoln's Inn. On 6 May 1752 he married his second cousin, nineteen-year-old Henrietta Catherine Graham.

Henrietta was the elder daughter of the Daniel Graham who had been apprenticed to his Uncle Malthus in 1709, when he was fourteen years old. He also had become a Royal Apothecary, in 1721, on the death of James Chase, and so he and his father Thomas Graham had together embalmed the body of George I and made up the anointing oil for George II and Queen Caroline; Daniel had five yards of scarlet cloth allowed him for the coronation.[19] Thomas Graham died in 1733, and was buried in Harrow church, in Middlesex; as he and his son were both governors of Harrow School, one assumes that the Grahams had a country house there. In any case, Daniel Graham resigned his post at court in 1740, in favour of his cousin, another Thomas Graham, with whom he was a partner in his private practice. Daniel Graham also had a post at the Chelsea Royal Hospital, and he became once more a Royal Apothecary - to George III - for just two years, before he died in 1778 at the age of eighty-three;[20] he was no doubt an excellent man, who fully deserved his Latin epitaph about his kindness to the sick, but his chief gift to posterity (apart from his grandson) is the picture of his children painted by Hogarth in 1742.

This is not the place to expatiate on that delightful masterpiece *The Graham Children*, which hangs in the Tate Gallery, and which few people can look at without smiling. The baby in the pull-along chair was soon to die, but Richard Robert carried on the family shop in Pall Mall until 1800; he lived to see his nephew become famous, and in 1816 died at the age of eighty-one; he too was buried at Harrow, although his domicile is given as Chelsea. The little girl in white embroidered satin was to become Mrs Ryves, and her daughter Georgina was to marry the elder son of her big sister in gleaming blue; it is difficult to realise that the smug little person holding the shiny red cherries is the mother of Population Malthus.[21]

But this is anticipating the future. I do not know where the newly-married Daniel Malthuses first set up house in 1752; the accession of George III probably found them in the neighbourhood of Dorking, in Surrey. In 1750 Daniel's sister Elizabeth had married Samuel Wathen, who was a well-to-do surgeon or physician (he is described as both); he had estates in Cumberland, but they lived near Dorking, where a road is named after him. Knapton painted an attractive group portrait of them in 1755.[22] Daniel's sister Catherine, who had married George Eckersall in 1745, was conveniently near at Leatherhead, as her husband had rented Thorncroft from the Dalton relations. There was a third sister, Anne, who made a childless and unsatisfactory marriage with a man called Humphrey Hackshaw, and whose financial position was a source of anxiety to her family until her death in 1793. Apart from her, Population Malthus's aunts provided him with an array of cousins who were to be very important to him throughout his life.

2 Family Circle

I have not discovered the birthplace of the Daniel Malthuses' first two children, Sydenham II and Henrietta Sarah; but the third, Elizabeth Maria (Eliza Maria for short), was christened in Wotton church on 21 July 1761. Sydenham I had died in 1757, and Daniel II must have found himself established, in Bishop Otter's words, in his Memoir of Robert Malthus, as 'a gentleman of good family and independent fortune'. At the age of twenty-nine he bought a farm called Chert Gate in the little valley of Mereden, just outside Dorking on the way to Guildford, and 'taking advantage of its beauties, hill and dale, wood and water, displaying them in their natural simplicity, converted it into a gentleman's seat, giving it the name of the Rookery'.[23] There is a photograph of it in the *Supplement* to *Country Life* of 28 September 1912, when the grounds extended to 175 acres in all.

The best description of this famous and extraordinary place is by John Timbs, who published at his own expense *A Picturesque Promenade Round Dorking*, of which a second edition appeared in 1823:

> The whole of the building is rough-cast, surmounted with battlemented parapets and gothic pinnacles ... The hill behind the house is clothed with a fine beech wood, extending a considerable distance, and intersected by serpentine walks, which formerly led to several romantic buildings with appropriate dedications.
>
> The foot-path (a public thoroughfare) passes the front of the tasteful residence. A bye-path branches off to the left, and winds on the brink of an extensive sheet of water ... In the centre is a small island, on which is a ruinous fishing house, partially hidden by trees and evergreens ... The hottest and most sunny season of the year seems the time for enjoying this place to full advantage. In dark and chilly weather it must, probably, appear to superabound in shade and water; yet the site of the house is tolerably cheerful and open. A boat-house, a rude ice-house, and a small corn-mill complete this enchanting spot, unparalleled in rusticity and picturesque effect.[24]

The reader will not be surprised to learn that Daniel Malthus had a passionate admiration for Jean-Jacques Rousseau.

It is possible that the Malthuses moved to the Rookery in the summer of 1761, after their second daughter's birth. The Wotton register shows that Anne Catherine Lucy was born at the Rookery on 8 September 1762, and Mary Catherine Charlotte on 16 July 1764. In his *History of Surrey* William Bray wrote that Daniel Malthus 'had travelled much in Europe and in every part of this island';[25] his increasing family does not seem to have prevented him from going abroad in the spring of 1764, when he spent, according to himself, six congenial hours with Rousseau at Motiers-Travers. Thus it was natural that he should send a welcoming letter to Rousseau as soon as that notable exile had landed in England, written in a schoolboy French which sounds painfully sentimental today.

Daniel Malthus assured Rousseau that, although he was neither milord, author, nor philosopher, his little country house was entirely at his disposal.[26] No one records how Mrs Malthus felt about this invitation, with her sixth child due in a month's time. On Thursday 13 February 1766 the baby was born, and on the 14th he was christened Thomas Robert.[27] We can imagine his mother's joy when she was told that she had a second son, after four daughters in a row; then her grief as she looked at the hideous little face, and wondered how she could explain to the other children about their new baby brother's hare-lip.

As for Robert's father, before the baby was a fortnight old he was offering to house-hunt for Rousseau and his mistress, for Thérèse le Vasseur had been brought over to England by James Boswell. The poor woman is always assumed to have been uncouth as well as ignorant, but Rousseau insisted on her dining at his host's table wherever they went. On 24 February 1766, apropos of his search for a suitable farm-house for them, Daniel Malthus again begged Rousseau to come and stay at the Rookery, that he might choose for himself his 'ideal refuge'. But when David Hume brought Rousseau and Thérèse to look at places in Surrey, on Saturday 8 March, they stayed the night with a Colonel Webb, and returned to their lodgings in Chiswick after spending only Sunday afternoon with the Malthuses. Did Thérèse take the ugly little baby into her arms, and tell his mother how she yearned for her own five, packed off to a foundling hospital?

Daniel Malthus was bitterly mortified; he had expected the party to stay at least one night in his house. He wrote to both Rousseau and Thérèse, offering his services in any capacity, and then was hurt again when he went to Chiswick on 29 March, and found that they had already left for the north without letting him know. But Daniel was persistent in his devotion, and in June there was a family excursion to Derbyshire - presumably the younger children were left behind - where Rousseau introduced him to the delights of botany.

The Malthus party, who stayed at an inn and not actually with Rousseau, included Jane Dalton; she was an orphaned cousin, a permanent member of the household. In 1766 she would have been twenty-four, and she seems to have taken to both Rousseau and botany with enthusiasm. Jane has been somewhat unkindly described by one of Daniel's granddaughters, Louisa Bray, in her 'Recollections', as 'a single lady related to Mr. Malthus, and had been his ward. She became romantically attached to him, and was his constant companion, more than his daughters. She had been handsome until the Smallpox spoiled her complexion, was very clever, had an excellent memory, and read much. This made her society much sought after.' But she was also 'enterprising and manoeuvering for herself and others, fond of power and admiration'. It is possible that Louisa Bray was biased by filial jealousy, for Jane Dalton was very attached to Louisa's mother - who had been the baby of the family - and Mrs Bray nursed Jane on her death-bed in 1817.

That Jane Dalton had much in common with her cousin Daniel is shown by the fact that she displayed, later on, 'remarkable taste in laying out grounds, or doing anything that required a picturesque effect, and everyone consulted her when they had gardens to make or improve. Her own Cottage and grounds at Albury were perfection.'[28] Her dinners may also have been perfection, for her French cookery books are included in the library of her cousin Robert at Jesus College, Cambridge. Her 'cottage', a house with two staircases and about ten acres of land, was left to Robert's elder brother, Sydenham.

But to return to the summers of 1766 and 1767. Daniel Malthus described to Rousseau the craze for botanising which he had inspired, on the hill behind the Rookery, with 'the little cousin' Jane aiding his researches, while his dear Henrietta and her children also played their part. He was horrified and miserable to learn of Rousseau's bitter quarrel with Hume, and then hurt yet again when Rousseau left England without telling him; he was in Wales at the time, and heard of Rousseau's departure through a newspaper. In what reads like a desperate love-letter, dated 6 August 1767, he describes how frantically he had tracked Rousseau's movements, through his banker, to get his address. On 14 December he sent a much shorter letter, very pained that Rousseau had not written to him, but 'Ce coeur qui vous aime si tendrement ne sait pas vous accuser' (This heart which loves you so tenderly does not know how to reproach you).

Was Rousseau touched by this, or did he merely want a supply of English botanical works? In any case he wrote for some, and Daniel was very happy to procure them, writing on 24 January 1768, 'I prefer your commissions to all the compliments in the world.' In this long letter he gives an account not only of his summer botanising but also of his winter fox-hunting, in which he joined partly from habit, and partly because it gave him some idea of 'la vie sauvage'. He assured Rousseau that he took no share in the quarrels of the landlords, with poachers and with each other, and that he spent more time in cottages than in castles.

Daniel Malthus concluded this letter, 'If ever I am famous, it will be as the friend of Rousseau.' How wrong he was! Yet his acquaintance with Rousseau gave him a sort of distinction in the neighbourhood; most people enjoy a connection with a celebrity, however tenuous, even a celebrity of whom they disapprove. By the time Bishop Otter came to write his *Memoir* of Daniel's famous son, Daniel had become 'the friend and correspondent of Rousseau and one of his executors',[29] which last he most certainly was not.

Some members of the family were unfavourably impressed. Daniel's granddaughter Louisa wrote in 1857: 'My Grandfather Malthus was a great admirer of Rousseau and his works, which no doubt contributed to his eccentricities. He would not allow his wife to wear her wedding ring. My Grandmother would not have been supposed a happy woman by those who knew her, yet towards the close of her life, she said she would willingly pass it over again.'

It is tantalising to know so little about Mrs Malthus. According to Louisa Bray, she 'was a most affectionate and indulgent Mother, and all her children loved her in the tenderest manner. She was likewise a devoted wife. They all took after her rather than Mr. Malthus, for never was there a set of more amiable and unselfish beings than my uncles and aunts.' Of Daniel she wrote further: 'My Grandfather's character was peculiar and his opinions on some subjects eccentric. With a highly cultivated mind and very fascinating manners, he was cold and reserved in his own family, except towards his eldest daughter, of whom he was very fond, and his youngest son [sic], whose talents probably early attracted his attention. I have heard Mama speak of him as a person whose will was imperative, and to whom everything gave way.'

Louisa is just, however: 'My Grandfather Malthus was not a religious man, but he had a respect for religion, and would never allow light conversation on such a subject in his presence. If any of his children had behaved ill in Church or talked of the persons they had seen there, remarked on their dress or anything of the kind (unhappily so commonly done by persons professedly religious) they would have been severely reprimanded. He would not allow his daughters to read the Old Testament, but encouraged their reading of the New.' And their niece had seldom met with women of more cultivated minds and pleasing manners than her Malthus aunts, all educated at home without a governess.

But we must go back to 1768, when possibly the Malthuses and their elder children went to Dijon in the summer, to join the George Eckersalls there, since that is what Daniel was planning when he wrote his last letter to Rousseau, in January. All we know for certain is that in 1768 the Rookery was sold, to a banker named Fuller. For the next nineteen years the family 'wandered about' - Miss Bray's expression - until 1787, when they returned to Surrey, to Albury and Shere, where descendants of Daniel Malthus still live.

Why did he sell the Rookery so suddenly? There is no obvious explanation, any more than there is of Daniel Malthus's leaving Oxford without a degree, or abandoning the law. Perhaps his disappointment over Rousseau, the baby's hare-lip, and what Timbs called the superabundance of shade and water, all had something to do with it. Robert Malthus's youngest sister, and the one most like him in looks and character, Mary Anne Catherine, was born in 1771, but such were her parents' wanderings that she herself never knew where this event had taken place.

What we do know for certain is that the family must have spent at least the spring and summer of 1773 at Claverton House in Somerset, near Bath. This information comes from the Rev. Richard Graves, who was to be Robert Malthus's first tutor outside the domestic circle, and a close friend of them all. He was born in 1715, was with the Methodist preacher George Whitefield at Pembroke College, Oxford, and became a Fellow of All Souls in 1736; he won a sort of second-hand fame through his intimacy with William Shenstone, a poet admired by writers as different as Dr Johnson and Robert Burns. Graves then offended his family by marrying a farmer's daughter, became rector of Claverton in 1749, and is said never to have been absent from his parish for more than a month.

In 1773 Richard Graves would have been fifty-eight years old. He had published in the previous year a satirical novel called *The Spiritual Quixote*, in which he recounted the adventures of a certain Mr Geoffry Wildgoose, who had travelled around the country as a free-lance saver of souls. Lest this should prejudice some readers against Mr Graves, I take the liberty of quoting a few verses he wrote at a later period, published in 1801, in a collection endearingly entitled *Senilities*:

> Survey the conduct of mankind,
>   Unless it too much shocks ye,
> His duty no one does, you'll find,
>   For all is done by Proxy.
>
> To every office should you go,
>   The Principal but mocks ye;
> He's at his country-seat, I trow,
>   His business done by Proxy . . .
>
> Pray, John, where does your Rector live
>   So fam'd for orthodoxy?
> At Lon'non master, I believe,
>   But preaches here by Proxy . . .
>
> Well, farmer, you sit by your fire,
>   Your man in dirty frock, see!
> Does all your work for slender hire,
>   You plow and sow by Proxy . . .
>
> In ev'ry post of Church or State,
>   Of deputies what flocks, see!
> Why should it then surprise create,
>   If t'heaven they go by Proxy?[30]

In addition to his literary activities, which included two more novels and a translation of Marcus Aurelius, Richard Graves took pupils, as did many

14

other clergymen of the period, and fortunately for him the Manor of Claverton was purchased by the philanthropist Ralph Allen, the original of Squire Allworthy in *Tom Jones*. According to Graves, 'after having repaired, improved, and built a gallery in the church; finding that the rector had several young gentlemen of family and fortune under his care; and a very indifferent old house for their accommodation, Mr. Allen offered to build him a room, which he immediately executed; building a room twenty-five feet by sixteen with two bed-chambers over it, which he observed would serve for a school, as long as he continued that employment.'[31]

That was in 1760, according to a note in the parish register, but even this addition was not enough for the increasing number of pupils. Ralph Allen left Claverton House to his niece, the wife of Bishop Warburton, and on 6 November 1766 the latter was writing to Bishop Hurd: 'But apropos of Mr. Graves. My Wife has let him the great house at Claverton, for which he gives £60 a year; and the great gallery-library is turned into a dormitory, so that where literature generally ends, it here begins.'[32]

Since Mr Graves's school lasted into the 1780s, one can only assume that he did not use the whole of the house, but sub-let part of it to Daniel Malthus. And in 1773 he wrote some lines to his tenant's wife, which were published in a miscellaneous collection called *Euphrosyne* in 1783; I quote from it at length, for it gives a picture of activity and sunshine very different from the sequestered gloom of the Rookery.

After comparing 'Mrs. M-lt-s' with Cynthia, or chaster Dian, he goes on:

> Well-pleas'd she sees her infant train
> Of nymphlins sporting on the plain
> Or dancing in the checquer'd shade,
> Like little Loves in masquerade.
> Whilst Harriet with Madona face,
> The rival of her mother's grace,
> Her novel flutt'ring in the gale,
> Hangs pensive o'er some moving tale;
> Or with expressive air attends,
> Whilst sprightly Delia cheers her friends,*
> (Not with wise comments on the weather,
> Or hints of 'who and who's together',
> But) with remarks on books profound,
> Or anecdotes of the gay monde:
> Then Manlius paints the toils and strife†

---

*This must be Jane Dalton.
†Daniel Malthus himself. Graves also wrote some verses especially for him; Manlius' 'poetic eyes' could appreciate the charms of 'Each primrose pale, that slighted blows, Each mossy stone that lies'.

The vain pursuits of public life:
Gently to lead, with art design'd,
In Virtue's paths the youthful mind;
Hence taught with innocence to rove,
Content, thro' life, the peaceful grove.

But when on serious studies bent,
I see the pygmy group intent
On books; with maps and globes surrounded
(By change reliev'd, but not confounded)
Their tutor's wise, parental care
Soften'd by love's more gentle air:
Whilst some amid' the studious quire
Touch the guitar or tune the lyre;
With dedal skill whilst Delia weaves
In threads of gold the mimic leaves;
Or decks with flow'rs the Brussels lace
To veil the beauties of her face –
When I behold this rural scene
So gay, so cheerful – yet serene:
What poets sing of nymphs and swains
Assembled on th' Arcadian plains: . . .
These scenes, methinks, so fam'd of yore,
Tho' fancy'd to exist no more,
Or deem'd by sceptics, fables all,
Are realiz'd at Cl-rt-n Hall.

June 1773.

N.B. this is a real though imperfect sketch of a worthy family, who
have happily united in their domestic economy, the elegant simplicity
of the pastoral ages with the refinements of modern life.[33]

3 Early Education

We do not know when the Malthuses resumed their wanderings, presumably
leaving Robert behind at Claverton to start his education in earnest. This
was to be the setting for important days in his life; he was at school here
until he was sixteen, and then at the turn of the century the great house was
taken by his first cousin, John Eckersall; in Claverton church Robert was
married to John's daughter Harriet, and the ramifications of the family were
united here for holidays until the house was sold over their heads in 1817.

It must have been a wonderful place; unfortunately, only fragments now remain of the terrace of the old honey-coloured manor house, which in 1819 was completely demolished. It was built in the first decade of the seventeenth century, in three storeys, with beautiful mullioned windows and ornamental gables. An architect's plan shows that the great gallery, as was characteristic of Jacobean mansions, ran the entire length of the very top of the house. Here forty little boys are said to have slept; there are no chimneys marked on the plan, so it would have been very cold in winter. Behind the great gallery were four bedrooms, all of which had chimneys, as did every other room in the house. On the floor below were four more bedrooms, one with a little dressing-room leading out of it; unexpectedly, a very large room is marked Dressing Room on the plan, which I feel could be a mistake for Drawing Room, with a small 'Library' adjoining it, communicating in turn with one of the larger bedrooms. On the ground floor was the great hall, a library as large as the kitchen, a small servants' hall, and the resident family's dining-room, used in the eighteenth century after they had ceased to have their meals on a dais at one end of the hall, while all the servants sat a little below them on long benches. There were, of course, no bathrooms or water-closets marked on the plan.[34]

Close by the great house, but deeper in the hollow, where the village lay, was the rectory, and then the little church. As Malthus's contemporary, John Britton, wrote: 'The scene is truly romantic, wild, and picturesque. An abrupt declivity, from the table-land of the Down, descends to a narrow ever-green valley, through which the river Avon meanders silently and sluggishly towards the west. This steep hill consists of rocks and woods, interspersed with natural terraces . . .'[35]

It would have been a good place for playing Cavaliers and Roundheads. When the present writer was exploring the village, she found herself in trouble through never having heard of the Battle of Claverton in 1643; those killed in it are buried in the churchyard, one Royalist and three Parliamentarians. A cannon ball was found embedded in the dining-room wall of the manor house - William Bassett, the owner, was an officer in the King's army - but it was after hand-to-hand fighting in the village that the Royalists won.

It is worth noting that the Prayer Book in use throughout Malthus's life contained a service for the annual commemoration of the death of Charles I, King and Martyr, on 30 January; on 29 May was celebrated the restoration of Charles II, in a service of 'praise and thanksgiving for the wonderful deliverance of these kingdoms from THE GREAT REBELLION'. On 5 November Richard Graves's pupils would have given thanks not only for deliverance from 'the most traiterous and bloody-intended Massacre by Gunpowder', in 1605, but also for 'the happy Arrival of his Majesty King William on this Day, for the Deliverance of our Church and Nation', in 1688, an event known as the Glorious Revolution.

Over the Down from seventeenth-century Claverton lay eighteenth-century Bath; here during four 'seasons', from 1777 to 1781, Sarah Siddons played all her great tragic parts. It was here that Malthus presumably acquired his love of the theatre, which lasted all his life; here, possibly, he also acquired his lifelong distaste for towns (Jane Austen disliked Bath so intensely that she fainted away on being told she had to live there).

Bath at this time was a brash new place, still being built – or rather, run up – by speculators. It was notorious for bad smells, which our less squeamish ancestors called stinks and stenches. Contemporary prints also show the beggars for which the city was equally famous, with their crutches and wooden legs; there are wandering vendors, too, of all kinds, with every sort of basket, and trays carried on the head; there seem to be children and stray dogs everywhere; one man is driving a single cow, another a small flock of sheep; it is almost as if the wheel had not been invented – the rich are carried in sedan chairs along the deeply rutted streets, and baggage is slung on pack-animals.[36] Drowsily turning over the pictures, one is astonished to find that eighteenth-century Bath is evoking memories of towns today which are far south and east of Suez.

In addition to the hypochondriacs and the truly sick who came, with their respectable families, to drink the waters, Bath also collected gamblers and adventurers. These sometimes came up to Claverton Down, since it was outside the jurisdiction of the Bath constables, to fight duels; the Down was also well-known for pick-pockets and highwaymen. More legitimately, it was the site of Bath race-course until it was abandoned in favour of Lansdown in 1784; the Claverton grandstand and stables were built in 1770, and the thirteen-year-old Bob Malthus might have been among the crowds in 1779 when the Duke of Cumberland attended the meeting, and took all the stables for his own horses. Bob would only have been eight at the time of the Down's most famous cricket match, Somerset against All England, in 1774, but he must have watched other matches; this was cricket played in three-cornered hats, shirts and breeches, with two stumps instead of three, bats resembling hockey-sticks, and a ball made by a local cobbler.

Richard Graves wrote at least two letters to Daniel Malthus about his son's progress. 'Don Roberto', wrote Graves, 'though most peaceably inclined, and seeming even to give up his just rights, rather than to dispute with any man, yet, paradox as it may seem, loves fighting for fighting's sake, and delights in bruising; he has but barely recovered his eyesight, and yet I have much ado to keep him from trying again the chance of war; and yet he and his antagonist are the best friends in the world, learn together, assist each other, and I believe love each other better than any two boys in the school.'[37]

In the second letter Don Roberto is referred to as Bob, and Graves is reporting on his progress in Latin. 'He has finished Horace, and has read five satires in Juvenal with apparent taste, and I never saw a boy of his age

18

enter more instantaneously into the humour of the fifth satire, which describes so feelingly the affronts and mortifications which a parasite meets with at a great man's table.' It is admittedly a puerile and crude form of humour: the sycophant, who cannot complain, being served some loathsome fish, while those at the head of the table enjoy every sort of delicacy with ostentatious pleasure. But the happy schoolmaster went on, 'I never saw a boy shew a quicker sense of the beauties of an author, or at least of any humorous and unexpected strokes': Bob was more responsive than two of his fellows who were fifteen years old.[38]

It is plain that Graves did not do his teaching by proxy, although the provision of cakes and pies was delegated to a kind but redoubtable Mrs B. She seems to have kept the boys clean and tidy, and thumped those with round backs to make them walk upright.[39]

But in 1782 this happy time came to an end, and Daniel Malthus indulged in what must have been regarded as one of his oddest eccentricities: he sent the sixteen-year-old Robert to read with Gilbert Wakefield, first at Warrington, in Lancashire, where the famous Dissenting Academy was just about to close down, and then at Wakefield's own home at Bramcote in Nottinghamshire. Younger readers, who cannot remember when small communities in England were still split between Church and Chapel, may have difficulty in understanding what an unusual step this was.

Since the Test Act of 1673, no one could hold any public office unless he received Holy Communion once a year according to the rites of the Church of England; moreover, only members of the Church of England could take a degree at either of the two English universities, Oxford or Cambridge.* This meant that Protestant Nonconformists, debarred from the services and the professions, naturally turned to industry and commerce. As they prospered, they set up their own establishments for higher education, with far wider curricula than the 'great schools' or grammar schools, or Oxford and Cambridge, training boys for practical managerial work as well as for the dissenting ministry.

Why Daniel Malthus sent his son to Warrington - roughly half-way between Liverpool and Manchester - we shall never know. His lifelong friend Bishop Otter remarked that Robert's character, when grown into maturity, bore few marks and signs 'of the scenes and persons to which he had been entrusted for the specific purposes of education'.[40] I am not so sure. Warrington may have given Malthus his dislike of what he called unwholesome manufactures, which was to bias his outlook as an economist for some years. It was a busy port, for ships of 70 or 80 tons could come up the Mersey, bringing, amongst other things, hemp from Russia, as about half the heavy sail-cloth used by the Navy was made in Warrington. There.

---

*In Scotland the position was different, and some English Dissenters received degrees from Scottish universities.

19

was an iron foundry and a sugar refinery, and workshops where locks and hinges were made; glass was manufactured there, and 'coarse linens and checks'. There was also an establishment for the manufacture of pins, so it is possible that Malthus saw for himself an example of Adam Smith's famous illustration of the division of labour.

John Aikin, MD (the son of one of the leading tutors of the Academy, John Aikin, DD),* described Warrington itself thus:

> The principal part of the town consists of four streets crossing at the centre, one of which runs directly from the bridge, and from its narrowness and mean buildings, gives but an unfavourable idea of the place to a stranger. But some of the other streets are much opener, and contain many good houses interspersed, the usual effect of commercial opulence rising in a place of antiquity. It has the common fault of being most straightened at the centre; a great inconvenience to a town which is one of the principal thoroughfares to the north.[41]

But if the town was unattractive, the Academy seems to have been a happy and lively place for many of the twenty-nine years of its existence. Joseph Priestley was a tutor for six years; it was there that he completed his *History of Electricity* in 1767, and in 1768 his *Essay on Government*, which contained that notable phrase 'the greatest happiness of the greatest number'; his discovery of oxygen came after he had left the Academy, in 1774. Gilbert Wakefield became classical tutor at Warrington because he could find nowhere else to go. The son of a clergyman, he became a Scholar of Jesus College, Cambridge, at the age of sixteen, and then Second Wrangler and one of the Chancellor's Medallists (the highest honour for classics) at the age of twenty. He was immediately made a Fellow of his college, and in 1778, when he was twenty-two, he was ordained deacon, and held curacies in Stockport and Liverpool. Most unfortunately for himself, he studied theology and became a Unitarian, although he was never attached to any specific dissenting sect - in fact, he disapproved of public or social worship altogether. His nonconformity, naturally, meant that he could get no living from the church, and he forfeited his fellowship through marriage in 1779.

In his *Memoirs*, Wakefield wrote of Warrington Academy, 'I pronounced the speedy downfall of this establishment soon after my arrival there.' He lists among his reasons 'the want of an established fund, secure from fortune and caprice', pointing out that they were bound to suffer from 'the death, sickness or declining zeal of subscribers, always more active in the *infancy*

---

*The Doctorate in Divinity was conferred on John Aikin the Elder, without notice, by the King's College, Aberdeen, in 1774. John Aikin the Younger, although he studied medicine for some time in Edinburgh, took his degree in 1784 at Leyden, in Latin.

of a scheme'. He also mentions 'the incapacity of preserving proper discipline from the untowardness of the situation and injudicious structure of the buildings'. However, he records that the trustees' behaviour to him 'was liberal and respectful on all occasions, worthy of gentlemen and dissenters'.[42]

I cannot find out to what extent Malthus was a member of the Academy, and how far he was a private pupil in Wakefield's household. Wakefield wrote to a friend of an arrangement with a young gentleman 'who attends some lectures at the Academy'. It is also confusing that both Lucy Aikin and her niece Mrs Le Breton speak as if Malthus had known John Aikin the Elder, although he died in 1780; it is possible that the family legend grew up through Malthus's having made some complimentary reference to the reputation of their grandfather and great-grandfather respectively. One of Lucy Aikin's brothers married Gilbert Wakefield's elder daughter, and we know that Malthus, ever a faithful friend, kept up the family connnection until his death.

It is exasperating that young Robert's letters home are lost: Dr Bonar tells us that he wrote to his father on 26 April 1782, which would appear to be the first in the series. According to Wakefield's *Memoirs*, Wakefield was 'fixt' in the autumn of 1783 at Bramcote, 'a most pleasant village within four miles of Nottingham on the Derby road'. He had written to all his friends ('real or pretended' - Wakefield's *Memoirs* are full of such animadversions) for recommendations to parents, but 'All my applications were answered only by a single pupil who had been a student under me at Warrington', which rather implies that Robert had gone home for a while and then travelled north again.[43]

Wakefield charged £100 a year, and liked his pupils to stay with him all the time, except for two months in the summer. In 1798 he wrote to a friend about his relationship with his young gentlemen:

> As every species of magisterial severity and distance is, and ever was, absolutely foreign to my thoughts, and inconsistent with my dispositions, an entire equality of association has ever taken place with all my pupils and my family, so that no more embarrassment as to any domestic enjoyment should attend them than if they were at home, and no affections prevail in me towards them but such as extend to my own children.
>
> On this account the whole family becomes moulded anew, and the same alteration takes place merely by the admission of one gentleman, as of half a dozen: nay, in some respects more; as the want of associates renders a much greater portion of friendly intercourse necessary to render their lives happy; without which no literary improvement can ever be expected to take place. Out of the intervals of study, therefore, I should neither expect nor wish a young gentleman to be insulated in his own room, but to have a free

21

communication with us all, as he finds agreeable, without any
hesitation or formality.

It is impossible not to speculate on how Robert regarded the household of
his tutor, who was but ten years older than himself, and often worried at
this period, as his letters show, by the illnesses of his little children.

His biographers point out that although Wakefield 'had a great dislike to
interruptions, especially in the morning, yet he never betrayed any incivility
or impatience when broken in upon by those who, perhaps, from their own
want of occupation, would intrude rather indiscreetly on his hours of study'.
In a paper entitled *Petty Moralities* Wakefield himself wrote, 'I never denied
myself to any visitor, of whatever rank or calling, on account of occupation,
or any other cause, to my knowledge, in all my life.'[44] Malthus was the
same. After his death his colleague Empson wrote of him: 'It is one of the
blessings of well-ordered natures to be always comparatively at leisure and
unconstrained. While [Mr. Malthus] was most deeply engaged in his philosophical speculations, he could pass at once from his study to his drawing
room with an elastic step and a placid countenance, to animate and share the
cheerfulness around him.'[45]

In another aspect of his character Malthus was not influenced by his tutor
at all. According to one of his descendants Wakefield was, 'in an age of
cock-fighting, bull-baiting, and almost universal indifference to the sufferings
of animals, so humane that he gave up fishing, of which he was exceedingly
fond, as well as shooting, because every form of cruelty was abhorrent to
him. He tried to persuade his friend, Charles James Fox, to do the same, but
was unsuccessful in the attempt.'[46] Malthus, like Fox, much enjoyed shooting
all his life.

How much of his liberal politics Malthus picked up from Wakefield is
a matter of conjecture. Robert wrote to his father on 16 March 1784: 'Mr.
Fox and his party have, it seems, at last given up the struggle, and by the
account of the papers Mr. Pitt is quite elated with his success. [He had just
gained a large majority in the general election, after three months of minority
government.] I really think he will ruin himself and will not be able to
stand it after all, for the rest of the Ministry have but very little ability. He
will never be so great a man as if he had shown a little more condescension
and less ambition. It appears ridiculous that so young a man should hold the
highest offices in the State.'

'Thank you for your politics,' his father replied on 5 April, 'but I am not
of your mind with regard to young ministers. They may have a little liberty
and a little of the fine enthusiasms caught from Athens, Lacedaemon, and
Rome, which Sir Robert Walpole used to say cost him a year or two to rid
some obstinate boys of. I am afraid that ... old men buy their political
experience with the loss of too many virtues.'

Robert answered on 15 April: 'I am by no means against young ministers,

22

but I think that general enthusiasm of youth which you mention is seldom found separated from a kind of modesty and diffidence in their own abilities. This, from the accounts I have always heard, seems to be by no means the case with young Pitt, who has taken upon himself the sole management of the State without any single person of any ability to associate in the arduous undertaking.' In the same letter he wrote: 'I think I shall never repent having been this little time at Bramcot before my going to college, for I have, if I am not deceived, got into a more steady and regular way of study.'[47]

Like other young gentlemen of eighteen, Robert sounds as if he could be insufferable at times, but the letters show a happy relationship between father and son. Of Robert's mother Bonar writes that 'only a few touches are recorded. She appears from the private letters to have been the oracle of the household in practical matters. There is one letter of Robert to her written on 11 December 1783, in which familiarity and affection and respect are properly blended. From a letter of Daniel to Robert (21 April 1784), it appears that she did not want Robert to go to either of the two great Universities. "I have myself" (adds his father) "a partiality for your taking degrees, and I prefer Cambridge." '[48]

Gilbert Wakefield seems to have made all the arrangements, and on 7 June 1784 he set out from Bramcote with his pupil, to enter him at his own old college, Jesus, as a pensioner (what is called at Oxford a commoner). After a brief stay in Cambridge, presumably at Jesus College, Wakefield returned to Nottingham, to combine domestic gentleness with bitter theological and academic controversy.[49] Robert, we imagine, went home for the long vacation.

'Home' at this period was Ferry House, at Cookham in Berkshire, on the river Thames. According to Eliza Berkeley, the daughter-in-law of the philosopher-bishop, Daniel Malthus had there become very fond of her son George, who was three years older than his own Robert. From her pathetic introduction to her posthumous collection of George's verse, it is possible to find out a little about the neighbourhood: some families, 'The polite Lord Conyngham's, the learned, accomplished Daniel Malthus's, the very sensible Thomas Forster's ... lived in the strictest harmony, perpetually meeting at each other's houses.' Mrs Malthus was in favour for having praised George's good looks, and he sent a sad poem to her when in the spring of 1781 he left Eton to go to the University of St Andrews. He wrote some equally conventional verses to the Misses Malthus, but the eldest seems to have been his idol, and on her death he composed an elegy which he had printed but 'never sold', although it is marked as costing 1s. 6d.

The Malthuses must surely sometimes have smiled at the Berkeleys behind their backs. Poor Eliza reminisced: 'It was a great diversion, when Mr. Berkeley was 17 or 18, to a lovely young lady [Henrietta Malthus] ... to wink on Mrs. Berkeley and say, "Aye, one day or other Berkeley will marry a girl with a hundred thousand pounds, and change his name to

Hickenbottom". . . . He used to storm, and say, "Harriet, hold your tongue: I will not change my name for a million." '[50]

When Henrietta Malthus died on 8 July 1785, George Monck Berkeley (1763-93) was about to be admitted a student of the Inner Temple. His elegy was dedicated to the surviving members of that 'truly amiable family of which Miss M —— was once a bright, a distinguished and a justly valued ornament'. According to this young man Henrietta, 'not satisfied with the attainment of every female excellence, and every human virtue, soared, on adventurous wing, into the regions of science and philosophy'. She was charitable, too, for the poet exhorts her father to look after her 'aged swains'.[51] Henrietta's niece, Louisa Bray, recalls her mother telling her that her eldest sister was 'very musical, and when they lived at Cookham on the Thames, they often went on the river, and she would sing the beautiful airs from the Messiah with only the accompaniment of a flute or guitar'.

It must have been a sad day when twenty-eight-year-old Henrietta was buried ('in Wool') at Harrow, like her Graham grandfather and great-grandfather. There seems no reason why this church should have been chosen unless she had been staying there before her death, possibly under the care of her uncle Richard Robert Graham, but this is conjecture. That she had been ill for a considerable time is indicated by some verses which her brother Robert is supposed to have written about her, beginning

> In pain and sickness tried, thou'st kissed the rod.
> Go, gentlest, purest spirit to thy God.[52]

So far as is known, the Malthuses had buried no other children.

Until this bereavement, the family circle sounds to have been both happy and enlightened, in spite of Daniel Malthus's eccentricities, or perhaps because of them; it is, of course, possible that outsiders like the Berkeleys were more conscious of his charm than his family were, and less affected by that 'imperative will' to which everything gave way. We would nowadays praise Daniel Malthus for his choice of schoolmasters for his gifted but severely handicapped son, so it is interesting to find a very different opinion expressed by a much younger man who only knew Robert Malthus for the last ten years of his life - William Empson (1791-1852). Empson was a Winchester man, and a school-fellow of Thomas Arnold, the famous headmaster of Rugby, with whose educational views he was in complete agreement.

Thus we find Empson, in 1837, writing disparagingly in the *Edinburgh Review* about 'the successive roofs of Richard Graves, the Warrington Academy, and Gilbert Wakefield'. Empson rejoiced that neither upon the surface of Malthus's mind

> nor in its depths was there anything to be perceived of the schools in
> which he had been brought up - nothing either of the wayward

father or the eccentric novelist, of the scrupulous nonconformist or the presumptuous polemic. Difficulties which would be ruinous to an ordinary disposition, may accordingly have been serviceable in the strengthening and perfecting of his. The early habit of having to think and decide for himself, would force on him a steadiness beyond his years. While the necessity, in which he was often placed, of differing from those whom he otherwise regarded with affection and esteem, doubtless contributed essentially to that combination of universal kindliness towards others, with strict personal self-respect, which met so happily in his character.[53]

Daniel Malthus could hardly have been better rewarded.

4 Cambridge

Robert Malthus arrived at Jesus College on 3 November 1784. His first concern would have been with furniture; we know from his friend Clarke that some of the beds in Jesus were 'not half long enough', and that it was important to make sure there were plenty of candlesticks.[54] Robert wrote home to his father on 14 November:

> I am now pretty well settled in my rooms. The lectures begin tomorrow; and, as I had time last week to look over my mathematics a little, I was, upon examination yesterday, found prepared to read with the year above me, though I believe I shall attend a few lectures at the same time with those of my own year. We begin with mechanics and Maclaurin, Newton, and Keill's *Physics*. We shall also have lectures on Mondays and Fridays in Duncan's *Logick*, and in Tacitus's *Life of Agricola* on Wednesdays and Saturdays. I have subscribed to a bookseller who has supplied me with all the books necessary. We have some clever men at college, and I think it seems rather the fashion to read. The chief study is mathematics, for all honour in taking a degree depends upon that Science, and the great aim of most of the men is to take an honourable degree. At the same time I believe we have some good classics. I am acquainted with two, one of them of this year, who is indeed an exceedingly clever man and will stand a very good chance for the classical prize if he does not neglect himself – I have read in chapel twice. It seems that it is the custom when the readers are absent that the two juniors should read the lessons, and I believe I am the junior of my year.[55]

All this sounds rather solemn, but there were other sides to Robert's career as an undergraduate. To begin with the most important: while he was at Cambridge he made four lifelong friends. Chief among these was William Otter of Jesus (1768-1840), who had also been educated by tutors, the son of a country clergyman who had parishes in Nottinghamshire and Derbyshire. Otter in due course became Bishop of Chichester and founded a teachers' training college, but we are particularly indebted to him for his *Memoir* of his celebrated friend; it was published in 1836 as a sort of preface to the posthumous second edition of Malthus's *Principles of Political Economy*.

Edward Daniel Clarke (1769-1822), known as Ned, another Jesus man, was also the son of a country clergyman. His father and grandfather had both been antiquaries of some note. Clarke had been to the Grammar School at Tonbridge, and in 1812 he wrote to Otter that he did not think anyone educated privately had been truly popular at the University: a belief hardly supported by the facts, but in due course the young Clarkes went to Eton and the young Otters to Rugby.

The other two men, who were close friends with each other although they were at different colleges, were John Whishaw (1764-1840) and William Smyth (1765-1849). Whishaw was from a well-to-do Cheshire family, and came up to Trinity College from Macclesfield Grammar School intending to go into the church; but the loss of a leg while he was at Cambridge made him 'canonically ineligible to the service of the altar' - he was not 'a whole man' - so he entered Gray's Inn in 1789, to be called to the Bar in 1794. Smyth, of Peterhouse, was the Etonian son of a Liverpool banker, and later became Professor of Modern History. Malthus seems to have known this pair of friends quite separately from the other pair, Otter and Clarke.

Since we shall follow the lives of these four men as we follow Malthus's, I need say no more about them here, except to mention Ned Clarke's balloon. It was sent up with great éclat from the lovely Cloister Court of Jesus, bearing a kitten in the basket: 'This balloon,' wrote Otter, 'magnificent in its size and splendid in its decorations, was constructed and manoeuvred, from first to last, entirely by himself.'[56] Malthus did nothing so dramatic, although according to his niece Louisa Bray he was extremely avant-garde in his hair-dressing. She heard that when he was an undergraduate 'he let his fair hair, which curled naturally, hang in ringlets on his neck, which in those days of powder and pig-tails must have looked singular.' Henry Gunning (1768-1854) observed in his invaluable *Reminiscences* that at this period in Cambridge 'All men wore powder, and many were the degrees of whiteness; I can well remember several who used it of a pink shade.'[57] Some ten years later, when George Pryme went up (he was to become the University's first Professor of Political Economy) the scene had changed: 'There were two or three undergraduates who wore powder ... The rest

26

of us wore our hair curled. It was thought very rustic and unfashionable not to have it so.'[58] Thus in some small matters, as well as great ones, Malthus was in advance of his age.

Otter did not describe Robert's personal appearance, but he had this to say about him:

> At this time, he was generally distinguished for gentlemanlike deportment and feelings, a polished humanity which remained with him through life, and a degree of temperance and prudence, very rare at that period, and carried by him even into his academical pursuits. In these he was always more remarkable for the steadiness than for the ardour of his application, preferring to exert his mind equally in the various departments of literature then cultivated in the college, rather than to devote it exclusively or eminently to any one, and evidently actuated more by the love of excellence than by the desire of excelling. For this happy disposition he seems to have been indebted next to his own gracious nature to the peculiar character of his education, which while it had employed higher motives with good effect, had rarely brought into action the principle of competition, so generally resorted to in colleges and schools; and the consequence was that he read in a better spirit, reflected more freely and more usefully and acquired more general information than any of his contemporaries.

Otter then went on with a little essay on the general necessity of competition in education, as 'a natural remedy for the natural evils of our youth, indolence and the love of pleasure'.[59]

In spite of his gentlemanlike deportment, Malthus seems to have been a buffoon on occasion. He had 'fitful bursts of fancy, which were wont to set the table in a roar'; his taste for humour, 'set off as it used to be by a very comic expression of features, and a most peculiar intonation of voice when he was in the vein, were often a source of infinite delight and pleasantry to his companions'. Again according to Otter, Malthus 'found sufficient time for the cultivation of history and general literature, particularly of poetry, of which he was always a great admirer and discerning judge'. He 'obtained prizes for declamations in Latin and English', which is unexpected, in view of his disability.[60]

Robert's general physical health was always good, although he apparently suffered from rheumatism during the winter of 1785-6. In a letter his father admonished him: 'Don't say *rhumatism*, but consider the derivation, and that no man should have a disorder which he can't spell, especially a man of Jesus.' Malthus was to be bad at spelling all his life.[61]

The attack of rheumatism occurred when Robert stayed for several inclement months continuously in Cambridge, as he did not go home for the Christmas vacation of 1785 - the family's first Christmas without Henrietta. His father sent him a long letter on 13 January 1786:

My dear Bob,

I find you are not yet in your new rooms. I heartily hope they will prove agreeable to you. We should have been truly glad to have seen you here in the leisure of Christmas, and would have subscribed to your journey; not that I used to think Oxford the less pleasant, and certainly not the less useful for being disburthened of some of its society: I imagine you will say the same of Cambridge.

I have always found that one of my greatest comforts in life was the delight I have ever taken in solitude - if, indeed, one can give that name to anything which is likely to happen to you or me. A true hermitage for any length of time is, I believe, an unnatural state; it would be a cruel deprivation of what we have both experienced to be the heart's dearest happiness. But even this at certain seasons will strengthen and refresh the mind, and suffer her wings to grow which

> In the various bustle of resort
> Were all too ruffled and sometimes impair'd.

The skating has been good this year. Did you go to Ely? By the way have you learnt the heart and cross roll? All the other tricks, such as skating backwards, &c. are absurd; but I like these as they amuse one upon a small piece of ice . . . The frost was harder than usual in England. January 2, at sunrise, 14 Fahr. January 3, at 9½ post merid 14 again. Ask Mr. — — how it was at Cambridge. My thermometer was upon a north wall at a distance from the house.

Did not I ask whether you had got my Theocritus with you? Have you got Rutherford's Philosophy, 2 vols. quarto? I would advise you to read something of that kind, while you are engaged in mathematical studies; and constantly to use yourself to apply your tools. I hate to see a girl working curious stitches upon a rag. [This may be a reference to Jane Dalton's embroidery, so much admired by Richard Graves. Jane Dalton's bookplate was a representation of an elaborately scalloped handkerchief, diamond shaped, with a coarse darn in the middle.]

I recommend Sanderson's Optics to you, and Emerson's Mechanics; Long's Astronomy you certainly have. There are papers of the mathematical kind in the Royal Society transactions which are generally worth reading. How do you manage about books? What good book on mensuration have you met with? Have you seen Bongner's mensuration of the degree in South America? I suppose Sir I's Principia to be your chief classical book after the elementary ones.

We are all pretty well; but Charlotte will write in a day or two. All send love. Adieu, my dear boy!

D.M.

Malthus kept all his life the copy of Sir Isaac Newton's *Philosophiae Naturalis Principia Mathematica*, which he bought second-hand, splendidly bound and embossed with his college arms. Few of us nowadays would take in our stride a scientific treatise in Latin, but this copy of the 1726 edition has been well used. Young Bob replied to his father very firmly:

The plan of mathematical and philosophical reading pursued at Cambridge is perhaps too much confined to speculation; the intention seems to be to ground you well in the principles, supposing you to apply them at leisure after your degree. In going through this course of study, if I read popular treatises upon every branch, it will take up my whole time, and absolutely exclude all other kinds of reading whatever, which I should by no means wish. I think therefore it will be better for me to pursue the general course adopted by the university, seeing the general application of everything I read without always descending to particulars.

When I mentioned popular treatises I did not mean to refer to the books you recommended in your last letter, but to what you said in a former one, expressing a wish to see me a practical surveyor, mechanic, and navigator; a knowledge of which kind would be difficult to obtain before I took my degree, while engaged in the plan of mathematical reading adopted by the university.

I am by no means, however, inclined to get forward without wishing to see the use and application of what I read. On the contrary I am rather remarked in college for talking of what actually exists in nature, or may be put to real practical use. With regard to the books you mentioned in your last, as it is absolutely necessary to read those which our lecturer makes use of, it is difficult to find time to apply to other tracts of the same nature, in the regular manner they deserve: particularly as many other books are required to be read during our course of lectures to be able to understand them as we ought. For instance, we have had no lectures of any consequence in algebra and fluxions, and yet a man would find himself very deficient in going through the branches of natural philosophy and Newton's Principia, without a decent knowledge of both. As I attended lectures with the year above me, and the course only continues three years, I shall be entirely my own master after the next summer vacation, and then will be my time to read different authors, make comparisons, and properly digest the knowledge I have taken in.

I believe from what I have let fall at different times, you have conceived the Senate House examination to be more confined to mathematical speculations than it really is. The greatest stress is laid on a thorough knowledge of the branches of natural philosophy, and problems of every kind in these as well as in mathematics are set during the examination; such a one as the ascertaining the distance of the Sun by a transit of Venus is not unlikely sometimes to be among the number.

If you will give me leave to proceed in my own plans of reading for the next two years, (I speak with submission to your judgment), I promise you at the expiration of that time to be a decent natural philosopher, and not only to know a few principles, but to be able to apply those principles in a variety of useful problems. I hope you will excuse me for detaining you so long upon this subject, but I thought I had not sufficiently explained myself in my last letter, and that you might possibly conclude from what I there said, that I intended to go on in the beaten track, without once reflecting on the use and application of the study in which I was engaged.[62]

These letters, quoted by Otter, speak for themselves. Possibly on account of his vacation work, Robert Malthus was made an Exhibitioner of his college in 1786: an exhibition at Oxford or Cambridge is an award lower than a scholarship, but for either to be conferred by the authorities in the course of an undergraduate's career is an honour worth having. It was in the spring of this year that Bob sent a letter to his father about his future; Bonar maintains that he had wanted to go into the church 'long before Cambridge', but he gives no reference for this statement. In any case, it was after a discussion with the Master of Jesus, Dr Beadon, that Robert wrote on 19 April 1786:

He seemed at first to advise against orders, upon the idea that the defect in my speech would be an obstacle to my rising in the Church, and he thought it a pity that a young man of some abilities should enter a profession without at least some hope of being at the top of it. When, however, I afterwards told him that the utmost of my wishes was a retired living in the country, he said he did not imagine that my speech would be much objection in that case, that, for his own part, when I read or declaimed in chapel he scarcely ever lost a single word. As to the business of getting into orders, he did not conceive there was any legal objection, but the bishops had it so entirely in their power to ordain whom they pleased that it was impossible to say how they would act; he thought there were some who might refuse, but that the generality would not.[63]

There is no evidence as to what Daniel Malthus thought about his son's decision, but it would have been very different from the views of an unorthodox parent today. In the eighteenth century at least one of the younger sons of a good family went into the church almost as a matter of course.

As was the custom of the time, Malthus did not have his final examination until January 1788, so that in 1787 he could enjoy his third Cambridge summer. His father wrote to him on 16 June:

> May I take the liberty of sending my compliments to Mr. Frend, with my most grateful thanks for the attention he has been so kind as to show you. You will guess the pleasure I have in returning thanks for that notice which you would not have had without deserving it.
>
> Everything I have heard of you has given me the most heartfelt satisfaction. I have always wished, my dear boy, that you should have a love of letters, that you should be made independent of mean and trifling amusements, and feel a better support than that of the next man who is idle enough to offer you his company. I have no doubt that you will be able to procure any distinction from them you please. I am far from repressing your ambition; but I shall content myself with their adding to your happiness. Every kind of knowledge, every acquaintance with nature and art, will amuse and strengthen your mind, and I am perfectly pleased that cricket should do the same by your legs and arms. I love to see you excel in exercises of the body, and I think myself that the better half, and much the most agreeable one, of the pleasures of the mind is best enjoyed while one is upon one's legs; - this is pretty well for me to say, who have little else left but my bed and my arm-chair. [He was fifty-seven.] May you long enjoy all the delights of youth and youthful spirits, of an improving mind, and of a healthful body, but ever and above all, my dear boy, with virtue and its best affections in your heart. Adieu![64]

The Mr Frend mentioned in this letter was William Frend (1757-1841), Robert's tutor at Jesus. Had he not still been alive when Empson criticised Malthus's teachers in his *Edinburgh Review* article, some harsh things might have been said about him too. William Frend was a year younger than Gilbert Wakefield; he had, like him, been Second Wrangler, taken orders, and become a Fellow of Jesus, although he had been at Christ's as an undergraduate; there his tutor had been that great Anglican William Paley (1743-1805). In addition to his fellowship, Frend was also given the living of Madingley, so that a competence and a career in the church were available to him against the time when he should marry and have to resign from his college. This Frend renounced in the summer of 1787, in a moving declaration which his pupils must have read:

> Whereas I, William Frend, did at several times, within the years 1780 and 1784, subscribe to the articles and doctrines of the church

of England, as by law established, being now convinced, by an attentive study of the holy scriptures, that many things contained in the said articles, have no foundation whatever in the holy scriptures, I do hereby declare my disbelief of many of the said articles and doctrines, particularly of the second, the fifth, and the eighth articles of that summary of faith, commonly called the thirty-nine Articles: and whereas from November 1780, till June 1787, I did officiate as a minister of the church of England, I do moreover declare, that there are many parts of its liturgy, to which I have insuperable objections, particularly to the prayers addressed to Jesus Christ, and to the Trinity; and as universal benevolence seems to be the striking character of the religion of Jesus Christ, I cannot conclude this declaration, without expressing my abhorrence of a tenet inculcated in one part of the said service, by which every person differing in opinion, as to some obscure points of an obscure creed, is doomed to everlasting perdition.[65]

Jesus College was to be proud of Frend, nearly two centuries later, as one of its famous Unitarians; but at this period Malthus's tutor must have been extremely unhappy. He followed up his declaration of disbelief with a pamphlet against the University's insistence on subscription to the Thirty-nine Articles, and on the treatment of Nonconformists in England generally. We know that full religious toleration, for both Roman Catholics and Protestant Dissenters, was one of the firmest tenets of Malthus's life, and it is impossible not to speculate on how he felt at this time about the position of the Church of England. My own guess is that Malthus was more or less in agreement with Archdeacon Paley: it is certain that he admired Paley's *Principles of Moral and Political Philosophy*, which appeared in 1785, and was much gratified to learn later that Paley had been converted to his theory of population.

Paley's attitude to the Thirty-nine Articles was well summed up by his biographer, G. W. Meadley:

The Articles of Religion [Paley] treated of as mere articles of peace, the whole of which it was impossible the framers could expect any one person to believe, as upon dissection they would be found to contain about two hundred and forty distinct and different propositions, many of them inconsistent with each other. They must therefore, he said, be considered as propositions, which, for the sake of keeping peace amongst the different sects of reformers, who originally united in composing the church of England, it was agreed should not be impugned or preached against.[66]

There is, I must stress, no evidence; but it seems likely that Malthus would have accepted this opinion. We shall see later that he did in fact share

Frend's abhorrence of the idea of everlasting perdition.

Whatever his views may have been, the young Robert duly went to the Proctor to pay his examination fees, and then to the Registry to subscribe to the Thirty-nine Articles. From the four-day ordeal which followed, he emerged with credit as Ninth Wrangler, the only Jesus man among the Wranglers. It should perhaps be explained that this extraordinary title for outstanding Cambridge mathematicians owes its origin to the fact that part of the examination consisted in 'Keeping an act', which meant a public argument defending a prescribed thesis, that is, 'wrangling'. It was a severe test, considered the hardest in Europe, and Pryme reminds us that 'the Senate House was not then artificially warmed'.

Henry Gunning, writing in about 1851, began his chapter on 1788 thus:

> On the 18th of January, we were admitted *ad respondendum quaestioni*. The admission of the Bachelors took place without the least interruption. Our University at that time prided itself that in this respect our practice was diametrically opposite to that of our sister University, at which on all public occasions the entrance of the University officers, and of persons distinguished by their rank and station, was greeted either by shouts of applause, or by hissing and hootings. Sorry am I to observe that for many years past the conduct of our undergraduates has become more outrageous than that of the Oxonians. It has not unfrequently happened that the Proctors have been obliged to clear the galleries entirely, and it *has* happened that the Vice-Chancellor has been under the necessity of adjourning the proceedings; for not only have the University authorities whose conduct has been thought to be marked by harshness and severity, been hissed and hooted, but even private individuals, whose supposed opinions (whether political or religious) were disagreeable to the majority, have been received with marked insult. On this account the election of Vice-Chancellor, which used to take place in the afternoon, is now constantly completed at an early hour in the morning. After admission to their degrees, the Bachelors generally assembled in large parties to dinner, when everybody was obliged to swallow a considerable quantity of bad wine.[67]

Malthus apparently stayed up at college after the jollifications to prepare for ordination and do some general reading. He wrote to his father on 17 April 1788:

> I have laid aside my chemistry for a while and am at present endeavouring to get some knowledge of general history and geography. I have been lately reading Gibbon's *Decline of the Roman Empire*. He gives one some useful information concerning the origin and progress of those nations of barbarians which now form the

polished states of Europe, and throws some light upon the beginning
of that dark period which so long overwhelmed the world, and
which cannot, I think, but excite one's curiosity. He is a very
entertaining writer in my opinion; his style is sometimes really
sublime, everywhere interesting and agreeable, though perhaps it may
in general be called rather too florid for history. I shall like much to
see his next volumes.[68]

They were published a few weeks later. Sometime that year Robert Malthus,
Esquire, became the Rev. Robert Malthus, and then, for a decade, we seem
to lose him. It was a decade of much drama, in this history of the world and
in the lives of Malthus's family and friends, but of his own doings, between
the ages of twenty-two and thirty-two, we know almost nothing.

5 Albury and Shere

From 1787 until 1939 the village of Albury, in Surrey, was to be the
headquarters of the Malthus family. One wonders whether Mr and Mrs
Daniel Malthus intended to establish themselves here permanently at last,
or whether they had always meant to settle down in each new home they
tried. Henrietta's death in 1785 had been followed by a year of anxiety over
their youngest child, Mary Anne Catherine, who was 'supposed to be going
into a decline, and for a whole year lived on vegetable diet, and was bled
every month, but she recovered entirely to go through fatigues few constitutions could have borne', dying at the age of eighty-one.[69] Some of her
descendants still live in Albury and the neighbouring parish of Shere.[70]

We know that in addition to the estate in Essex purchased by his
grandfather, Daniel Malthus owned land in Hertfordshire and Cambridgeshire; but Surrey then, as now, was the favourite county of the well-to-do
who wished to be within easy reach of London.

Daniel's nephew John Eckersall (whose parents had settled near Leatherhead) had married Daniel's Dorking niece Catherine Wathen, in 1774,
and built himself a house called Burford Lodge, near Box Hill, in the same
part of Surrey. John Eckersall had gone up to Christ Church from Westminster School in 1766, and took his BA in 1770, the year his father died.
He made the Grand Tour in some style, with the Hon. John Trevor, also
of Christ Church, and like so many Englishmen he was painted in Rome
by Pompeo Batoni. The portrait, three-quarter length, his head turned to
his right, shows him rather unflatteringly: he looks too fat for a man of
twenty-five, his lips are too much of a Cupid's bow; one is reminded of Jane

Austen's immortal phrase 'a strong, natural, sterling insignificance', which it were utterly false to apply to the truly delightful old gentleman into which John Eckersall developed after he had had eleven children.[71]

Catherine Wathen, soon after she became Catherine Eckersall, was painted by Reynolds; sittings began in 1775, stopped some time before the birth of her daughter Harriet (on 1 May 1776, at St James's Square, London) and were resumed again afterwards. It is a lovely picture in the traditional grand manner, half length, with the bride's hair piled and coiled, ermine at her neck, a flower at her waist, the pensive left profile resting on her hand, a hint of a windswept tree in the background. We can well believe that Catherine had a beautiful voice and played the harp; it is harder to visualise her as the happy and lively matriarch she was later to become.[72]

We do not know whether a visit to the older Wathens or the younger Eckersalls inspired the Malthuses to return to Surrey; we do know that in 1786, on Friday 10 October - a cloudy day - William Bray met Mr Malthus at Albury Park. The house was then owned by Captain (later Admiral) Finch, and the Rector of Albury, Mr Polhill, was the third visitor.

We know this from William Bray's diaries, never published in full, and one of the treasures of Guildford Muniment Room.[73] They are little more than engagement books, but a most useful source for Malthus's biographer, since Bray did not die until 1832, at the age of ninety-six. The Brays had been the principal family in Shere since Tudor times; we must distinguish between the Brays, who were 'landed', and the Malthuses, who bought land in different parts of the country for investment. William Bray, being a younger son, became a lawyer, with his headquarters in London, in Great Russell Street; by the time he inherited the Surrey estate from his elder brother George, a bachelor clergyman, he was far too immersed in his practice to give it up. His activity was remarkable, for in addition to a large legal practice, which involved incessant travelling - on horseback as well as by chaise and coach - he wrote the major part of Manning and Bray's *History of Surrey*. According to his granddaughter Louisa he was 'a cold dry man', but it is impossible to read his diaries without admiring his energy and sympathising with his intense grief at the deaths of his children and grandchildren - grief perhaps the more intense because he was unable to express his affection for them while they lived.

Possibly William Bray arranged for the purchase by Daniel Malthus of 'Captain Schaw's house'. The descendants of both these men (keen local historians) have not been able to identify the site, but it was in that part of Albury which belonged to the parish of Shere.

Whatever his religious views, a parish document, dated 28 September 1787, shows that Daniel Malthus rented seats in Shere church appropriate to his position. His 'Maid Servants' apparently needed more than one row: some sit behind those of George Bray, of Tower Hill, and others with those of Mr Duncomb the Rector, just in front of the row allotted to 'Women and Children' from the establishment of Edmund Lomax, Esq., of Netley Place. Behind these 'Mr. Maltiss at Weston' has another row of seats, presumably for his men-servants. There is no doubt but that the Malthuses were people of substance.

The village of Albury itself has completely changed since Malthus's time. What he knew as Albury church was closed in 1841, and stands now among the beeches in the grounds of Albury Park, quite close to the house. When the Malthus family first came to this attractive place, Captain Finch had done no more than take off a corner of the churchyard and put it into his garden. He had become wealthy through capturing 'a rich Spanish ship' during the American War of Independence, and died suddenly in 1794.

The next owner of Albury Park was Samuel Thornton (1755-1838), of the well-known Yorkshire family 'in the Russian trade', members of the Clapham Sect of prosperous Evangelicals. Samuel Thornton was a director of the Bank of England and a Member of Parliament; his brother Henry disapproved of his buying Albury Park and trying to pretend they were not 'all City people and connected with merchants, and nothing but merchants on every side'.[74] But Louisa Bray wrote that they were 'a most amiable and agreeable family, and no-one who has lived there since, has appeared to enjoy the place so much, or opened it so freely for the enjoyment of others'.

It would appear that the Malthus family moved to Albury in the early summer of 1787, for Daniel wrote to Robert on 16 June: 'You must find your way to us over bricks and tiles, and meet with five in a bed, and some of us under hedges; but everybody says, they will make room for Robert.'[75]

By Saturday 25 August (which was 'fair, cloudy, showery, windy') they were sufficiently established for William Bray to drink tea with them on his way back to Shere after dining in Guildford. The following Tuesday 'Mr. R. Malthus' and an unknown number of 'Miss Malthus's' drank tea with Mr and Mrs William Bray, and presumably met - if they did not know them already - their son Edward and their three daughters, Catherine, Mary, and Caroline (who was to die some two years later).

Possibly through the Brays the Malthuses met the Godschalls, another well-established family. William Man Godschall, LLD, FRS, was a learned old gentleman and a Justice of the Peace; most unfortunately, we only have his diary for the last eighteen months of his life. His only surviving child, Samuel, was a clergyman; after being at 'the Rev. Mr. Gilpin's, Cheam School, near Croydon', he went up to Cambridge, to Trinity Hall; he was ordained, like Robert Malthus, in 1788.

The Malthuses quickly became connected by marriage with both the Godschalls and the Brays. The Godschalls lived in the parish of Albury, so presumably that was why it was in Albury church that Samuel Godschall was married to Lucy Malthus on 10 August 1789. She would have been nearly twenty-seven, and her husband had celebrated his twenty-fifth birthday a week before, on 2 August. Louisa Bray's description of this couple is naturally a child's eye view (she was not born until 1800), and she would not have known what they were like when they were first married, but I give her account of them here, since it is all we have:

> Aunt Godschall was dark, but must have been very attractive when young. I have seldom met with any women of more cultivated minds and pleasing manners than my Aunts. Aunt Godschall was from her position, the more of a woman of the world, and had the talent of conversation, by no means common even among men of education, and rare in ladies, who are more apt to talk than *converse*!
>
> [Her husband] was descended from the Godschalls by his Mother (Mr. Mann having taken the name on his marriage with Miss Godschall) and by the death of his elder brother became heir to the extensive property of Weston with its beautiful woods, heaths, and dells. He had a more than ordinary share of abilities, a good memory, and had read much of general literature, and poetry for which he had a great taste; a naturally feeling heart, much sensibility, a great admirer of the beauties of Nature; romantic and imaginative in a high degree, and remarkably graceful high-bred manners – yet, with all this he had neither religious nor moral principles, and a temper over which he had no control. He truly loved and respected my Aunt, who made him an inestimable wife, but he must have given her many a heartache. He was very fond of my 3 elder brothers, and treated us all with the utmost kindness and affection, yet I invariably shrank from him as a girl, without knowing why. The depression that affected his spirits in his latter days, was painful to witness. With him ended the Godschall family.

Louisa Bray may not have known that her Uncle Samuel left an illegitimate son, for whom provision was made in his will, of which his wife was the sole executrix.[76]

The second Malthus wedding took place at Shere church, when Mary Anne Catherine, who was only nineteen, married Edward Bray, who was twenty-two and, like his father, a lawyer. The wedding was on Tuesday 28 September 1790, and the Malthuses' first grandchild was born in February 1792. This baby, Reginald, died in his fourth year, which (according to her daughter) made young Mrs Bray 'an anxious mother'. His birth had been rapidly followed by those of Edward and Henrietta, and he was replaced by another Reginald in 1797, who lived to carry on both the family and the firm. By the time her brother wrote his *Essay on Population*, Mary Anne Catherine had already borne four children.

We do not know what Robert thought of his supposedly delicate little sister's marriage, to a man two years younger than himself, but we are told by Edward Bray's daughter Louisa that he 'was a handsome man, gentle and gentlemanlike in his manners and of a very affectionate disposition. As a lawyer he was equally respected for his talents and highly honourable principles.' Edward sounds the most agreeable member of the family, for according to Louisa, 'My two Aunts Bray were so unlike Mama in education and habits, that there could not be any real intimacy between them'; in another place she says that they were 'uncongenial and unsympathetic to Mama, but she had her own kind brothers and sisters'.

She was to need them, for in 1814 Mrs Bray was left a widow with nine surviving children (she had eleven in all), 'the eldest not 21, the youngest 3 years ... with an income scarcely sufficient to keep her large family with the strictest economy. Many would have been overwhelmed in such a case, but it only roused her energies.' Louisa Bray adored her mother, yet it is possible that there is some truth in her panegyric, for it sounds very similar to what innumerable people have said about Robert Malthus. Like him Mrs Bray was painted by Linnell in her old age, left three-quarter-face, so that it is a companion portrait to that of Malthus, and the resemblance between the brother and sister is very marked. There is something about Mrs Bray's portrait which makes one understand why a descendant wanted to call her own daughter Mary Anne Catherine.[77] Louisa wrote of her Uncle Robert, 'He, like Mama, was loved by everyone who knew him,' and both seem to have had that quality, deeper than what is called charm, which made them keep their good looks all through life.

According to Louisa, no servant, whether good or bad, ever left Mrs Bray without regret, 'though this was not from indiscriminate indulgence, for she required to be obeyed, and was always treated with respect. The poor were particularly charmed by her kindness. She did not sit in judgment on their faults, forgetting, as many do, that they have much more excuse for theirs than the educated and upper classes have for faults which may differ in kind because the temptations differ, but are equally wrong. When Mama lived in London, she frequently made friends with street beggars, and always found her kindness appreciated.' In one way she differed from her younger brother, for 'To go without her dinner was a matter of perfect indifference, if circumstances made it convenient to do so'; we know from his travel diaries that Malthus (like most men) needed his meals at regular intervals.

Louisa, naturally, had less to say about the rest of the family. There were two unmarried Malthus aunts. Charlotte 'was not handsome, but had a pleasing countenance, pretty figure and lively manners, which made her a general favourite'. Eliza Maria, the eldest sister after Henrietta's death, 'was faultlessly handsome in face and figure, with a beautiful fair complexion'; later her niece writes of her: 'She was a truly excellent person, and her death was peaceful and happy. Devoted in her attachments there was nothing she would not or did not do for Mama that was in her power. Her temper was warm, and always intent on doing what was right and reasonable herself, she had not perhaps much patience with the faults and follies of others; but

38

her indignation subsided as quickly as it was roused, and in action she was invariably kind.'

Sydenham, the elder son and heir, seems less marked in character than the younger Malthuses, but when he died Robert wrote of him as a brother he 'tenderly loved' and Mary Anne Catherine had hysterics; it was the only time her daughter had seen her 'quite overcome by her feelings'. Sydenham, after the Napoleonic Wars, lived much abroad; he gave his younger brother power of attorney to manage his affairs, and very tiresome they sometimes were, for Sydenham had six step-children as well as four surviving children of his own; there was also a 'natural daughter, Mary Walker', who received £30 a year under his will in accordance with the terms of her marriage settlement; Mary's mother was left £8 a year.[78]

Although he did not marry until 1799, which is outside the decade we are considering, it might be as well to give an account of Sydenham's wife now, since her affairs would have been worrying the family throughout the 1780s and '90s. She was born Marianna Georgina Ryves, and was the daughter of Mrs Malthus's younger sister, Anna Maria - the little girl in white in Hogarth's picture of the Graham children. Georgina was born six months after her cousin Robert, on 25 August 1766, and in 1783, at the age of seventeen, she ran away with William Leigh Symes, who was the same age as herself; after they were married he 'behaved ill to her, spent all his fortune', according to Louisa Bray. They had three sons and three daughters who survived infancy; the youngest child, George Frederick, was born in 1794, a year before his father's death in Jamaica.[79]

We do not know what Daniel Malthus and his wife thought about the affair, when their forty-five-year-old son decided to marry this much encumbered widow, but Mrs Ryves must surely have felt relieved. What we do know, with hindsight, is that all this family background - if 'background' be the appropriate word - was to be of supreme importance to the warm-hearted Robert, of whom his niece wrote that 'in private life few could equal him'.

CHAPTER II

The Principle of Population

1 The Curate of Okewood

During Robert Malthus's fallow decade, from 1788 to 1798, we can pinpoint little except for two events in the year 1793. On 10 June his college made him a Fellow: this was not simply an honour, it provided him with a small income, without any obligations, as long as he remained unmarried. At about the same time, he was appointed perpetual curate of Okewood, a chapel of ease at the southernmost tip of the parish of Wotton in which he was born. Okewood became an ecclesiastical parish in 1853, but before that date the remote little church was not licensed for marriages, and the curate was not instituted or inducted, merely nominated by the patron who had the gift of the rectory of Wotton - the illustrious Evelyn family. Daniel Malthus refers to both these landmarks in his son's life in the following letter, beginning with the fellowship:

> I heartily congratulate upon your success; it gives me a sort of
> pleasure which arises from my own regrets. The things which I have
> missed in life, I should the more sensibly wish for you.
>   Alas! my dear Bob, I have no right to talk to you of idleness, but
> when I wrote that letter to you with which you were displeased, I
> was deeply impressed with my own broken purposes and imperfect
> pursuits; I thought I foresaw in you, from the memory of my own
> youth, the same tendency to lose the steps you had gained, with the
> same disposition to self reproach, and I wished to make my
> unfortunate experience of some use to you. It was indeed, but little
> that you wanted it, which made me the more eager to give it you,
> and I wrote to you with more tenderness of heart than I would in
> general pretend to, and committed myself in a certain manner which
> made your answer a rough disappointment to me, and it drove me
> back into myself. You have, as you say, worn out that impression,
> and you have a good right to have done it; for I have seen in you the
> most unexceptionable character, the sweetest manners, the most
> sensible and the kindest conduct, always above *throwing little stones*

40

into my garden, which you know I don't easily forgive, and
uniformly making every body easy and amused about you. Nothing
can have been wanting to what, if I were the most fretful and
fastidious, I could have required in a companion; and nothing even to
my wishes for your happiness, but where they were either
whimsical, or unreasonable, or most likely mistaken. I have often
been on the point of taking hold of your hand and bursting into tears
at the time that I was refusing you my affections: my approbation I
was precipitate to give you.

Write to me, if I could do any thing about your church, and you
want any thing to be done for you. Such as I am, believe me, dear
Bob, yours affectionately, Daniel Malthus.[1]

It is impossible not to conclude from this letter that dear Bob had been
wasting his time, however delightfully he made everybody about him easy
and amused. The only excuse one can make for him is that this was his first
experience of a settled home, where he saw his mother happy in a house she
was fond of, with long-established neighbours and connections whose roots
they could share, and with whom they could put down roots of their own.
Robert Malthus had been given an extremely liberal education, but because
of the family wanderings he could have had no knowledge of the day-to-
day working of the community; this he would probably have acquired,
almost without knowing it, had his father practised law or medicine, or
been a settled country squire or parson, one who conscientiously performed
his duties - and such there were, even in the eighteenth century. This
knowledge - or perhaps experience would be a better word - is what I think
Robert was assimilating during these ten years in Surrey, and they were to
give him a love of country ways which lasted all his life.

The diaries of both his sisters' fathers-in-law show 'Mr. R. Malthus' as
a constant visitor. One cannot imagine William Bray being indiscreet over
whist about his clients' affairs - and he had an imposing Whig practice -
or about the transactions of the Board of Green Cloth, or even the Society
of Antiquaries, but he must have opened Robert's eyes to what might be
called the basic mechanics of the administration of property and the administration of justice.

We are, in Malthus's time, a long way from the feudal system, but it
must be remembered that this is the period in which Jane Austen, in
Persuasion, could write contemptuously of Sir Walter Elliot exchanging for
'the littlenesses of a town' (it was Bath) 'the duties and dignity of the
resident land-holder'. The diaries of William Man Godschall, more fully
kept than Bray's, give us a glimpse of them, interspersed with his own
affairs. For an octogenarian (he married very late) they are impressive, and
I list some characteristic quotations; I have expanded and modernised the
spelling, which is difficult to follow in the original:

41

Sent William to Mr. Cornwall's about the Botany Bay plant.

Invited Mr. Polhill to dine upon the turbot that came last night.

Translated the introduction to Necker.

Dick Baker cleaned the bottom of the Pillars in the Vestibule.

Mr. Woods came about prosecuting Hersey.

Sent Necker's introduction to Mrs. Dalton for explanation.*

Committed a disorderly girl to the House of Correction.

Up in Billiard Room found an old edition of Chaucer.

The venison from Windsor Park remarkably fine.

Lambert, Overseer of the Poor, came about Ansell's wife. Ordered them 5s. a week.

Mr. Edward Bray came about . . . the Slyfield Charity in Herfordshire.

Resolved to brew a pipe of strong beer.

Fished the new pond - a great stock of small trout.

Read First Epistle of St. Peter.

Taylor the Millwright came to look at the Engine.

Wrote to Mr. Schweppe [sic] for a dozen of his artificial Seltzer.

Mr. Polhill came - talked about Laborers' Wages.

Mr. Thornton & Callingham came - Settled Laborers' Wages at 10s per week.

Caught three large eels.

Began setting in Order the Books in my Den - collected all Acts of Parliament.

Finished the bound Books in the Den - carried Physick and Agriculture into the Gallery.

Received Wild Fowl and Oysters from Colchester.

Elliott and John went to Guildford for livery cloth &c.

The Rev. Mr. Polhill his year's tithe £24.

Could not find list of the Poor for Meat in the hard weather.[2]

*This was 'sprightly Delia', clever Jane Dalton. Her 'Mrs' was a courtesy title in view of her advancing age.

It is hardly surprising that the list was lost, or that the old gentleman constantly entered in the diary much time spent 'setting my table to rights'. But it is surely to him, old as he was, that Malthus owed much of his insight into the ways of English landowners, who still seemed a more important class in the life of the country than either the manufacturers of Warrington or the scientists of its former Academy.

At Okewood Malthus would have seen something very different. From the introduction to the copies of the Registers of Abinger, Wotton, and Okewood, printed by the Surrey Record Society, we learn that 'these three parishes form a fairly complete geographical unit in the hill district of mid-Surrey ... At various times there have been disputes as to the boundaries, but it seems clear that Oakwood, a woodman's little chapel in the heart of the forest area, was always considered inferior to the mother churches of Wotton and Abinger, both of which parishes claimed certain rights in Oakwood.' After stating that the Evelyns were the principal landowners in these three parishes, the writer lists the armigerous families in Abinger and Wotton, and concludes, 'In Oakwood there appear to be none, nor in the whole of that Register is any person described as Esquire.'[3]

This is so. When Malthus left Albury for the nine-mile ride to Okewood, along narrow bridle-paths, he entered a world as remote from books as it was from turbot and artificial Seltzer. Here he learned, as he wrote in 1798, that 'The sons and daughters of peasants will not be found such rosy cherubs in real life, as they are described to be in romances. It cannot fail to be remarked by those who live much in the country, that the sons of labourers are very apt to be stunted in their growth, and are a long while arriving at maturity. Boys that you would guess to be fourteen or fifteen, are, upon enquiry, frequently found to be eighteen or nineteen.'[4]

They must have seemed like a different race from the lads who played cricket at Cambridge, and in a sense they were. They lived almost entirely on bread; bread was their staple; Malthus later computed from the figures of Sir Frederick Morton Eden, whose work on *The State of the Poor* was published in 1797, that two-fifths of the entire income of a labourer's family was spent on bread alone; one-fifth was spent on other forms of food, which left two-fifths for everything else – house-rent, fuel, soap, candles, clothing, and the luxuries of tea and sugar which were not classified as 'food' at that time.

Small wonder that many went without shoes or stockings, especially the women and children. Malthus would have seen them walking steadily for long distances, possibly using a staff for support in this hilly country, with perhaps a basket of apples or a tub of skimmed milk, or a bundle of clothes washed in the brook and dried on the bushes, all carried on the head, the natural way to bear such burdens along a rough and narrow track. They were tough, these people.

When he visited his parishioners in their homes, the curate would have seen them living in a different kind of house from his own friends; they often inhabited not merely much smaller versions of brick or stone houses, but dwellings made of quite different materials – various forms of mud and plaster daubed on to wattle, made from the 'underbrush' of the woods. Sir F. M. Eden wrote: 'The cottage of wattle and dab, as it is called, is perhaps the warmest; that of brick, the driest; and that of stone the strongest dwelling.'[5] There would have been no upper floor. At this period, in southern England, there would always have been a stone or brick chimney, not just a hole in the roof, as in Ireland or the Highlands of Scotland, and some sort of glass in such small windows as there were; a modern visitor might have been surprised by the hardness and smoothness of the earth floor, once he had recovered from the immediate impression of smelliness and dark. Gainsborough's sketch for the scene of *Love in a Cottage* shows a labourer's hut with the thatched eaves coming right down to the top of the low door, and a window about a foot square.[6]

Inside there would have been some sort of bed, benches, and a table, from which the people ate off trenchers, all of wood. There could be very little in the way of shelves or cupboards; valuables were kept in a chest, ordinary garments and utensils hung on hooks attached to the supporting posts or cross-beams. It is worth pausing to consider how a mud hut could be made burglar-proof, for we shall then better understand the savage laws of the time against theft; stealing anything above the value of five shillings (25p) was a capital offence, and to rob an empty dwelling was 'the worst of all', because, if not checked, such thieving would destroy all incentive to industry and a better standard of life among the cottagers. Our ancestors were like most primitive people in this, but we would be horrified today to see what Malthus must have seen many times – the gibbets outside Guildford, with corpses blackened by sun and rain, held together by chains until they rotted away.

So much has rotted away that we are inclined to forget that the labourers' leaky huts ever existed, and to visualise instead a golden age when all English country folk lived in picturesque two-storey cottages. These parishioners of young Robert have vanished too; the names of their descendants can be found in the local churches, on memorials to the dead of two world wars, but they themselves have left us no letters or memoirs, journals or account-books; only their scratchy marks remain like multiplication signs, sometimes splodgy and smudged, in the neighbouring marriage registers. Throughout his life Malthus was to see signatures substituted for marks, as Sunday schools became established, and he was later to help forward this work himself.

After a visit to the church, one feels convinced that Malthus must have loved Okewood. It is still easy to get lost in the lanes which wind through the woodland. Let other writers shudder at 'pagan practices', long continued in this part of Surrey; if Okewood were a magic place before it became holy

THE PRINCIPLE OF POPULATION

(and there are traditions of Druid and Roman temples), it must have been
a good, white magic. The thirteenth-century chapel stands in a circular
clearing, on a little knoll, surrounded by tall oaks; such trees, one feels, at
any time of the year, as Malthus had in mind when he wrote his warm-
hearted reply to William Godwin's denigration of 'the passion between the
sexes'. Then there are the flowers by the way; perhaps the loveliest are the
white wood anemones, which hang like little bells before the early service
on a spring morning, and after it are discovered to have transformed
themselves into wide-awake stars. Inside the churchyard are wild daffodils,
primroses, bluebells creeping in from the woods; but they may not have
been there in Malthus's time, for the eighteenth-century register contains
a bad-tempered scribble to the effect that 'The Grass of the Yard belonging
to the chappel is worth ten shillings per year at least, though now let for
but five.'[7]

There are birds everywhere, and some may even fly into the church with
us. The north aisle was not there in Malthus's time, nor the small vestry on
the south side, and the wooden bell-tower was not quite like the present
one; but the porch between the two stocky buttresses was much the same,
and so were the three south windows; these are all different and uneven and
asymmetrical, even the white-washed splays, on which the morning light
gleams with a beauty that is somehow both homely and unearthly.

This is a well-loved church. Malthus would have known of the strenuous
efforts of the local yeomen in the sixteenth century to preserve it from being
destroyed on the false assumption that it was a chantry chapel; he would
have read, as we do today, the marble slab which commemorates the
early-eighteenth-century benefactors who provided three farms to endow
the chaplain. In 1745 the yearly revenue was £104. 6s. 8d. (£104.33); I cannot
find what it was at the end of the eighteenth century, but by the first quarter
of the nineteenth century increased rents and the sale of timber had made
the value of the curacy between £300 and £400 per annum, better than
many vicarages and rectories. Yet there was still no house for the curate in
1829.

The chapel was originally supposed to hold 200 people, some of whom
would have sat in the gallery. The curate was to preach once and read
Divine Service twice every Sunday throughout the year. By 1809 William
Bray is reporting on Okewood in his *History of Surrey*: 'The chapel is kept
in good repair; but the service on Sunday afternoon in the winter half year
has been discontinued by the present possessor of the Chapel, till whose
time it was always regularly performed, and well attended.'[8] One can
sympathise with this unknown back-slider, possibly called John Graves,
when one realises that there was no stove in the church until 1852. Nor was
there a font until then. Malthus must have christened the babies from a
pewter bowl. We learn from the Register 'That at Easter the Clerk of the
Chapel makes out a Bill for washing & mending the Surplice of the Chapel

& for washing the Table Linnen & scowering the Pewter & delivers it to the church Warden of Wooton, who always pays it.' The Register is very muddled, for the clerks were almost illiterate, but I hope Malthus enjoyed an entry for 1791, when Louisa Jenner was christened 'Luezer'.

It was the eighteenth-century baptisms in the Okewood Register which so much astonished subsequent clergymen, who knew nothing whatever about Malthus. They noted with amazement that there were so many pages and pages of baptisms, and that the baptisms were so greatly in excess of the burials. Of course, this was not of any statistical significance, as the Ninth Wrangler would have known, but one can hardly deny that it must have been these poor cottage babies, in the 1790s, who first set the curate thinking about the principle of population.

2 Revolution, War and Pamphlets

The year 1793, which saw Malthus a Fellow of Jesus and curate of Okewood, was also the year in which - in January - Louis XVI was guillotined; the new Republic of France declared war on England in February. The true 'Reign of Terror' under the Committee of Public Safety did not start until the autumn of 1793, but well before that there had been fierce reaction in England against the Revolution.

We must briefly recall that the traditional enmity between England and France had become almost global. The British successes against the French in Canada and India, under Wolfe and Clive,* had to a certain extent been offset by the loss of the American colonies, and the word 'Republic' had for many Englishmen an unhappy connotation when associated with the United States. By the end of the century Republicanism had come to mean rather what, in certain circles, Communism did later - bloodshed and confiscation under the aegis of an alien tyranny. As Henry Cockburn (1779-1854) wrote in his *Memorials*: 'Everything rung, or was connected, with the Revolution in France; which for about twenty years was, or was made, the all in all. Everything, not this or that thing, but literally everything, was soaked in this one event.'[9]

There is no doubt that Malthus shared Burke's reverence for the traditional liberties of Englishmen as established by the Glorious Revolution of 1688. It seems strange to us that a jumble of Magna Carta, Habeas Corpus and the Bill of Rights should be called the British Constitution, so schooled have we been by nineteenth-century writers on England's good fortune in having

*During the Seven Years' War (1756-63), which terminated in the Peace of Paris.

no written constitution at all. But the possibly mis-called constitutional liberties of the British are worthy of twentieth-century respect, for the equality of all citizens before the law, and the iniquity of imprisonment without trial, are not taken for granted all over the world today, any more than they were in pre-revolutionary France. Absurd though it now appears, many who in 1789 hailed with enthusiasm the storming of the Bastille thought that the French were about to establish a constitutional monarchy of checks and balances on the English pattern; it seemed to some the natural outcome of the visits to England of Montesquieu and Voltaire; Samuel Romilly, then a rising young barrister in London, sent to his friends in Paris a summary of the Riot Act and an account of the Rules of the House of Commons for the benefit of the French National Assembly.

The Revolution Society, before whom Richard Price preached his famous sermon on 'Love of Our Country', in November 1789, was a most respectable association, established for nearly a century, to commemorate the expulsion of James II in 1688; that Price should congratulate the French must have seemed to his listeners a matter of course. Burke's classic answer to Dr Price, *Reflections on the Revolution in France*, was the first intimation, for many English people, that this was a political upheaval far more fundamental than even their own Civil War in the seventeenth century.

Burke's *Reflections* were followed by a host of other works; we might note James Mackintosh's reply, in 1791, *Vindiciae Gallicae*, for we shall hear more of him later. Tom Paine's *Rights of Man*, which was far more violent, appeared in 1792; he had to flee to France (where he was elected to the National Convention) and the citizens of Cambridge burned him in effigy on Market Hill on 31 December. William Godwin's *Enquiry Concerning Political Justice* was published in February 1793; as it cost three guineas (£3.15) it was considered too expensive to corrupt the masses, and no prosecution followed; later Godwin was to write with pride of this book, and his subsequent *Enquirer*, inasmuch as they 'gave the occasion, and furnished the incentive, to the producing so valuable a treatise' as the anonymous *Essay on the Principle of Population*.[10]

But I feel that the publication which concerned Malthus most in February 1793 was not Godwin's, but a pamphlet written by his old Cambridge tutor, William Frend: the title was *Peace and Union recommended to the Associated Bodies of Republicans and Anti-Republicans*. This appeared on 16 February, and a week later the proceedings against Frend began; they continued all through the spring and summer, in his own college and in the Vice-Chancellor's Court, much of them in Latin of unbelievable caninity. Frend published an account of the whole affair. He described how on 2 August he 'received an intimation in writing from the master that the College servants were prohibited from supplying him in future with necessaries'; on 27 September, when he 'intended to revisit the College', he found the gates shut and an iron chain across the great door.[11]

Some younger members of the University had behaved differently. Coleridge joined other sympathisers - including two who later took orders, one who was knighted, and one who became Lord Chancellor Lyndhurst - and they worked briskly until 'hardly was a Wall of a College left unmarked by "Frend for Ever". We were at it three or four Hours.'[12]

After his expulsion from the University, Frend went to London, where he became secretary and actuary of the Rock Assurance Company (with which Malthus insured his own life) and taught mathematics to the girl who was to marry Lord Byron. Malthus kept up with Frend at least to the extent of sending him a copy of the anonymous first *Essay on Population*, and three weeks later he called on his former tutor to acknowledge the authorship.[13]

It is interesting to see that Frend, although excluded from his college, was not deprived of the emoluments of his fellowship, which he kept until he married in 1808. A fellowship, once bestowed, was inalienable property as long as the Fellow remained a bachelor. Residence in college was irrelevant; some Fellows resided, and some became tutors, for which they received fees, but this was a separate arrangement altogether; there was no question of Richard Graves lampooning non-resident Fellows as teachers by proxy (see p. 14). This is important to remember in Malthus's case, for it would appear that he hardly resided at Jesus at all, merely signing the Conclusion Book of the College once in each academic year at the meeting at which he was given his annual leave of absence.

Why was this? A number of reasons come to mind: his dislike of towns, his affection for his family, the claims of Okewood. His friends were scattered. William Smyth (who was Eighth Wrangler in 1787) was made a Fellow of Peterhouse in 1793, but seems hardly to have resided at all until he became a tutor in 1806. John Whishaw was reading for the Bar at Gray's Inn. Ned Clarke, who for ten years had a successful career as a private tutor, was in Italy with one of his titled pupils. William Otter (who had been Fourth Wrangler in 1790) was a curate at Helston, in Cornwall, and teaching at the Grammar School; he and Clarke were to become Fellows of Jesus in 1796. Edward Otter, William's elder brother, was already a Fellow of the College, and one of the three who supported Frend. Malthus would have had no opportunity to do this, but it seems likely that the whole episode distressed him, and there is a strong probability, to my mind, that his becoming a Fellow at such an unhappy time took from both honour and emolument much of the pleasure he might have had in them.

Frend's pamphlet contained one passage which would certainly have hurt his ordained pupils' feelings: 'The same passions will every where produce on certain minds the same effect; and the priest in every age, whether he celebrates the orgies of Bacchus, or solemnizes the rites of the Eucharist, will, should either his victims or his allowance fail, oppose in either case every truth, which threatens to undermine his altars, or weaken his sacerdotal authority.'[14] This any Christian could be justified in regarding as offensive, but otherwise the pamphlet was an innocuous hotch-potch of suggestions for reform, from the abolition of the game laws to the civil registration of births.

In general, Frend thought the British government the best in Europe, and did not consider that the republican constitutions of America or France would suit the United Kingdom. He felt that his own elaborate plan for gradual parliamentary reform must wait until the minds of men were more enlightened, and the lower classes better instructed, but that meanwhile there could be a number of improvements in the law. He wanted the more rational punishment of criminals, and (like all his contemporaries) made suggestions for revising the Poor Laws. He attacked legal training and legal language, and urged reforms in the Established Church which have long since taken place. Here he was not altogether conciliatory; when pleading for toleration for Dissenters he wrote that their power need not be feared since, once their disabilities had been removed, they would 'retire to their different camps, and be separated from each other by the usual marks of theological hatred'.[15]

Frend summed up the situation in 1793 as he saw it:

> The trite argument, that this is not the time to reform, can no longer have any weight on the minds of englishmen. It has been repeated in periods of publick commotion and the profoundest peace. The natural indolence of many may plead for the support of abuses, but the example of a neighbouring nation must surely produce an effect in the cabinet of every monarch. From neglecting to examine and correct the abuses, prevailing through length of time in an extensive empire, we have seen a monarch hurled from his throne, the most powerful nobility in Europe driven from their castles, and the richest hierarchy expelled from their altars.[16]

Far from correcting abuses (of which Pitt had been most intelligently aware), the government was stricken with panic. The country seemed ringed with enemies and riddled with traitors. We must remember ill-used Ireland, and recall that 'the '45', when Bonnie Prince Charlie's army had straggled as far as Derby, was still a lively memory. (Prince Charles Edward, the Young Pretender, did not die until 1788.) Malthus was fourteen when, for seven long, hot summer days in 1780, the whole of London had been at the mercy of a drunken, looting, fire-raising mob under the leadership of a madman, Lord George Gordon, and 285 people had lost their lives before the military succeeded in restoring order. It is impossible not to deplore repressive measures, but we must try to understand them, and push through the haze of the late-nineteenth-century myth that the English never really lost a battle, and were a top nation for whom everything always came right in the end. In Malthus's era, as we shall see again and again, this myth was far from established; fears of bloody revolution and invasion may have been groundless, but they were none the less terrifying at the time.

January and February 1793 saw the passing of the Aliens Act and the Traitorous Correspondence Act, aimed at societies who exchanged views on political philosophy with their French counterparts. Royal decrees enjoined severity on all magistrates in case of tumults, prosecution after prosecution was directed against the press, a bill against seditious assemblies restricted the liberty of public meetings, and in 1794 the Habeas Corpus Act was suspended. In Scotland the persecution of supporters of the Whig opposition went to outrageous lengths; in England, in the autumn of 1794, Hardy, Thelwall, and Horne Tooke, leaders of a Corresponding Society sympathetic to France, were acquitted after a treason trial which ought to be better known as a landmark in the annals of the English jury system.

Yet persecution and prosecution went on, with the usual paraphernalia of agents and counter-spies. Perhaps the most amusing episode was the serious following-up (at considerable public expense) of rumours about Wordsworth and Coleridge, who in 1797 had aroused suspicion in Somerset by wandering abstractedly up and down the romantic countryside with notebooks in their hands; they were, of course, at work upon *Lyrical Ballads*, which was published the following year.[17]

But before this, in 1796, Malthus himself had written a pamphlet. It was never published, and all that we now have of it are a few fragments quoted by Otter and Empson, who had both seen the manuscript. It was called *The Crises, a View of the Present Interesting State of Great Britain, by a Friend to the Constitution*. It is sad that we have Malthus's first completed work only at second hand, as our approach to it would almost certainly have been quite different from that of his contemporaries.

According to Empson, Malthus's 'first object was, as a friend of freedom, to protest against Mr. Pitt's administration. His second, as the friend of order and moderation, to arbitrate between extreme parties. The allies whom he looked to in the patriotic cause, were to come from the camp of penitent country gentlemen; the means which he recommended were the redress of grievances.' But, wrote Malthus, 'In the country gentleman of 1796, it is impossible to recognise that old and noble character, the jealous guardian of British freedom.' Malthus went on:

> It appears to me that nothing can save the Constitution but the revival of the true Whig principles in a body of the community sufficiently numerous and powerful to snatch the object of contention from the opposing factions. In the Portland party, it is in vain to look for a revival, fettered with blue ribbands, secretaryships and military commands:* freedom of action may be as soon expected

*The Duke of Portland, with Burke and Sheridan, had joined Pitt, leaving Fox and Grey to lead the true Whigs in opposition to the war and the repression and high taxation which resulted from it.

from prisoners in chains. Where then are we to look for the principles that may save us? the only hope that Great Britain has, is in the returning sense and reason of the country gentleman, and middle classes of society, which may influence the legislature to adopt the safe and enlightened policy, of removing the weight of the objections to our constitution by diminishing the truth of them.

What Malthus's detailed plans for reform were we may never know, but Empson quotes an interesting passage on 'the policy of religious exclusions', in which Malthus wrote:

An instance of the evil effects of this kind of policy occurs in the present state of the Dissenters in England. As a body, though there are certainly many individual exceptions, they may now almost be considered as professed enemies to the State as well as the Church; yet at the revolution of 88, when the constitution was fixed in its present state, the nation was greatly indebted to them for their assistance; and since that time, till of late, they have been among the firmest friends of the constitution. If during this period, the tests that related to them had been removed, and they had been admitted to equal privileges with the rest of the community; we should never have seen the present violent opposition from them to the established government. And perhaps if the mother church prompted by an universal charity had extended her pale to admit a set of men, separated by such slight shades of difference in their religious tenets, such a conduct, so far from endangering the holy building, I must ever think would have added strength and safety both to the Church and the State. Admitted to equal advantages, and separated by no distinct interests, they could have no motives peculiar to themselves for dislike to the government. And as neither religious nor political principles are born with men, the next generation, educated at the same seminaries, and mixing indiscriminately in other society, would quickly be lost and undistinguished in the great mass of the community. An observation on this subject which is given to Mr. Courteney, though it has at first the air of one of his usual witticisms, is founded on the justest reasoning, and a knowledge of mankind. 'For my part, I hate the Dissenters and I vote for a repeal of the tests that I may hear of them no more'.

There is no evidence that Gilbert Wakefield or the Aikins saw this manuscript, but if they did they must have enjoyed it.

After a short digression, Empson continues:

The part of the *Crisis*, which, with reference to Mr. Malthus's literary history is the most curious - that is, its political economy - remains to be mentioned. In the course of his argument, he enters at

large into the distresses and dissatisfactions of the labouring classes of
1796, and discusses the nature of the relief which he conceives poor
laws might and should supply. Many persons have been desirous of
tracing the source and current of Mr. Malthus's doctrines. A passage
in this essay contains the earliest intimation which exists, of his
having already begun to think upon the principle of population. But,
from all the observations, by which the passage is surrounded,
concerning the condition of the poor and the means by which
poverty may be most effectually alleviated, it is evident that as yet he
was only at the threshold. At this time he was as little aware, as any
other writer who had stumbled upon the principle before him, of the
immense importance of the practical applications which it involved.
'On the subject of population', he observes, 'I cannot agree with
Archdeacon Paley, who says, that the quantity of happiness in any
country is best measured by the number of people. Increasing
population is the most certain possible sign of the happiness and
prosperity of a state; but the actual population may be only a sign of
the happiness that is past'.

Empson goes on:

> Mr. Malthus owed the discovery, which will immortalize his name,
> mainly to his benevolence. Instead of his speculations on population
> having hardened his heart against the interests of the poor, it was the
> earnestness and the perseverance with which he set himself to work
> on behalf of those very interests, that first fixed his attention upon
> these particular speculations. In the same manner, his progressive
> conviction of the extent to which the interests of the lower orders
> were comprised in them, alone gave them, in his sight, the value
> which he so justly set upon them. The consideration of the several
> schemes for reducing the hardships of the poor within the smallest
> compass, was the task which he originally undertook. He brought to
> it a resolute purpose and a philosophical mind; and he never quitted
> it, until, by degrees, the whole subject of population in all its
> relations and consequences had spread itself out before him. The
> consequence was, that his views as to the means by which the pains
> of poverty might be most effectually relieved were completely
> reversed. It was not that his humanity became narrowed, but that his
> knowledge became enlarged. If popular declaimers ever put
> themselves in the way of learning humility and charity, it might do
> something towards teaching them these virtues, to be informed, that
> when Mr. Malthus first entered upon the enquiries among which he
> passed the remainder of a retired and thoughtful life, he entertained
> most of the erroneous opinions in which they are immersed at
> present. He had to do what they refuse to do - to unlearn false

THE PRINCIPLE OF POPULATION

knowledge, and to master the prejudices of his age and country. This
made him frequently remark that there was no science in which first
impressions were so generally wrong as in political economy. We
have repeatedly heard him say that the two converts of whom he
was most proud, were Dr. Paley and Mr. Pitt. It will be seen,
however, that he had had to begin with himself - the great victory of
all.[18]

To understand this, we must turn to two paragraphs from *The Crisis* which
are quoted in Otter's *Memoir*, in which Malthus defends the policy of
relieving the poor in their own homes rather than sending them to
workhouses.
   Malthus wrote in 1796:

But though it is by no means to be wished that any dependent
situation should be made so agreeable, as to tempt those who might
otherwise support themselves in independence; yet as it is the duty of
society to maintain such of its members as are absolutely unable to
maintain themselves, it is certainly desirable that the assistance in this
case should be given in the way that is most agreeable to the persons
who are to receive it. An industrious woman who is left a widow
with four or five children that she has hitherto brought up decently,
would often gladly accept of a much less sum, than the family would
cost in the work-house, and with this assistance added to her own
exertions, might in all probability succeed in keeping herself and her
children from the contamination of a society that she has surely just
reason to dread. And it seems peculiarly hard upon old people, who
perhaps have been useful and respectable members of society, and in
their day, 'have done the state some service', that as soon as they are
past their work, they should be obliged to quit the village where they
have always lived, the cottage to which time has attached them, the
circle of their friends, their children and their grand-children, and be
forced to spend the evening of their days in noise and unquietness
among strangers, and wait their last moments forlorn and separated
from all they hold dear.
   It is an old saying that home is home, be it ever so homely; and
this sentiment certainly operates very strongly upon the poor. Out of
the reach of most of those enjoyments that amuse the higher ranks of
society, what is there that can attach them to life, but their evening
fire-side with their families in a house of their own; joined to the
consciousness that the more they exert themselves the better they
shall support the objects of their affection. What is it but a sentiment
of this kind that tempts many who have lived in the ease and luxury
of [domestic] service, to forego these advantages, to marry, and
submit to the labour, the difficulties, the humbler condition and hard

fare, that inevitably attend the change of situation? And surely no wise legislature would discourage these sentiments, and endeavour to weaken this attachment to home, unless indeed it were intended to destroy all thought and feeling among the common people, to break their spirit, and prepare them to submit patiently to any yoke that might be imposed upon them.[19]

We shall hear much of the Poor Laws, and of Malthus's harsh suggestion to abolish them altogether; but I quote these passages here not only because Malthus (like all of us) had to live his life in chronological order, with a kaleidoscopic content of subject matter, but also because they throw light on how the curate regarded his humble and prolific community at Okewood.

For some reason Otter believed that Malthus refrained from publishing *The Crisis* at his father's request, which was certainly not the case. Bonar quotes a letter from Daniel to Robert of 14 April 1796 in which he wrote, 'I cannot reconcile myself to your not publishing your pamphlet. I am sure it will never do you discredit, though I cannot answer that it will get you a Deanery.'

'The truth is,' Daniel wrote, 'that the market overflows, and, if there is not some particular abuse or known name, the booksellers are not willing to risk their money. I would give very little for Debret's judgment with regard to the pamphlet, but I believe that what he said to you was a pretty good picture of the farce of publick affairs. If any warning voice can awake us from this apathy there never was a time when it was more wanted. What you have done appears to me to be extreamly well done and to be perfectly adapted to the occasion.'[20]

We must notice one more pamphlet in this overflowing market, in which known names and particular abuse were not lacking; it is that of Malthus's former Warrington tutor, Gilbert Wakefield, replying with scornful wit to the Bishop of Landaff's *Address to the People of Great Britain*. He wrote it in Hackney, where he was once more teaching at a Dissenting Academy, and it is dated 30 January 1798; on 30 May 1799 Lady Holland was to write in her journal, 'Gilbert Wakefield was this day condemned to two years imprisonment in Dorset jail; the sentence is severe; one cannot but regret severities should fall upon a man of learning.'[21]

Wakefield had indeed by now a European reputation as a classical and Hebrew scholar. All the same, one is inclined to agree with Sir James Mackintosh's opinion of his 'seditious libel': 'But let the pamphlet be read; let the terrible danger of the kingdom be remembered . . . There never was an age or nation in which Gilbert Wakefield's pamphlet would not have been thought punishable.'[22] At a time of threatened invasion, Wakefield had impugned the courage and ability of the troops: 'No great expectation will be formed of English prowess on its own ground, with all our swaggering pretensions, by those who recollect the adventures of about 9,000 ragamuffin

54

breechless loons from Scotland, but a few years ago.' Even worse was his allegation that the 'lower orders of the community' would not fight the French because 'they cannot well be poorer, or made to work harder, than they did before.'[23]

His two dreadful years in prison in Dorchester proved fatal, and Wakefield died of typhus in 1801, shortly after his release. He was forty-five.

It is not known how Malthus felt. He ket up with Wakefield's family connections, and he had been to Wakefield's celebrated Unitarian publisher, Joseph Johnson, with his own little volume, of which the preface was dated 7 June 1798. It was called *An Essay on the Principle of Population, as it affects the Future Improvement of Society, with Remarks on the Speculations of Mr. Godwin, M. Condorcet, and Other Writers*. It was anonymous and the price was six shillings (30p) 'in boards'. The author had intended writing 'a kind of second part to the essay', on the theme that 'The first great awakeners of the mind seem to be the wants of the body'; but 'a long interruption, from particular business, has obliged me to lay aside this intention, at least for the present.'[24]

With this enigmatic footnote we come to the end of the unknown decade of Robert's life. Although the first version of the *Essay* was published anonymously, its author may be regarded from now on as Population Malthus.

3 Arguments and Utopias

Before considering the first *Essay on Population*, modern readers must face three difficulties.

The first is the air of unreality which, for us, pervades all early British works on the subject, since the writers argue as if there were no such thing as contraception. For all practical purposes this was truly the case: it simply would not, *could not*, have occurred to more than a handful of men that contraceptives might ever be in general use as a means of controlling the size of families.

The second difficulty is that Malthus was born before the age of specialisation. The Everyman edition of the 'very much enlarged' second version of the *Essay on Population* was appropriately classified with 'Philosophy and Theology'. We must remember that in the earlier years of Malthus's life the words 'literary', 'philosophical' and 'scientific' were all used more or less synonymously: a literary man was an educated person, not necessarily a writer, who could - let us say - enjoy botany philosophically, with Linnaeus; what we would now call mathematical or scientific instruments

THE PRINCIPLE OF POPULATION

were then called philosophical apparatus. We must not, therefore, think of Malthus as we would think of a modern economist, still less as a demographer. We have to make an effort to banish from our minds all comprehensive theoretical economic literature other than Adam Smith's *Wealth of Nations*, which appeared when Malthus was ten years old.

Our third difficulty with the early writers is not merely the complete absence of the statistics we take for granted today, but an attitude of mind which set a low value on ascertained facts. Dr Johnson is a good example. 'The truth is', he wrote,

> that the knowledge of external nature, and the sciences which that knowledge requires or includes, are not the great or the frequent business of the human mind ... I have Socrates on my side. It was his labour to turn philosophy from the study of Nature to speculations upon life; but the innovators whom I oppose are turning off attention from life to nature. They seem to think that we are placed here to watch the growth of plants, or the motions of the stars. Socrates was rather of opinion that what we had to learn was how to do good and avoid evil.[25]

Three years before this was written, Thomas Coke had succeeded to his estates at Holkham, in Norfolk, where his enthusiasm for watching plants and animals grow is generally considered to have 'done good'; the agricultural improvements of Coke and others were later to demonstrate to pessimistic economists that scientific methods could increase food production on even the most unpromising land. And at the actual moment that Samuel Johnson was penning these famous words, published in 1779, a noted star-watcher was on board the *Resolution*, on Captain Cook's last voyage, working on astronomical aids to cartography and navigation. He was William Wales, FRS (1734-98). After his return to London in 1780, he plunged into a literary battle then being waged between two learned gentlemen, as to whether the population of England was increasing or declining; no one, of course, had any precise idea of the actual size of the population at the time.

That well-known dissenting minister Dr Richard Price (1723-91) held that the population of England and Wales, in 1780, was about five million. We now think it must have been approximately seven and a half million. Price held further that the population had fallen dramatically by as much as a quarter since the Glorious Revolution of 1688. The Rev. John Howlett (1731-1804), a Church of England parson, took exactly the opposite view, and maintained that numbers were steadily rising. He is now known to be right: it had been calculated that during the latter half of the eighteenth century the population of England and Wales was growing more rapidly than ever before, with an average increase of about 8 per cent per decade.

The only figures Price and Howlett could work upon were culled from the unsystematic study of a few parish registers. Price had a sound reason

56

for pessimism with regard to mortality in large towns: he was concerned with insurance, annuities and the like, and knew how many benefit schemes (such as that of the Laudable Society for the Endowment of Widows) could easily become bankrupt through inaccurate forecasts of expectations of life. The full title of the first edition of his two-volume miscellany, published in 1780, is revealing:

> Observations on Reversionary Payments; on Schemes for providing Annuities for Widows, and for Persons in Old Age; on the Method of Calculating the Values of Assurances on Lives; and on the National Debt, also Essays on different Subjects in the Doctrine of Life Annuities and Political Arithmetic; a Collection of New Tables, and a Postscript on the Population of the Kingdom.

Known for short as Dr Price's *Reversionary Payments*, this book went into innumerable editions – later rearranged by Price's nephew, William Morgan – and remained a standard work for almost half a century. We shall hear of it again.

William Wales alone seems to have tried to investigate the size of the population in a spirit of scientific detachment. With the help of friends, he set about conducting a sample census of his own, in parishes up and down the country. He was innocently astonished by what happened; he must have forgotten the rejection by the Commons of Mr Potter's Enumeration Bill of 1753; Mr Thornton, the member for York, had violently opposed it as subversive of the last remains of English liberty. Mr Wales's friends 'were assailed not only with persuasions, but by threatenings of every kind; such as loss of employment, prosecutions, and even blows'.[26] Needless to say he was reminded of the twenty-first chapter of the First Book of Chronicles, in which we are told of the pestilence that fell upon the Israelites when King David attempted to number his people.

The clergy, however, co-operated kindly, and Wales published in 1781 *An Inquiry into the Present State of the Population in England and Wales*. He was convinced that the population of the country had increased between 1750 and 1780, and that it was more than the seven or eight million which was the estimate of 'our enemies'. But he was sufficiently unsure of himself to doubt the advisability of 'a public census', in case 'the smallness of our numbers' should depress the spirit of the nation.[27] John Howlett, who also published an attack on Price in 1781, was more confident: 'Great-Britain and Ireland, which at most contain not above twelve or fourteen millions, were yet, in the last glorious war, more than a match for France and Spain, which have at least three times that number. Nay, what is greater and more extraordinary still, we seem at this very day to maintain our ground with firmness against these perfidious enemies, aided by the unnatural alliance of our revolted colonies, and our mercenary neighbours the Dutch.'[28]

In 1786 Howlett again took up the cudgels against Price. This time

England was at peace, and the emphasis was more on Price's view of the depopulating effect of enclosures. The controversy was well summed up by Sir Frederick Morton Eden; his *Estimate of the Number of Inhabitants in Great Britain and Ireland* was published in 1800, after Malthus's anonymous first *Essay on Population*, but it expresses the feelings of the period:

> That our numbers have increased, since his majesty ascended the throne, there can, now, be little doubt. Our towns are confessedly larger, and more populous, than they were forty years ago; but, even in this enlightened age, there are political economists, who gravely lament, that great cities are inimical to the multiplication of the species; that a devouring metropolis drains the country of its inhabitants; that the consolidation of small farms lessens the number of cultivators; and that, though trade and manufactures may flourish, the hardy stock of independent yeomen, and industrious peasants, decays. Such complaints, to say the least of them, are unwarrantable, if not mischievous.[29]

Eden trusted that the proposed enumeration would prove, 'beyond the possibility of doubt, that, among the distresses of the times, we have not to deplore a declining population'.[30]

In short, before the first British census of 1801, there was a strong feeling in favour of increasing numbers for military reasons. But in addition to the pamphlets of the 1780s, Malthus possessed, or found in his father's study, the works of two British writers fully aware that an increase of population could not be continued indefinitely. They were Robert Wallace and William Godwin, and it is important to appreciate that they were concerned solely with the distant future of an ideal state.

Dr Wallace (1697-1771) was a Scots minister who had been interested in David Hume's *Political Discourse* 'Of the Populousness of Antient Nations'. Wallace published in 1753 *A Dissertation on the Numbers of Mankind . . . in which the Superior Populousness of Antiquity is maintained*, but his most influential work, which appeared in 1761, was called *Various Prospects of Mankind, Nature, and Providence*; he writes in his 'Advertisement' that 'the following Speculations are chiefly designed for the Free-thinkers . . . whom he would rather convert than irritate.'[31] It is impossible not to wonder whether Daniel Malthus was given this book by a pious relation; certainly its influence on young Robert went very deep indeed, for parts of his first *Essay* seem to be remembered echoes of Dr Wallace's own words.

After a general View of the Imperfections of Human Society, Dr Wallace describes his model of a perfect Government, not for a single Nation only, but for the Whole Earth, and never was there a system more oppressively totalitarian. What we are concerned with, however, is Prospect IV, in which Wallace points out that his Utopia is 'inconsistent with the Circumstances of Mankind'.

'Under a perfect government,' wrote Wallace, 'the inconveniencies of having a family would be so intirely removed, children would be so well taken care of, and every thing become so favourable to populousness, that though some sickly seasons or dreadful plagues in particular climates might cut off multitudes, yet in general, mankind would encrease so prodigiously, that the earth would at last be overstocked, and become unable to support its numerous inhabitants.' Quite apart from the question of food, 'There would not even be sufficient room for containing their bodies upon the surface of the earth.'[32]

He could devise no regular expedient to restrain the number of citizens within reasonable bounds which was not either inhuman or unnatural; he considered at some length, and rejected, compulsory celibacy, castration, infanticide and euthanasia. Therefore Wallace argued that the tranquillity and blessings of the Utopian governments would come to an end: 'Force and fraud must prevail, and mankind be reduced to the same calamitous condition as at present.' It did not seem to worry him very much, for 'our present distresses may be easily explained. They may even be called natural, being the natural consequences of our depravity. They may be supposed to be the means by which providence punishes vice; and by setting bounds to the encrease of mankind, prevents the earth's being overstocked, and men being laid under the cruel necessity of killing one another.'[33]

William Godwin (1756-1836) had read Wallace, and was therefore well aware of this difficulty when he planned his own Utopia. Chapter IX of Book VIII of the *Enquiry into Political Justice* is headed 'Objection to this system from the Principle of Population'.

I must admit to finding Godwin's 'system' uncongenial. To take but one example: 'Shall we have theatrical exhibitions? This seems to include an absurd and vicious co-operation. It may be doubted, whether men will hereafter come forward in any mode, formally to repeat words and ideas that are not their own? It may be doubted, whether any musical performer will habitually execute the compositions of others? We yield supinely to the superior merit of our predecessors, because we are accustomed to indulge the inactivity of our faculties. All formal repetition of other men's ideas, seems to be a scheme for imprisoning, for so long a time, the operations of our own mind.'[34]

Godwin's remedy against the destruction of his Utopia by over-population is even more uncongenial than the Utopia itself. He was obsessed by the idea of mind over matter. In his ideal world mind is so to triumph over body that the passion between the sexes will gradually become extinct, and health will develop into individual earthly immortality: 'The men therefore whom we are supposing to exist, when the earth shall refuse itself to a more extended population, will probably cease to propagate. The whole will be a people of men, and not of children. Generation will not succeed generation, nor truth have, in a certain degree, to recommence her career every thirty years. Other improvements may be expected to keep pace with those of health and longevity. There will be no war, no crimes, no administration of justice, as it is called, and no government. Every man will seek, with ineffable ardour, the good of all.'[35]

It is not astonishing that Godwin's *Political Justice* should have been popular, in spite of its high price of three guineas. No one could produce nearly nine hundred pages – over a thousand in the third edition – without some good in them, and Malthus himself wrote in his refutation of Godwin that 'it is impossible not to be struck with the spirit and energy of his style . . . and particularly with that impressive earnestness of manner which gives an air of truth to the whole.'[36] At a time when ardent humanitarians were disillusioned by the internecine quarrels and massacres of the French Revolution, Godwin held out the possibility of something better. Not everyone would like the sort of life we should have to lead if each man only did half an hour's manual work a day; but the idea might well have appealed to 'young Bowler the baker' of Neasden who, Reginald Heber noticed, had Volney, Voltaire and Godwin in his cart. 'These', wrote the seventeen-year-old Mr Heber, 'are the fruits of circulating libraries.'[37]

Political Justice went into three editions in five years. Malthus must have used the first, published in 1793, and the third, published in 1798, with all four volumes heaped round him as he wrote. Rather meanly, perhaps, young Robert refers to an absurd passage about sleep in the first edition, which Godwin later omitted: 'Before death can be banished, we must banish sleep, death's image. Sleep is one of the most conspicuous infirmities of the human frame. It is not, as has often been supposed, a suspension of thought, but an irregular and distempered state of the faculty.'[38] Godwin was to be avenged: Malthus's paragraph about those for whom there is no room at life's feast, which appeared in only one edition of the *Essay on Population*, and was omitted from all the others, is still bitterly remembered and quoted against him.

But we must, once more, refrain from looking ahead, and return to the curate of Okewood in 1798, with his pile of books. Malthus tells us, in the introduction to the quarto edition of 1803, the sources from which his principle of population derived: they were the works of David Hume, Robert Wallace, Adam Smith, and Richard Price, which would all have been for some years on the shelves of most literary gentlemen's libraries. 'The speculations of Mr. Godwin and M. Condorcet', which figure on the title-page of the first *Essay*, were the publications then being reviewed and discussed, as opposed to these four standard 'classical' writers.

There is little to say of Condorcet's posthumous *Sketch for a Historical View of the Progress of the Human Mind*, except that his belief in our perfectibility shows a remarkably optimistic view of human nature from a man in hiding with a price on his head. Shortly after the work was finished, Robespierre threw him into prison, where he was found dead in his cell on

28 March 1794. Nonetheless, his book was openly published in Paris, and a second edition was needed in 1795 - or, as the title-page has it, 'L'An III de la République, Une et Indivisible'. Joseph Johnson brought out an English version in the same year, truly disgraceful in its badness: Malthus used the original French and made his own translations.

Malthus's most significant reference to Condorcet is, I think, on page 154 of the first *Essay*. Condorcet, perhaps because he was French, did not believe that the population problem of the perfect world should be solved by the extinction of sexual passion; what he looked forward to - I give my own free translation - was a time when the ridiculous prejudices of superstition should cease to imbue our morals with a discipline which did not purify and elevate them, but was in itself corrupting and degrading; he wanted men to be concerned not merely with the existence, but the happiness, of potential beings; they should consider the general welfare of the human race, of the society in which they lived, and of their own families, and so not cumber the earth with useless and miserable people.[39]

We, with our modern contraceptives, can understand Condorcet's vision. It is hardly fair to criticise Malthus for dismissing this as an allusion to 'either a promiscuous concubinage, which would prevent breeding, or to something else as unnatural. To remove the difficulty in this way, will, surely, in the opinion of most men, be, to destroy that virtue, and purity of manners, which the advocates of equality, and of the perfectibility of man, profess to be the end and object of their views.'

It is essential to remember that in eighteenth-century London condoms were used solely for the protection of men against venereal disease. James Boswell, for example, refers to the 'armour' he used with prostitutes, but it would never have occurred to him to take steps to protect his wife against pregnancy. Malthus's opposition to deliberate sterility in conjugal intercourse - which he maintained all his life - is unsympathetic to most modern readers; they forget that it was no more possible for this young man to envisage twentieth-century family planning than it was for him to envisage a successful flight to the moon.

4 The First *Essay* of 1798

Malthus himself tells us that the first *Essay on Population* was sparked off by an argument - he calls it a conversation - with a friend; they were talking about Godwin's essay on 'Avarice and Profusion' in *The Enquirer*, which 'started the general question of the future improvement of society'.[40] Bishop Otter tells us that the friend was Robert's father, and that the tendency of population growth to prevent the perfectibility of the human state, by always increasing faster than subsistence, 'had been often the subject of animated discussion between them'.[41]

This is confirmed by George Pryme (1781-1868). As a young man reading for the Bar, Pryme met Malthus in 1805, at the home of another member of Lincoln's Inn, Edmund Lomax of Netley Place near Shere; as a neighbour and fellow-parishioner he had, of course, known the Malthus family since he was a little boy. Some sixty years after this visit Pryme was to dictate to his daughter that 'the author of the celebrated work on *Population* ... said that his theory was first suggested to his mind in an argumentative conversation which he had with his father on the state of some other countries.'[42] It sounds as if old Professor Pryme was confusing the first and second versions of the *Essay*, but it hardly matters, for Malthus stuck to his basic theory all his life.

Fundamentally, Malthus's theory was simply that 'the power of population is indefinitely greater than the power in the earth to produce subsistence for man.' He put his argument thus:

> That population cannot increase without the means of subsistence, is a proposition so evident, that it needs no illustration.
>
> That population does invariably increase, where there are the means of subsistence, the history of every people that have ever existed will abundantly prove.
>
> And, that the superior power cannot be checked, without producing misery or vice, the ample portion of these two bitter ingredients in the cup of human life, and the continuance of the physical causes that seem to have produced them, bear too convincing a testimony.[43]

Where there were no such checks, as in the United States of America, where morals were pure and food abundant, the population doubled itself in twenty-five years; this rate of increase could there be safely continued for some time, because of the great extent of uncultivated land.

Unfortunately, Malthus propounded as a general rule: 'That population, when unchecked, goes on doubling itself every twenty-five years, or increases in a geometrical ratio,' while 'the means of subsistence increase in an arithmetical ratio.' That is to say,

> Taking the population of the world at any number, a thousand millions, for instance, the human species would increase in the ratio of - 1, 2, 4, 8, 16, 32, 64, 128, 256, 512, &c. and subsistence as - 1, 2, 3, 4, 5, 6, 7, 8, 9, 10, &c. In two centuries and a quarter, the population would be to the means of subsistence as 512 to 10.[44]

As far as his own country was concerned:

> The population of the Island is computed to be about seven millions

[in fact it was about 10½ millions]; and we will suppose the present produce equal to the support of such a number. In the first twenty-five years the population would be fourteen millions; and the food being also doubled, the means of subsistence would be equal to this increase. In the next twenty-five years the population would be twenty-eight millions, and the means of subsistence only equal to the support of twenty-one millions [and so on].[45]

Increased population led not only to starvation but also to overcrowding and epidemics. After a plague there would be vacant houses and food to spare, but such was the strength of 'the passion between the sexes' that the empty places left by disease would speedily be filled up again, and then overfilled, until vice and misery once more reduced the population to the level of subsistence.

As the author himself wrote in his preface, 'The view which he has given of human life has a melancholy hue; but he feels conscious that he has drawn these dark tints, from a conviction that they are really in the picture; and not from a jaundiced eye, or an inherent spleen of disposition.'[46] It is precisely this lack of spleen which I think made the little book so successful. The subject-matter is indeed depressing, but it is treated with such verve and good nature that one cannot but enjoy the two or three hours required to read it. The work combines two of the mainstreams of literary discussion of the period, in that it is concerned with both populousness and theories of government inspired by the French Revolution, but it has an auroral sincerity all its own. The young man's direct, almost cruel, approach to the unpleasant realities of life is tempered by his first-hand compassion for the girl who has an illegitimate baby ('so natural a fault'),[47] or the labourer's wife with six children, sometimes in absolute want of bread, who is unable 'to give them the food *and attention* necessary to support life' (my italics).[48]

This *Essay* is, in fact, a medley from which we may cull a number of biographical details - good horsemanship, long walks with a gun, and 'a very bad fit of the tooth-ache'[49] - for Malthus dashed it off in the first person almost as though he were writing a letter. It is as if he had to pour out all at once a synthesis of his youthful experience and his solid reading, as if, quite suddenly, his quill could communicate freely what his cleft palate and hare-lip prevented him from talking about. The modern reader will disagree with many of Robert's conclusions, but he will not be bored, as he most certainly would have been by *The Crisis*.

It is not surprising that Mary Berry, cultivated and sociable, when she was faced with a long journey took with her 'to read in the chaise' both Kotzebue's *Lovers' Vows* and the anonymous *Essay on Population*. She considered the latter 'uncommonly clearly written, and contains much curious and uncontrovertible reasoning on the subject in question'. A month later she re-read Condorcet, and declared that the author of the *Essay* had not only the best of the argument in a philosophical light, 'but is absolute *conviction* on the subject of the different ratios in which population, and the means of subsisting that population, increase'.[50] Other people, including William Frend, were to find these geometrical and arithmetical ratios quite without significance[51] - truly nonsensical - but Joseph Johnson's *Analytical Review* accepted them, as Miss Berry did, without question.

The writer in the *Analytical Review* also accepted Malthus's very crude theory of oscillations in the supply of labour according to the demand for it, more children being produced when real wages were high and subsistence plentiful, and vice versa. That people should marry younger, that more babies are born and fewer die in relatively prosperous times and regions, is what one would expect, given a certain standard of conventional necessities, and this view is confirmed by modern statistical studies of the late eighteenth century. We may perhaps need a reminder of the speed with which, in this period, newly produced workers could pour into the labour market. Not until 1833, the year before Malthus's death, was the first effective Factory Act passed; this only prohibited the employment of children under the age of nine in textile factories - other than silk mills, for which special arrangements were made. Children of any age could be set to domestic tasks, to help in any kind of shop or workshop other than a textile factory, to run errands, and so on, until the Elementary Education Act of 1870. Not until 1868 was it illegal to employ children under eight years old in field gangs: 'Only think of stooping for six, eight, ten hours a day,' wrote Miss Mitford, 'drilling holes in the earth with a little stick, and then dropping in the beans one by one.'[52]

Before we condemn this state of affairs too harshly, it is important to remember the general demographic structure of the country. Accuracy is impossible, but the high birth-rates and high death-rates prevailing during Malthus's youth meant that very roughly a quarter of the whole population of Britain could have consisted of children under the age of ten, and nearly half the population might have been under the age of twenty. It was not until the census of 1821 that attempts were made to record the ages of the people enumerated.

In all these circumstances it is not surprising that the curate of Okewood in the 1790s should have been obsessed by the thought of too many children and too little food. He saw the problem in simple terms of physical scarcity, not economic distribution; he believed that there was not enough food to go round. 'Suppose', wrote the thirty-two-year-old Malthus, 'that by a subscription of the rich, the eighteen pence a day which men earn now, was made up five shillings, it might be imagined, perhaps, that they would then be able to live comfortably, and have a piece of meat every day for their dinners. But this would be a very false conclusion. The transfer of three shillings and sixpence a day to every labourer, would not increase the quantity of meat in the country. There is not at present enough for all to have a decent share.' All that could happen would be an increase in the price of meat, which would put it beyond the reach of the poorest, and lead to the rearing of more cattle at the expense of corn, which would in turn rise in price to the detriment of 'the lowest members of society ... They must at all events be reduced to live upon the hardest fare, and in the smallest quantity.'[53]

We shall return to this question when we consider Malthus's pamphlet on *The Present High Price of Provisions* and also his scheme for the gradual abolition of the Poor Law. It is worth noting here, however, his remarks on 'Mr. Pitt's poor bill' which were supposed to have led to the dropping of the measure:

> I entirely acquit Mr. Pitt of any sinister intention in that clause of his poor bill which allows a shilling a week to every labourer for each child he had above three. I confess, that before the bill was brought into Parliament, and for some time after, I though that such a regulation would be highly beneficial; but further reflection on the subject has convinced me, that if its object be to better the condition of the poor, it is calculated to defeat the very purpose which it has in view. It has no tendency that I can discover to increase the produce of the country; and if it tend to increase population, without increasing the produce, the necessary and inevitable consequence appears to be, that the same produce must be divided among a greater number, and consequently that a day's labour will purchase a smaller quantity of provisions, and the poor therefore in general must be more distressed.[54]

This passage was not remarked by the writer in the *Analytical Review*, although he commended the sixteenth chapter, in which 'our author' respectfully criticises 'an important part of Dr. Adam Smith's work on the Wealth of Nations; and shows that every increase of wealth does not better the condition of the labouring poor'.[55] I quote what I think is Malthus's most significant paragraph on this issue:

> The commerce of this country, internal, as well as external, has certainly been rapidly advancing during the last century. The exchangeable value, in the market of Europe, of the annual produce of its land and labour, has, without doubt, increased very considerably. But, upon examination, it will be found, that the increase has been chiefly in the produce of labour, and not in the produce of land; and therefore, though the wealth of the nation has been advancing with a quick pace, the effectual funds for the maintenance of labour have been increasing very slowly; and the result is such as might be expected. The increasing wealth of the nation has had little or no tendency to better the condition of the

labouring poor. They have not, I believe, a greater command of the necessaries and conveniences of life; and a much greater proportion of them, than at the period of the revolution, is employed in manufactures, and crowded together in close and unwholesome rooms.[56]

The young man who wrote that paragraph could not justly be described as an enemy of the poor.

Those familiar with economic terms will light at once on the phrase 'the effectual funds for the maintenance of labour'. The Wages Fund Theory was to be interpreted in various ways by the British classical economists of the nineteenth century, but for Malthus in 1798 it meant 'the yearly stock of provisions in the country'.[57] In the next chapter he wrote: 'The consumable commodities of silks, laces, trinkets, and expensive furniture, are undoubtedly a part of the revenue of the society; but they are the revenue only of the rich and not of the society in general. An increase in this part of the revenue of a state, cannot, therefore, be considered of the same importance, as an increase of food, which forms the principal revenue of the great mass of the people.'[58]

Like the notice in the *Analytical Review*, those in the *Monthly Magazine* and the *New Annual Register* were more concerned with the overthrow of Godwin's system than with the positive implications of Malthus's principle of population. The *Monthly Magazine* gave the *Essay* a brief review under the heading of 'Political Economy'. In the *New Annual Register* the *Essay* received nearly two columns under the heading of 'Philosophy and Ethics'; this critic speaks warmly of the pleasure the book gave him, but concludes:

> In the latter part of his work the author advances certain notions which many will pronounce to be no less fanciful than the hypotheses of his opponents. Such are his sentiments, that the moral situation of man in this world is not a state of trial, according to the common acceptation of that expression, but 'the mighty process of God for the creation and formation of mind, necessary to awaken chaotic matter into spirit, to sublimate the dust of the earth into soul', and that 'those beings that come out of the process of the world in lovely and beautiful forms, shall be crowned with immortality, while those who come out misshapen, those whose minds are not suited to a purer and happier state of existence, shall perish, and be condemned to mix again with their original clay'.[59]

This strange theory Malthus proposed as an alternative to Hell. He could not value that virtue which is virtuous only through fear of everlasting punishment, nor could he conceive that any creatures of God's hand would be condemned by Him to 'eternal hate and torture'; he thought it better, therefore, that God should consign 'to their original insensibility those beings that, by the operation of general laws, had not been formed with qualities suited to a purer state of happiness'.[60]

Malthus was drawn to this unorthodox conclusion by the need to reconcile the cruel general law of his principle of population with his belief in an omnipotent and loving God. This was something which was later brought up against him by adversaries innumerable, with all the thunder of biblical eloquence; here it is sufficient to remark that Malthus was fully aware of the theological problems of the existence of vice and misery. He justified the necessity of vice as the antagonist of virtue, which 'could not be generated without the impressions of disapprobation which arise from the spectacle of moral evil'.[61] The misery of suffering engendered tenderness and sympathy, all 'those kind and amiable affections, which dignify the human character, even more than the possession of the highest talents'.[62]

But Malthus's great defence of his principle on moral grounds is summed up in the sentence 'Evil exists in the world, not to create despair, but activity'[63] – and activity is an essential element in the formation of mind. Without the stimulus of necessity, the mass of mankind would be sunk to the level of brutes in a general and fatal torpor. More than this, 'Some of the noblest exertions of the human mind have been set in motion by the necessity of satisfying the wants of the body. Want has not unfrequently given wings to the imagination of the poet; pointed the flowing periods of the historian; and added acuteness to the researches of the philosopher.'[64]

Did Sydenham, sure of his inheritance, smile as he read 'that talents are more common among younger brothers, than among elder brothers'? Robert was certain that 'the difference, if there really is an observable difference, can only arise from their different situations. Exertion and activity, are in general absolutely necessary in the one case, and are only optional in the other.'[65]

In *Pride and Prejudice* Jane Austen makes Elizabeth Bennet blush when Colonel Fitzwilliam tells her, 'Younger sons cannot marry where they like.' I think it possible that Malthus may have had experience of this; in his defence against Godwin of 'the passion between the sexes' (which Malthus thought showed no signs of weakening as civilisation advanced) he writes like someone who has loved and lost:

> Perhaps there is scarcely a man who has once experienced the genuine delight of virtuous love, however great his intellectual pleasures may have been, that does not look back to the period, as the sunny spot in his whole life, where his imagination loves to bask, which he recollects and contemplates with the fondest regrets, and which he would most wish to live over again.[66]

There is also the possibility that Malthus was thinking of himself when he wrote of 'a man of liberal education' with an income only just sufficient to enable him to associate with his own kind on equal terms. Were he to marry and have a family, could such a man 'consent to place the object of his affection in a situation so discordant, probably, to her tastes and inclinations? Two or three steps of descent in society, particularly at this round of the ladder, where education ends, and ignorance begins, will not be considered by the generality of people, as a fancied and chimerical, but a real and essential evil . . . These considerations undoubtedly prevent a great number in this rank of life from following the bent of their inclinations in an early attachment.'[67]

Perhaps Robert showed some youthful ignorance of life in believing that cultivated 'tastes and sentiments' were a matter of income. Education and taste are certainly less dependent on income today than they were in Malthus's time, but even in that period these things were often a question of choice rather than money. Jane Austen began *Sense and Sensibility* in November 1797; it is noticeable throughout that the Middletons, though far richer than the disinherited Dashwood ladies, were surprised when they called on their tenants to find them 'always employed', with their music and drawing and serious reading.

Rather inconsistently Malthus said in a letter to Godwin that he could 'conceive that a period may arrive when the baubles that at present engage the attention of the higher classes of society may be held in contempt'; presumably he was thinking of such things as the gold plate and gambling debts of Devonshire House. It is a charming letter, sticking to his guns, but courteously deferential to an established author ten years his senior. Malthus and Godwin must have met within a few weeks of the publication of the anonymous *Essay* – one imagines through their publisher – for Malthus wrote on 20 August: 'I went out of town almost immediately after I left you on Wednesday morning, and therefore did not receive your obliging letter till I arrived at Albury, whither Mr. Johnson was so good as to send it.'

With regard to 'political justice', it is interesting to find Malthus setting out to Godwin in this letter the views which he held all his life: 'Great improvements may take place in the *state* of society; but I do not see how the present form or system can be radically and essentially changed, without a danger of relapsing again into barbarism.' And, 'In speaking of the present structure of society, I do not in the least refer to any particular form of government, but merely to the existence of a class of proprietors and a class of labourers, to the system of barter and exchange, and to the general moving principle of self-love.' He agreed with Godwin as to the desirability of abolishing all unnecessary work, and the equal sharing-out of the necessary labour amongst the community; but surely people would want more than bare necessities? And no man could be prevented from working as many hours as he liked (to obtain a few luxuries or other advantages) 'without the interference of Government, which I know you would reprobate as well as myself'.

As far as the development of Malthus's theory of population is concerned, the most important passages in this letter are those in which Malthus comments on Godwin's 'system of prudence':

> The prudence which you speak of as a check to population [wrote Malthus], implies a foresight of difficulties; and this foresight of difficulties almost necessarily implies a desire to remove them ... With the present acknowledged imperfections of human institutions, I by no means think that the greatest part of the distress felt in society arises from them. The very admission of the necessity of prudence, to prevent the misery from an overcharged population, removes the blame from public institutions to the conduct of individuals.[68]

Those who know the second edition of Malthus's *Essay* will recognise in these words his alternative to vice and misery as checks to over-population. Since it involved more than mere prudence, he called it 'moral restraint', and its practical application was the postponement of marriage, which would limit the number of children each couple might be expected to produce. Thus population growth could be kept within bounds not merely by the positive checks of vice and misery, but also by the preventive check of delayed marriages.

5 The First Foreign Tour

An anonymous pamphleteer who criticised the second version of the *Essay on Population* wrote rather unkindly of Malthus in 1803: 'Having tried the experiment of an anonymous treatise, and emboldened by success, in its rapid circulation and increasing fame, he has in this latter publication avowed his name in the title page, and thus appropriated the merit of his speculations.'[69]

This is unfair, for the first *Essay* was certainly not a calculated experiment. We have every reason to believe Malthus when he tells us: 'It was written on the spur of the occasion [Malthus changed 'spur' to 'impulse' in 1806], and from the few materials which were within my reach in a country situation.' He then goes on to say, in the preface to the great quarto, that the principle of population 'appeared to account for much of that poverty and misery observable among the lower classes of people in every nation, and for those reiterated failures in the efforts of the higher classes to relieve them.* The more I considered the subject in this point of view, the more

---

*Those who brand Malthus a snob for using the then current terms, higher and lower classes, might pause to reflect on what our descendants may think of our own jargon, especially when we talk about a Higher Standard of Living.

importance it seemed to acquire; and this consideration, joined to the degree of public attention which the Essay excited, determined me to turn my leisure reading towards an historical examination of the effects of the principle of population on the past and present state of society.'[70]

This phrase 'leisure reading' is an unsolved mystery. 'Leisure' then, as now, meant time not occupied with regular work; if the tremendous amount of reading which Malthus got through before publishing his quarto was the fruit of his leisure, what could have been his non-leisure reading? The only explanation I can think of is that for some of the time he was reading the classics with one or more pupils, but I have no evidence for this.

There is evidence that he got down to the detailed study of demography (though the word was not then in use) soon after the publication of the first *Essay*. Bonar quotes a letter from Robert in Albury to his father in London, dated 4 February 1799, in which he asked for a formidable list of books; they range from Dr Styles's *Discourse on Christian Union* - 'hard to get' - to Dr Haygarth on the population and diseases of Chester. Robert very much wanted Süssmilch's *Göttliche Ordnung*, extensively quoted by Richard Price, if there was an English or French translation: as far as I know there still is none, which is sad, for Malthus would have enjoyed it.[71]

It certainly seems that his son's success had aroused Daniel Malthus, at sixty-nine, from the arm-chair to which he had consigned himself at the age of fifty-seven. One can imagine him being as enthusiastic in equipping Robert for his first journey abroad as he was in hunting for the books he wanted.

Robert Malthus would probably never have made his Scandinavian tour had not a young man in Sussex called John Marten Cripps 'come into possession of a large fortune - about two thousand five hundred a Year' - and, in March 1798, asked Ned Clarke 'to be his private Tutor for three Years, on any terms'.[72] Cripps was nineteen, and according to Otter his previous education had been 'indifferent'; this indeed seems to have been the case, judging from his postscripts to Clarke's letters, which are reminiscent of Jane Austen's Lucy Steele (in *Sense and Sensibility*); but he was very likeable, enthusiastic, generous, and devoted to his eccentric tutor.

Edward Daniel Clarke is difficult to describe in a few paragraphs. According to his biographer, William Otter, the natural state of Clarke's spirits was, 'at least, upon a level with the half-intoxication of his friends'. To this day his manuscript letters seem to emit sparks of the energy and excitement with which he pursued - and with Clarke 'pursued' is the only appropriate word - his multiplicity of activities. He did not do well as an undergraduate, since he was not interested in mathematics. Although a competent classical scholar, his real concern was with what we should now call science: as a small child, on a visit, he contrived so completely to stuff every part of his mother's carriage 'with stones, weeds, and other natural productions of that country, then entirely new to him', that the poor lady, 'upon entering, found herself embarrassed how to move; and . . . she was constrained, in spite of the remonstrances of the boy, to eject them one by one from the window'.[73]

Psychologists may be amused to learn that Clarke returned from his longest tour with seventy-six packing-cases, containing botanical and mineralogical specimens galore, as well as the usual books and antiquities.

The carriage episode did not cloud Clarke's deep attachment to his mother. After he had been travelling for ten years, with different pupils, all over Britain, Switzerland, the Rhine, and Italy (twice), Otter found him in 1798 quite content to remain with her in Uckfield, until he found he might be called upon to serve in the Sussex Militia; then he wrote frantically to Otter, at this time in residence at Jesus as Senior Tutor: 'Seriously I beg of you to request the Master to appoint me bursar without delay, that I may go to Lewes, and tell the justices that I am exempted by a College office, and only here upon a visit.'[74]

'Accordingly he was appointed bursar', Otter wrote, although strictly speaking this was not the case, as the College records show: Clarke was Steward and Rustat Bursar, and the Master (Dr Pearce) performed his duties for him during his long absence abroad.

For a year, however, Clarke and Cripps resided at Jesus, from the spring of 1798 until May 1799. Clarke's 'love of travel still showed itself to be the ruling passion of his mind'; Otter wrote frankly that 'he was never less disposed to be at ease in the whole course of his life, and if they who knew him best were desired to point out that period of his history, in which he appeared least amiable to others (and it is only of the degree of which there can be any question), it would certainly be this year of his residence at Cambridge. On these accounts he often urged upon the author of this memoir . . . the immediate execution of a scheme they had long had in contemplation of going abroad together . . . and as no part of the Continent was then open to English travellers, but the north of Europe, it was determined, after various plans had been proposed and rejected, that they should visit Norway and Sweden, with as much of Russia besides, as could be comprehended within the extended limits of a long summer vacation.'

Otter goes on:

> Mr. Cripps, his pupil, was of course of this party from the beginning [it was his money that was paying for Clarke], and with it was afterward associated a gentleman, since highly distinguished in the literary world, Professor Malthus. He was at that time Fellow of the College, and having been occasionally resident during this year, and often present at the discussions to which the scheme had given birth, was easily persuaded to embark in an expedition, which, besides the many obvious inducements it held out to him in common with the rest, afforded a prospect of information peculiarly desirable to himself. He had lately published his first work, an octavo volume,

upon the Principle of Population; and although it was quite impossible for him to anticipate the deep and extensive interest, which the peculiar circumstances of the country have since given to the subject, it is certain that he was at that time exceedingly impressed with the practical evils to which the prevailing errors respecting population had given rise ... But being certain that a theory so adverse to all the rooted prejudices and received opinions of mankind, was not likely to make its way by argument alone, however logically supported, he was anxious for the sake of truth as well as of public happiness to collect from every quarter of the habitable world all the prominent facts which could fairly be supposed to bear upon the question.

Somewhat inaccurately, Otter ends his immense paragraph about Malthus:

To this tour, therefore, the public are indebted for all that curious statistical information respecting Norway and Sweden, with which his quarto volume is enriched, and for many of those facts and documents by which the truth of his former demonstration is so triumphantly supported and confirmed.[75]

Dear, loyal Otter. These words were first published in his *Life* of Clarke in 1824, and it is to be hoped that they comforted Malthus in the sorrows of the last ten years of his life.

But on 20 May 1799 the four men who set out from Cambridge for Bury St Edmunds, where they spent the night on the way to Yarmouth, were eager and happy. We know from a letter Clarke sent to his mother from Hamburg (which they reached on the 25th) that Otter suffered most on the voyage and Malthus bore it better than anyone. We know from Malthus's own journal that the packet *Diana* had about sixteen passengers: 'French, German, Swiss & Italian. They all talked french well. Most of them had travelled & were well informed & entertaining.' On the boat from Cuxhaven to Hamburg their sociability had to be of a different kind: the master 'was a very good natured man. We amused ourselves with talking to him in English & found that there were many words which we could make him understand.'[76]

So they went on all through their tour; nothing could be less like the image of the stand-offish travelling English gentleman who talks to nobody. Malthus did, however, show one trait which is regarded as typically English, and that was his carelessness or downright anglicisation where foreign proper names are concerned. Perhaps non-English readers will be mollified when they hear that he was equally unreliable over British names, as is shown in his letters to Ricardo and his later travel diaries. When I first read Malthus's Scandinavian Journal in manuscript I was rather rude about his frequent crossings-out and slips in spelling - 'poll' for pole, 'bean' for been - and so on; since then I have tried to keep travel diaries myself, in countries where waiting for repairs or spares, beside a murram road through the bush, can be just as tiresome as waiting for horses in eighteenth-century Europe, and I have now nothing but admiration for his persistence and objectivity.

Like all travellers seeking information, Malthus found that gentlemen in general were 'either unable or unwilling to answer the questions I have asked; but very willing to run on into long discussions of their own'. I think it is possible that he had the naïve outlook common to those who possess what Robert Louis Stevenson called 'honourable curiosity' - seeking truth for its own impersonal sake; it simply did not occur to Malthus that some of the people with whom he talked might have found his questions impertinent. Perhaps it was considerations of this sort that made their servant-interpreter show 'a little unwillingness to repeat' the torrent of questions with which Malthus might otherwise have overwhelmed the nomadic Laps in their birch-tree hut, rather than that he 'thought so many questions trifling and foolish'.

Then, of course, his informants were always telling him contradictory things; anyone who has taken part in any sort of survey will understand. But it would be quite wrong to describe this holiday as a survey in the modern sense, although Malthus did attach importance to two aspects of life in Norway which he thought delayed marriage, and therefore led to a slow growth of population and the consequent prosperity of the common people. These were the custom whereby a farm servant did not take a wife until a 'houseman's' or cottar's place was vacant for them, and the obligation to serve in the army; in theory, men were expected not to get married before or during their military service, and permission to do so was only granted when there was some sort of provision for the maintenance of their families while they were away.

Practice is different from theory. Malthus wrote of the lonely milkmaids in the little huts of the summer pastures who were comforted by visits from their sweethearts. He noted, 'In general however, it is not thought right to have more than one Sweetheart at a time,' and then changed 'right' to 'creditable'. He was also told at Trondheim that 'A marriage seldom takes place but when a child is about to appear.' Surely some babies must have given notice of appearance before their fathers were called up for military service or a cottage became vacant?

Malthus himself seems to have been extremely susceptible to pretty girls; but I am told that any man would remark, as he did, the bare bodies that were occasionally visible because the women wore shorter shifts than those in England, or the lamentable apparent absence, in some Swedish villages, of 'young women that looked to be from 17 to 22' - obviously the most desirable age-group. But he noticed also, near Lübeck, 'a very picturesque mother walking with short petticoats & bare legs & neck, with ten children round her'. He knew about the care of babies: in the Österdal they saw 'a child about 5 weeks old swaddled & bound up almost like a mummy. The mother told us that she kept them in that state for nearly a year, & we were much surprised therefore to hear that she had had 12 children, 9 of which were alive.' Everywhere he noted the condition of the labourers, their homes and families; it is obvious that the writer of this journal was a good curate who knew his poor.

He also met the rich, and found Bernt Anker 'very polite & obliging tho rather great', and his brother's house at Bogstad 'quite princely'. Like all travellers who are hospitably entertained, they had sometimes to admire and to eat rather more than they felt inclined to do, but were 'determined to accommodate themselves to the customs of the country'. They could not control their English passion for fresh air, however, and at Elstad a good-natured landlord employed four or five men for half an hour in removing the frame of a window which would not open.

On one occasion a 'lost' portmanteau was (I think) stolen during a fracas about paying for horses, and of course they were sometimes overcharged at inns. At Moss a young Norwegian army officer was astonished at what they had to pay, and Malthus wrote very naïvely: 'We were glad, in this instance, to know from good authority, that the very high charges that had been made to us during our journey, did not arise from the actual dearness of provisions in the countries thro which we had passed; but from the desire of people not to lose an opportunity of making as much of strangers as possible ... We had before been at a loss to conceive how people of small fortunes, & all are certainly not rich in Sweden & Norway, could contrive to live.'

In general, however, the travellers were kindly treated wherever they went, even if they arrived at their inns long after the household had gone to bed. I was interested to hear a Norwegian lady comment on this in 1968; only about fifty years before, people living in the remote parts of Norway still regarded a hare-lip with superstitious horror, and she thought that the courtesy with which Malthus was treated everywhere was a notable tribute to his innate charm and goodness. The only difficulties he records with the ladies he danced with at balls or sat next to at dinner parties were language problems – with some he could 'converse only by signs'. It is impossible not to wonder how he felt about his affliction, fancy-free and abroad for the first time, and at a stage in his life when normal lips seem so expressly formed for kissing.

No such regrets are apparent in the journal. His happy curiosity extends from the French minister at Copenhagen, with his national cockade – Malthus appears surprised that 'he seemed to be perfectly well bred in his manner' – to the details of copper mining in Röros and his daily thermometer readings of the temperature. Modern Norwegians delight in these, confirming as they do their legends of 'good old-fashioned summers'. It was a

74

common habit of diarists of this period to record the weather; harvests, if not a matter of survival, were of immediate financial concern to everyone, from the careful tradesmen and craftsmen, whose customers' rents and profits depended upon the price fetched by their crops, to the spendthrift worried over his horses' keep.

We feel, as we read Malthus's diaries, that the price of the horses' hay was comparable to the price of petrol in modern times; he was much interested in prices and wages, but not markedly more so than other travellers of the period. He collected facts wherever he could, about the size of the farms, improved methods of agriculture, the common people's diet; and he set it all down along with his embarrassment at making 'a very awkward figure' at the Walse, his intense delight in landscape, as distinct from cultivation or geology, his pleasure in swimming, and strawberries and cream, 'some difficulties about our passport, which we thought we had lost' - in short, his diaries are the mixture of detailed information, reported opinion, description and personal trivia, which make up any authentic serious journal of a holiday abroad.

When Malthus's *Travel Diaries* were first published in 1966 some critics found them extremely dull: others exclaimed, 'What a delightful fellow he must have been!' Everyone felt a little cheated that there was not more in them about the principle of population.*

There is certainly no sparkle about Malthus's Scandinavian Journal, and no literary flourish; it was not written for publication, and one can feel how he forced himself to keep it up, when he was tired out after travelling all day, or after parties at which difficult subjects, such as the judicial system or land tenure, had to be discussed in French (which was not the mother-tongue of anyone present) or varying degrees of imperfect English. But he must have been a good travelling companion - and not simply because he gave Otter, as the worse sleeper of the two, the only bed at a small inn, while he himself slept on a box of moss, 'which was not so soft in reality, as a mossy couch generally is in idea'. On a similar occasion Malthus writes, 'having laid a cow's skin upon the dresser & spread a great coat over it, & taken another for a pillow, I laid myself down not uncomfortably & slept at intervals till half past 3 - when we rose, took our milk & oat cake for breakfast, & at 4 mounted our horses in pursuit of the Lapfins.'

This sounds quite strenuous travelling, but it was nothing for Clarke, who once for eighteen days on end was never in bed more than four hours out of forty-eight. There was no quarrel, but after they had been together for a month, in Hamburg, the Duchies, Denmark, and south-east Sweden, the party split up. Malthus and Otter went on to spend just over two months in Norway; they stayed in Halden (then called Fredrikshald) and Christiania (now Oslo), visited the silver mines at Kongsberg, and went up the

*For a detailed essay about 'Malthus on Norway' see Michael Drake's article in the *Journal of Population Studies*, Vol. 20 (1966), p. 175.

Gudbrandsdal to Trondheim, then on to Röros and down the Österdal to Kongswinger. The diaries for their time in central Sweden, Uppsala and Stockholm, are lost, but we know they crossed the Gulf of Bothnia to Finland, and came home by sea after a very brief sojourn in Russia, probably reaching England in November, having been away about six months.

Clarke and Cripps travelled on from Scandinavia right through Russia, to Turkey, the Holy Land, Egypt and Greece, for three and a half years in all. Otter met them in Paris at the beginning of September 1802; he had been asked to bring with him Cripps's servant, John, and also his favourite mare, if he liked, though Clarke thought it would 'hardly be worth while to be bothered with a Horse in your Journey'. They may all still have been in Paris, with or without the mare, when Malthus arrived there on 25 September, with a large family party, after touring in France and Switzerland.

But much had happened in the meantime, before the short interval of the Peace of Amiens. A few weeks after Robert's return from his Scandinavian travels, on 5 January 1800, Daniel Malthus died, 'instantaneously', according to Louisa Bray. His wife, who had been ailing for some time, survived him for just three months; she died on 5 April, and was buried beside her husband. Their graves are on the very edge of the churchyard at Wotton, facing outwards, as though they might wish to look beyond the sloping fields and bare trees towards the Rookery.

The choice of burial-ground was in accordance with Daniel Malthus's will, which he had made on 4 January 1779, more than ten years after the Rookery was sold.[77] He wrote: 'If it happens to be equally convenient, [I wish] to be buried in Wootton Church Yard with a plain stone and Daniel Malthus upon it in the manner of the country people' - which could well have been regarded as eccentric in an age of elaborate epitaphs. He wanted his coffin 'to be carried by my old friends' and 'a suit of plain clothes to be given to them'.

His bequests were perhaps even more unexpected than the instructions for his burial. To begin with, his wife was sole executrix and legatee, but he then added a paragraph requesting her to give £20 each to his sisters Wathen and Hackshaw, and £600 to General Morrison. George Morrison (1704-99) was an outstanding professional soldier, but I can find no reason for this legacy, which in any case he did not live to receive. More pathetic is the bequest 'to my daughter Harriot any little memorial of me she shall chuse'. He left nothing at all to his other children, apart from Sydenham; in a codicil dated 9 April 1799, the year of Sydenham's marriage, Daniel Malthus bequeathed to him the income derived from the sale of his land in Cambridgeshire, at Little Shelford, Hauxton, Hewton and Harston. The most intriguing legacy is 'To Mrs. Jane Dalton all my Botanical Books in which the Name of Rousseau is written, likewise a Box of Plants given me by Monsr. Rousseau, A white Cedar Box marked "Papers & c" to be delivered to her unopened.' Surviving members of the family have no knowledge of this box or what it contained.

Daniel Malthus's life has another mysterious postscript, which gave occasion for Robert's first appearance in print over his own name. The *Monthly Magazine* of February 1800 remarked in the obituary section that 'Mr. Malthus was the admired, though hitherto unknown, translator of "The Sorrows of Werter"; of an Essay on Landscape, from the French of the Marquis d'Ermenonville; and of the elegant translation of "Paul et Virginie", published by Mr. Dodsley, under the title of "Paul and Mary". His works evince that Mr. Malthus was a man of taste and learning, though certainly an eccentric character in the strictest sense of the word.'

Robert dashed back a denial, and both obituary and contradiction were recorded in the *Gentleman's Magazine*: 'We feel pleasure in correcting our own errors as well as those of others, and shall make no apology for transcribing from the *Monthly Magazine* of March last, the following letter, respecting the character &c. of Daniel Malthus, esq.

> "Sir, I shall esteem it a particular favour, if you will allow me to correct an erroneous paragraph, which appeared in your Obituary for last month. Daniel Malthus, esq., is there mentioned as the translator of some pieces from the French and German. I can say, from certain knowledge, that he did not translate them. The turn of his mind very little disposed him to imitation, or to the copying, in any way, the works of others. Whatever he wrote was drawn from the original source of his own fine understanding and genius; but, from his singular, unostentatious and retired character, and his constant desire to shun every thing that might attract notice, will probably never be known as his.
>
> T. Robert Malthus".[78]

The last statement is indeed true, but we have no difficulty in checking that the *Sorrows of Werter* was in fact translated by the Malthuses' old friend and tutor Richard Graves; it was first published by Dodsley in 1779, and ran through five editions in six years. It seems strange that no one writing in 1800 troubled to look at a copy, or they would have seen that Mr Graves was perfectly candid about having used a French version of 'a German story', 'to exhibit a picture of that disordered state of mind too common in our own country'. 'Mr. Goethé' is described in a footnote as 'Doctor of Civil Law, and author of some dramatic pieces which are much esteemed'.

With regard to the English versions of the Vicomte d'Ermenonville's *Landscape*, and Saint-Pierre's *Paul and Mary*, I can only speculate. *Paul and Mary* was published, not by Dodsley, but by a Dublin consortium, in 1789; in the 'Advertisement' the Translator says that 'The Linnaean names of animals and plants are added at the bottom of the page, where it seemed requisite, and it could be done with tolerable certainty.' This work is still listed as Daniel Malthus's in the Bodley and British Library Catalogues. His Surrey neighbours could as justifiably have attributed to him d'Ermenonville's *Essay on Landscape, or the Means of Improving and Embellishing the Country round our Habitations*; it was published by Dodsley in 1783, with a frontispiece showing Rousseau's tomb on the Island of Poplars at Ermenonville.

My guess is that Robert knew, with 'certain knowledge', that both these publications were the work of Jane Dalton. After all, old Mr Godschall sent her his translation of the Introduction to Necker 'for explanation' (see p. 42); and as we have seen she was devoted to Rousseau and was herself an enthusiastic botanist whose own cottage and grounds at Albury were perfection, and 'everyone consulted her when they had gardens to make or improve.' Her anonymity may be ascribed to feminine delicacy, then fashionable, but it might also have had some psychological connection with her romantic attachment to her guardian.

Robert Malthus was clearly on good terms with his elderly cousin; Jane Dalton's bookplate can be found in some of the works which he consulted for the second version of the *Essay on Population*,[79] and he asked Murray to send her a set of his *Rent* and *Corn Law* pamphlets.[80] When she died on 10 December 1817, at the age of seventy-five, he must have made the arrangements for her funeral, as he was one of her executors,[81] and Sydenham was abroad at the time. She lies in Wotton churchyard on Daniel Malthus's right hand, not so close to him as his wife, but with the same pattern of plain headstones. They were later to be joined by the two unmarried Malthus sisters, who were buried side by side at their parents' feet.

CHAPTER III

The Great Quarto of 1803

1 'My Garret in Town'

We know from William Bray's diary that he went with Sydenham Malthus to Doctors Commons on 29 January 1800, to see about Daniel Malthus's will. Sydenham presumably inherited the family house, and the two unmarried daughters, Eliza Maria and Charlotte, moved to a cottage of their own in Albury; it was conveniently near one which had been built for their youngest sister and her husband, Edward Bray, so that the children could spend every summer in the country, their father riding down from London at week-ends.

One might have thought that Robert would have taken up residence in his college on a permanent basis. Instead, he chose a 'garret in Town', or rather, a series of garrets, since he wrote to a friend in November that he had a temporary lodging 'till I can fix upon one that will suit me for the winter'.

Malthus's address for letters was 57 Great Russell Street, where William Bray, his son and his clerks carried on the work of a busy solicitor's office, and where the whole family lived in the winter: Grandfather William, Edward and Mary Anne Catherine, and their ever-increasing brood of children. We must remember that we are in the pre-Victorian age: life had not as yet become fragmented, any more than knowledge had become specialised. Middle-class families were not, at this time, invariably divided between the nursery and the drawing-room; later, in 1815, when his own three children had joined his widowed sister's more numerous flock for Christmas, Malthus was to apologise to Ricardo for the incoherence of a letter, because 'I am writing from Town and among all the children who are reading aloud so I hardly know what I say.'[1]

For Edward Bray there was no essential split between home and office, for lawyer or merchant, any more than there was for doctor, parson, or country squire. Just as James Eckersall, the early-eighteenth-century Clerk of the Kitchen, had made no clear distinction between his public and private duties, so for a hundred years after him business and domestic affairs were bound up with each other; this was a matter of law, as well as tradition, since what we now think of as an ordinary limited liability company could not be established before the Act of 1855.

London in 1800 contained about a million inhabitants – roughly one-tenth of the total population of Great Britain. It was not surrounded by residential suburbs, but by market gardens, dairy-farms and abattoirs. The fresh meat, for those who could afford it, had perforce to come trudging and pattering in from the country, in lowing, bleating, grunting droves. Only grain and dry goods and imperishables generally came by barge or waggon. Not until the middle of the nineteenth century did the Express Dairy Company send milk to London by express trains, and in Malthus's time London was full of cow-houses as well as stables. In 1802 there were 1,100 hackney cabs, and the drivers must sometimes have had difficulty in finding their fares' destinations, as the numbering of houses in a street was not compulsory until 1805.

Malthus's London is difficult to imagine. There were only three bridges over the Thames; Westminster, Blackfriars, and London Bridge itself. The river was thronged with little rowing-boats, for going up and down as well as crossing it, later to be made unsafe by the advent of 'steamers'. The smell of the river could be overwhelming, at low tide in hot weather, until late in the nineteenth century. During the first half of the eighteenth century the death-rate in London was 50 per cent above the national average; when Malthus took up residence in his garret it was still about 20 per cent above that for the rest of the country.

The capital was far from idyllic in other ways too. Malthus probably never went to watch a hanging, but he could hardly have avoided such a sight as nearly made Miss Berry hysterical when she saw a man in the pillory on the corner of North Audley Street and Oxford Street; she 'looked out of the window for the instant that the wretched man was putting in, and for one instant afterwards, when he was assailed by such a shower of every sort of mud, filth, and horrors, as to give every part of him and the machine one and the same hideous composition'.[2] Charles Lamb loved London, but even he conveys the impression that most nights were disturbed by cries of 'Fire!' and 'Stop thief!'

We might have felt squeamish about some of the shops, whose windows were beginning to be glazed 'with large panes of plate glass, at a great expense'. Southey makes his fictitious Don Espriella describe a few of them as they were in 1802:

Here you have cages of birds of every kind, and on the upper story live peacocks are spreading their fans . . . Here a painted piece of beef swings in a roaster to exhibit the machine which turns it; here you have a collection of worms from the human intestines, curiously bottled, and every bottle with a label stating to whom the worms belonged, and testifying that the party was relieved from it by virtue of the medicine which is sold within.[3]

And here Malthus, in his unknown garrets, worked on the second edition of the *Essay on Population*.

The difference between the first and second editions is so great that it is hard to believe they are separated by only five years. The principle, the tendency of unchecked population to outrun subsistence, is of course the same, and a few passages from the first edition appear verbatim in the second; but one's general impression is that these two books are the work of two different men, and in a sense I think this impression is a true one. Malthus is not somebody about whom one can be patronising or clinical, and it would be anachronistic to apply to him the language of modern amateur psychology; nonetheless I do find it helpful to think of him as what we should now call 'a late developer'. This may be attributed to his hare-lip, his peripatetic childhood, his unconventional home and tutors, his rural seclusion, as the reader pleases. The fact remains that he seems to have grown up in his garret in town or, more accurately, away from it, when he left his books for his friends.

And what friends they were! One must make allowance for the rosy spectacles of reminiscence and the shameless omissions of Victorian biographers, but one is still left with happy envy of Malthus's interlocking circles. It is difficult to make out who was in London on any precise date, or who introduced him to whom. I can sympathise with Malthus's friend William Smyth, a cunning old historian, who omitted dates altogether when he wrote, for his nephews and nieces, in 1840, his farcical account of his period as tutor to the elder son of Richard Brinsley Sheridan - a period which was for Smyth 'one eternal insult, mortification and disappointment'.[4] Before he knew of Sheridan's drunkenness and debts, the young Smyth had idolised him as dramatist, orator, and reforming Whig, and thus he had applied for this uncomfortable post when his father's Liverpool bank was 'totally ruined' by the war with France. According to his own account, Smyth was unfit for any employment 'but to go tutor to some family', on account of 'a nervous affection in the retina', which prevented him from reading 'more than two or three hours in the day, and not at all at night'.[5]

In Liverpool, Smyth had been intimate with three remarkable men, all about ten years older than he was: William Rathbone IV (1757-1809), William Roscoe (1753-1831), and James Currie (1756-1805). The first two were men of business; Currie, a doctor of medicine, published in 1800 a *Life and Collected Works* of Robert Burns, to raise money for the poet's widow and children. All three were men of wide culture though little formal education, and with young Smyth from Eton and Cambridge they founded the Liverpool Philosophical and Literary Society, which had to fade away in the early 1790s because of the proclamations against seditious meetings.

All were philanthropists and ardent for the abolition of the slave trade. We know that Dr Currie sent Wilberforce information about conditions in Liverpool, and that Smyth, when he was in London, sent Currie accounts of the parliamentary debates; he described Pitt as 'vulgar'.[6]

Thus Malthus had, through Smyth, links with Sheridan and the dissolute Prince of Wales on the one hand, and Wilberforce and his friends of the Clapham Evangelical group on the other. But there were more connections: William Roscoe knew the Aikins, and Gilbert Wakefield's daughter stayed with the Roscoes when the attentions of the gaoler's son made it impossible for her to remain in Dorchester near her father. And Samuel Thornton from Clapham, as we saw, had bought Albury Park.

The Aikins, for their part, also knew Samuel Rogers. John Aikin, MD, whose work I have already quoted, left Warrington to settle with his family in Yarmouth, until he saw his practice dwindle, and his 'children persecuted by children', during the agitation for the repeal of the Test Act, in 1792, by Protestant Nonconformists - John Aikin's sister, Mrs Barbauld, was prominent among them. After some wandering, the Aikins established themselves among the Dissenters of Stoke Newington, a village to the north-east of London; here young Samuel Rogers had attended the Academy and listened to the sermons of Dr Richard Price in the Presbyterian chapel.

Samuel Rogers (1763-1855) early left this world of distinctly plain living and high thinking; but John Aikin's granddaughter recorded that he 'never forgot his old friends', even after he 'had built a house in the Green Park and lived chiefly in the highest society'.[7] Rogers had become a bank clerk at the age of sixteen, and by the age of twenty-five was believed to be making more than £5,000 a year. When he was twenty-nine, in 1792, he published a long poem called *The Pleasures of Memory*; it is unreadable now, but in 1816 the nineteenth edition was brought out with some éclat.

Dr Burney was to write of Rogers in 1804: 'He is a good poet, has a refined taste in all the arts, has a select library of the best editions of the best authors in all languages, has very fine pictures, very fine drawings, and the finest collection I ever saw of Etruscan vases; and moreover, he gives the best dinners to the best company of men of talents and genius I know; the best served, and with the best wines, liqueurs, &c.'[8] But it would be unfair to write off Rogers as a sybaritic bachelor: he visited Gilbert Wakefield in prison in 1800, and he had the most serious and intimate discussion of religious problems with at least three of his friends. One of them was Malthus. The other two were James Mackintosh and the Rev. Sydney Smith's brother Robert, always known by his nickname of Bobus.

James Mackintosh (1765-1832) came to London after studying medicine in Edinburgh, staying with a relative of his mother's who was a wine merchant. At the Society for Constitutional Information he met his lifelong friend Richard Sharp (1759-1835), who had early made a fortune as a manufacturer of hats; he was known as Conversation Sharp, but had a reputation 'quite peculiar to him among town-wits and diners-out. He never talks scandal. If he can say nothing good of a man he holds his tongue.'[9]

The 'novelties and distractions' to which Sharp introduced the young Scots doctor were too much for him. According to Mackintosh's son, 'The unexciting tenor of life, which the medical profession holds out, had no chance in the struggle with the stirrings of ambition, which the political excitement, in which he was already immersed, could hardly fail to cherish.'[10] In short, Mackintosh turned first to journalism and then to law. In 1791 he published his *Vindiciae Gallicae* in answer to Burke on the French Revolution; this was much praised not only by Fox and Sheridan, but also by Dr Parr, a famous pedagogue as renowned for his outspoken liberalism and Latin epitaphs as he was for an outsize wig and a reprehensible tobacco pipe. In 1795 Mackintosh was called to the bar at Lincoln's Inn. In 1796 we find him writing to Edmund Burke that since the publication of *Vindiciae Gallicae* the shocking outcome of the French Revolution 'has undeceived me on many subjects on which I was then the dupe of my own enthusiasm',[11] and he visited Burke for a few days at Beaconsfield.

The following year, when he was thirty-two, Mackintosh's first wife died, leaving him with three little girls. Twelve months later he married Catherine Allen, who was known in some circles as the bluest of bluestocking ladies; she was one of nine daughters whose father is alleged to have thrashed them (afterwards) if they did not talk sufficiently brilliantly at dinner to amuse his guests.[12] With his brother-in-law, 'honest John Allen', of Cresselly in Pembrokeshire, Richard Sharp, Samuel Rogers, Bobus Smith, and a fellow-barrister James Scarlett, later Lord Abinger, Mackintosh founded a dinner-club, which Bobus christened 'The King of Clubs', and which became famous for good talk. Then, in 1799, Mackintosh became more widely known for his thirty-nine lectures on 'The Law of Nature and Nations'; they were delivered from February to June in the Hall of Lincoln's Inn, and he remarked with satisfaction that his 150 pupils included six Peers and twelve Members of Parliament.

These discourses clearly gave a new impetus to the King of Clubs, for on 27 April 1799 a list of seventeen members was drawn up; it contained the name of one of Malthus's Cambridge friends, the blunt and stocky John Whishaw who had lost a leg. And as Bobus Smith had been a close friend of Lord Holland since they were contemporaries at Eton, it may have been through this connection that Whishaw became such a mentor to the Fox family that he was later known as the Pope of Holland House.[13] This beautiful little palace - for so foreigners regarded it - was then just outside London, and was generally considered as the headquarters of the Whig party in opposition.

Other early members of the club whom Malthus was often to meet later on were the Genevese Étienne Dumont, closely associated with Jeremy Bentham; Lord Henry Petty (the future Lord Lansdowne), who had been

Dumont's pupil; and Whishaw's great friend Samuel Romilly. Malthus himself did not become a member until 1812, but he must certainly have attended earlier as a guest.

Nobody (as one might expect) ever records Malthus as a shining conversationalist at a party, but we get an attractive glimpse of him in London at the house of his publisher, Joseph Johnson. Shortly after printing the first *Essay on Population,* Johnson had been fined £50 and sent to prison for nine months for his part in the publication of Gilbert Wakefield's seditious libel; but as he was only confined 'within the Rules of the King's Bench', his sufferings were not great, and he bore them philosophically. We get a glimpse of him, too, through the eyes of twenty-four-year-old Thomas Campbell, who had achieved instant fame with his poem *The Pleasures of Hope* in 1799. On 13 April 1802 Campbell wrote to Dr Currie:

> Mr. Roscoe's introduction to Johnson has gained me the acquaintance of a very sensible and good man. I have met at his table some literary characters exceedingly interesting; in particular, Mr. Malthus, author of an Essay on Population – a most ingenious and pleasant man.[14]

How we wish we could have been there, at one of Joseph Johnson's renowned weekly three o'clock dinners.

It must not be imagined that the new London life made Malthus neglectful of his relations in Surrey. William Bray's diaries show a constant exchange of visits, and to some extent the circles overlapped: William Bray knew Whishaw, and later called on Romilly at Tanhurst, 'on the side of Leith Hill', and on Scarlett at Abinger Hall. Conversation Sharp also had a house in Surrey, near Dorking, at Fredley Farm, and Sydney Smith visited him there so often that he was called the Bishop of Mickleham. We must try not to be prejudiced against these people because they became prosperous. No amount of flattery in posthumous memoirs can alter the fact that they worked extremely hard, rising strenuously to plenitude from impecunious and often very humble beginnings; they spent their money on art and learning and intelligent foreign travel. Rather we should be astonished that so many of them did not remain in their ivory towers – the charming country houses they rented – but drove themselves ever harder as the years went by in the causes of civil liberty and the improvement of the poor.*

Nor should we be prejudiced by our Whigs' attitude to the poor whose lot they wished to 'improve'. It is distasteful for us to read how some of Malthus's friends refused to enter the House of Commons until they could

---

*This phrase, in common use throughout Malthus's life-time, perhaps needs some explanation for modern readers. It meant, quite literally, the improvement of the poor themselves, through education, training, and religious instruction, so that they could by their own efforts get the best out of life, here and hereafter. Improving the condition of the poor, through model cottages or better fireplaces for cooking, was something quite different.

do so 'independently' - that is, by purchasing a seat, or finding a patron who would give them one without strings - rather than face a popular election; it is reminiscent of Shakespeare's Coriolanus. But we must remember the drunkenness and downright bribery of the so-called free elections; so rough were the crowds that before the railway age mothers with young children took care never to travel through any counties in which elections were being held.

Once in Parliament, the integrity and persevering altruism of these reformers was as remarkable as their physical stamina. That great lawyer Sir Samuel Romilly is a good example. I have unfortunately found no correspondence between him and Malthus, but that they knew each other quite well is obvious from contemporary letters and memoirs; it was at the Romillys', for example, that Richard Lovell Edgeworth met Malthus at a party with Dumont and Dr Parr.[15] Apart from their mental affinity, Malthus and Romilly had close personal ties: two of Romilly's sons became pupils of William Otter at his Shropshire rectory (one of them, like Malthus's son, Henry, later married one of Otter's daughters), and before Romilly committed suicide in 1818, on his wife's death, he had appointed Whishaw as the guardian of his children.

Romilly was born in 1757, of Huguenot stock; his friend Jean Roget, the Genevese minister of the French Protestant Chapel in London, became his brother-in-law, and the father of Dr Peter Mark Roget of *Thesaurus* fame. With a touch of historical irony creditable to all concerned, Romilly was given the pocket borough of Horsham in Sussex by the Roman Catholic Duke of Norfolk - for whom, incidentally, William Bray did a fair amount of business. When he happened to be unseated on a technical point, Romilly bought the borough of Wareham in Dorset for £3,000, in the sincere belief that he was making a sacrifice of his private property 'merely that I may be enabled to serve the public'.[16] After Curwen's Act had made illegal the practice of purchasing seats, the Duke of Norfolk gave Sir Samuel Romilly his borough of Arundel in 1812, the sole condition being that he should dine with him at Arundel Castle once a year.

Romilly's first concern was with popular education, 'not to give knowledge to the poor, but to qualify them to acquire it ... To enable men to read and write is, as it were, to give them a new sense.'[17] He was Solicitor-General in the Whig ministry of 1806-7, but is chiefly remembered for his struggle to reform the penal code with bill after bill rejected by the Lords if they did happen to pass the Commons, except for one memorable exception in 1811: stealing from bleaching grounds was removed from the list of capital offences, at the cloth manufacturers' request, because the death penalty made it impossible for them to get information about such depredations. Romilly thought in 1814 that the punishment of the pillory should be abolished, but wrote, 'There is not, however, the least probability that, if a bill were brought into Parliament for that purpose, it would pass into law.'[18] The pillory was not abolished until 1837, having been last used in 1830. In fairness to the House of Lords, we should note that in 1814 they did concede that the body of a man convicted of treason need not be disembowelled while he was still alive; they insisted that it should be quartered, according to custom, after his death. In practice, after the public hanging, the corpses were merely beheaded.

2 *The Cause of the High Price of Provisions*

We must now get back to August 1800, when the poor of England were near starvation. Reginald Heber wrote to his friend John Thornton (the son of Samuel Thornton of Albury Park) about the general anxiety over the harvest, 'which will undoubtedly be a late one', so that –

> the distress for a month or two longer will, I fear, be terrible. It was a shocking consideration, which I had an opportunity of observing when in Yorkshire, that the number of robberies was very great, no less than three taking place in the neighbourhood of Harrogate during my stay there, and that food alone was stolen. For instance, an inn there was broken open, but all that was taken was a joint or two of meat. That want must surely be dreadful, which would brave the gallows to obtain a single meal.[19]

It is quite likely that this intelligent seventeen-year-old had read a sizeable pamphlet of eighty-six pages called *The Question of Scarcity Plainly Stated*, by Arthur Young, Esq., FRS, Secretary to the Board of Agriculture, which had appeared in March 1800. Young gave an extremely good factual account of grain yields and shortages throughout the country, reminding his readers that as early as 1771 he had advocated a census of the population and annual returns of the acreage sown with wheat. 'What farmer', he wrote, 'sees his flocks and herds augmenting, without paying any attention to increasing their food? Had the people and acres been numbered in 1788, and again in 1798, and the one found to increase nothing, but the other one-third, who would be surprized at scarcity?'

Arthur Young pointed out 'that the return of similar situations may be expected, with so increasing a population', and suggested 'that the best prevention is to render as general as possible the system of cottagers having land for potatoes and cows'. This is an unexpected long-term solution from a traveller who had seen in France and Ireland the distress caused by the continual splitting up of smallholdings as families multiplied, and who was an advocate of the improved methods of large high-yield farms as against a subsistence agriculture. Malthus took issue with this point about the 'cow system' in the second edition of the *Essay on Population*, but letters show that the two men were on friendly terms. Malthus might also have had his private reservations over the final sentence of Young's pamphlet on *Scarcity*: 'It may not be in the councils of the Almighty, that this nation should be conquered by foreign arms, or destroyed by internal commotion; but it evidently is His will that it should be chastized; or the punishment we feel at present would not have taken place.'[20]

Malthus's attitude in 1800 was completely different from Young's. He described how the idea for his own pamphlet on the subject came to him, in a letter to a Cambridge friend, George Turner, who was then a curate at Kettleburgh in Suffolk, where he afterwards became rector. The letter is dated 28 November, from London:

> My dear Turner;
>   Your letter was sent to me to Bath, where I have been on a visit to a family of pretty cousins, and could not therefore look down long enough to write a letter. On my return I made a short packing up excursion to Albury, and am now got into my garret in Town . . . Before I went to Bath, I had been to Hastings for some time with my sisters, and in my ride to Town, an idea with regard to the present high price of provisions struck me so strongly, that in the day or two that I remained in Town, previous to my Bath Expedition, I determined to write down a few thoughts on the subject. I send you the result, which would have come to you sooner but from a mistake of Johnsons. I sat up till two o clock the evening before I went to Bath to finish it, that it might come out before the meeting of parliament. You will see that it was written in a hurry . . .[21]

It certainly was, and Malthus had to add a footnote to the second edition of his pamphlet (otherwise a reprint of the first) to make himself clear: 'It will be observed that I am not now speaking of the causes that may have contributed to the actual scarcity; but of the cause of the very high price of provisions in proportion to the actual degree of that scarcity.'[22]

Others besides Arthur Young and Malthus had realised that it was actual shortage, not the speculation of dealers, which had occasioned the dramatic rise in the price of wheat, and that the judiciary were powerless to stabilise the prices of scarce commodities through medieval edicts against 'forestalling' and 'regrating'.* Romilly wrote to a friend in September 1800, when

---

*'Forestalling' meant buying up goods privately, before the vendor had brought them to a public market; this was an indictable offence, because it deprived a town of market dues and tolls, as well as giving the purchaser an opportunity of retailing forestalled commodities at a monopoly price.

Basically a 'regrater' was simply a middleman, but 'regrating' was illegal when it involved selling at an enhanced price goods purchased on the same day or in the same market - or, in some cases, within four miles of it.

commotions were becoming serious:

> The poor misguided wretches who engage in these riots are greatly to be pitied. They feel the scarcity and the high price of the necessaries of life most severely; great pains have been taken by persons in high authority to persuade them that what they suffer is not to be ascribed to those natural causes which were obvious to their senses, but to the frauds and rapaciousness of the dealers in provisions. . . . I cannot find that the least attempt has been made to undeceive the people.[23]

Malthus at any rate hoped to enlighten Parliament. He wrote in his pamphlet that when he was passing through Sweden in July 1799 (it was in fact August) the distress was considerably greater than any hitherto experienced in England; the people were 'reduced to two most miserable substitutes for bread; one, made of the inner bark of the fir, and the other of the common sorrel, dried and powdered'. Yet the price of rye, from which Swedish bread was made, was not more than double the usual average; wheat in England was more than three times its former price, which was quite disproportionate to the actual physical shortage of grain. This Malthus attributed not to the roguery of middlemen, who were 'absolutely necessary in the complicated machinery that distributes the provisions and other commodities of a large nation', but to what we should now call inflationary welfare payments: 'the attempt in most parts of the kingdom to increase the parish allowances [to the poor] in proportion to the price of corn, combined with the riches of the country, which have enabled it to proceed as far as it has done in this attempt'.

He then went on to his famous arithmetical example; fifty people, but only enough for forty: 'If the fortieth man from the top have two shillings, the thirty-nine above more, the ten below all less . . . the actual price of the article, according to the genuine principles of trade, will be two shillings.' Then the ten poor men, previously excluded, are each provided with two shillings; we now have fifty people able to pay two shillings for the article, but still only enough of it for forty. Ironically Malthus points out the obvious: 'If we interfere to prevent the commodity from rising out of the reach of the poorest ten, whoever they may be, we must toss up, draw lots, raffle, or fight, to determine who are to be excluded. It would be beyond my present purpose, to enter into the question whether any of these modes would be more eligible, for the distribution of the commodities of a country, than the sordid distinction of money.' The price of the commodity must rise to a point which will put it beyond the power of ten out of the fifty to buy it.[24]

We go back to Albury and Shere, 'the neighbourhood where I then lived', for meetings similar to those which took place elsewhere, when the magistrates were 'aided by the united wisdom of other gentlemen of the county; but the result was merely the continuation and extension of the former system of relief; and, to say the truth, I hardly see what else could have been done. In some parishes this relief was given in the shape of flour; in others, which was certainly better, in money, accompanied with a recommendation not to spend the whole of it in wheaten bread, but to adopt some other kind of food.'

This in turn led to increases in the price of butter, cheese, bacon, pickled pork, rice and potatoes. The poor's rates had risen in some parishes from four to fourteen shillings in the pound;* wheat at the end of the year was nearly £40 a load, when Malthus felt that its 'natural' scarcity price, on Adam Smith's principles, should have been about £20 or £25.

But he said very firmly that he did not consider the parish allowances had been prejudicial to the state: they had prevented starvation among 'the poorest inhabitants', and 'by raising the price of provisions so high, caused the distress to be divided among five or six millions, instead of two or three, and to be by no means unfelt even by the remainder of the population'.[25]

In addition to stressing the desirability of spreading out the hardship and sharing it among the nation, by means of the Poor Law, Malthus also put in a good word for those who had spread it over a period of time by holding grain back from the market; they had certainly consulted their own interests, but they had also 'consulted the true interest of the state: for, if they had not kept it back, too much would have been consumed, and there would have been a famine instead of a scarcity at the end of the year'.[26] This is virtually a recollected quotation from Adam Smith's famous 'Digression concerning the Corn Trade and Corn Laws'.

Malthus was never afraid of writing in the first person, and I must quote in full a passage which calls to mind young Mr Robert, the curate of Okewood, and his happy knack of getting on with everybody:

> I know that I differ from some very respectable friends of mine, among the common people, who say that it is quite impossible that there can be a real scarcity, because you may get what quantity of corn you please, if you have but money enough; and to say the truth, many persons, who ought to be better informed, argue in exactly the same way. I have often talked with labouring men on this subject, and endeavoured to show them, that if they, or I, had a great deal of money, and other people had but little, we could undoubtedly buy what quantity of corn we liked, by taking away the shares of those who were less rich; but that if all the people had the same sum, and that there was not enough corn in the country to supply all, we could not get what we wanted for money, though we possessed millions. I never found, however, that my rhetoric produced much impression.[27]

*The pound at this period contained 20 shillings, and each shilling contained 12 pence.

After discussing the inflationary rise in prices due to attempts to increase the purchasing power of the poor, Malthus turned to those who 'have attributed the dearness of provisions to the quantity of paper in circulation'. The quantity of bank-notes had naturally become much larger since February 1797, when the Bank Act was suspended. The 'suspension of cash payments', as it was called, meant that the Bank of England was no longer obliged to pay out gold, on demand, in exchange for its own notes of the equivalent face value. The immediate cause of the crisis was a run on some banks after rumours of a French invasion; but gold reserves had been seriously depleted before this by the demands of the war and France's return to a metallic currency after the inflationary collapse of her paper *assignats*. Malthus believed that

> There was undoubtedly great reason for apprehension, that when, by the stoppage of the Bank to pay in specie, the emission of paper ceased to have its natural check, the circulation would be overloaded with this currency; but this certainly could not have taken place to any considerable extent without a sensible depreciation of bank notes in comparison with specie. As this depreciation did not happen, the progress of the evil must have been slow and gradual, and never could have produced the sudden and extraordinary rise in the price of provisions which was so sensibly felt last year, after a season of moderate cheapness, subsequent to the stoppage of the Bank.

He went on to point out that the circulation of a given quantity of commodities at a high price must require more of the circulating medium (whether notes or specie) than if the price were lower, and it was therefore probable either that the Bank of England had found it necessary to issue a greater number of notes on this account, or that the country banks had supplied the deficiency. 'If the quantity of paper, therefore, in circulation, has greatly increased during the last year, I should be inclined to consider it rather as the effect than the cause of the high price of provisions. This fulness of circulating medium, however, will be one of the obstacles in the way of returning cheapness.'[28]

Malthus concluded with a reference to the growth of population. He could hardly have done otherwise, since the full title of his pamphlet was *An Investigation of the Cause of the Present High Price of Provisions by the Author of the Essay on the Principle of Population.*

> Of late years, even in the best seasons, we have not grown corn sufficient for our own consumption; whereas, twenty years ago, we were in the constant habit of exporting grain to a very considerable amount. Though we may suppose that the agriculture of the country has not been increasing as it ought to have done during this period; yet we cannot well imagine that it has gone backwards. To what

then can we attribute the present inability of the country to support its inhabitants, but to an increase of population?

He finished by saying that the *Essay* had 'been out of print above a year, but I have deferred giving another edition of it in the hope of being able to make it more worthy of the public attention'. He had previously referred to two years' reflection on the principle of population since the *Essay* was published, which convinced him of its truth, and continued, 'Particular engagements in the former part of the time, and some most unforeseen and unfortunate interruptions latterly, have hitherto prevented me from turning my attention, with any effect, towards this subject. I still, however, have it in view.'[29]

Also in November 1800 there appeared a jumbled little pamphlet by one Edward Gardner, printed in Gloucester, anti-commerce and pro-agriculture, entitled *Reflections upon the Evil Effects of an Increasing Population upon the Present High Price of Provisions*. He does not refer to Malthus's *Essay*, but it is significant that Gardner wrote, 'The subject is certainly new. The utility of an increasing population has I think never yet been questioned ... We are certainly misled by the craft of an interested policy, if we believe for a moment, that national aggrandizement or national wealth, can atone for the distress of the *bulk* of the people.'[30]

Gardner's small work is now a forgotten straw in the wind. Malthus's letter to Turner shows that his own pamphlet was read in high places:

Such as it is, it has obtained some little notice. A friend of mine gave it to the Chancellor, who called it the best that had appeared on the subject, and sent it to Mr. Pitt. I know not the opinion of the latter about it; but whether from that or from some other source, you will see that in the first report of the committee of the house of commons, now just published, much of the same kind of reasoning has been adopted.

It is amusing to recall what the eighteen-year-old Bob had written to his father about the young Prime Minister in 1784. One could also twit Malthus about the Lord Chancellor, Loughborough, who as Alexander Wedderburn had been one of the most notorious trimmers and turncoats of the second half of the eighteenth century; he was one of those whom Robert himself had castigated in *The Crisis*, in 1796, for joining the Duke of Portland's Pittite group, and thereby ceasing to be a true Whig.

Malthus went on with his letter to Turner:

I expect your thanks as a farmer; and if I am ducked by the mob I hope the monopolizers and forestallers will give me some dry cloathes. The circulation of this pamphlet, and the prevailing conversation about the population of the country [arrangements were proceeding for the first British census the following year] has caused enquiries to be made about the Essay which is now no where to be bought. This I hope will animate me to proceed in another edition, though to say the truth I feel at present very idle about it.

After giving the address of his brother-in-law Edward Bray, Malthus concludes:

Pray never make an apology for talking·of yourself and your family, as it is information that will always most interest me. I am sure I ought to apologize for talking of myself in this letter but I wish to encourage you to return it in kind. [Two lines are then heavily crossed out, with a different ink. The first sentence appears to begin with the words *Destroy this*.] I am inclined to think that those which open the soonest are not always the best. I am sorry to hear so indifferent an account of Mrs. Turner, my best respects.
                                    Yours most sincerely,
                                    R. Malthus.

George Turner seems to have faded out of Malthus's life. All I know of him is that he edited Forby's *Vocabulary of East Anglia* and had a son, another George, who followed his father to Jesus College, Cambridge, in 1811, and to the rectory of Kettleburgh in 1840. Somebody clearly felt guilty about not destroying the letter; one cannot help being grateful for this act of disobedience to a friend's request. I think Turner realised the letter was of historical importance. He may even have heard that Malthus was particularly noticed by Pitt, in December, at a supper-party in Jesus Lodge, when the Prime Minister was 'upon a sort of canvassing visit in the University'.[31]

3 Reading and Travelling

Malthus must quickly have shaken off the idle fit which he mentioned in his letter to his friend Turner. The second edition of the *Essay on Population*, a quarto volume of 610 pages, was completed on 8 June 1803. For the whole of the previous summer, like so many other English people after the Peace of Amiens, he had been travelling with a large party of relations in France and Switzerland; they crossed from Dover to Calais on 2 May and returned to London on 13 October.

This tour must therefore have cut over five months out of Malthus's writing time. The enlarged version of the *Essay* is divided into four Books, and it would appear that the two first were almost complete by the spring of 1802. The chapter on 'The Checks to Population in France', which comes towards the end of Book II, he says 'was written in 1802, and refers to the state of France before the peace of Amiens'; this implies that he did not expect to have an opportunity of visiting the country before his great work was published. After his return from France he added an enormous footnote to this chapter, instead of re-writing it; he must have been feeling rushed by the autumn of 1802, and there were, as we shall see, harrowing emotional complications, but it is quite possible that he added the footnote to save expense as well as time, because the type for the chapter had already been set up; Malthus may have been sending his manuscript to his publisher, Johnson, piecemeal, as was customary at this period. The chapter on Switzerland, although bound before that on France, was obviously written later, after the party's return. So probably was Chapter III of Book I, on 'The Checks to Population in the Lowest Stage of Human Society', since it was based mainly on the Appendix to Collins's *Account of New South Wales*, which was not published until 1802.

On any reckoning, Malthus must have worked like the proverbial beaver. The first two Books are the more factual: I, *Of the Checks to Population in the Less Civilized Parts of the World and in Past Times*, and II, *Of the Checks to Population in the Different States of Modern Europe*. For this half of the *Essay* Malthus consulted 102 authorities, and many of them were works in considerably more than one volume.

I have not been able to find quite all of them, and some are not easily accessible in the actual editions which Malthus used. I have pored over enough, however, to realise the truth of Otter's statement that Malthus 'read in a better spirit, reflected more freely and more usefully and acquired more general information than any of his contemporaries' at Cambridge, contemporaries who had been reading solely for prizes. Here is a man with tremendous powers of assimilation and intellectual metabolism, integrating facts and ideas so that they become essential parts of his own mental and spiritual being; one feels that he would not have been content merely to understand a difficult passage; he had to absorb it into himself, correctly related to all the rest of his knowledge, indeed to all the rest of his very existence.

There was nothing unscholarly in this approach to his task. I have been able to check most of his references, and have found very few slips; some are probably printers' mistakes, which those who have had to proof-read footnotes will more readily forgive than those who have not. There is only one inconsistency: a reference to 'Note XXVIII' in Robertson's *History of America*, in one place, becomes 'Note 28' in another, which suggests rough scribbles in which Malthus used Arabic numerals because they were quicker to write than the Roman used by Robertson.[32]

The material in itself is enthralling; I wonder nobody has ever produced an annotated edition of the second version of the *Essay* simply as an excuse for the pleasure of thoroughly studying the sources. For the checks to population in Greek and Roman times, Malthus went right back to his childhood reading with Richard Graves - Caesar's Gallic wars and Livy, Tacitus, Plutarch, Pliny, Juvenal, Aulus Gellius and Dionysius of Halicarnassus. He was perhaps less acquainted with Greek than he was with Latin, using John Gillies' *History* (published in 1786) and also his Aristotle; Malthus pointed out, however, that 'some passages he has wholly omitted, and of others he has not given the literal sense, his object being a free version.'[33] It is worth noting that the greatest Greek scholar of his time, Richard Porson, was among the earliest members of the King of Clubs.

Malthus would certainly have been familiar with Plato, and Hume's *Dissertation* 'On the Populousness of Ancient Nations'; Gibbon's *Decline and Fall of the Roman Empire* we know he read at Cambridge. What we cannot guess is how many of the historical and topographical works of his contemporary world he had read before, and how many he had to seek out for this particular purpose, and then go through them, volume after volume, in college libraries or those of his friends, and in his own garret.

Some of these travellers' tales are classics, cheaply available in modern editions; but we must bear in mind, as we follow Captain Cook's *Voyages*, that Malthus was already thirteen at the time of the death of this - to us - almost legendary explorer. James Bruce, of Abyssinian fame, died only four years before the publication of the first *Essay on Population*, and it is possible that Malthus met both Sir George Staunton, who was Lord Macartney's secretary on his embassy to China, and Mungo Park, whose accounts of his travels in West Africa were later to be edited, with a biography, by Whishaw.

I found the lesser-known works more exciting, the leather-bound books with the long *s*, the maps mounted on fine linen, showing gaps marked 'Great Space of Land Unknown', and the engravings which somehow give an eighteenth-century air to both Le Vaillant's naked Hottentots[34] and the elaborately dressed mandarins of Duhalde's China. Possibly the most fascinating of all the books which Malthus read were those of the Jesuit missionaries; the Society had been suppressed in 1773 (it was revived in 1814), and I have a suspicion that contemporary papal disapproval gave these works a respectability in Protestant England which they might not have had otherwise. Paradoxically, Malthus's admiration for these learned, hardy, compassionate and resourceful men may well have contributed to his liberal attitude towards Catholic Emancipation.

Apart from Duhalde's *History of China*,[35] of which he quotes the English version, and du Creux's *Historiae Canadiensis*,[36] which is in delightful seventeenth-century Latin,* Malthus read the works of the Jesuit Fathers in French; one of the little duodecimo volumes of their *Lettres Édifiantes et Curieuses*, of which he possessed a complete set, could well have been

---

*Of the Red Indian women, 'aequam lignaque comportant ... canoas reficiunt', and so on. (They carried the wood and water ... repaired the canoes.)

slipped into a pocket or saddle-bag, or propped up on the table to accompany a solitary meal.[37] French was the only modern foreign language he knew; of the many Spanish sources quoted by Robertson in his *History of America*[38] (Robertson took it for granted he should cover the whole continent) Malthus was only able to chase up one for himself, the *Voyage* of Don Antonio Ulloa, of which a French translation had been published in Amsterdam and Leipzig in 1752.[39] Malthus made use of three demographic works in German, those of Süssmilch,[40] Crome,[41] and the Danish Thaarup:[42] from those of Süssmilch and Thaarup he only took data which were tabulated; he quotes from Crome's actual text, so he must somewhere have picked up either an English or a French translation – both were available.

The second half of the great *Essay*, Books III and IV, are in effect concerned with what has been or should be done to mitigate the evils arising from the principle of population. Some of the authorities quoted in the first two Books are, naturally, referred to again, but Malthus names in addition twenty-six other works which he had consulted. Several of these he had read before – Wallace's, Condorcet's and Godwin's are obvious examples – just as we know he was already familiar with Montesquieu and Adam Smith, Richard Price and Paley, Sir Frederick Morton Eden, Tom Paine and Arthur Young, whose publications are referred to throughout the second *Essay*. But he must have been reading hard, up to the very last minute, keeping abreast of all the latest books and pamphlets; we almost see him as historian and periodical writer combined.

How much information Malthus collected informally from contemporary travellers can only he conjectured. Clarke's letters to him from St Petersburg, Aboukir, and Constantinople, later published by Otter, show how much Malthus relied on him. Clarke was asked for details about the Russian foundling hospitals, and passed on to Professor Pallas Malthus's 'queries respecting the peculiar checks to population among the Nomades'. In Chapter VII of Book I of the quarto Malthus quotes extensively from Pallas's contribution to 'a general abridgment of the works of the Russian travellers ... entitled *Découvertes russes*',[43] since he could not procure his work on the history of the Mongol nations; he must have been interested to learn that Clarke stayed some time with the renowned Peter Simon Pallas. He was a German traveller and naturalist whom Catherine the Great had settled on rich estates in the Crimea, and, according to Clarke, was 'troubled with a gay wife'; but she no doubt helped to make their hospitality 'a continued feast, intellectual as well as sensual'.[44]

The most informative of Clarke's letters is one from Aboukir Bay, dated 9 September 1801, in which he states, 'You are to give full credit to Bruce.' Malthus might well have hesitated to quote James Bruce as an authority, for Bruce's description of Christian Abyssinia's customs had appeared so extraordinary, so utterly inconsistent with Dr Johnson's imaginary *Rasselas*, that his account of his travels had been openly disbelieved and ridiculed. Clarke had, however, found 'a native of Abyssinia' who 'in all things strictly confirmed what Bruce had written', as did French travellers in Upper Egypt, 'the captains of the ships in the Red Sea, and the officers of the Indian Army'.[45]

Malthus would probably not have contemplated an expedition such as Bruce's, but it is easy to understand how eagerly he must have welcomed the Treaty of Amiens and the prospect of travelling in France and Switzerland. We get a glimpse of the general joy at this short-lived peace from old Mr Godschall in Surrey; here are two entries from his diary for 1802:

> Tuesday 30th March: Last night at 12 o'clock Sammy came to say the **DEFINITIVE TREATY** was signed at Amiens on the 27th Instant between England, France, Spain and Holland, he came into my Chamber just as I was a-bed.

> Tuesday 6th April: Mr. and Mrs. Samuel, Mr. Robert and Miss Charlotte Malthus came to tea & brought Fireworks which were let off in the Garden - staid to Supper . . .[46]

I find I have a lively mental picture of the servants' and villagers' delight in the fireworks, and the younger gentry afterwards discussing over supper their plans for going abroad as soon as they could.

Unfortunately, Malthus's journal of this extended family holiday (if he wrote one) does not survive, and we are dependent on that kept by his future wife, his first cousin once removed, Harriet Eckersall. The diary consists of only fifty-four octavo pages, but we can see in five minutes how pleasant she was; a Frenchman has described her, from her portrait by Linnell, as 'bonne et souriante' (goodnatured and smiling), and so she must have been always. She was, moreover, the perfect wife for Malthus. Her journal, possibly written for the younger brothers and sisters at home, gives a conscientious account of their sight-seeing. Like Malthus, she loved pictures more for the story they had to tell, the expressions of the people depicted, than for pure aesthetics. Like him, she loved a good play well acted, and here they were both interested in professional technique. The party only went to one concert in Paris, about which Harriet says nothing at all; and at the Tivoli public gardens she saw what were probably her first 'Walz's', and wrote, 'These last appeared to us ridiculously awkward.'

The party - or some of them - twice went to what Harriet called a 'Sèance of the Legislative Body'; on their second visit they heard 'the grand projet pour la formation d'un legion d'honneur . . . laid before the legislators by Lucien Buonaparte in a clear & eloquent speech, delivered in so distinct a manner that we did not lose a word - notwithstanding the Echo of ye Hall'. They attended 'a lecture on Chemistry at the Jardin des Plantes', 'were very much gratified by viewing the curious manufacture' of the Gobelin tapestries, and at the Institut des Sourds et Muets listened to a most interesting lecture from the Abbé Secard, 'in which he developed in an intelligible manner his Method of instructing the Deaf and Dumb'.

But the tour was also a holiday. There was nothing affected about Robert's and Harriet's delight in the Swiss scenery - cheerfully fertile, or mountainous in the grand manner - and they did not mind facing discomfort to get it. She describes how, when they were crossing the Col de Balme in a long cavalcade of mules, there was a shortage of side-saddles, so that 'Myself and another of the Ladies' were obliged to ride astride: 'The seat was very comfortable upon an ascent but on any at all steep descent we thought we should fall over the Mules head.'

I think the turning point in their lives came early in July. Harriet describes an episode which Malthus made use of in his chapter on Switzerland, when on Sunday 4 July they made an excursion to a 'delightful glen' somewhere near the Lac de Joux.

> We found in our way quantities of the finest wood strawberries & at the source bought an immense provision of them of some young girls. While we sat on the grass to eat them, were much entertain'd with the Philosopic discourse of the driver of our char on the over-population of his country, he complain'd much of the extreme early marriages, which he said was the 'vice du pays', & a custom that had originated in a prosperous time & when a good deal of money could be earn'd by polishing stones & that now when the case was altered & the means of subsistence less, they still continued, 'de se marier au sortir de l'Ecole':* they had large families of children which owing to the extreme healthiness of the air never died but from actual want - he concluded with observing 'qu'on ne devoit se marier qu'a quarante ans, et encore alor's qu'a des vielles filles'† - les *jeunes* filles who were sitting near us were much diverted but did not look as if they would take his advice. The Author of a late Essay on Population with whom he held the conversation was greatly interested to hear many of his own ideas in the mouth of a Swiss peasant - Some of our party wishing for milk to drink after their strawberries, rather shamefully it must be own'd, seiz'd upon one of ye Cows by force & milked her - no bribe being able to corrupt the fidelity of the little Boy who kept them, they did not belong to him he said & he could not sell any of the milk - he endeavour'd to drive his cows away - even after the mischief was done & the cow milk'd, they could hardly make him take any money for it - the milk was not his & it would do him no good - The theives while they robbed him praised his honesty & commended his conduct, but his example

---

*'To marry as soon as they left school.'
†'Men should not get married until they were forty, and then only to old maids.' The *young* maids nearby were amused.

produced no effect - those who had no concern in the seizure of the Cow shared her milk.

The following Monday:

> Coming through Signerol this time we had a compleat view of Mont Blanc unobscured by clouds, rising considerably above the other mountains notwithstanding its infinitely greater distance. While the horses rested Mr. M. and I walked down to the bridge over the Orbe to which Mr. Ricardon had conducted us when we passed through Signerol 3 weeks ago - we met him on our return, he offered to conduct us by a very curious foot way to Orbe, he ran himself up to the Inn to desire our companions would go on to Orbe without us in the Carriage. While he was gone we examined the remains of an old Castle ... though one must not in general trust much to the Swiss idea's of Beauty, Mr. R. had not deceiv'd us ... we found our walk well worth the fatigue.

In August, exploring round Vevey, their ramblings seem to have been associated more with the seductively romantic Rousseau of *La Nouvelle Héloïse* than with the philosophical Rousseau of *Du contrat social*. They were very calm about Switzerland's miniature war: the party got out of Berne at noon on 17 September, when the gates 'were allowed to remain open for an hour', and General d'Erlach's army of peasants captured the town on the following day. By 25 September they were back in Paris, where they stayed for ten days at the Hotel Richelieu, in which 'Mr. Fox had appartments' at the same time. They went to more theatres, and to the Louvre again, but this was obviously all written up very cursorily after Harriet had returned home.[47]

It must have been apparent to everybody, servants and all, what had happened: Mr Malthus and Miss Eckersall, at the ages of thirty-six and twenty-six respectively, had fallen passionately in love. But since the gentleman must lose his income from his Cambridge fellowship on his wedding day - for only professors and the heads of colleges were allowed to have wives - how could they be married?

4 The Walesby Rectory

When Malthus got back to his garret, the first number of the *Edinburgh Review* had appeared. Sydney Smith (anonymously, as was the custom) had referred in very flattering terms to Malthus's controversy with Godwin.

Poor Godwin! Malthus had set on him in the first *Essay on Population* in 1798, Mackintosh in 1799 in *The Law of Nature and Nations*, and then on Easter Tuesday 1800 Dr Parr had joined in the cry against him in what was known as the *Spital Sermon*; this Dr Parr, in a new wig, had preached at the invitation of the Foxite Lord Mayor of London before the Court of Aldermen and the Governors of the City Hospitals; his text was St Paul's 'As we have therefore opportunity, let us do good to all men, especially unto them which are of the household of faith.' The published version contained erudite notes more lengthy than the sermon itself.[48]

Godwin produced in 1801 his *Thoughts Occasioned by the Perusal of Dr. Parr's Spital Sermon*, 'being a reply to the attacks of Dr. Parr, Mr. Mackintosh, the Author of an Essay on Population, and Others'. He wrote movingly that 'universal philanthropy' need not conflict with 'domestic and private affections'. 'While I educate my child judiciously for himself, I am rendering him a valuable acquisition to society ... by contributing to the improvement of my countrymen, I am preparing for my child a society in which it will be desirable for him to live.' Godwin wrote further, 'I would have men, in proportion to the faculties they possess, not omit to devote part of their energies to the natives of different climates, and to ages yet unborn,' and he pointed out that Christ had not merely justified, but applauded, the Good Samaritan.[49]

I think that Godwin had the advantage over Dr Parr here; so thought Thomas Robinson, in a letter to his well-known literary journalist brother, Henry Crabb Robinson, in Germany. Tom wrote on 20 October 1801: 'I am however decidedly of opinion now that I *have read* Godwin's Pamphlet, that he has not answered the Essay on Population – Indeed he makes large concessions to the Author, and allows that his notion of population is correct, he likewise treats the author with great respect.'[50]

The *Edinburgh Review* adopted a similar attitude in Article IX, reviewing the published sermons of a then much respected divine, the Rev. Dr Thomas Rennel, 'who seems to think it more useful, and more pleasant, to rail than to fight'. Rennel should have followed Malthus's example: 'While everybody was abusing and despising Mr. Godwin, and while Mr. Godwin was, among a certain description of understandings, increasing every day in popularity, Mr. Malthus took the trouble of refuting him; and we hear no more of Mr. Godwin.'[51] This is rather ridiculous, as Article II of the same number reviewed Parr's *Sermon*, and Article III Godwin's *Reply* to it; but it is certainly true that in 1812 Shelley (who became Godwin's son-in-law) was surprised to find him not, as he had assumed, 'among the honourable dead'.

It is impossible to guess how much satisfaction Malthus derived from all this. Certainly he must have gone on with his second edition with fresh vigour, aware that the world was waiting for it, aware that he must do something in the world if he were to marry Harriet. His subject he believed to be one of great importance, and it was of absorbing interest to him, an interest that must have been stimulated by over five months of foreign travel; yet I am convinced that he rushed at the work, at times, with feelings of overwhelming bitterness.

Malthus, I believe, enjoyed the company of babies for their own sake. His *Travel Diaries* indicate that his interest in the care of infants was not wholly scientific, and there is a footnote in the 1798 *Essay* in which he comments on 'the extraordinary difference of susceptibility in very young children',[52] which suggests that he observed them more than many men would do. In the 1803 edition he described parental affection as 'one of the most delightful passions in human nature'.[53] Possibly it was his warmly domestic temperament which made him prefer the company of his relations to the communal bachelor life of a college. Yet there he was, elaborating the implications of his principle of population, with no settled home, no secure income if he married, approaching middle age and deeply in love.

It was surely his personal suffering which prompted the passage in the quarto that is still quoted against him. I give the paragraph in full:

> A man who is born into a world already possessed, if he cannot get subsistence from his parents on whom he has a just demand, and if the society do not want his labour, has no claim of *right* to the smallest portion of food, and, in fact, has no business to be where he is. At nature's mighty feast there is no vacant cover for him. She tells him to be gone, and will quickly execute her own orders, if he does not work upon the compassion of some of her guests. If these guests get up and make room for him, other intruders immediately appear demanding the same favour. The report of a provision for all that come, fills the hall with numerous claimants. The order and harmony of the feast is disturbed, the plenty that before reigned is changed into scarcity; and the happiness of the guests is destroyed by the spectacle of misery and dependence in every part of the hall, and by the clamorous importunity of those, who are justly enraged at not finding the provision which they had been taught to expect. The guests learn too late their error, in counteracting those strict orders to all intruders, issued by the great mistress of the feast, who, wishing that all her guests should have plenty, and knowing that she could not provide for unlimited numbers, humanely refused to admit fresh comers when her table was already full.[54]

This paragraph was cut right out of the third edition of the *Essay*, which appeared in 1806 (it did not in the least affect the argument), but it could not be expunged from the memories of those who read it and hated it.

Malthus referred to the excision of this paragraph in his 'Advertisement' to the 1806 edition. He also stated that 'a passage of some length, relating to a comparison of the married and unmarried, has been omitted, and an observation added on the propriety of not underrating the desirableness of marriage, while we are inculcating the duties of moral restraint.'[55] This omission is too long to quote in full, but the passages which naturally gave offence - we must remember that we are in the pre-contraceptive era - are the following:

> The merits of the childless, and of those who have brought up large families, should be compared without prejudice, and their different influence on the general happiness of society justly appreciated.
> The matron who has reared a family of ten or twelve children, and whose sons, perhaps, may be fighting the battles of their country, is apt to think that society owes her much; and this imaginary debt, society is, in general, fully inclined to acknowledge. But if the subject be fairly considered, and the respected matron be weighed in the scales of justice against the neglected old maid, it is possible that the matron might kick the beam. She will appear rather in the character of a monopolist, than of a great benefactor to the state. If she had not married and had so many children, other members of society might have enjoyed this satisfaction; and there is no particular reason for supposing that her sons would fight better for their country than the sons of other women. She has rather subtracted from, than added to, the happiness of the other parts of society. The old maid, on the contrary, has exalted others by depressing herself. Her self-denial has made room for another marriage ... She has really and truly contributed more to the happiness of the rest of the society arising from the pleasures of marriage, than if she had entered in this union herself ... Like the truly benevolent man in an irremediable scarcity, she has diminished her own consumption, instead of raising up a few particular people, by pressing down the rest. On a fair comparison, therefore, she seems to have a better founded claim to the gratitude of society than the matron.[56]

What can the Brays have thought, or the writer's future mother-in-law?

The second edition of the *Essay on Population* appeared about midsummer 1803, and on 4 July of that year John Whitcombe died. This was an event of great importance to Malthus, since John Whitcombe was rector of Walesby, a Lincolnshire village in the Division of Lindsey, some four miles north-east of the little town of Market Rasen. Whitcombe had received this living early in 1767 from Richard Dalton; in 1787 another of the innumerable Malthus cousins, Henry Dalton of Knaith, near Gainsborough, became the patron of Walesby; he was Jane Dalton's brother, and a few years later the possibility of Robert Malthus becoming rector on Mr Whitcombe's death might well have been under discussion in the family.[57] I base this suggestion on two entries in one of William Bray's letter-books, in which his clerks made abstracts of all his out-going correspondence.[58] Most exasperatingly, but understandably, confidential letters were given to the clerks already sealed, so that only the addressees' names were recorded. Thus we find that on 10 August 1792 a sealed letter was sent to George Tennyson, Esq., at Lincoln; he was a prosperous lawyer who acted for Henry Dalton. This would tell us nothing were it not that three days before, on 7 August, another clerk had scribbled out this letter:

> Mr. Geo Tennyson Att[y] at Law Lincoln
> I take the liberty to trouble you as Mr. Dalton is out of Town & he forget to beg you wd. say for what the Rents are pd. whether house Land & in what parish each. Is Walesby *within reach* of the sea so as to be subject to be flooded.

Mr Tennyson and his clerks must have laughed heartily at the last question, for Walesby is sixteen miles from the sea as the crow flies, and the church itself stands high up on a ridge of the Lincolnshire Wolds. This letter, of course, may not relate to the benefice at all; but if it does, this promised living would explain why Malthus took the curacy of Okewood in 1793 - I do not know how long he kept it - as a sort of stop-gap until Walesby became vacant.

However that may have been, Malthus was duly admitted and instituted rector of Walesby on 21 November 1803, and held the living without residing there until his death. It was worth just over £300 a year, from which Malthus paid a curate £70, increased to £80 in 1828. The number of parishioners grew from about 170 to 250 in thirty years; according to Rivington's *Clerical Guide* of 1836, the net value of the benefice had increased by 1831 to something over £440.

One cannot help wondering what might have happened had Mr Whitcombe died sooner; I calculate that he was sixty-nine in 1803. Had John Whitcombe died earlier, the great quarto on the principle of population might have been written by an author comfortably married, or one whose domestic happiness was assured. The book would certainly have been different, and it might not have been so widely noticed. It could never have been anything but a great work, but it is arguable that it would have received less attention had it not been rushed through its final stages by an impassioned and frustrated man, who relieved his feelings by writing with almost sadistic gusto of smallpox and famine, babies exposed and children starving.

It is perhaps impossible to contemplate the fundamental problems of population without some kind of emotional bias, emotions which require recognition but not apology. Any excuses which are made for Malthus's disturbed state must also be applied to his detractors, such as Southey, grieving with 'sore eyes' beside his 'almost heart-broken' wife over the death of their first baby when she was about a year old; he was ashamed to be so deeply wounded by 'so common a calamity', but to her father Margaret was 'not a common child', and when he goes on to 'Malthouses rascally metaphysics' in the same letter, he urges his friend John Rickman to set his foot upon such a mischievous reptile and crush him.[59]

Much of Southey's attack on Malthus in the *Annual Review* of 1804 was inspired by Coleridge, himself most wretched in his marriage, and obviously unbalanced in his approach to the subject, as may be seen from his furious marginal comments on the quarto in the British Library. But possibly a mental picture of Margaret Southey's small grave is the best aid to keeping a sense of proportion as we read the cruel gibes of those who launched out at Malthus so venomously.

5 Three Pre-Malthusians

The bitterness of Malthus's opponents is the more astonishing when we discover that a number of other writers had reached much the same conclusions as he had without arousing a storm. Their remarks on population had, indeed, been included in works with other titles, chiefly concerned with other subjects; they did not write as well or as dramatically as he did; they did not, the cynical might say, dine with the King of Clubs or have friends who could bring their pamphlets to the attention of Mr Pitt. Above all, they were not writing at the time of the first British census, when the population was shown to be far higher than most people had expected, and that shortly after months of near-famine.

In his preface to the second edition of the *Essay on Population*, Malthus wrote: 'I found that much more had been done than I had been aware of, when I first published the Essay. The poverty and misery arising from a too rapid increase of population had been distinctly seen, and the most violent remedies proposed, so long ago as the times of Plato and Aristotle. And of late years the subject has been treated in such a manner by some of the French Economists, occasionally by Montesquieu, and among our own writers, by Dr. Franklin, Sir James Stewart, Mr. Arthur Young, and Mr. Townsend, as to create a natural surprise that it had not excited more public attention.'[60] Many of us can appreciate his feelings: a theory is spun spontaneously from our own minds and experience and then, when we come to investigate, we find that we are merely part of a trend.

The writers I would like briefly to discuss in this connection are Stewart - usually spelt Steuart - Franklin and Townsend. Summaries of the classics (Montesquieu and Mirabeau as well as Plato and Aristotle) are not hard to come by, and Arthur Young's remarks on the constant subdivision of farms in Ireland and France will be remembered by all who have enjoyed his *Travels*. These other three writers are less well known today, but I believe they are of great significance in Malthus's approach to his subject. It is very important to remember that he had not read them when he dashed off the *Essay* of 1798. After he had read them, his whole outlook changed; the possibility of Utopia is no longer a starting point; with the great quarto of 1803 Malthus began the global population controversies which are still going on.

Sir James Steuart (1713-80) had the advantage of a cosmopolitan outlook. He was an exiled Jacobite, who between 1746 and 1763 wandered all over Europe, and who spoke French, Spanish, Italian and German. In 1763 he returned to Scotland to find that he was still legally a traitor, although his only child was a cornet in the British army, but he put his estates in order and worked on unmolested at his *Principles of Political Oeconomy*; in all, he was eight years writing it, and it was the result (admittedly somewhat muddled) of eighteen years of travel and reflection. It was published in 1767, was well reviewed, and sold 370 copies. In 1772 Steuart was finally pardoned and presented at court; the East India Company consulted him, and in the same year he added to his long list of pamphlets *The Principles of Money Applied to the State of the Coin in Bengal*. In 1776 Adam Smith published the *Wealth of Nations* without so much as mentioning Sir James, and that was the end of him for thirty years. His son, General Sir James Steuart-Denham, with whom the line became extinct, published his father's *Collected Works* in 1805, but Malthus had discovered somewhere a well-bound though battered copy of the first edition of the *Political Oeconomy* (it may still be found today in his library at Jesus College).

The relevant writers who preceded Steuart had been concerned with population as a source of national wealth and power; little Holland was great and prosperous because she had so many inhabitants to the square mile. Steuart pointed out that the quality of a population was as important as its quantity: 'Every one knows that the labour of mankind is not in proportion to their numbers, but to their industry.'[61] He maintained 'That mankind have been, as to numbers, and must ever be, in proportion to the food produced; and that the food produced will be in the compound proportion of the fertility of the climate, and the industry of its inhabitants.' *But* - and one wishes that Malthus in the early days had paid more attention to this *but* - 'It is sometimes of ill consequence to fix one's attention too much upon any one object, however important. Nobody can dispute that agriculture is the foundation of multiplication [of the human race], and the most essential requisite for the prosperity of a state. But it does not follow from this, that every body almost in the state should be employed in it; that would be inverting the order of things, and turning the master into the servant. The duty and business of man is not to feed; he is fed, in order to do his duty and to become useful.'[62]

Commercial interdependence, for Steuart, was an essential part of a free civilisation: 'If we can suppose any person entirely taken up in feeding himself, depending upon no one, and having no one depending upon him, we lose the idea of society, because there are no reciprocal obligations between such a person and the other members of the society.'[63]

If there is no trade, the farmers' superfluity 'will perish like their cherries in a year of plenty; and consequently the farmers will immediately give over working'; it is the duty of 'the statesman' to 'contrive different employments for the hands of the necessitous, that, by their labour, they may produce an equivalent which may be acceptable to the farmers, in lieu of this superfluity; for these last certainly will not raise it, if they cannot dispose of it'.[64]

Money was obviously the best 'equivalent' of all, since 'Every person becomes fond of having money.'[65] Steuart wrote (in italics) as one of his Principles, that 'Agriculture among a free people will augment population, in proportion only as the necessitous are put in a situation to purchase subsistence with their labour.'[66] He stressed the practical importance of easy transport, the harm done by artificial barriers to trade, and maintained that population 'cannot augment without an increase of food on the one hand, and of industry on the other, to make the first circulate. These must go hand in hand: the precedence between them is a matter of mere curiosity and speculation.'[67]

Sir James's idea of industry was cottage and workshop craftsmanship rather than 'unwholesome manufactures', although he has some pertinent comments on machinery: 'The ancients held in great veneration the inventors of the saw, of the lathe, of the wimble [the brace and bit], of the potter's wheel; but some moderns find an abuse in bringing mechanism to perfection ... The great Montesquieu finds fault with watermills, though I do not find that he has made any objection to the use of the plough.' Steuart agreed that sudden innovations cause inconvenience, and 'the statesman' must deal with unemployment arising from inventions, or peace after a war; but 'nobody, I believe, will allege that, in order to give bread to soldiers, sutlers, and undertakers, the war should be continued.' He went on, 'Machines therefore I consider as a method of augmenting (virtually) the number of the industrious, without the expence of feeding an additional number.' Later he was to point out the advantages of mechanisation in keeping down the prices of a country's exports.[68]

With regard to human numbers, Sir James Steuart marvelled at 'the generative faculty, which from one pair has produced so many millions';[69] he apparently accepted Adam and Eve, although Malthus himself did not take this couple as an instance of what the principle of population could accomplish. But he must often have gasped, as he read Steuart's great work, to find his own thoughts in another man's words: 'Several kinds of animals,' wrote Steuart, 'especially insects, multiply by thousands, and yet the species does not appear annually to increase. Nobody can pretend that particular individuals of any species have a privilege to live, and that others die from a difference in their nature. It is therefore reasonable to conclude, that what destroys such vast quantities of those produced, must be, among other causes, the want of food. Let us apply this to man.'[70]

Benjamin Franklin (1706-90) Malthus presumably counted 'among our own writers' because at the time of his birth there, Boston, Massachusetts, was still a British colony. From this almost superhuman statesman and scientist Malthus quotes an essay of ten and a half pages, 'Observations concerning the Increase of Mankind, Peopling of Countries, etc.', which was written in Pennsylvania in 1751; Malthus found it in a volume of Franklin's *Political, Miscellaneous and Philosophical Pieces* which Joseph Johnson had published in 1779. The essay is reminiscent of Bacon in its logical brevity: Malthus must have felt, as he read it, that almost all his ideas and discoveries had been compressed into this one exquisite nutshell years before he himself was born.

I think Sir James Steuart may have read Franklin's essay, and that it was partly against Franklin's strictures that Sir James felt he must defend manufacture and commerce. Like Dr Price, Franklin had a poor opinion of town life, and wrote of people remaining single in cities because the cost of raising a family in a town was so much greater than in the country. Franklin held that 'cities do not, by natural generation, supply themselves with inhabitants: the deaths are more than the births.' Sir James Steuart could retort that in Paris the births were more than the deaths. Franklin, as might be expected, wanted more people, to fill the vast territory of North America, and so advocated the encouragement of early marriages and plain living: 'The greater the common fashionable expence of any rank of people, the more cautious they are of marriage. Therefore luxury should never be suffered to become *common*.'[71]

But Franklin and Malthus agreed on the basic facts, including the filling of 'occasional vacancies' by 'natural generation'. I quote from Franklin's three final paragraphs:

> Who can now find the vacancy made in Sweden, France, or other warlike nations, by the plague of heroism 40 years ago; in France, by the expulsion of the Protestants; in England, by the settlement of her colonies; or in Guinea, by a hundred years exportation of slaves, that has blackened half America? . . .
>
> There is, in short, no bound to the prolific nature of plants or animals, but what is made by their crowding and interfering with each other's means of subsistence. Was the face of the earth vacant of other plants, it might be gradually sowed and overspread with one kind only; as for instance, with fennel; and were it empty of other inhabitants, it might, in a few ages, be replenished from one nation only, as for instance, with Englishmen . . .

106

In fine, a nation well regulated is like a polypus; take away a limb, its place is soon supplied; cut it in two, and each deficient part shall speedily grow out of the part remaining. Thus, (if you have room and subsistence enough) as you may, by dividing, make ten polypuses out of one; you may, of one, make ten nations, equally populous and powerful; or rather, increase a nation tenfold in numbers and strength.[72]

The American Declaration of Independence did in fact split Franklin's political polypus into two nations. Our three pre-Malthusians were indeed unfortunate as regards their theories of population: Steuart was obliterated by Adam Smith, Franklin's gem was temporarily lost with the revolted colonies, and the Rev. Joseph Townsend (1739-1816) seems for a time to have obliterated himself through eccentricities which bordered on the insane.

According to the *Gentleman's Magazine*, Joseph Townsend 'distinguished himself as a preacher among the Calvinistic Methodists, and occasionally officiated at Lady Huntingdon's Chapel in Bath; but of late years his zeal on that side was considerably abated'. He was rector of Pewsey in Wiltshire, where his congregation dwindled markedly from two hundred communicants to two or three; he neglected them for the affairs of the Kennet and Avon Canal, of which he was one of the principal projectors and shareholders, and also for his researches in geology, etymology, and the authenticity of Mosaic legend, all of which appear to have become obsessive. As a young man he had studied medicine in Edinburgh, and his works include *Free and Despotic Governments* and *The Physician's Vade Mecum*, which were both published in 1781. In 1786 came his *Dissertation on the Poor Laws* (to which we shall refer later), but his most popular book was his three-volume *Journey Through Spain*, of which the first edition was published in 1791.

Townsend is still a good bedside companion, especially on a Spanish holiday. Malthus thought so highly of him that, in his account of the checks to population in the different states of modern Europe, he omitted Spain altogether, referring the reader 'to the valuable and entertaining travels of Mr. Townsend in that country, in which he will find the principle of population very happily illustrated'.[73] 'Happily' was perhaps an unfortunate adverb to apply to Townsend's description of 'the poor, naked, and half-starved, inhabitants' of the 'wretched village' of Cullar de Baza, through which he rode on his way from Granada to Carthagena:

> The little valley, which supplies this village, is about a quarter of a mile in breadth, inclosed by barren gypseous mountains; and although it is well watered, and consequently fertile in flax, hemp, and wheat, with vines on the more elevated spots, yet the population bears too great a proportion to the extent of land susceptible of cultivation.

Looking down upon so rich, yet such a contracted spot, we instantly and evidently see that the human race, however at first, and whilst their numbers are limited, they may rejoice in affluence, will go on constantly increasing, till they balance their quantity of food. From that period, two appetites will combine to regulate their numbers. Beyond that period, should they continue to increase, having passed the natural limits of their population, they must suffer want.[74]

In his index, Townsend has 'Population, principles of', so that anyone who wished could accuse Malthus of plagiarism, or of taking a quarto to elaborate a dilemma which Townsend had summed up in a few pages. Townsend named eight causes which retarded the propagation of the species: 'Want of food' and 'Diseases' headed the list; third came 'Want of commerce for the promotion of industry, and of a market for the surplus of its produce'. 'War' was the fourth check on population, and '5th, Superstitious vows imposed on the monastic orders, and celibacy enjoined on the priesthood'. It is interesting that he gives 'Emigration' as an evil, resulting 'from a vicious form of government, and the want of that security of person and property which can be enjoyed only where freedom reigns'. 'Want of land' and 'Want of habitations' are his seventh and eighth hindrance to population. He goes on:

Now in proportion as you remove these obstacles, your population will advance. When, therefore, it is your object to increase the number of your people; the way to accomplish this will be obvious, and the task in Spain, under a wise government, would be easy; but when the question is, how to banish poverty and wretchedness, *hoc opus, hic labor est*. Yet in the investigation of this question we have one general principle to guide us: increase the quantity of food, or where that is limited, prescribe bounds to population. In a fully peopled country, to say, that no one shall suffer want is absurd. Could you supply their wants, you would soon double their numbers, and advance your population *ad infinitum*, which is contrary to the supposition. It is indeed possible to banish hunger, and to supply that want at the expence of another; but then you must determine the proportion that shall marry, because you will have no other way to limit the number of your people. No human efforts will get rid of this dilemma; nor will men ever find a method, either more natural, or better in any respect, than to leave one appetite to regulate another.[75]

6 The Book and its Readers

After this brief account of Townsend's views on population, it hardly seems necessary to remind ourselves, once again, that we are considering a period without contraceptives. Yet we must make a renewed effort to keep this in mind if Malthus's alternative to the misery of over-population - the prudently delayed marriage - and all the contemporary objections to it, are not to appear utterly meaningless. In 1797, in Young's *Annals of Agriculture*, Jeremy Bentham had indeed published an article on the Poor in which he made an allusion to the use of a 'spunge' for soaking them up, as it were, before they came into existence; but his language was so allegorical that hardly anyone could have received practical help from it.[76]

In general, even a whispered hint of such an idea was regarded as unspeakably immoral. Yet in spite of all these circumstances, Malthus's quarto represented what would now be called a break-through. His book is a landmark because he affirmed that population - procreation - was something which man not only could, but should, as a duty, attempt to control.

It is difficult to appreciate the fact today, but Malthus initiated a new era when he maintained that population growth should be limited by prudence, rather than dramatically checked by disease and famine. He never said (and did not believe) that a time might come when the poor would not be always with us, but he insisted that the condition of the poor could be ameliorated if, through education and self-respect, they were induced to postpone marriage until they could provide decently for their families; and, of course, the older they were when they married, the fewer children they would have. With hindsight, we can see that John Stuart Mill was right when he wrote in 1844 of 'the appearance of Mr. Malthus's Essay on Population. Though the assertion may be looked upon as a paradox, it is historically true, that only from that time has the economical condition of the labouring classes been regarded by thoughtful men as susceptible of permanent improvement.'[77]

Malthus's 'very much enlarged' second edition cost, unbound, one and a half guineas - that is, 31s. 6d., or £1. 11s. 6d., or £1.57½p in the present decimal currency. It was entitled:

AN ESSAY ON THE PRINCIPLE OF POPULATION
OR
A VIEW OF ITS PAST AND PRESENT EFFECTS
ON HUMAN HAPPINESS
WITH AN INQUIRY INTO OUR PROSPECTS RESPECTING

THE

FUTURE REMOVAL OR MITIGATION OF THE EVILS WHICH
IT OCCASIONS

This title-page in itself reveals how Malthus's outlook had changed in the five years since he wrote the first *Essay*; then he was somewhat negatively concerned with 'the Principle of Population as it affects the Future Improvement of Society, with Remarks on the Speculations of Mr. Godwin, M. Condorcet and Other Writers'. The title-page of 1803 also explains why Malthus's name has been linked with those of the Benthamite Utilitarians and the pursuit of the greatest happiness of the greatest number. A little reflection will show that subsequent works on population have followed much the same pattern, with surveys and statistics replacing the travellers' tales; the inquiries respecting the mitigation of the evils of excessive numbers are now concerned with technical questions of food production and transport, contraception and communication, utterly beyond the range of the most visionary of the Whig and Radical reformers of the early nineteenth century.

Since the second version of the *Essay on Population* has been summarised so often, I do not think yet another résumé will serve any useful purpose. The book deserves a first-hand perusal. Modern readers should not be daunted by its length; an hour or so of skimming and skipping will give them enough of the atmosphere of the work for a general understanding of Malthus's application of his main - and very simple - theses. Malthus's contemporaries, of course, were in a different position, and it will be worth while to see how the book first appeared to them, before we consider some of the controversies it started.

One can sympathise with the writer for the *Monthly Review*, whose article appeared in two sections, in the issues of December 1803 and January 1804; he affirmed of Malthus that 'wherever, in future, any positions in political economy are discussed, his name will be associated with those of Montesquieu and Turgot, of Hume and Smith,' but he could not commend Mr Malthus 'on the score of brevity and method'.[78] The *British Critic*, on the other hand, which also reviewed the quarto in two parts, in January and March 1804, was more charitable: 'A desire to leave nothing unsaid upon a subject of so much importance, has certainly led Mr. Malthus to be rather diffuse. A more concise view might have been more pleasing to some persons, and better adapted for general reading. For ourselves, we can truly say that we found every part of the work so curious, and so ably treated, that it did not appear to us too long.'[79]

The *Monthly Magazine* and the *Imperial Review* both gave the book excellent but not uncritical notices in single articles in January 1804, and Southey was to write to John Rickman on 9 March: 'Malthus is as great a favourite with the *British Critic* as with the other voiders of menstrual pollution. I shall be very glad to lend a hand in some regular attack upon this mischievous booby, and if you will put your shoulder to the work we may in a few evenings effectually demolish him.'[80]

In fact it was in this month that the tide began to turn, for the anonymous *Remarks on a Late Publication* . . ., although dated 1803, actually appeared in March 1804. Joyfully the hack working for the *Gentleman's Magazine* must have seized upon this pamphlet of 62 pages, as compared with Malthus's 610, and in April 1804 he produced a review which is a précis of the Remarker rather than of Malthus. Some of the Remarker's general criticism is, I think, valid. He stated that the novelty of Malthus's speculations 'appears to have drawn him into the great error of all system-formers; and by confining his attention to one object solely, he has neglected the operation of all the other wheels in the great machine of society. Pursuing his hypothesis, I had almost said with the ardour of discovery, he endeavours to establish the principle of population, as the master-spring in this social and political machine; and to its favourable or unfavourable action attributes at least one half of the goods or ills of society.'[81]

With regard to the general tenor of the work, the Remarker thought 'the author has given the most gloomy and exaggerated view.' Tom Robinson, on the other hand, writing to his brother in 1803, just after Christmas, thought that Malthus threw out 'some very useful ideas on the improvement of society - and although his theories do not delude us with the expectation that men are to become *immortal angels*, yet he does not discourage the expectation of bettering society to a certain extent . . . Since Adam Smith, so able a writer has not appeared on the subject of political economy, and in one respect he improves upon Smith, by proposing plans not only to increase the *wealth* of the state but the *happiness* of the community, and particularly the poor.' Malthus himself, of course, never saw this letter.[82]

Tom Robinson's reference to 'immortal angels' is another hit at Godwin, and it is astonishing to find how many reviewers were interested in the comparatively unimportant chapter in the quarto in which Malthus repeated the arguments he had used against *Political Justice* in 1798. The same preoccupation is noticeable in a review in the Philadelphia *Literary Magazine and American Register* of August 1804, which is otherwise largely lifted from the London *Monthly Magazine*.

Perhaps the saddest story about the quarto is that told by Dr Currie in a long letter from Liverpool to his student son in Edinburgh. It is dated 19 February 1804, and concerns a mental patient whose reason gave way after his indulgence in speculations on the perfectibility of man. Dr Currie (who had praised the *Essay* of 1798 in his Prefatory Remarks to Burns' *Life*) explained to his patient the principle of population; his reaction was to produce 'a scheme for enlarging the surface of the globe, and a project for an act of parliament for this purpose, in a letter addressed to Mr. Pitt'. To show that even this measure could not solve the problem, Dr Currie gave the young man Malthus's quarto. This he read twice, aloud the second time, not omitting a single word, and then, after a few distressing days, he quietly lay down and died. Dr Currie added, 'At the moment that I write this, his copy of Malthus is in my sight; and I cannot look at it but with extreme emotion.'

Emotion did not, however, prevent Currie from asking his son what Dugald Stewart, the most influential professor of philosophy at this period, thought about 'Malthus's principles and deductions from them, which are of the most important kind. I wish to see an able article in the Edinburgh Review on this curious, interesting, and melancholy subject.'[83]

No article specifically on Malthus's quarto on population ever did appear in the *Edinburgh Review*. The work was entrusted by the editor, Francis Jeffrey (1773-1850), to the brilliant and lovable Francis Horner (1778-1817). Both men were later to become close friends of Malthus, but Horner embarked on reviewing the book before either of them had met the author. The Lord Lyell, to whom it belongs, has allowed me to see Francis Horner's own copy of the quarto; his pencilled comments are scribbled everywhere, often with a query mark in the margin, as though he doubted many of Malthus's statements.

Jeffrey continually urged Horner to get on with the review. On 14 September 1803 he begged, 'May I *entreat* you now to do Malthus, if possible, for this number?' On 6 May 1804 he was more insistent:

Now, my most trusted and perfidious Horner, I earnestly conjure you to think how necessary it is to set instantly about Malthus ... I do think it of consequence that we should begin, if possible, with this article, both because it is more important, and more impatiently expected than any other.[84]

On 5 August he wrote again:

For our sake, for my sake, for your own sake, and for God's sake, do set about Malthus immediately, and by the labour of one week save yourself from the penitence and reproaches of many months. I cannot vary my exhortations more; you have worn out my whole stock of obtestations.[85]

Nonetheless, a month later, on 3 September, he was still begging:

My dear Horner - Will you take compassion upon me, and rise five mornings at seven o'clock, and let me have Malthus to begin with. Upon my honour, I would do that for you, horribly as I detest rising, if it would relieve you half as much as you can do me.[86]

The last of these requests was made on 20 January 1805:

Will you, or will you not, do Malthus for April? Is it fair to the

Review, or kind to me, or well for yourself, to keep up an article of this kind for so enormous a time?[87]

We do not know how Horner replied, but the article was never written. I think the reason was that this young Scots lawyer, who had migrated south to Lincoln's Inn, disagreed strongly with Malthus's views, but was too much in the same 'set' to write against him. Horner's versatility was remarkable, and deplored by some of his friends, but I cannot accept the suggestion that he failed to apply himself to the review of Malthus simply because he was overwhelmed by other activities. When he was a law student in Edinburgh he had pursued chemistry and jurisprudence simultaneously, and wrote of poetry, 'Scarcely a day has passed in which I have not melted away an hour or two in this luxurious reading.'[88] He had written a paper on population for a university society founded by Henry Brougham.

Visits to Edinburgh from Sydney Smith and James Mackintosh had intensified Horner's desire for public life in London, and he therefore decided to read for the English bar. He met Whishaw in the spring of 1802, and also had a letter of introduction from Dugald Stewart to Samuel Romilly. On 10 April he had his first dinner with 'the King of Clubs, which meets monthly at the Crown and Anchor in the Strand', and thereafter we find the names of its members recurring in his letters and journal. I think he met the Evangelicals later, after his article on Henry Thornton's *Paper Credit* had appeared in the first number of the *Edinburgh Review*, a piece of work which established Horner as an economic expert. We know that he met Wilberforce in May 1803, at Charles Grant's house in Russell Square, whither he had recently moved after being the Thorntons' neighbour in Clapham. Thus the twenty-six-year-old aspirant with 'two glorious visions, historical reputation and professional eminence',[89] may have felt it impossible to review Malthus's quarto as his conscience dictated without the risk of abusing hospitality and offending the influential.

Attached to Francis Horner's copy of the quarto on *Population* is a letter which Malthus sent to him, through Whishaw, for insertion in the *Edinburgh Review*; it was never published, as the *Review* did not deal in that sort of correspondence. The letter itself is undated, but the covering note from Whishaw to Horner is headed 'Monday Nov 19', and the year must have been 1804. Malthus's purpose in writing was to explain that Otter's brother Edward - 'an able mathematical friend' - had pointed out that he was wrong in assuming that the proportion of annual marriages to annual births 'expressed . . . the proportion of the born which lives to be married'. The statistical aspects of this letter are discussed by Professor Petersen and need not detain us here;[90] what is interesting from a biographical point of view are Malthus's motives for writing it.

The letter begins with the sentence 'As it would always be my wish to acknowledge an error as soon as it was known to me, I should esteem it a particular favour if, in your widely-circulating review, you could find room for the following remarks.' This tallies with what we already know of Malthus; the pursuit of accurate statistics and their correct interpretation were among the intellectual passions of his life. But one cannot help wondering whether he was acting altogether disinterestedly in sending the letter to Horner, or whether he hoped it would stimulate this notable young man into writing the article which he must have been anxiously awaiting: by this time, not to be reviewed in the *Edinburgh* was a disagreeable slight. It is also possible that Malthus's friends talked him into it.

In any case, Whishaw's note begins familiarly, 'Dear Horner', and the first paragraph concerns the postponement of an engagement with Smyth, called away to a sister who was ill in the country. In the second paragraph he refers to Malthus's 'Papers', and concludes in a way which might have made the recipient uncomfortable:

> As you are engaged in reviewing the work, I send you the Papers in
> order that you may judge what use shd be made of them. You will
> be kind enough to give me your opinion when I next see you, which
> I hope will be soon.
> Yrs truly
> J. Whishaw

What excuses did Horner make?

All that can be said with certainty is that Malthus entirely re-wrote the chapter 'On the Fruitfulness of Marriages' for the third edition of the *Essay*, which was published in 1806. There had been some correspondence about it in the *Monthly Magazine*, between September 1804 and March 1805, in which the conflicting views of Richard Price and Malthus were discussed.[91] The conclusions to be drawn from the data in parish registers were an obvious field of controversy; Malthus's original statistical chapter was attacked even after the appearance of the revised version in the third and fourth editions, by people who had only read the quarto - the Rev. Robert Ingram, whose book was published in 1808, was the most notable.

In general, of course, it was not Malthus's statistics which interested the public, but his religion and morals. After the eulogy of the monthly periodicals came Southey's blistering assault in the *Annual Review* for 1803, published the following year. We shall refer to it again, but the tone of the whole may be judged from the two concluding paragraphs:

> What then is the purpose of this quarto volume? To teach us, first,
> that great misery and great vice arise from poverty; and that there
> must be poverty in its worst shapes wherever there are more mouths
> than loaves, and more heads than brains. Secondly, that the only
> remedy is, that the poor should not be encouraged to breed. There is
> not a man in England who was ignorant of the first fact, nor a

mistress of a family who does not advise her servants not to marry. No wonder that Mr. Malthus should be a fashionable philosopher! He writes advice to the poor for the rich to read; they of course will approve his opinions, and, understanding with perfect facility the whole of his profound reasonings, will of course admit them with perfect satisfaction.

The folly and wickedness of this book have provoked us into a tone of contemptuous indignation; in affixing these terms to the book, let it not be supposed that any general condemnation of the author is implied, grievously as he has erred in this particular instance. - Mr. Malthus is said to be a man of mild and unoffending manners, patient research, and exemplary conduct. This character he may still maintain; but as a political philosopher, the farthing candle of his fame must stink and go out.[92]

Southey was very quickly proved wrong. As early as 1 January 1805 the *Monthly Magazine* informs us that 'A new edition of Mr. Malthus's Essay on Population is preparing for publication.' It appeared in March 1806, and was followed a year later by the fourth edition; both the third and fourth editions were in two octavo volumes. There was then a gap of ten years before the fifth edition of 1817; the sixth, the last which Malthus was to correct, was published in 1826. The *Essay* was translated into French and German in Malthus's life-time, and since then reprints, translations, extracts, explanations and elaborations have filled many library catalogues, in alphabets as well as languages incomprehensible to his present biographer.

To make amends for the *Edinburgh's* neglect of the *Essay on Population*, Jeffrey, in August 1810, unfavourably reviewed two of Malthus's critics, Ingram and the anonymous Hazlitt. He had written twice to Horner in 1809, 'I wish you could put your notes and notions of Malthus together at last,' and then, 'If I am to think of reviewing Malthus myself, could you give me any notes or ideas?'[93] Perhaps the notes were not forthcoming, but the article certainly reads very like Jeffrey's spontaneous work, with the famous dictum that the *Essay on Population* was a book more generally talked of than read. It is possible that it has also been more written about than studied.

CHAPTER IV

The Population Controversies Begin

1 Religion

Malthus added an *Appendix* to his third edition of 1806. In it he wrote: 'I should feel greatly obliged to those who have not had leisure to read the whole work, if they would cast their eyes over the few following pages, that they may not, from the partial and incorrect statements which they have heard, mistake the import of some of my opinions, and attribute to me others which I never held.'

This *Appendix* was also printed separately on quarto sheets - it occupies thirty-five such pages - and sold for half a crown (12½p), for the benefit of those who already possessed the quarto second edition. Books, like clothes, were meant to last in those days, with alterations and patches; most copies of the quarto I have seen have the 1806 *Appendix* bound up with them. The supplement is entitled *Reply to the Chief Objections which have been urged against the Essay on the Principle of Population.*

Malthus began his *Reply* with what was to him the most important issue: 'The first grand objection that has been made to my principles is, that they contradict the original command of the Creator, to increase and multiply and replenish the earth.'[1] This is not how we would regard the main religious difficulty today; once more we must adjust our historical perspective, and remember that Malthus's mentors and friends, and from 1805 onwards his employers in the East India Company, were many of them either Dissenters or Evangelicals who attached supreme importance to the literal interpretation of the Bible. He had little difficulty in pointing out that later marriages and smaller families were in no wise contrary to Jehovah's command to increase and multiply: according to God's own law, men could not live without food; an attempt to increase the number of people without a proportionate increase in the supply of food would simply not succeed in replenishing the earth; the result could only be misery and premature death.

The fundamental psychological religious difficulty lies much deeper than this notion of obedience to a scriptural command. People with no professed religion can still be found today who deny with a vehemence beyond reason the tendency of unchecked population to exceed supplies. Partly due, I think, to indolence, and partly to insecurity, there is a human need to be able to say, 'It is bound to work out all right in the long run,' or, 'Whatever God wills is best,' or as Dr Jarrold wrote in 1806, 'A wise and benevolent Creator has his eyes constantly upon us.'[2]

No one said in so many words that Malthus had demolished religious Providence as he had demolished political Utopias, that nothing could be achieved without hard thinking and hard work, but that was the uncomfortable truth. It was not a new idea; none of Malthus's opponents would have impugned the goodness of the Deity because we must exert ourselves to provide clothes against the cold or shelter against the rain, any more than they made a grievance of the need for constant exertion to obtain food, which had, in any case, a biblical sanction. In these, and in many other spheres, the difference between an active faith in God and a lazy trust in Providence was fully recognised; man was, after all, to subdue the earth as well as replenish it. To Malthus belongs the credit for being the first to open up for man an entirely new sphere in which continuously to exert his intelligence - with, of course, the added strength and serenity of divine aid, should he believe in it.

But how his adversaries went for him! Malthus's main antagonists at this time were Southey, helped by Coleridge, and Hazlitt, supported by Cobbett. There were also a well-known physician, Dr Thomas Jarrold (1770-1853); the Rev. Robert Acklom Ingram (1763-1809), a philanthropic Leicestershire parson; and three anonymous writers. These were the Remarker, whom we have already met; an Edinburgh man who styled himself Simplex; and the author of a book printed at Hawick in 1807, entitled *A Summons of Wakening or the Evil Tendency and Danger of Speculative Philosophy*; we will call him the Awakener.

On the practical contemporary problem of the Poor Laws, Malthus was to cross swords with many more antagonists, but this subject must be left to another section. We must also defer consideration of his views on food production and free trade, since he thought of such questions in contemporary terms, within the framework of the Corn Laws of the period.

Naturally it was on the theological issue that writers were most violent. 'The religious mind revolts', wrote Mr Ingram, 'at the apparent want of intelligence, and contrivance, in the Author of the creation, in infusing a principle into the nature of man, which it required the utmost exertion of human prudence and ingenuity to counteract.'[3] 'Is there no law in this kingdom for punishing a man for publishing a libel against the Almighty himself?' demanded the Awakener.[4]

Simplex stuck to the infallibility of biblical texts: 'Trust in Jehovah, and do good; so shalt thou dwell in the land, and VERILY thou shalt be FED.'[5] Mr Ingram pointed out from his Old Testament studies that 'Judah and Israel were many as the sand which is by the sea in multitude ... eating and drinking and making merry'; he computed that in King David's time

the population of Palestine was more than 500 to the square mile.[6] Like Dr
Jarrold, Ingram held that after the Flood God had made human beings live
longer and breed more, so that the earth should be rapidly re-stocked with
men and women; thereafter our lives were gradually shortened to three score
years and ten, and our breeding proclivities adjusted accordingly. Both these
men - and they were not stupid - assumed that divine guidance of human
fecundity (utterly divorced from general natural laws) would prevent an
excessive number of births. They agreed with the Awakener in condemning
'this impious and atheistical assertion, *that the Almighty brings more beings
into the world than he prepares nourishment for*'.[7]

It was a position difficult to defend rationally: for our transgressions, or
for our development, there could quite properly be every kind of
emergency - wars, plagues, famines, droughts, tempests, earthquakes, even
thunderbolts, with which the virtuous were to cope to the best of their
ability - but God would not allow a population problem. Dr Jarrold stated
firmly that war, famine, and pestilence were not 'natural'; famine should be
averted by foresight, and diseases investigated and eradicated; yet he found
Malthus's plea for a population policy blasphemously monstrous: 'The
representation given, makes the Almighty much more unwise in planning,
and weaker in executing, than man.'[8]

None of Malthus's opponents denied that the poor were often short of
food, but Mr Ingram made the astonishing suggestion that Malthus was
exaggerating when he wrote as if he 'regarded the distress, which is sometimes
experienced by large families of the lower classes, as that species of misery,
which is the most deplorable of any, to which human nature is exposed'.
Ingram wrote that 'Death must, sooner or later, overtake all, and is commonly
preceded by pain and suffering; and if the lives of some few are shortened
by a deficiency of nourishment, or the want of other comforts, that are
denied to the poor, their sufferings are, probably, not more acute than those
by which their dissolution would, otherwise, have soon been effected; and,
on the contrary, if the lives of the affluent are sometimes prolonged by
assiduous attention and good nursing, it often amounts only to a prolongation
of misery and torment.'[9] The sufferings of the wealthy, if they were the
result of their own misconduct, would of course be far more acute than
those of the virtuous poor.

The problem of innocent suffering, indeed, remains unsolved; it is difficult
to believe that a benevolent and omnipotent deity consents to the suffering
of those too young, too old, or too incapacitated to learn from it. Towards
the end of his life, Samuel Rogers pondered: 'Why there should be evil in
the world is indeed a mystery. Milton attempts to answer the question; but
he has not done it satisfactorily. The three acutest men with whom I was
ever acquainted, Sir James Mackintosh, Malthus, and Bobus Smith, were all
agreed that the attributes of the Deity must be in some respects limited, else
there would be no sin and misery.' The Rev. Alexander Dyce, who edited

Rogers' *Table Talk*, put in a footnote: 'I cannot help remarking, that men whom the world regards as far greater "lights" than the three above mentioned have thought very differently on this subject.'[10]

Rogers' statement may not be true: old people are inclined to forget or muddle proper names. But if it is true, Malthus must have endured much spiritual distress.

There are two other theological points - Hell, and Utilitarianism - which are of biographical interest, though perhaps not generally relevant today. We recall that in the 1798 *Essay* Malthus had taken up a most unorthodox position for a clergyman of the Church of England when he wrote, *inter alia*, that he could not conceive of a loving God condemning any of his creatures to 'eternal hate and torture'. Various reviewers of the first *Essay* had commented on this at the time, and in September 1805 a correspondent in the *Christian Observer*, who signed himself Unus, raised the matter again:

> It is true, indeed, that in the larger edition of this Essay some
> passages are omitted which held a conspicuous place in the original
> outline. In the quarto volume we read no reflections upon the
> Christian doctrine of the everlasting punishment of the impenitent;
> nor are entertained by the theory of the grand operation of nature for
> exciting mind out of matter. The omission was just and prudent: but
> some rigid censors would be apt to insinuate that it was the duty of
> Mr. Malthus to retract as well as omit, unless he is still determined
> to afford to the world an example of the most acute intellectual
> powers joined with the imbecility of a visionary.[11]

I cannot help wondering whether Unus missed an enigmatic sentence on page v of Malthus's preface to the second edition: 'I should hope that there are some parts of it [the first *Essay*] not reprinted in this, which may still have their use; as they were rejected, not because I thought them all of less value than what has been inserted, but because they did not suit the different plan of treating the subject which I had adopted.'[12] In the third edition of 1806 this sentence no longer appears. In every other respect but one the 1803 preface was reprinted as it stood in all subsequent editions. The other alteration was very minor: Malthus said that the 1798 *Essay* was written on 'the impulse of the moment' and not the 'spur'. Such a small verbal correction is a very different matter from the deletion of a whole sentence, since this cut implies that his views had changed between 1803 and 1806, and that he in fact thought that 'some parts' of the first *Essay* were now of less value. Whether or not he intended this omission as a retraction of his former heterodox opinions we shall never know.

The main concern of Unus, however, was not with everlasting punishment, but with Malthus's conception of right and wrong. Malthus, according to this writer, had adopted the noxious principle of Expediency or Utility, stating that the general consequence of vice being misery 'is the precise reason why an action is termed vicious'; he had, after all, on the title-page of the great quarto declared that he was concerned with the past and present effects of the principle of population on human happiness.

Unus quoted page 560 of the quarto, where Malthus had written: 'Though utility, therefore, can never be the immediate excitement to the gratification of any passion, it is the test by which alone we can know, whether it ought, or ought not, to be indulged; and is therefore the surest foundation of all morality which can be collected from the light of nature.' With this Unus most fundamentally disagreed, and went to some length to support his contention that 'Moral obligation can have no foundation but the will of an intelligent superior possessing supreme authority. If such a will has been declared, it is the duty of man to obey it, in the face of consequences apparently the most inexpedient, in the face of any consequences whatever.'*[13]

The *Christian Observer* ('conducted by members of the Established Church') was virtually the monthly organ of the Clapham Evangelicals, and Henry Thornton was one of the chief contributors. Malthus must have had this letter pointed out to him, and in the third edition of 1806 the offending passage was amended as follows: 'Though utility, therefore, can never be the immediate excitement to the gratification of any passion, it is the test by which alone we can know, independently of the revealed will of God, whether it ought or ought not to be indulged; and is therefore the surest criterion of moral rules which can be collected from the light of nature.'[14]

Marriage and success had, I think, combined to make Malthus sincerely more orthodox; they often do. I cannot imagine him, merely for respectability's sake, making these alterations in his text, and especially in his preface; he must have realised that they would pass almost unnoticed. That he might have done so for friendship's sake is more likely. We cannot know, we cannot even probe.

Otter here, as elsewhere, is not very clear, but he wrote of Malthus that 'being always deliberate in composition, and habitually disposed to weigh well every opinion before he submitted it to the public, he was rarely called upon to retract, but whenever the case required it, no one could do it with more candour, or with a better grace. He expunged two whole chapters from his first work, in deference to the opinions of some distinguished persons in our church.' Otter also wrote of his friend's sermons, after his death: 'It is now particularly pleasing to record, that they became more earnest and more edifying every year he lived.' In all ordinances of religion,

*Unus may have been Thomas Gisborne (1758-1846), an Evangelical whose *Principles of Moral Philosophy*, first published in 1789, were read with approval by Jane Austen after she had overcome a prejudice against him; his brother John was a minor poet, the husband of the Maria Gisborne to whom Shelley wrote a memorable letter in verse.

'his manner was uniformly serious and devout; nor could he ever say grace at his own table, without inspiring those present with a sense of his piety.'[15] To say grace at meal-times is now regarded as old-fashioned, but I like to think that Malthus, in a hungry world, did not take his dinner for granted.

2 Sex

His opinions on what he called 'the passion between the sexes' affected Malthus's detractors in surprisingly different ways. The idea of prudently delayed marriage appalled the pious: God had created Eve because it was not fit that man should live alone. Simplex gives this point of view: 'But, it may be urged, Mr. Malthus does not forbid, but only inculcates, a *temporary* abstinence from marriage. I say in reply, that they who inculcate, and they who adopt *abstinence* (without absolute necessity) from what God the Creator hath commanded, are alike guilty of *resisting* his ordinance, and, of course, equally liable to damnation.'[16]

It is perhaps worth noting that celibacy seems to have been derided in some circles because it was connected with popery - Catholic Emancipation was an important contemporary issue - and so St Paul's advocacy of continence was conveniently forgotten. Simplex maintained 'generally speaking, that *ninety-nine* of *one hundred* of the human species will find the *must-be* of Mr. M. a *physical impossibility*'. A bachelor who tried to remain chaste 'must *counteract nature*. He *must*, then, of course, *burn*, as the apostle terms it; and self-pollution, and debauchery of mind, though no overt act should take place, must be the inevitable consequence.'[17]

Southey, with Coleridge behind him, and Hazlitt, attacked Malthus for exactly the opposite reason. Southey castigated him for assuming 'that lust and hunger are alike passions of physical necessity, and the one equally with the other independent of the reason and the will. If this were true, chastity could not exist; fornication would be as indispensable as food.'[18] Hazlitt wrote, 'Mr. Malthus's whole book rests on a malicious supposition, that all mankind (I hope the reader will pardon the grossness of the expression, the subject is a gross one) are like so many animals *in season* ... But I hope things are not quite so bad.'[19] Actually Southey was more gross than Hazlitt, with references to John Ox being more tractable than John Bull, and the ironic suggestion 'we should rear our own opera-singers, and reform our church-music according to Italian taste.'[20]

On a more serious plane, however, Southey was partially justified in writing of the second edition that Malthus at the end of the volume admits every thing which he has controverted in the beginning, and is clearly and confessedly a convert to the doctrine of the perfectibility of man! He draws a picture of christian society, in which the well being of all is founded upon this very virtue of chastity, the non-existence of which was to destroy all the theories of Godwin and Condorcet ... The latter part of the book therefore palpably confutes the former, and he perishes by a stupid suicide, like the scorpion who strikes his tail into his own head.[21]

Another criticism of Malthus's logical position was made by the Remarker:

> The existence of vice and misery to a very considerable extent, is a fact which neither Mr. Malthus nor myself are inclined either to palliate or deny. But the author, by setting out with the supposition that these are the principal checks to population, has progressively in his work involved himself so far in the hypothesis, that at the close, when he comes to consider the remedies to be employed against these evils, he assumes as undeniable the converse of this proposition, that vice and misery principally arise out of the operation of the principle of population.

The Remarker thought that Europe was not over-peopled - remote agricultural provinces needed more labourers - and went on:

> Frequent and considerable variations in the price of labour, the precarious demand for labourers, sickly seasons, bad crops, the prevalence of vicious morals, idleness, drunkenness, and debauchery, are great and teeming wombs of evil, which neither marriages at the age of forty, nor even unrelenting celibacy can destroy.[22]

Mr Ingram, like the Remarker, favoured early marriages for their own sake, and not simply because bachelors were inclined to be sexually promiscuous. Marriage and a large family steadied a young man, and gave him an incentive to industry. In fact, both writers thought that there was too great an indisposition to marry in England, too much taste for luxury, too little inclination among young gentlemen to live quietly in the country, with their wives and children, and improve their estates. As for Malthus's 'young man of liberal education', who did not want to deprive himself or his wife of congenial acquaintance by marrying on too low an income, he was thoroughly trounced by Mr Ingram and, most properly, urged to do some useful work to earn what he needed.[23] The Remarker had a different point of view:

> If we enquire what is the chief outcry of these simpering mortals, we shall find it to be only this, that they are deterred from entering into the matrimonial state, by the dread of stepping a rank lower in life. Let them reflect upon the circumstances of the large class of the labouring community, who are prevented from stepping lower, only

122

because they already occupy the lowest rank, and they will find that they enjoy privileges in this respect, at least superior to those of one half of their brethren.[24]

The periodical reviewers wrote more soberly than those who felt impelled to produce books or pamphlets, and were more inclined to take up practical points, such as that a man who married late would not only be denied the pleasure of seeing his children grow up, but was also in more danger of leaving a widow with an unprovided family. One is reminded of the actuarial calculations of Dr Price, 'for the Endowment of Widows', but Malthus in a footnote to the 1806 *Appendix* gives what is surely the *reductio ad absurdum* of prudential foresight: 'The lowest prospect with which a man can be justified in marrying seems to be, the power, when in, health, of earning such wages, as at the average price of corn will maintain the average number of living children to a marriage.'[25]

The sentence is obviously carefully thought out; one can, perhaps, forgive Malthus's lack of sense more easily than his lack of humour. Other clever people obsessed with one idea - even a good idea - have lost touch with reality in the same way, but this sentence strikes me as the perfect example of well-meaning academic nonsense. Malthus's contemporaries joyfully seized on it, but on the whole they were more interested in sex than in sick and hungry children, and vice, to begin with, got more attention than misery.

Naturally those against Malthus interpreted what he said in the most sensational way. The word 'vice' at this period, like 'immorality' later, was used loosely to cover what we more accurately term 'extra-marital sex'; strictly speaking the words 'vice' and 'immorality' should include all conduct believed to be wrong - murder and robbery, lying and breaking promises, deliberate unkindness, and so on. Malthus wrote, 'I certainly cannot think that the vices which relate to the sex are the only vices which are to be considered in a moral question; or that they are even the greatest and most degrading to the human character.' This was controversial enough, but Malthus made it worse by going on with the Utilitarian argument, that sexual offences 'ought always strongly to be reprobated' because 'they can rarely or never be committed without producing unhappiness somewhere or other'. It was hardly an attitude to be approved by those who regarded the Seventh Commandment ('Thou shall not commit adultery') as sacrosanct. Malthus followed this up with a moving account of the temptations to every sort of crime which beset the children of abject poverty, bred up in filth and rags, which he drew from the experience of Patrick Colquhoun, a well-known London magistrate; the inference was that a little unchastity caused less sin and misery than the breeding of needy children - children who, as Malthus pointed out, were not in any case likely to be chaste themselves.[26]

123

It is easy to see how this was twisted into the idea that Mr Malthus preferred vice to babies, just as he was accused of approving famine and smallpox, because they cut down our numbers. The anonymous critic who discussed the *Essay* of 1798 in the *Analytical Review* opined that 'Without knowing it ... we think the author, in this essay, has furnished the best apology for prostitution that has ever been written.'[27]

I do not think the position was made any easier by the *Monthly Review*. The first part of the article on the quarto appeared in December 1803, and the critic wrote of Malthus, after quoting his basic propositions, 'He afterward denominates moral restraint, the *preventive* check on population; and vice and misery the *positive*.'[28] The number for January 1804, which carried the second half of the article, also contained the following note, headed 'Correspondence':

> From a communication with which we have been favoured by Mr. Malthus, we learn that we have misconceived and therefore incorrectly represented his classification of the checks on population: but he is so polite as to ascribe our mistake to a want of clearness in his own language. Be this as it may, it is beyond all doubt that the corrected statement is the just one, and that which best harmonizes with the author's system.
>
> The reader, then, is to understand that Mr. Malthus, instead of confining the preventive check to moral restraint, extends it to promiscuous intercourse, unnatural passions, and improper acts intended to conceal the consequences of irregular connection [abortions], which come under the head of vice: while excesses, wars, &c. which range under the same head, together with misery, constitute the positive check. Thus it appears then that vice comes in part under the preventive, and in part under the positive check. If we now rightly comprehend his meaning, he regards whatever operates to the prevention of births as belonging to the preventive class of checks, and whatever takes away human beings prematurely as belonging to the positive.[29]

No wonder Malthus felt it necessary to declare in the *Appendix* of 1806: 'It is an utter misconception of my argument to infer that I am an enemy to population. I am only an enemy to vice and misery, and consequently to that unfavourable proportion between population and food which produces these evils. But this unfavourable proportion has no necessary connection with the quantity of absolute population which a country may contain. On the contrary, it is more frequently found in countries which are very thinly peopled, than in those which are populous.'[30]

Also in the *Appendix*, at the end, in a huge footnote, Malthus described how 'While the last sheet of the Appendix was printing, I heard with some surprise, that an argument had been drawn from the principle of population in favour of the slave trade. As the just conclusion from that principle appears to me to be exactly the contrary . . .' and for two quarto pages of minute print he rams home his objections to this vile institution. He concludes with the words, 'As long as the nations of Europe continue barbarous enough to purchase slaves in Africa, we may be quite sure that Africa will continue barbarous enough to supply them.'[31]

The misunderstanding about slavery was possibly due to a malicious thrust of Cobbett's. It is hardly necessary to point out that homosexuality prevailed among the Africans in the West Indies, since comparatively few women were imported; in a leading article in his *Political Register* for 16 February 1805, headed 'Jamaica Complaints', Cobbett wrote:

> But, as to the Africans, it is not pretended, I believe, that the constant fresh supply is rendered necessary by the destructiveness of the climate, so much as by the effects of *celibacy*, and other circumstances therewith connected. And, is this an *evil?* A question not to be settled without a discussion, into which, I should think, that even Mr. Wilberforce would not be inclined to enter, at least not very minutely. If he were, however, it might be quite sufficient to refer him to the profound work of Mr. Malthus, who has not scrupled to recommend *checks to population*, as conducive to the *good* of mankind.[32]

Eleven months later, on 18 January 1806, Cobbett quoted Malthus's quotation from Mungo Park about the Africans voluntarily selling their children into slavery, to each other, when food was short. This would have been while the *Appendix* was printing, and was probably what immediately induced one of Malthus's friends to tell him how he was regarded on this issue.[33]

He seems to have found that the footnote to the 1806 *Appendix* was not enough to clear him. In a letter to Clarke written on 27 February 1807 Malthus told his friend:

> I went to Town on Monday with the intention of being present at the debate on the abolition, but was too late; I was just in time however to see Mr. Wilberforce before he went into the house, and to furnish him with data to rescue my character from the imputation of being a friend to the slave trade. I should have been much distressed if the accusation had been made without being contradicted.[34]

Trading in slaves was prohibited in 1807, but it was not until the Whigs' next period in power, in 1833, that slavery itself became illegal in all the British dominions.

It is perhaps worth noting here that a certain amount of the Sydenham Malthuses' money probably came from slave labour. Some of the fortune of Marianna Georgina's first husband, William Leigh Symes, consisted of property in Jamaica, the principal part of which was called the Oxford Plantation. She had great difficulty in getting all that she and her children were entitled to, and when their step-father was abroad, their Uncle Robert had to continue the struggle (with William Bray's help) on the young Symeses' behalf. Their family ended with them, so the Jamaica Estates reverted to the Malthuses, and were a source of vexation rather than profit for another hundred years.

3 The Poor

Empson commented in 1837 that Mr Malthus was 'far from being indifferent to fame'. I can imagine that as he rode or walked alone, down country paths, Malthus might well have wondered how the literary men of the future would write about him, in their histories of political economy. Yet it is important to remember that he was sometimes entirely preoccupied by what could be called the latest short-term news, *this* session of Parliament, *this* Bill, *this* Speech. To quote Empson again: 'Mr. Malthus was not fond of storms, as the petrel is said to be, for their own sake. But it will be seen, on looking at the date and nature of his pamphlets, that he usually turned out in one. At these times, the opportunity of being useful was excitement enough: and his spirits rose with the occasion.'[35]

This was certainly true of the *High Price of Provisions* and the *Letter to Samuel Whitbread* on the Poor Laws. Whitbread's great speech on 'how to reduce the sum of human vice and misery, and how to augment that of human happiness and virtue', was made in the House of Commons on 19 February 1807. On 27 February Malthus was writing to Clarke about newspaper reports of it, adding, 'I want to get however, the genuine speech, which I hear is to be published, before I determine on the merits of his plan.' Malthus's *Letter* on Whitbread's proposed Bill for the amendment of the Poor Laws was dated from Hertford just a month later, 27 March 1807.

But before we look at this we must go back to the quarto on *Population*, in which Malthus made his grim attack on the system of poor relief in England. It is worth noting that at this time writers still talk about 'the poor', rather than about 'poverty'. It jars on the modern ear: there is something authoritarian in such phrases as 'the management of the poor', or 'the improvement of the poor'. Yet the poor were regarded as individuals, towards whom the 'better classes of society' felt a personal responsibility, which was perhaps lacking among some of those who later analysed poverty as an abstraction.

The foundation of the English Poor Law was the Act of the forty-third year of the reign of Elizabeth I, which made each parish responsible for its own poor. From the earliest years four classes of poor were distinguished: (1) the aged, chronic sick, and very little children, constitutionally unable to work; (2) those temporarily unable to work through illness or accident; (3) those who could find no employment; and (4) the idle, who might be roughly treated according to local custom.

As time went on, it became harder to differentiate between the third and fourth categories, and the Laws of Settlement hampered the mobility of labour. Basically, these laws made it difficult for a newcomer to 'settle' in a parish, and thereby possibly become a burden on the poor-rates. Not unnaturally, strangers - especially women about to have babies - were cruelly hounded from one parish to the next. If the parish was small and unprosperous, useless mouths to feed were understandably resented, and proud and timorous poor alike avoided having to ask for parish relief at the expense of their neighbours. Some records show that relief was given with sympathy and imagination, but there was also much inefficiency and corrupt administration up and down the whole country, especially when the poor-houses were farmed out to contractors, who had no incentive to care for the sick and the aged.

Towards the end of the eighteenth century, with the rapid growth of population, a new category of 'poor' began to be recognised. These were the families of men who were fully employed, but whose wages were too low to keep their children from starvation. It was a situation not envisaged by the Elizabethans, and possible contributory causes were rising prosperity, which enabled people to marry younger, and inoculation against smallpox, which meant that a higher proportion of sucklings than ever before could live to become bread-eaters. Those who would have scorned to claim relief for themselves accepted it for their children, and the practice gradually arose of giving what we should now call a family allowance, on a sliding scale fixed by the price of bread; this became known as the Speenhamland System, since the most popular scale was one drawn up in 1795 by some magistrates in the Berkshire village of that name. It is easy to see that low wages and a high poor-rate might have suited some farmers very well, and that this system made it difficult to ascertain the workers' average weekly earnings from their ordinary paid employment.

This is not the place to discuss the merits of children's allowances. What we must note is that by the 1780s 'the poor' had become synonymous with 'the lower orders' or 'the labouring classes', and the literate were obsessed by what they thought of as the enormous national cost of demoralising the peasantry by turning them all into paupers.

Here again Malthus was anticipated by Joseph Townsend. As a low churchman, Townsend was prejudiced against Popery, and in his *Journey Through Spain* he constantly deplored the Roman Catholics' large-scale almsgiving. Two quotations will suffice:

127

[In Seville] I was struck with the multitude of beggars clothed in rags; and was at first inclined to attribute this to the decay of trade; but, upon examination, I found a more abiding cause in the distribution of alms at the archbishop's palace, and at the gates of twenty convents [he used this word to include monasteries], daily, and without distinction to all who make application for relief. Such misplaced benevolence is a bar to industry, and multiplies the objects of distress, whose numbers bear exact proportion to the provision made for their support.[36]

The town of Leon, destitute of commerce, is supported by the church. Beggars abound in every street, fed by the convents, and at the bishop's palace. Here they get their breakfast, there they dine. Besides food, at San Marcos they receive every other day, the men a farthing, the women and children half as much. On this provision they live, they marry, and they perpetuate a miserable race.[37]

Before he left for Spain, Townsend had published his *Dissertation on the Poor Laws* in 1786, under the pseudonym of 'A Well-Wisher to Mankind'. Here are some typical extracts:

The poor know little of the motives which stimulate the higher ranks to action - pride, honour, and ambition. In general it is only hunger which can spur and goad them on to labour; yet our laws have said, they shall never hunger ... Hunger is not only a peaceable, silent, unremitted pressure, but, as the most natural motive to industry and labour, it calls forth the most powerful exertions ... Hunger will tame the fiercest animals, it will teach decency and civility, obedience and subjection, to the most brutish, the most obstinate, and the most perverse ... Indeed it is the general complaint of farmers, that their men do not work so well as they used to do, when it was reproachful to be relieved by the parish.

It seems to be a law of nature, that the poor should be to a certain degree improvident, that there may always be some to fulfil the most servile, the most sordid, and the most ignoble offices in the community. The stock of human happiness is thereby much increased, whilst the more delicate are not only relieved from drudgery, and freed from those occasional employments which would make them miserable, but are left at liberty, without interruption, to pursue those callings which are suited to their various dispositions, and most useful to the state. As for the lowest of the poor, by custom they are reconciled to the meanest occupations, to the most laborious works, and to the most hazardous pursuits ... The fleets and armies of a state would soon be in want of soldiers and of sailors, if sobriety and diligence universally prevailed: for what is it but distress and poverty which can prevail upon the lower classes of the people to encounter all the horrors which await them on the tempestuous ocean, or in the field of battle?

Now a fixed, a certain and a constant provision for the poor weakens this spring; it increases their improvidence, but does not promote their cheerful compliance with those demands, which the community is obliged to make on the most indigent of its members; it tends to destroy the harmony and beauty, the symmetry and order of that system, which God and nature have established in the world ... [The Poor Laws] say, that in England no man, even though by his indolence, improvidence, prodigality, and vice, he may have brought himself to poverty, shall ever suffer want. In the progress of society, it will be found, that some must want; and then the only question will be this, Who is most worthy to suffer cold and hunger, the prodigal or the provident, the slothful or the diligent, the virtuous or the vicious?[38]

To do Townsend justice, he was extremely sympathetic towards his good poor: 'The quiet and the cleanly dread the noise and nastiness even more than the confinement of a work-house.' Moreover, the pauper who could manage with £4 a year in his own home cost £12 annually in an institution: 'But whilst the expence is so enormous, are they happy? Far from happy, they are wretched ... They eat, they drink, and they are miserable.'[39] Townsend suggested that those who needed care and had no relatives should be boarded out among cottagers, the workhouse being used only as a deterrent. He wanted the Poor Laws repealed and replaced by compulsory subscriptions to Friendly Societies, the unmarried man paying one-quarter of his wages weekly, and the father of four young children not more than one-thirtieth of his income.[40]

On the positive side, Townsend advocated greater food production, and proposed a tax on horses, which 'would be apparently a tax on husbandry, but in reality it would only be a tax on pride and prejudice'. A horse needed four acres to keep it, an ox but two: 'The land which now supports one horse, in proper working order, would bear two oxen for draft and for the shambles, if not also one cow for the pail; or any two of these, with a man, his wife, and his three children.'[41]

Townsend also objected to the hedges with which the new agricultural improvers were enclosing their fields: 'Hedgerows consume much land, stint the growth of corn, cause it to lodge, prevent its drying, and harbour birds.'[42]

Malthus does not remark on these details, but he approved of Townsend's general conclusion, that the relief of real distress should be left to voluntary charity, Christian benevolence. Townsend pointed out that there was no virtue in compulsory giving, which was what the poor-rate amounted to;

he also thought it unjust that the frugal, hard-working small farmer or tradesman should have to feed and clothe the children of the idle and the profligate before his own. Other people thought the same, especially when Pitt's Poor Bill was under discussion. 'Peter Pindar' (John Wolcot, 1738-1819) wrote a lampoon called *Visit to Weymouth* in 1796, in which George III is confronted by a sailor, 'On crutches borne - an object of despair'. After hearing the beggar's story the king exclaims,

> Wife and nine children, hae - all, all alive.
> No, no, no wonder that you cannot thrive.
> Shame, shame to fill your hut with such a train!
> Shame to get brats for others to maintain.[43]

Against this background, Malthus's concern for 'the causes which affect the happiness and comfort of the lower orders of society' seems more humanitarian. The Poor Laws, according to him, were bad because they diminished both the power and the will to save, and thus weakened 'one of the strongest incentives to sobriety and industry, and consequently to happiness'. 'Hard as it may appear in individual instances,' wrote Malthus, 'dependent poverty ought to be held disgraceful. Such a stimulus seems to be absolutely necessary to promote the happiness of the great mass of mankind.'[44]

But the crux of the matter for Malthus was the physical impossibility of providing for all the poor, on account of the principle of population. The argument he used in the tract on *The High Price of Provisions* in 1800 was repeated in the great quarto. He wrote in 1803: 'I confess it appears to me strange that so many men, who would yet aspire to be thought political economists, should still think that it is in the power of the justices of the peace or even of the omnipotence of parliament to alter by a *fiat* the whole circumstances of the country; and when the demand for provisions is greater than the supply, by publishing a particular edict, to make the supply at once equal to or greater than the demand.'[45] 'In this we act too much in the same manner as if, when the quicksilver in the common weather-glass stood at *stormy*, we were to raise it by some mechanical pressure to *settled fair*, and then be greatly astonished that it continued raining.'[46]

Since the indiscriminate giving of parish relief merely spread distress by an inflationary rise in the price of provisions, Malthus came naturally to his conclusion that no one could have a right to subsistence, since no one could have a right to what it was impossible to procure: 'It must be allowed that we have practised an unpardonable deceit upon the poor, and have promised what we have been very far from performing.'[47]

Malthus obviously thought that he had not made himself clear in 1803, for in 1806 he inserted a further short passage to this effect before stating his plan for the gradual abolition of the Poor Laws: 'We are bound in justice and honour formally to disclaim the *right* of the poor to support.' His scheme was very simple: 'I should propose a regulation to be made, declaring

130

that no child born from any marriage, taking place after the expiration of a year from the date of the law; and no illegitimate child born two years from the same date, should ever be entitled to parish assistance.'[48] He explained in the 1806 *Appendix* that 'According to this plan all that are already married, and even all that are engaged to marry in the course of the year, and all their children, will be relieved as usual; and only those who marry subsequently, and who of course may be supposed to have made better provision for contingencies, would be out of the pale of relief.'[49]

Many of Malthus's contemporaries, Sir Frederick Morton Eden as well as Townsend, believed that it would be beneficial to abolish the Elizabethan Poor Law and its accretions; but Malthus damaged his own proposal (a bad one anyhow) by a stroke of utter silliness; one can only say that it was kindly meant.

After the sentence describing his scheme, in the great quarto, Malthus went on:

> To give a more general knowledge of this law, and to enforce it more strongly on the minds of the lower classes of people, the clergyman of each parish should, previously to the solemnization of a marriage, read a short address to the parties, stating the strong obligation of every man to support his own children; the impropriety, and even immorality, of marrying without a fair prospect of being able to do this; the evils which had resulted to the poor themselves, from the attempt which had been made to assist, by publick institutions, in a duty which ought to be exclusively appropriated to parents; and the absolute necessity which had at length appeared, of abandoning all such institutions, on account of their producing effects totally opposite to those which were intended.
>
> This would operate as a fair, distinct, and precise notice, which no man could well mistake; and, without pressing hard on any particular individuals, would at once throw off the rising generation from that miserable and helpless dependence upon the government and the rich, the moral as well as the physical consequences of which are almost incalculable.

One can hardly blame Coleridge for scribbling in the margin opposite this passage: 'Clergyman! Mr. M. you must send for the Sow-gelder.' While some laughed, others were horrified at Malthus's impiety. In 1806 he amended a sentence: the parson was to read the address not 'previously to the solemnization of a marriage', but 'after the publication of banns'.[50] It could hardly have made much difference in practice, for by the time a couple were 'cried on Sunday' they would have been determined to get married in any case, even if a baby were not already on the way. Presumably Malthus thought his warning might impress younger members of the congregation,

131

as yet unattached, but he never said so, and the absurd paragraph was repeated in all subsequent editions.

After a passage expunged in 1806, about the conservatism of the poor in their dietary habits, Malthus continued:

> After the publick notice which I have proposed had been given, and the system of poor laws had ceased with regard to the rising generation, if any man chose to marry, without a prospect of being able to support a family, he should have the most perfect liberty to do so. Though to marry in this case is, in my opinion, clearly an immoral act, yet it is not one which society can justly take upon itself to prevent or punish; because the punishment provided for it by the laws of nature falls directly and most severely upon the individual who commits the act, and through him, only more remotely and feebly, on the society. When nature will govern and punish for us, it is a very miserable ambition to wish to snatch the rod from her hand and draw upon ourselves the odium of executioner. To the punishment therefore of nature he should be left, the punishment of want. He has erred in the face of a most clear and precise warning, and can have no just reason to complain of any person but himself when he feels the consequences of his error. All parish assistance should be denied him; and he should be left to the uncertain support of private charity. He should be taught to know that the laws of nature, which are the laws of God, had doomed him and his family to suffer for disobeying their repeated admonitions; that he had no claim of *right* on society for the smallest portion of food, beyond that which his labour would fairly purchase; and that if he and his family were saved from feeling the natural consequences of his imprudence he would owe it to the pity of some kind benefactor, to whom, therefore, he ought to be bound by the strongest tied of gratitude.
>
> If this system were pursued, we need be under no apprehensions that the number of persons in extreme want would be beyond the power and the will of the benevolent to supply. The sphere for the exercise of private charity would, probably, not be greater than it is at present; and the principal difficulty would be to restrain the hand of benevolence from assisting those in distress in so indiscriminate a manner as to encourage indolence and want of foresight in others.[51]

Many of Malthus's readers took a different point of view. As Mr Ingram wrote, 'To be sure it is a little hard on the poor children, who came into the world by no fault of their own'; on Malthus's principle, men should not marry until they could be certain of leaving provision for widows with a train of dependent infants, 'or, what would most effectually prevent the shameless urchins from intruding "at nature's mighty feast" ... they had better be dissuaded or prevented from marrying at all, except when there was no prospect of a family'.[52]

Malthus was popularly misinterpreted on this question. Simplex exclaimed 'Is it humane or benevolent to confine the comforts and endearments of conjugal life to the more wealthy or independent, and to compel, *by law*, the *most numerous* class of the community to live in a state of uncleanness and distraction of mind, merely because their prospects are less fair in this life than those of their neighbours!'[53] So Malthus became known as the man who wanted an Act of Parliament to prevent the poor from marrying.

In the third edition of the *Essay on Population* a passage was added to the 1803 version, about alleviating hardship due to war or a bad harvest: 'We must not forget that both humanity and true policy imperiously require that we should give every assistance to the poor on these occasions that the nature of the case will admit.'[54] Yet he did not believe that both humanity and true policy required the community to care for children, already born, whose parents were unable or unwilling to do so.

It is here that we see Malthus the economist at his worst. In 1803 he wrote:

> If the parents desert their child, they ought to be made answerable for the crime. The infant is, comparatively speaking, of little value to the society, as others will immediately supply its place. Its principal value is on account of its being the object of one of the most delightful passions in human nature - parental affection. But if this value be disregarded by those who are alone in a capacity to feel it, the society cannot be called upon to put itself in their place; and has no further business in its protection, than in the case of its murder or intentional ill-treatment, to follow the general rules in punishing such crimes; which rules, for the interests of morality, it is bound to pursue, whether the object, in the particular instance, be of value to the state or not.[55]

This last sentence was modified a little in the 1806 third edition. All one can say is that we are no better than hypocrites if we criticise Malthus for his cruel words and then, through our own cruel inertia, condemn neglected children to lives of crime or apathy.

Contemporary writers took up the issue. The *Imperial Review* was typical: 'Is there an Englishman that could see a child perish for want without holding out his hand to prevent the suffering? Admitting, which we are not very ready to do, the immorality of marrying at a time when the prospect of maintaining six children be not quite clear, still the religion, which we profess, recommends the duty of forgiveness to the offenders, and calls for the most extensive acts of benevolence towards the helpless and unfortunate.'[56]

The case of the labourer was well expressed for him in December 1804 by an anonymous letter-writer to the *Monthly Magazine*, who called himself Philander:

> I ask nothing (says he) to feed and clothe a family but what these hands, if employed, can procure, while at the same time their labour is a fruitful source of emolument to others. If, however, I am thrown out of work by any accident, you must take upon you to do for them what I am prevented from doing; and in case of extraordinary scarcity, you must deduct somewhat from your superfluities, to enable me and mine to procure necessaries. Moreover, I must have a little help when we are visited by sickness; and if you think a little instruction will render us more useful to you, it will be your part to provide the means. Upon these terms I will rear girls to be your domestic servants, your semstresses, and laundresses; and stout boys to fight for you, navigate your ships, till your land, make your cloathing, build your houses, work your machines, in short, do every service that can be required from them.

Philander went on to say that the table of nature was not full, and 'Worse than shame on him who can argue, that the rich man's horses have a better right to be fed than the poor man's children!' He concluded:

> Nothing can be more contrary to the spirit of our laws than this abandonment of such of our fellow-subjects as come into the world without property. The law instantly takes them under its protection, and in return claims from them all the duties of allegiance, upon the mere ground of being natives of the soil. Their country appropriates them to her service, and summons them from the remotest parts of the earth, when in need of their arms for her defence. Nay, she has made it a crime against herself for them to use the natural liberty of withdrawing from the world when life is a burden; for suicide is considered as felony, because 'it deprives the king of a subject'. If then the poor man has not a right to die, surely he has a right to live![57]

Possibly the anonymous Remarker's criticism of Malthus's plan for the abolition of the Poor Laws was the most pungent and perceptive. He expressly mentioned the old, as distinct from the children, and was quite unsentimental about them. They should be given parish relief, and not be allowed to burden their families, 'clogging the great machine of society', and preventing the thrifty labourer from doing his best for his own offspring; such relief would encourage industry 'by diminishing the oppression of unproductive idleness'.

The Remarker did not accept Malthus's thesis that the Poor Laws created the poor which they maintained: 'Such a self-increasing system, proceeding in the geometrical series described by the author, must long ago have swallowed up at least nine-tenths of the population of this country.' He agreed that the Poor Laws 'directly tend to encourage idleness, to reward want, and to cherish a spirit of prodigality and dependence', but 'I am very far from coinciding with him in opinion, that the poor in a flourishing, and more especially in a commercial country should be left altogether to nature and chance for subsistence in all the vicissitudes of life and fortune.'[58]

After showing from the example of Scotland the inadequacy of private charity in real famine, the Remarker went on to recommend hospitals for the sick and public works for the unemployed. He wrote:

> In the manufacturing towns of Birmingham, Manchester, Leeds, &c, the injury done to the morals, the industry, and the prosperity of the lower orders, by the precarious demand for labour in the different manufactories, is an evil incalculably great and pressing. Every new war, every continental disturbance, every suspicion upon foreign or domestic credit, the abolition of old manufactories, the introduction of new ones, improvements in machinery, and, finally, the unbounded spirit of speculation, alternating the acquisition and loss of immense capitals, are dreadful instruments constantly to impede the motions of the great commercial machine.[59]

I do not think Malthus, at this period, realised that the hardship caused by the dreadful instruments of commerce were analogous to those caused by a broken leg or a bad harvest, and that both humanity and true policy dictated liberal help at such times. He did note that 'The weavers of Spitalfields were plunged into the most severe distress by the fashion of muslins instead of silks; and numbers of the workmen in Sheffield and Birmingham were for a time thrown out of employment, from the adoption of shoe-strings and covered buttons, instead of buckles and metal buttons';[60] but it was not until the general depression which followed the Napoleonic Wars that Malthus appreciated the vulnerability of industry to circumstances more intricate and far-reaching than a mere change in fashion. He was, of course, aware of the disorganisation of trade caused by the wars with France, but he had not yet fully realised that a complex monetary economy might of itself generate distress worse than that caused by the failure of crops or the loss of ships in a storm.

We shall return to this when we examine Malthus's *Principles of Political Economy*, but it is worth noting here, as Professor Hayek has pointed out, that Adam Smith and his followers gave comparatively little attention to 'the economic crises which appeared with surprising regularity in 1763, 1772, 1783 and 1793'.[61]

But if the trade cycle as one cause of poverty had not yet been analysed, the condition of the poor was indeed a recognisable contemporary problem. In 1803 nearly one-seventh of the population of England and Wales was receiving some parish relief (there were 15,000 parishes), at a total annual cost of £4¼ million, raised from local rates on the value of land. This was a large sum for a country at war, when the gross national revenue from taxation and the Post Office was only about £41.2 million.[62] What was more worrying than the sum itself was the rapidity with which the poor-rates were increasing; in 1803 they were double the average annual expenditure for 1783-5, and more than treble that for 1776, figures truly horrifying to people at the time. In this situation Malthus's quarto made a great impact on serious politicians.

4 The *Letter to Samuel Whitbread*

Among the best-known of the multitude who wrote about the Poor Laws was George Rose (1744-1818), a Pittite Member of Parliament. To put it crudely, Rose wanted a large population for the fighting services, and low wages - subsidised by poor-rates - for the benefit of competitive exports. But he thought Malthus harsh, since the most prudent marriage might be followed by ill-luck, and Rose felt it was unfair that all the relief of the poor should fall on the charitably generous. The stingy should be made to contribute as well: 'In the same way they might refuse contributing to the national defence, if that were left entirely to the voluntary offerings of individuals; they might leave it to others more apprehensive, or more impatient than themselves of foreign subjugation; whether it would be just or safe to allow this, it is surely unnecessary to enquire; and yet the two cases appear to be exactly analogous.'[63] The pregnant significance of this argument as regards the need for compulsion in the modern state does not seem to have been remarked by Rose's contemporaries. Basically his pamphlet was a commentary on Malthus; he was in favour of education and Friendly Societies, and thought that paupers might be profitably employed on such tasks as plaiting straw for hats, since this would only put Italians out of work, not English people![64] He was certainly no economist as far as theories of international trade were concerned.

Rose's pamphlet appeared in 1805. In 1806 came the brief interlude of Whig government, under Lord Grenville, known as the Ministry of All the Talents, because it was a coalition of all such politicians as could be induced to work together after the death of Pitt; Fox was Foreign Secretary, but died in September after some six months of office, during which he had attempted to negotiate a peace treaty. Romilly was Solicitor-General, and liberal hopes were high. At that time Napoleon was supreme on the Continent (Pitt had rolled up the map of Europe) and it is a tribute to Malthus's friends that at this critical period they could abolish the slave trade within the British dominions, and produce such a comprehensive scheme of social reform as Samuel Whitbread's Bill 'for promoting and encouraging industry amongst the labouring classes of the community, and for the relief and regulation of the criminal and necessitous poor'. Francis Horner, now a Member of Parliament, was one of the people who helped to draw up the schemes.

Whitbread's speech, in which he asked leave to bring in his Bill, came to nearly a hundred pages when it was printed as a pamphlet. Like Rose, he took Malthus as his starting point, and like Rose he respectfully disagreed with him. By the time Malthus leapt to his own defence the ministry had already resigned, on the issue of Catholic Emancipation, which George III could not reconcile with his coronation oath; but so great was the general public interest in the subject that Whitbread's and Malthus's pamphlets both went into second editions.

Whitbread hurt Malthus's feelings by saying, after some obviously sincere compliments, that any man who read his works 'ought to place a strict guard over his heart, lest it become hardened against the distresses of his fellow creatures; lest in learning that misery and vice must of necessity maintain a footing in the world, he give up all attempt at their subjugation'.[65] In his *Letter to Samuel Whitbread* Malthus replied: 'I am sure your own feelings will tell you, that though I must be prepared to hear unmoved all those accusations of "hardness of heart" which appear to me to be the result of ignorance or malice, yet that any remark of the same kind coming from an enlightened and distinguished member of the British Senate cannot but give me pain, although accompanied by expressions of respect for my understanding.'[66]

In fact, Samuel Whitbread had begun his speech by using Malthus's own cutting arguments against Arthur Young, which had occupied considerable space in the *Appendix* to the third edition of the *Essay*. Poor Young was unhappily married and inconsolable after the death of his favourite child, overworked and afflicted with religious near-mania; he had rashly advocated in his *Annals of Agriculture* a scheme which he had previously ridiculed some twelve years before in his *Travels in France*. This was the voting by the French National Assembly of an immutably fixed annual sum for the relief of the poor, quite regardless of their numbers or the extent of their distress. As Whitbread pointed out, 'it would be difficult to distinguish between the right to relief possessed by those who should have received it before the fund was exhausted, and those who might make application for relief after it was gone.'[67]

Whitbread then proceeded to demolish Malthus's plan for the gradual abolition of the Poor Laws on much the same principle, describing to the faithful Commons 'what a scene of confusion would ensue during the interval which must elapse, till the present generation should have all passed away, and the condition of all your people should have become the same.

Divided as they would be into two distinct classes, the one possessing a claim upon you, the other none; what end would there be to their discontent, jealousies, and quarrels! What jarring, wrangling, and conflict!'[68]

I am sure Whitbread was right. He went on, 'If you were to say to men, that they had no right to any assistance or support from you under any circumstances, you could not impose any restraint upon them as to settlement. You could not condemn them to starve, and therefore you must allow those in need to beg. Are you prepared to encounter that host of sturdy and valiant beggars? ... Your metaphysical positions may be unquestionable, but you would create a set of dangerous enemies.'[69] This must have been a home thrust for Malthus. Whitbread had also toured in Norway - Malthus had read his tutor's account of their journeys - and he too had seen this country where there were no Poor Laws, and the labourers were better off than in Britain, yet where the streets of the towns swarmed with beggars to an extent unknown in England.

Whitbread's all-embracing proposals we cannot notice in detail here, fascinating though they are to anyone interested in the evolution of the Welfare State. He wished to retain the Poor Laws, for emergencies, but he hoped they would fall into disuse through the increased prosperity of the lower classes as the result of his schemes for parochial schools, a national savings bank and insurance office for the poor, a more equitable assessment of local rates on all productive capital, not only on land, and the provision of parochial cottages for couples wishing to marry, to be let at what we would now call economic rents. He deplored institutions except for special cases, and is so 'modern' in outlook that we are pulled up with a jerk when he suggests rewards and badges of honour for men who have brought up six or more children without parish relief, and badges of infamy ('the name of the parish, in large letters on his outer garment')[70] for a man who has become a burthen upon others through his own idleness or extravagance.

With regard to the Poor Laws and population, Malthus was by this time in an awkward position. Rudimentary as the 1801 census appears to us, it had enabled some pioneer statisticians - including Southey's friend John Rickman - to produce figures which showed that England's unique Poor Laws did not in fact precipitate an overwhelming number of feckless marriages. Malthus admitted this, both in his 1806 *Appendix* and in his *Letter to Whitbread*, in which he wrote: 'In England it appears that the proportion of births and marriages to the whole population is less than in most of the other countries of Europe; and though this circumstance is principally to be accounted for from other causes, yet it affords decisive evidence that the poor laws do not encourage early marriages *so much* as might naturally be expected.'[71]

Later in 1807, in the *Appendix* to the fourth edition of *Population*, he added a footnote to the effect that the returns of the Population Act seemed to warrant the assertion that the Poor Laws, 'under all the circumstances with which they have been accompanied', do not encourage marriage. 'Should this be true, many of the objections which have been urged in the Essay against the poor laws will of course be removed; but I wish to press on the attention of the reader, that they will in that case be removed in strict conformity to the general principles of the work.'[72]

However, if the old Poor Law did not positively encourage early marriages, Malthus was quite certain that Whitbread's new scheme for the provision of cottages would do so, since this would remove 'the difficulty of procuring habitations'. Under the famous Act of Elizabeth I the overseers of the poor had been empowered to build cottages for them, but this clause had not been operative, which Malthus considered 'the principal reason why the Poor Laws had not been so extensive and prejudicial in their effects as might have been expected'.[73] It is not surprising to find the word 'prejudicial' underlined, with sundry quill marks in the margin, in several copies of this pamphlet. All the world loves a lover, and there is something particularly unattractive about Malthus's attitude towards young couples seeking a home.

To do Malthus justice, he was not concerned with the cost of the poor-rates; as he said in the *Letter to Whitbread*:

> I should indeed think that the whole, or a much greater sum, was well applied, if it merely relieved the comparatively few that would be in want, if there were no public provision for them, without the fatal and unavoidable consequences of continually increasing their number, and depressing the condition of those who were struggling to maintain themselves in independence. Were it possible to fix the number of the poor and to avoid the further depression of the independent labourer, I should be the first to propose that those who were actually in want should be most liberally relieved, and that they should receive it as a right, and not as a bounty.[74]

What troubled Malthus was the danger of the supply of labour exceeding the demand, and therefore falling in price, with hunger, disease and death following in the wake of low wages:

> We should soon see a most unfavourable change take place in the present small mortality, which we justly consider as one of the great tests of our national happiness; and a large proportion of deaths would invariably accompany the large proportion of births. The births however might still exceed the deaths, the population might still be increasing, but the character of it would be greatly changed; it would consist of a much larger proportion of persons not capable of adding by their exertions to the resources of the state; each generation would pass away in a more rapid succession; and the greatness of the mortality would sufficiently indicate the misery of the state of society.[75]

Today this paragraph can be illustrated by television cameras.

139

What is sometimes uncongenial to modern readers is the emphasis which Malthus and all his contemporaries placed on individual effort and private property; industry and thrift, with some authors, seem to be synonymous with moral perfection. This should be less surprising when we reflect that Britain was at the stage of painfully 'taking off' into a modern industrial society. Accustomed to labour according to the demands of season and weather, the ex-peasants in the towns found it difficult to adapt themselves to a regular working week; manufacturers cursed the absenteeism derisively ascribed to the festivals of St Monday and St Tuesday. The desire for respectability and comfort, as contrasted with debauchery, seemed to be the only incentive that would make the lower orders work sufficiently to acquire, say, enough furniture for a decent life, or a few pennies for their children's schooling.

Through his study of primitive peoples, and later through letters from India, Malthus realised how hopeless it was to expect men to have any incentive to hard work if the fruits of their labours were to be snatched from them by rapacious tax-farmers or brigands – it was often hard to distinguish between the two. Hence the sacred security of private property was a logical part of a liberal's creed, and not the excuse for selfish accumulation which it afterwards became. It is also not difficult to understand why saving was regarded as a prime virtue by a rapidly developing country in need of capital and engaged in a desperate war at the same time.

Against this background Malthus shuddered at the prospect that 'we should in time see the greater part of our villages consisting of parish tenements, as well as the greater part of our labouring classes dependent on parish relief'.[76] He could not possibly have foreseen modern contributory and egalitarian social services, or a fully literate 'working class' in his beloved Norway running their own co-operative housing estates.

What Malthus did foresee was the difficulty of the inevitable halfway stage in the education of a developing state. He heartily approved of Whitbread's plan of general education: 'Should you only be able to accomplish this part of your Bill, you will in my opinion confer a most important benefit on your Country.' Later in the pamphlet Malthus wrote: 'The principal objections which I have ever heard advanced against the Education of the poor would be removed if it became general. A man who can read and write now may be discontented with his condition, and wish to rise above it; but if all his fellow labourers possessed the same advantage, his relative situation in society would remain the same as before, and the only effect would be that the condition of the whole mass would be elevated and improved.'* He also remarked that he believed the English and Irish

---

*Malthus would have enjoyed the company of the Norwegian guard on a train from Trondheim to Röros who examined my travel-pass in 1965. In good English he told me what he had learned at school about Adam Smith, Jeremy Bentham, and Malthus himself.

peasantry to be the most ignorant in Europe, but wrote of Napoleon; 'Our formidable neighbour certainly does not think that education is likely to impede his subjects either in fighting or working.'[77]

Cobbett, of course, would have none of it. He recorded gleefully the collapse of Grenville's ministry in the *Political Register* of 21 March 1807; it pleased him 'to see Mr. Whitbread who, after years of study upon feeding the hungry bellies of the poor, had, at last, come forward with his spelling-books and his badges and his *bank* (lord save us!) for depositing their fortunes, while Mr. Malthus was in the lobby with his auxiliary scheme for the *checking of all population*, except that of placemen and pensioners; to see the number, the swarms, of new dependants and expectants, who were, but yesterday, the most blithe of God's creatures: to see these, all these, hurled at once from their enjoyments and their hopes'.[78]

Two of Malthus's friends, however, were not hurled from their enjoyments by the resignation of the government. The Whigs' brief tenure of office gave Whishaw and Smyth appointments which established them for life. Their benefactor was Lord Henry Petty (1780-1863), Chancellor of the Exchequer and Member of Parliament for the University of Cambridge in succession to William Pitt; he moved to the Upper House when he became Marquess of Lansdowne on the death of his half-brother in 1809.

In October 1806 Lord Henry gave John Whishaw a post as a Commissioner for Auditing Public Accounts. He served conscientiously in what was then 'a very large department', and according to one of his junior colleagues, J. L. Mallet, 'no man was oftener consulted, or gave kinder and better advice.' It was not all plain sailing for Whishaw to begin with: 'The instincts of reform followed him into his new office. He strove, but strove in vain, to abandon the use of Roman numerals and bad Latin for Arabic figures and English words. Lord Grenville would hear of nothing so revolutionary as writing "hair powder duty" instead of *debitum super pulverem crinalem.'*[79]

William Smyth's turn came a little later, early in 1807, when Lord Henry obtained for him the post of Professor of Modern History at Cambridge. His published lectures are so good that it is easy to understand why he would sometimes read them 'elsewhere than at Cambridge for the gratification of his friends'. One pupil recorded that 'his conversation was very agreeable, and well seasoned with humour.'[80] This is apparent in the book-list he compiled for his students in 1817: such a book 'should be read', another 'may be looked at', and Chalmers's *Legal History of the Colonies* 'may be consulted, but cannot be read'.[81] He delighted in music, and at his parties allowed no whispering during the playing of Haydn and Mozart, although he welcomed his guests 'with a genial pleasantry peculiarly his own and which diffused a feeling of ease and enjoyment over all of them'.[82]

It is impossible to think of Whishaw and Smyth, 'placemen' though they were, as the villains Cobbett imagined them to be.

5 The Wrongs of Ireland

In September 1804 Jeffrey sent a begging letter to Horner, who was by this time well established in London. It was on behalf of an impecunious young man, the poet Thomas Campbell, whom Jeffrey did not think good enough to contribute to the *Edinburgh Review*, but he hoped that something 'could be done for him in India, Ireland, or anywhere'.[83] There was nothing facetious about this request. Francis Horner, indeed, all his life, regarded sinecure posts as 'an additional security given to the democracy, for the efficacy of what we justly reckon one of the best marks of our freedom, that a man may rise from the humblest rank to the highest office - with the financial help of a sinecure to free him from worry and put him on a level with those born to more affluent families'.[84]

The attitude of some Englishmen towards the Indians and the Irish was, in fact, very similar: they 'abhorred the natives for their religion and despised them for their misfortunes . . . The English have the disposition of a nation accustomed to empire; anything that compromises their own dignity appears quite out of the question. But the dignity of any other nation never makes an obstacle to their measures, either in theory or practice.'[85]

These words were written in a pamphlet published in 1804, called *An Inquiry into the Causes of Popular Discontents in Ireland* by an Irish Country Gentleman. He was William Parnell; his better-known younger brother was Henry Brooke Parnell (1776-1842), a prominent Whig Member of Parliament, and a Commissioner of the Treasury for Ireland in Grenville's ministry, who became in 1841 the first Lord Congleton.

Here we can do no more than touch on Anglo-Irish relations. After 1690, when William of Orange defeated the Irish supporters of James II, who were helped by the French, Ireland gave no more assistance to the Jacobite cause; the risings of 1715 and 1745 were entirely Scottish affairs. In 1782, following the American revolt, Ireland was allowed a subordinate legislature of her own, known as Grattan's Parliament, because Henry Grattan (1746-1820) was instrumental in bringing it about. It could not last. As John Wilson Croker wrote, 'It was in nature that the greater should rule the less; it was in nature too that, intoxicated with fancies of freedom, Ireland should revolt at the reality of dependence; too powerful for a province, too weak for a rival; the consequences were inevitable, Rebellion and Union.'[86]

The rebellion came in 1798, and General Lake had actually to surrender to a combined Irish and French force, smaller than his own, at Killala. The Irish still sing -

> And hist'ry can tell how we routed
> The red-coats through old Castlebar.

142

There was dreadful bloodshed, but never any looting, drunkenness or rape in Irish rebellions; they were the outcome of 'the desire of vengeance, the love of destruction, from which no authority, no persuasion, could divert them', as William Parnell put it.[87] The patriots' triumph in '98 was short-lived; Lord Cornwallis restored order. The sentiments of the people were not even consulted by 'the common decent appeal of a dissolution of Parliament'; after the most scandalous bribery with sinecures and pensions, Grattan's constitutional assembly voted itself out of existence. A hundred Irish members joined the 450 for England and Scotland (Wales was considered part of England), and the Parliament at Westminster became once again the sole legislature of the British Isles. It must be added, in justice to all concerned, that the choice for Ireland appeared to be union with England or union with the Directory of France. At the time, as Croker exclaimed, 'Whatever is not England, must be France!' He thought that 'the honest preferred England to France; the base, possession to expectancy'.[88]

Why the honest Irish should have preferred England to France is difficult to imagine. William Parnell was an Etonian from a Cheshire family which had migrated to Ireland in the reign of Charles II; there was no reason for him to be unduly biased in favour of the natives. Yet he wrote, 'The English government, in order to steel its heart against all the sufferings of the Irish, concluded that the nature of the Irish was different from that of any other people.'[89] Elsewhere he says:

> Notwithstanding the magic of the Union, a stranger can readily distinguish the race of the conquerors from that of the conquered, in the imperious insolence of the former, and the sullen deference of the latter.
>
> It has not been unusual in Ireland for great landed proprietors to have regular prisons in their houses for the summary punishment of the lower orders.[90]

As Croker said, 'The law has never thoroughly mingled itself with Ireland.'[91]

Pitt's Act of Union would have failed to pass even a corrupt parliament had he not promised free trade between the two countries and, most important of all, Catholic Emancipation. It was on this issue that Pitt had to resign in February 1801, just after the meeting of the first Parliament of the Union, because George III regarded the toleration of Papists as a breach of his solemn coronation oath; this was not altogether blameworthy, since the Hanoverian dynasty had been established expressly to ensure the Protestant succession, but it meant that one of England's greatest prime ministers was replaced by a comparative nonentity, Addington (later Viscount Sidmouth), at a critical time for the country.

When Pitt was recalled as First Lord of the Treasury in 1804, he promised the King that he would not raise 'the Catholic question'. After Pitt's death in January 1806, Lord Grenville's government were in an impossible position, being pledged to a policy of religious freedom, although we should today regard it as extremely limited.

Under an Act of 1793, Roman Catholics could hold Irish commissions up to the rank of colonel, and as the military situation became more serious there was a proposal to extend this concession to England. Lord Howick's attempt to open to Catholics all ranks in the army and navy caused the fall of the Grenville ministry in March 1807, but the Whigs in this one year had established themselves as the party sympathetic to Ireland. Thus when William Parnell wrote under his own name *An Historical Apology for the Irish Catholics*, in 1807, he dedicated it to the Whig Duke of Bedford, the termination of whose 'wise and conciliating administration' he regretted 'in common with every other Irishman'. This cannot have been strictly true, since the Duke, unlike other Lord-Lieutenants, refused to watch the processions of the Protestant Orange Lodges, described by Parnell as 'notoriously intended by the one party, and felt by the other, as a parade of insulting domination'.[92]

The most outrageous penal laws against the Roman Catholics had been repealed but, as Parnell said, 'as long as the Catholics are treated as a subservient sect, the recollection of former injuries will have almost as great an effect as the suffering from actual grievances.'[93] Catholics could still not sit in Parliament or hold any office under the Crown, nor could they be directors of the Bank of Ireland, which had been established in 1783. Thus, said William Parnell, they 'lose all political consequence in the country; so that a Protestant of seven hundred a year is more looked up to than a Catholic of seven thousand a year'.[94]

Thomas Newenham (1762–1831), a Shropshire man of whom we shall hear more, had a different but equally down-to-earth point of view with regard to unpopular officials such as tax-collectors: 'Had the Roman Catholics been permitted to participate in the odium, ordinarily attached to the exercise of several of the subordinate functions of the executive power, it is highly probably that the Protestant establishment would have been equally secure, and very certain that much less envy and much less hatred would have subsisted among Irish Christians.'[95]

The worst grievance, however, was the ecclesiastical tithe. This traditional levy of a tenth of the produce of the soil to support the church had naturally been much modified in the course of time, particularly after Henry VIII's breach with Rome; the right to collect tithes had sometimes been given to secular landlords along with the extensive possessions of dissolved religious houses. In Ireland, as in England, the legal position was extremely involved, but in many cases pasture was exempt from tithe, so that a farmer who turned from cereals to grazing could drastically cut his tithe-owner's income, be he squire or parson. The poor Irish peasant, whose little piece of land was perforce all in tillage, to grow potatoes, had no way out. Henry Parnell stressed how oppressive this system was: in England the labourers could work for wages, in Ireland a family would starve without their potato patch; thus in Ireland tithes were exacted from men who in England might be receiving assistance from their parish.[96]

What made matters even worse in Ireland was that the tithe was chiefly used to support the religion of a very small minority. The position at the turn of the eighteenth and nineteenth centuries was that roughly four million Catholics and half a million Presbyterians were supporting an Anglican establishment of about half a million Episcopalian Protestants. The unfairness of this is best described by good-hearted William Parnell, who was himself a member of the Church of England and Ireland, as it was then called:

> Are these men supposed to have no sense of justice, that in addition to the burden of supporting their own establishment exclusively, they should be called on to pay ours; that where they pay sixpence to their own priest, they should pay a pound to our clergyman; that while they can scarcely afford their own horse, they should place ours in his carriage; that where they cannot build a mass-house to cover their multitudes, they should be forced to contribute to build sumptuous churches for half a dozen Protestants to pray under shelter?

In a previous paragraph he had described the peasants submitting to a voluntary tax 'that the old and infirm part of their Sunday congregation may have a mass-house to shelter them from the weather; the great crowd, the young, and those that come late, kneel without doors'.[97]

The Irish tithe question, although obviously related to Catholic Emancipation, was yet sufficiently distinct from it to be raised in Parliament again and again without reference to the King's conscience. The redress of this grievance had also been promised at the time of the Union. Henry Parnell hammered away in the House of Commons with requests for a Select Committee, and it is interesting to find the same names again and again in the minority who supported him: Grattan himself, Sheridan, Wilberforce, Brougham, Romilly, Whitbread, Conversation Sharp, Francis Horner, James Abercromby, who had introduced Horner to Whishaw, Ricardo's friend Pascoe Grenfell, Tierney, and Thomas Bernard of the Society for Bettering the Condition of the Poor, with which Maltus was much concerned.

Malthus himself paid disgracefully little attention to Ireland in the great quarto. In the chapter 'Of the Checks to Population in Scotland and Ireland', Scotland had fourteen pages and Ireland only one paragraph, although the population of Scotland was about one and a half million as compared with over five million in Ireland. I give this paragraph in full:

> The details of the population of Ireland are but little known. I shall only observe, therefore, that the extended use of potatoes has allowed

a very rapid increase of it during the last century. But the cheapness of this nourishing root, and the small piece of ground which, under this kind of cultivation, will, in average years produce the food for a family, joined to the ignorance and barbarism of the people, which have promoted them to follow their inclinations with no other prospect than an immediate bare subsistence, have encouraged marriage to such a degree, that the population is pushed much beyond the industry and present resources of the country; and the consequence naturally is, that the lower classes of people are in the most depressed and miserable state. The checks to the population are of course chiefly of the positive kind, and arise from the diseases occasioned by squalid poverty, by damp and wretched cabins, by bad and insufficient clothing, by the filth of their persons, and occasional want. To these positive checks have, of late years, been added the vice and misery of intestine commotion, of civil war, and of martial law.[98]

Not until after his visit to Ireland, in 1817, did Malthus expunge the words 'barbarism' and 'filth of their persons' from the final edition of the *Essay*. In the chapter on the plan for abolishing the Poor Laws he also changed 'the wretched and degraded state of the common people' of Ireland to their 'depressed state'.[99]

As far as I know, the only man really to hit back at Malthus on this issue was the Rev. William Richardson, DD, (1740-1820), rector of Moy and Clonfele in County Tyrone. He was mainly a writer on geology, but for Malthusian purposes his chief concern was the cultivation of fiorin grass (*Agrostis alba*, var. *stolonifera*), sometimes called bent-grass, which could grow on bad land, and be used for feeding livestock when potatoes were scarce; when potatoes were plentiful they were themselves fed to the animals. Richardson thought that he had benefited humanity when he found that an Irish grass would provide food for cattle 'on lands hitherto neglected and completely barren'; after reading the *Essay on Population* he found, as he facetiously put it, ' that by adding to the food of man ... I was only laying the foundation of future evil, aggravating impending calamity, and preparing a wider range of the horrors and depredations of *vice* and *misery*'.[100]

He then proceeded

with great reluctance to a most unpleasant subject, the discussion of Mr. Malthus's observations upon Ireland.
I am compelled to enter upon this topic; for having spoken on so many occasions (and with great sincerity) most respectfully of Mr. Malthus, were I to stop now, I corroborate his assertions, and confirm his statements, in which my country is exhibited in the most odious and disgusting points of view.[101]

Richardson quoted extensively Malthus's frequent references to the 'rags

146

and wretched cabins of Ireland' which occur throughout the *Essay*, usually in connection with 'the disadvantageous effect of a low relative price of food on the condition of the poor'. With plain truth Richardson wrote:

> On other occasions Mr. Malthus seems quite alive in the pursuit of information; we can trace him in most countries of Europe, especially its wildest parts, examining records, consulting professors, taking every opportunity of communicating with the lower orders of people; yet, though he introduces Ireland so often, it does not appear that he ever saw the country, consulted a document, or asked a simple question about so important a part of the United Kingdom.[102]

Malthus cannot be defended against this charge. Like almost all Englishmen, he seems to have held that 'the nature of the Irish was different from that of any other people': hearsay evidence and prejudiced opinions were good enough for a paragraph about Ireland. He was to learn better, but he never altered what he had written in the quarto, apart from the small verbal changes I have mentioned. Richardson's pamphlet was dated 'Moy, Ireland, May 1811', and was printed in 1816 in *The Pamphleteer*. Malthus may never have seen it, and Richardson presumably never read Malthus's sympathetic articles about Ireland in the *Edinburgh Review* for July 1808 and May 1809.

It is possible that Malthus came to write these Irish essays as a consequence of the controversy between himself and Arthur Young (1741-1820). Their debate started with general schemes for the improvement of the lot of the poor, but became increasingly a discussion about the condition of Ireland, and especially about what Malthus regarded as the peril of cheap food, with THE POTATOE as the villain of the piece. Young knew the country well (the account of his extensive *Tour in Ireland* was published in 1780) and was far less prejudiced against potatoes than Malthus: he particularly re-marked that as these were fed to the cattle, pigs and poultry of the Irish peasants, their children were better nourished than their English counterparts reared on bread and tea.

Young, like many others concerned with the welfare of the poor, wanted cottages to be built in England with parcels of land inalienably attached to them, enough for the keep of a single cow, with some pigs and poultry. A Mr Robert Gourlay, who surveyed 'The State of the Cottagers in Lincoln and Rutland' in 1801, had found - not unexpectedly - that those with a field and a bit of garden had suffered less than those without, although even some of these smallholders had been sold rations of flour at a reduced price during the scarcity; there was one man who also needed a shilling a week from the parish in spite of possessing three acres and a cow, but the reason for this was succinctly given: 'The children young [there were five of them], the man rather indolent, the wife a trollop'.[103]

On this sort of evidence Arthur Young attacked Malthus in the *Annals of Agriculture* for 1804:

I contend that cottages ought not to be built without land, to render the inhabitants comfortable. Mr. Malthus says, that *with land* they will increase, who doubts it? They certainly will, though perhaps not more than without it. The superfluity must emigrate: so they must in every case, and if there is not a demand for this superfluity, misery is the consequence ... But will any man contend that you shall not render 500,000 families comfortable because they will increase? Seeming to assume the false supposition that if they are *not* comfortable they will not increase; though the proofs to the contrary are to be seen by millions.[104]

Back came Malthus in the 1806 *Appendix*:

I am quite sure I have never said that it is not our duty to do all the good that is practicable ... Who could ever have doubted that if without lowering the price of labour, or taking the labourer off from his usual occupations, you could give him the produce of one or two acres of land and the benefit of a cow, you would decidedly raise his. condition? But it by no means follows that he would retain this advantage if the system were so extended as to make the land his principal dependance, to lower the price of labour, and in the language of Mr. Young, to take the poor from the consumption of wheat, and feed them on milk and potatoes. It does not appear to me so marvellous as it does to Mr. Young, that the very same system which in Lincolnshire and Rutlandshire may produce now the most comfortable peasantry in the British dominions, should in the end, if extended without proper precautions, assimilate the condition of the labourers of this country to that of the lower classes of the Irish.[105]

I do not know whether Malthus himself especially wanted to write more about Ireland, or to contribute to the *Edinburgh Review* (which paid well), or whether he was asked to do so. It is certain that during 1807 he grew more closely acquainted with Francis Horner, who had become a Member of Parliament in October 1806; Horner and Whishaw had adjacent chambers in Lincoln's Inn, and the link between the *Edinburgh Review* and the reforming Whigs was firmly established through personal friendship as well as the united causes of peace and reform.

Francis Horner wrote about Malthus to his friend Lord Webb Seymour, on 6 July 1807, in a way which suggests he had not known him well before this:

Since you left us, Malthus has been a day or two in town, and gave me a little of his society, enough to enable me to judge him; and I am happy to say that a more philosophic candour, calm love of truth, and ingenious turn for speculation in his important branch, I have seldom met with. It is quite delightful to find how closely he has taught himself to examine the circumstances of the lower classes of society, and what a scientific turn he gives the subject. There is a new speculation of his, about the importance of the people being fed dear, which I wish you were here to discuss; it has the look of a paradox, and, like most of his views, is revolting to the common belief; but I have not yet detected the fallacy, if there is one.

This was high praise from a young man of thirty-one (Malthus was a decade older) who just two years previously, on 9 July 1805, had written to the same friend that he was meeting new people every now and then, but reckoned 'that about one in ten is worth seeing a second time, and about one in fifty worth adding to the permanent list'.[106]

6 Malthus's Irish Reviews

A book published in 1805 launched Malthus's first *Edinburgh Review* article; it was by Thomas Newenham, and called *A Statistical and Historical Inquiry into the Progress and Magnitude of the Population of Ireland*. Malthus also noticed with it Henry Bate Dudley's *Address to the Primate of All Ireland on Tithes*, and John Wilson Croker's anonymous *Sketch of the State of Ireland Past and Present* from which I have already quoted. The essay appeared in the *Edinburgh Review* for July 1808, but Malthus must have finished it early in April. A letter which Horner wrote to Jeffrey on 17 February 1808 suggests that he was a little anxious about Jeffrey's reaction to Malthus's work:

> Since Malthus has begun to contribute, I hope it will not be for want of solicitation on your part, if he does not continue to supply you with articles. Of all subjects, political economy is at present the most productive of useful publications, and though his general views are sometimes imperfect, he is always candid, and an advocate for what he believes to be most liberal and generous.[107]

Jeffrey responded by sending Malthus a letter whose formal flattery contrasts amusingly with the familiar style with which he was later to address 'My dear M.' On 21 April 1808 Jeffrey wrote from Edinburgh to Malthus:

> My dear Sir,
> I have just read your review of Newenham. It is admirable, and to my taste and feelings beautiful and irresistible. I feel a great degree of pride in saying that the manly and temperate tone of your patriotism - the plain and enlightened benevolence of your views - as far

149

removed from faction and caprice, as from servility or affectation, - are more consonant to my own sentiments and impressions than anything I have yet met with in the writings of my contributors. I honour and almost envy you for the dignity and force of your sentiments, and feel new pleasure in the thought of being soon permitted to see you. I think I shall set out from this on Sunday in the mail, and expect to be with you some time early on Wednesday.[108]

Horner was more critical of the article, writing to a friend that he would find in it the fault which affected all Malthus's work: 'a want of precision in the statement of his principles, and distinct perspicuity in upholding the consequences which he traces from them'.[109]

Most unfortunately, there is no complete edition of the collected works of Malthus; the miscellany edited by Bernard Semmel consists of photographic reproductions which are extremely trying to modern eyesight.[110] I must therefore summarise this review of Newenham's book as best I can, but no précis or string of quotations can convey the forcefulness - one might almost say the punch - of Malthus's indignation 'at the late debates on the Catholic petition'.

> If it be really true [he wrote] that the middling and lower ranks of society in this country are by no means prepared to consider the Irish Roman Catholics as fellow Christians worshipping the same God, and fellow subjects entitled to the same civil privileges; if they are really so bigoted as to wish to deny the benefits of the British constitution to above a fourth part of the population of the empire, and so ignorant as to imagine they can do it with safety . . . they are not only violating the genuine spirit of Christianity, but blindly endangering their own security, and risking the subjugation or dismemberment of the empire.[111]

This was not an idiosyncratic exaggeration. Jeffrey himself wrote to Horner in December 1808. 'My honest impression is, that Bonaparte will be in Dublin in about fifteen months; perhaps sooner.'[112]

Against this background one can understand the heinousness of the 'friends of the Protestant ascendancy in Ireland' who concealed the real magnitude of the Catholic population and the rapidity of its increase. Ireland was not included in the 1801 census, but Newenham estimated the population in 1804 to be 5,400,000, roughly quadruple what it had been a century earlier. He based his calculations on a poll tax and the later hearth-tax, and Malthus thought that - allowing for evasions and inaccuracies - this 'cannot be on either side far from the truth'. Malthus continued:

> The *causes* of this rapid increase, among a people groaning under a penal code of singular severity, and oppressed for three fourths of the

period in a manner of which history does not furnish a second
example, cannot fail of exciting our astonishment and curiosity. We
are at a loss to reconcile such an instance to those causes of increase
laid down by Hume and Smith, - 'wise institutions', and an
'increasing demand for labour'. Under circumstances apparently the
most opposite, Ireland has increased with extraordinary rapidity; and
this fact affords so striking an illustration of the doctrines which Mr.
Malthus has advanced in his late Essay on Population, that we are
surprised that he did not enter into it in more detail. Nothing,
however, that this author has said tends really to contradict these
positions of our illustrious countrymen. It is still true that wise
institutions, and an increasing demand for labour, are most powerful
promoters of population; because, in all ordinary cases, they most
effectually tend to produce the means of its support. But in any
particular case, where such means could be produced and distributed
without the aid of these advantages, population would still make a
rapid progress under circumstances in other respects the most
adverse.[113]

According to Malthus the POTATOE seemed to be 'the single cause which
has produced the effects which excite our astonishment'. We need not go
into the particulars of the relative nutritional value of one pound of bread
and 'three pounds of good mealy potatoes', but Malthus did, and compared
Newenham's figures with those given by Arthur Young in his *Tour of
Ireland* twenty-seven years before. Nor need we spend any time on the
comparison of yields - whether one acre of potatoes provides the same
nourishment as three or four acres of wheat depends on a number of variable
factors. What was relevant to the economist was that Irish farmers, by
leasing a relatively small portion of their land to be cultivated by potato-
eaters, could obtain an enormous supply of cheap labour.

But 'Something else besides food is required to make life comfortable.'
Malthus noted that furniture and clothing were as dear in Ireland as in
England (one of Ireland's principal imports was 'old drapery') whereas the
'pecuniary wages of the Irish labourer are not equal to half the wages of the
Englishman'. Hence the cabin -

hardly superior to an English pigstye; - its furniture confined almost
exclusively to the pot in which the potatoes are boiled; and the
clothing of its human inmates as deficient in quantity as it is
wretched in quality. Mr. Young observes, that an Irishman and his
wife are much more solicitous to feed than to clothe their children;
but the fact is, that they have the power of doing the one, and not
that of doing the other.[114]

Thus it was natural that there should be much emigration, and also that
Ireland should supply Europe, more especially France and Spain, with

mercenary soldiers. Newenham himself comments, although Malthus does not, on the absurdity of the situation: from 1691 to 1745 almost half a million Irishmen perished in the service of France.[115] Malthus merely says that he thinks this figure exaggerated, without disputing the point that the English connived at the Irish escaping to join their French enemies, although they refused to have them in the British army unless they were Protestant.

It is interesting that in spite of his 'geometrical ratio' Malthus was truly astonished not only at the absolute increase, but at the accelerating rate of increase of the population of Ireland since 1777. This seems to us so obvious, that it is perhaps worth while to point out that Hazlitt criticised Malthus's own principle from the same standpoint, being unable to envisage a situation in which population could advance in a way similar to compound interest on money, something well understood at the time. On any reckoning, if the increase continued at the present rate, Ireland would 'contain *twenty millions* of people in the course of the present century', and Malthus went on to say that 'With such a physical force, it is quite impossible that it should remain united to Great Britain without sharing, in every respect, the full benefits of its constitution.'

Malthus could not foresee the catastrophic tragedy of the potato blight of the 1840s. There is therefore a grim irony in his next two paragraphs. The population of Ireland could obviously not go on growing indefinitely, and Malthus considered two main causes which would check the rate of increase:

> The cause first generally felt, will be the dearness of land; and the advance of rent will continue, till the usual quantity of land, considered as necessary to support a large family, cannot be obtained for the amount of the average earnings of a year's labour ... The cottar system will be gradually destroyed, and give place to a set of labourers earning their pecuniary wages like the peasantry of England, but still living upon potatoes as their principal food. These potatoes will then be raised by the farmers, and will become a principal object of cultivation for the market, as the great staple food of the country.
>
> The other and ultimate cause of retardation will be such a rise in the price of potatoes, compared with the price of labour, as will give the labourer no greater command over subsistence in the shape of potatoes, as he has at present over corn, in some of the stationary or slowly-increasing countries of Europe. When the Irish peasant can only earn the maintenance of five, instead of ten persons, the habit of early marriages will necessarily be checked; the rearing of families will be impeded; and the cabins will cease to swarm, as they do at present, with overflowing broods of healthy children.[116]

The cabins did indeed cease to swarm, but not because the birth-rate fell by imperceptible degrees as the gradual decline of real wages 'slowly and almost insensibly' generated prudent habits and delayed weddings. But even if we forget the horror of the famine of 1846, it is difficult for modern readers to follow Malthus here; they can sympathise wholeheartedly with his attitude towards religious toleration and civil liberty, but find it hard to understand his *laissez-faire* approach to the economic situation. When he referred to Dudley's pamphlet, Malthus agreed 'that every effort should be used to relieve the people from the pressure of tithes ... but that any man of common sense should talk as Mr. Dudley does about *rents* is quite inconceivable'. With what seems to us absurd inconsistency, Malthus thought that the Legislature might interfere to prevent the undue pressure of rents paid in kind, but the rise of pecuniary rents 'which takes place from the principles of free competition in the progress of wealth and population ... is in the natural and necessary order of things; to clamour against it is folly – to interfere in it would be madness'.[117]

The same applied to falling wages; like increasing rents, these were beyond the Legislature's power to relieve *directly*. This did not, however, absolve the Legislature from responsibility. The causes of such distresses 'cannot be made intelligible to every poor peasant who suffers from their effects; but the Catholic poor readily see that a marked line of distinction is drawn between them and the Protestants'.[118] *Indirectly*, therefore,

> Government has great influence on the causes of distress here particularly alluded to. Universally it will be found, that political degradation is accompanied by excessive poverty; and that the opposite state of society is the most efficient cause of the general spread of comforts among the lower classes.

Over and over again he makes the point, a little quaintly perhaps, in his emphasis on diet:

> The exclusion of the lower and middle classes of society from all share in the government, by annihilating in a great degree individual importance and dignity, would have a strong tendency to make the poor submit to the lowest and cheapest kind of sustenance; and it is quite certain, that if they once consent to produce an adequate supply of labour on the cheapest sort of food, they never will be able to obtain any thing better.[119]

The first step (these are Malthus's italics) to ameliorate 'the present moral and political degradation of the mass of the Irish poor' must be 'the full and complete emancipation of the Catholics'. Croker had put ignorance and poverty at the head of the list of his country's misfortunes, which Malthus said 'was manifestly to begin at the wrong end and to labour in vain'; the abolition of the Catholic Code and the improvement of the government must come first.[120]

It is impossible not to speculate on how Malthus's Evangelical friends regarded his ecumenical outlook, and especially the passage 'Every year the proportion of the Catholics to the Protestants is rapidly augmenting, - a circumstance which might be contemplated without fear if they were once conciliated.'[121] The Clapham Sect may well have thought that a clergyman of the Church of England should take a less calmly objective and practical view of the proliferation of Popery.

In 1808 Newenham followed his *Population of Ireland* with *A View of the Natural, Political and Commercial Circumstances of Ireland*, and Malthus wrote about this in the *Edinburgh Review* for April 1809. He found the book disappointing, largely because, although Newenham was 'the first who brought together all the facts relating to the population of Ireland', on other aspects of the country's life he had had 'most able precursors, particularly Arthur Young and the two Mr. Parnells'.[122] For us, however, this second article of Malthus's is perhaps more interesting than the first, since it provides some of the meaty evidence on which he based his loathing of mercantilism, and his firm belief that the duty of government 'is to stand by and see fair play, and not to be actively assisting - first one party, and then another, as its caprice may direct'.

Malthus quoted Newenham at length on all the natural advantages of Ireland, her situation 'so eminently favourable to foreign commerce', safe and capacious harbours, navigable rivers, good materials for road-making, productive fisheries, the richest soil in Europe, a temperate climate; 'How did it happen', asked Newenham, 'that a spirit of industry and a spirit of commercial enterprize became completely extinguished among the active, quicksighted and adventurous people of Ireland?' Malthus wrote, 'It is of course impossible in this place to go through the disgusting detail of the various commercial regulations which, aided by the penal laws, have produced this melancholy effect,' and then gave the famous answer of William III to the petition of the English manufacturers of woollen cloth: 'Gentlemen, I will do all that in me lies to discourage the woollen manufacture of Ireland.'

This, Malthus went on,

> was the answer of the most liberal and enlightened prince of his age; and was spoken, not of an enemy's country, as from the language one might naturally suppose, nor even of a distant colony likely to be separated from the parent state, - but of a part of the dominions of the crown of England ... It was in this manner that, even without the plea of religious animosity, the interest of British and Irish consumers, involving the whole population of the two countries, was sacrificed to a few English traders ... The same system was uniformly pursued; and the monopolizers of England alone listened to, not only with regard to many other manufactures

peculiarly situated to Ireland, but even with regard to the raw produce of its land, and its trade in provisions. The poor resource of a poor country in the neighbourhood of a rich one was denied to it; and by the 18th of Charles II, which was not repealed till the reign of George III, the importation into England of great cattle, sheep and swine, beef, pork and bacon, and, shortly after, of mutton, lamb, butter and cheese, was declared a common nuisance, and forbidden on pain of forfeiture.

Hateful as religious animosities are, their connexion with the greater passions renders them perhaps less uniformly disgusting than that mean and pitiful jealousy of trade which is thus allowed to crush the industry, and repress the wealth, of those who ought to be considered as friends and brothers.[123]

In this context, it should be pointed out that not everyone shared Malthus's ideas about Newenham's book. Mr Richard Bligh, for instance, in the *London Review* for May 1809, attributed the poverty of Ireland to 'the uncommercial spirit of her people', and approved of the suppression of the wool trade, since the country's scarce capital could then be more advantageously employed in the manufacture of linen.[124] The classical economist's reply to this, of course, would be that under free competition capital would always flow to the most profitable industry of its own accord.

Apart from mercantilism, 'government interference' in Malthus's world often meant what was called jobbing; he bitterly quoted a speech in the Commons a month before, with reference to the half-million pounds voted by Parliament at the Union for the improvement of the inland waterways of Ireland; in the past eight years only about £27,000 had been spent, of which £6,000 had gone in salaries.[125] (By the time he read over this article, Jeffrey had probably forgotten his plea for a sinecure for poor Campbell, 'in India, Ireland, or anywhere'.)

Ireland's roads had a good reputation, presumably better than the waterways, but Malthus thought that the county grand juries levied the taxes for their upkeep with an inequitable lack of uniformity. 'The peculiar state of Ireland', he wrote, 'calls upon the Legislature, by every principle of justice and policy, to remove the burden of the partial and oppressive county rates, and the still heavier and more oppressive burden of tithes, from the poor tenantry to the rich landlords. Such a measure would be an effective and permanent encouragement to agriculture.'[126] In Ireland, as elsewhere, good farming meant much to Malthus. It was not simply that he wanted the Irish to improve their own diet and produce a vendible surplus to exchange for clothes and furniture; he was also concerned with Irish farms as a source of food for England. Even as things were, Malthus thought that

> There can be little doubt, from the progressive state of the Irish exports of corn, that if things remain quiet some years, the empire

will be entirely independent of foreign supplies, except in times of scarcity; and for this independence it will be indebted to Ireland ...

And yet this is the country the loss of which is daily risked by the inhuman cry of no popery – by the bigotry and littleness of one part of an administration, and by the tergiversation and inconsistency of the other. It is really sickening to think, that at a period when every heart and hand is wanted to rally round the last remains of liberty in Europe, a set of men should be found at the head of affairs who are either absolutely incapable, from narrowness of intellect, of profiting by the great lessons of experience that are daily unfolding themselves; or whatever their opinions may be, are willing to sacrifice them and their country at the shrine of present place and emolument!

...Before the conquering legions of France return from the Danube, let us, by a great and generous act, prepare the hearts of the Irish for their reception ... Let the Irish Catholics have all that they have demanded; for they have asked nothing but what strict justice and good policy should concede to them. Let them not only enjoy all the civil advantages of the British constitution, but give them a church establishment, like Scotland.[127]

Malthus does not elaborate this idea, and it would be interesting to know if he did so in private discussion. He was surprised and gratified to learn from Newenham that 'in point of literary attainments' the Catholic poor were 'far above the level of the same classes in England', which was attributed to the care and industry of the Catholic clergy, 'of whose general conduct, politeness, erudition, and pastoral exertions as a body, he speaks in the highest terms'.

Newenham also surprised other English readers by showing how low was the rate of crime in Ireland. Francis Horner, when he visited the country in 1810, wrote to his mother in astonishment that in spite of idleness and dirt and nakedness, the Irish 'look a much happier people than I have seen in any part of England or Scotland; the English peasant is a torpid animal, and the Scotch one eaten with care, compared with the light-hearted cheerful people of this country'.[128] Well-meaning economists! It must have seemed strange to disciples of Adam Smith that a nation of no wealth, and little opportunity to truck or barter, could still be merry, virtuous and literate.

Horner also sent a letter to Malthus from Killarney in September 1810, chiefly about the Report of the Bullion Committee, but he wrote too of the mountains all round, 'so great and rude', and the exquisitely beautiful islets 'covered with the richest heaths, arbutus, and hollies'. Such was the impression made by Malthus's Irish articles, that Horner assumed he had been there, and wrote, 'I forget whether you came so far as this when you visited Ireland.'[129]

Malthus certainly did not set himself up as an authority. Rather surprisingly, we find him writing to Henry Parnell in May 1808, just after he had finished his review of Newenham's first book, 'I have not been in the way lately of acquiring information relating to Ireland.' Presumably he meant recent information from private sources, unless this was an attempt to preserve his anonymity as an *Edinburgh* reviewer, which seems unlikely; the authorship of the articles was an open secret in the social circles in which both men moved.

By this time Malthus was married and living in Hertford, and Parnell gave Smyth some papers to take with him on a visit there, for Malthus's advice or suggestions. The subject under discussion was 'the best substitution for tithes' in Ireland, and Malthus wrote to Parnell on 4 May 1808:

> With a view to a land tax Adam Smith has proposed a plan of registering leases, and if such a plan could be adapted so as to prevent collusion, I think that a fifth or some such portion of the actual rents paid according to these leases, would be the most natural and least violent change that the attainment of the object would admit. I do not know, however, whether the very small portions of land into which estates are divided in Ireland, and the consequent great number of tenants, may not occasion objections to this system which cannot readily be got over; and I conclude that this is your opinion from your local knowledge, as you have not yourself suggested it. Would it be possible to get over the difficulty by valuing the estates (which must in fact be done when tithes are valued) and assigning a certain portion of the neat rents of the whole in lieu of tithes? In this case the landholders, whether Catholic or Protestant, would be the direct contributors, and not the Catholic tenantry. The worst of this plan perhaps is that you would require new surveys and valuations at certain intervals [Malthus had started to write 'occasionally'], which might be both expensive and unpopular.
>
> A general prejudice seems to have prevailed against giving land to the clergy, though not I think with sufficient reason; but on account of this prejudice I should fear that the proposal of such a substitution was not likely to be favourably received. And I should also be apprehensive that in many parishes it would be necessary to pay a very exorbitant sum in order to get a contiguous quantity of land fit for the purpose. In other respects the assignment of land would in my opinion possess many advantages, particularly that which you justly state as so important, that of removing the idea of the direct contribution of the Catholic to a Protestant church.

Malthus had possibly encountered the 'general prejudice' at first hand, since his incomes at both Okewood and Walesby were derived from farmers' rents for land which had been given to the church. He continued his advice to Henry Parnell:

> On account of the numerous objections which would certainly be started to any particular substitute for tithes, Smyth and I were both of opinion that in discussing the Catholic petition, it would be most prudent to avoid at first the proposal of a specific plan for the commutation of tithes, and to dwell only on the extreme oppression and distresses to which the lower classes of the Irish are subject in the present mode of levying them, in order to get, if possible, an assent to the absolute necessity of some change in this particular, before the specific mode of doing it came under consideration. The peculiar oppression to which the lower classes of Irish are exposed in the collection of tithes, you have stated in the clearest manner, and we were both inclined to think that the subject on the whole would have the fairest chance in the House, by your dwelling almost exclusively on that part of it; but of this, of course, from knowing the temper of the House, you can have better means of judging than we have.

Henry Parnell obviously studied this letter very carefully, underlining much of it, but it is clear that he found it impossible to follow Malthus's advice to postpone the discussion of specific remedies. On 12 May Malthus wrote to him again:

> Dear Sir,
>   Smyth and I, as you justly suppose, were by no means aware of the particular situation in which you were placed with regard to tithes, by the wishes of your constituents. This situation alters the state of the case entirely; and I fully agree with you in thinking, that as it will probably be expected of you, that you should make some specific propositions on the subject, it will be best to make up your mind to that plan of commutation which appears on the whole to be least objectionable.
>   I have not been in the way lately of acquiring information relating to Ireland, and have besides at present but little leisure, so that I fear I can be of little or no use to you; but any suggestions that may occur to me I shall be most happy to communicate, and I shall have great pleasure in seeing you at Hertford at any time that you can make it convenient to call. We shall have a well-aired bed at your service, which I hope you will do us the favour to make use of.
>   I forgot to notice in my last letter an objection to the plan of raising the amount of the tithes in Ireland by general taxes, which I fear may occasion considerable opposition to it. You have no land tax I believe in Ireland, and there is no tax but a land tax which would

affect the same persons who pay, or ought to pay, the tithes at present; and very strong opposition may naturally be expected from all those persons who may be called upon to pay a commutation for a species of impost to which they were not before subject. I just throw out this hint for your consideration. You will be able to judge what weight ought to be attached to it; and whether, in particular, an Irish Chancellor of the Exchequer would not make such a circumstance a strong ground of objection, as it would diminish the powers of certain classes of the society to contribute to the expences of the state, while without an entire new system of taxation, the loss could not be compensated by the proportionably increased contribution of those who had been relieved from tithes.

Hoping to have the pleasure of seeing you soon, I shall not enter further on the subject at present. I have the honour to be

> Dear Sir,
> Your very obed' humble S'
> T. Rob' Malthus

It is possible I may have business in Town for a couple of days, either quite at the beginning of next week, or quite at the end of it, in which case I will have the pleasure of calling on you in Baker Street.[130]

There is no evidence that Mr Parnell ever slept in the well-aired bed, but these letters are sufficient to indicate that Malthus's influence with the opposition party in Parliament might by now have been quite considerable. One cannot but smile at the contrast between his private style of writing, for those with practical responsibilities, and his anonymous propagandist journalism; yet in neither case do I think he was acting a part: he operated with different sides of his nature as circumstances required, and whatsoever he did, he did heartily. This made him occasionally rather absurd, sometimes inconsistent, often incomprehensible, but never insincere.

CHAPTER V

A Married Professor (1804–10)

1 Mainly about Weddings

When Malthus wrote to Clarke in February 1807 he concluded his letter with a post-script: 'Wish you joy of your boy. I hope you will never go to Town without calling.' The main purpose of the letter was to commiserate with Clarke on the Professorship of Modern History having been given to William Smyth. Malthus wrote:

> Though Smyth is not rich, yet as he is an unmarried man I think he does not want the professorship so much as you, and I should have been still more happy to hear that it had fallen to the lot of you and your rib and your little one. However as you have not got it, I am glad that he has. As he has been so old a friend of Lord Henry's, it was rather to be expected, that he would have it.
>
> I am delighted to hear that you are going on so brilliantly with your lectures, and I most sincerely hope that you will find them profitable, though I am told that I have no occasion to be fearful on that score, as you now seem to be rolling in wealth.[1]

Clarke's lectures were on mineralogy, which, as Otter wrote, 'next to his *Travels*, obtained him his highest distinction as a literary man'. Of mineralogy itself Otter informs us, 'Low at that time, as was this branch of literature in our Universities, it had risen under a variety of encouragement and patronage - the result of policy as well as taste - to a high degree of importance in every public establishment of education on the Continent.'[2] In 1808 Clarke became Cambridge's first Professor of Mineralogy.

Clarke's 'rib' was born Angelica Rush, a cousin of the pupil who had succeeded Cripps (Cripps himself married one of Angelica's sisters). Before his wedding could take place, Clarke had to resign his fellowship and enter the church; he was ordained at Christmas 1805, and married in March 1806; it should be recorded that he was an exceptionally good parish priest. In the early days of his courtship his friends were apprehensive; Otter summed up their views: 'Making every fair allowance for the chances of life, and for that powerful stimulus to exertion which the wisdom of Providence has happily annexed to a prolific marriage, it was impossible to regard the match,

160

or to represent it to himself in any other light than as a most imprudent one.'[3] In fact the marriage was extremely happy, and Mrs Clarke fully deserved her pet-name of Angel.

Otter himself was married on 3 July 1804 to Nancy Bruere, three days after he had been instituted as rector of Colmworth in Bedfordshire. The benefice was in the gift of his father-in-law, William Bruere, a former member of the Supreme Court at Calcutta who had retired to Leatherhead in Surrey. The living was worth less than £200 a year; a little later Otter also became rector of Sturmer in Essex, which would have brought him in about another £170. No wonder he took pupils, and then in 1810 accepted the rectory of Chetwynd in Shropshire, which was worth over £700; when he had the neighbouring parish of Kinlet as well, he would have been receiving some £1,000 a year for the cure of about the same number of souls. Mrs Otter seems to have got on very well with both Clarke and Malthus, who would often write to her instead of to her husband, on the grounds that she answered letters more promptly and in a more legible hand.

As for Malthus himself, when he started the population controversies in 1803 he was an unsettled bachelor who (in the words of the *Monthly Magazine*) found the moral restraint of his virtuous inclinations a palpable infelicity. By the time the fourth edition of the *Essay* was published in 1807 he was, as proclaimed on the title-page, Professor of History and Political Economy at the East India College, and he had begotten his three children. He had himself committed, as Hazlitt facetiously put it, the sin of matrimony.

As we saw, he was able to do this thanks to a secure income as rector of Walesby, where he was instituted on 21 November 1803. He stayed in Cambridge on his way to Lincolnshire, and Clarke - then in residence at Jesus - wrote to a friend on 15 November: 'Malthus left me this morning, but still new lions pour in ... certainly we must have a new table in the hall - we have not room even for the members of the college, and still less for lions, who always occupy considerable space.'[4]

Malthus was not, by all accounts, that sort of lion. On his first visit to Walesby he seems to have stayed with Mr and Mrs George Clayton Tennyson (he spelt them 'Tennison') at the old Bayons Manor, just above the village of Tealby, some three miles away. Throughout Malthus's life George Tennyson (1750-1835), the grandfather of the poet, was to act as his Lincolnshire agent. The earliest letter in the Lincoln Archives which Malthus wrote to Tennyson is dated from Claverton, 5 April, and the year must have been 1804. The first paragraph refers to the officiating curate, who was also vicar of the parishes of Tealby and Corringham, and who had been acting on Mr Whitcombe's behalf since 2 July 1797, when the rector was presumably too unwell to carry out his duties himself.

> Dear Sir,
>   I have received rather a strange letter from Dr. Hodgson in which he continues his charge of a guinea a sunday to Easter day inclusive,

and begs particularly for prompt payment. I was guilty certainly of an omission in not entering into a specific agreement with him when in Lincolnshire; but as I did not do this, though I think his taking advantage of it unhandsome, I do not think it worth while to contest the matter, and have a reference to the Bishop. I should be much obliged to you therefore to pay him his demands, which he says are £20 18s including Easter Sunday. He tells me that he made an attempt to get a guinea and a half a sunday, but was unsuccessful. This conduct naturally diminishes much the regret I should otherwise feel at depriving him of the curacy, though I am still very sorry for him as a man with so large a family and so small an income.

I expect to be in Lincolnshire soon after the 20th. When you and Mrs. Tennison were so good as to invite me to your house you were not of course aware what the invitation might include. I now believe that I shall bring a lady with me. Tell Mr. Robinson if you see him that I felt so hurt at his airs of superiority on account of being a married man that I determined before I saw him next to put myself on a par with him. I hope to be able to get the lodgings you spoke of at Otby, or others at Market Rasen; and I dare say that Mrs. Tennison will have the goodness to extend her hospitality to us, till we can find something that will do. The lady is not difficult - so little so, that I believe we shall even travel without a servant. Her name is Eckersall of a family formerly known to the Lockes.

I expect to call at Mr. Dalton's about the 20th where I should like to find a letter from you.

I wish I had settled with the tenants when in Lincolnshire. I fear this will be an exceedingly bad time for the purpose.

Best respects to Mrs. Tennison & all your family.

> Yours sincerely,
> T. Robt. Malthus.

I would wish you to pay Dr. Hodgson at the time he wishes it. [P.S.] Pray let the tenants know if you have an opportunity, that I hope their rents will be ready.[5]

Poor Population Malthus - there must have been jokes innumerable about his marriage. Fourteen-year-old Marianne Wathen wrote some verses in her cousins' honour:

> 'Twas at the op'ning of the vernal year,
> When violets and primroses appear . . .
> Forth from his rosy bower in the grove,
> With hasty step advanced the god of love:
> 'Awake! my little troop of smiling loves,
> Prepare my car, put to my fleetest doves;

162

We're bidden to the marriage of a pair
Who long have been my most peculiar care ...'
He spoke, and graceful waved his little hand,
The doves obey the imperial Boy's command,
Who thus resumes, - 'Yes, 'tis well worth our while
To gladden this fair wedding with a smile;
Endow'd with sense, with truth, with polished air,
And with a manly heart to guard the fair,
The youth, - no flutt'ring coxcomb of the day,
Who laughs at mine and Hymen's gentle sway.
The maid, - unlike the light coquettish dame
Of fashion, who disclaims all but the name
Of wife, - is soft and gentle as the dove,
The pride of virtue and the pride of love.
Sweet temper fills her breast, illumes her eye,
And on her lip hangs fair sincerity;
Health's vernal tints her modest cheeks adorn
With all the beauty of the blushing morn.
For such as these, my torch burns bright and pure,
And shall to life's last hour so endure.
Yes,' cried the god, 'each year shall, on its wing,
Unfading and substantial pleasures bring ...'[6]

Mr Malthus and Miss Eckersall were married by licence at Claverton church on Thursday 12 April 1804 by a family friend, Robert Cropp Taunton. According to Mary Russell Mitford, he was 'a most popular person at all times, and certainly the favourite marrier of the county'; during what she called an epidemic of weddings, he was once 'wanted to tie the hymeneal knot the same morning by two couples who live forty miles apart'.[7] On this early spring day he must have been just beginning his career, since he was only twenty-four. A year later he was to become Malthus's brother-in-law, so we may pause to investigate the circumstances of the young man who conducted the marriage service of the thirty-eight-year-old Population Malthus just when the *Essay* was receiving its initial burst of publicity.

Robert Cropp Taunton was the son of a learned divine who had married an heiress; his eldest brother did the same, for he married the 'daughter and heiress' of the Rev. Joseph Townsend, the eccentric rector of Pewsey whose reflections on population and the Poor Law had anticipated those of Malthus. This William Leonard Taunton in due course became Lord of the Manor of Ashley in Hampshire, and his brother naturally had the living. According to an anonymous work, *The Tauntons of Oxford*, by One of Them, published in 1902: 'The Rev. Robert Cropp Taunton, Rector of Ashley, always wore Hessian boots and drove a tandem to the Bishop's Visitations ... When up

163

at Oxford [he was at Corpus] he sent a challenge to Cambridge of a triple nature, backing himself against any Cambridge man in driving a coach, writing Greek verses, and a Latin sermon. His challenge was not taken up ... His brother, Edmund Taunton, wine merchant, of Birmingham and Palermo, was a great authority on bi-metallism (not the one that went mad but the one that died).'[8] There was a fourth brother, who went into the army and died of cholera in India in 1819.

After their wedding Mr and Mrs Robert Malthus were driven northwards from Claverton to the Lincolnshire Wolds. In the words of a contemporary account of the Division of Lindsey, 'The whole is under a high state of management, and wonderfully productive in cattle, sheep, wool and corn; there is much picturesque scenery to be found in it, and many ancient residences of nobility and gentry.'[9] It would seem, however, that the Malthuses never liked Walesby or stayed for very long in this attractive part of Lincolnshire.

Walesby had in those days a large rectory with a big kitchen-garden and orchard. The old church of All Saints, now no longer used, stands on a spur of the Wolds; the tower, forty-five feet high, with fifteenth-century buttresses, gives a fine impression of aspiration and sturdiness, dominating the skyline as one approaches from the south. Inside, it is still very much as Malthus knew it. Standing at the west end, one notices at once that the three little arches of the north arcade are rounded – they are late twelfth-century – while those of the south are pointed; on each side of the nave are three double clerestory windows, with faces on the corbels. It is light and fresh and rustic, and the memorial tablets with their homely epitaphs date from the time when the proxy rector was the hare-lipped Mr Malthus so famed in far-away London. Even the 'pulpit' made in 1636 is still there; it is best described as a little octagonal wooden box, raised one step from the floor, with a wooden canopy over it, all now painted white.

Malthus solemnised two marriages at Walesby in 1804, on 21 and 22 May. For the first, the entry in the register, in Malthus's handwriting, starts with a muddle of deletions; then he made exactly the same mistake as he had made at a wedding in Albury on 3 October 1793, writing 'by me, Thomas Robert Malthus', where he should have written 'by Banns', so that he had to cross it out and sign all over again in the proper place. Malthus was obviously not used to marrying people, and it is possible that he did not officiate at weddings as much as he might have done on account of superstitions about his deformity; it would have caused real apprehension if the bride were pregnant.

Both the Walesby pairs Malthus married in May 1804 were illiterate. One couple left the parish, but one remained, so we can learn from the register that their first child was christened on 2 September; let us hope his mother did not spend a miserable summer expecting a baby with a hare-lip; she had thirteen children in all, of whom four died under the age of six months.[10]

On 9 June 1804 Mr and Mrs Malthus were in London, dining with William Bray and other members of the family; on 25 July they dined with him at Shere, with Jane Dalton. We know from William Bray's invaluable diary that Robert and Harriet were staying in Albury with the Samuel Godschalls, whose home was to be their Surrey headquarters until Samuel's death in 1821. Old Mr Godschall had died in December 1802, so Malthus's sister became mistress of the imposing Weston House fondly recollected by Louisa Bray: 'It was built of stone in the Italian style ... A handsome portico was in the centre of the garden front, where we often dined in Summer ... The Entrance Hall was spacious and lofty, opening into another, where was the great staircase leading up to the gallery over the portico. This was a delightful room in Summer, with its fine large windows looking East over a beautiful lawn to fine trees and fields beyond. In the centre of the courtyard was a pond with a fountain, round which the pigeons sat cooing ...'

Malthus's first child, Henry, was born in Bath, in a terraced house in New King Street. (When the Austen family were looking for a home there in 1801, Miss Jane had rejected the entire row as being much too cramped, and one house they saw was 'quite monstrously little ... the second room in every floor about capacious enough to admit a very small single bed'.[11]) Henry Malthus was born on Sunday 16 December 1804, eight months after his parents' marriage. It is not difficult to guess the ribald comments that must have been made, and some writers have politely confused Henry's birth with his baptism, which took place at Claverton on 16 April 1805. But the date of his birth ('in ye parish of Walcot') is clearly entered in the register, and is confirmed by the following letter which Malthus wrote to the publishing firm of Cadell and Davies about a new edition of Adam Smith's *Wealth of Nations*:

December 16th, 1804   Bath.
                                      37 New King Street.

Dear Sir,

    I have looked over the packet that you sent, though from being at present very particularly engaged I have not been able to give it the attention I could have wished. Some of the notes appear to have merit, others not, and some of the most important points are not discussed at all. It is difficult however to pass any fair judgement upon the work as a whole; because the supplementary chapters evidently contain the discussion of those subjects which the writer thinks of the greatest consequence, and none of these supplementary chapters are sent. With regard to myself I can have no manner of objection to your publishing this edition before mine, as it would give me more time, which the more I think on the subject the more I feel is necessary, in order to produce an edition that would have any thing like the effect of giving you a new copyright. I had much rather that you would rely on the advice of any other friend respecting the eligibility of publishing the edition now offered, than on mine, particularly as I have not had leisure to read the manuscript very attentively, and this you will not be surprised at when I tell you that in addition to the engagements, I have been in a state of considerable anxiety about Mrs. Malthus, who was brought to bed this morning before her time, but is now happily pretty well. Should the present offer that you have received or any other, make you wish to alter your plans, I beg that you will not consider yourself as tied by anything that has passed between us.

> I am Dear Sir
> Your obe' huml St
> T. R. Malthus

In the advertisement, the last paragraph and the manner in which the French economists are spoken of do not give a favourable impression. The style is not very correct, and is written without punctuation; but such little errors may be easily amended.

The Author of the original work is always called *Mr*. Smith; but Adam Smith, Dr. Smith, or Smith are all preferable.

I am writing in the dark - Excuse great haste.[12]

On the following day, 17 December 1804, a single quarto sheet was posted in Bath, hastily addressed to Messrs 'Cadill & Davies', and containing other slips of the pen. The letter read:

> Dear Sir
> I have just recollected that I ought to have given you a line to say that I yesterday booked your parcel by the mail, which left Bath at 5 oclock.
> Do not be prejudiced against the Edition by any thing that I have said. I really think that some of the notes are of value.

> Yours & c
> T. R. Malthus[13]

It is impossible not to feel grateful to the autograph-collector who cherished and preserved a scrap of paper so characteristic of the writer.

The edition of the *Wealth of Nations* to which these letters refer, with notes by William Playfair, duly appeared in 1805; there were to be many more, by other writers, in several languages, but none by Malthus. We shall see later for how many years he kept in mind a scheme for his own annotated edition of Adam Smith. The very particular engagements he mentions would have included the visit to London when he dined with William Bray on 8 November. In the autumn of 1804 the Directors of the East India

Company were planning to establish a college in England, and it seems likely that the possibility of Malthus's becoming a member of the staff was considered at this time. He may also have been discussing with Joseph Johnson the third edition of the *Essay on Population* which was 'preparing for publication' in January 1805.

Malthus would also have been concerned with the death of his first tutor, Richard Graves, on 23 November at the age of ninety-one. According to the *Bath Chronicle* for 29 November 1804, 'His physical and intellectual vigour was prolonged to him, almost unimpaired and unclouded, till within a short period of his departure . . . On the day preceding his dissolution, he received the sacrament from the hands of a neighbouring clergyman, and awaited the approaches of death with that earnest spirit of religious peace and cheerfulness, which gave the characteristic form to his conduct and manners, and distinction to every part of his life.' There is a tradition that the neighbouring clergyman was his most famous pupil, the erstwhile Don Roberto.[14]

We also get a glimpse of Malthus at this period through the eyes of Dr Currie, who was in Bath for his health in December 1804; he died the following year. He wrote to William Roscoe: 'I had one or two evenings, at my lodgings, uncommonly good society. Earl Selkirk, just come from America, Lord Henry Petty, Sir William Watson, Malthus the economist and writer on population (a very profound and modest pleasing man) Parry Okeden, Colonel Barry, de Barry the clergyman, Hoare the London banker, and Dr. Crawford.'[15]

'Malthus the economist' must surely have found the distance between Bath and London a great inconvenience, but he had no home, and Harriet would understandably have wished to be near her family and their old nurse, Catherine Orts, during the first baby's first difficult months. The Eckersall sisters were all very devoted to each other, and to each other's children, as is apparent from the miscellaneous collection of memoranda and little portrait sketches which their descendants have kindly allowed me to see. In the spring of 1805 the sister next to Harriet in age came over from Ireland on a visit to Claverton with her husband, the Rev. Henry Wynne, and a flock of children and nurse-maids reminiscent of Isabella Knightley's arrival at Hartfield (in Jane Austen's *Emma*). They were there for Henry Malthus's christening, when he was exactly four months old, and for the wedding of his aunt Lucy Eckersall to Robert Cropp Taunton on 25 April; Henry Wynne performed the ceremony, and the witnesses were the bride's father, the bridegroom's eldest brother, and Thomas Robert Malthus.[16]

Less than a month later, on 17 May 1805, Malthus must have been in London, for on that day he dined with Joseph Johnson, and met both Godwin and Richard Lovell Edgeworth, the father of 'the great Maria'. Edgeworth wrote home to his daughter, 'Godwin is less presumptuous - and more agreeable than I expected - he however talks paradoxically . . .

Mr. Malthus is much more of a gentleman than the other author - he is a sensible modest man.'[17]

By this time Malthus was probably aware of the pattern of his life. In the course of three years he had published his *magnum opus*, he had married and had a son, and he was secure both in the possession of a rectory and in his appointment at the East India Company's college, of which the Principal had already been named. With all his modesty, he must have realised that Adam Smith's mantle had fallen upon him, and that in spite of his critics he was regarded as the country's foremost living political economist.

2 The Founding of the East India College

Elizabeth Grant was two, her sister Margaret only ten months old, when they died of smallpox in Calcutta in 1776. Their deaths at first prostrated their father, then caused him to be suddenly converted to active Evangelical Christianity. It is difficult to estimate how much can be attributed to any one man, but from Charles Grant's conversion stemmed the prominent part he played in the foundation of the British and Foreign Bible Society, the Church Missionary Society, the Church of England's establishment in India, the setting up of the East India Company's College, and - from this - a new idea of a hard-working, full-time Civil Service, educated, salaried and incorruptible. Whatever reservations one may feel in approving any or all of these institutions, their influence on world history cannot be denied.

The seventy-eight years of Charles Grant's life, from 1746 to 1823, seem to cover a much longer span of evolution. He was christened after Bonnie Prince Charlie, in the presence of a number of his clansmen on their way to Culloden; each took the baby's right hand, laid it on his sword, and swore fealty on the infant's behalf to his rightful king. When Charles Grant died, after collapsing over his desk at the India House, gentlemen carried not swords but umbrellas.

Grant's father was badly wounded at Culloden, but lived to join a Highland regiment and die of fever at the siege of Havana in 1762. His children were brought up largely by his brother, and young Charles went out to India to make his fortune; he was one of the last of the Company's servants to do so by private trading, mainly in silk. There was never any slur on his integrity, but for two years before his conversion he was supposed to have gambled heavily in Calcutta, where British expatriate society does indeed seem to have touched rock bottom for avarice and triviality. In 1780 Grant was made Commercial Resident at Malda; after seven years he came back to Calcutta as Fourth Member of the Board of Trade, and with his friend John Shore (later Lord Teignmouth) did all he could to encourage Protestant missions, such as there were, at this time mostly Danish or German.[18]

Charles Grant returned to England in 1790, and at once met other Evangelicals – Wilberforce, the Thorntons, Hannah More. He also worked at Wimbledon with Lord Grenville, Pitt himself, and Henry Dundas (later Lord Melville) on the Revenue Settlement of Bengal. In 1794 he set up house in Clapham and became a Director of the East India Company; very soon he was 'not a Director, but the Direction'.[19]

There were thirty Directors in all, but as six went 'out of Direction' annually in rotation, only twenty-four functioned at any given time. This Court of Directors, as it was called, was nominally responsible to the Court of Proprietors, which consisted of the holders of East India stock, whose voting strength was proportional to the amount of stock they held; there were between two and three hundred of them, and they normally met four times a year in the General Court Room at India House, in Leadenhall Street. The standard of debates was high, and the General Court had close links with the House of Commons. During the period 1784–1834 about sixty to a hundred Members of Parliament would be proprietors of East India stock, and of the 110 Directors who held office during this half-century, forty-five were MPs at one time or another. Well over half the Directors had lived in India. The Court of Directors met weekly on Wednesdays, more often if the occasion required, and they were split up into committees to manage different aspects of the Company's affairs, Accounts, Correspondence, Shipping, and so on; the most important was the Secret Committee, of which 'the Chairs' of all the other committees were *ex officio* members. The Company employed four hundred clerks in Leadenhall Street, and from 1792 until 1825 Charles Lamb was one of them.[20]

India had long been regarded as a Tom Tiddler's ground where the adventurous might pick up gold and silver, bring it back to England in early middle age – if they survived climate and fever – and live happily ever after. Fox's India Bill led to the fall of his government in 1783 because he proposed in effect to transfer the powers of the Company to the Crown, which would have meant such extensive patronage of lucrative posts as to keep his party in office for ever – or so it appeared to his opponents. The position was a difficult one, for what had started in 1600 as a chartered monopoly trading company was now the only effectual government of vast alien territories, supported by the King's troops as well as the Company's own forces. What were originally trading stations had become involved in the ubiquitous war with France which began in George II's reign; the Peace of Paris in 1763 had made Britain the supreme European power in India even though she did not then administer the whole peninsula, and there could be no putting the clock back.

Since public money was involved in the defence of British interests in

India (the Company was heavily in debt to the Exchequer), some sort of regulation by Parliament was essential, and Pitt's India Act of 1784 (amended in 1786) achieved a compromise. A ministerial body of Commissioners for the Affairs of India was set up, known as the Board of Control, with general supervisory powers, who communicated with the Court of Directors mainly through the Secret Committee. Supreme power in India was vested in the Governor-General in Calcutta, the Presidency of Bengal being given authority over those of Madras and Bombay, and all senior appointments were ministerial. But the appointment of the fifteen-year-old apprentice civilians, who were called Writers, remained with the Directors, and such nominations were eagerly sought by parents and guardians; once a boy became a covenanted Writer he was provided for, for life.

Nominations for Writerships could not be purchased, and were intended to be restricted to boys personally known to the Directors, their families and friends; for these and other obvious reasons British India was the property, so to speak, of a closely-knit group. A contemporary of Charles Grant, Richard Chichele Plowden, is a good example. He too returned to England in 1790, with £33,550, 'not a bad little fortune after ten years' service in India', according to the family historian Walter Chichele Plowden, who continues: 'In 1803 Richard was elected a Director of the Honourable East India Company, and he was enabled to put his sons Richard, Trevor, George and William, and his nephew William, into the same service, and his son Charles into the India Board at home. In addition to his sons, he was able to provide for his grandsons, Richard and Augustus, sons of Richard, and Trevor and George, sons of Trevor, all in the Bengal Civil Service, as well as to place his great-nephew James and others in the Company's Army.'[21]

Five of these lads passed through the East India College in Malthus's time, undistinguished either there or in their subsequent careers, but it is easy to see how a mere professor might have difficulty in disciplining an unruly member of such a dynasty.[22]

The idea of an East India training establishment in England had been discussed half-heartedly for about a decade. Boys destined for China spent time in British warehouses learning about the tea trade, and there were suggestions from Canton that a more systematic course of instruction was desirable. Then in the summer of 1800 the Governor-General of India, Lord Wellesley (brother of the future Duke of Wellington), set about establishing a college at Fort William without consulting the Court of Directors. He annoyed them further by saying that his Calcutta College should train all Indian civil servants, before they were posted to the Presidencies of Bengal, Madras, or Bombay, which made the Directors fear that the Governor-General was exalting himself at the expense of their patronage.

Wellesley was unpopular with the Directors on two other counts: he wished to break the Company's monopoly and open India to private traders, and he pursued an expansionist military policy which terrified the Court on financial grounds, and of which Grant also disapproved morally. He lamented 'the bloodshed, miseries and devastation' of Wellesley's Mahratta wars, and wrote, 'We rule over a greater Empire than Akbar held. But is this a change to exult in? Truly I think very much otherwise.' In another letter he wrote of Wellesley's conquests, 'I have great fears that they will prove only a splendid road to ruin.'[23]

To say that the immediate cause of the founding of the East India College was an intense desire to snub Wellesley would be an over-simplification amounting to a perversion of the truth; the fact remains that a letter was sent to India on 27 January 1802 formally abolishing the College at Fort William, except as a limited establishment for teaching Oriental languages in Bengal, and Charles Grant started to prepare a scheme for a college at home. In the same year he became a member of the House of Commons and moved from Clapham to 40 Russell Square, where he entertained Francis Horner and Sir James Mackintosh; Jemmy Mackintosh had been knighted on his appointment as Recorder of Bombay, and some of his Whig friends were a little perturbed at his accepting such a post from a Tory government. Grant, like Wilberforce, was more concerned with causes than parties; we know they discussed the proposed college together in 1804. In Leadenhall Street the Directors' Committee of Correspondence laid their Plan before the Court on 3 October, and on 26 October 1804 the Committee of College held its first meeting.[24]

The result was a remarkable memorandum. The Committee decided that henceforth nominations should be made to the College, not to the Company, and that those gentlemen who do not 'pass with credit the final examination . . . shall not be appointed into the Civil Service of the Company'. Lest time and money should be wasted on unsuitable applicants, the fifteen-year-old gentlemen were to be tested before admission: they must be 'not only able to write fairly and well, but to be well grounded in Arithmetic, and qualified to be examined in Caesar and Virgil, the Greek Testament and Xenophon'. In our own exam-ridden days it is hard to realise what a revolutionary innovation this was; thereafter the relations of 'a tormenting boy' were to find it increasingly more difficult to pack him off to India in the Company's Civil Service unless he were prepared for grinding work.

The Committee's first object was that the students 'should be imbued with reverence and love for the Religion, the Constitution, and Laws of their own Country'. Their formal education was to be considered under four headings.

Classical literature came first, partly because it was the basis of all liberal education, partly because 'in India so much of all the business, public, and Private, is carried on in Writing (a circumstance of vast importance to the due superintendance at home of the affairs of our Empire there,) that the Art of Composition ought to be studied in early life, by every Person who

171

is to Act on that Scene'. Whatever we may think of studying Latin and Greek in order to write English, it should be remembered in this connection that a voyage from England to Calcutta, round the Cape, took from four to six months; it was expected that a whole year would elapse between the despatch of a letter and the receipt of an answer to it.

Second, 'A good acquaintance with Arithmetic and Mathematics will also be indispensible. In almost every situation in which a man can be placed in India, a ready use of Figures will be found of greater value than those who may be apt to regard this as merely a Vulgar attainment would suppose. Mercantile Accounts are not here particularly intended.'

Third came Elements of General Law, Politics, Finance and Commerce, instruction provided by 'no existing Establishment in this Country'.

Oriental Learning came fourth. 'It could not but seem preposterous to exclude from a System of Education for India, the elementary study of Oriental Languages.' Yet this preposterous state of affairs had long continued; when John Shore went out to India in 1768 the languages he set himself to learn before his departure were Portuguese and French.[25] The Committee of College noted in 1804 that the French set 'high value' on regular institutions for Eastern languages. 'Their present government affords distinguished encouragement to the study of Oriental literature; it is pursued with ardour, and Paris so much abounds in proficiency in Persian, Arabic, Turkish and even Sanskrit, that a gentleman detained there, an Eastern scholar of our own, and from that character admitted into their free society with their savants, has written that he conversed with them more frequently in Persian than in French.' All this was bad politically, for French diplomats could negotiate independently of interpreters, while the English were quite at their mercy.

The Committee added a significant sentence to their memorandum on the scope of the College courses: they suggested that part of the students' vacations 'might be usefully employed in Viewing the great Public Works in England, Docks, Arsenals, Manufactories and the like, of which else they will know nothing but by report, before a late period of Life'. The first tour of service could be as long as seventeen years, followed by three of furlough in Britain before going back to India again.

The Committee of College went on to recommend 'That a suitable House in a healthy convenient situation at a proper distance from the Metropolis be provided and decently furnished by the Company', and in December 1804 they decided on Hertford Castle, which they rented from Lord Salisbury on a twenty-year lease. *The Times* at first did not get it quite right: among the snippets of 8 January 1805 we read that 'The Directors of the East-India Company have purchased Hertford Castle, to be converted into a College for the education of the children of the Civil Servants of the Company.' On 26 February, however, they published an informed and approving letter from 'An Old Proprietor', and on 2 March they printed the formal Resolution setting up the Establishment.[26]

Meanwhile the Committee must have been canvassing for staff, and we know that Malthus was in London in the first half of November 1804. Samuel Henley was appointed Principal in April 1805, and on 13 June, under the chairmanship of Charles Grant, the Committee of College confirmed the other initial appointments. They had found a wide choice of classical professors, but 'in other cases, as in the Professorships of Mathematics, Natural Philosophy, and Political Economy, the Candidates were so few, and at the same time so distinguished as to Academical Reputation as to render the Selection easy.'[27]

Malthus's formal letter accepting his post as 'Professor of General History, Politics, Commerce and Finance' is dated from London, 10 July 1805; it is addressed personally to Charles Grant, and concludes:

> I am fully sensible of the importance of the charge which they [the Honourable Court of Directors] selected me to fill, and it will be my earnest endeavour not to disappoint their choice.
>
> I beg you, Sir, to accept my particular thanks for the interest you have taken in my favour.[28]

The Oriental Department was to be in the charge of Jonathan Scott (1754-1829), who had gone out to India, with his two elder brothers, at the age of twelve; when he was eighteen he became an ensign in the 29th Native Infantry of the Carnatic. Warren Hastings recognised his ability and made him his Persian Secretary, and it would appear that Scott returned to England with Hastings in 1785. He set to work on scholarly translations and histories, and would have been the ideal man for the post but for his touchiness. He had been appointed in April at the same time as Henley, 'having offered his services', and there being no other applicant 'but one Gentleman who has never been in India'.[29] Yet Scott resigned in a huff on 3 December 1805, after he had been in Hertford Castle for some weeks. He wrote: 'Had I not supposed that in the formation of the College Oriental Learning would have been a primary object and therefore have born a distinction, I should not have applied for the appointment. I did expect it would have been made secondary to that of the Principal in emolument and honour.'[30]

The Principal, the Rev. Samuel Henley (1740-1815), had been Professor of Moral Philosophy at Williamsburg, Virginia, but was forced to return to England on the outbreak of the War of American Independence. He became an assistant master at Harrow, held a living in Suffolk, and wrote a number of innocuous and scholarly oddments on *Controverted Passages . . . concerning the Angels that Sinned,* the *Fourth Eclogue,* the *Elegies* of Tibullus, and an *Inscription on a Brick from the Site of Ancient Babylon.* But what he is chiefly remembered for is the English translation of the Arabian nightmare fantasy *Vathek,* which William Beckford originally wrote in French; Henley was accused in the *Gentleman's Magazine* of writing the fairy-tale himself, in order to show off in his notes on Persian folklore. This was in 1784, and the French version was not published until 1787; it has been suggested that Henley took advantage of Beckford's persecution by scandal-mongers for a homosexual affair.[31]

Perhaps Charles Grant knew nothing of the matter - he was in India at the time - and he seemed to have picked the right man at this juncture. The folios of the old India Office Records still seem to throb with Henley's harassing activity. In September 1805 he started arranging for deal partitions to make up thirty-nine students' rooms, in such a way as not to damage Lord Salisbury's walls and ceilings; accommodation had to be furnished in the Castle for two bachelor professors, and suitable houses found 'within a mile of Hertford' for the married ones. The Committee of College were very slow in making up their minds about the catering contract, and allowances for coal and candles and 'stationary'. Then they dropped a bombshell.

Although the College was not to be opened until February 1806, there were several Writers of the 1804-5 intake who had not been posted to India, and their parents were 'very desirous of sending them for some time into the College'; so the Committee decided that a Table should be kept for them at the expense of the Company, until the Writers appointed for 1805-6 should enter the College, 'against which time an experience will be gained of the expense of keeping the Table'. The papers reflect the chaos: it is impossible to discover how many students moved in at the end of October, or when any work was begun in the makeshift lecture-rooms and the library with no books in it which also served as a sitting-room for the professors.[32]

On 9 October 1805 the Committee of College decided it would cost too much to make the Castle satisfactory, with only a twenty-year lease to run, so they resolved to buy land near Hertford, 'and thereon to raise from the Foundation a neat structure in the Collegiate Form according to a Plan to be made for the Purpose'. There were two suitable estates up for auction, but on 22 October they decided to purchase the lovely fields on which Haileybury now stands; the following day (Trafalgar Day, though they did not know it) they bought the land - just under sixty acres - for £5,900. A house with '16 airy Bed-chambers' was included, which the Company let to a Dr Lushcomb, to set up a school for the under-fifteens.[33]

The architect chosen to make the Plan was William Wilkins (1778-1839), and copies of his drawings are preserved in Sir John Soane's Museum in London. To begin with, Wilkins must have thought of the College as a school, for he designed it with three huge dormitories and seven classrooms, with rooms for the Head Master. These are altered to make the Principal's Lodge; masters' rooms become professors' dwellings; classrooms are re-named lecture-rooms, and individual studies replace the dormitories. Discussions must have gone on for months as changes were made: the Committee of College - presumably - cut down the architect's provision of thirty

174

water-closets in three rows of ten to a 'Cloaca' with but twelve closets in all, and so on.[34]

Principal Henley was thus simultaneously occupied with the new building - it was he who found a field with clay suitable for brick-making - supervising the school, and getting the College itself established. In the midst of all this he had to move out of the Castle, just after he and his family had moved into it, in order that sixty students might be accommodated instead of the thirty-nine originally intended. Never can a man of his age have worked harder, or a historic institution begun in a more uncomfortable muddle. The first terms of both the new College and the school were to start on Monday 3 February 1806, and as late as 10 December Henley was reminding the Committee that neither the Drawing Master, the French Master, nor the Fencing Master had as yet been appointed. Even more serious, there was no Oriental Professor; the two men the Directors had in mind were Major Charles Stewart, who was still in Calcutta, and Captain Alexander Hamilton, who was nearer home but not then available, being an honoured prisoner of war in Paris. Dr John Gilchrist, who undertook to fill the breach, was a friend of Jonathan Scott's and something of a mischief-maker.[35]

The last document of the Records for 1805 is a letter dated 28 December in which the Archbishop of Canterbury (Charles Manners-Sutton) complies with the East India Company's request to make Mr Samuel Henley a Doctor in Divinity. The Archbishop took great pleasure in giving this proof of his respect for the East India Company and his opinion of Mr Henley's merits.[36]

3 Colleagues and Pupils

Probably Malthus moved to one of the Company's houses in Hertford, with Harriet (just pregnant again) and baby Henry, at the beginning of November 1805. From William Bray's diary it is clear that they spent October in Surrey; Malthus officiated at a wedding in Shere on the 16th - possibly of family servants - and we have George Pryme's word for it that he dined with the Lomaxes of Netley Place in this month. One of Bray's clerks, S. T. Adams, wrote respectfully to Sydenham Malthus on 24 October, about inquiries he had made for Mr Robert Malthus's saddlebags and a parcel, lost between Guildford and Saffron Walden; there is a strong supposition that Robert had sent them either by the wrong coach, or to the wrong address, or both. One fears that Malthus was not very practical.

I cannot find out from the records when he began to receive his salary from the East India Company. Henley was paid £1,000 a year, the same as

Sir Charles Wilkins, who was the chief Oriental scholar in England and the Company's first Librarian. The other professors had £500, which was a good income for the period, better than almost all parsonages. The Committee of College agreed

> that men of distinguished name in the Universities have prospects of emoluments and advantage open to them, both in those Seats of Learning and in the Church; if they go out of the road in which they are advancing to connect themselves with an insulated establishment like that now proposed they must renounce other hopes and therefore will expect in their immediate benefits some inducement to make such a sacrifice.[37]

Henley's and Scott's salaries were paid from 10 April 1805; next on the list came the Rev. Bewick Bridge of Peterhouse (1767-1833), whose salary as Professor of Mathematics dated from 26 June. The Rev. Edward Lewton (1769-1830) began to draw his on 1 October; he was the only Oxonian on the staff, and is described as Vice-Principal and Tutor of St Alban's Hall (later Wadham College).[38] Malthus joined these four men at 'A Convention of the Principal and Professors' arranged by Charles Grant at the India House on 30 August 1805, when they drew up a code of regulations which were later embodied in a prospectus.

The College year was to be divided into two terms, each consisting of twenty weeks, from 2 February to 19 June and 1 August to 21 December. Later this was changed to allow about a month's vacation at Christmas and two months in the summer. The fee for each term was to be fifty guineas (£52.50). Parents were warned that 'All extravagance among the students will be discouraged; and on this account it is much to be desired that their pecuniary allowances may be moderate.' Everything was compulsory; the wearing of caps and gowns, attendance at divine service and prayers, lectures from 10 a.m. till 2 p.m., and 3 o'clock dinner in hall. No student was to be allowed out before dinner or after evening prayers (8 o'clock in winter and 9 o'clock in summer); they were forbidden to ride at all, or even to walk two miles from the College without permission; the little towns of Hoddesdon and Ware - and later Hertford itself - were out of bounds. The keeping of animals, wines and spirits, firearms, billiards and games of chance were all prohibited. It is interesting to note that it never occurred to the Convention to prohibit smoking, which was then completely out of fashion. George Pryme remarked of the turn of the century in Cambridge, 'Smoking was allowed in the Trinity Combination Room after supper in the twelve days of Christmas, when a few old men availed themselves of it, among *us* undergraduates it had no favour.'[39]

The Convention laid much emphasis on competition. The results of the annual December examination were to be published, with the students' names listed in order of merit; four lists were to be made, corresponding to the four divisions of subjects studied, and it was hoped that no *one* student should be found at the bottom of all of them. Expulsion was to be only for misdemeanour, not for inferior intellect, provided that the student worked hard: 'Where fatuity actually exists, no appointment could in the first instance have been made.'[40] This sentence, of course, was in the minutes but not in the prospectus.

In the prospectus Oriental Literature came first in the curriculum, since Jonathan Scott had helped to draft it:

1 Practical Instruction in the Rudiments of the Oriental Languages, more especially the Arabic and Persian.
2 A Course of Lectures to illustrate the History, Customs, and Manners of the People of India.

Second came Mathematics and Natural Philosophy, and parents were told, 'It is here of importance to observe, that the more abstruse parts of pure Mathematics will be utterly excluded from these Lectures, as altogether inconsistent with the object of the Institution. The Mathematical Lectures will be made entirely subservient to the purposes of Natural Philosophy.' Natural Philosophy comprised Mechanics, Hydrostatics, Optics, and Astronomy, and the lectures 'will have for their scope and end, the arts and objects of common life'.

There were to be two courses on Classical and General Literature:

1 A Course of Lectures to explain the Ancient Writers of Rome and Greece, more particularly the Historians and Orators.
2 A Course of Lectures on the Arts of Reasoning and Composition; and on such other subjects as are generally understood by the 'Belles Lettres'.
These lectures will be altogether plain and practical. Peculiar care will be taken to make the Students well acquainted with the English Language, and with the merits of its most approved Writers. They will be exercised also in every species of composition appropriate to their future occupations.

Finally came:

4 Law, History, & Political Oeconomy.
1 A Course of Lectures on general History, and on the History and Statistics of the Modern Nations of Europe.
2 A Course of Lectures on Political Oeconomy.
3 A Course of Lectures on general Polity, on the Laws of England, and Principles of the British Constitution.[41]

I think Charles Grant went to the Convention with the concluding passages of the prospectus already drafted: the cultivation and improvement of the students' intellectual powers 'should be accompanied with such a course of moral discipline as may tend to excite and confirm in them habits of application, prudence, integrity, and justice ... An Institution conducted upon these principles may reasonably be expected, under the favour of Providence, to be productive of a benign and enlightened policy toward the Native Subjects of British India, to improve their moral condition, and to diffuse the happy influence of Christianity throughout the Eastern World.'[42]

It is easy to understand why Grant had bitter opponents, not only among the commercially-minded Directors and Proprietors, but also among the Writers' parents, who had hoped that 'the least manageable of their sons' might be 'at once swept out of the way', at no expense to themselves. Charles Grant wrote to Sir James Mackintosh in Bombay on 17 September 1805: 'Simple as the idea is of this Institution, I have found it to be no easy matter to carry it into execution. What with opposition to the design, the settlement of details, and the choice of persons for Professors, it has proved a tedious work.' It is significant that Grant used the first person singular instead of the usual committee 'we'. He went on about the professors: 'I have found it, on the whole, safer in a new Institution, respecting which the public opinion was to be conciliated, rather to choose academical men versed in the art of teaching, and reputable in their several lines, than men of, perhaps, more powers, but withal more eccentric.'[43]

When we look at the appointments, this statement is puzzling. As far as I know, Malthus had no experience of teaching, and Lewton seems to have been quite unable to keep boys in order; his colleague in the Classical Department who came a little later, the Rev. Joseph Hallet Batten (1778--1837), was a much stronger character, although possibly eccentric in some ways, as we shall see. The Rev. William Dealtry (1775-1847), who was appointed to help Bridge with the Mathematics and Natural Philosophy as numbers increased, was also made of sterner stuff than poor Lewton. But the most extraordinary of all the initial appointments was that of Edward Christian (1758-1823) as Professor of General Polity and the Laws of England.

To begin with, he was the brother of Fletcher Christian, the leader of the mutiny on the *Bounty*; Grant would have been in England in 1792 when Fletcher Christian was court-martialled in his absence. Edward Christian was notorious for having tried to obtain a sinecure office with the aid of three hired bullies and his own fists; he did in fact collect several part-time appointments, and derived 'considerable gain' from an edition of Blackstone's *Commentaries*. But worse than Christian's unfortunate family connection and his bad temper was his incompetence; it was so widely known in the legal profession that I wondered whether his imposing testimonials from the Lord Chancellor, the Lord Chief Justice, the Master of the Rolls, and so on, were not part of a conspiracy to play an unkind practical joke on John Company's Evangelical Chairman.[44] It must have been trying to work in double harness with Christian; according to Gunning 'his society was avoided by every one whose time was of any value.'[45] Poor Malthus had to put up with him, as their two departments were regarded as one for examination purposes until 1810.[46]

On the other hand Alexander Hamilton (1762-1824), after the French had courteously released him in the spring of 1806, became a cherished friend. He was known as Sanskrit Hamilton or the Pundit, and is described by Cockburn as 'a little amiable person, of excellent conversation'. After youthful military service with the Company in Bengal, he returned to Scotland and became a close friend of Francis Jeffrey during his impecunious days, when Edinburgh was an unprosperous place for young Whig lawyers; they planned a visit to Germany in 1800, but found they had only money enough for a tour of the Highlands. Jeffrey contemplated going to India with Hamilton (he went back as soon as his father died) and had even toyed with the idea of becoming Professor of Moral and Political Science at Wellesley's Calcutta College.[47]

Another Scot, Charles Stewart (1764-1837), was also an Orientalist who had started his career as a soldier; he used to be called Major rather more often than Hamilton was called Captain. Stewart was designated Professor of Arabic, Persian and Hindustani, while Hamilton was Professor of Hindu Literature and the History of Asia. Both men seem to have established themselves in Hertford towards the end of 1806. Later they were given Asiatic assistants called 'moonshees', whose financial and family difficulties, beautifully penned in their own scripts, the professors translated and forwarded to the Committee of College. Stewart and Hamilton had a hard time of it with the Committee, who jibbed at the expense of importing books, and suggested that the moonshees might copy those in the Library at the India House![48] With the doggedness of their race and their original calling the two Scots battled on, with the result that even today Messrs Stephen Austin of Hertford are still pre-eminent as printers of Asiatic languages.

Until 1818 there was a French master, M. de Foligny; he was described as a Protestant and paid £200 a year; when he retired, to return to his native Switzerland, his salary had risen to £350, and the company gave him a pension of £150. It is clear from the minutes that he was not good at keeping order, and no more French masters were appointed. Drawing was also compulsory in the early days, unless the boys were quite hopeless at it; ability to make accurate sketches was of real importance in the era before photography. Thomas Medland was on the staff as drawing master, and later as Oriental writing master, until 1833; to him we are indebted for pictures of capped and gowned students in the grounds of Hertford Castle.

Dancing and fencing were optional. The dancing master attended no more after 1810, but Henry Angelo (1756-1835) gave fencing lessons until 1816. In his reminiscences he not unnaturally looked back sadly to the days when 'every person having the least pretensions to gentility wore his sword', and wrote of the elegance of Ranelagh: 'There were no cropped heads, trousers, or shoe-strings seen here - such dresses would not have been admitted.' Then there were the Vauxhall Gardens, where the Rev. Mr Bate Dudley, the Fighting Parson, chastised immediately and in person an Irishman who had insulted the actress on his arm: 'Alas', wrote Angelo in his memoirs, 'we have no such glorious *kick-ups* now to relate in these insipid times!'[49]

The East India Company's students did what they could. The first kick-up which came to the Committee's notice was in October 1808; on Thursday October 27 Mr Lewton reprimanded some lads for being in a pastry-cook's shop after 8 p.m., and ordered them to return at once to the Castle. They withdrew jeering to the back of the shop, and later assembled outside Lewton's rooms with newsmen's horns and whistles. Such was the laughter and shouting and banging on doors and windows that, when the racket was repeated on Friday night, poor Lewton took refuge in the apartments of Mr Bridge. Not all the disturbers of the peace could be recognised in the dark, so there was a general admonishment at a College meeting on the Saturday, when the principal and Professors were assailed with groans, hisses and hootings.[50]

This insubordination gave rise to secret Directors' meetings and pages and pages of minutes, but nobody confessed and nobody would betray his fellows. The boys won. An unknown leader amongst them thought of a simple way out of the deadlock: if everyone apologised no one could be punished, and an impressive document was produced on 13 November.[51]

> The Students of the East India College beg leave to express to the Honourable the Committee of College their very sincere contrition for the insult; which from a momentary impulse they offered to the Principal and Professors, and of the great impropriety of which they are fully sensible from subsequent reflection.

There were eighty-three signatures; nothing more could be said in Leadenhall Street.

The following year, on 21 and 22 October 1809, there were more serious disturbances, two months after the College had moved into the new buildings at Haileybury, and Dr Lushcomb's school into the students' old quarters at Hertford Castle. Women and children were truly frightened as stones were thrown - one hit Sanskrit Hamilton - and so many windows, gates and bannisters were broken, and other damage done, that the neighbouring country-people came sight-seeing to inspect it. The Mayor of Hertford prepared warrants for the arrest of two of the band of students who (for a reason never given) had gone to the town and violently assaulted the servants of Dr Lushcomb at the Castle entrance.[52]

It is worth remembering that the year 1809 had been a difficult one for the Company, and especially for Charles Grant, who had been Chairman for the year from 12 April. The repercussions of the mutiny among the

Sepoys at Vallore in 1806, when nearly a hundred British officers and soldiers had been killed, were still before the public; news was just coming in of more trouble in the Madras Presidency, the so-called White Mutiny of 1808, when the military officers of Fort St George defied the Civil Governor. In the spring of 1809 the press was able to seize on a scandal at home, where there was less of a time-lag in communication, the alleged corrupt practices regarding 'the sale of Writerships, Cadetships and of Voyages to Bombay and China'. *The Times* devoted a whole page on 30 March to the Report of the Select Committee on these accusations, from which it transpired that three Writerships had indeed been sold, for over £3,000 each, through the agency of a solicitor called Tahourdin. The Company's arrangements were shown to have been extremely lax, nomination cards with names left blank having passed from hand to hand 'like pawnbrokers' duplicates'. On a motion of Mr Randle Jackson, the Company's Parliamentary Counsel, regulations were made to ensure that in future each Petitioner for a Writership should be personally 'interrogated' with his nominating Director.

Naturally there was a stir, especially as this was the year of the Mary Anne Clarke disclosures - the sale of patronage in the Army through the Duke of York's mistress. The pamphlet literature is revealing: why, it was rhetorically asked, should there be so much indignation over these Indian Writerships and Commissions in the Army, when seats in Parliament itself were openly bought and sold?

In this atmosphere, the destructive exuberance of a few young men was treated with a solemnity out of all proportion to its importance. *The Times* of 6 November 1809 reported the first evening's disturbance as follows:

On the night of Saturday the 21st, two or three of the students who, contrary to the regulations of the College, had been amusing themselves all day in the country, without leave obtained for that purpose, on their return seized the watchman, who was particularly obnoxious to them, and treated him very roughly. They afterwards summoned all their adherents, who took their stand in the Courtyard, calling out 'No Watch'; and keeping up a perpetual volley of stones, added to the firing of pistols and blunderbusses (which, however, since appear to have been only loaded with powder), set all opposition at defiance. Apprehensions were at length entertained that they intended to fire the building; in consequence of which, the Professors were induced to enter into a negociation which was speedily followed by a treaty on the following bases - that the rioters should be exempt from corporal punishment; that their grievances should be redressed; and that the too vigilant watchman should be dismissed. At the commencement of the disturbance, intelligence had been transmitted by express to the Board of

Directors; several of whom arriving when tranquility was restored, three of the misguided young men, who had acted as ring-leaders in this alarming affair, were brought to an examination before the College Council, and finally expelled; the remainder, on expressing their contrition, were severely reprimanded, and suffered to pursue their studies.

Again, *The Times* was not quite correct. The College chapel must have sibilated with resentment and accusations of betrayal, and on the evening of the 22nd more pandemonium broke out. One student, Edward Marjoribanks, in a written statement, said that Hamilton sent him 'to the Boys who were rioting to ask what they wanted, and that they would state their grievances upon paper . . . They replied, the Professors had not kept their promise, and therefore they would have nothing to do with them, unless they would come forward and say the three dismissed Boys should be recalled.'[53]

After this second night of confusion, all the students were rusticated by the Committee, and then allowed back as their names were cleared. Inquiries went on at the India House for weeks, during which time - as Malthus remembered later - the lads were kept hanging about in London and got into more mischief. There were reprimands from the Chairman for the less culpable, 'in suitable and impressive terms', and seven boys were expelled, two being nominees of Charles Grant. Like the three other Directors involved, he was allowed to appoint substitutes, and selected a younger brother of one of the rioters to take his place; they were nephews of his wife, and their mother was a widow.

There seems to have been no explanation for the sudden outbreak of violence after the isolated attack on the watchman. Edward Christian sent a letter to the Committee of College on 8 November claiming that 'the first combination to behave ill was aimed at me personally and individually; but by the assistance of Mr. Dealtry those who had combined to insult me were reduced to submission.'[54] No one paid any attention to this, in spite of a note that Professor Dealtry had 'been some time absent from the College through indisposition'. What greatly concerned Charles Grant were the basic causes of discontent, of which the most obvious was the lack of any provision for recreation. The Committee quickly set the Company's Surveyor to work on a Fives Court and a Cricket Ground, and £800 was voted to equip a laboratory, that the students might have some evening lectures, 'easy and amusing, at the same time useful, and requiring no deep attention . . . Some subjects of Natural Philosophy and Chemistry seem most suitable for this purpose, and Experiments might be exhibited, which would entertain and instruct without fatiguing them.'[55]

It is extraordinary how much detailed management was left to the Committee. The Principal, now sixty-nine, was preoccupied with finishing the building, laying out the grounds, and such concerns as the exemption of his staff and pupils from service in the local militia. The professors' time was taken up with procuring books and equipment and planning courses of study quite new to any academic institution; years later, in 1823, Stewart was to write 'Neither Mr. Malthus nor myself understood, when appointed, that we were to be employed in the *discipline*.'[56] There is no doubt that, at least to begin with, these learned gentlemen were inclined to lecture over their students' heads, and, as one of the boys put it, 'but few of the Professors were men that could manage youth.'[57]

The youths themselves at this time could be unpromising material for any pedagogue, with Writerships being so frequently regarded as means of disposing of the troublesome or the penniless, many of whom hated the thought of exile to India. Those from 'Indian' families were sometimes such text-book deprived children that it is an effort to read their reminiscences without tears. They were sent 'home' from India at the age of five or six, to relatives who did not always want them, frequently unable to speak English properly, having learned to talk in the vernacular of their ayahs. School-masters could easily exploit children whose parents were dead or twelve months away, and at one establishment the food was so bad that eight boys 'advanced far into the habits of a Robinson Crusoe sort of life – could catch all sorts of animals; serve up a pigeon, a hedgehog, or a squirrel; bake, boil, &c; and make fruit-pies (ourselves the judges) with Gunter'.[58]

It is hardly surprising that the writer of these memoirs, Augustus Henry Bosanquet, was among those found at the pastry-cook's after hours in 1808, and caught 'shooting and poaching Game in the Grounds of the neighbouring Gentry' in 1809.[59] Not that the Company fed the students badly; they were each allowed a pound and a half of meat a day, a pint of milk and three ounces of butter with bread, vegetables, puddings, tea, coffee, and table beer.

The attitude of the boys' parents who were in England was not always conducive to discipline; the middle classes had yet to become accustomed to regulations and exams. 'Too indulgent mothers' sent wine to their sons, but more serious were continual demands for young men to be allowed to leave the College early, so that they could sail for India on a particular ship, often with a friend or relation. It was an understandable request, but fatal to systematic work, especially in Oriental languages, where courses were carefully arranged so that the lads could profitably continue their studies by themselves during the long voyage out.

Underlying all Grant's problems was the fundamental dislike of his innovation, and naturally the children reflected their families' attitudes. It was hard to accept that an official post could not be filled without qualifications, that it was no longer regarded as a piece of property, possibly bestowed as a reward upon a boy whose father had gallantly fallen at Seringapatam. At the General Court of 6 July 1809 Charles Grant had stressed this; he was applauded for saying that there was no service in the world in which greater attention was paid to the welfare of the servants and their families, but not when he added that he 'thought it would degrade and sink the character of the service, if it were supposed that any one was born with a sort of hereditary right to be employed by the Company'.[60]

Many people did cling to this supposition, and for the next twenty-five years there were to pour into the College Office in Leadenhall Street copies of hurt and bewildered letters from the relatives of unintelligent or lazy boys: how could these so-called professors be allowed to expel a young gentleman whose father and grandfather, uncles and cousins, had lived and died in the Company's service?

4 Home and Family

That Malthus was conscious of Charles Grant's difficulties is apparent from the two pamphlets in defence of the East India College which he wrote in 1813 and 1817; but during the early years in Hertford he must have been preoccupied with his own affairs. In 1806 came the third edition of *Population*, and baby Emily on 5 July; in 1807, there was the fourth edition of *Population*, the forty-page pamphlet on the Poor Law, and baby Lucy in December. In the summer of 1808 and the spring of 1809 his articles on Ireland were published in the *Edinburgh Review*. Then there is a gap of two years before Malthus appears again in print, and I think we may say that the students' rebellion of October 1809, just after he had moved into his permanent home, marked a turning point. When Malthus next contributed to the *Edinburgh Review*, in February and August 1811, it was on contemporary currency problems, nothing whatever to do with population, but basic to monetary theory. In the period between these two sets of reviews he was turning his attention from population to other economic matters, and it seems more than likely that the requirements of a lecture syllabus, as well as public affairs, influenced both his thought and his reading.

Haileybury was perfectly situated for Malthus's work, only eighteen miles from London, yet surrounded by the undulating, wooded landscape which he loved. His views on the College buildings themselves are not known. A later generation thought them too plain, typical of John Company's meanness, but for those who enjoy the beauty of proportion the great sloping quadrangle at Haileybury is a source of delight each time one enters it.

On three sides were rooms for about a hundred students and 'residences' for four professors (each slightly different) on two floors, with lecture-rooms, a reading-room, and a fencing-room. On the south side, which had a terrace with three classical porticoes facing the fields, were the Principal's residence, chapel, library, council room and dining hall; there was a cluster of domestic offices round the horse-operated pumping engine which replaced the well - kitchen, tea house, 'shoe cleaning', and so on; a brew-house was added in 1810 after complaints about the local beer. In addition to the row of twelve water-closets alongside the coal-yard, each professor had one in his residence, as well as a privy in his garden; the Directors were often occupied with matters cloacinal, and there are repeated edicts against the emptying of pots into the sinks of the bed-makers' pantries.

Much is changed now, but it is not hard to imagine what a glorious substitute for a kick-up there must have been when, at the last stroke of midnight, on auspicious occasions, all the students sent their iron coal-scuttles crashing down the stone stairs, a Haileybury custom apparently condoned by the authorities as time went by.

The Malthuses would not have been disturbed, since they shared with the Battens the original Hailey House. It is possible that Malthus owed this preferential treatment to his fame and his acquaintance with Charles Grant; Joseph Hallet Batten had married a Miss Maxwell, 'a Scottish lady of good family', related to Dr Henley. On the occasion of the riot, both these professors 'explained, as to their not having taken minutes of the proceedings, from not residing in the College'.[61] Nowadays the house is part of the campus of an up-to-date public school, but in 1809 it must have seemed pleasantly private.

The building was basically late Tudor, four floors high, and too tall for its bulk. It must have been mid-way between a farm and a gentleman's residence, and the auctioneers in 1805 called it 'an excellent Freehold Family House'.[62] Inside it seems quite different, with well-proportioned rooms lit by tall windows, some dark heavy timber on the staircases, and that indefinable charm with which generations of boys and their house-masters' young families always seem to endow their dwelling-places.

According to the minutes of the Committee of College, the house was easily and conveniently divided at a cost of £1,500. All the professors got £100 each towards 'painting, papering, and whitewashing their respective residences', any excess to be borne by themselves. The gardens were laid out by Repton, as part of the general scheme, and he contrived that Malthus and Batten should each have a south wall in their kitchen gardens, as well as an oak paling round the whole.[63]

After Malthus died, his house was occupied by William Empson, the younger colleague who was so fond of him; in May 1841 Empson was visited by his father-in-law, Francis Jeffrey, who wrote thus to a Scottish friend:

This house is in a cluster of tall shrubs and young trees, with a little bit of smooth lawn sloping to a bright pond, in which old weeping willows are dipping their hair, and rows of young pear trees admiring their blooming faces ... There are young horse-chestnuts with flowers half a yard long, fresh full-clustered white lilacs, tall Guelder roses, broad spreading pear and cherry trees, low thickets of blooming sloe, and crowds of juicy-looking detached thorns, quite covered with their fragrant May flowers, half open, like ivory fillagree, and half shut like Indian pears ... and resounding with nightingales, and thrushes, and sky-larks, shrilling high up, overhead, among the dazzling slow sailing clouds. Not to be named, I know and feel as much as you can do, with your Trosachs, and Loch Lomonds, and Invernays; but very sweet, and vernal, and soothing, and fit enough to efface all recollections of hot, swarming, whirling and bustling London from all good minds.[64]

I was shown at Haileybury a little wooden summer-house, then set up by the swimming bath, which I was told had belonged to Malthus, who used to work in it in his garden. We can guess, from the minutes of the College Committee, that this 'garden house' was originally Dr Henley's, and that Malthus bought it from him in 1815, when Henley retired; the Company had refused to buy in the departing Principal's domestic effects,[65] and the Henleys were notorious for being always hard up.

There is a legend that Malthus at one time lived 'under the clock tower' in the centre of the north range of the quadrangle. This is not true; all his correspondence, as well as the minutes of the Committee of College, show conclusively that the eastern half of Hailey House was Malthus's only home from 1809 until his death.

From the minutes we can also see that the Malthuses were not without their practical domestic worries; indeed, what with defective gutters and ill-fitting skylights over the stairs, it would appear that their house was hardly ever completely water-tight. After they had been in residence for only a year, the local surveyor was asked to 'Inspect Mr. Malthus' House, and to report upon the steps necessary to be taken to prevent the Rain from penetrating certain parts of the Premises'.[66] In 1814 it was decided that 'the outside plaistering ... be cased with weather Tiles',[67] and in 1828 Hailey House was given an entirely new roof, the old tiles being replaced by slates; the roof had been in 'a very dilapidated state'.[68] In the autumn of 1824 the ponds were cleaned out, having become 'extremely offensive and dangerous to health'.[69] At intervals the stables and coach-house nearby, shared by all the professors, required the attention of one or all of the College contractors, Mr Clifton the Carpenter, Mr Stallibras the Plumber, Mr Chuck the Painter and Glazier (who did well out of the riots), and Mr Caleb Hitch, usually designated the College Bricklayer, but obviously a general builder.

It is from some estimates of these last two, in the summer of 1817, that we learn that the Malthuses had five bedrooms, front and back stairs, and a study, parlour and nursery in addition to their dining-room and drawing-room. There were seven stone chimney-pieces and 1,095 feet of skirting board. All these, and an upstairs pantry, needed 426 yards of Dead White and 85 yards of French Gray. Most of the professors had French Gray, except Lewton, who perhaps characteristically chose Dove Colour. The Malthuses' 'Kitchen, Scullery, Larder, Pantry, &c' were 'Common Colour'. All this cost £54. 8s. 3d., but before it could be done Mr Hitch had completed £44. 12s. 8d. worth of 'Sundry Plasterers Works', making good the ceilings and cornices, repairing, cleaning and colouring 'Old Walls which are generally bad', and cleaning and lime-whiting the cellar.[70]

Whatever its occasional inconveniences may have been, Malthus and Malthusia, as Jeffrey called them, made Hailey House a very happy place. In his long letter to Godwin of 20 August 1798 Malthus had written, 'Moderate cloathing, moderate houses, the power of receiving friends, the power of purchasing books, and particularly the power of supporting a family, will always remain objects of rational desire among the majority of mankind.'[71] Now he had them all. As the years passed, his home 'was frequently the resort of men of cultivated minds in every department of literature, and the warm but simple and unpretending hospitality that reigned there was not more pleasing than it was remarkable to all who partook of it'. Otter described Malthus as 'habitually cheerful and playful', and 'as ready to engage in all the innocent pursuits and pleasures of the young as to encourage them in their studies'.[72]

That Malthus was less well off than many of those with whom he associated undoubtedly troubled him at times. One gets a hint of this in a letter to Ricardo dated 14 October 1819, refusing an invitation to Gatcomb, his country seat in Gloucestershire: 'You forget that Mrs. Malthus is governess to her own girls, and that I am preceptor to my own boy, when he is at home, which will be at Xmas. It so happens, further, that we shall have a nephew with us about that time . . .'[73]

No anecdotes of the children survive, and it is difficult to get much impression of Harriet as a mother. Maria Edgeworth wrote of her in 1813, 'Mrs. Malthus is a charming domestic amiable woman with a pleasing voice and manner - well dressed and well looking - perfectly a gentlewoman.'[74] Maria's half-sister, Harriet Edgeworth, gives a less complimentary picture of Harriet Malthus: of a party in London in 1822 Miss Harriet wrote, 'Mr. Malthus and his crawky voice was there & Mrs. Malthus who was remarkably awake & really knew a little what she was saying.' Twenty-one-year-old Harriet had, some three months previously, spent a few days at 'Mr. Malthus's house, close to Hertford College'; she wrote of her host that he was 'so truly good, so sensible and gentle, that one forgets even the hairlip and stopped pronunciation when he really converses - He has a red-faced little wife & two red-haired little daughters.'[75]

Harriet's high colour was clearly notable. Marianne Wathen wrote flatteringly that 'Health's vernal tints her modest cheeks adorn'; a little water-colour sketch made on a Malthus-Wynne-Wood-Eckersall family holiday in Bangor, in 1814, suggests that Harriet's complexion was a sisterly joke: she is shown as having just fallen over a breakwater (she is easily recognisable from Linnell's portrait) and her cheeks are two red blobs like those of an old-fashioned Dutch doll.[76] But there must have been more to Harriet. Robert Owen, for instance, reminiscing in extreme old age, wrote that in his discussions with her husband 'Mrs. Malthus always took and defended my side of the argument.'[77] Her servants all stayed with her until they married, and her tact and good nature must have contributed, after the inauspicious beginnings, to make Haileybury the agreeable community it later became.

We have a chance glimpse of the early married life of the Malthuses, while they were still at Hertford, through a letter written to Basil Montagu (1770-1851). He was the illegitimate son of the fourth Earl of Sandwich and an actress called Martha Ray, who was shot dead by an unsuccessful suitor outside Covent Garden Theatre when Basil was nine years old. The boy was properly brought up and educated by his father, and would have been at Christ's College, Cambridge, for two of Malthus's undergraduate years. In 1797 he sustained the heartbroken William Godwin throughout the fatal illness of his first wife, Mary Wollstonecraft. Then, in the course of his travels as a barrister on the Norfolk circuit, Montagu established a warm friendship with James Mackintosh; Jemmy (according to the *Dictionary of National Biography*) converted him 'to political common sense and the study of Bacon'. Montagu would have had a further personal link with Malthus as Clarke's senior brother-in-law: he had married as his second wife the eldest of Sir William Rush's daughters in 1801, but she died not long afterwards. In 1805 he applied for the post of Professor of Law at the East India College, and was rejected in favour of Edward Christian's 'more mature experience'.[78] This must have been a disappointment to Malthus, as his letter to Montagu shows that they were on pleasant terms. It is dated 8 February 1808 and runs:

Dear Montagu,

I am much obliged to you for your valuable present, which I always take up with great satisfaction; and Mrs. Malthus desires me to add her thanks to you, for introducing to her acquaintance some very able and agreeable men with whom she was not much in the habit of conversing before.

I called upon you the last time I passed through Town, but had not the pleasure of finding you at home. We have always been hoping that you would fulfil your promise of coming to see us, but begin to think now that you have put it off sine die. I need not I hope repeat that we shall always be most happy to see you, when you can spare a few days from your occupations in Town.

The letter ends, 'Believe me, Yours most sincerely', and Malthus signs his name with some neatly convoluted decoration that I have seen on no other correspondence.[79]

Montagu wrote much about bankruptcy law, also on the death penalty and the emancipation of Jews in Britain, but the 'valuable present' must have been the second edition, published in 1807 in two pretty duodecimo volumes, of his *Selections from the Works of Taylor, Hooker, Hall & Lord Bacon, with an Analysis of the Advancement of Learning*. Basil Montagu shows himself as a man of taste and well-assimilated experience in his choice of extracts; that perceptive divine, Jeremy Taylor, is the most quoted; Harriet might well have found this book a good introduction to all the learned and eccentric men to whom she was to act as hostess for the next quarter of a century.

CHAPTER VI

Paper Money

1 English Pounds and Guineas

At one of the last Haileybury Visitation Days, on 28 June 1852, the Duke of Cambridge caused uneasy amusement by proposing the health of the Governor and Directors of the Bank of England, instead of the Chairman and Directors of the East India Company;[1] he persisted firmly in his mistake, regardless of courteous efforts to put him right. We might sympathise with him more readily today than did his fellow-diners, since from our point of view the two organisations had much in common. Each had a Court of twenty-four Directors, and a General Court of the Proprietors of Stock, with quasi-parliamentary debates; speeches made in both General Courts were reprinted as pamphlets. Each was initially a straightforward profit-making enterprise which came gradually to assume functions that are now regarded as belonging solely to government.

The East India Company was nearly a hundred years older than the Bank, and had greater prestige: when Henry Thornton (1760-1815), the author of *Paper Credit*, took to banking at the age of twenty-four, his mother thought that 'to cease being a merchant in order to become a Banker was to descend in life'.[2] It is shameful that throughout European history money-lenders were usually treated with contempt by the kings and aristocrats whom they served, but so it was. The Bank of England was established by Act of Parliament in 1694 as a Chartered Company to raise money for William III's struggle against Louis XIV of France, and it acquired a reputation for integrity with remarkable speed; this it never lost, however much its mistaken policies and high dividends might be criticised.

After the breaking of the speculative South Sea Bubble in 1720, the Bank became the only joint-stock bank in England - Scotland had more - because both government and public jumped to the conclusion that all joint-stock companies were hazardous affairs unless each was separately incorporated by a special Act of Parliament, as were all the turnpike road and canal trusts, and later the railways. Thus all English banks other than the Bank of England had to be private concerns of six partners or less, and they were liable to the whole extent of their fortunes in the event of a failure, like any other business-men of the period. At the end of the eighteenth century there were about 400 country banks in England and Wales, playing an important part in the development of agriculture and industry by acting as outlets for the investment of local savings and providing short-term loans to farmers and manufacturers for the purchase of stock and the payment of wages.

The media through which these transactions took place may seem complicated today, but it is impossible to understand contemporary ideas about money without some knowledge of the state of English currency and credit at this time. To begin with, it was generally taken for granted that 'It is the essence of money to possess intrinsick value', and (since Sir James Steuart's *Complete Works* had been published in 1805) Huskisson and other pamphleteers referred to money as 'the common and universal equivalent'. Money was therefore much more than 'the common measure and common representative of all other commodities'; it was regarded in itself as part of the nation's capital.

This form of capital consisted largely of golden guineas, so called because they were first minted in 1663 from gold brought by the Royal African Company from the Guinea Coast. Yet the unit of account in England was not the guinea at all, but the pound sterling, which was theoretically made up of twenty silver shillings; each shilling was worth twelve copper pennies - written *d.* from the Latin *denarius*. Silver had long been a monetary standard, in Britain as elsewhere, which led Sir Isaac Newton, when he was Master of the Mint, to fix the value of a guinea at twenty-one silver shillings in 1717. Paradoxically, this decision was to set England on the gold standard, and by 1774 the silver currency had become so debased as not to be legal tender, except by weight, for sums over £25. From 1816 silver coins were legal tender only for sums under £2.

A minted guinea was made of eleven parts of gold to one of alloy, and it weighed 5 pennyweights 9 grains.* If, through clipping or wear, a guinea weighed less than 5 dwt 8gr it ceased to be legal tender. On this basis, the Mint price of an ounce of standard gold ($\frac{39}{89}$ 'pure') was £3. 17s. 10½d, and a Troy pound of standard gold cost £46. 14s. 6d, or 44½ guineas. The weight and fineness of the coin was 'publickly proclaimed to all the world by the stamp which it bears' - the sovereign's head - and to counterfeit coin was a capital offence. Thus it was perfectly logical, although unpopular, that people should be hanged for forging Bank of England notes; the number of executions for the forgery of paper money - comparatively easy at this period - was a strong argument in favour of the return to 'real' metallic money after the Napoleonic Wars.

*The Troy Weight of precious metals is as follows:

4 grains (gr)	=	1 carat
6 carats or 24 grains	=	1 pennyweight (dwt)
20 dwts	=	1 ounce (oz)
12 oz	=	1 pound (lb, from the Latin *libra*)

The Royal Mint charged no seignorage, and anyone who wished could bring gold to be coined, which was, of course, only profitable when the Mint price of gold was above its market price as a commodity. Conversely, it would be profitable to melt and export coin when the Mint price was below that of the world's markets; this was permitted in the case of coins too worn to be legal tender, but the melting or export of full-weight guineas was illegal. However, as Ricardo wrote, 'It is by all writers indiscrimately allowed, that no penalties can prevent the coin from being melted when its value as bullion becomes superior to its value as coin.'[3]

Long before Adam Smith's time, merchants had realised the expense, inconvenience and danger of carrying bags of gold. Debts were frequently discharged through the purchase of bills of exchange, whereby a merchant in London could pay a creditor in Edinburgh or obtain a remittance from Hamburg without any 'money' travelling at all; these bills were also extensively circulated as short-term loans, usually for sixty or ninety days, passing from hand to hand at a discount until they became due. For local transactions the promissory note was also used, and the traditional formula can still be found on Bank of England notes today. In Malthus's time many banks printed their own notes for making interest-bearing loans, which was extremely profitable provided that too many note-holders did not try to redeem the promise simultaneously and demand gold which was not there. The Bank of England had the monopoly of note issue in London.

Cheques, known sometimes as 'drafts' upon such-and-such a bank, were slowly coming into use; but William Bray's office correspondence shows that as late as 1830 it was common for well-to-do and educated people to send bank-notes through the post, cut in half as a precaution against theft, in separate letters; bank clerks with quill pens laboriously numbered the notes on both sides of the face to facilitate this. There were, however, complications when the notes of one district did not circulate in another, especially when it came to sending back some change because the note originally despatched was for too large a sum. Malthus sent a 'check', as he spelt it, to Linnell in 1834, but long before this the cheque and the overdraft had become well known in commercial circles. Henry Thornton in his *Paper Credit of Great Britain*, published in 1802, described how 'by the transfer of debts in the books of the banker a large part of what are termed cash payments are effected',[4] and explained the procedure of the London Clearing House (one room, then) which was established in about 1775. In 1797, when Bank of England notes ceased to be redeemable in gold, there were sixty-nine private banks in London, almost all of which were linked through 'correspondents' with banks throughout the provinces; these country banks normally kept their reserves partly in specie and partly in Bank of England notes.

It must be stressed that the issue of notes was regarded as the crucial factor in monetary policy at the time, because - to the uncommercial classes who formed the majority of both Houses of Parliament - it appeared not only the most obvious form of inflation, but also the one most susceptible to central control. The Bank of England could not at this period restrict credit on a national scale (without regard to the 'soundness' of individuals) by the simple expedient of raising the rate of interest it charged borrowers: the maximum rate had been fixed at 5 per cent by an Act of 1714, the last under the medieval Usury Laws designed to thwart money-lenders, which were not finally repealed until 1833. The Scots had long been familiar with small notes, but in England none under £10 had been in use until the crisis of 1793, when £5 notes were brought into circulation. After the panic of 1797, the Court of Directors had to appoint six clerks to set to work at once to sign the first Bank of England notes for £1 and £2.

Malthus, in the 1803 quarto *Essay on Population*, refers to the issue of £1 and £2 notes as a 'pernicious custom', although on his own showing it is a little hard to see why. He repeated what he had said in the pamphlet on *The High Price of Provisions*: the soaring price of wheat in 1800 was due both to its scarcity and to the inflationary effect of the extraordinary expenditure on poor relief to supply the labourers' families with bread. In the quarto Malthus estimated this at £7 million. As the Bank of England's additional notes were probably not much above what was needed to replace the gold withdrawn from internal circulation, he believed this sum must have been provided by the country banks, whose increased note issue, he repeated, was 'rather a consequence than a cause of the high price of provisions', and 'it could not be expected that they should hesitate in taking advantage of so profitable an opportunity'. But:

> If the circulation of the country had consisted entirely of specie,
> which could not have been immediately increased, it would have
> been impossible to have given such an additional sum as seven
> millions to the poor without embarrassing, to a great degree, the
> operations of commerce ... The nature of the medium then
> principally in use was such that it could be created immediately on
> demand ... And with regard to the effect of the circulating medium
> on the prices of all commodities, it cannot be doubted that it would
> be precisely the same, whether this medium were made up
> principally of guineas, or of pound-notes and shillings, which would
> pass current for guineas.[5]

'The great mischief of the system' was that, being once absorbed into the circulation, these new notes 'must necessarily affect the price of all commodities, and throw very great obstacles in the way of returning cheapness'. On page 404 of the quarto Malthus had a footnote here:

> It does not appear to me that Mr. Thornton in his valuable
> publication on paper credit, has taken sufficient notice of the great

paper issues of the country banks, in raising the price of
commodities, and producing an unfavourable state of exchange with
foreigners.

This note was excised in 1806 and in all subsequent editions; possibly
Malthus cut it out after discussing the subject with Henry Thornton, which
he might easily have done either with the Samuel Thorntons at Albury
Park or the Charles Grants in Russell Square. But he may simply have come
round to the view, between 1803 and 1806, that the country bank issue was
self-regulating on account of its convertibility to Bank of England notes.
This view was expressed by Lord King in 1803 and quite commonly held
in 1810 by those who believed the Bank of England to be solely responsible
for the depreciation of the pound. Yet Malthus never altered the passage,
in which he wrote that private bank notes would be generally acceptable,
'from the little preference that many people might feel, if they could not get
gold, between country bank paper and Bank of England paper'.

Malthus then goes on, thinking aloud, almost to contradict himself. This
is something which happens to all of us when we are anxious to get at a
complicated truth, but Malthus was perhaps over-inclined to noncommittal
honesty in public, in a dogmatic age enamoured of systems. After expressing
the fear that 'a lasting evil might be entailed upon the community, and the
prices of a time of scarcity might become permanent, from the difficulty of
reabsorbing this increased circulation', he went straight on to say:

> In this respect, however, it is much better that the great issue of
> paper should have come from the country banks than from the Bank
> of England. During the restriction of payment in specie, there is no
> possibility of forcing the Bank to retake its notes when too abundant;
> but with regard to the country banks, as soon as their notes are not
> wanted in the circulation, they will be returned; and if the Bank of
> England notes be not increased, the whole circulating medium will
> thus be diminished.[6]

Fortunately the two years of scarcity were followed by an abundant harvest
and the Peace of Amiens, but although the immediate crisis had passed, the
discussion of monetary depreciation continued. The fate of the French
assignats, with which people were alleged to have papered their walls, was
an example of the horrors of inflation and the collapse of 'unnatural money',
of which Fox and Sheridan made good use when they attacked Pitt's policy.
It should also be remembered that debasing the coinage was a common
device of monarchs in difficulty. Newspaper readers would have known
about 'the barbarous policy of the Turkish government', who 'made three
great adulterations of their coin in 1770, 1787 and 1796'. 'Before these frauds'
Turkish piastres exchanged at eight to the pound sterling, but now their
value was halved, being sixteen to the pound.

Thus the literate public were familiar with the idea that a depreciated currency caused rising prices and unfavourable exchange rates; they were also familiar with the obvious facts that high prices could be caused by scarcity and an adverse rate of exchange by an excess of imports over exports. What they argued about were the degrees of blame, so to speak, to be attached either to an excessive note issue or to the large payments for foreign corn, subsidies to allies, and the cost of maintaining British forces abroad. Walter Boyd, a bitter opponent of the Bank, fixed the entire blame on the note issue, and Thornton probably wrote his *Paper Credit* in answer to Boyd, although the importance of this classic far exceeds that of a topical pamphlet.

2 The Bullion Controversy

After reaching £4. 6s. an ounce in January 1801, the price of standard gold fell to £3. 19s. in 1803, not much above the pre-war £3. 17s. 10½d., so the controversy died down for a time. The pamphlet literature almost dried up, except for Lord King's *Thoughts on the Effects of the Bank Restrictions*, of which the first edition appeared in May 1803, the second in March 1804. Peter King (1776–1833) had been at Eton with Henry Parnell, and they remained close friends. Lord King lived at Ockham in Surrey, where Malthus's brother-in-law Samuel Godschall was rector; there is evidence that Malthus met him while staying with the Godschalls at Albury in 1815, but it is impossible to guess how well the two men knew each other.[7]

Lord King in 1803 attacked the Bank Restriction Act as 'a law to suspend the performance of contracts', and in this connection he drew attention to two important facts. First, 'By a wise forbearance on the part of the legislature Bank notes have not been made legal tender',[8] even though they were valid for the payment of taxes, and no one who offered notes instead of gold could be imprisoned for debt. Second, he pointed out that this was understood in Belfast and its neighbourhood, and although the much depreciated notes of the Bank of Ireland were accepted elsewhere, many in the north insisted on 'payments in gold coin or in the notes of private banks payable in specie'. In a footnote to the second edition, Lord King elaborated this:

> The manufacturers of the North of Ireland have . . . exhorted the land owners of that part of Ireland from *patriotic motives* to accept bank notes at par in payment of their rents. But the land-holders have very wisely refused to listen to advice, by which they would lose more than 10 per cent. upon all rents payable under existing

contracts, and expose themselves to additional loss by further depreciation. They do not chuse to submit to an income tax, which is levied not for the benefit of Government, but of the proprietors of Irish Bank stock. The manufacturers who urged this request, have the means of indemnifying themselves against the loss which may be sustained by their support of the Irish Bank, by an additional charge upon their goods . . .[9]

In March 1804 the exchange against Dublin (as compared with London) was so unfavourable that the Commons appointed a Select Committee on the Circulating Paper, the Specie, and the Current Coin of Ireland. Sheridan, still Smyth's employer, sat on this Committee, and must surely have been an amusing contrast to Henry Thornton; the Bank of Ireland denied Thornton's assertation that bankers could do much to stabilise exchange rates by contracting or expanding credit. The Committee reported in June, but by then the Irish exchange was moving back to par, and Parliament and the nation were preoccupied with other matters until, five years later, the whole discussion was re-opened in a pamphlet by Robert Mushet and – with results more far-reaching – a letter to the *Morning Chronicle* from David Ricardo on 29 August 1809.

Mushet's contribution was called *An Enquiry into the Effects Produced on the National Currency and Rates of Exchange by the Bank Restriction Bill; explaining the Cause of the High Price of Bullion with Plans for Maintaining the National Coins in a State of Perfection*. His concern for the coinage was natural, since he worked at the Mint, and in July 1809 the price of standard gold had reached nearly £4. 13s. an ounce. According to Mushet, this meant a depreciation of 16 per cent, £100 was now worth only £84, and 'It seems an unheard of evil that the Bank of England should possess the power of diminishing, *at her pleasure*, the value of all the moneyed interest in the Kingdom!' It grieved Mushet professionally that a 'light guinea', which was not legal tender, had become more valuable than a full-weight guinea which could not legitimately be melted.[10] The shortage of silver coins was now such that some bankers were issuing notes for a crown (five shillings), a half-crown, and even one shilling.

This was the year in which Napoleon allowed the French to dispose of their surplus grain, under licence and in neutral ships, to feed their British enemies, on the principle that he would simultaneously benefit his own farmers and injure Britain 'by draining her of her gold'. Also in 1809, Napoleon's Continental System, blocking European outlets for British trade, was beginning to have serious effects. There was a short-lived speculative boom, and re-exported coffee, sugar and other colonial goods could find purchasers; but two-thirds of British exports were home-produced, and her textiles, ironware and cheap pottery were becoming harder to sell, in unfamiliar markets much further afield.

The full title of Ricardo's first work, following the correspondence in the *Morning Chronicle*, was *The High Price of Bullion, a Proof of the Depreciation of Bank Notes*; it contains quotations from Adam Smith, Henry Thornton and Sir James Steuart, and is notably more of a miniature economic treatise than a polemical pamphlet. About a month after it appeared, Francis Horner made a speech on the question in the House of Commons, on 1 February 1810, and on 19 February a Committee was appointed to inquire into the Cause of the High Price of Gold Bullion. Of the twenty-four members, six had served on the Irish Currency Committee, including Thornton, Sheridan, and Tierney; other representatives of Malthus's circle were Henry Parnell, Richard Sharp and Davies Giddy; William Huskisson was an active member, but Horner was pre-eminent.

The Bullion Report was formally laid before the House in June 1810, but was not printed until the middle of August, and not debated by the Commons until May 1811. Its recommendations were opposed to the views of almost all the men who had been asked to give evidence, especially the bankers, and they were rejected by the government to whom they were addressed; then, a decade later, this document of just over seventy octavo pages became the foundation of British monetary orthodoxy for nearly a century. In brief, the Committee blamed the Bank of England, rather than the country banks, for the excessive issue of notes, which they declared was the cause of rising prices at home and falling exchange rates abroad; the only way to remedy this was gradually to return to the convertibility of paper into gold, on demand, within two years, regardless of whether the war was over or not.

Two subsidiary points are worth noting. The Committee were concerned solely with what they regarded as the 'unnatural' superfluity of the Bank's note issue; there was never any question of loss of confidence. Second, they were quite aware that 'imperious necessity' might justify such steps as the government had taken.

Modern authorities agree that Spencer Perceval, then both Prime Minister and Chancellor of the Exchequer, and the majority in Parliament, were right not to act on the Committee's recommendations. Professor Court sums up:

> From a broad political point of view, it was clear that to abandon the paper pound, even to escape inflation, and return to a gold basis for the currency without regard to the issue of the war, would have increased the risks to public credit at a time of grave national danger, when the struggle with Napoleon was reaching its height. It would have made that credit depend upon a given quantity of gold, which might at any time be diminished by alarms and hoarding at home, by the violet fluctuations of war-time trade or sudden military need abroad. The practical case for suspension [of the Bank Charter Act] was that public spending must go on until the war was over, that suspension had become a part of the system of war finance, and that

the evils of inflation must be put up with in the interests of national security.[11]

Francis Jeffrey's chief worry over the Bullion Report was to find somebody to 'do' it for the *Edinburgh Review*. It was very much part of the literature of the day, and Professor Fetter estimates that ninety pamphlets were written on the subject in two years.[12] The obvious choice was Ricardo himself, but he took fright at the notion of writing in the *Review*, according to a letter of 3 December 1810 which Jeffrey received from Horner. Horner went on: 'Malthus has given me hopes that he will be able to scramble up an article this week; and I am very anxious to have the subject in his hands, and to engage him in the discussion, both because he agrees with me upon the fundamental principles of the doctrine, and because we have some differences, or rather difficulties which we try to solve differently, in some parts of the Theory.'[13]

It is tantalising that Horner does not expatiate further on this distinction between the doctrine and the Theory. We do, however, know that Malthus's view of the self-regulating nature of the country bank issue was confirmed in the summer of 1810. He made a tour to Scotland, by way of Northumberland, where he stayed with Otter's brother Edward, at that time rector of Bothal-with-Hebburn. In the course of his holiday Malthus jotted down odd facts in a small note-book; he gave no dates, but as he could hardly have left Haileybury before 28 May, the date of the Directors' Visitation, and was a witness at his sister-in-law's wedding at Claverton on 13 July, he must have written the following paragraphs round about midsummer 1810:

> Heard from Mr. Otter that the jobbers of Cattle from their extensive communications, immediately hear of the slightest variations in the prices of cattle at the different fairs, which they are accustomed to frequent, and arrange their purchases and sales accordingly, so as to buy where they are cheap, and sell again almost immediately at some distance where they are dearer.
>
> It is probably from practices of this kind that the level of currency is so accurately kept, and any country bank is prevented from filling its district of circulation too full. If for instance the Lincoln district was too full of notes and prices had experienced the slightest rise in consequence, cattle and other commodities would be purchased with Lincoln notes in the neighbouring districts, and these notes, which will be received by other banks, will be immediately sent to be exchanged for Bank of England notes, and reduce the circulation of the Lincoln notes to their proper level.
>
> It is the custom for the bankers of neighbouring districts to send their clerks once a week or oftner mutually to exchange their notes. In general, probably, the balances will be nearly equal, but if one

issues a greater proportion than the rest, he will have to pay a greater number of Bank of England notes, and on notes returned thus soon, he can make no profit.[14]

It should be remembered that not everyone held this view. The number of banks outside London probably doubled in the first decade of the nineteenth century, rising from 400 to 800, of which 755 were licensed to issue notes, so it was not difficult to find evidence of their unreliability.

Francis Horner, however, like Lord King, also approved of the country banks, and mentioned them in a letter to Malthus dated 15 September 1810 from Killarney; Malthus had obviously sent appreciative comments on the Bullion Report, and asked Horner to spend some days at Haileybury. Horner wrote:

> I have no doubt that, at no distant time, the evils, proceeding from the want of responsibility in the Bank, will get to such a pitch as to force upon parliament a recurrence to the old system; I am only afraid, that some mischief may be done in the mean time by interfering unwisely with the country banks, & with that diffused & subdivided credit afforded by their means to the enterprises of small capitalists in remote parts of the country.

By this time Malthus and Horner were good friends, as the letters show, and it is, I think, to the credit of both that Malthus accepted Horner's criticism and advice in the composition of his bullion article, which was by no means scrambled up in a week. It must have occupied most of the Christmas holiday, which the Malthus family spent in Surrey; a manuscript sent to Jeffrey at the turn of the year was passed on to Horner who posted it back to Malthus, early in January 1811, with such remarks as occurred to him in perusing it. Horner sent as well, 'by the Guildford coach which goes from the Golden Cross', a copy of the Report itself, and Mushet's article, at Malthus's request; he added to the parcel on his own initiative Ricardo's *Reply to Mr. Bosanquet's Observations*, with the suggestion that Bosanquet should also be noticed in the article. There must have been considerable patching and re-arranging, and one regrettable excision, for Horner asked:

> Will it not be expedient to wrap up a little, in more general & less obvious expressions, the truth which you state in p. 33 as to the pay of the army & navy? I am afraid of telling it nakedly, for no other reason but because it is so true, & true to such an extent. Perhaps you will consider this timidity on my part somewhat prudish and unnecessary. But I own, that I should not like to have such allies in the argument, as we might obtain by such a proclamation . . .[15]

The mystery will never be solved, for Malthus clearly found it easier to cut out this passage altogether than to wrap it up a little.

3 Malthus as a Monetary Economist

Malthus's article in the *Edinburgh Review* for February 1811 was printed to follow the titles of six pamphlets, not the Bullion Report itself; the page-headings were 'Depreciation of Paper Currency'. Malthus led off with 'the general principles of supply and demand, which are unquestionably the foundation on which the whole superstructure of political economy is built', and 'the doctrine that every kind of circulating medium, as well as every other kind of commodity, is necessarily depreciated by excess, and raised in value by deficiency, compared with the demand, without reference either to confidence or intrinsic use'.[16]

After praising Mushet and Ricardo for proving the fact of the depreciation of the pound, and having their opinion endorsed by a Committee of the House of Commons, Malthus threw down the gauntlet:

> The great fault of Mr. Ricardo's performance is the partial view which he takes of the causes which operate upon the course of Exchange.[17]
>
> ... He attributes a favourable or unfavourable exchange *exclusively* to a redundant or deficient currency, and overlooks the varying desires and wants of different societies, as an original cause of a temporary excess of imports above exports, or exports above imports.[18]

This was the crux of their different approaches to political economy, Ricardo throughout being more concerned with production and supply, Malthus with consumption and demand.

In this article, Malthus quoted Ricardo's famous criticism of a section of *Paper Credit*:

> Mr. Thornton [wrote Ricardo] has not explained to us, why any unwillingness should exist in the foreign country to receive our goods in exchange for their corn; and it would be necessary for him to show, that if such an unwillingness were to exist, we should agree to indulge it so far as to consent to part with our coin.
>
> If we consent to give coin in exchange for goods, it must be from choice, not necessity. We should not import more goods than we export, unless we had a redundancy of currency, which it therefore suits us to make a part of our exports. The exportation of the coin is caused by its cheapness, and is not the effect, but the cause of an unfavourable balance: we should not export it, if we did not send it

to a better market, or if we had any commodity which we could export more profitably.

Malthus's riposte is equally well known; it must be quoted at length as it marks a stage in Malthus's development as an economist on subjects not directly concerned with population:

> Now, we would ask, what necessary connection there is between the wants of a nation for unusual importations of corn, occasioned by a bad harvest, or its desire to transmit a large subsidy to a foreign power, occasioned by a treaty to that effect, - and the question of redundant or deficient currencies? Surely, such wants or desires might occur in one of two countries where, immediately previous to their existence, the precious metals circulated as nearly as possible on a level. And the unwillingness of the country to which the debt is owing, to receive in payment a great quantity of goods, beyond what it is in the habit of giving orders for, and consuming, stands much less in need of explanation than that a bad harvest, or the necessity of paying a subsidy in one country, should be immediately and invariably accompanied by an unusual demand for muslins, hardware and colonial produce in some other.[19]

The debt would be paid partly by the increased export of commodities, but also by the transfer of bullion,

> owing precisely to the cause mentioned by Mr. Thornton - the unwillingness of the creditor nation to receive a great additional quantity of goods not wanted for immediate consumption, without being bribed to it by excessive cheapness; and its willingness to receive bullion - the currency of the commercial world - without any such bribe ... The prices of commodities are liable to great depressions from a glut in the market:- whereas the precious metals, on account of their having been constituted, by the universal consent of society, the general medium of exchange and instrument of commerce, will pay a debt of the largest amount at its nominal estimation, according to the quantity of bullion contained in the respective currencies of the countries in question.[20]

The third pamphlet reviewed was *Observations on the Principles which regulate the Course of the Exchange,* by William Blake (the FRS and economist, not the mystic poet and painter), whom Malthus was also to know personally later on. Here Malthus thought that the writer did not sufficiently recognise the effect which a depreciated currency could have on exchange rates, and after a highly technical discussion summed up with typical realism: 'All that can be done, as it appears to us, is to rank among the causes of the real exchange, not only the varying desires and necessities of different nations, but every such alteration in their currencies as tends to affect the bullion prices of commodities.'[21]

Huskisson's publication was reviewed next, in chronological rather than logical order; it was called *The Question concerning the Depreciation of our Currency stated and examined*, and Malthus lauded 'the liberal and manly spirit which prompted him to undertake the task', since Huskisson was 'a practical statesman bred in the school of Mr. Pitt'. In some of his comments Malthus shows himself a practical economist bred in the school of Adam Smith, as in this passage:

> It is true that, in the healthy state of our circulation, Bank notes are and always should be exchangeable for coin at the option of the holder; but it is found by experience ... that a bank-note is not considered as valuable only because it enables him to obtain a given quantity of the precious metals. The holder is in general satisfied if he feels quite sure of always obtaining for his note a quantity of commodities *equal in value* to the quantity of the precious metals specified in it. This is in fact what, ninety-nine times out of a hundred, he really wants; and what alone, in reference to the whole body of notes in circulation, the country possesses the means of effecting.[22]

Malthus thought that neither Huskisson nor the Bullion Committee had sufficiently recognised that the wartime difficulties, 'thrown in the way of commercial intercourse, may have operated something like a return to a less advanced period of civilization, and occasioned the necessity of employing a greater quantity of the precious metals, in proportion to the number of exchanges to be transacted'. But even so, the Bank directors cannot 'urge the argument of a great demand for gold on the Continent, to justify the comparative depreciation of their notes. Whatever may be the variations in the value of the precious metals, their business is to regulate the issue of their notes so as always to maintain them of the same value.'[23]

He was able to continue his attack on the Bank when making fun of Charles Bosanquet's *Practical Observations on the Report of the Bullion Committee*: 'Even the assignats of France rested upon a better foundation than that on which it is now proposed to place the paper circulation of Great Britain. In fact, what security have we, except in their integrity, that the Bank Directors may not agree to create and divide 24 millions in notes among them for their private fortunes?'[24] The final pamphlet discussed was Ricardo's *Reply* to Bosanquet, in which Malthus again censured him for 'considering redundancy or deficiency of currency as the mainspring of all commercial movements. According to this view of the subject, it is certainly not easy to explain an improving exchange under an obviously increasing issue of notes; an event that not unfrequently happens.'[25]

Having thus done his duty as a reviewer, Malthus proceeded to give some thoughts of his own, which were to be developed later, in the 1817 edition of *Population*, and in his *Principles of Political Economy,* which appeared in 1820. Horner's interest in this part of the article was such that he plunged straight into it in the letter of 4 January 1811 from which I have already quoted:

> My dear Malthus,
> I send today the rest of your MS; in this part of it there is a great deal of very important discussion. Your account of the operation of paper credit, in distributing capital among those who will employ it productively, coincides entirely with the view I have long taken of that question, so much agitated, whether paper credit gives a real or fictitious capital. And I am disposed to think that you have given a true solution of the difference between Hume and Smith, as to the rise of prices in Scotland.[26]

In order fully to understand Malthus's position, it is advisable to read Adam Smith's famous chapter 'Of the Accumulation of Capital, or of Productive and Unproductive Labour', in which he wrote:

> That portion of his revenue which a rich man annually spends, is in most cases consumed by idle guests, and menial servants, who leave nothing behind them in return for their consumption. That portion which he annually saves, as for the sake of the profit it is immediately employed as a capital, is consumed in the same manner, and nearly in the same time too, but by a different set of people, by labourers, manufacturers, and artificers, who reproduce with a profit the value of their annual consumption.[27]

The idle guests included 'some of the most respectable orders in the society', whose labour, like that of menial servants, is

> unproductive of any value, and does not fix or realize itself in any permanent subject, or vendible commodity, which endures after that labour is past, and for which an equal quantity of labour could afterwards be procured. The sovereign, for example, with all the officers both of justice and war who serve under him, the whole army and navy, are unproductive labourers ... In the same class must be ranked, some of the gravest and most important, and some of the most frivolous professions: churchmen, lawyers, physicians, men of letters of all kinds; players, buffoons, musicians, opera-singers, opera-dancers, &c ... Like the declamation of the actor, the harangue of the orator, or the tune of the musician, the work of all of them perishes in the very instant of its production.[28]

This extraordinary point of view was wittily trounced by Henry Brougham in the *Edinburgh Review* for July 1804 when he wrote about Lord Lauder-

dale's *Public Wealth*; we shall hear more of this later on. What is relevant
here is that, as the pamphleteers pointed out, the depreciation of the pound
was beneficial to the sellers of commodities, who could take advantage of
rising prices, but extremely hard on those with fixed incomes who were
buyers only; into this category came not only Peter King's landlords with
long leases, but the salaried public servants, and the holders of the 3 per cent
Consolidated Government Stock. These last, whose capital and income were
alike diminishing in purchasing power, were much written up by journalists
and pamphleteers; some thought of them as though they were all genteel
widows and similar pitiful cases; others, like Cobbett, fulminated against
them as parasites.

But Malthus wrote in his article on the 'Depreciation of Paper Currency':

> A merchant or manufacturer obtains a loan in paper from a bank;
> and with this loan he is able to command materials to work upon,
> tools to work with, and wherewithal to pay the wages of labour; and
> yet he is told that this transaction does not tend, in the slightest
> degree, to increase the capital of the country.
>
> The question of how far, and in what manner, an increase of
> currency tends to increase capital, appears to us so very important as
> fully to warrant our attempt to explain it. No writer that we are
> acquainted with, has ever seemed sufficiently aware of the influence
> which a different distribution of the circulating medium of a country
> must have on those accumulations which are destined to facilitate
> future productions . . .
>
> It is quite certain that anything like an equal distribution of the
> circulating medium, among all the members of the society, would
> almost destroy the power of collecting any considerable quantity of
> materials; - of constructing proper machinery, warehouses, shipping,
> &c; - and of maintaining a sufficient quantity of hands, to introduce
> an effective division of labour. The proportion between capital and
> revenue would evidently, by this distribution, be altered greatly to
> the disadvantage of capital; and in a few years, the produce of the
> country would experience a rapid diminution. On the other hand, if
> such a distribution of the circulating medium were to take place, as
> to throw the command of the produce of the country chiefly into the
> hands of the productive classes, - that is, if considerable portions of
> the currency were taken from the idle, and those who live upon
> fixed incomes, and transferred to farmers, manufacturers and
> merchants, - the proportion between capital and revenue would be
> greatly altered to the advantage of capital; and in a short time, the
> produce of the country would be greatly augmented . . .
>
> We cannot help thinking, that an effect of this kind took place in
> Scotland in the interval of two periods alluded to by Hume and

Smith. In 1751 and 1752, when Hume published his Political
Discourses, and soon after the great multiplication of paper money in
Scotland, there was a very sensible [noticeable] rise in the price of
provisions ... attributed by him in part to the abundance of paper.
In 1759, when the paper currency had probably not been diminished,
Dr. Smith notices a different state of prices; and observes that, for a
long period, provisions had never been cheaper. The dearness at the
time that Hume wrote he [Smith] attributes carelessly, and without
any enquiry about the fact, to the badness of the seasons ... The
probability, however, seems to be, that the high prices of 1751 and
1752 were influenced by the paper ... but that the new stimulus
given to industry by this increase of capital, had so increased the
quantity of commodities in the interval between 1752 and 1759, as to
restore them to the level with the increased currency.[29]

Having made this point, however, Malthus referred with disapproval to
those who might be said 'to gamble in trade', and to the 'injustice committed
towards one portion of the society', those with fixed incomes; he concluded
with a solemn reminder that Parliament was trusted to 'attend equally to the
happiness of all classes of the community'.[30]

Ricardo published a fourth edition of his first pamphlet almost immediately
after Malthus's essay had appeared, with an Appendix 'containing some
Observations on some Passages in an Article in the Edinburgh Review'. In
this, again, one can see the beginnings of the controversies which were to
occupy the two men so happily for the twelve years before Ricardo's
untimely death in 1823. Specialists will study them in Sraffa's incomparable
volumes, but for the purpose of following Malthus's life-story it is sufficient
to note that even at this stage Ricardo was upholding what later became
known as Say's Law. The first edition of Jean-Baptiste Say's *Traité
d'Économie Politique* was published in 1803; in this he had expounded the
theory that all trade is fundamentally barter, product exchanging for product,
so that demand must essentially always equal supply in the aggregate; thus
what was then called 'a general glut' or superfluity of unsaleable commodities
could not exist. Sir James Steuart's 'Every person becomes fond of having
money' had been forgotten: the concept of liquidity preference had not been
developed.

Thus Ricardo could write in his Appendix in reply to Malthus:

No mistake can be greater than to suppose *that a nation can ever be
without wants for commodities of some sort.* It may possess too much
of one or more commodities for which it may not find a market at
home. It may have more sugar, coffee, tallow, than it can either
consume or dispose of, but no country ever possessed a general glut
of all commodities ...

No nation grows corn, or any other commodity, with a view to realise its value in money ... Money is precisely that article which till it is re-exchanged never adds to the wealth of a country: accordingly we find, that to increase its amount is never the voluntary act of any country any more than it is that of any individual. Money is forced upon them only in consequence of the relatively less value which it possesses in those countries with which they have intercourse.[31]

On 7 April Malthus wrote to Horner:

I have this moment been reading Mr. Ricardo's observations on the Review, but remain quite unconvinced - indeed there is no point on which I feel more sure than of the incorrectness of attributing the variations of the exchange exclusively to redundancy or deficiency of currency. I was sorry to find a small monosyllable put into the article, either by Jeffrey or by accident, which made a considerable alteration in the sense, and may have offended Mr. Ricardo in some degree justly. I had said 'We do not think these facts are all satisfactorily explicable upon the principles of M Ricardo alone', - it is printed *at all*, which makes a good deal of difference. By the by, have you heard any other critiques on the article? Jeffrey thinks it is not popular enough and probably he is right.[32]

Horner was immersed in preparing for the full-dress Commons debate on the Bullion Report the following month, but he replied on 8 April:

Dear Malthus,

I promise myself the pleasure of coming to see you for a day with Whishaw; he has not fixed what day, whether Friday or Saturday, but I will contrive to make either of them suit me. I wish very much to have a conversation with you upon the subject which engrosses me at present.

Your article is very popular in London. Tierney spoke to me in particular commendation of it, as giving what he thinks the most correct view of the subject ... The Governor of the Bank also mentioned the article to me, and praised it for candour and fairness; upon which I took the liberty of telling him by whom it was written. So that you see you have the rare fortune, in this instance, of pleasing both sides. I have a still better judgment to report in your favour; Hallam [Henry, the historian, 1777-1859] who has a great knowledge of the subject, & no bias whatever, said in a letter I had from him lately that he thought your view of the question the most sound as well as comprehensive he had yet read.

Ricardo's reply to your objections is not so well written, in point of clearness, as his usual style. I suspect that upon that dispute the truth lies between you, and that a mode of expressing and stating what takes place might be hit upon, to which you would both assent.[33]

On the same day that he wrote to Horner - 7 April 1811 - Malthus also wrote to Jeffrey. He did not mention the *contretemps* of 'all' and 'at all', which he perhaps thought could be more easily dealt with in person. The letter shows how much Jeffrey, in three years, had become a family friend: 'the ladies' are Harriet and her sister Fanny; it would appear from their correspondence that Malthus and Malthusia were hardly ever without a visitor. Malthus wrote:

Dear Jeffrey,

The ladies say that if you come to Haileybury, and pay a visit of a decent length, they are determined that I shall write another article on the Bullion question in your next number, but that if you disappoint us, be the cause what it may, they are equally determined that I shall not draw my pen in your service. As you see by this that I am not master of my own determinations, it will be useless for me to give you any further answer. I am only sorry that the debate does not come on before the 29th of April, as in the case of my being asked to write, College business may prevent my being able to get the article finished in time for you to take it back.

You are probably right in thinking my article not sufficiently popular; but I own that on such a subject I cannot but despair of the incapables; and generally speaking I am rather inclined to be of opinion that in reviewing scientific subjects, more good is likely to be done by explaining the errors of the most popular writers, than by attempting to restate in different words principles that have been repeatedly laid down with sufficient clearness before.

I have received your pamphlets ... but I have not leisure to go into the subject now. The greatest part of the article in the British Review appears to me to be very erroneous - but we will talk of these matters when we meet, which I hope will be very soon. Do not fail, and I will endeavour not to fail you.

Ever truly Yours
T. R. Malthus

I am writing in the dark.

The only address necessary for sending this letter through the ordinary post was 'F. Jeffrey Esqr, Edinburgh'.[34]

4 The Meeting with Ricardo

On 16 June 1811, Malthus wrote to Ricardo 'that as we are *mainly* on the same side of the question, we might supersede the necessity of a long controversy in print respecting the points in which we differ, by an amicable discussion in private'. Ricardo on 17 June was actually drafting in pencil a letter to Malthus in almost the same words: 'As we are so nearly agreed on the principles which regulate the value of money in the countries which have constant commercial intercourse with each other, I am desirous that we should endeavor [*sic*], by amicable discussion in private, to remove the few objections which prevent us from being precisely of the same opinion.' In the letter which he copied and posted to Malthus, this sentence was omitted.[35]

A plan for Ricardo to spend the week-end at Haileybury fell through, so the first meeting took place at Ricardo's house on Saturday 22 June; Malthus wrote on Friday, 'I will therefore have the pleasure of breakfasting with you tomorrow, but it will be out of my power to stay dinner.' I find it moving that such a scrap should have been carefully preserved, along with later letters which read like contributions to a learned periodical.[36]

David Ricardo was thirty-nine, an extremely successful stock-jobber, but with none of the unlovable qualities popularly associated with a man who makes money quickly. His family had migrated to Holland from Portugal, and then in about 1760 his father, Abraham Ricardo, a stock-broker from Amsterdam, settled in London; in due course Abraham became one of the twelve 'Jew Brokers' allowed to practise in the City. The economist's mother was Abigail Delvalle, from a family who traded in tobacco and snuff, and David spent two years in Holland with her relatives, from the age of eleven to thirteen. Ricardo was always conscious of his limited education, but his clear head and happy temper are reflected in his straightforward euphonious writing; his modest deference to the patronising literary instruction of James Mill, then at work on his *History of British India*, is as incomprehensible as it is endearing.[37]

In 1805 Ricardo had become a foundation member of the London Institution, of which Richard Sharp and Henry Thornton were on the original committee. In 1808 he joined the Geological Society, founded the year before; Leonard and Francis Horner were also members, as were Dr Alexander Marcet, William Blake, FRS, and Henry Warburton, who all had links with Malthus. The aged Rev. Joseph Townsend was one of the forty-two honorary members elected at the Society's inception, and so also – and with more justification – was Professor E. D. Clarke of Cambridge.

The list includes, too, Maria Edgeworth's brother-in-law, Dr Beddoes of Clifton, and Francis Horner's friend Lord Webb Seymour. Other acquaintances of Malthus were to join later, 1813 being a notable Whig year for the Geological Society, with the Duke of Devonshire, Lord Lansdowne and John Whishaw added to the roll of ordinary members.[38]

With so many overlapping social connections, as well as their common interest, Malthus and Ricardo were bound to have met sooner or later. It is easy to see how they became friends in spite of differences of background, education and wealth – Ricardo died worth about £¾ million – and also in spite of Ricardo's success in Parliament, and his fame and influence as an economist, which eclipsed that of the older Malthus. Empson records that the only time he ever saw 'an approach to anger on the countenance of Mr. Malthus' was when he mentioned attempts which had been made to cause or represent a jealousy between him and Ricardo. Malthus said, 'I never loved any body out of my own family so much.'[39]

Apparently Malthus was on friendly terms with Ricardo's large growing-up family, but Mrs Malthus cannot, I think, have found Mrs Ricardo, loud-voiced, 'neither polished nor literary',[40] a congenial companion. Priscilla Wilkinson was the daughter of a Quaker surgeon, and Ricardo left the Jewish community in order to marry her, when he was twenty-one, much to the grief and rage of his parents. Although they had, by law, to be married in an Anglican parish church, Priscilla kept up her connection with the Society of Friends, and was much 'admired as she swept grandly and proudly up the meeting, followed by her fine, elegant daughters. At the death of her husband Mrs. Ricardo was left with a handsome income, £3,000 per annum, but to her, who had lived in a princely style, beyond what this jointure would afford or permit her to continue, it seemed a great change, and she angrily declared that she should not have money enough to keep her from the workhouse!' Charlotte Sturge, who wrote that, might have had more to say had she been correctly informed, for the widowed Mrs Ricardo was in fact left £4,000 a year.[41]

Such a story could never have been circulated about Harriet Malthus, nor could her husband ever have written to their children as Ricardo did to his in November 1822: 'We arrived at Autun about 6, to a very tolerable Inn, but your mother could not divest herself of the idea that it was not the very best in the place, and that never fails to discompose her for the first half hour.'[42]

At the time of the Bullion Controversy the Ricardos were still living at Mile End, a part of London by no means fashionable, with nursery gardens on one side and cattle-pens on the other, although the place was well within the sound of Bow bells. They moved to 56 Upper Brook Street, off Grosvenor Square, in 1812. The counting-house where Ricardo conducted his business was in the City, at 16 Throgmorton Street, and it was to this address that Malthus first wrote. The initial letter was followed by others continuing the discussion, requests for particulars about the rate of exchange with Jamaica, and another invitation to Haileybury after the summer vacation, on 14 August, 'as I am about the Review, and should like to consult you on some points'.[43] Jeffrey must have paid his promised visit to the East India College.

Malthus's second *Edinburgh Review* article on the state of the Currency, which was number X in the issue dated August 1811, also appeared under the titles of six topical publications, and was headed 'Pamphlets on the Bullion Question'; this was misleading, since he never once mentioned any of them, and 'Depreciation of the Currency' would, in fact, have been far more appropriate. The excuse for a second article was that the parliamentary debates in May had not ended the Bullion Controversy. In June it was carried into the law courts: the King's Bench ruled that a man called de Yonge had committed no crime when he dealt in full-weight guineas at a premium against bank-notes, and this clearly contradicted the government's assertion that in all legal transactions a bank-note was on a par with gold. In the same month Lord King brought a test case against a tenant (a Director of the Bank of England) for £45, to be paid in gold or 'Bank notes of a sum sufficient to purchase the weight of standard gold requisite to discharge the rent'.

It is impossible for modern readers not to feel cynical at the horror of our ancestors, Malthus included, over the injustice caused by the depreciation of money - 'this violent and unfair transfer of property' - since inflationary prices are now almost taken for granted. Much of this article, therefore, has an unrealistic air about it today, especially as Malthus thought it necessary to spell out the proofs of depreciation - stationary bullion prices in other countries, a marked rise in paper prices at home, and an increase in the note issue equal to one-fourth of the amount in circulation three years before. Changes in the velocity of circulation were not yet regarded as a separate factor for analysis, although Malthus and other writers, as we have seen, were fully aware that increased commercial activity would involve an increase in the media of exchange. He wrote: 'We entirely agree with those who are of opinion, that no positive conclusions are to be drawn respecting an excess of currency, from the mere quantity of notes in circulation, independently of other circumstances; and think, that the market price of bullion, and the state of the exchanges, are the only certain criterions of depreciation.'[44]

A great deal of this essay is statistical rather than theoretical, giving the numbers of notes in circulation, and so on, but in one paragraph Malthus sums up the prevailing attitude towards the forces which were believed automatically to maintain economic equilibrium:

One of the certain effects of a really unfavourable exchange, and the precise cause which prevents the possibility of its permanence, is its

tendency to raise the price of foreign commodities, and lower the
price of home commodities ... We ought therefore to see a very
marked fall in the price of our home produce, and a marked rise in
the price of foreign commodities; instead of which, our home
produce has experienced a marked advance in price, and our imported
commodities are stationary. Nothing, we conceive, could have
produced effects so opposite to those which were to be expected, and
of the duration and extent actually observed, except an issue of notes
not only insufficient to prevent that compression of the currency,
which is at once the natural effect and natural remedy of an
unfavourable exchange, but greatly to enlarge the medium of
circulation, at the very moment when circumstances required it to be
contracted.[45]

To us, there is something almost comically pathetic about Malthus's use of
the word 'natural' in this connection, just as there is in his reference to
Napoleon's stranglehold of Europe as 'the present unnatural state of the
Continent'.

Yet as we read on, we can today appreciate the germ of a theory which
must have made his contemporaries raise their eyebrows. Adverting to rising
prices as a stimulus to industry, Malthus wrote:

To this principle we gave its full weight in a former Number. It
appears to us, indeed, a very important one; as explaining the reason
why severe taxation is not so prejudicial to the resources of a state, as
might naturally be expected; and why great public prosperity is not
incompatible with much individual distress.

After his fashion, Malthus immediately modified this 'principle' with further
reference to David Hume, in whose opinion

the natural check to the continuance of great commercial prosperity
in any one country, is the rise of corn and labour, necessarily
occasioned by that prosperity itself; and that, for fear of accelerating
the period of this check, he entertains great doubt of the benefit of
banks, even without reference to any depreciation of their paper
below the value of bullion ... Is not that period, contemplated by
Hume as so unfavourable to industry, already arrived? And do not
our ruined merchants, our impoverished manufacturers, and the
severe check that our capital and revenue have of late suffered, amply
testify that, even in the first application of the stimulus, it was
administered in much too large a dose?[46]

The essay ended with a compliment to Ricardo in the scheme outlined in
his appendix in which he had attacked Malthus's first currency article; this
plan Ricardo later developed in his *Proposals for an Economical and Secure*

Currency (1816), and the idea was virtually adopted in Peel's Bill for the Resumption of Cash Payments in 1819. 'The valuable suggestion of Mr. Ricardo' was that after two years notes for £20 and over, only, should be payable in guineas, standard bar gold, or foreign coin, at the option of the Bank Directors. 'Its great object', concluded Malthus, 'is to maintain, steadily, the bullion value of our paper currency, at a very small expense of the precious metals; and this object it seems calculated to answer.'[47]

It did answer, and was destined to be the basis of British monetary policy for nearly a hundred years. Owing to the popular demand for 'real' money, notes were not issued for less than £5, and the new unit of specie was not the golden guinea but the golden sovereign, worth twenty shillings. Such is the force of tradition, however, that gentlemanly fees and subscriptions, as well as the prices of works of art and pedigree livestock, have continued to be estimated in guineas, even after two world wars and the decimalisation of the British currency in 1971, when the sum of £1.05 became of no significance at all.

CHAPTER VII

The Haileybury Champion (1811–17)

1 The College under Fire

Between the two bullion articles came the summer vacation of 1811. Malthus spent ten days in Lincolnshire, after a visit from Mr and Mrs Eckersall, his first cousins and parents-in-law, who went on from Haileybury to stay with their daughter Anne Eliza; she was now married to her 'amiable and beloved' Henry Wood, the heir to Hollin Hall, near Ripon. According to family legend, the couple had met in Bath over amateur theatricals. Colonel Wood's account books show that he gave his daughter-in-law a set of jewels which cost £252; he also gave her a quarterly dress allowance of £15, although his unmarried daughters only had £10; but perhaps they did not do too badly, for on 19 October 1810 he noted that he gave the two of them £5 each 'for their Expenses at Doncaster Races and the Music Meeting at Derby'.[1] Colonel Wood died in 1815, and beautiful Hollin Hall became in due course a lively place for the seven young Woods and their Wynne and Malthus cousins.

One of the social events of the summer of 1811 was the installation of the Duke of Gloucester as Chancellor of the University of Cambridge on 29 June, followed by several days of festivities. Malthus appears to have stayed there for a week. Reginald Heber, by this time vicar of Hodnet in Shropshire and on a visit to Cambridge, thought the quite exceptional celebrations 'fell short of even the *annual* splendour of Oxford',[2] but I doubt if Oxford could have produced anything like the *Ode* performed in the Senate House, music by Dr Hague, words by Professor Smyth.

Not unnaturally, Malthus's old friend took Napoleon's devastation of Europe as his theme, with an inspiring chorus:

> Britannia rise! – 'tis thine, – 'tis thine!
> To roll the thunders of the blazing line!

A recitative then asked the Duke why

> 'Mid states in flames, and ruins hurled,
> Why England yet survives the world?

213

The answer came in a martial air:

> From hardy sports, from manly schools,
>   From Truth's pure lore, in learning's bower,
> From equal law, alike that rules
>   The people's will, the monarch's power ... [3]

This must be one of the earliest references to the fetish of the 'public school' which was to dominate for so long the education of the well-to-do British. Inevitably the East India College was to play a part in the extension of this system, in spite of having begun as a unique institution to fill the special needs of British India.

The year 1811 saw the third of Haileybury's notable rebellions. One student, Benjamin Guy Babington, was to confirm years later what was said in *The Times* of 18 November: 'The insubordination was noticed on the 4th inst. when the Masters reprobated the practice of firing off pistols, &c. on the anniversary of Guy Faux.' Babington thought that the prohibition of the traditional fireworks was injudicious, and 'actually increased the evil it was meant to remedy; and there is every probability that if it had never existed, there is not a student in the establishment who would not have thought it infinitely beneath his dignity to find amusement in such childish sport'.[4] There were other grievances too, including 'bad dinners', but that does not appear in the minutes until Dr Batten recalled the fact in 1816, when praising the improved catering.[5]

The 'unjustifiable Disturbances' of 1811 followed the usual pattern of rowdiness and destruction, which appears to have gone on for five days; they were reported by Malthus and Batten to the Committee of College on 13 November, and on the 15th the Committee met at Haileybury, to see for themselves where the rioters had been 'tumultuously assembling before Mr. Lewton's door', and to learn that 'An opinion prevailed, as to the existence of a Combination among the students.'[6]

It is worth noting here that it was the Combination or Conspiracy that troubled the authorities; the use of firearms, which would be regarded with horror today, was not considered particularly serious by the Directors, although they were prohibited at Haileybury. Swords were going out of fashion, but the possession of pistols by gentlemen, as well as sporting guns, was taken for granted. There was no police force in the modern sense of the term. This was the age when the 'guard' on a mail-coach really was an armed guard, on the look-out for thieves at the inns where horses were changed, as well as the more picturesque highwaymen.

We should also remember that the 'great schools' like Westminster and Winchester, Eton and Harrow, had their 'great rebellions' too, which simply became part of the institutions' folklore. What worried Charles Grant was the opportunity which these 'disgraceful outrages' gave to the financially interested enemies of the East India College. These enemies within the

Company itself had no scruples about fighting their battles in public through the columns of *The Times*, where 'A Proprietor of East India Stock' attacked Haileybury with gusto on 28 November 1811, giving reasons for 'the very apparent necessity for its dissolution'.

The Proprietor pointed out that boys usually went to public schools at the age of nine, and were 'immediately subjected to corporal chastisement mingled with literary impositions', which meant that by the time they were fifteen fear and habit had induced them to look on their teachers with respect. At such an age it was preposterous to expect boys to submit to unfamiliar instructors, yet this was demanded at Haileybury 'for no other reason than because you have written down rules which ordain that they shall do so'.

As for the instructors themselves, he noted that 'One of these tutors has written a book which . . . has acquired its author a considerable share of celebrity' (an asterisked footnote explained that this was 'Mr. Malthus, the author of the Essay on Population'). 'It were better that the rest had never meddled with the profession of authorship; but yet, their moral conduct being irreproachable, they are probably more competent to the management and instruction of boys than abler men, who would feel impatience on being withheld from the important business of life, to toil incessantly in the same round of scholastic discipline and elementary drudgery. No blame, therefore, attaches to the tutors at Hertford, personally; to the Institutions under which they act, much.'

The Proprietor then went on to make a point which was to be gleefully laboured in editorial articles for the next twelve years - the absurdity of a master and ushers calling themselves Principal and Professors. Then came what must have been the most bitter part of the letter to those who knew the truth of it only too well: 'Do you suppose that it has never occurred to these boys that, while their instructors are seeking by foolish titles, to impose an idea that they are something more than school-masters, they are in reality something less?' They could not punish without the Directors' permission, and the Proprietor doubted whether discipline could ever be maintained at the College 'except a Committee of Directors or Proprietors be regularly stationed at Hertford, to preserve order, while the Professors are exempt from every other duty than that of reading lectures'.[7]

On 13 December 1811 *The Times* printed a long letter approving of Haileybury in general terms, signed 'A Friend to the Good Government of India'.[8] On the 20th the 'Proprietor of East India Stock' returned again to the charge: What was wrong with Eton and Westminster 'and the hundred other excellent endowed schools in the Kingdom? In these, the rest of our youths of respectable birth are trained for every department of Church, Law, State, Diplomacy; but these, it seems, are incompetent to the instruction of boys who are sent out to India, in the same arts.' Expulsion from these seminaries did not mean blasted prospects for the pupil and great financial loss to his family, as it did in the monopolistic East India College; the obvious answer to the disciplinary problem at Haileybury was amending legislation to enable Writers to qualify from other institutions: 'So do I maintain, if the tutor at Hertford is armed with the power of expulsion, ought the parent to be provided with the corresponding option of admission.'[9]

Malthus and his colleagues must have pored over this correspondence, while the Committee of College and the Court of Directors held a series of Secret Meetings. The Directors who went down to Haileybury had suspended immediately the thirty-nine rioters 'who voluntarily confessed themselves implicated in the late Outrages', after an appeal to their honour by an unknown member of the Committee 'not to involve the Innocent in a punishment which should attach only to the Guilty'. This was obviously more satisfactory than rusticating the whole College, as was done in 1809. According to The Times the rebels were sent off at once: 'Carriages, and change of horses on the road, had previously been provided at the expence of the East India Company, to bring them to London, whence several of them will have to proceed to distant parts of Scotland.'

This cannot have been the case, as all thirty-nine were to be 'examined' in Leadenhall Street on 9, 10 and 11 December. There followed an acrimonious battle, the Directors beating down the College Council over the number of expulsions, of which eleven seemed to be indicated; finally, at a meeting on 14 January 1812, 'The Principal replied for himself and the rest of the Professors [Batten, Dealtry and Malthus were present] that the number could not, with Security to the College, be reduced lower than five.'[10] These five expulsions were duly enforced by a Resolution of the Court of Directors on 22 January.[11] Then, while Charles Grant was 'out of Direction' according to the rota, the Court on 8 April, without any further proceeding, or any previous public notice, passed another Resolution re-instating all the expelled students! So, far from having suffered for their misdeeds, they had benefited, since they were appointed as Writers and sent out to their posts in India without having to take the qualifying tests.

Charles Grant joined with six of his friends in a dignified 'Dissent' from this scandalous Resolution. They wrote: 'The sacrifices made in the year 1809 to the cause of discipline by the expulsion of Students nearly connected with Members of the Court are thus rendered worse than useless; and provision is made for new scenes of riot and rebellion, for which the present indemnity will be pleaded, and pleaded successfully, to the contempt and ruin of all further pretences to the exercise of Discipline.'[12]

As it happened, comparative order reigned at Haileybury for the next three years, largely owing to the necessity for all concerned to maintain a solid front against attacks on the Company from outside. The complete history of the renewal of the East India Company's Charter in 1813 is a fascinating example of bargain and compromise in politics, and of the apparently accidental influence on world events of particular individuals, but here we can only touch on what relates to Malthus. It is doubtful whether at this juncture the government could in practice have refused to renew the charter altogether, and have transferred the entire administration of India to the Crown, but there was real anxiety that it might; this hurdle passed, the terms of the new charter (to apply for the next twenty years) were matters of intrigue as well as debate.

In the enthusiastic pioneering era of free trade ideology, disciples of Adam Smith naturally shared his distaste for the East India Company as an instrument of monopoly. On the other hand the monopoly was sincerely defended by both Evangelicals and Benthamite Utilitarians, on the grounds that if India were open to all who might settle there, the natives could be insulted and exploited in a manner detrimental to their welfare and dangerous to British rule; there had been unfortunate experiences with indigo planters. It should be remembered that the possibility of growing tea in India was not realised until the year of Malthus's death: tea was brought from China, mainly in exchange for Indian opium.

For many years it had been increasingly difficult to sell Indian textiles in world markets. Charles Grant thought that this was due to high freight charges, and wanted the Company's shipping monopoly to be thrown open to competition, but he illogically defended the trading monopoly as a form of Property, acquired 'through a long course of dangers and vicissitudes and at the expense and hazard of the Company themselves'.[13] Merchants' petitions to the contrary effect poured into Parliament.

But more than anything else Grant wanted an Anglican establishment in India and the recognition of missionaries. He and Wilberforce had lost their 'pious clause' in the Charter debates of 1793, but this became a counter to bargain with in 1813. Most of the Directors had no objection to a bishop and some extra clergy (the shortage of chaplains sometimes made it extremely difficult for the respectable English in India to be properly married) but - especially after the mutiny at Vellore - they dreaded any attempt to disturb the religious beliefs and traditions of the natives. To do Grant justice, he equated Christianity with well-being; he wrote movingly of the husbandman of Bengal, who thinks he is destined to suffering, 'and is far more likely to die from want than to relieve himself by any new or extraordinary effort . . . We might communicate information of material use to the comfort of life and to the prevention of famine. In silk, indigo, sugar, and in many other articles, what vast improvements might be effected by the introduction of machinery. The skilful application of fire, of water, and of steam, improvements which would thus immediately concern the interest of the common people, would awaken them from their torpor, and give activity to their minds.'[14]

Another friend of Malthus's, less religious, also supported the Company's rule in India from first-hand knowledge - Sir James Mackintosh, who had returned to England in April 1812. He had written of a journey from

Bombay to Madras, 'I went through the Passes, by which Hyder Ally's army entered to lay waste the Carnatic ... Peaceable and solitary travellers now travel through these Passes with more security than they could ride from London to Windsor.' On another occasion he wrote, 'Nothing can more show the infernal character of the Asiatic governments, than that the English power really seems to me to be a blessing to the inhabitants of India ... and I conscientiously affirm that the most impartial philanthropist ought to desire its preservation.'[15]

It is against this background that we must think of Malthus among the 'Strangers' in the House of Lords on the evening of 9 April 1813, listening to Lord Grenville, for whom, according to Mackintosh, India was 'a subject on which he has more interest and information than any other public man. He is, in the highest degree, adverse to the Company.'[16]

A fortnight later Rowland Hunter, Joseph Johnson's successor, brought out Malthus's pamphlet of forty pages, *A Letter to the Right Honourable Lord Grenville occasioned by some Observations of His Lordship on the East India Company's Establishment for the Education of their Civil Servants*. It was never reprinted, but much of it was incorporated in Malthus's second pamphlet in defence of the College, which appeared in 1817 and caused considerable public stir. The 1813 pamphlet is remarkable for its moderation and brevity. With so much he could have enlarged upon about Indian affairs in 1813, it is interesting to find that Malthus was more than capable, when he chose, of remaining within narrow terms of reference.

Lord Grenville's case was that

> the college at Hertford ought to be suppressed as a baneful
> institution, which separated young persons from their friends and
> companions at an early age, and formed them into a class resembling
> an Indian caste; that the young men to be sent out to India ought to
> be selected from the public schools of the country, where they
> would learn British feelings and British habits; that this selection
> should be founded on good acquirements and good conduct; and
> should take place at an age not earlier than the usual age of leaving
> England from the East India College.[17]

Grenville's plan, as Malthus pointed out, was based on the assumption that the East India Company's Charter would not be renewed, and if this were the case he felt that the suggestions of his lordship 'were of high value and, with some modifications, might be adopted with great advantage'. 'But as', wrote Malthus, 'in the present temper both of his Majesty's government and of the Company, there is every reason to believe that it will be renewed, your lordship's observations do not apply to the actual state of things.'[18] According to Malthus, education for the Company's Civil Service was

> not a question about the general merits of public or private

education. It has nothing to do with any general innovation in the modes of instruction to be recommended in this country. It is one of those practical questions, which must often come before a statesman – how to accomplish a particular object in the best manner – how to supply a particular want most effectually, as well as most economically. In the consideration of such a question, it is impossible to form a correct judgement by taking only one view of it. A public school and three years' residence at one of our universities may be decidedly the best education for an English statesman; but for an Indian statesman, who must be acquainted with the oriental languages, and habituated to Indian customs and manners before he loses his pliability, there is evidently not time for such a course. The oriental languages are best taught in the East; but languages alone are not a sufficient qualification for the administration of the British government in India, and general knowledge is best taught in the west.[19]

Malthus answered Grenville's specific arguments against the College by pointing out that with boys destined to become naval or military officers,

We do not hesitate to separate them, for a time, from other boys, trusting, and trusting I think justly, that while they are living under the British constitution, and seeing continually their parents and friends, and hearing their conversation, they are not likely to lose the habits and feelings of British citizens.[20]

He also felt that many parents would be 'unable to undergo the extravagant expense of a long residence at a public school', although they could manage to 'give their sons a good education in their own neighbourhood', and pay for two or three years at Haileybury.[21]

Only once does Malthus become controversial, when he accuses his lordship of inconsistency; Grenville had supported the Marquis Wellesley's collegiate establishment at Fort William, to which boys would have gone at the age of fifteen, thus being cut off from their families earlier than under the Haileybury system. In Calcutta at this tender age they would be exposed to all 'the temptations to indolence and sensual indulgencies peculiar to a warm and luxurious climate and a city nearly as large as London', with 'the power of borrowing almost any sum of money from particular natives who speculate on their future prospects in the service'.[22] The circumstances would indeed 'operate as formidable discouragements to begin a course of law, history, political economy, and natural philosophy, or to continue a course of classical studies'.[23] As things were, Malthus could say that in the opinion of Lord Minto and other authorities in Calcutta there had been 'a marked improvement in the conduct and attainments of the young men who have arrived since the establishment of the college in England'.[24]

There are two interesting paragraphs on the wide range of the curriculum of Haileybury:

> At the commencement of the institution, it was feared by some persons that this variety would too much distract the attention of students at the age of sixteen or seventeen, and prevent them from making a satisfactory progress in any department; but instances of distinguished success in many of these studies at the same time have proved that these fears were without foundation, and that this variety has not only been useful to them in rendering a methodical arrangement of their hours of study more necessary, but has decidedly contributed to enlarge, invigorate and mature their understandings.
>
> It was also imagined that some of the pursuits that contribute to form this variety were of too difficult a nature for young men of the age above mentioned; and the subject of political economy was considered as one. I confess that I once thought so myself. But the particular examples, which I have witnessed, of distinguished progress in this study at the East India College, and the numerous instances of very fair progress, enable me to say with confidence that a youth of seventeen (and this is the most usual age at which the study is begun, as it is generally confined to the last year or year and a half) with a good understanding, is fully able to comprehend the principles of political economy, and is rarely inclined to think them either too difficult or too dull to engage his attention.[25]

Possibly the most historically significant passage is that in which Malthus describes the procedure of a competitive examination, for those to whom both the idea and the method were quite unfamiliar:

> The answers are, in all cases which will admit of it, given in writing, in the presence of the professors, and without the possibility of a reference to books. After the examination in any particular department is over, the professor in that department reviews at his leisure all the papers which he has received, and places, as nearly as he can, each individual in the numerical order of his relative merit, and in certain divisions implying his degree of positive merit. These arrangements are all subject to the controul of the whole collegiate body. They require considerable time and attention, and are executed with scrupulous care and, I firmly believe, with singular impartiality. If the lists of many successive years were examined with the most scrutinizing eye, I doubt if the slightest trace of general connexion could be found between the places of the students in these examinations and the rank or supposed influence of their patrons.[26]

The last sentence would not have startled contemporary readers in the same way that it startles us today. When the College was founded – and long before – a young man's Rank in the Company's Civil Service was determined by the seniority of the Director who had nominated him; complicated discussions about Rank (always so spelt) occupied many hours of the Committee of College, especially when patronage was exchanged, and students transferred from one Presidency to another. Much time was to elapse before the Court of Directors took for granted an order of Rank based on the list of Writers passing out of Haileybury, arranged straight-forwardly in order of merit.

Malthus became more rhetorical when he reviewed the disadvantages of the College, 'a new institution uncongenial to the prevailing prejudices of the public':

> It has to contend with the evil of an appeal, in all cases of
> importance, to a body of men whose individual interests could hardly
> fail to be always in opposition to the interests of the discipline. It has
> had to contend with a party connected with Indian affairs, from the
> first decidedly hostile to the College, and indulging themselves, as
> there is too much reason to believe, in a sort of language respecting
> it, of a nature to produce the very worst effects on the temper and
> conduct of the students connected with them. And it has had to
> contend with an impression of instability, arising from the two
> preceding causes, necessarily tending to generate disturbances, and to
> produce the very evils which it prognosticates.
>
> But let these disadvantages be removed, let the discipline be placed
> on a proper footing, by giving full powers to the Principal and
> Professors, with an appeal only to some one individual of high rank,
> not immediately connected with the patronage of the students. Let
> the stability of the College be secured by some legislative sanction,
> which will prevent it from depending upon the variable wills of a
> fluctuating body of Directors . . .[27.]

The Act of 1813, which renewed the East India Company's Charter for another twenty years, did in fact give statutory recognition to the College. Henceforth no person could be sent as a Writer to any of the Presidencies of Bengal, Madras or Bombay who had not passed four terms (two years) at the College; and not even then, unless he produced a certificate of his good conduct under the hands of the collegiate authorities. Rank was to be determined by the classification of the students in order of merit on leaving Haileybury, according to industry, proficiency and general good behaviour, and powers of expulsion were granted to the College Council, with an Appeal to the Visitor, the Bishop of London.

Charles Grant won his religious establishment and £10,000 annually for native education; in practice the Evangelicals found it difficult to recruit either clergy or missionaries for India, and the education provision (unused for ten years) was later to cause much controversy as to whether the Indians were to be taught in English or their own vernaculars. The Company lost the monopoly of the Indian trade, but kept that with China, largely because it was unlikely that the Chinese would have traded at all with any other merchants.

It is impossible to estimate how much this parliamentary triumph for the East India College was due to Malthus's pamphlet and, presumably, his personal influence in London. Before he had read the *Letter*, Horner wrote to him on 20 April 1813:

> I am anxious to see your defence of the College, which cannot but prove of great service not only at the present moment but to the future character of the institution. Nothing is so much to be regretted as the view which Lord Grenville has taken of it; I think unjustly, after the best consideration I am able to give the subject. The general question of the education of those whom we send to govern India is one of the first importance, and what you are going to publish cannot fail to obtain a more deliberate attention for it, than has yet been bestowed upon it by any body else.[28]

There is nothing explicit to show why Malthus and not one of his colleagues was entrusted with the responsibility of defending the College. Dr Henley was seventy-three, and possibly the other professors thought that Malthus, as the most celebrated among them, was their most appropriate public champion. But it is also possible that they thought he had more leisure than anyone else, far more than the overworked members of the Oriental Department. Certainly Malthus seems to have written little during the six years 1808-13, and it is round about this period that we find him most engaged in what would later have been called good works and social life.

2 Outside Activities

I cannot estimate how much time Malthus spent on the Bible Society, Lancaster's Committee for educating poor children, and workers' savings banks, but he was involved with all three.

To begin with the last mentioned, Malthus's name, with those of Ricardo, Torrens, and Wilberforce, is among those of the sixty-one Gentlemen listed as 'Managers' of the Provident Institution for Savings, established in the Western Part of the Metropolis. Such societies were being founded all over the country, and in Horner's phrase gave 'birth to a new host of pamphlets', often surprisingly and savagely controversial over the details of accounting and organisation. This particular Institution was 'to afford to the labouring Classes, to Servants, Mechanics, and Tradesmen, and all other persons, a secure Investment in the Public Funds for such Sums of Money as they may wish to deposit at Interest; leaving them at liberty to withdraw the whole, or a part, whenever they require it'.[29]

The regulations were set out by Joseph Hume (later a noted radical politician) in a booklet of sixty-four pages; many of these were taken up with attacks on rival systems, including that of Professor Christian, who 'should have been cautious of measuring the ability of the ablest men in the country by his own standards'.[30] Hume's Institution had an Office open to Depositors 'every Monday from *Twelve* o'clock till *Three*, and every Saturday Evening, from *Seven* till *Nine* . . . when the Actuary, with one or more of the Managers, shall attend'.[31] I do not know whether the Rev. Mr Malthus ever did.

Malthus's connection with the Bible Society and Lancaster's schools may simply have been due to his friendship with Clarke and Otter in the former instance and Francis Horner in the latter; both these organisations were frowned on by many of the more rigid members of the Church of England.

For some months the Cambridge branch of the British and Foreign Bible Society was one of Ned Clarke's enthusiasms, and Otter wrote that it 'absorbed for a while every feeling and every faculty of his soul'.[32] According to Gunning's *Reminiscences*, its foundation originated with the undergraduates in 1811, and the scheme 'was carried out by their zeal and perseverance; for it met with strong opposition from the leading members of the University, who considered that if the young men assumed the character of a deliberating body, it would be productive of great mischief in the discipline of the University'.[33] Perhaps the authorities knew better where they were with students like the young gentleman of Trinity who, according to the second Lord Teignmouth, 'won a bet that he would stand on his head during the entire divine service in our chapel'.[34]

Gunning recorded that the zeal of the Bible Society undergraduates

> was unabated, and they seemed determined to struggle against all
> difficulties. They at length succeeded in obtaining the sanction of the
> Vice-Chancellor who, although he did not patronise the measure,
> gave his consent that a meeting should be called of the University,
> Town, and County of Cambridge, for the purpose of establishing a
> society.
> At this crisis the opposition became very great, and the expressed
> opinions of Dr. Marsh most injudicious. He stated how highly
> improper it was to circulate the Bible without the Book of Common
> Prayer. This unprotestant mode of opposing the meeting disgusted
> many persons who were not originally friends to the Society, but
> who in consequence gave it their support.

Clarke and Otter both published pamphlets against the learned Dr Marsh, who opposed the Bible Society largely because it sanctioned co-operation with Dissenters; as these pamphlets were printed by Watts of Broxbourne (who also printed for the East India College) 'Malthus could read every sheet as it issued from the Press.' This was in February 1812. By August Clarke was writing to Otter, 'Malthus will "read the sheets, and mention anything that strikes him: but he will neither correct nor transpose" - Those are his Words.'[35] We cannot know the inside story; Otter rather slurs over it in his *Life* of Clarke, and stresses that Clarke 'was always a zealous supporter of the Church, and afterwards an active member of the Society for Promoting Christian Knowledge'.[36] It is certain, however, that in 1812 Clarke was instrumental in founding several more branches of the Bible Society, and Malthus helped at a meeting of one of these, at Chelmsford.[37]

What Frend had called 'the usual marks of theological hatred' also distinguished the dispute between the two associations designed to promote the education of poor children in large numbers; both systems involved teaching the brightest pupils one stage ahead of the others, and then setting each little 'monitor' to impart the lessons of the day to his fellows, in groups of ten or a dozen.

Joseph Lancaster (1778-1838) had a school with a thousand boys in 1803, when he published a *Report* of his progress. His organisation was the British and Foreign School Society, and Joseph Hume was a member of the Central Committee. The religious side of the work was based on simple Bible readings. Because Lancaster had become a Quaker, he was attacked by the Established Church, whose champion was the Rev. Andrew Bell (1753--1832). Bell was famous for having held eight army chaplainships simultaneously in India, probably due more to the death-rate among chaplains than to his machinations as a pluralist, and he introduced a system of instruction by monitors into the Madras Male Orphan Asylum in 1789. He published an account of this in 1797, when he was back in England, and in 1811 he became 'Superintendent' of the National Society for the Promotion of the Education of the Poor in the Principles of the Established Church, with religious teaching based on the Anglican prayer-book Catechism.

The religious issue was to be a stumbling block in British education for years, but without the stimulating malevolence of sectarian controversy many poor children might have had no education at all for another half-century. All we know of Malthus's views is what can be deduced from a letter which Horner wrote to him:

London, 8th February, 1812

My dear Malthus,

I am very glad it occurred to you, to offer Lancaster's committee the sanction of your name as a steward at our meeting; and I have written to Joseph Fox, telling him, that I have reason to believe you would not refuse to serve in that capacity, if it were proposed to you.

I entirely concur in your sentiments upon the subject, that both societies ought to be encouraged; nay I go a little farther, for if I could be convinced that the church would sincerely and zealously set themselves to accomplish the work of national education, the church should have the best of my wishes by preference; inasmuch as I regard the establishment as our best preservative against fanaticism, though I am persuaded it can only operate effectually to that end, or indeed subsist long as an establishment, by acting upon the true principles of the Reformation, of which educating the common people is the most important ... In the mean time, they cannot crush the system of Lancaster, whose zeal is as unconquerable as that of John Knox; the only thing to be regretted is, that that zeal should have so large an admixture of polemic irritability which begins, I fear, to disgust some of those persons whose taste is fastidious, and who cannot, for the sake even of the good that is effected, overlook the rudeness of the means by which such good has, almost in every instance of the sort, been accomplished.

> Most truly yours,
> Fra. Horner.[38]

But Malthus and Horner were not always corresponding about economics and education. Horner was much interested in the strategy of the campaigns against Napoleon, and - like the whole of London society - in the poetry of Lord Byron. On 14 September 1813 he wrote to Malthus, 'There is a new edition of our friend the Giaour, in which it exceeds 1200 lines. How he has grown since we saw him first!'[39] Malthus and Byron had met a few months before, on 12 May, at a party for seventy or eighty people, given by Lady Davy. The party is well described by both Mary Berry and Maria Edgeworth. Maria knew Sir Humphry Davy because he had been an assistant to Dr Beddoes, the husband of one of Maria's half-sisters, who established what was called the Pneumatic Institution at Clifton, near Bristol, for the treatment of tuberculosis. The widowed Anna Beddoes was a close friend of Mrs Leonard Horner, and thus Maria also saw 'the great man', as her brother-in-law Francis had now become.

History is so much concerned with the great Whig Landlords, with Holland House and Lansdowne House, that the interlocking families of the Whig intelligentsia are sometimes overlooked. The year 1813 seems to have been a particularly social one for Malthus and his friends, or perhaps one gets this impression from a plethora of published letters and journals describing the memorable visits to London first of Miss Edgeworth and then of Mme de Staël (Malthus met her at a party too). Among the men conspicuous in Whig society in 1813 were Sir Samuel Romilly and Sydney Smith entertaining Dr Parr, with his old-fashioned wig and his obnoxious pipe; Sir James Mackintosh, just about to become MP for Nairn, who had stayed with the Malthuses for a fortnight in March, suffering from a high fever and erysipelas of the face, and had 'experienced the kindest hospitality';[40] Dr Marcet, the famous physician and chemist from Guy's Hospital, one of whose daughters was to marry one of the Romilly boys; and young Dr Holland (his second wife was to be Sydney Smith's daughter Saba), who was surprised to find that the author of the *Essay on Population* had such a 'genial, even gentle expression of features'.[41]

The first two cantos of *Childe Harold* had appeared the year before, in 1812, and Byron was still the lion of lions, although when she saw him at Lady Davy's Maria Edgeworth wrote that 'his appearance is nothing that you would remark in any other man'. After Lord Byron, the second lion whom Maria described to her cousin Sophy was Malthus: 'plain and sensible in conversation and agreeable notwithstanding a sad defect in his pronunciation'.

A few days later Whishaw, who had met the family in Dublin, brought Malthus to call at the Edgeworths' lodgings, and subsequently they all met again at the Marcets', on which occasion Harriet came too. Jane Marcet (1769-1858), of Swiss origin, had published a popular work called *Conversations on Chemistry* in 1806, which had been the basic text-book of a youngster who was then helping Davy at the Royal Institution; his name was Michael Faraday, and he was only three years Dr Holland's junior, but he was not invited to parties. According to Maria Edgeworth the evening at Mrs Marcet's was 'very agreeable', and it was then that she wrote to her half-sister Fanny, 'Mr. Malthus is a perfectly unaffected amiable, gentlemanlike man, who really *converses*; that is, listens, as well as talks, and follows the ideas of others as well as produces ideas of his own.'[42]

The splendour of the London season of 1814 greatly surpassed that of 1813 as far as the non-literary were concerned. With 'General Buonaparte' exiled to Elba, Romilly wrote to Dumont in August that the capital had 'for a long time been half crazy with emperors, and kings, and shows, and illuminations, and fireworks'.[43] Then came the news of Napoleon's escape, and his triumphant arrival in Paris on 20 March 1815. On 28 March Malthus wrote in the course of a letter to Brougham:

> What a change in our political horizon!!! and what a phenomenon is this same Buonaparte!!! There is nothing at all resembling it in history. I should not care about it, if it does not promise to lead to almost eternal war. It would be wise to give up Belgium, if peace could be purchased by it. But I suppose in the first place that we are not likely to make the cession, and in the next place that it would by no means be sufficient.[44]

It is still extremely difficult for many English people to realise not merely that Napoleon could possibly have won the battle of Waterloo, but also

226

that numbers of patriotic and intelligent Englishmen felt at the time that it might have been better for Europe had he done so. This was partly because they saw Napoleon as a reformed hero, renouncing the idea of empire, framing for France a free constitution with liberty of the press, promising the abolition of the slave trade, and so on, and partly because they dreaded and detested – Dr Parr's words – the despotic monarchs of the Holy Alliance.

With regard to France herself, Horner wrote to Lord Grey on 28 March that it seemed wrong to force upon that country a royal family 'who, in a year's possession of the throne, could not secure a dozen bayonets to keep them in it; and who were so utterly insignificant, that they were not molested in their flight'. To his father Francis Horner repeated the same theme on 18 April, condemning 'the unjustifiable principle of interfering with the right of the French to choose their own government'.[45] In his *Diary of his Parliamentary Life* Romilly recorded that on 28 April Whitbread proposed a Motion praying the Prince Regent 'would not involve the country in war on the ground of the government of France being in the hands of any particular individual, or to that effect; for I do not recollect the precise words of the motion. I voted for the motion, in a minority of 72 against 273.'[46]

Malthus held the same Whig views, and after the battle of Waterloo wrote to Ricardo from Claverton on 16 July 1815:

> I hope the victory of the Duke of Wellington will be the means of giving Europe some permanent repose. It has been purchased by a tremendous sacrifice, and I do not quite like the idea of imposing the Bourbons upon France by force, but if it leads to a lasting peace, it will be worth all that it has cost. I think Louis in order to be safe himself must disband nearly the whole army, and this must powerfully contribute to the safety and repose of Europe, though this second successful combination of Sovereigns will I fear be unfavourable to its liberty and improvement.[47]

Before this, however, Malthus had shown a lack of confidence in both the government and the army which would have sunk his reputation still lower among his detractors had they known about it. Ricardo used to buy small parcels of new issues of government stock on his friends' behalf, and had reserved £5,000 for Malthus from a loan of £36 million which he, with others, was to contract for on 14 June 1815. But on 11 June Malthus wrote to Ricardo from the Godschalls' that the proclamation of the new French constitution

> has passed off so well for Buonaparte, and I am so much inclined to think that he will make a formidable resistance, that I expect the Stocks will be rather lower than higher some months hence. I may very likely be quite mistaken; but under this impression I should

227

naturally be disposed to take an early opportunity of realising a small profit on the share you have been so good as to promise me. I will not however do this if it is either wrong, or inconvenient to you, and whatever may occur, you may depend upon it, that I shall always be sensible of your kindness, and not disposed to repine.

Sraffa thinks Ricardo probably sold Malthus's share on the day the stock was issued, when the Omnium bore a premium of 2½ to 3¼ per cent. On 21 June, the morning after the news of Waterloo reached London, the premium rose to 6 per cent, and touched 13 per cent a week later; Ricardo, only a little more optimistic than Malthus, had sold his stock at a premium of 5 per cent.[48]

3 The College Before and After Waterloo

The Minutes of the Committee of College reflect nothing of European affairs between 1813 and 1817.

There were a number of staff changes, important for Haileybury, which would also have affected Malthus's everyday life. His Evangelical and mathematical friend William Dealtry resigned in August 1813 on 'accepting the valuable Rectory of Clapham, at which it was necessary that he should reside', as Malthus wrote to Sir James Mackintosh. He was replaced by Charles Webb Le Bas (1779-1861), whom Malthus did not know, but he understood that 'he bore a high character at Cambridge'.[49] In the minutes for 1 March 1814 Le Bas' 'matrimonial engagement' is reported, and that 'he is prevented from fulfilling the same, on account of the insufficiency of his present residence at the College for the accommodation of a Family'. The Committee recommended the Court to spend £650 on amalgamating four students' rooms with Le Bas' quarters,[50] and thus he was able to marry Sophia, the daughter of Mark Hodgson of the Bow Brewery, inventor of the famous India Pale Ale. 'There was a large family', according to the *Dictionary of National Biography*; a practical example of the connection between housing and population.

Le Bas' paternal grandfather, of Huguenot stock, had also been a brewer, and his maternal grandfather was a captain in the East India Company's mercantile marine. His father kept a linen draper's shop in London, in Bond Street, and from a private school Charles became a Scholar at Trinity College, Cambridge, where he won the Chancellor's Medal for classics as well as becoming Fourth Wrangler in 1800. He was called to the bar in 1806, and then had to abandon the law on account of 'constitutional deafness'.

He took orders in 1809, in 1811 became rector of St Paul's, Shadwell, and in 1812 a prebendary of Lincoln, where he had been tutor to the Bishop's sons. Although he was Professor of Mathematics and Natural Philosophy, his published works were all theological, or else the biographies of churchmen; after his death his old pupils founded the Le Bas Prize for an essay on 'an historical subject'.

Dealtry's partner, Bewick Bridge, resigned in March 1816 for his health, with a pension of £200 a year from the Company; he became vicar of Cherry Hinton, near Cambridge, where he founded the village school, and lived until 1833. His successor was the Rev. Henry Walter (1785-1859), who had produced for the Committee's perusal no less than twenty-one testimonials including three from bishops. In spite of the College's reputation for disorder, it must have had some advantages, as two of the applicants for Bridge's post were mathematical instructors at Sandhurst and Addiscombe. At the bottom of the list was Mr Charles Babbage, supported solely by a letter from John Herschell.[51]

Henry Walter, a Fellow of St John's, Cambridge, was the son of a Lincolnshire parson and had been educated at Brigg Grammar School. He was Second Wrangler in 1806, and approved of by his cousin Jane Austen, who in 1813 was pleased to hear that he was 'considered as the best classick in the University'. Within a year of his appointment the Committee granted him, at his request, more apparatus for his evening lectures on experimental philosophy, and his pupils remembered Mr Walter as 'one of the cleverest and most genial of men', who inspired his students with a 'taste for the study of beasts and birds'.[52] He was later to publish a history of England in seven volumes, and edit the works of William Tyndale for the Parker Society.

But the most notable change at this period was the replacement of Dr Henley by Dr Batten - as he shortly became by royal mandate - on 1 February 1815. Batten, at thirty-seven, was exactly half Henley's age. One is inclined to believe Charles Grant when he wrote in a memorandum on the lack of discipline at Haileybury, 'It may perhaps be also true, that there has too long been a want of efficiency in the Superior Department of the College.'[53] The Rev. Joseph Hallet Batten was the son of a Congregational minister in Penzance; he spent some time at St Paul's School in London, but it was from Truro Grammar School that he went up to Trinity College, Cambridge; he was Third Wrangler in 1799. He never lost a strong Cornish accent, in which he displayed what were described as 'brilliant conversational powers'. The Batten family moved into the Principal's Residence, and that pleasant Orientalist Major Stewart became the Malthuses' new neighbour in Hailey House.

The Principal's house had to be enlarged several times at the Company's expense to accommodate the Battens; their precise number can no more be ascertained than can that of the Le Bas family. Malthus followed the common practice of having his children christened and their names entered in the appropriate parish register when they were small babies; Batten must have baptised his infants at home and then listed their names in the register at Great Amwell in batches, with a fine disregard for both legal claims and demographic statistics. Thus Catherine and John Hallet were entered on 7 June 1811, and Priscilla, Charlotte and Maria on 10 September 1816; Susan, William Henry, Joseph Gordon, and Georgina Henrietta were added nine years later, on 10 September 1825; Charles Hamilton had an entry all to himself on 24 May 1827.[54] Yet this list is not complete, since George Maxwell Batten was nominated a student at the College in January 1825, but allowed by the Committee to remain in his father's house, as there was no room for him elsewhere.[55]

Two requests from Dr Batten are repeated constantly throughout the Minutes: for an additional water-closet for his children, and a new colleague to take over his duties as a classical professor. He got the first after four years, but was never granted the second, and he continued until the end to give lectures to the older students on classics and divinity. All the work was better organised than it had been in Henley's time, however, with Le Bas acting as Dean and the long-suffering Lewton as Registrar, a position analogous to that of a modern bursar, each having an extra £100 a year for his services.

Disciplinary problems remained, and there were disturbances on 17 May 1815, but not of a nature to be reported in *The Times*. The difficulty was that the students who misbehaved disguised themselves with fencing masks, and slipped away in the darkness, while the whole College 'combined' - the word had a sinister connotation - 'for the purpose of screening and protecting offenders'. This matter ended with only one expulsion, but anxious discussion went on all through the summer. Batten thought that students should sign a declaration every term, to the effect that 'it is with the free choice and liking of the student that he goes to the College, and is ultimately destined for India', and 'disavowing the principle of maintaining an obstinate silence and refusing to speak even to his own innocence'.

There were arguments over the principles of Decimation and Selection. The new Principal favoured the former, threatening arbitrarily to expel or punish one boy in ten after a disturbance, in the hope that this would persuade the innocent to declare themselves and that the guilty, if they did not confess, could then be discovered by elimination. His colleagues thought this might cause injustice, and that Selection was preferable, allowing the College Council 'to select for punishment the persons of the worst character'; Professor Christian put forward a scheme of his own, but the clerk does not give details and no one paid any attention.[56] That feeling ran very high throughout the whole Court of Directors is shown by the address of Charles Grant, then Chairman, to the students on 3 August 1815 at the beginning of a new term. His theme was that no Individual or Combination of

Individuals could destroy the Establishment: 'they might destroy themselves, but he wished to say once for all, the Establishment they could not destroy'.[57]

Behind the scenes, helped by the Bishop of London, Grant tried to get the President of the India Board to agree to raising the age of entry from fifteen to sixteen, which the professors - except for Sanskrit Hamilton - had long been urging; but the Earl of Buckinghamshire would not yield. The Bishop consecrated the chapel and held a confirmation on 24 August 1815,[58] and on 28 October the Council reported that they had permitted the students to establish a Debating Society: they required some Evening Amusement, this was one of their own Choice, and the Members of it had conducted themselves extremely well.[59] The Society was to last as long as the College, and the recollection of its earnest and well-informed debates was to give pleasure for almost a century after its foundation.

But this could not be known in 1815, and on 16 November Horner was writing to Malthus about the most serious riot in the College's history:

I am very much grieved to hear that the peace of your College has been again disturbed by your young men. From your letter to Whishaw, which he has shown me, it would seem that they have proceeded farther lengths this time than ever, and the attack upon the servants appears to have been attended with circumstances which require the interposition of some stronger authority than college discipline. It struck me, last time, that there was no certain remedy for outrages of this description, except in the ordinary process of the criminal law; and I apprehend there can no longer be any hesitation in resorting to that same expedient. If you cannot punish your pupils as boys, you must subject them to the punishments by which other men are kept in order; and as the particular plan of your Institution, together with the situation of most of the lads, make rustication and even expulsion nugatory as correctives, you have nothing else left but recourse to the law.

The servants attacked ought to be directed to prefer indictments, and in my opinion there ought to be no false delicacy about the employment of the most effectual means which Bow Street and the Old Bailey can furnish you with, for tracing out evidence. A conspiracy and riot is one of the offences that have been committed; and the wounding of the servants with the sharp instrument which you describe is, by the law, a capital felony in all who were concerned.

There is something quite unintelligible in the conduct of these young men. A multitude of men, and especially young men, is rarely so much and for so great a while in the wrong. In nine out of ten school riots, the youngsters have some justice originally on their side. I cannot help being persuaded that, in the present instance, the very

231

object of the instigators of all this violence must be to draw upon themselves the rustication or expulsion which you have supposed all along to be a punishment, but which in truth is any thing but that. By *you*, I mean the Directors and ruling authorities.[60]

Further light is thrown on the affair by a letter which Batten sent to the Earl of Buckinghamshire on 26 November 1815:

My Lord,
　　Your Lordship must have heard of the late unfortunate scene at the East India College. Fourteen students engaged in an unmanly attack, at night, disguised in masks, & armed with sticks, upon two of the College Servants - obnoxious to them, not from any incivility or officiousness, but for the faithful discharge of their known duty.[61]

The servants concerned were the steward and his assistant; it is not clear whether the obnoxious duties for which they were assaulted on 9 November were the prevention of a Guy Fawkes celebration or the performance of their nightly round of the students' rooms. The object of this intrusion was to discourage drinking parties, and arguments about it went on for years, some members of the Committee of College even wanting the professors to inspect their pupils' rooms in rotation. This interference with the students' privacy was later modified, probably through Canning's influence at the India Board, but until the College came to an end in 1857 the servants went round 'every night at eleven o'clock, knocking at every door and asking in solemn tones: "Are you alone?"'[62]

Batten's letter to Lord Buckinghamshire continued:

After trying in vain to procure the disclosure or surrender of the parties, we had recourse to the new Statute of Selection, & sent away nine, pledging ourselves to expel a portion of them. It has since appeared that we were right in six instances out of the nine; but altho' 3 of those sent away were innocent of the actual outrage, the risk which they ran of losing their appointments failed to have the effect of extorting the guilty. In the meantime a general outcry was raised against the College for not calling in the Civil Magistrate at once. The Servants were therefore directed to make their complaint before the Magistrate at Hertford. The consequence was an examination of students before the Bench, which led to the discovery of the 14 who had united to assault the men.

Even in that violent age, the prospect of hanging must have subdued the most rebellious, but in fact only three boys were sent for trial, 'as a warning to the rest'; they spent a day or so in prison in Hertford before being released on bail, and were later discharged by a Grand Jury. One of them, George Dallas, died some weeks later, while the formalities involving the expulsion of all fourteen conspirators were still in progress. It was an unhappy episode which was to have repercussions.

The Company paid the two servants' legal expenses, amounting to £83, on account of 'the circumstances which occasioned the Assault and consequently the Prosecution being the performance of their duty positively required of them by the statutes'.[63] Yet Batten could write naïvely to Lord Buckinghamshire:

> Notwithstanding the clamour which this affair will excite amongst the enemies of the College, it is distinguished from all former scenes of an unpleasant nature there, 1st, From its involving no possibility of blame upon the authorities, to whom no insult was offered & against whom no grievance was alleged. 2, From its leading to no *rebellion*, the great body of the Students continuing throughout to conduct themselves with order and obedience. 3, From its authors being accurately ascertained and adequately punished.

Batten was fortunate that the enemies of the College never found this letter.

It is difficult to tell exactly how far Malthus was involved, but a letter to Ricardo dated 22 December 1815 is revealing: 'I should have written before but have been over whelmed with College business and able to do nothing, on account of these foolish disturbances, and the necessity of constant councils, Reports, &c: The term is ended now, and I can breathe again.'[64] Yet not for long; six days later he was writing to Ricardo refusing an invitation to Gatcomb:

> I shall be so behind hand with regard to my own business, and so likely to be involved in College affairs, that I fear it will be quite impossible for me to leave this neighbourhood. I have been so much interrupted already by College business, that I have made very little progress in my edition since I saw you ... I much fear I shall be called upon to write something about the College, which will be very inconvenient to me.[65]

The 'edition' was the fifth of the *Essay on Population*, 'which Murray wishes to have finished before anything else is done', as Malthus had written to Ricardo on 1 October 1815;[66] it did not appear until June 1817, by which time the College had passed its worst crisis.

In April 1816 Charles Grant, having been Chairman for a year, went 'out of direction', and his opponents embarked on a policy of harassment which must have sorely tried the College Council. They insisted on detailed 'reports' on each student at the end of every month, 'Similar to the Report furnished at the End of each Term'; they tried to cut down the purveyor's catering allowance, and Batten had to fight hard for 21s. per head per week for professors and students, and 10s. 6d. for servants; most extraordinary of all, they refused to renew the insurance policy for £10,000 on the buildings, 'as the Committee have every reliance on the care of the Members of the College Council to prevent accidents from happening at the College'.[67] Then they started an onslaught on the use of rustication as a punishment, which (if he lost a term) inevitably delayed a student's going to India and added to his parents' expense; the College Council were making a practice of sending away tiresome lads for an indefinite period, and there were envenomed debates as to the legality of this.[68]

Meanwhile, after the death of Lord Buckinghamshire as the result of a riding accident on 4 February 1816, George Canning became President of the Board of Commissioners for the Affairs of India. There is no evidence that he knew Malthus, but they would have had a personal link in Wilberforce and an idealogical one in Catholic Emancipation. Malthus had complained to Ricardo on 9 February 1816 that he had almost determined to extend *Population* to three volumes, 'but I have been doing nothing at it lately, having been compelled to be thinking of drawing up something about the College'.[69] On 6 August he wrote after a holiday at Claverton: 'I have been returned now near ten days, and have been busy as usual in College matters - indeed I am drawing up a paper relating to the College, which is to be sent to Mr. Canning.'[70]

Possibly this paper was behind a Memorandum from the India Board to the Court of Directors in November 1816, 'earnestly recommending not only a liberal confidence on the part of the Court in the Principal and Professors, but also an abstinence from any minute and habitual interference in the internal management of the College'.[71]

4 The Battle for the College

The enemies of the College must have realised early in December 1816 that they had only four months in which to destroy it before Charles Grant returned to the Court of Directors. The pretext they seized upon for a full-dress debate in the Court of Proprietors was the appointment of an assistant professor in the Oriental Department. He was Lieutenant Graves Champney Haughton (1788-1849), 'of the Bengal Military Establishment, now in England upon a Sick Certificate', with a reputation (seven medals, a sword of honour, and several handsome pecuniary donations) for his proficiency in Arabic, Bengali, Hindustani, Persian and Sanskrit, although he was still under thirty.

Because this appointment involved the creation of a new post, and not the mere filling of a vacancy, it had to be approved by a Resolution of the Court of Proprietors at a meeting held on 18 December 1816. Joseph Hume and Randle Jackson opposed the motion in long, set speeches of great bitterness, on the grounds that the matter should be 'postponed altogether, until the question of the existence of the college itself were considered'. After the Chairman had intervened, however, Hume agreed that 'if the establishment were suffered to exist, a professor was necessary to be appointed', and the resolution was carried by a majority, but it had to be confirmed at the next General Court on 8 January 1817.[72]

It is not clear why Hume and Jackson wished to become the mouthpieces of the anti-college faction in the Company. Randle Jackson (1757-1837) was a successful barrister, and parliamentary counsel to the Corporation of the City of London and the Bank of England, as well as to the East India Company. He had made an able and lively speech in the Bank's General Court defending their conduct during the bullion controversy, which was printed as a pamphlet, and for which, according to Whishaw, he received 'an handsome present from the Bank'. He would also have been known to Malthus as one of the Proprietors who had originally been favourable to the establishment of the College, and who had framed the regulations to prevent the sale of Writerships in 1809.

Joseph Hume (1777-1855) had a more adventurous career than the Oxonian Jackson. His widowed mother had kept a crockery stall in the market place of Montrose, Forfarshire, and apprenticed her son to a local surgeon when he was thirteen. There followed a meteoric career in the East India Company, first as a ship's surgeon and then in the army during the Second Mahratta War (1802-5); Hume's rapidly acquired Hindustani enabled him to act as interpreter to his commanding officer, and to obtain lucrative posts in the paymaster's and prize agency offices, and also in the commissariat; he returned to England in 1808 with £40,000. Thereafter we find him very often on the same side as Malthus (he became a Whig MP in 1818) particularly in his advocacy of Catholic Emancipation and, as we have seen, in the promotion of savings banks and popular education. He was well known for 'his nature's plague of spying into abuses', and I cannot help wondering if his zeal for rooting out financial chicanery in the annual balance sheet of the East India Company might not owe its origin to his failure to get himself elected as a Director.

Be that as it may, on 18 December 1816 Hume attacked the College with surprising ignorance as well as virulence: it was the pest of the whole neighbourhood, a place where morality was regarded as a vice. Rather inconsistently, he then went on to cite the disconsolate letter of a father whose son had been expelled from this college of wickedness and was now an outcast upon society and shunned by all who knew him. According to *The Times*, Hume said 'the Eastern language was scarcely attended to, but the study of French and other languages supplied its place', which he must have known to be nonsense. It is perhaps significant that he devoted much of his speech to that cantankerous and not very learned Oriental scholar Dr

Gilchrist, who had tried to set everyone by the ears at Hertford Castle before Stewart and Hamilton arrived, and was now dissatisfied with his pension from the Company. We can see from the records that Gilchrist applied unsuccessfully for two posts at Haileybury in 1818;[73] had he perhaps wanted Haughton's job in 1816?

On general grounds, Randle Jackson was even more absurd than Hume. He referred to Lord Wellesley's famous 'Minute in Council' of 18 August 1800. In this the Marquess stressed repeatedly how completely non-mercantile in character the duties of the Company's civil servants had become: their task was 'To dispense justice to millions of people of various languages, manners, usages and religions:- to administer a vast and complicated system of revenue, throughout districts equal in extent to some of the most considerable kingdoms in Europe:- to maintain civil order in one of the most populous and litigious regions of the world.' Randle Jackson must have known this passage by heart, yet he played up to the Proprietors by saying:

> Young men provided with masters in philosophy, political economy, jurisprudence, mathematics, natural philosophy, the law of nations and other high branches of human knowledge, and stimulated to literary ambition by rewards and honours, could not be expected to descend from their exalted eminence of literary glory, and to leave the rostrum of declamation to count bales and to measure muslins. (*A laugh*) It was not proper to make the young men doctors and magistrates before they acquired a knowledge of trade, or of the Company's concerns and interests, nor could profound learning or great eloquence be required in the counting-house.

Having made this jibe, Jackson then changed his tune and alleged that in fact the students learned nothing at all: 'Several had not been able to pass the test of their examination in the Eastern languages ... they declared classical learning a great bore, they did not appreciate mathematics very highly, they therefore put on their cap and gown and marched to Hertford for society and amusement.' The caps and gowns seem to have infuriated everyone, and Jackson wondered why Oxford and Cambridge did not object, 'through the legislature, to the usurpation of these distinctions'.

A Mr Lowndes followed racily and at length. *The Times* reported his words thus: 'What could the country think of a college under the India Company where two staircases were pulled down, and the boys threatened to shoot their professors from the windows? ... They held the people of the neighbourhood in perpetual terror and bondage ... If they went out to India they would throw every thing into disorder and confusion. They were more riotous than the populace of this great city, without the same excuse from ignorance and want. Here the honourable proprietor, who had resisted a long time, was obliged to put an end to his speech, from the overpowering impatience of the Court.'

The Court adjourned for three weeks, but *The Times* did not let the matter rest. On 20 December 1816, the day after it had reported this remarkable meeting, it published a third leader on the 'variety of letters' received about the College, to the effect that 'amputation was the only cure'.[74] On Christmas Day it printed a long letter from an anonymous writer called Maro; he defended the College quite sensibly, but obviously knew nothing of its affairs, since he thought that Haughton was to replace the lately deceased Dr Henley. *The Times* took up the subject for its principal leading article, reiterating the view 'that boys of the age of the Hertford students should be placed under schoolmasters, instead of professors; and should be punished, if necessary, with the rod, instead of being either left in total impunity, or having all their hopes in life at once blasted by expulsion'. For Malthus there was a special sting in the final sentence: 'Some of the gentlemen employed there, we understood to possess high literary reputation; and all, we have no doubt, are men of talents and learning; but if eminent scholars and ingenious men are placed where they can do no good, and where their presence gives a sort of sanction to evil; then, without at all blaming the individuals, we think we have but the stronger reason for holding up the system to general reprobation.'[75]

On Thursday 26 December Harriet's brother Charles, an Oxford undergraduate, left Haileybury for London. He was given a packet to deliver to Malthus's new publisher, John Murrary (who was already negotiating terms for the fifth edition of the *Essay on Population*), with the enclosed letter:

> E. I. Coll.
> Dec. 26, 1816.
>
> Dear Sir,
>
> You would oblige me very much by putting to the press without the loss of a moment, the Manuscript respecting the East India College, which I have sent to you by my brother in law Mr. Eckersall. It is of the greatest importance that it should [*it should* crossed out] come out as soon as possible, and I wish most particularly that it should be finished, and actually published by the end of next week. Pray let me have the first proof sheet if possible by friday nights post, or two on Saturday night.
>
> I will trouble you to advertise it immediately and extensively [*and extensively* crossed out] as in the press and speedily to be published - in three or four papers at least.
>
> There is another section to be added relating to the proceedings in the Court of Proprietors, which you shall have monday or tuesday, and probably I shall be in Town next week. Let me have a line by fridays post to say how soon it can be finished.
>
> Truly yours
> T. Robt. Malthus

237

After his signature Malthus wrote, 'I am sorry for this interruption to our other business, but it [is] unluckily necessary and I hope will soon be over.'[76]

On Friday 27 December *The Times* was at it again, with an even longer article. It began with the usual arguments against treating schoolboys as if they were undergraduates, and then went on to protest against the Principal's being made a Justice of the Peace, as were the heads of houses at Oxford and Cambridge. Reading between the lines, it would seem that the writer had gone into the background of Maro's letter more thoroughly than he had had time to do before, and picked up a number of half-truths; Batten's appointment as a magistrate was linked, quite unjustifiably, with the assault on the servants in November 1815. Then came an unforgivable reference to the death of George Dallas:

> We have hitherto treated Maro with some respect, and really because we have thought his talents deserved it: he has done the best he could for a bad cause: but there is one sentence in his letter that indicates so gross a want of feeling, that we must deal out our strongest reprobation upon it. Maro says, speaking of the seminary at Hailey, 'that he positively does not see why any parents *but those of criminals* should object to the introduction of the criminal law!'
> Good God! is the man who wrote this a father? and can he tell us as such, that it is indifferent to him whether his son, at the age of 16, is admitted of a school where his offences are to be visited by the ordinary correctives of flogging and imposition, or by the rigorous sentence of the criminal law, in open court; by solitary confinement in a common gaol, for example; by the pillory, or public whipping? Proh pudor! If we are to trust to the anonymous mass of information now before us on this subject, a lamentable case has actually occurred. Was there ever a boy from Hailey went to the common gaol of Hertford for an offence committed in the precincts of the school; let out upon bail, presented to the grand jury of the county, had his bill ignoramused, and *is that boy now no more?*
> As to the abolition of the establishment, we are aware that it cannot be puffed away by a breath of wind; but that which has made may with equal ease unmake it, on the now undeniable conviction of its worse than inutility.[77]

Here the article concluded.

In *The Times* for Saturday 28 December there was an anonymous letter of almost a column with a mixed bag of accusations against the College, deploring the waste of public money, 'for such it must be considered, as long as the public shall continue to uphold the pecuniary engagements of the Company', and leaving no doubt as to the writer's belief in the educational merits of 'a sound flogging'.[78] So the acrimonious controversy went on, almost daily, repetitiously, while forces were mustered for the General Court's next debate on 8 January.

Murray had played his part. Malthus received on Saturday the proof sheets of the manuscript sent to London on Thursday. The rest of the pamphlet was sent to Albermarle Street by 'monday nights post' - 30 December - and it was on sale on Saturday 4 January 1817. It was fairly summarised in the *Morning Chronicle* of Monday 6 January, the Editor affirming that the debate had 'produced much discussion in one of the daily prints', but that he was concerned that the public should see both sides of the case.[79] *The Times* was vitriolic to the point of absurdity.

The pamphlet, of 105 pages, was called *Statements respecting the East India College, with an appeal to facts in refutation of the charges lately brought against it in the Court of Proprietors*. A great deal of it was the same as that of 1813, including the detailed account of the conduct of an ordinary written examination, which Jeffrey thought of sufficient interest and importance to quote verbatim in the *Edinburgh Review*, in a twenty-page article. Much of Malthus's second pamphlet must have been written at odd times after the renewal of the Charter, and only the final section (VII) concerns 'the charges brought in the Court of Proprietors on 18 December' - which section, naturally, was the most vehement and the most quoted.

In the penultimate section, on Disturbances, Malthus wrote, 'It is generally allowed that the age from fifteen or sixteen to eighteen is the hardest to govern'; he then went on to discuss the peculiar difficulties of the College in this respect - many of the lads not wanting to go to India, and above all the 'spirit of direct hostility in a considerable body of the Directors and Proprietors'.[80] He stated his own position in a way that sounds conceited if the paragraph is read without knowledge of the personal attacks made on him in both *The Times* and the General Court:

> I certainly would have no connexion with an institution which could *justly* be considered as the disgrace of England; but I should think it a pusillanimous desertion of a good cause if I were to allow myself to be driven away by a clamour which I know to be founded either in interest and prejudice, or in utter ignorance of what the college really is.

Malthus went on to answer Joseph Hume about

> the ebullitions of disappointed fathers who, however justly they may be pitied, are the very last persons who should be heard as authorities, particularly as it is known that there have been persons of this description who, after having vainly attempted by misrepresentations and menaces to intimidate the college authorities, have most imprudently and rashly, as well as wickedly, vowed to pursue them with the most determined hatred and hostility.

239

He did not mince his words over the case 'about which Mr. Hume seems to have made so silly a parade', of the expelled boy who had become a social outcast: 'Let it be seen, by *an appeal to facts*, whether he was not much more likely to corrupt others than be corrupted himself.'[81]

As regards the country gentlemen of Hertfordshire, 'I feel much indebted to them for the uniform personal kindness and attention they have shewn me', but 'with one or two splendid exceptions, they have been from the very first enemies of the college'. Malthus sympathised with them: 'I can most readily enter into their feelings, in not liking an establishment of eighty young men, from sixteen to twenty, in their immediate neighbourhood. Had I the choice of settling in a country residence, I should certainly avoid the vicinity of Oxford or Cambridge, Eton or Harrow.'[82]

What he could not forgive the country gentlemen for was their inspiring *The Times* to protest at the Principal's 'being made a justice of the peace without a foot of land in the county'. With his friends' advice behind him, Malthus could say categorically that 'Dr. Batten, as a clergyman having a considerable benefice in Lincolnshire, is as legally qualified to become a justice of the peace as any magistrate on the bench.' It is in this context that he slashed at *The Times* of 27 December, in a way which shows how far he and Horner were in advance of many of their contemporaries:

> I could not have conceived it possible that any English writer, with the slightest pretension to character, would have dared to avow that a lad of seventeen or eighteen, who offends against the criminal laws of his country, is not amenable to those laws because he happens to be a gentleman's son, and to be resident at some school or college . . .

and is therefore to be let off with a private flogging instead of public whipping, pillory, or imprisonment.[83]

As far as the rod was concerned, 'One would really think that the people who talk about the wonderful effects of corporal correction had not only never been at a great school themselves, but had never seen a man who had been at one.' More seriously Malthus wrote:

> Those who go out to India must and will be men the moment they reach the country, at whatever age they may be; and there they will be immediately exposed to temptations of no common magnitude and danger. To prepare them for this ordeal, Mr. Jackson and the silly writers in the *Times* recommend their being whipped till the last hour of their getting into their ships. I own it appears to me that the object is more likely to be attained by a gradual initiation into a greater degree of liberty, and a greater habit of depending upon themselves, than is usual at schools, carried on for two or three years previously, in some safer place than Calcutta.[84]

PLATE 1

(*a*) Claverton Manor and Church, 'from the south,' in 1790,
by Samuel Hieronymous Grimm

(*b*) Okewood Chapel in 1849, by Thomas Allom

PLATE 2

'The Revd T. R. Malthus, M.A., F.R.S.
Professor of History & Political Economy at the East India College
and Author of an Essay on the principle of Population, &c. &c.'

PLATE 3

Harriet Malthus, painted by John Linnell in 1833

PLATE 4

(*a*) Edward Daniel
Clarke, painted in 1804
by John Opie

(*b*) William Smyth,
Professor of Modern
History at Cambridge,
in 1830

(*c*) William Otter, as seen
by Linnell in 1840

PLATE 5

(*a*) Charles Grant, by an unknown artist

(*b*) David Ricardo, from the portrait by Thomas Phillips

(*c*) John Murray, by H. W. Pickersgill

PLATE 6

(*a*) The East India College, Terrace Front, by T. Picken

(*b*) The East India House in 1817, by Thomas Hosmer Shepherd

PLATE 7

(*a*) Menial servants: *The Squire's Kitchen,*
by Thomas Rowlandson

(*b*) A skilled craftsman: Rowlandson's *Country Cobbler*

PLATE 8

(*a*) Francis Horner,
as seen by Raeburn in 1812

(*b*) Francis Jeffrey,
by Colvin Smith

(*c*) William Empson,
from Linnell's portrait

(*d*) William Bray at ninety-six,
by John Linnell

At the end of the pamphlet Malthus referred again to the difficulties of the College Council, with the students knowing perfectly well 'from the avowed wish of many of the proprietors of East-India stock to destroy the college, that a rebellion would be agreeable to them':

> For my own part, I am only astonished that the college has been able to get on at all, under these overwhelming obstacles; and that it has got on, and done great good too, (which I boldly assert it has), is no common proof of its internal vigour, and its capacity to answer its object.[85]

Malthus could hardly have foreseen the consequences of this battle as he sat in the General Court Room, near Charles Grant's son Robert, on 8 January. Naturally quotations from his pamphlet were frequent, but the arguments went over the same old ground, still nominally concerned with the appointment of the Assistant Oriental Professor; Randle Jackson combined this with the suggestion that if parents should be allowed to educate future civilians where they wished, the military seminary (there was no question of freedom of choice here) might well be removed from Addiscombe to the more commodious and spacious building at Haileybury.[86]

In the event, Haughton's appointment was confirmed, and Jackson's suggestion became a formal motion to be discussed at four special meetings of the Court of Proprietors, on 6, 20, and 25 February and 4 March. Malthus told Ricardo that he was unable to leave the College on 6 February - term had started - but he would have read in the papers an abstract of Randle Jackson's speech, which lasted nearly three hours. According to the *Morning Chronicle*, 'the Worthy Gentleman at some length attacked some opinions of Mr. Malthus, shewing their futility',[87] while *The Times* went into more detail. Only one new point was raised: Jackson doubted whether an appeal to the Bishop of London over an expulsion could be effective, since he would naturally support 'his brother clergymen' on the College Council.[88]

Ricardo was at the Court of 20 February, and wrote that he fully expected to see Malthus there, 'as I thought the subject of debate at the India House was of too much interest not to make you desirous of hearing it'.[89] Malthus in fact wrote to Murray, 'I had some thoughts of being in Town for the debate at the India House today but was prevented. I hope it will go off well, and that I shall not be further interrupted by business relating to the College.'[90]

Robert Grant's speech on behalf of the College, according to *The Times*,[91] lasted over three hours, and according to Ricardo 'left nothing unsaid which might assist the cause which he so ably defended'. Byron's friend Douglas Kinnaird also 'spoke at great length' according to the *Morning Chronicle*, and was, as might be expected, amusing about Haileybury's collegiate pretensions: 'There were quadrangles, and chapels, and plots of grass not to be walked across.' Ricardo wrote to Malthus:

Mr. Kinnaird began by speaking in the most respectful manner of you, and indeed in terms of great eulogy - but afterwards I think absurdly dwelt on your being an interested party, and an advocate for the college ... In what manner could we have any correct account of the college and its concerns but from an interested party? Who could speak of its management, attainments and discipline but those who were acquainted with it? ... His main argument was built on the general principle that a supply of intellectual attainments will as surely follow an effectual demand for it, as the supply of any material commodity will follow effectual demand.

Ricardo had a few minutes' conversation with Kinnaird after the debate, and Kinnaird 'finished by assuring me that my friend had a bad cause - that it could not be defended and must fall'.

Neither Malthus nor Ricardo appear to have attended the Court on 25 February, when Joseph Hume made 'a very long speech', in which 'he deprecated the insubordinate language to the Directors by Mr. professor Malthus, who was paid by the Company, and ought to have conducted himself with more decorum to his employers'. This debate was chiefly notable for a phrase of the eloquent (but sometimes long-winded) Mr Lowndes. The College had been described on various occasions as the child of Charles Grant, and Lowndes, after complimenting 'the ex-Director Mr. Grant' on his son's speech at the previous meeting, declared that 'while he admired the real child, he must insist that the adopted one was a ricketty, squint-eyed, stupid brat', which 'kind of eccentric humour' much pleased his audience, and was applied frequently to Haileybury thereafter.[92]

Ricardo was at the decisive General Court on 4 March, when Jackson's motion was lost on a show of hands, 40-62.[93] Jackson possibly sensed the opinion of the meeting before the vote was taken, for Ricardo wrote to Malthus that he 'said every thing of you that your most partial friends could wish'.[94]

Two serious comments on Malthus's position are worth noting. His plan for a new system of recruiting civilians (characteristically tucked into a footnote in the pamphlet) was criticised by Jacob Bosanquet, a Director who supported the College and sympathised with the professors' difficulties. Malthus had written:

Little other change is wanting than that an appointment should be considered, in spirit and in truth, not in mere words, as a prize to be contended for, not a property already possessed, which may be lost. If the Directors were to appoint one-fifth every year, beyond the number finally to go out, and the four-fifths were to be the best of the whole body, the appointments would then really be prizes to be contended for, and the effects would be admirable.[95]

According to *The Times* Jacob Bosanquet had said that with all his respect for Malthus as a 'distinguished writer and scholar, he could not approve of his plan of adding six more students for the purpose of plucking an equal number, in order to excite competition. The tendency of such a regulation must be, among other evils, to transfer the civil patronage of the company to the professors of the college.'

In the circumstances of the time, Malthus's proposal would hardly have been fair, as the Haileybury course was not suitable for any other employment; but Bosanquet's reaction is interesting in that it shows how remote from the feelings of the period was any scheme which involved open competition and impartial examiners.

The second comment touched Malthus more nearly, and he dealt with it earnestly in a letter to Ricardo dated 7 March 1817. Another Director, William Elphinstone, had been reported thus in *The Times* of 5 March:

> He believed the college was capable of being easily improved, and
> that the direct means of accomplishing this end, was a due discharge
> of their duty by the professors. (Hear, hear). With a great respect for
> their character and acquirements, and with nothing to complain of in
> their conduct in the lecture-room, he must declare his opinion, that
> some attention to the students was incumbent on them at other
> times, and in other places. (hear, hear, hear). He believed that they
> had been wanting in facility of intercourse, and general kindness of
> demeanour: that they had carried themselves too high, and with too
> much disposition to treat their pupils as boys rather than as men. Mr.
> Malthus, he was aware, had described this sort of treatment as
> wrong; but he would ask, had he never practised it? (Hear, hear).

As Malthus wrote, this charge 'does not admit of an appeal to facts, but is nevertheless essentially unfounded'.[96] Years later he was supported in this assertion by the reminiscences of a student who was at Haileybury during the years 1816 and 1817, Brian Houghton Hodgson; he was born in 1800 and died in 1894, and as an old man he told the story of his life to a younger friend, William Wilson Hunter, who published it in 1896.

Hodgson's father was an 'easy-going country gentleman' who ruined himself through trying to add to his fortune by banking; his mother was a life-long correspondent of William Smyth.[97] It was Smyth who obtained an East India nomination for the boy, and then took him to Haileybury and 'settled him as a guest in the house of Malthus ... until he should pass his entrance examination'. This would have taken but a few days, yet 'the foundation of an intimacy was thus laid which for the first time turned the young student into a thinker'. Hodgson remembered Malthus at work on the fifth edition of *Population* (he thought it was the seventh) 'and full of the ideas to be embodied in his crowning work on Political Economy published in 1820', as well as the pamphlet in defence of the College. In young Brian's opinion, Malthus was 'both the favourite and the hero' of his fellow-students.[98]

According to Hunter:

> In the hands of Malthus political economy became a living science, dealing with the actual facts and needs of humanity, and quickening young minds with ideas instead of cramming them with formulae.
>
> Malthus was, in fact, the dominant influence in Hodgson's intellectual horoscope. He found him a young aristocrat in social feelings and sympathies; he left him an advanced liberal in politics. But for the inspiration of Malthus, the youthful civilian would scarcely have embarked on a comprehensive study of the institutions and constitutional problems of Nepal, or struck into the great conflict over popular education in India with a scheme of his own . . .
>
> The love of liberty and the generous respect for the liberties of others, with a belief in their capacity for exercising those liberties aright, which Malthus impressed on Hodgson's awakening mind, resisted the effacing influences of time and of a bureaucratic career.[99]

Allowance must be made for the roseate spectacles of a very old gentleman recalling his late teens; but I do not think Sir William Wilson Hunter would have published this tribute to Malthus, at a time when it would have been of no fashionable interest, had not Hodgson in his reminiscences repeatedly expressed his admiration for him

One should not pay too much attention to the response of an exceptional pupil, yet it is possible that Malthus's influence on the East India College - and all that stemmed from it - was far greater than has hitherto been suspected. There is naturally no correspondence with his colleagues, since they all saw each other almost every day, and therefore no evidence of his part in the deliberations of the College Council, except for one important sentence which occurs almost by chance in the 1817 pamphlet: 'I believe even that I was the first that proposed the present test in the Oriental languages, as the absolute condition of a final appointment to India.'[100] In this context it is perhaps permissible to quote from a letter written by the bluestocking Lucy Aikin shortly after Malthus's death:

> For the honour of the Whig ministry one may wish they had conferred some mark of esteem on such a man as Mr. Malthus; but what could it have added to him? He possessed a competence, and there was so much of the true philosopher about him that I should have grieved to see him a clerical sinecurist, instead of the useful and respected head of a college.[101]

Miss Aikin was not ignorant of public affairs, and her mistake is revealing.

CHAPTER VIII

Literary Misfortunes (1812–15)

1 Notes on Adam Smith

It is an exercise in empathy to appreciate the quasi-biblical character of the *Wealth of Nations* during Malthus's life-time. Cadell and Davies, after Playfair's edition of 1805, about which they consulted Malthus, had brought out another *Wealth of Nations* in 1812, without notes; it was in three volumes, contained a brief anonymous life of Smith, and 'A Short View of the Doctrine of Adam Smith as compared with that of the French Economists by Germain Garnier'. Malthus had bought a copy of Garnier's annotated French translation of the *Wealth of Nations* when he was in Paris in 1802. Cadell and Davies had also published, in 1810, 'the compleat edition' of all Smith's works (now almost forgotten) with a biography by Dugald Stewart.

Malthus's desire to produce an up-to-date edition of the *Wealth of Nations* with notes of his own must have been intensified by lecturing on it week after week at the College, as well as by its lucrative possibilities, but he seems to have set about arrangements for its publication with his usual lack of practical acumen. The following letter from him to Messrs Cadell and Davies is dated from the East India College, on 28 August 1812:

> Gentlemen,
>   I am sorry you did not think it worth while to notice the communication which I made to you through Mr. Whishaw before. As a matter of civility and attention on account of our former intercourse on the subject of a new edition of the Wealth of Nations, but by no means as a matter of obligation on my part, I made known to you the proposal which I had received from Edinburgh; but not receiving any kind of proposition from you in consequence, and having waited ten days after I had seen Mr. Whishaw subsequent to his calling upon you, I naturally considered your silence as an indication of your indifference towards the subject of my communication, and wrote the other day to a friend at Edinburgh to talk further to the gentleman who had made me the proposal,

respecting the plan of the edition, the time in which it might be accomplished, and the terms, preparatory to my entering into a definitive agreement with him. Under these circumstances, it may not be very easy for me now to indulge any preference which I should naturally have felt for your House.

I was I own not a little surprised at the intimation in your letter of my having given you reason to expect, that as soon as I could find leisure I should hold myself bound to execute the undertaking in question on the terms originally talked of. On what grounds you could form these expectations I cannot readily conjecture. When before any specific agreement had been concluded between us, I found myself in a situation which prevented me from accomplishing what I had intended, in any definite time, I naturally and very properly in my opinion declined the undertaking. I had refused to enter into any regular agreement precisely because, not being certain respecting my future situation, I could not be certain either of my time or my inclinations for such a task. And if you recollect, when you endeavoured to remove my objection with regard to time, by saying that if I would enter into an agreement with you I should be allowed to accomplish it entirely at my leisure, I distinctly and positively refused. I have ever since of course considered both myself and you as entirely freed from any kind of engagement to each other, either express or implied; so much so that on the return of some leisure when I began to balance whether I should resume my former plan, or publish a volume of original essays, it certainly never occurred to me that I was not entirely free to chuse which I liked. I had in consequence rather inclined most to the original essays, and I have no hesitation in saying that it was the handsome offer of the Edinburgh bookseller, with an apparent readiness even to give time, if it was required, that decided me in favour of a new edition of Adam Smith, thinking that I could put the substance of the essays that I had projected in an additional volume of notes and dissertations. I am sorry that the new edition should be brought forward by strangers, but cannot consider myself in any degree to blame. I do not at all know whether anything in the shape of partnership might be proposed; but at all events the intimations in your letter which I consider as improper and unfounded must not be renewed, or I must beg to decline all further correspondence on the subject.

> I am Gentlemen
> Your obed[t] humble Servant
> T. R. Malthus[1]

There is here much that cannot be explained without further documents coming to light; it would indeed be interesting to know how Whishaw in London and Jeffrey in Edinburgh regarded each other's activity on behalf of their dearly loved but unbusinesslike friend. Cadell and Davies obviously did all they could to make peace, for less than a week later Malthus was writing to them again, on 3 September 1812:

Gentlemen,

I most decidedly wished to give you the preference in any engagement I might form for notes to Adam Smith, both on account of your being the original publishers of the work, and on account of what formerly passed between us on the subject; and I did in consequence postpone giving an answer to the proposal made to me for six weeks. I called at your house in my way through Town from the neighbourhood of Bath to talk to you about it, and not finding you at home, left the commission with Mr. Whishaw. Unfortunately he had not an opportunity of seeing you for some little time, and the impression which he received when he did see you was that you were not very anxious on the subject. Under these circumstances I really thought I had done all that could be expected from me when I had waited the time I mentioned. But I am now sorry that I wrote so soon; and would do what I could with propriety to continue the work in your hands.

I have no objection to state to you exactly the proposal which I made to the gentleman at Edinburgh, through my friend Mr. Jeffrey. It was to accept the offer of 1500£ with the addition of an interest in the subsequent editions, or without such interest £2000.

The amount of the interest in the subsequent editions I left to be the subject of a proposal from the bookseller, as the agreement was not to be settled definitely by Mr. Jeffrey. The work was to consist of foot notes where only short remarks were required, [with] an additional volume of longer notes and dissertations, - to be finished in about two years.

Should you wish to engage with me upon these terms, I shall be happy to do anything towards it which I can do with propriety but you will readily see the difficulty in which I am placed. I have not yet heard the result of Mr. Jeffrey's communication of my proposals, but should any thing occur which will allow me the liberty of giving you the preference which I wish, I shall be very happy to do it. Would it answer to you to share the publication?

> I am, Gentlemen,
> Your obed' humble Servant
> T. Rob' Malthus[2]

These suggestions came too late, for by the time Jeffrey approached 'the

gentleman at Edinburgh' negotiations were already completed for the publication of David Buchanan's four-volume edition of the *Wealth of Nations*,
which appeared in November 1814. This was published jointly by Oliphant,
Waugh and Innes in Edinburgh and John Murray in London. The introduction to the fourth volume (which consisted solely of original writing by
Buchanan) was dated 14 September 1814, yet as late as 23 May of the same
year Davies wrote to Murray:

> Mr. Cadell, as well as myself, is fully sensible of your handsome and
> very friendly conduct towards us, relative to Buchanan's Edition of
> Adam Smith's Wealth of Nations; and we beg that you will put us
> and our interests out of the question, when forming your
> determination on the subject of that publication.[3]

Buchanan's forthcoming work had been announced a year in advance, and
on 10 November 1813 Malthus was writing to Horner:

> I have lately seen the advertisement of the new Edition of Adam
> Smith. It is to be sure precisely upon the same plan as that which I
> had projected, and if it is done tolerably well the author must
> anticipate me in some points. Under these circumstances I am not
> sure whether it may not be necessary for me to change my plan and
> to publish only a volume of essays instead of a new edition of Smith.
> I suppose I had better however wait to see what sort of work it is,
> before I finally make my determination. The circumstance on the
> whole is rather unfortunate.[4]

Malthus's highly topical pamphlet, *Observations on the Effects of the Corn
Laws*, which was published in the spring of 1814, seems to have been
regarded by his friends as a side-line.

On 24 November 1814 James Mill wrote to Ricardo, 'What is Mr.
Malthus doing with his notes on Adam Smith? I see Buchanan's book is
out', which suggests that Malthus's edition of the *Wealth of Nations* had
been discussed as a *magnum opus* in active preparation. Ricardo wrote to
Malthus on 13 January 1815, when the latter was working on *Rent* and the
second Corn Law pamphlet: 'I hope your notes on Adam Smith are in great
forwardness, and that they will soon follow the smaller publications which
you are now preparing.' Yet nearly three months before, on 28 October
1814, Whishaw had written to Horner from Lincoln's Inn: 'Malthus is very
well, and was here a few days ago. He seems to have relinquished his plan
of editing Adam Smith (in consequence of being forestalled by Buchanan);
and seems disposed to publish a volume or two of essays on distinct branches
of political economy.'[5]

There are two ways of interpreting this confusion, and possibly there is
truth in both of them; first, that Malthus did not quite know his own mind,
and second, that his friendship with Ricardo was of a unique character, quite

unlike his friendships with other people. There is no question here of more or less: any analysis of the complicated relationships of a lively mind must be qualitative rather than quantitative, since the many facets of each individual will strike different sparks of affinity or stimulus from the equally multitudinous facets of those around him. I do not doubt that Malthus was sincere when he said that he loved Ricardo more than anyone else outside his own family; on Ricardo's part, Malthus was one of only three people outside his family who benefited under his will. But theirs was the tie of a passionate and specialised intellectual curiosity, rather than the daily organisation of even their public lives, much though they had publicly in common. Thus Malthus would tell Whishaw of his plans, and receive some practical help, but would perhaps not want to waste time on them with Ricardo. It is noteworthy that Malthus and Ricardo addressed each other for seven years as 'My dear Sir', and that Malthus used only one exclamation mark at a time when writing to Ricardo about Napoleon's escape, whereas to his 'Dear Brougham' he dashed them off in batches of three.

I can find no evidence that Malthus ever met Buchanan, but he referred to the work which had ruined his own project as 'a very respectable edition of the *Wealth of Nations*',[6] even though he disagreed with some of Buchanan's views. David Buchanan (1779-1848) was a journalist rather than an economist - he edited the *Caledonian Mercury* and the *Edinburgh Courant* - and possibly for this reason gives useful insight into popular Whig views at the time when Malthus entered the Corn Law debate. Buchanan admired Malthus: 'Since the publication of Dr. Smith's work, Mr. Malthus is the only Author who can be said to have extended the boundaries of political science.'[7]

2 The First Corn Law Pamphlet

We have noted before that the common people of England, at this period, were regarded as living almost on bread alone; 'the price of corn' was virtually synonymous with 'the price of food' or 'the cost of living' in popular argument. According to Adam Smith, 'Countries are populous, not in proportion to the number of people whom their produce can cloath and lodge, but in proportion to that of those whom it can feed. When food is provided, it is easy to find the necessary cloathing and lodging.'[8] It seems extraordinary to us now that this latter sentence passed without editorial comment.

We have seen how Malthus took issue with Adam Smith in the 1798 version of the *Essay on Population*, maintaining that not every increase of the wealth of a nation was necessarily of benefit to the labouring poor. 'Silks, laces, trinkets and expensive furniture', wrote the young Malthus, 'are undoubtedly a part of the revenue of society; but . . . an increase in this part of the revenue of a state cannot . . . be considered of the same importance as an increase of food, which forms the principal revenue of the great mass of the people.'[9]

Therefore it did not appear inappropriate to Malthus, or to any of his readers in his unspecialised age, that four chapters of Book III of the quarto on *Population* should be entitled thus:

Chapter VII   Of Increasing Wealth as it affects the Condition of the Poor.

Chapter VIII   Of the Definitions of Wealth. Agricultural and Commercial Systems.

Chapter IX   Different Effects of the Agricultural and Commercial Systems.

Chapter X   Of Bounties on the exportation of Corn.

Malthus re-wrote a number of pages in 1806, and altered a few paragraphs in 1807, but these chapters remained substantially the same until the great revision of 1817. There was no need in the quarto to have a chapter about duties on the importation of foreign corn, because since 1773 the price had to all intents and purposes been well above that at which imports were restricted.

Malthus's concern for agricultural production, his native caution, one might say his anxiety, is apparent as early as 1803. He advocated bounties (what would now be called a subsidy) on the export of grain, so that farmers should not be discouraged by low selling prices at home in years of plenty, and would be able profitably to keep enough land under tillage to provide food for the whole country in years of war or bad harvest. As Malthus wrote in 1803, 'We have now stepped out of the agricultural system, into a state in which the commercial system clearly predominates'; the commercial part of British society - manufacturers and traders - had increased 'beyond the surplus produce of its cultivators', which meant that England, which used to export grain, would now become a corn-importing nation.

In a passage which his forebears, the royal apothecaries, might have deplored, Malthus argued that the imbalance between urban and rural production would not have occurred had things been left to take their natural course:

> but the high profits of commerce from monopolies, and other
> peculiar encouragements, have altered this natural course of things,
> and the body politick is in an artificial, and in some degree diseased
> state, with one of its principal members out of proportion to the rest.
> Almost all medicine is in itself bad; and one of the great evils of

illness is the necessity of taking it. No person can well be more averse to medicine in the animal economy, or a system of expedients in political economy, than myself; but in the present state of the country something of the kind may be necessary to prevent greater evils. It is a matter of very little comparative importance, whether we are fully supplied with broadcloth, linens, and muslins, or even with tea, sugar, and coffee; and no rational politician therefore would think of proposing a bounty upon such commodities. But it is certainly a matter of the very highest importance, whether we are fully supplied with food; and if a bounty would produce such a supply, the most liberal political economist might be justified in proposing it; considering food as a commodity distinct from all others, and pre-eminently valuable.[10]

In 1806 Malthus felt it necessary to add to this a passage professing his general adherence to the theoretical ideals of free trade and perfect competition:

In discussing the policy of a bounty on the exportation of corn, it should be premised, that the private interests of the farmers and proprietors [of land] should never enter in the question. The sole object of our consideration ought to be the permanent interest of the consumer, in the character of which is comprehended the whole nation.

According to the general principles of political economy, it cannot be doubted that it is for the interest of the civilised world that each nation should purchase its commodities wherever they can be had the cheapest.

According to these principles, it is rather desirable that some obstacles should exist to the excessive accumulation of wealth in any particular country, and that rich nations should be tempted to purchase their corn of poorer nations, as by these means the wealth of the civilised world will not only be more rapidly increased, but more equally diffused.

It is evident, however, that local interests and political relations may modify the application of these general principles; and in a country with a territory fit for the production of corn, an independent, and at the same time a more equable supply of this necessary of life, may be an object of such importance as to warrant a deviation from them.

It is undoubtedly true that everything will ultimately find its level, but this level is sometimes effected in a very harsh manner. England may export corn a hundred years hence without the assistance of a bounty; but this is much more likely to happen from the destruction of her manufactures, than from the increase of her agriculture; and a

251

policy which, in so important a point, may tend to soften the harsh corrections of general laws, seems to be justifiable.[11]

As we have seen, the main preoccupation of political economists after the publication of the 1807 edition of *Population* was not so much the import of corn as the export of bullion; it was over this question that Malthus and Ricardo first met, and with it the earlier letters of their correspondence are concerned. By the summer of 1813 the emphasis is shifting to what we can, with hindsight, recognise as the beginning of Ricardo's theory of profit, which was linked with the Malthusian doctrine of population always rising to 'meet' subsistence, and the supposed inevitability of diminishing returns from the application of capital to land. There is no direct reference in the Ricardo letters to the first appearance of Malthus's first pamphlet on the Corn Laws, possibly because the two men were seeing each other frequently, but possibly also because this was what Empson called one of Malthus's 'stormy petrel' productions – when he flew head-on into a public controversy – as distinct from the 'scientific' discussions in which he thought aloud *tête-à-tête* with Ricardo.

Earlier contentions and riots about the Corn Laws have been eclipsed by those which raged during the 'hungry forties', after Malthus was dead, so it is important to remember that the debate which he entered in the spring of 1814 had begun in the time of Richard II, who reigned from 1377 to 1399. The controversy in more or less its modern form dates from the reign of William and Mary (1689-1702) and perhaps gave rise to a larger and more heterogeneous pamphlet literature than any other single issue. There had been an outburst in 1804, when an attempt was made to ensure supplies and stabilise prices through a sliding scale of duties on imported corn, the duty becoming progressively less as the home price increased. It was the public discussion which this subject had 'lately received', and its 'present importance', which made Malthus insert the new paragraphs in the 1806 edition of *Population* which I have already quoted.

It is as well to recall the capriciousness of even a temperate climate. The British Isles do not often suffer from drought, but excessively cold or wet weather at unpropitious times can lead to bad harvests which, in the past, meant semi-starvation. So great was the fear of scarcity and of profiteering that there were even restrictions on what was called 'the internal corn trade', the movement of grain from one district to another; these restrictions were not formally removed by Act of Parliament until 1772, when Malthus was six years old.

By the time David Buchanan published his edition of the *Wealth of Nations* there was, of course, a strong body of Whig opinion against any restriction or regulation of economic activities; he wrote in his notes on Adam Smith's chapter 'On the Restraints on Particular Imports': 'It would surely be both extremely unjust and impolitic to stop the importation of corn, and thus to distress the community at large, in order to increase the profits either of the farmers or proprietors of land. An attempt of this sort, made during the year 1813, was abandoned in consequence of the general and formidable opposition which its obvious injustice provoked.'[12] This 'attempt' was a proposal for a prohibitive duty on the importation of wheat until the average home price reached 105 shillings a quarter (£5.25 for 28 lb, roughly 12½ kilos).

The government then reduced the price at which importation would be allowed to 80 shillings a quarter. According to Lord Holland it was Lord Lauderdale (nominally a Whig) who had been the secret instigator of this bill, and Lord Grey's real opinion leant towards any measure that kept up the price of corn and prevented any sudden reduction of rents: 'Lord Grenville and Mr. Horner were decidedly friends to a free trade; and the authority and sound philosophy of such men, coinciding with the natural prejudices of the populace and the mischievous clamour of some seditious writers, constituted a formidable opposition to a very questionable, as well as unpopular, policy.'[13]

Lord Lauderdale explained his position in a *Letter on the Corn Laws* which preceded Malthus's pamphlet by a few weeks. He listed all the usual protectionist arguments, including the high rate of taxation in Britain which enabled the Foreign Adventurer to undersell the Home Trader, referred to the decline of the Roman Empire as soon as the Romans imported grain and neglected their own tillage, and quoted Adam Smith. Lord Lauderdale's most interesting point for modern readers is in connection with agriculture suffering from lack of investment, since 'every other branch of industry' made higher profits because they had been given 'the exclusive possession of the Home Market':

> You have only to look into the Agricultural Reports, or to go to any Parish in the Kingdom, to learn from the one, and to hear in the other, that nothing is wanting but additional Capital to ensure the improvement, and increase of produce, of almost every part of the Country; whilst no one ever heard of an order for Cotton Goods, or for any of our Manufactures, however extensive, suffering even delay from a similar cause.[14]

Malthus's first Corn Law pamphlet, published by Johnson's successors in the spring of 1814, was called *Observations on the Effects of the Corn Laws, and of a Rise or Fall in the Price of Corn on the Agriculture and General Wealth of the Country*. It consisted of forty-four octavo pages, and went into a second edition almost immediately, with minor alterations bringing it up to forty-seven pages. Its popularity was partly due to the fact that the author did not come down on either side of the fence, but stated explicitly that it was not his intention to express his own views. In his second pamphlet, which appeared about 10 February 1815, Malthus wrote of the first: 'Some of my friends were of different opinions as to the side towards which my arguments most inclined. This I consider as a tolerably fair proof of impartiality.'

The arguments are indeed fairly balanced. National security is even more important than wealth, but 'If Holland, Venice, and Hamburgh had declined a dependence upon foreign countries for their support, they would always have remained perfectly inconsiderable states, and never could have risen to that pitch of wealth, power and population which distinguished the meridian of their career.'[15] On the other hand, 'Wealth, population and power are, after all, only valuable as they tend to improve, increase and secure the mass of human virtue and happiness.' Malthus is worth quoting at length here, at his contradictory best, compassionate, forward-looking, and – for his period – extremely democratic:

> It may be said that an *excessive* proportion of manufacturing
> population does not seem favourable to national quiet and happiness.
> Independently of any difficulties respecting the import of corn,
> variations in the channels of manufacturing industry, and in the
> facilities of obtaining a vent for its produce, are perpetually
> recurring. Not only during the last four or five years, but during the
> whole course of the war, have the wages of manufacturing labour
> been subject to great fluctuations . . . and even during a peace they
> must always remain subject to the fluctuations which arise from the
> caprices of taste and fashion, and the competition of other countries.
> These fluctuations naturally tend to generate discontent and tumult,
> and the evils which accompany them; and if to this we add that the
> situation and employment of a manufacturer and his family are, even
> in their best state, unfavourable to health and virtue, it cannot appear
> desirable that a very large proportion of the whole society should
> consist of manufacturing labourers . . .
>
> Yet though the condition of the individual employed in common
> manufacturing labour is not by any means desirable, most of the
> effects of manufactures and commerce on the general state of society
> are, in the highest degree, beneficial. They infuse fresh life and
> activity into all classes of the state, afford opportunities for the
> inferior orders to rise by personal merit and exertion, and stimulate
> the higher orders to depend for distinction upon other grounds than
> mere rank and riches. They excite invention, encourage science and
> the useful arts, spread intelligence and spirit, inspire a taste for
> conveniences and comforts among the labouring classes; and, above
> all, give a new and happier structure to society, by increasing the
> proportion of the middle classes, that body on which the liberty,
> public spirit and good government of every country must mainly
> depend.[16]

Some Tory squires must surely have snorted over this, and exclaimed that it was what might be expected from a servant of the East India Company who associated with Jews and Dissenters. We can hark back to 1796 and Malthus's unpublished tract *The Crisis*; then, according to Empson, 'the allies whom he looked to in the patriotic cause were to come from the camp of penitent country gentlemen.'

But as far as the general welfare of the inferior orders was concerned, the relationship between the price of corn and the wages of labour was the crux of the matter. It is an over-simplification to assert that the landlords and farmers wanted a high price for their wheat, while the poor wanted cheap bread, and the manufacturers sided with the poor because cheap bread meant low wages, and therefore competitive prices for their artefacts in the world's markets; yet there was a widespread belief that wages rose when the price of corn was high and fell when it was low, based partly on the tendency for general prosperity to be marked by a certain amount of inflation, and partly on the truism that wages could not fall below the rate needed to keep alive such workers as were 'in demand'.

We should note in this connection that, long before the Speenhamland magistrates deliberately tried to adjust a labourer's income according to the price of bread, the county justices (like old Mr Godschall) had been empowered in 1563, by the Statute of Artificers, annually to fix wage rates for every kind of workman; they were supposed to vary them in accordance with the general level of prices, in order to allay pauperism and discontent. It could not be done without further inflation, as Malthus had pointed out in his pamphlet of 1800 on *The High Price of Provisions*, but Buchanan repeated the argument in 1814, in the treatise which he wrote as a supplement to his edition of the *Wealth of Nations*. According to Buchanan:

> It is an opinion indeed adopted by Dr. Smith, and most other writers, that the money price of labour is regulated by the money price of provisions, and that when provisions rise in price, wages rise in proportion. But . . . it is to be observed that the high price of provisions is a certain indication of a deficient supply, and arises in the natural course of things for the purpose of retarding the consumption.
>   . . . The English poor laws have been justly found fault with, for giving money to the labourer in proportion to the price of corn. But do we not charge nature with a similar error, when we maintain that wages keep pace with the price of provisions; that when the price of provisions rises to curtail the consumption of the labourer, wages rise for the opposite purpose of still leaving him the same abundant supply?[17]

As we smile at Buchanan's reference to nature, we might reflect that we are far from hearing the last of the doctrine that wages must be related to the 'cost of living', regardless of the state of the economy of either a single country or the world as a whole.

Malthus was not thinking in terms of what would later be called productivity or growth rates; for him wages were fixed by the 'demand' for labour as compared with the supply; if there was 'too much' labour for existing capital to employ, wages would fall, and in his *Observations on the Effects of the Corn Laws* he pointed out that the withdrawal of labour from the market due to diminished demand was slow and painful: 'the same supply will necessarily remain in the market, not only the next year, but for some years to come.' At the same time he was working in a roundabout way to the conclusion that cheap food meant too many babies, and therefore starvation in the long run, while dear food meant fewer children and a higher standard of living.

He took as his starting point 'that mine of information, for every thing relating to prices and labour, Sir Frederick Morton Eden's Work on the Poor'; it did not occur to Malthus (or anyone else) that the budgets of the poor might have changed in the eventful seventeen years that had elapsed since Eden made his inquiries, although he pointed out that there must be considerable variations arising from the size of the family and the amount of their earnings. But even if Eden's findings only approximated towards the truth, Malthus thought they proved that

> a rise in the price of corn must be both slow and partial in its effects upon labour. Meat, milk, butter, cheese and potatoes are slowly affected by the price of corn. House-rent, bricks, stone, timber, fuel, soap, candles and clothing still more slowly; and as far as some of them depend, in part or in the whole, upon foreign materials (as is the case with leather, linen, cottons, soap and candles) they may be considered as independent of it; like the two remaining articles of tea and sugar, which are by no means unimportant in amount.
>
> It is manifest therefore that the whole of the wages of labour can never rise or fall in proportion to the variations in the price of grain.[18]

Having written this at the beginning of the pamphlet, Malthus wrote at the end in another connection, 'The wages of labour in this country, though they have not risen in proportion to the price of corn, have been beyond all doubt considerably influenced by it.' In the second and third editions of the tract he went further, adding a footnote to this sentence which read: 'It appears from the evidence before parliament that wages, when they have not been obviously and purposely kept down by parish allowances, have risen about in the same proportion as the price of corn.'[19]

Malthus seems to have taken it for granted that *post hoc* was *propter hoc*, and the supposition of a causal connection between high corn prices and high wages implied that Corn Laws would be advantageous to the labourer.

If only two-fifths of his income were spent on bread or flour, but his whole income advanced in proportion to the price of grain, the increased three-fifths not so spent would, *ceteris paribus*, buy more of other things. Malthus and his contemporaries had, of course, no conception of a cost of living index, with each commodity given a weighting. In the times in which they lived they could not have acquired the data for compiling such an index, any more than they could obtain precise information about the nation's wages; nor were there figures to show how unemployment might offset the benefit which the working classes as a whole could otherwise have derived from a fall in the real price of food.

One cannot stress too often the absence of statistics at this period. Although the Customs Office could provide some figures for the overseas corn trade since 1697, there were no agricultural returns at all in the modern sense until the 1840s in Ireland, the 1860s in the United Kingdom, and so no certain knowledge of how much food was produced in Britain. There was no agreement, even, as to whether a particular year's harvest had been under or over average, unless the season had been markedly wet or favourable throughout the whole country. Sir Edward West (1782-1828), in a pamphlet published in 1826, enjoyed himself very much collating Adam Smith's account of cycles of bad crops with Edmund Burke's *Thoughts and Details on Scarcity* (1795) and Thomas Tooke's Evidence before the Commons' Select Committee on Agriculture in 1821:

> Mr. Tooke's bad cycle commences four or five years before the termination of Mr. Burke's, and Mr. Burke's bad cycle commences a year before the termination of Dr. Smith's, so that from the year 1766 to the year 1820 there have been three cycles of bad crops, and those without any intermission.*[20]

It is only just to say that Sir John Sinclair and Arthur Young at the Board of Agriculture collected all the information they could, but the Board itself was regarded as a war-time body - it had been established in 1793 - and was wound up in 1822.

Meanwhile, Malthus's *Observations* were a great success, and Jeffrey sent him an affectionate and admiring letter, regretting that he had not let him have the tract in the form of an article for the *Edinburgh Review*, where it would have been read 'by twice as many people as ever see pamphlets. And for your glory and credit it might have been as well known to all that you care about, as if your name had been on the title.'[21]

The Corn Law controversy went on all through 1814, and Malthus

*West turned the whole argument about corn and wages upside down. It was *not* the price of corn that determined the wages of labour: it was the grand total actually paid in wages (not the rate per man or per hour) which constituted the effective demand for bread, and therefore determined the price of corn. Malthus admired West's pamphlet, having in due course reached a similar conclusion himself, as will be seen in the next chapter.

followed it closely, but his correspondence with Ricardo throughout this period was chiefly concerned with their basic differences over supply and demand, production and consumption. There were other topics. Malthus, in 'a large and agreeable family party', wrote from the Penryn Arms, Bangor, and Ricardo said in his reply: 'I expect that your eye will be quite weary of the bare mountains of Wales and you will hail with pleasure the more fruitful country of England.' Malthus's answer was that with his company and 'many delightful excursions' he did not expect 'to be very soon tired of the mountains, particularly as we do not absolutely live in the midst of them, but only see them at such a respectful distance, as to make them lose all their terrors, and shew only their beauties'.[22]

This was the year in which Ricardo bought Gatcomb Park, a lovely 'gentleman's seat' in Gloucestershire. In the summer of 1813 he had looked at a house in Hertfordshire, near the East India College, but it would appear from the correspondence that Mrs Ricardo turned it down because it was too small. I do not think it could have compared with Gatcomb, and Malthus wrote to Ricardo perhaps a little enviously on 11 September 1814:

> I dont wonder that you find your time much engaged in walking and riding about your beautiful place, and in the general pleasures and cares of a Country gentleman, particularly at first, when the change from your London life must be so striking. Perhaps another year you will find a little more leisure; but I have no idea of your finding too much, or of your being tired of your retirement.[23]

Malthus seems to have paid only three brief visits to Gatcomb, during the summer vacation of 1816, from Claverton, and the Christmas holidays of 1818 and 1820, from Bath. Maria Edgeworth stayed with the Ricardos at Gatcomb in November 1821, and found 'all the luxuries that riches can give without the ostentation'; she wrote that she 'never was in a more *comfortably* splendid house 110 feet of rooms opening into each other in front all perfectly well warmed so that you never want to go to the fire but may sit to read or write in any part of them'.[24]

Possibly Malthus felt a little painfully the contrast between Gatcomb and Hailey House, with its dilapidated roof and leaky skylights, but these did not worry Ricardo. He paid a number of week-end visits from his London home, frequently enough for him to write to Malthus of his arrival on a Saturday 'at the usual hour'; Malthus stayed with Ricardo in Upper Brook Street sufficiently often to be able to regret that one visit 'must be for a shorter, rather than a longer time than usual'. In one letter Malthus remarked that 'With a view to any discussion on subjects of Political Economy, it is difficult to proceed with a party of more than three or four.'[25] Most of us would agree with him; a greater number requires a chairman.

3 The Second Corn Law Pamphlet

In February 1815 his new publisher, John Murray, brought out almost simultaneously two new pamphlets by Malthus: the 'philosophical' *Inquiry into the Nature and Progress of Rent* on the 3rd, and on about the 10th the political *Grounds of an Opinion on the Policy of Restricting the Importation of Foreign Corn*; this was designated an Appendix to the popular *Observations on the Corn Laws*, of which Murray published a third edition at the same time. To the astonishment and consternation of his Whig friends, Malthus's 'Opinion' was that the importation of grain should be restricted, on the lines proposed by the government. It says much for all concerned that Malthus's outrageous heresy and disloyalty - for so it was regarded - did not affect his private friendships. Jeffrey, however, could never ask him again to contribute to the *Edinburgh Review*, except for an article on Population in 1821.

We know from Malthus's letters to Murray that a copy of the *Grounds* (his own abbreviation) was sent to Lord Liverpool, the Prime Minister. Copies of both the *Grounds* and *Rent* were to be sent to Lord John Townshend, of Balls Park in Hertfordshire, one of Haileybury's few friends among the neighbouring landowners, then 'at Brighton', and to Sir Henry Parnell 'if he is in Town'. Sir John Sinclair was also to have them, in return for his giving Malthus a copy of his *General Report of Scotland*; from Malthus's letter to Sinclair of 31 January 1815 it looks as if Sir John had sent him a note inquiring about the work's safe arrival, for he writes, as he often did, 'I am quite ashamed of having so long delayed thanking you for your very valuable present.'[26] Copies of the *Grounds* only went to Lord Cowper in George Street and 'Lady Melbourn' (Malthus's spelling) in White Hall; these last also had seats in Hertfordshire, at Panshanger and Brocet respectively, within visiting distance of the East India College. Poor Lady Melbourne, now in her sixties, was at this time much troubled by family affairs, since she was both the mother-in-law of Lady Caroline Lamb and the aunt of the newly married Lady Byron. Perhaps Malthus's pamphlet pleased her especially, as 'her friends noted with irritation that she was the only woman who made her garden a paying concern'.[27]

Malthus's *Grounds of an Opinion* in favour of the Corn Laws was a pamphlet of roughly the same length as his *Observations* on them, forty-eight pages. He explained that three additional factors had influenced him during the past year. The first was the evidence laid before Parliament as to the large amount of capital invested in agriculture during the past seven years, especially for the improvement of inferior land; this had enabled the country to survive 'in 1812 when, with the price of corn at above six guineas

259

a quarter, we could only import a little more than 100,000 quarters'. It would not only be unfair to the agricultural interest, but a loss of national capital, if this recently improved land were to revert again to rough pasture because its cultivation was no longer profitable. According to Malthus, 'There never, perhaps, was known a year more injurious to the interests of agriculture' than 1814, with 'the unusual combination of low prices and scanty produce'.[28] This failure of the price of corn to rise, according to the laws of supply and demand, was attributed by other writers to the anticipation by the dealers of an inflow of cheap foreign grain; therefore they did not bid against each other to lay in stocks of the scarce British Wheat.

The second factor was the improved position of the pound on the foreign exchanges, and the fall in the price of bullion. Malthus's reasoning on this point is as incomprehensible to the present writer as it was to his younger contemporary, the economist Robert Torrens (1780-1864). Malthus believed that falling corn prices were inevitable, and 'it certainly does not seem a well-chosen time for the legislature to occasion another fall still greater, by departing at once from a system of restrictions which it had pursued with steadiness during the greatest part of the last century'.[29]

The third new factor in the situation was an illustration that the corn trade could never be *really free* - Malthus's italics - and 'that it is entirely out of our power, even in time of peace, to obtain a free trade in corn, or an approximation towards it, whatever may be our wishes on the subject'. France, 'our nearest neighbour, possessed of the largest and finest corn country in Europe, and who, owing to a more favourable climate and soil, a more stationary and comparatively less crowded population, and a lighter weight of taxation, can grow corn at less than half our prices, has enacted that the exportation of corn shall be free till the price rises to about forty-nine shillings a quarter, and that then it shall entirely cease'. This meant that 'all assistance would be at once cut off, in every season of only moderate scarcity'.[30]

Malthus, as we know, was fully cognizant of the advantages to be obtained from the principle of the division of labour between countries; but he stated firmly:

> I protest most entirely against the doctrine that we are to pursue our
> general principles without ever looking to see if they are applicable
> to the case before us; and that in politics and political economy we
> are to go straight forward, as we certainly ought to do in morals,
> without any reference to the conduct and proceedings of others.

In short, 'it is not in the power of any single nation to secure the freedom of the foreign trade in corn'.[31]

Here Malthus's general argument is valid, but it was most unfortunate that he should take France as an example. In a hurried letter written to Malthus on 12 February 1815 Horner referred to the witnesses giving parliamentary evidence, many of them experienced corn factors: 'In stating the various countries from which we are to look for imports of grain, during the subsistence of peace, none of them ever name France, or seem to think of it.'[32] Other critics were to make the same point: at this period Poland and America were regarded as Britain's principal suppliers of foreign grain.

Malthus then turned to 'the resources of Great Britain and Ireland for the further growth of corn, by the further application of capital to the land'. Since both he and Ricardo formulated theories, of population and profit respectively, based on the diminishing returns obtained from applying successive 'doses' of capital to agriculture, it is interesting to find that Malthus could be pragmatically optimistic, and believed that Britain might be kept 'in average years, nearly independent of foreign supplies of corn'. His detractors will find the qualifications typically Malthusian. With cautious optimism he wrote:

> There is even a chance (but on this I will not insist) of a diminution in the real price of corn, owing to the extension of those great improvements, and that great economy and good management of labour, of which we have such intelligent accounts from Scotland. If these clay lands, by draining, and the plentiful application of lime and other manures, could be so far meliorated in quality as to admit of being worked by two horses and a single man, instead of three or four horses with a man and a boy, what a vast saving of labour and expense would at once be effected, at the same time that the crops would be prodigiously increased![33]

This was obviously relevant to the labouring classes of society, 'the foundation on which the whole fabric rests; and, from their numbers, unquestionably of the greatest weight in any estimate of national happiness'. He went on, 'If I were convinced that to open our ports would be permanently to improve the condition of the labouring classes of society, I should consider the question as at once determined in favour of such a measure.' But Malthus was not so convinced, and reverted again to the argument that a high money price of corn, although hard on the 'very poorest', would be an advantage to the labourers in the purchase of other commodities. At the time he was writing, wages were low and there was much unemployment among farm workers; with his usual honesty (what was then called his candour) Malthus put in a footnote: 'I was not prepared to expect ... so sudden a fall in the price of labour as has already taken place. This fall has been occasioned not so much by the low price of corn, as by the sudden stagnation of agricultural work, occasioned by a more sudden check to cultivation than I foresaw.'[34]

Malthus went on to produce statistical evidence which he felt showed that corn laws helped to smooth out harmful fluctuations in the price (Horner thought that his figures proved nothing of the kind), and then considered 'the next most important class of society, those who live upon the profits of stock'. By these he meant active entrepreneurs, not idle rentiers living on their investments. Half of these entrepreneurs would be farmers, half 'of the commercial and manufacturing part of the society'. Of the commercial half, Malthus thought that only a quarter were engaged in foreign trade, and therefore liable to suffer from the Corn Laws: 'It may be said, perhaps, that a fall in the price of our corn and labour affords the only chance to our manufacturers of retaining possession of the foreign markets.' But, for Malthus, decreasing exports seemed less ruinous than a decline in demand at home. He stressed, as did other pamphleteers again and again, the superior importance of the home market for commodities, as compared with the export trade; falling prices might favour the sale of British goods abroad, but at home they meant cumulative depression with an accelerating fall in purchasing power.

According to Malthus, 'in all the country towns, this diminution of demand has been felt in a very great degree; and the surrounding farmers, who chiefly support them, are quite unable to make their accustomed purchases.' That the manufacturing towns might be prospering from increased exports was possible, but Malthus felt that the transfer of wealth and population from country to town would be 'slow, painful, and unfavourable to happiness'.[35] He had to use the same sort of argument when he came to consider the third class of the community, the landlords, justifying their rents for providing 'the most steady home demand for the manufactures of the country, the most effective fund for its financial support'.[36] Here he referred in footnotes to his *Inquiry into the Nature and Progress of Rent*, which must be discussed separately.

Malthus's fourth class of society were those who lived upon the interest of money invested in loans to the government (his term 'stockholders' can be misleading to modern readers) and those who earned fixed salaries. In this class he included himself in a footnote: 'Much the greatest part of my income is derived from a fixed salary and the interest of money in the funds.'[37] This was to show the disinterested impartiality of his views, but perhaps he also did not want people to think that he made a handsome living from the sale of his books. He would seem to have under-estimated his income from the rectory at Walesby. It is interesting that Malthus regarded the fixed-income group as 'small in number, compared with those who will be affected in a different manner'; it is a reminder of the extremely uncertain hand-to-mouth existence of 'the poor' at this period. Day-labourers, as their name implies, were paid by the day; both their employment and their remuneration fluctuated with their employers' circumstances in a way that their descendants would find intolerable.

Naturally those with fixed incomes would suffer from a general rise in prices, but Malthus repeated the argument of his first Bullion article in the *Edinburgh Review*, with regard to the great stimulus which rising prices had given to industry and capital accumulation; this stimulus enabled the country to support 'with almost undiminished resources, the prodigious weight of debt which has been accumulated during the last twenty years', which would have been impossible without some depreciation of the currency. He then produced figures and calculations which purported to show that a reduction in the price of corn, 'even supposing that corn does not effectually regulate the prices of other commodities', would be so deflationary as to mean that the interest on loans to the government during the war would be paid at a much higher rate of purchasing power than had been contracted for, 'which increased interest can, of course, only be furnished by the industrious classes of society'.[38] This Malthus regarded as manifestly unfair.

The final pages of the pamphlet are a summing-up. In comparing the effects of a free trade in corn, as opposed to one that is restricted, Malthus rather quaintly lists the disadvantages of each system, instead of the advantages, which is the more common practice in a dispute on policy, however much the antagonists may acknowledge that there are difficulties on both sides. He wrote that he himself was not acquainted with the details of the subject, but thought that the government's proposal to restrict the import of corn until the price reached eighty shillings a quarter was appropriate 'in the actual state of things'.

The pamphlet concluded with a warning against the appearance of partisan legislation:[39]

> But, in future, we should endeavour, if possible, to avoid all discussions about the necessity of *protecting* the British farmer, and securing to him a *fair living profit*. Such language may perhaps be allowable in a crisis like the present. But certainly the legislature has nothing to do with securing to any classes of its subjects a particular rate of profits in their different trades. This is not the province of a government; and it is unfortunate that any language should be used which may convey such an impression, and make people believe that their rulers ought to listen to accounts of their gains and losses.

The final sentence was,

> I firmly believe that, in the actual state of Europe, and under the actual circumstances of our present situation, it is our wisest policy to grow our own average supply of corn; and in so doing, I feel persuaded that the country has ample resources for a great and continued increase of population, of power, of wealth, and of happiness.

4 The Aftermath

It was useless for Malthus to write that he was not concerned with the prosperity of a particular class; he appeared as the ally of the agricultural interest against the community, an apostate from the basic tenets of economic liberty.

Francis Horner wrote to his great friend John Archibald Murray on 30 January 1815: 'The most important convert the landholders have got is Malthus, who has now declared himself in favour of their Bill.' He went on: 'to be sure, there is not a better or more informed judgment, and it is the single authority which staggers me. But those who have looked closely into his philosophy will admit, that there is always a leaning in favour of the efficacy of laws; and his early bias was for corn laws in particular.'[40]

In more homely terms Whishaw wrote to a friend of his, Thomas Smith of Easton Grey in Wiltshire, on 16 February: 'I do not know whether you interest yourself much in the Corn Laws, which occupy all conversation here. Our friend Malthus has published a pamphlet in favour of restrictions which is not at all relished by his friends here, but will gain him a great name among the clergy and landed interest. Indeed we, the poor corn consumers, are no match against these powerful bodies ...'[41]

Malthus's two pamphlets were trounced together in the *Edinburgh Review* for February 1815, which gave an orthodox Whig view of the dangers of any sort of government interference:

> At present corn is abundant and cheap; and we are called upon for
> an artificial rise of price. But supposing, in the event of a scarcity and
> a high price, that we are required, by a discontented and infuriated
> populace, to pass a law for the purpose of reducing the price, what
> satisfactory answer can be made to this apparently just demand? ...
> Formerly, indeed, we might have replied, that the freedom of trade
> was a sacred principle which we dared not presume to violate ...
> Government, by tampering with the price of provisions, becomes
> responsible, in the eyes of the people, for all subsequent variations of
> price; and, in the event of scarcity, the sufferings of the community
> are universally ascribed to its maladministration.[42]

With regard to the risk inherent in dependence on foreign supplies of food, the *Review* was optimistic. Corn had been imported since 1793, and foreign supplies had been most drastically cut in 1811 and 1812, when Britain was at war with both France and the United States, but the country had survived: 'We have had experience of the calamity; and we find that it is in no respect different from that produced by a deficient crop - an evil against which no system of restrictions will be found to afford any security.'[43]

Agriculture had no special sanctity about it for the *Edinburgh* reviewers:

> The price of corn, as it is fixed by the voluntary contract of the
> buyer and the seller, we consider to be the natural standard by which
> the agriculture of the country should be regulated ... If cultivation
> is extended to lands of which the produce at this standard price will
> not repay the original cost, these lands *ought* to lie waste ...
> According to our notions, in short, there never was a more idle
> alarm, than that a nation, noted for capital, industry and enterprize,
> should blindly pursue trade and manufactures at the expense of
> agriculture - in other words, should be anxiously providing a supply
> of luxuries, and be in the meantime starving for want of necessaries.[44]

Malthus's tract was naturally also seized upon by a flock of sympathetic
pamphleteers, some of whom supported the Corn Laws for reasons less
philanthropic than his. He must have read with mixed feelings Lord
Sheffield's eulogy, for instance: on perusal of the *Grounds* for restricting
imports, his 'admiration of Mr. Malthus's work was raised to the highest
degree', but the impartial *Observations* were not to the taste of this octogenarian peer, for 'such a mode of treating it has the effect of perplexing,
rather than enlightening the question.'[45] Sales of both pamphlets, however,
were enough to justify Murray in asking Malthus to revise them for
reprinting.

Robert Torrens's *Essay on the External Corn Trade*, which also appeared
early in 1815, was not a pamphlet but a book of 348 octavo pages. In this
work Torrens made his famous pronouncement: 'It is a singular fact, and
one which it is not improper to impress upon the public, that, in the leading
questions of economical science, Mr. Malthus scarcely ever embraced a
principle which he did not subsequently abandon.' But the criticism, whether
justified or not, makes Torrens's subsequent praise of Malthus all the more
valuable:

> If these fluctuating and contradictory opinions, however, do not
> indicate that, in the science of political economy, Mr. Malthus has
> attained any very clear conceptions, or arrived at any certain
> conclusions, they at least must serve to convince us that he possesses,
> in a very eminent degree, a spirit of candour and the love of truth.
> Though his works cannot, perhaps, in any instance, be safely
> consulted for practical authorities, they may always be
> advantageously referred to as furnishing materials for speculation, and
> suggesting hints for inquiry. The spirit, too, in which his essays are
> written, forms a pleasing contrast to that which pervades the
> publications of certain economists, patrician and plebian, who, having
> lost themselves in the labyrinths of erroneous theory, with disdainful
> pertinacity reject the clue of facts.[46]

Meanwhile, Horner was sedulously opposing the Eighty-shilling Corn Bill, then being steered through the House of Commons by Frederick John Robinson, later Viscount Goderich.

It is amusing to compare the diaries of Miss Berry and Sir Samuel Romilly. On Monday 6 March 1815 the lady wrote calmly: 'They are beginning to assemble in the streets, and to break the windows, and to knock in the doors, on account of the Corn Bill.'[47] Romilly sounds more alarmed: his journal entry for the same day was: 'Great outrages have been committed against the Members of both Houses of Parliament who are supposed to be friends to the Corn Bill. The populace broke into the houses of the Lord Chancellor and of Mr. Robinson, and destroyed part of their furniture ...' On the following day he wrote, 'The same outrages and riots in different parts of the town, and a few persons killed or wounded by the soldiery.'[48] It is hardly surprising that on the day after, Wednesday 8 March 1815, Miss Berry should write, 'In the evening we expected a few people, but most of them were in fear of the crowds which still continued.'

More responsible citizens, all over the country, protested through petitions to Parliament; this was the only way in which the unenfranchised could make their opinion known, other than through the press, a medium which most of them were insufficiently educated to use. According to Lord Grey, 'the greatest number of petitions had been presented, that had ever, perhaps, been known in the history of parliament, the petitioners uniformly stating that the measure would have the effect of preventing a cheap supply of food to the labouring classes.'[49]

On the day Miss Berry was disappointed of her party, 8 March 1815, Malthus wrote to John Murray:

I have been so very much engaged since I returned from Town that I have hardly been able to look at the pamphlets. I ought however to have sent you the *Observations* before, in which I do not mean to make any alterations, except the correction of one or two slight typographical errors. It may be as well to begin reprinting this first, and in three or four days I hope to let you have the *Grounds*.

I am quite sorry for these riots. Of course they should not be attended to in the decision. But it is unpleasant for the Parliament to go against such a prodigious weight of petitions. I am fully persuaded that all the trading classes, not immediately connected with Foreign commerce, will feel very severely the loss of home demand, and the increased pressure of taxation, occasioned by the fall in the price of corn; but if the nation is almost unanimous against restrictions, I fear that the passing the act under such circumstances will be a perpetually reviving cause of discontent.

Two days later, on 10 March 1815, Malthus ended a letter to Ricardo with similar sentiments:

The Post is here, and I have only time to say that tho I think the
country will feel considerable inconveniences, from a great fall in the
price of corn, yet I should be sorry to see the measure carried in
spite of such a crowd of petitions. The mob of course should not be
regarded; but a neglect of such numerous petitions may in many
respects be a bad precedent.[50]

On 14 March he wrote to Horner:

I remain firm in my opinion as to the Policy of some Restrictions,
but tho I would not yield to the mob, I should be disposed to yield
to the prodigious weight of petitions, and let the people have their
way.[51]

One is left wondering whether Malthus's chief concern was simply for the
harmful effects of general discontent, or whether he believed that it was
morally wrong for a Bill to be passed so contrary to the expressed wishes
of the people, even though he himself was certain that the Bill would be for
the people's own good. It sounds as if he were doubtful of the issue of the
debate.

In fact Mr Robinson's Bill became law, but its passage was completely
overshadowed by 'the fearful news', as Miss Berry put it, of Napoleon's
escape from Elba and landing in France.

As far as Malthus was concerned, the timing was inopportune. He wrote
to Murray on 29 March 1815:

What with business in the College and company in the house, I have
had little or no leisure lately, and have not been able to execute what
I intended. I suppose however, from what Mr. Whishaw says, who
has just left us, that it is of little consequence at present, and that no
publications can be attended to, while the public mind is so entirely
occupied by one great object. The corn question seems indeed to
have fallen at once to the ground, and it is natural on many accounts
that it should do so. I had begun a kind of answer to Mr. Torrens,
but it was likely to be longer than I wished, and as I was quite in
doubt in what form to put it, whether in a note at the end of the
Grounds, or separated in different notes at the bottom of the pages.

If you think the discussion is for the present over, on account of
the new events that have occurred, perhaps it might be as well to
incorporate the observations I have to make on the subject at my
leisure in the Rents; but if not, I think it would be best to add a long
note, almost amounting to another pamphlet, to the Grounds. What I
shall have to say is of some importance; - not merely of a
controversial nature; but explaining some points which Mr. Torrens
has overlooked, and calculated to make an essential difference in his
conclusions.

Pray let me know what you think will be the most adviseable
plan, and what degree of haste is required.

Poor author! To understand the pathos of this letter we must look back a
little over the month of March 1815. Malthus would have seen Torrens's
Essay on the External Corn Trade at about the same time that he heard of
Napoleon's escape. He mentioned it in a letter to Ricardo on 12 March,
generously saying, 'It is ably written, tho I think there are some important
errors in it, and as it is likely to be generally read, I believe I must say
something about them.' Ricardo replied on the 14th that Torrens was an
adversary worthy of Malthus's pen.[52]

Malthus and Ricardo then exchanged four more letters, on the subject
which was engrossing them, agricultural rent in relation to wages and
profits, before Malthus, on 24 March, told Ricardo:

> I have written part of an answer to Torrens for a new Edition of the
> *Grounds*, but I think it would be too long, and as I hear of more
> attacks [another pamphlet], I fear if I begin to answer I shall be led
> too much into publick controversies, which I had rather avoid. Do
> you know whether Torrens is much read [?] I think he has treated
> me unjustly in the preface and that the instances of inconsistency
> which he produces, even if established, would by no means warrant
> his sweeping accusation.[53]

Ricardo replied on 27 March. Like Malthus, he left Torrens until the end
of a long letter on their own theoretical discussion. He thought that Torrens
had treated Malthus unjustly, that instances of inconsistency in Malthus's
theories (even if Torrens were right about all of them) were 'much too few
to justify his severe observation'. But, 'At the Geological Club his book was
spoken of the other day with great approbation'; two members whose
opinions Malthus would have respected thought that Torrens 'has exhausted
the subject and that his arguments cannot be controverted. - I should think
that he is very generally read.'[54]

It was this news which no doubt inspired Malthus, in spite of his
asseverated dislike of public controversy, to write Murray the unhappy letter
of 29 March. The letter was never answered. A week after it had been
posted, when Ricardo was planning one of his week-end visits to Haileybury,
Malthus asked him to call on Murray before he left town, and find out how
matters stood; should he say what he had to say in a new edition of *Rent*,
without directly answering Torrens, or should he reply to the *External Corn
Trade* in a long note at the end of the *Grounds*?[55]

Clearly Murray's answer must have been a very decided negative to all
Malthus's propositions. The next letter in the archives, from Malthus to
Murray, is dated 22 April 1816, over a year later. The *Inquiry into the Nature
and Progress of Rent* was reprinted, with some alterations, in the *Principles*

of Political Economy in 1820, but the *Observations* and *Grounds* simply faded away, as far as their sales were concerned. They were not forgotten, any more than was the cancelled paragraph in the quarto about the guests who were turned away from Nature's feast. After his support of the Corn Bill, it was even easier than it had been before to make Mr Malthus seem like an ogre who wanted large families of little children to be starved into extinction.

According to Empson, who was very close to him in his last years, Malthus when he wrote his Corn Law pamphlets

> was quite aware of the risk which his reputation was running by the course of argument he pursued on that occasion. He said that he well knew that nothing he had ever written had injured it so much. On the whole, too (to use his favourite summing up), he was not on this occasion as sure as usual of the soundness of the judgment which he had pronounced. He continued to think that the friends of truth and of fair-dealing had received considerable provocation by the one-sided manner, as well as by the insolence of personal imputations, with which the discussion had been conducted against the landlords. He deemed it highly useful that inflammatory declamation should be met by cool argument - that both sides of the question should be heard with patience, and unreasonable expectations, one by one, exposed. These are invidious duties which it demands a certain spirit to discharge. Of these, he felt it to be one, to put people upon their guard - that they were not to expect from the repeal of Corn Laws, advantages of a kind which no repeal of measures of this nature could possibly confer. This duty he never regretted that he had performed. But his general principles in favour of freedom of trade were so absolute that, at times, doubts came over him whether any exception ought to be admitted . . .[56]

Poor Malthus!

5 Unanswered Questions

Among the authorities whom Malthus quoted in Book I of the quarto on *Population* was the Scots explorer of West Africa, Mungo Park (1771-1806). His *Travels in the Interior of Africa* was published in 1799, a classic true adventure story, and in 1805 he set out on a second expedition to the Niger, from which he never returned. No definite account of his fate reached Europe until 1812, by which time the slave trade was abolished in all British possessions, and the African Institution had been established to promote and watch over the operation of the famous Act of 1807. The relevance of all this to Malthus's story is that John Whishaw, being a good Whig and a kind man, was a director of the African Institution: he decided to write, anonymously, a life of Mungo Park, to be published with the explorer's own account of his journeys for the benefit of his widow and four children – all of whom Park had acquired in the five years which elapsed between his two voyages to Africa.

John Murray was the obvious publisher to approach. Murray's large brown letter-book – less complete than William Bray's – shows that on 6 February 1814 Murray wrote to Whishaw expressing his gratitude for a biography of Mungo Park, as his journals, however interesting, were 'so scanty in quantity'. This entry is followed by what is headed an 'Extract' of a letter to the Revd. T. R. Malthus dated 3 January 1815. It runs as follows:

> If it be agreeable to you to allow me to print one Thousand Copies of the Improved 'Observations on the Corn Laws' and Two Thousand Copies of your new tract on the 'Origin and Nature of Rent' – I shall have much pleasure in giving you the sum of One Hundred Pounds. – In this arrangement the Copyright will remain entirely your own. –
>
> I submit to you a more extended proposition – If I understand Mr. Whishaw correctly – it is your intention to publish a Volume of detached remarks upon the more interesting topics of political Economy meaning to incorporate in that Volume the two tracts on 'Rent' and on 'Bullion' –
>
> For the Copyright of this Volume, to form if printed in the same manner, as much in quantity, as the second Volume of Buchanan's recently published edition of Smith's Wealth of Nations, including the Copyright of the Tract on Corn Laws, and of one or two other Tracts published for you by Johnson (and which I mention only* that I may have the whole without interference) – I will pay you the Sum of One Thousand Pounds, in Six, Twelve, and Eighteen Months from the day on which the Volume shall be compleated. I wish to be allowed to publish all the leading subjects – Rent – Bullion – & say two others in Tracts – separately – at intervals before or, not later, than May – after which they may be arranged, connected & Systematized with such additions as you think proper, for forming them into the Volume to be published perhaps at the meeting of Parliament next year. –
>
> *I mean that as their subjects were temporary – they can possess no very great Commercial Value at this time –

It is hard to avoid platitudinous statements about the unpredictability of human affairs. We know that a 'Volume of detached remarks upon the more

270

interesting topics of political economy' never appeared, but the tract on Bullion is a complete mystery. Murray writes as though it were actually in existence, and it is of course possible that it does still exist, anonymously hidden in some collection; at that period there would be no question of off-prints of the *Edinburgh Review* articles. Another explanation may be that Malthus never wrote (or meant to write) such a pamphlet and that Whishaw, acting on his friend's behalf, had got things wrong. To me this seems unlikely, and I doubt if the matter can be cleared up until more documents come to light. The Malthus correspondence still preserved in John Murray's congenial house, in Albemarle Street, begins with the letter of 6 February 1815, in which he made arrangements for the despatch of the new pamphlets that Murray had just printed; Napoleon was already planning the events which would effectively prevent any orderly issue of small tracts during the spring of that memorable year.

What is extant, however, is a letter which Malthus wrote two days after Murray's 'Extract', on 5 January 1815. It was addressed to Rowland Hunter, who was either Joseph Johnson's nephew or adopted as such, and who carried on the business as 'bookseller' in London at 72 St Paul's Church Yard; he published in due course quite a number of well-known short works on political economy. Malthus's letter runs:

Dear Sir,

I believe I mentioned to you when I was in Town, that having given up the Edition of Adam Smith, which as my income is chiefly a life income, I could hardly quite justify to my children, I wished to make my other plan approach in some degree to it in point of profit. My friends have been for some time mentioning to me Mr. Murray as a person able and inclined to make very liberal offers. And understanding that it was not your intention to continue the line of Extensive publication, I mentioned my plans in a letter to Mr. Murray with a request that he would tell me what he might be inclined to give. He has proposed 100£ for one edition only of the Inquiry into rent of 2000 copies, and one edition of the Observations on the Corn Laws of 1000 copies, and has further proposed a thousand pounds for the Copy right of a good sized octavo volume consisting of the subjects I had mentioned, including the Essay on Rents, together with the copy right of the few small tracts I have published on my own account.

I am quite sure you will not think that I act unhandsomely towards you in accepting these offers, if it does not suit you to give me the same, and I should really think that it would not answer to you to do it. Mr. Murray has I understand now great means of pushing a work and probably is able on that account to give more

than many other booksellers. I shall be very happy still [to] continue
my connection with your shop.

I am dear Sir
Sincerely Yours
T. Rob' Malthus[51]

This letter also raises tantalising questions. The first sentence must mean
that Malthus thought he was not justified in spending time, and perhaps also
his own money, on an edition of the *Wealth of Nations* which would be
unlikely to sell so soon after Buchanan's. With regard to 'the few small
tracts I have published on my own account', he is presumably referring to
The High Price of Provisions, the *Letters* to Whitbread about the Poor Law
and to Lord Grenville about the College, all printed by Johnson or Hunter;
yet it is quite conceivable that there are anonymous pamphlets by Malthus,
in addition to a tract on Bullion, long lost among bound volumes in basement
stacks - pamphlets whose reprinting Murray knew perfectly well would
not be profitable in 1815. I doubt if Malthus would have published anything
without telling his family and friends about it, but there is always the
possibility that the letters concerning these 'small tracts' were mislaid or
thrown away.

The hit-or-miss nature of written evidence is only too obvious. It can be
argued that we over-emphasise the importance of Ricardo in Malthus's life
because this friendship is so fully documented: Malthus may have had
relationships with other people which were of great significance to him but
about which we know nothing, either because they were not orderly keepers
of letters or because the letters at a later date were used as curl-papers, or
rolled up into spills to light candles from an open fire. They may even have
been used to light fires, by a housemaid like Martin Tupper's, who told her
master, 'I never burns no papers but what is spoilt by being written on.'[58]

These considerations apply very much to Malthus's friendship with
Henry Brougham (1778-1868). He had come from Edinburgh to Lincoln's
Inn like his childhood play-fellow, Francis Horner, but was initially less
successful, and did not enter the House of Commons until 1810, four years
after Horner; he would at first have been hard put to it to live in London
were it not for what he earned from his contributions to the *Edinburgh
Review*. He became a member of the King of Clubs in 1805, and the sole
extant letter from Malthus to Brougham suggests that they knew each other
quite well. It is dated from the East India College on 28 March 1815, and
shows how Malthus - after the pamphlets on the Corn Laws and *Rent* -
was regarded as a practical authority by 'improving' landlords.

Dear Brougham,
I have looked over your friend's 'hints for the improvement of
landed property,' and should have written to you before on the
subject, but that by some unaccountable accident I mislaid your note,

272

and had quite forgotten that *Northern Circuit* was a sufficient address to you. Whishaw who is here has set me right; and as I am not going to Town very shortly, he has promised to take care that the book shall be sent safely to Mr. Walker.

I think that certainly landed property might be much improved, and much good might be done in various ways both moral and political, as well as economical, by the adoption of Mr. Walker's hints; but I should fear that it might be very difficult to acquire such an influence over landed proprietors as to persuade them to put such plans in execution. I should think it would be adviseable for him to attend at first principally to those modes of laying out capital upon the land which will be the most profitable in a pecuniary point of view; and the other more benevolent objects might be introduced subsequently. If he begins by stating the whole of his views at first, he will I apprehend run some risk of being considered as too visionary for a practical adviser. Much more however might certainly be done by Landlords, both with regard to their own interest, and the happiness of those around them, than is done at present. Most of the principal improvements which have taken place on the land during the last 20 years have been effected I believe chiefly by tenants; yet it is certain that they improve comparatively to a great disadvantage; and every attempt to introduce a more general spirit of improvement among landlords ought to be encouraged. I feel some doubt I confess respecting the success of your friend's plan; but I think it a most benevolent and desireable one, and if he does not depend upon it in a pecuniary view, very well worth the trial.[59]

I have been unable to trace the philanthropic Mr Walker, so his visionary plan is another unsolved mystery. After this long paragraph, presumably meant for transmission to Brougham's friend, Malthus breaks out with the lines I have already quoted about Napoléon's escape from Elba, with the exclamation marks in clusters.

Whatever his relationship with Brougham, this letter is a useful reminder of how much Malthus was a man of his period, closely in touch with all that went on, and with apparently more correspondence than he could fit in with family and visitors, college life and teaching, his own work, and what Jane Austen called all the latest publications and States of the Nation. It is well to remember this before embarking on the theory of rent, so much taken up by later writers all over the world that we are inclined to think of the subject in a vacuum, 'right' or 'wrong' like a mathematical exercise. It was, in fact, an idea which came to four men simultaneously in one small country where the system of land tenure was unusual, in exceptional post-war circumstances, combined with an unprecedented long-term economic mutation.

CHAPTER IX

The Principles of Political Economy

1 The Nature and Progress of Rent

Up to now, Malthus's books and articles have been considered roughly in chronological order, but with the publication in 1815 of his *Inquiry into the Nature and Progress of Rent* this method is no longer appropriate. Here we come to what Brougham called 'the pure metaphysics of political economy',[1] and it seems best to give a simplified account, in one chapter, of the inter-related theoretical discussions which occupied more than a decade. This involves quoting from both the first edition of Malthus's *Principles of Political Economy*, published in 1820, and the second edition of 1836; this posthumous edition was constantly worked over by Malthus himself, and possibly even more by the anonymous Editor, Le Bas' 'mercantile friend' John Cazenove (who became Malthus's friend too), so that one cannot be certain whose views are represented. The controversies between Malthus and Ricardo about land, labour and capital can appear slightly unreal to modern readers, but they were to have dramatic and concrete results, the outcome of long hours spent in what was then the Reading Room of the British Museum by the refugee Karl Marx, who lived in London from 1849 until his death in 1883.

In this context Malthus is less important than Ricardo, for the three editions of Ricardo's *Principles of Political Economy*, published in quick succession, quite eclipsed Malthus's. The *Essay on Population* remained an established classic, and the foundation on which other men built, Ricardo most of all; but in the economic debates of 1815-25 Malthus's was no longer the paramount name, just as he himself was no longer a pioneer with a single message. In the *London Magazine* for December 1823 De Quincey gives a contemporary view:

It is remarkable at first sight that Mr. Malthus, to whom Political Economy is so much indebted in one chapter (viz. the chapter of Population), should in every other chapter have stumbled at every step. On a nearer view, however, the wonder ceases ... What is the brief abstract of his success? It is this: he took an obvious and familiar truth, which until his time had been a barren truism, and showed that it teemed with consequences ... Not logic but a judicious choice of his ground placed Mr. Malthus at once in a situation from which he commanded the whole truth at a glance - with a lucky dispensation from all continuous logical processes. But such a dispensation is a privilege indulged to few other parts of Political Economy ... [2]

The irony for us today is that, making due allowance for the conditions of his period, Malthus's economic analysis is often more congenial to modern readers than Ricardo's, although the latter's brilliantly logical 'system' may compel the suspension of disbelief as we read him; so consistent and forceful are his assertions that we forget they are not truths, only statements.

Ricardo's noetic system originated in the extremely practical disagreements over the Corn Laws. As that campaign reached its climax, three pamphlets and a book appeared in one month, February 1815, which all incorporated what became known as the differential theory of rent. That the same idea should occur simultaneously to four men is not altogether surprising, when one remembers the supreme importance of agriculture in Britain at this time, with what was called the 'high farming' of newly enclosed fields everywhere visible. Before looking at Malthus's views it might be helpful to study, in the accompanying table, a modern estimate of the structure of the nation's capital in 1812; the figures for 1912 are given for comparison.

The structure of the national capital of Great Britain
(as percentages of the total national capital)[3]

	1812	1912
Land (excluding standing timber, which is included in industrial capital)	54.2	6.9
Buildings	14.9	25.9
Farm stock	9.3	2.5
Overseas securities	—	12.0
Domestic railways	—	9.3
Industrial, commercial and financial capital	19.8	33.7
Public property, excluding roads and military	1.8	9.7
Total national capital, excluding the national debt and movable property	100	100

The table may make the British classical economists' preoccupation with land more comprehensible. What it does not explain is why they should have theorised about land as though it had but one use, which was to grow

275

corn to feed labourers. The *Annals of Agriculture* and other sources show that farmers were having an ever-widening choice between different sorts of crop and stock, and each year a larger number of landlords were finding - as was said at the time - that bricks and mortar were the most profitable seed to sow. But in general the wicked landlord of popular imagination lived in sylvan luxury on an inherited estate, his rent-roll swollen by the high price which the poor workers were forced to pay for their loaves of bread, and therefore indirectly by the high wages which their employers were forced to pay to prevent them from dying, as some put it, rather than to enable them to live. The rich farmer was also a regular character in cartoons of the time, but according to classical theory he was prevented by the competition of other capitalists from making more than 'ordinary profits'; thus the landlord alone was assumed to benefit from the rising price of corn.

Malthus in the 1803 edition of *Population* showed that he then shared, more or less, this widely held opinion. In the chapter on the 'Different Effects of the Agricultural and Commercial Systems' he wrote:

> During the late scarcities, the price of labour has been continually rising - not to fall again; the rents of land have been every where advancing - not to fall again; and of course the price of produce must arise - not to fall again; as, independently of a particular competition from scarcity, or the want of competition from plenty, its price is necessarily regulated by the wages of labour and the rent of land.[4]

In the following chapter, 'Of Bounties of the Exportation of Corn', he is equally explicit: 'One of the principal ingredients in the price of British corn is the high rent of land.'[5]

After the publication of the great quarto came the Walesby rectory, marriage, and the professorship at the East India College; Malthus had lectures to prepare, and Bonar considers that these led him to think about rent, and Adam Smith's inconsistency on the subject, more carefully than he had done before. In any case, there is a complete *volte-face* in the 1806 edition of the *Essay*: in the re-written chapter on export bounties, Malthus affirms that 'universally, it is price that determines rent, not rent that determines price.'[6]

In order to understand fully the implications of this concern over theories about rent, we must go back to mid-eighteenth-century France, to the physiocratic *Économistes*; they were often called in Britain simply 'the Economists', to the great confusion of later students. Briefly, the *Économistes* regarded rent as a net surplus, attributable not to the productivity of labour and capital but to the productivity of nature. Thus this school, of which François Quesnay (1694-1774) was the chief exponent, held that land was the sole source of the wealth and revenue of any country; the only truly productive workers were those on the land, because only labour on

THE PRINCIPLES OF POLITICAL ECONOMY

the land yielded a surplus, that is to say, something over and above what the cultivators themselves needed to consume in order to continue production. This surplus provided food and raw material for the artificers and manufacturers, who were designated the sterile or unproductive classes, because their industry did nothing but replace the capital which had employed them, together of course with the customary profit, without which no enterprise of any kind would ever be undertaken.

The *Économistes* were blind to the fact that no profit could come into the picture at all unless the coat made from woollen cloth was of more value to the consumer than the fleece on the sheep's back. Agriculture, from the physiocratic point of view, produced something from nothing; manufacturers merely changed one form of matter to another. The profit of the tailor was not an increase of value which arose naturally in the course of production, because an effective demander was prepared to pay more for a coat than for a piece of cloth; the profit arose simply because the coat was *sold*. This is called the theory of profit upon alienation: according to the physiocrats, the tailor had produced nothing, merely changed cloth to coat, and then exchanged it in the market for something else.

In 1803 Malthus had agreed with this view, writing that 'manufactures, strictly speaking, are no new production, no new creation, but merely the modification of an old one.'[7] When he revised the quarto three years later, all five pages in which he appeared sympathetic towards this general maxim of physiocracy were omitted. There is nothing to show what caused him to change his mind.

The importance of physiocratic doctrines in support of the political power of landed proprietors is obvious; there was renewed discussion of them in England during the Napoleonic Wars, when food was scarce and foreign trade impeded. William Spence's *Britain Independent of Commerce*, published in 1807, provoked two replies: one was Robert Torrens's *The Economists Refuted* (he meant *Économistes*), and the other James Mill's *Commerce Defended*, which appeared in 1808 and marked the beginning of his friendship with Ricardo. Mill pointed out that foreign trade was not a swapping of commodities of equal value, to the benefit of no one but the profiteering merchant; exchange would not take place at all unless each party gave up something he valued less for something he valued more; thus trade, as well as agriculture, did increase national wealth.

This very brief summary of current discussion will explain why David Buchanan, when he published his notes on the *Wealth of Nations* in 1814, felt it necessary to affirm that

> Agriculture adds no more to the national stock than any other sort of industry. In dwelling on the reproduction of rent as so great an advantage to society, Dr. Smith does not reflect that rent is the effect of high price, and that what the landlord gains in this way, he gains

at the expence of the community at large. There is no absolute gain to the society by the reproduction of rent; it is only one class profiting at the expence of another class. The notion of agriculture yielding a produce, and a rent in consequence, because nature concurs with human industry in the process of cultivation, is a mere fancy. It is not from the produce, but from the price at which the produce is sold, that the rent is derived; and this price is got, not because nature assists in the production, but because it is the price which suits the consumption to the supply.[8]

In an earlier note Buchanan had put the same point of view a little differently, and I quote both passages to indicate how widely current was the discussion of agricultural rents at this period. Adam Smith had written: 'As soon as the land of any country has all become private property, the landlords, like all other men, love to reap where they never sowed, and demand a rent even for its natural produce', such as the wood of the forest and the grass of the field; of the three component parts of the price of corn, 'one part pays the rent of the landlord, another pays the wages or maintenance of the labourers and labouring cattle employed in producing it, and the third pays the profit of the farmer.'[9] Buchanan comments:

> Other men love also to reap where they never sowed; but the landlords alone, it would appear, succeed in so desirable an object . . . In another part of this work Dr. Smith, with great perspicuity, states rent to be the effect not the cause of high price. It is rather inaccurate, therefore, to call rent a component part of the price; nor is this inaccuracy merely verbal, since it is calculated to encourage a very general mistake, namely, that because high rents are paid for land, high prices will therefore be got for its produce. The very reverse, however, is the case, according to Dr. Smith's own clear statement. It is because high prices are paid that high rents are got.[10]

With this last statement Malthus in 1815 fully concurred, but it was with an attack on Buchanan that he launched the original part of *An Inquiry into the Nature and Progress of Rent and the Principles by which it is regulated.* He began, as he had to, with the *Économistes* and Adam Smith, and referred briefly to his two famous contemporaries who were writing in French, Say and Sismondi; Malthus then turned to 'Mr. Buchanan, of Edinburgh', pointing out that 'while former writers, though they considered rent as governed by the laws of monopoly, were still of opinion that this monopoly in the case of land was necessary and useful, Mr. Buchanan sometimes speaks of it even as prejudicial, and as depriving the consumer of what it gives to the landlord.'[11] A mild summing-up.

According to Malthus, land and its raw produce had three outstanding characteristics for the student of political economy:

First, and mainly, That quality of the earth, by which it can be made to yield a greater portion of the necessaries of life than is required for the maintenance of the persons employed on the land. [Agricultural apologists of the period wrote that four-fifths of the nation were living on the backs of the fifth who were farm labourers.]

2ndly, That quality peculiar to the necessaries of life of being able to create their own demand, or to raise up a number of demanders in proportion to the quantity of necessaries produced. [This was, of course, an essential ingredient of the principle of population, that a country was peopled up to the limits of its subsistence.]

And, 3dly, The comparative scarcity of the most fertile land. [This was the only point truly relevant to the differential theory of rent.][12]

Malthus himself was to realise the shortcomings of this analysis of the properties of land within the next five years: the great distress which followed the end of the war showed painfully that the empty stomachs of the unemployed did not constitute an effective demand for the necessities of life, while farmers and manufacturers alike were being ruined by falling prices and a general stagnation of trade. Thus when Malthus incorporated the pamphlet on *Rent* in the *Principles of Political Economy* he qualified his second characteristic feature of agricultural produce: 'That quality peculiar to the necessaries of life, *when properly distributed*, to create their own demand' (my italics).[13]

Other alterations were made when the pamphlet was expanded into a long chapter, but they did not affect Malthus's theory that rent is the result of the infinite gradations in the fertility of land; or, more accurately, the profitableness of land, since he appreciated diversities of location as well as soil: 'All land cannot be the most fertile; all situations cannot be the nearest to navigable rivers and markets.'[14]

The differential theory of rent was based on the axiom that there could be but one market price of corn; this was where the effective demand met the cost of production (the 'usual' wages of labour plus the 'normal' profits of stock) on the worst land which it was worth the farmers' while to cultivate - what would later be called marginal land. On that more fortunate land which was exceptionally fertile or well placed, this selling price where supply and demand coincided would clearly be well below the costs of production; there would therefore be a surplus over and above the current profit on agricultural capital, and this surplus was rent. It was a gift of Providence to the owners of land better than that at the margin of cultivation, and since it arose because their fields were able to produce corn at less than the market price, a high rent could obviously not be a component part of that price; thus the landlords might receive it with a clear conscience.

It will be apparent to modern readers that the differential theory of rent could never have been formulated except by economists writing in early-nineteenth-century Britain, where the land was almost entirely cultivated on a three-tier system practised nowhere else, except on a small scale in parts of Holland and Belgium. The work was done for wages, by labourers, directly employed by farmers, who provided the capital and made profits, while the land was owned by proprietors who received contractual money rents, regardless of individual good or bad harvests, although leases were usually only for terms of seven years. Thus it was natural for Malthus and Ricardo to follow Adam Smith in equating the three factors of production - land, labour and capital - with 'the three great divisions of society', landlords, labourers and capitalists.

Malthus thought that 'The effect of transferring all rents to tenants, would be merely the turning them into gentlemen, and tempting them to cultivate their farms under the superintendence of careless and uninterested bailiffs, instead of the vigilant eye of a master, who is deterred from carelessness by the fear of ruin, and stimulated to exertion by the hope of a competence. The most numerous instances of successful industry, and well directed knowledge, have been found among those who have paid a fair rent for their lands; who have embarked the whole of their capital in their under-taking; and who feel it their duty to watch over it with unceasing care, and add to it whenever it is possible.'[15] This passage was repeated verbatim in *Political Economy*, and presumably made a number of hard-headed farmers frown in bewilderment when it was translated into French; why, they must have wondered, were Englishmen allegedly so much more diligent when their capital was employed on other people's land than on their own?

It is also difficult not to smile when Malthus makes an affirmation concerning rent reminiscent of his unpopular statement about the laws of nature which are the laws of God, and which decree that the children of the poor should suffer starvation for their parents' imprudence. Rents must inevitably rise as more and more 'inferior land' is cultivated, at an ever-increasing cost, to feed a growing population. 'Therefore', wrote Malthus, it may be laid down

> as an incontrovertible truth, that as a nation reaches any considerable degree of wealth, and any considerable fullness of population ... the separation of rents, as a kind of fixture upon lands of a certain quality, is a law as invariable as the action of the principle of gravity. And that rents are neither a mere nominal value, nor a value unnecessarily and injuriously transferred from one set of people to another; but a most real and essential part of the whole value of the national property, and placed by the laws of nature where they are, on the land, by whomsoever possessed, whether the landlord, the crown, or the actual cultivator.[16]

This is no sudden conversion on Malthus's part, inspired by the Corn Law controversy. Over six years before, in his *Edinburgh Review* article on Ireland in July 1808, he had written of a rise in pecuniary rents as in the

natural and necessary order of things, in the progress of wealth and population. He appears again to be guilty of arguing that *post hoc* is *propter hoc*
when he repeats enthusiastically in 1815 'that a progressive rise of rents
seems to be necessarily connected with the progressive cultivation of new
land, and the progressive improvement of the old: and that this rise is the
natural and necessary consequence of the operation of four causes, which
are the most certain indications of increasing prosperity and wealth - namely,
the accumulation of capital, the increase of population, improvements in
agriculture, and the high price of raw produce, occasioned by the extension
of our manufactures and commerce'.[17] Ricardo put the matter much more
neatly in his *Principles*, when he stated that a rise in rents was a symptom
but never a cause of wealth.[18]

Malthus wrote, 'It is not of course meant to be asserted, that the high
price of raw produce is, separately taken, advantageous to the consumer';
but in the same pamphlet he repeated his assurance that for the poorer
consumers a high price for corn was 'a positive and unquestionable advantage
to them'. 'With regard to all the objects of convenience and comfort (and
there are many such consumed by the poor) their condition will be most
decidedly improved.'[19] In a footnote he showed his compassion for the
workers which was so often remarked by his friends:

> With regard to the unusual exertions made by the labouring classes
> in periods of dearness ... they are most meritorious in the
> individuals, and certainly favour the growth of capital. But no man
> of humanity could wish to see them constant and unremitted. They
> are most admirable as a temporary relief; but if they were constantly
> in action, effects of a similar kind would result from them, as from
> the population of a country being pushed to the very extreme limits
> of its food. There would be no resources in a scarcity. I own I do
> not see with pleasure the great extension of the practice of task work
> [piece-work]. To work really hard for twelve or fourteen hours in
> the day, for any length of time, is too much for a human being.
> Some intervals of ease are necessary to health and happiness ...

This note was omitted from the *Principles of Political Economy*; it was, after
all, not relevant to rent.

Another point in Malthus's favour is that he did not consider the landlord's
income from rent as the most important part of the whole economy, the
largest section of the home demand for manufactured goods, and the chief
source of national revenue, as was implied or expressed in many contemporary pamphlets in support of the Corn Laws. In a passage which shows
his foresight he wrote that 'in the progress of a country towards a high state
of improvement, the positive wealth of the landlord ought, upon the
principles which have been laid down, gradually to increase; although his
relative condition and influence in society will probably rather diminish,

owing to the increasing number and wealth of those who live upon a still more important surplus - the profits of stock.'[20] Here Ricardo was to disagree fundamentally with Malthus; Ricardo's thesis was that with a growing population and an ever-increasing scarcity of food, wages would rise with the rising price of provisions to such a point that profits would disappear altogether, while the rents of fortunately placed landlords would continue to augment to the disadvantage of the whole community.

Malthus himself, ever trying to be practical, warned landowners not to be too hasty in raising their rents when prices rose sufficiently to enable farmers to pay more: 'In the progress of prices and rents, rent ought always to be a little behind; not only to afford the means of ascertaining whether the rise be temporary or permanent, but even in the latter case, to give a little time for the accumulation of capital on the land, of which the landholder is sure to feel the full benefit in the end.'[21]

This is indeed practical advice, but in his letter to John Murray of 13 February 1815 Malthus obviously adverts to criticisms of the pamphlet as being too theoretical; they came, presumably, from the simple-minded protagonists of the Corn Law debate. He was then preparing a second edition of *Rent* (split into sections) which was not in fact ever published except as a chapter in the *Principles of Political Economy*. In the letter to Murray, Malthus wrote:

> I cannot do anything essential towards writing the tract to the *meanest capacities* without casting it quite anew, and running the risk of spoiling the whole, which would not be worth while. The fact is that the subject, tho it may appear quite easy before it is considered, is one of the most curious and difficult in the whole range of political economy ... Sir James Mackintosh writes me word, that he sees no other fault in it, other than that of its being too philosophical for the form in which it is published.

Malthus himself had been aware of this fault, and in the 'Advertisement' which served as a preface to the tract on *Rent* he wrote that 'if the nature of the disquisition should apppear to the reader hardly to suit the form of a pamphlet, my apology must be, that it was not originally intended for so ephemeral a shape.' He had previously explained that the tract contained the substance of some notes which, with others collected in the course of his professional duties, he was meaning to publish, but 'the very near connexion of the subject ... with the topics immediately under discussion, has induced me to hasten its appearance at the present moment. It is the duty of those who have any means of contributing to the public stock of knowledge not only to do so, but to do it at the time when it is most likely to be useful.'

It is impossible not to feel that Malthus was his own worst enemy.

There is of course some truth in the law of diminishing returns, especially in the application of successive doses of exactly the same sort of capital to a given area of land. But advances in technology can alter the whole situation. Both Malthus and Ricardo admitted the importance of agricultural 'improvements' but, perhaps because they were not even gardeners themselves, they underestimated their effects. Indeed, it seems clear from Ricardo's correspondence with Hutches Trower that he was deliberately resolute against becoming 'more enamoured of the vegetable part of the creation' at Gatcomb. In July 1815 Hutches Trower hoped his old friend would devote a portion of his time and attention to farming, 'and especially to that most interesting and important branch of it, the growth and culture of trees'. By September, in reply to a letter from Ricardo now lost, Trower had changed his tune, and wrote that he would 'regret exceedingly' if Political Economy 'were to give way to the humbler pursuits of farming and planting'.[22]

On the other hand the Rev. Richard Jones (1790-1855), Malthus's successor at Haileybury, was a passionate rose-grower; he is the only economist I know who took a square yard of earth as an example, and Maria Edgeworth addressed him as 'My dear King of Roses'.[23] Thus he knew in his bones, as the saying goes, that in real life farmers and market-gardeners were not concerned with applying to the land continual doses of a homogeneous abstraction called capital: those who embarked on 'improvements' were concerned with several different methods of field drainage; with the advantages of separate animal manures, spread in varying quantities; with a choice of procedures in harrowing or hoeing; with the economic as well as the climatic importance of timing the order of operations, the introduction of new hybrids, and so on. Jones may be said to have demolished the classical theory of rent in 1831. We cannot pursue the discussion here, but it would not be giving a true picture of Malthus - who was concerned above all things with the truth - if I did not point out his lack of historical sensibility.

In 1820 Malthus wrote of the labourers' 'decided elevation in the standard of their comforts and conveniences', and could almost *en passant* (and quite accurately) attribute this to a large extent to 'the improving cultivation of the country after 1720'.[24] Yet in his *Measure of Value*, an eighty-page essay published in 1823, he referred to 'an early period of society, when the soil was very fertile and the labour of 7 men only was necessary to produce 100 quarters of corn on land which paid little or no rent', and then to 'a more advanced period, when the last land taken into cultivation was less fertile, and the labour of 8 men was necessary to obtain the return of 100 quarters'.[25] Malthus cannot be expected to have known of the discoveries of modern archeology, which show that the poorest soil was the first cultivated, because no heavy loam could be scratched up with primitive tools; but two quotations from Richard Jones's *Essay on Rent* will demonstrate that it was possible even at this period (especially for someone who was himself an experimental cultivator) to have a truly historical approach to the subject:

The average corn produce of England at one time did not exceed 12 bushels per acre; it is now about double. Are we to believe that there is a law of nature which makes it inevitable that the cost of getting 24 bushels from one acre is really more than the cost of getting the same quantity from two?

The turnip and sheep husbandry, and the fresh capital employed to carry it on, produced a greater alteration in the fertility of the poor soils, than in that of the better; still it increased the absolute produce of each, and therefore it raised rents, while it diminished the differences in the fertility of the soils cultivated.[26]

Jones's *Rent* was not reprinted during his life-time. The *magnum opus* of which it was to form the first part was never written, possibly because he combined his appointment at Haileybury with posts on the Tythe and Charity Commissions. The differential theory of rent remains firmly established in all histories of economic thought, and rightly so; as Jones wrote of Malthus, 'It is the perilous privilege of really great men that their errors, as well as their wisdom, should be fertile in consequences.'[27]

What is tragic in the case of Malthus is that at times his common sense, his capacity for 'seeing things as they are', did break through his theorising. In 1820, in the second chapter (Section IV) of his *Principles of Political Economy*, he repeatedly contradicted what he wrote about rent in 1815.

'It is still true', wrote Malthus in 1820, 'that the cost of the great mass of commodities is resolvable into wages, profits, and rent . . . A very few may be resolvable into wages and profits, or even wages alone. But, as it is known that the latter class is confined to a very small proportion of the country's products, it follows that the payment of rent is an absolutely necessary condition of the supply of the great mass of commodities, and may properly be considered as a component part of price.' A little later on, Malthus showed appreciation of the different uses to which farming land may be put, as well as more inconsistency;

All cattle pay rent . . . In this respect they are essentially different from corn. By means of labour and dressing [with manure] a good crop of corn may be obtained from a poor soil, and the rent paid may be quite trifling compared with the value of the crop; but in uncultivated land the rent must be proportioned to the value of the crop, and, whether great or small per acre, must be a main ingredient in the price of the commodity produced.

As to the value of urban property, it 'is greatly affected by the strict monopoly of ground rents; and the necessity of paying these rents must affect the prices of almost all the goods fabricated in towns'.[28] And finally, 'no error seems to arise from considering rent as a component part of price, after we have properly explained its origin and progress.'[29] This must have been rather confusing for any readers unfamiliar with current economic discussion, as the chapter explaining the origin and progress of rent did not begin for another thirty pages.

None of the passages I have quoted in the paragraph above appear in the 1836 edition of the *Principles of Political Economy*; there is no evidence to show whether Malthus himself returned to the belief that rent was not a component part of price, or whether John Cazenove made these cuts, for the sake of theoretical consistency, after 'the Master' was dead. The master only inserted minor verbal alterations here when he was revising the book for the 'second edition' of 1823 which was never printed. In the article he wrote for the *Quarterly Review* of January 1824, attacking Ricardian economics as expounded by McCulloch, Malthus can only be described as sitting on the fence: 'If the price of a bushel of corn be the same, whether it be resolvable into more or less rent, rent cannot have much influence in determining its exchangeable value; and we think, on the whole, that satisfactory reasons have been given why, in tracing the causes of exchangeable value, in reference to the most important commodities, rent may be considered as having only a very inconsiderable effect.'[30]

It is impossible not to sympathise with the exasperation of Torrens and De Quincey, and also with later writers, infuriated by Malthus's changes of mind and, consequently, by what might be called his satyagraha to classification by historians of economic thought. But surely his pursuit of truth and his aversion to dogmatism are both admirable and endearing?

2 Rent, Wages and Profits

As has been noted, three writers contemporary with Malthus were also concerned with the law of diminishing returns on land. They were Ricardo, Torrens (his *Essay on the External Corn Trade* has already been quoted) and a 'Fellow of University College Oxford'. The latter was soon identified as Edward West (1782-1828), who was later knighted and became Chief Justice of Bombay, where he died; an anonymous biographer wrote that West, finding Oxford 'did not possess competent instructors for the more abstruse parts of mathematics', studied for a time in London with Malthus's former tutor William Frend.[31]

For Malthus and his contemporaries, it was irrelevant whether, as prices rose, successive 'layers' of labour or capital were applied to the same land to increase output, or whether an additional acreage of what had formerly been sparsely grazed waste land was enclosed and cultivated; as West put it, 'an equal quantity of work extracts from the soil a gradually diminishing return.' This was, as we know, an integral part of Malthus's principle of population, and it is important to bear in mind that by 1815 this principle was taken for granted by almost all the political economists.

Of this quartet of like-minded authors in February 1815, Malthus was the only one to be preoccupied with rent, and the only one to use the differential theory of rent to support the Corn Laws. Sir Edward West's title is self-explanatory: *Essay on the Application of Capital to Land with Observations shewing the Impolicy of any great Restriction of the Importation of Corn.* It probably appeared on 13 February, Malthus's forty-ninth birthday. Torrens's *External Corn Trade* and Ricardo's pamphlet were published on the 24th: the latter was called *An Essay on the Influence of a low Price of Corn on the Profits of Stock; shewing the Inexpediency of Restrictions on Importation: with Remarks on Mr. Malthus's two last Publications.* (These were *Rent*, which had appeared on 3 February, and the *Grounds* for approving the Corn Laws, which came out on the 10th.)

Ricardo and Malthus had been corresponding about the accumulation of capital and the rate of profit since the summer of 1813; by the end of 1814, as his letters show, Ricardo had virtually developed his 'system'. Thus he could very quickly produce his pamphlet in 1815, accepting as axiomatic a subsistence theory of wages based on the principle of population, and beginning both his introduction and his text with complimentary references to Mr Malthus and his 'very correct' definition of rent. At the insistence of his 'school-master' James Mill, Ricardo followed up his *Essay on Profits* with his *Principles of Political Economy*, which was published by Murray in April 1817; there was a second edition in 1819 and a third in 1821.

Richard Jones was very severe on Ricardo. According to Jones, Ricardo took Malthus's theories of population and rent, and

> overlooking altogether the limited extent of the field to which these principles were really applicable, undertook from them alone to deduce the laws which regulate the nature and amount of the revenue derived from land at all places, and under all circumstances; and not content with this, proceeded from the same narrow and limited data, to construct a general system of the distribution of wealth, and to explain the causes of variations which take place in the rate of profits, or amount of wages, over the surface of the globe.[32]

Very briefly, Ricardo's thesis was that the prices of commodities were determined by demand on the one hand and by the cost of production on the other. Rent was a surplus, not a part of true production costs; production costs therefore consisted of wages and profits. Owing to the principle of population, wages could not rise much above what was regarded as an acceptable subsistence level, according to the customs of the country; nor could they fall below it, if the 'race of labourers' were to be maintained and continued. Wages, consequently, were determined by the number of labourers in the market and the cost of producing corn on land at the margin of cultivation which paid no rent. Profits were what was left over from wages; or, as Ricardo put it: 'Profits, it cannot be too often repeated, depend on wages.' 'Whatever raises the wages of labour, lowers the profits of stock.'[33] 'Low wages are another name for high profits.'[34]

These statements are, of course, truisms, if everything else is assumed to be equal. David Buchanan put the matter in his usual lively way in one of his notes: 'The commodity fetches its just price in the market, and the two partners interested quarrel about the division of the spoil . . . What is it to the public whether the thing at issue goes into the pockets of the servants or the masters? . . . It is of no moment, as far as the community is concerned, how the price is divided between wages and profit.'[35]

It is important to remember Buchanan, in order that Ricardo may not be the sole scape-goat for the origin of the belief that wages may rise indefinitely at the expense of nobody but the wicked profiteering capitalist. It should also be remembered that Ricardo was perfectly consistent within the limitations of his own theory; all wages being regulated by the cost of subsistence from marginal land, 'a rise of wages equally affects all producers; it does not raise the price of commodities because it diminishes profits; and, if it did raise the price of commodities, it would raise them all in the same proportion, and would not therefore alter their exchangeable value.'[36] De Quincey proved this proposition with irrefutable chop-logic in the closely printed columns of the *London Magazine*, in April and May 1824, in a series of 'Templars' Dialogues' between Phaedrus, Philebus and the omniscient X.Y.Z. Unaccountably, readers of that generation appear to have found them good entertainment, and they inspired Samuel Bailey to write his anonymous *Critical Dissertation on Value*, which is today regarded as a minor economic classic.

More significant of the way Ricardo's doctrine of wages and profits had taken hold of the public was Francis Place's evidence before the Select Committee of the House of Commons on Artizans and Machinery. On 20 February 1824 Place was asked,

> 'Do not the masters, in consequence of a rise of wages, raise their prices?'
> 'No,' replied Place. 'I believe there is no principle of political economy better established than this of wages; increase of wages must come from profits.'[37]

Place was, of course, concerned to convince the Committee that combinations or unions of workmen to secure fair wages would not raise prices, but his thorough-going Ricardian principles were sincerely held. Later, on 7 May, McCulloch made the same point at much greater length. Responsible trade unionists today are as fully aware as anyone else that one man's pay-rise may be another man's price-rise, but it is impossible to deny that

287

Ricardo's doctrine has caused much mischief.

In justice to Ricardo, he was not concerned with profit for profit's sake. Like Adam Smith, he believed that it was accumulation with a view to profit that set in motion the greater part of the useful labour of every society; England at this period was 'taking off' as an industrial country, and heavy capital investment was essential to further progress. Incredible as it may seem, Ricardo thought that profits provided the only source of investment funds. As the price of corn rose, owing to the pressure of population and the need to cultivate inferior soils, so wages would have to rise too, and profits would dwindle to nothing; then no further investment could take place – and it was, of course, on the continuous accumulation and investment of capital that the demand for labour depended: Ricardo was therefore being quite sincerely philanthropic when he wrote that 'Nothing contributes so much to the prosperity and happiness of a country as high profits.'[38] It was true that as more marginal land was taken into cultivation, rents would automatically increase; but since, according to Ricardo, landlords never invested their revenue ('All savings are made from profits') this was of no advantage to the community.

Small wonder that with such a theory Ricardo maintained that 'the interests of the landlords are opposed to those of the other classes of society',[39] and advocated the importation of cheap corn.

Malthus's whole approach to his subject could not have been more different. The early parts of the chapter 'On the Wages of Labour' in his *Principles* have a pedagogic air about them, as though unconnected jottings, based largely on Adam Smith, had been strung together for the benefit of students; Ricardo in his 'Notes on Malthus' has little on which to comment. Nor can much be said about Malthus's painstaking attempt to give the history of wages in England during the past five centuries; he takes the wages of a labourer, where records were available, and compares them with the known price of wheat: when the labourer earned twopence a day, early in the reign of Edward III, he could purchase a peck, and so on, a daily peck of wheat being regarded as the appropriate remuneration for 'a good labourer in good times'.*

What is interesting is the use Malthus makes of this train of thought. It will be remembered that in the very first *Essay on Population* in 1798 he distinguished between the wealth of the nation, which he thought had been 'advancing with a quick pace', and the happiness of the poor, which depended upon the 'effectual funds for the maintenance of labour', and these he considered had been 'increasing very slowly'; basically, these funds consisted of the country's 'stock of provisions'.[40] He enlarged upon this in the great quarto: increased demands for labour from prosperous manufacturers might raise wages, but the labourers would be no better off if the price of food

---

*A peck is a measure of capacity, but a peck of wheat would weigh about 15 lb.

rose too, as it would do if the yearly stock of provisions in the country were not increasing; indeed, it might even diminish if men were enticed into industry from agriculture.[41]

By 1820 Malthus had experienced what was later to be called a slump, and was much influenced by what he saw: an abundance of wage-goods in the country was of no use to 'the poor' if they lacked the money to buy them. The labourer's 'corn wages' might indeed be high, estimated in pecks of wheat; but this did not necessarily mean that he was well off, for if the price of a peck of wheat was very low, the purchasing power of the worker's wage would be low too, in reference to other commodities. Moreover, if the price of corn were low, the farmer's profit would be low, and he would be unable to employ as many labourers as before; those he did employ might have to work short time, there would be fewer jobs available for their wives and children; 'after a period of great distress', wages in general would probably fall too. This would involve less effectual demand by both farmers and labourers for manufactured goods, so there would be further falls of prices, profits and employment. All this had been made painfully obvious in 1816, when the price of wheat was lower than it had been for twelve years, and the farmers and the poor had suffered together.

Thus, in 1820, Malthus thought that what mattered with regard to the demand for labour and the increase in population was not the bulk of provisions available, but 'the rate at which the whole *value* of the capital and revenue of the country increases annually; because, the faster the *value* of the annual produce increases, the greater will be the power of purchasing fresh labour, and the more will be wanted every year' (my italics).[42]

This is a highly significant passage in connection with the nature of profitable enterprise, which we touched on in sketching the physiocratic attitude to the tailor who increased the value of a piece of cloth by turning it into a coat, and this approach to profit will be referred to later. But the astonishing thing is that sometime after 1820 Malthus changed his mind again, with an important new development. There are in the Marshall Library at Cambridge three quarto sheets of paper watermarked 1822, folded to make an octavo booklet inscribed 'To be inserted page 261' in the 1820 *Principles*; unlike the other addenda which Malthus slipped into this volume, these are held together with a black pin. Cazenove used this manuscript, with some verbal alterations, on page 234 of the 1836 edition, and scrupulously followed Malthus in some dozen places on other pages where 'the resources of the country' were corrected to 'the funds for the maintenance of labour'. These funds 'consist principally in the necessaries of life, or in the means of commanding the food, clothing, lodging and firing of the labouring classes of society'.

'What in most cases', runs Malthus's manuscript, 'is principally necessary to a rapid increase of population is a great and continued demand for labour, and this is proportioned to the rate of increase in the *value* of those funds, whether arising from capital or revenue, which are actually employed in the maintenance of labour.' (Here and in the second paragraph of the manuscript the italics are Malthus's.) He goes on:

It has been sometimes thought that the demand for labour is in proportion only to the circulating, not to the fixed capital of the country. But strictly speaking the demand for labour is not proportioned to the increase of capital either fixed or circulating nor even to the increase of the exchangeable value of the whole annual produce. It is proportioned only as above stated to the rate of increase in the *value* of those funds which are actually employed in the maintenance of labour.

The next two paragraphs Cazenove prints almost exactly as Malthus wrote them, to the effect that if all the capital now employed in the production of material luxuries and conveniences were spent on the maintenance of servants and soldiers, a far greater population could be supported. Ricardo made the same point in the third edition of his *Principles*, in the new chapter 'On Machinery':

If a landlord, or a capitalist, expends his revenue in the manner of an ancient baron, in the support of a great number of retainers, or menial servants, he will give employment to much more labour, than if he expended it on fine clothes, or costly furniture; on carriages, on horses, or in the purchase of any other luxuries.[43]

Cazenove gives the reference to Ricardo in a footnote, but altogether leaves out of the text a long paragraph in the manuscript in which Malthus illustrates this proposition:

This will be made strikingly clear if we refer to any approximating calculations relating to the value of the whole produce of a manufacturing and mercantile country. Mr. Colquhoun estimated the value of the whole annual produce of the United Kingdom of Great Britain and Ireland in 1812 at [£] 432 millions supporting 3,500,000 families and 17 millions of persons. If this value in money were converted into necessaries, at the average prices of the time, then taking the full allowance of 60£ a year for each family as representing the wages of common labour, the whole of the new value created every year would be adequate to maintain more than double the actual population. - It is obvious however that this value is not so convertible, that the half of it consists in the value of conveniences and luxuries consumed by the possessors of rents, profits, government annuities and by those classes of labourers who earn very much more than the wages of common labour, and consequently that the value of the funds directly appropriated to the maintenance of the labouring classes, or the demand for labour, cannot have increased in proportion to the value of the whole produce, and might have been as great with a very much less capital.

It would be interesting to hear John Cazenove's reasons for not inserting this paragraph in the 1836 edition. Was he afraid of the obvious but completely mistaken political inferences? Malthus's basic analysis had gone far beyond the idea of a heap of produce of unvarying size to be divided out in ever-smaller shares amongst a growing population. The rigid distinction between wage-goods on the one hand, and the conveniences and luxuries consumed by the upper classes on the other, has ceased to be of major importance; what matters now is that whether Malthus is thinking of 'the funds for the maintenance of labour', or of the total resources of the country, he is thinking in terms of monetary value in a monetary economy, and no longer of a physical stock of provisions for the poor and trinkets for the rich.

With over another century of economic theory behind us, we can see how confused Malthus was, but most of us would agree that Malthus was more nearly 'right' than his friend in the following passage:

> Mr. Ricardo always seems to think that it is quite the same to the labourer, whether he is able to command more of the necessaries of life by a rise in the money price of labour, or by a fall in the money price of provisions; but these two events, though apparently similar in their effects, may be, and in general are, most essentially different. An increase in the money wages of labour generally implies such a distribution of the actual wealth as to give it an increasing value, to ensure full employment to all the labouring classes, and to create a demand for further produce, and for the capital which is to obtain it. In short, it is the infallible sign of health and prosperity. Whereas a general fall in the money price of necessaries often arises from so defective a distribution of the produce of the country, that the general amount of its value cannot be kept up; in which case, under the most favourable circumstances, a temporary period of want of employment and distress is unavoidable; and in many cases, as may be too frequently observed in surveying the different countries of the globe, this fall in the money price of necessaries is the accompaniment of a permanent want of employment and the most abject poverty, in consequence of a retrograde and permanently diminished wealth.[44]

With regard to Ricardo's doctrine of the inverse relationship between wages and profits, the allegedly muddle-headed Malthus saw the obvious difficulty as clearly as any writer professedly logical. Ricardo's detractors pointed out, as did the reviewer in the *British Critic* (probably Cazenove), that a Derbyshire iron-master or a Yorkshire clothier would assuredly exclaim that in their experience wages and profits always rose and fell together; in other words, 'when they could afford to give their men most they had most to themselves.'[45] Malthus explained, assuming that it was he who wrote the conclusion to the chapter on wages in the 1836 *Principles*:

> Profits, indeed, and interest, had always been and must always be estimated by proportions; but wages had always been, and always should be, estimated by quantity, either by the quantity of money which the labourer earns, or by the quantity of the necessaries and conveniences of life which that money enables him to purchase...
> ... Consequently, according to the ordinary and most correct language of society, we frequently see high profits and high wages, low profits and low wages going together; in using which expressions, *high* and *low*, as applied to profits, always refer to their *rate* or *proportion*, and as applied to wages, to their *quantity* or *amount*.[46]

When it came to what Buchanan called the quarrel over the spoils, between masters and men, Malthus agreed with Ricardo. In his article in the *Quarterly Review* for January 1824, after the statement about rent already quoted, Malthus affirmed that 'Of all the truths which Mr. Ricardo has established, one of the most useful and important is, that profits are determined by the proportion of the whole produce which goes to labour. It is, indeed, a direct corollary from the proposition, that the value of commodities is resolvable into wages and profits.' But 'it is, however, only one important step in the theory of profits',[47] and Malthus goes on to attempt to prove that labour's share of the spoils is determined not so much by the employers' demand for labour *per se*, when compared with the supply of it, as by a rising or falling demand for the products of labour.

Malthus's friend and Hertfordshire neighbour William Blake had put the matter more simply in a pamphlet published the year before: when there was an urgent demand for produce, as there had been during the war, it was clearly to the capitalist's advantage to go all out with longer hours and extra pay for his men.[48] With hindsight, it seems obvious that the 'demand for labour' depends upon the consumers' demand for its products or services, but at the time this approach to the subject marked a distinct advance from the early *Population* days; then Malthus urged the working people to limit their numbers in order that their labour might have a scarcity value relative to the employers' demand for it. Now the 'demand for labour' has been transferred from the capitalist to the consumer; the capitalist has become, in theory at least, a middle-man or manager, to raise funds and organise production on the consumers' behalf.

All the implications of this changed outlook could hardly have been apparent to Malthus himself, and it is perhaps dangerously anachronistic to think in these terms. It is also important to remember that at this period the unreformed House of Commons was still dominated by landowners, to the exclusion of capitalists as well as labourers, and - as we have seen - it was over his defence of the Corn Laws and the landlords' place in society that Malthus publicly clashed with Ricardo and his Whig friends.

In 1820 Malthus added three new sections to the original *Nature and Progress of Rent* in open opposition to Ricardo; two were on 'The strict and necessary Connexion of the Interests of the Landlord and of the State', and the last consisted of 'General Remarks on the Surplus Produce of the Land'. Most of the argument is familiar, from the Corn Law pamphlets, but Malthus scored a point, I think, when he said that 'the mode in which Mr. Ricardo estimates the increase or decrease of rents is quite peculiar; and this peculiarity in the use of his terms tends to separate his conclusions still farther from truth as enunciated in the accustomed language of political economy.' In applying Ricardo's language to our own country, 'we must say that rents have fallen considerably during the last forty years, because, though rents have greatly increased in exchangeable value ... it appears, by the returns to the Board of Agriculture, that they are now only a fifth of the gross produce, whereas they were formerly a fourth or a third.'[49]

Malthus's main thesis in these sections was that the great increase in rents during the past century had been due to increased productivity, and he went on to illustrate from the example of Ireland how closely linked were the fortunes of farming and manufactures. With more regard for truth than for his theory of rent, Malthus wrote that 'an operose and ignorant system of cultivation, combined with such a faulty distribution of property as to check the progress of demand, might keep the profits of cultivation low, even in countries of the richest soil ... The great source of the future increase of rents will be improvements in agriculture, and the demand occasioned by a prosperous external and internal commerce, and not the increases of price occasioned by the additional quantity of labour required to produce a given quantity of corn [on progressively inferior soils].'[50]

Malthus, as was noted earlier, had visited Ireland in 1817, and his reactions should dispel the myth that his delight in country scenes had given him the outlook of a bigoted physiocrat. He wished to see an Ireland where all kinds of property were secure, and an improved system of agriculture would 'raise the food and raw materials required for the population with the smallest quantity of labour necessary to do it in the best manner', and the remainder of the people 'instead of loitering about upon the land', should be 'engaged in manufactures and commerce carried on in great and flourishing towns'.[51]

This seems quite inconsistent with the early Malthus, and Torrens, apt as ever, followed up his previous criticism: his *Essay on the Production of Wealth* appeared in 1821, after Ricardo and Malthus had both given the world their *Principles*. Torrens's comment was: 'As presented by Mr. Ricardo, Political Economy possesses a regularity and simplicity beyond what exists in nature; as exhibited by Mr. Malthus, it is a chaos of original but unconnected elements.'[52]

One unconnected element was concerned with Ricardo's attitude towards rent as a by-product of the niggardliness of Nature, who had not made all land equally fertile; for Malthus it was a bonus, on an ascending scale, on lands which yielded progressively more than those at the margin. Malthus was inclined to confuse the 'surplus' economic product which gave rise to rent with the 'surplus' physical product which enabled a relatively small proportion of the labour force to grow food for a whole community - but that does not detract from the following passage:

> If any person will take the trouble to make the calculation, he will see that if the necessaries of life could be obtained [here Malthus added 'and distributed'] without limit, and the number of people could be doubled every twenty-five years, the population which might have been produced from a single pair since the Christian aera, would have been sufficient, not only to fill the earth quite full of people, so that four should stand in every square yard, but to fill all the planets of our solar system in the same way, and not only them, but all the planets revolving round the stars which are visible to the naked eye, supposing each of them to be a sun, and to have as many planets belonging to it as our sun has. Under this law of population, which, excessive as it may appear when stated in this way, is, I firmly believe, best suited to the situation and nature of man, it is quite obvious that some limit to the production of food, or some other of the necessaries of life, must exist ... It is not easy to conceive a more disastrous present - one more likely to plunge the human race in irrecoverable misery, than an unlimited facility of producing food in a limited space.[53]

One must regret that Malthus did not enlarge upon this idea in the *Essay on Population*. It is interesting that the British classical economists were concerned only with food, with this one digression to standing-room. Although Ricardo was very conscious of the varying degrees of 'fertility' in gold and silver mines, as was natural in a society still thinking of money in terms of the precious metals, he was insistent that the doctrine of rent applied only to 'the surface of the earth'. As he wrote to Malthus on 18 December 1814, he believed that if there were no increasing difficulty in obtaining food, 'profits would never fall, because there are no other limits to the profitable production of manufactures but the rise of wages'.[54] It seems extraordinary to us that neither he nor Malthus saw any limit to profitable manufacture through the increased difficulty of obtaining such raw materials as coal, or iron ore, brick or china clay, tin or slate; but it has been estimated that at this period only about 20 per cent of everything consumed came from mines or quarries; today in industrial countries mineral resources may account for as much as 70 per cent of total consumption.[55]

Malthus made many alterations to his chapter headed 'Of the Profits of Capital'. But like his contemporaries, he accepted throughout the Smithian concept of the capitalist 'advancing' to the labourers their daily supply of necessities, for the cost of which he would recoup himself at the end of the farming year, when the crop was harvested and sold. It was all in 'corn'. Corn was advanced from stock for the labourers to eat while the bare fields were ploughed, seed corn was put into the ground, whence more corn was duly garnered. It is easy to see how in a rural background wages could be considered as the workers' share of the produce in a palpably hylic sense, while the farmer's profit might be gauged in material terms by the amount of wheat produced from a given quantity of seed.

With this in mind, Malthus went to some length, with arithmetical examples, to show that the farmer's profit, like the labourers' total remuneration, did *not* depend on the physical yield of the grain, but on the price which could be obtained for it in the market, as compared with the monetary outlay on seed and other production costs; thus he might make a small profit after a bumper harvest if the price of wheat fell sharply, and a high profit from poor yields if prices rose disproportionately, as they often did in times of scarcity. Malthus was then able to go on to 'manufacturing and mercantile employments' and make the point again, that profits must be measured by monetary values and not by quantities of output: 'The varying rate of profits, therefore, in the production of every commodity, depends upon the excess of its value when sold above the known value of the advances, determined in all cases by the state of the supply and the demand.'[56]

Malthus agreed with Ricardo that the general rate of profit must be limited 'by the powers of the soil last cultivated', since capital would theoretically 'flow' between industry and agriculture until the returns from both were equal. But limitation was not the same as regulation; although profits could rise no higher than this, Malthus maintained that they might easily fall lower. In fact,

> in the actual state of things in most countries of the world, and within limited periods of moderate extent, the rate of profits will practically depend more upon the causes which affect the relative abundance or scarcity of capital, and the demand for produce compared with the supply, than on the fertility of the last land taken into cultivation.[57]

It was this stress on the demand for produce that was to mark the greatest difference between Malthus on the one hand and Ricardo and almost everybody else on the other.

3 Labour and Profits

We have touched on Ricardo's doctrine of the inverse relationship between wages and profits, which was to have important historical results; even more seismic was what became known as the Labour theory of value. It was with this that Ricardo began the third edition of his *Principles of Political Economy*:

> The value of a commodity, or the quantity of any other commodity for which it will exchange, depends on the relative quantity of labour which is necessary for its production, and not on the greater or less compensation which is paid for that labour.[58]

It is important to bear in mind that by 'labour' Ricardo meant physical labour itself, muscular exertion, not the remuneration or wages of the workers. In modern everyday speech we refer to labour costs and wage costs indiscriminately in monetary terms; the labour cost theory of value was concerned solely with the amount of human energy needed in production.

Adam Smith had given the labour cost theory of value a plausible start:

> In that early and rude state of society which precedes both the accumulation of stock and the appropriation of land, the proportion between the quantities of labour necessary for acquiring different objects seems to be the only circumstance which can afford any rule for exchanging them for one another. If among a nation of hunters, for example, it usually costs twice the labour to kill a beaver which it does to kill a deer, one beaver should naturally exchange for or be worth two deer.[59]

Ricardo took this as applying to all stages of society, and the political charms of the labour cost theory of value are still proof against its attackers in some circles.

Malthus attacked the theory on three grounds. First, an article could not have exchangeable value if it had no value in use or esteem. Wild strawberries were not valuable *because* they had taken a day to collect; someone had stooped for a day to gather them because of their intrinsic value as a pleasant form of food, without which there would have been no demand for them in the market. The labour the strawberries had cost in picking was not, therefore, the sole cause of their value.

Second, even in the most primitive societies some form of capital was necessary; Malthus does not make the point, but a disposable quantity of strawberries could not have been amassed without a basket or some other kind of container. The example Malthus used was the bow and arrow necessary to hunt the deer. Proponents of the labour cost theory tried to resolve this difficulty by calling these aids to production hoarded, accumulated or indirect labour, but here again the limitations of the theory are obvious: how much of the value of a sack of flour should be attributed to the miller's immediate labour, and how much to the accumulated labour embodied in his grindstones and his wheel? This point was taken up by writers opposed to what became known as Ricardian Socialism. Samuel Read in 1829 protested that 'the labourers have been flattered and persuaded that they produce all ... It is truly astonishing that this doctrine should have been maintained till this time of day in a country where the effects of capital [in increasing the productive power of labour] are so remarkably conspicuous.'[60]

The third difficulty, allied to the problem of the rudimentary capital necessary to make labour effective, was the time factor. This worried Ricardo. He wrote to McCulloch a few weeks before he died, 'I cannot get over the difficulty ... of the oak tree, which perhaps originally had not 2/ expended on it in the way of labour, and yet comes to be worth £100.'[61] Even more awkward was the wine which increased in value as it matured. James Mill attempted to sidestep this embarrassment by assuming a theoretical quantity of labour at work in the process of fermentation, which was delightedly seized upon by Samuel Bailey: it is indeed ridiculous to contemplate that additional labour which, 'in defiance of bars and bungs, pertinaciously settles upon a cask of wine which has been scrupulously preserved from human hands in the security of a well locked cellar'.[62] As Whishaw wrote to a friend about James Mill, 'He is clever and ingenious, but by no means a sensible man.'[63]

Malthus's solution was the adaptation of another of Adam Smith's ideas, known as the labour command theory of value. Having dismissed rent as a component part of price, Malthus attributed the exchangeable value of a commodity to the 'labour and profits' combined in it. Some commodities, like a straw bonnet or a piece of Brussels lace, were of a high labour and low profit content; others, which involved heavy machinery, embodied little labour but much 'profit', as did Ricardo's timber, owing to the decades which must elapse before any reward for the initial outlay could be obtained. In most cases it was impossible to ascertain the proportions to be attributed to labour and profit in any given article, but with the labour command theory this was irrelevant. Malthus for years attempted to prove (to nobody's satisfaction) that the combined value of the labour and profit embodied in a commodity must be equal to the quantity of labour which that commodity could command in the market.

It does not sound a very helpful concept. In general, however, it is considered an improvement on the labour cost theory, since it relates value to purchasing power. In everyday language, in a free society with a market economy, the value of anything is what you can get for it. As Malthus wrote to Pierre Prévost (who translated *Population*): 'The reason why I have not taken the invariable sacrifice of the labour as the measure of value, is, that I consider this sacrifice as *cost* of the labour to the labourers, and not its *value in exchange*, which must refer to the estimate placed on this by others.'[64]

As always, Malthus is concerned with demand. The value of a commodity is not what it cost the supplier, but what the demander is prepared to give for it. It is the current market value of the crop, not the hours worked or the quantity of corn produced, which determines the farmers' profits and the labourers' wages.

Where we cannot follow Malthus is in equating this exchangeable value, or price of a commodity, with the quantity of *labour* which it will command. One immediately asks, 'What sort of labour?' Both the labour cost and labour command theories assume that labour is homogeneous; both Malthus and Ricardo admitted that it was not, yet both believed that all other forms of labour could be evaluated in relation to 'the great mass of day labour', which 'is of the same character in regard to physical strength and duration'. Thus Malthus could write:

> In every country this sort of labour . . . may be considered as the standard into which every other kind of labour is resolvable, and no difficulty will arise from the acknowledged fact that a great part of the labour of every country is of a higher value than the standard. If the labour of a common journeyman watchmaker be paid at the rate of ten shillings a day, and that of a common agricultural labourer at twenty pence, the only effect will be that each day's labour employed on the watch, will communicate to that watch a value in exchange arising from intrinsic causes equivalent to that of six days of the standard labour; and the power of the standard labour to measure the difficulty of obtaining the watch will in no degree be impaired.[65]

Before we are too hard on Malthus, it must be noted that this extraordinary belief was actually put into practice during his life-time. In 1832 Robert Owen set up the National Equitable Labour Exchange in London, in the Gray's Inn Road. It dealt mainly in clothing and household goods, and beautifully engraved notes were issued similar to the bank-notes of the period: 'Deliver to Bearer Exchange Stores to the Value of Five Hours'. The smallest tokens were circular cards for one-sixth of an hour, which was the equivalent of a penny, sixpence an hour being taken as the standard wage;[66] adjustments had to be made to cover not only the cost of materials, but also the remuneration of skilled craftsmen whose wages were above this rate. There were various complications and, as G. D. H. Cole pointed out, nothing would have been either lost or gained by this translation or re-translation of pence into labour-time 'if the goods had really been worth the sums asked for them. But some were worth more and some less ... One man might take twelve hours to make what another would make in six; and while for some articles it was fairly easy to fix a standard time allowance, for others there was nothing for it but to accept the estimate of the maker ... When the Exchange opened, naturally people bought what was cheap and left what was dear on the hands of the promoters.' This Exchange, like those in South London, Birmingham and Liverpool, closed down in 1834.[67]

There is no evidence that Malthus, or any other member of the Political Economy Club, ever heard of this experiment; but there is no doubt that he was obsessed by labour theories of value. It is also obvious from J. L. Mallet's diaries that the Club, as such, was quite aware that the labour force consisted of motley workmen, and not a homogeneous liquid which flowed in such a way that all wages were equalised, at one level, like the unruffled surface of a reservoir.

As early as April 1824, when the laws against Combination were being discussed, the Political Economy Club debated 'the reason why the labourer absorbs a larger proportion of what is produced than he did ten or twelve years ago'.[68] In 1831, 1832 and 1833 the matter came up repeatedly. There was admittedly 'great want of employment and suffering'; but the skilled men, mechanics or shoemakers, bookbinders, plumbers, and so on, were more prosperous than they had ever been before, since their money wages had not fallen with falling prices. This was attributed largely to the trade unions, who would strike and live miserably on poor relief rather than accept lower wages, and also to 'the greater weight of public opinion and popular feeling which supported them against the capitalist'.

Mallet wrote in his account of a meeting held on 9 February 1833: 'Mr. Malthus and myself coincided in this opinion, and also thought that although the wages of all persons employed had been kept up, somewhat artificially, the consequences had been to limit employment, and to throw on the poor rates and on the charitable funds of society a large mass of individuals whose labour was thus precluded from entering into competition with the mass of privileged labourers ...'[69] Mallet might not have known that Malthus and Ricardo had touched on this subject in July 1821. Malthus maintained, 'We know from repeated experience that the money price of labour never falls till many workmen have been for some time out of work.' Ricardo contradicted him: 'I know no such thing ... for why should some agree to go without any wages while others were most liberally rewarded?'[70]

It is astonishing that Malthus, since he appeared to perceive clearly the emergence of a new situation, should have been concerned for so long with Adam Smith's labour theories of value; these theories related to 'perfect competition' amongst agricultural workers who, by 1831, amounted to only a quarter of the employed adult males in the United Kingdom. Malthus's attempt in 1823 to make such standard labour an invariable measure of value will be referred to in a later section.

Meanwhile we must revert to Malthus's preoccupation with what he regarded as the source or cause of exchangeable value, and which he made the subject of two papers read before the Royal Society of Literature. The first (4 May 1825) was entitled *On the Measure of the Conditions necessary to the Supply of Commodities*; the second, read on 7 November 1827, he headed *On the meaning which is most usually and most correctly attached to the term 'Value of a Commodity'*.[71] This was the last piece of original writing of Malthus's to be published during his life-time: the *Summary View of the Principle of Population* which appeared in 1830 was merely a reprint of an article he had written for the *Encyclopaedia Britannica* seven years earlier.

I can find no record of the size of Malthus's learned audience at the Royal Society of Literature, nor how they reacted to his papers, which a recent Fellow dismissed as 'very dry'. But for anyone wishing to understand Malthus's doctrine that the value of a commodity is composed of labour and profits, these short essays can be recommended for their comparative simplicity. As is so often the case, enlightenment comes from a footnote - in this instance, at the beginning of the first paper (with Malthus's italics):

> *The natural and necessary conditions of the supply of commodities* are precisely the same as *the natural and necessary costs of production*, when reduced to their simplest elements; but I have preferred the former expression, because the term *cost*, if not well guarded, is too apt to convey the idea of *money* expenditure.[72]

This I found illuminating. In thinking of a profit as a monetary percentage gain on capital invested, it is easy to lose sight of what is meant in non-economic terms by 'a profitable activity'; that is, an activity which is beneficial, advantageous, or worth while. Thus, money apart, it is often advantageous to turn rectangles of cloth into coats; a piece of cloth can indeed be draped around the body for warmth, but for many occupations a fitted garment with buttons and sleeves is infinitely more convenient. Yet the profitableness of an activity depends upon a host of variables summed up by the word 'demand': under certain conditions it might be more beneficial, advantageous, or profitable to hem the cloth for use as blankets, rather than to make it up into thick coats for which there is no demand in the tropics or among the bed-ridden. Thus, apart from seasonal variations, miscalculation on the producers' part, or monopoly conditions (natural or artificial), Malthus held that the value of commodities depended on 'not only the quantity of manual labour required to produce them, but the quantity and rate of profits necessary to continue the application of this labour to the production of these commodities'.[73]

It is this preoccupation with demand that distinguishes Malthus from the other classical economists: there will not be a continued supply of goods unless their production is profitable; whether production is or is not profitable depends on effective demand; therefore effective demand is a necessary condition of supply. Thus Malthus came to affirm that with regard to 'a class of commodities of the greatest extent, it is acknowledged that the existing market prices are, at the moment they are fixed, determined upon a principle distinct from the cost of production . . . the great law of demand and supply is called into action to determine what Adam Smith calls natural prices, as well as what he calls market prices'.[74]

This does not mean that Malthus had gone back to the physiocratic theory of profit upon alienation. Obviously there could be no profit in a monetary economy unless a product were sold; but the price at which the product was sold was determined by the increased value the raw material naturally acquired in the course of the production of the finished article - and that value was dependent on the effective demand for it. The implications of this led to the greatest purely economic debate in which Malthus was involved.

4 Production and Consumption

Journalists have always been quick to pick out what makes a headline, although at the beginning of the nineteenth century their readers would have felt badly cheated had they wasted expensive paper-space on letters several inches high; people then expected their money's worth, in dense columns of sonorous literary English. Both press and pamphleteers fell at once on the same point in Malthus's *Principles of Political Economy*. It is summed up in the title of an anonymous work of 130 pages published by Rowland Hunter in 1821:

> An Inquiry into those Principles, respecting the Nature of Demand and the Necessity of Consumption, lately advocated by Mr. Malthus, from which it is concluded, that taxation and the maintenance of unproductive consumers can be conducive to the progress of wealth.

To the simple-minded there must have seemed no end to the wicked absurdities of Mr Malthus. First he wanted to prevent the poor from marrying, and to let them starve for lack of parish relief; next he defended the Corn Laws, which were again before the public eye in 1820; now he was asserting that the maintenance of a body of consumers whom he himself called 'unproductive' was essential to national prosperity, and if the public did not voluntarily support enough of these parasites they must be sustained from taxation.

It is necessary to remember that Malthus's under-consumptionist theory was not connected with what would later be called the trade cycle. It arose quite logically from his belief that the value of a commodity consisted of the labour and profits worked up in it; the workers, with their labour, could buy the labour part of the nation's total product, but who could buy the profit part? John Cazenove made the point briefly and clearly in a footnote in 1836: 'The demand created by the productive labourer himself can never be an *adequate* demand, because it does not go to the full extent of what he produces. If it did, there would be no profit, consequently no motive to employ him. The very existence of a profit upon any commodity presupposes a demand *exterior* to that of the labour which has produced it.'[75]

The unproductive labourers were to provide this exterior demand. As we have seen (pages 203-4) Malthus stuck to Adam Smith's distinction between productive and unproductive labour. This again was the logical outcome of Malthus's definition of wealth as 'the *material* objects necessary, useful or agreeable to man, which have required some portion of human exertion to appropriate or produce' (my italics).[76] Before the invention of sound-recording the song, in Adam Smith's words, really did perish in the instant of its production, on the lips of the singer. Indeed, Francis Horner had regretted in 1801 that these things, such as songs and reels, could not be bottled up or kept in a drawer, ready for use when one longed to hear them.[77] Thus the beautiful voice of Madame Catalani (1779-1849) was not wealth, because her songs could not be stored in a warehouse; but her earnings at the height of her fame, which amounted to about £16,000 per annum at the time Malthus was writing, made her an excellent effective demander.

The debate is not quite over. Brougham trounced Lord Lauderdale's antagonists in 1804 for the paradox of calling the makers of musical instruments 'productive' when the performers who were to use them were 'unproductive', and so on.[78] In the discussions on the British Selective Employment Tax (SET) in 1966 analogous arguments were used about the makers of hairdressing equipment, who were a 'manufacturing industry' and exempt from the tax, and the hairdressers themselves, who were a 'service industry' and therefore liable to it. By 1971 a new Chancellor of the Exchequer could declare, regardless of party politics, that 'the distinction between manufacturing and services is in fact quite untenable.'[79]

It is important here not to read too much in to Malthus. To begin with, he makes no distinction between unproductive consumers with fixed incomes and those whose incomes might be expected to rise and fall with a nation's general prosperity and adversity, such as musicians or prize fighters; he was not concerned with what later economists called 'ironing out the trade cycle'; he believed that over-production was inherent in a free monetary economy all the time. And second, his productive labourers expressly included 'carriers and shopmen', who in 1966 would in the majority of cases have been liable to SET because they provided services rather than goods.

What was relevant to Malthus in this connection was not what people did, or how their pay fluctuated, but where their money came from. If men were employed by a capitalist with a view to profit, they were productive. If they were not paid from capital, but from revenue, they were unproductive: they might be private domestic servants paid from their master's income (however acquired) or they might be generals and judges paid from the national revenue; from the standpoint of economic analysis they were all unproductive labourers because they did not reproduce, with a profit, the equivalent of what they consumed. Later Malthus decided that 'the term unproductive is unfortunate'. In a letter to Dr Chalmers he wrote on 6 March 1832 that he was going 'to change it for *personal services*', and this is the phrase used in the 1836 edition of the *Principles of Political Economy*.[80]

Malthus distinguished between those whose personal services were, so to speak, paid for compulsorily out of taxation, and those upon whom a man might voluntarily expend his revenue, a category which included teachers, doctors and lawyers as well as footmen and opera singers. But he also included in his list a third class of unproductive consumers, who did no work at all, those whose incomes were derived from the interest on money previously lent to the government, the fund-holders or stock-holders. Other economists were to point out that these people were living on capital amassed by labour and abstinence as legitimately as anyone else, and that the loans which they or their predecessors had made to their country had saved the day against Napoleon; but their unpopularity during the hard post-war years is understandable, and their numbers and importance as a class were greatly exaggerated. Far less defensible were the holders of sinecures, or those who had pensions for no better reason than that they were well-bred and indigent with powerful connections, and the navy and army officers who were able to retire on half-pay after a nominal period of service.

It is not difficult to imagine the outcry, and to sympathise with those who railed at Malthus for wanting, on the one hand, to abolish the Poor Law, while affirming on the other hand that 'splendid paupers', living 'in idleness, pomp and luxury' were indispensable to the progress of wealth. Their indignation seemed reasonable: it was surely inconsistent of Economist Malthus to say there were too few demanders for the products available, when Population Malthus had insisted that there were too many. As a pseudonymous writer put it in 1825: 'We beg our readers' permission to appropriate the title of Humbug School of Political Economy to those writers and orators who maintain the co-existence of excess of population and over-production.'[81]

These issues had, in fact, been taken up before Malthus's *Principles of Political Economy* was published, by a clerk in the War Office called Simon Gray. In 1815 he produced a quarto even longer and heavier than Malthus's, entitled *The Happiness of States, or, an Inquiry concerning Population, the Modes of Subsisting and Employing it*. Later he said that the book was actually written in 1804, the year after Malthus's great second edition of *Population*, and the year in which the distinction between productive and unproductive labour was a source of argument in connection with Lord Lauderdale's *Nature and Origin of Public Wealth*. Gray was to write in 1840 that in *The Happiness of States* 'I had, as I conceived, fully established in what wealth, or the medium of procuring the necessaries and comforts of life, consisted. That is, CHARGEABILITY. Whatever species of circuland or article, whether solid or intangible, possesses this quality, is a portion of wealth.'[82]

Gray is only just beginning to receive the attention he merits, in an age perhaps less worried by jargon than his own. In his time he was laughed at for describing farmers as 'manufacturers of agricultural circuland' and physicians as 'medical circulators'.

Most unfortunately, Gray also made himself ridiculous by publishing in 1817 and 1818 two books (far more readable than his great work) under the name of a mythical Dr George Purves. The first was *All Classes Productive of National Wealth; or the Theories of M. Quesnai, Dr. Adam Smith and Mr. Gray Analysed and Examined*. The second was *Gray versus Malthus: the Principles of Population and Production Investigated*.

Ricardo treated Dr Purves, 'if there be really any such person in existence',[83] as nothing but a joke. Malthus, I think, may have taken Gray more seriously. Early in 1823 he was visited by Alexander Everett, the United States ambassador to the Hague, who had occupied himself during the previous winter with the composition of a little book called *New Ideas on Population*. Everett was enchanted by Malthus: he had 'rarely met with a finer specimen of the true philosophic temper, graced and set off by the urbanity of a finished gentleman'. In the course of their discussion on Everett's pamphlet, Malthus suggested that 'the leading principle maintained in it, is the same in substance with that of a work on Population by Mr. S. Gray.' Everett had not read Gray, but did not agree with Malthus's opinion after 'a hasty reference to some passages of his book at the house of Mr. Malthus'.[84]

Malthus can hardly be accused of plagiarising Gray, since he stuck to his guns about productive and unproductive labour, and to his principle of population, both of which theories Gray believed he had refuted. Gray held specifically against Population Malthus that it was not true that in the case of subsistence supply regulated demand:

> The universal law of nature with respect to circulation is, that the demand regulates the supply in the case of subsistence, as of all other things dependent on the will of man ... Our farmers have lately (and often before) found to their cost that subsistence may increase beyond the demand for it, so as to lower the price, just as in the case of manufacturers, to such a degree that, far from leaving them any profit, it subjects them to a ruinous loss.[85]

In such a case the material solidity of their product, without chargeability, was of no consequence whatever. Gray could scarcely have anticipated that here Economist Malthus would more or less agree with him.

With regard to Adam Smith, Gray bewailed the social rancour caused by what he called the Unproductive Theory. 'It is gloomy and malevolent, and calculated to set the various classes of society against one another, as well as to inspire general discontent and a spirit hostile to subordination among the lower classes.'[86] Yet these lower classes were inconsistent: they protested that the rich rioted in abundance on the fruits of their labours, and then complained of absentee squires 'who spend their money elsewhere, which would give us employment and make us all more comfortable'; that was 'virtually to acknowledge that the rich are productive with respect to them'.[87] The rich, according to Gray, commanded more circuland solely because their talents, possessions or output were of higher chargeability than those of the poor.

No doubt because he was himself a public servant, Gray was very conscious that taxes were odious to the multitude, since they represented money taken from them 'for which they receive nothing tangible or visible in return. They do in fact, however, receive in return something most truly valuable, which is protection from foreign enemies and from lawless, dishonest and ferocious men at home.'[88] Apart from this benefit, wise government expenditure was an important factor in creating demand: 'Retrenchment is always a fine topic for a public orator . . . But nothing can be clearer in statistics than that, *in point of wealth*, retrenchment is almost uniformly injurious to the *working* classes, though they cry out loudest for it. Retrenchment is, in fact, equivalent to a diminution of employment.'[89]

One must stress here that whereas Malthus needed his unproductive consumers to take up the slack, as it were, in the effective demand for the annual produce of the country, Gray also saw the public servants, professional classes and entertainers as prime suppliers of disposable capital: their savings could flow freely into the most profitable channels, being locked up neither in land nor in machinery.[90] Gray was, indeed, very little troubled by the orthodox economists' rigid distinction between capital, which was 'employed', and revenue, which was 'consumed'.

This is shown clearly in Gray's treatment of domestic servants, a class of 'unproductive' consumers of recognised importance in Europe at this time. The prevalent opinion, regardless of whether they were productive or not, was that they were paid out of their employer's revenue, and were therefore in a completely different category from the workers in his cotton-mill, who were paid from his circulating capital. Malthus was particularly emphatic that the wages of domestic servants 'have no tendency to increase cost and lower profits'.[91] But from Gray's point of view there is no labour 'which is *charged for and paid for* which does not add a value to the subject on which it has been bestowed . . . The charge is made as fully by the master for his house-servant as for his servant in the manufactory. Both these charges alike enter into the price of what he sells, and alike are drawn from the public or his customers.'[92]

Malthus himself was much interested in the position of 'menial servants', as he called them, and on 6 March 1826 he opened a discussion at the Political Economy Club with the question 'What would be the effect on the Wealth and Capital of a country of an increasing taste for menial servants and attendants compared with material products foreign and domestic?'[93]

We can only guess at the way the debate would have gone, with the usual references to Adam Smith and his legendary chiefs and barons, in an isolated subsistence economy, surrounded by crowds of idle retainers because there was no other form of wealth. Malthus probably admitted that the desire for a display of liveried footmen, like a fondness for the theatre, could stimulate the Georgian industrialist to greater exertion in the manufacture of goods, and thus allow that attendants and actors were indirectly productive. He might also at this meeting have developed the characteristically negative approach to the subject which appeared in the posthumous *Principles of Political Economy* ten years later (the passage does not occur in the 1820 edition):

> It is also very important to observe, that menial servants are absolutely necessary to make the resources of the higher and middle classes of society efficient in the demand for material products. No persons possessing incomes above five hundred pounds a year, would be inclined to have such houses, furniture, clothes, carriages and horses, and such eatables and drinkables in their houses as they have at present, if they were obliged to sweep their own rooms, brush and wash their own furniture and clothes, clean their own carriages and horses ... [94]

We may smile, but the fact remains that the number of people employed in domestic and similar services, expressed as a proportion of the total British labour force, was to rise fairly steadily throughout the nineteenth century: it reached its peak in 1891, when such service probably accounted for 15.8 per cent of the total occupied population; thereafter it sharply declined, with dramatic drops after each of the two world wars. From 1801 to 1831 the estimated percentage rose from 11.5 to 12.6, so Malthus was not mistaken in thinking that these 'unproductive labourers' played a significant part in the national economy.[95]

All this was irrelevant to Ricardo. Since on his system the value of commodities was dependent on labour alone, all labour was, so to speak, swapped or bartered for labour, production for production, inevitably balanced in accordance with Say's Law (see page 205). As far as Malthus's under-consumptionist theory was concerned, Ricardo wrote that 'A body of unproductive labourers are just as necessary and useful with a view to future production, as a fire, which should consume in the manufacturer's warehouse the goods which those unproductive labourers would otherwise consume.' And again, 'What power has an unproductive consumer? Will the taking 100 pieces of cloth from a clothier's manufactory, and clothing soldiers and sailors with it, add to his profits? - yes, in the same way as a fire would.'[96]

This popular, almost vulgar, reaction to what Malthus was trying to say seems unworthy of Ricardo's intelligence. He knew perfectly well that cloth for military uniforms was not requisitioned but paid for. But to be consistent within his own system he had to deny the possibility of universal over-production or, as it was called at this period, a general glut. The Ricardian school admitted that as the result of miscalculations on the part of merchants or manufacturers there might be too much of one particular commodity in one particular time or place; but that was only because there was too little of another commodity for which to exchange it. Both Malthus and Ricardo were enthusiasts for hard work, and deplored the lazy inhabitants of Central America (as newly described by Humboldt), who lived solely on bananas, and therefore had nothing with which to trade in return for all the goods that British exporters were frantic to sell them. But whereas Ricardo thought in terms of deficient supply, Malthus was preoccupied by the natives' deficient demand: 'Wants produce wealth'; people must be inspired with new wants, educated to form new and civilised tastes, 'to excite their exertions in the production of wealth'.[97]

This was an attitude typical of the age, it will be noted, and applied equally to the lazy Irish: 'The potatoe', wrote the British Critic reviewing Malthus, 'has proved their banania.'[98]

Where Malthus was in open conflict with his age was over the question of saving; parsimony, as Adam Smith called it, or thrift, as the Victorians were to say, was a virtue as important as hard work. It was easy to ridicule a simplified version of Say's Law; when British cotton goods were being sold below cost price in Kamchatka,* the remedy for such over-production was certainly not still more production, as far as Manchester was concerned. It was not so easy to accept Malthus's remedy - that there should be less saving and more spending in Britain, less capital accumulation by manufacturers, and more widely spread purchasing power among those who did not themselves manufacture anything.

We cannot here go fully into the discussions of the period as to the possibility of capital and labour both being redundant at the same time. Malthus's chief contribution to the debate was that capital might accumulate too quickly relative to the effective demand for its products; therefore

---

*Malthus spelt it Kamtschatka (Population, Everyman edn, Vol. I, pp. 101-2). Interest in this distant region of eastern Russia had been inspired by Baron Jean-Battiste Barthélemy de Lesseps's Travels in Kamtschatka, of which Joseph Johnson published an English translation in 1790. Writers of the period, including Jane Austen, used the name to mean the back of beyond, as later generations were to speak of Timbuctoo.

taxation to discourage saving, and government expenditure to stimulate demand, were both conducive to the progress of wealth.

Ricardo and others accepted the logic of Malthus's position: if people really were insufficiently lavish in their expenditure, it was quite rational to call in the tax man to help them get rid of their money. The opportunities for facetious comment were endless. Looking back on it all, it is astonishing how the Ricardians could have closed their eyes to the obvious cause of the distress which followed the sudden cessation, after twenty years, of naval and military demands for every kind of equipment and material, stores and weapons, and - above all - for men. We can sympathise with Malthus for writing that 'Public works, the making and repairing of roads, and a tendency among persons of fortune to improve their grounds and keep more servants, are the most direct means within our power of restoring the demand for labour.'[99]

Malthus gave no definition of 'persons of fortune', but he believed that for those of moderate means to save in order to provide for one's family was 'a most sacred and binding *private* duty';[100] he knew that the East India Company would give Harriet no pension. But as far as public policy was concerned, it was a duty of government to try and preserve a balance between saving and spending. He wrote in the introduction to the *Principles*:

> If consumption exceed production, the capital of the country must be diminished, and its wealth must be gradually destroyed from its want of power to produce; if production be in a great excess above consumption, the motive to accumulate and produce must cease from the want of an effectual demand in those who have the principal means of purchasing. The two extremes are obvious; and it follows that there must be some intermediate point, though the resources of political economy may not be able to ascertain it, where, taking into consideration both the power to produce and the will to consume, the encouragement to the increase of wealth is the greatest.[101]

I think Malthus's ideas might have made more headway had he not linked them with the distinction between productive and unproductive labour - had he, in short, accepted Gray's theory of chargeability: Malthus's concept of intensity of demand, of such a will to consume as would absorb all that was produced at a profitable price, is so obviously an advance on Say's doctrine that everything produced must ultimately be consumed, regardless of financial gain or loss to the producer. With hindsight, it seems incredible that intelligent people could have accepted James Mill's categorical simplification of Say's thesis that men only laboured to produce in order that they might consume: 'Production can never be too rapid for demand. Production is the cause, and the sole cause, of demand. It never furnishes supply without furnishing demand, both at the same time, and both to an equal extent.'[102]

Just as James Mill tried to get round the obvious difficulties of the labour theory of value by making imaginary labour mature the cask of wine in the well-locked cellar, so he tried to dodge the contention that Say's Law (if it were valid at all) could only apply to a barter economy. He said that money was a commodity to which the law applied in the same way as to all other commodities. In this part of the controversy Ricardian economics might have taken a more realistic turn had Henry Thornton not died in 1815; he would have pointed out that the paper credit which sets in motion both trade and production could not possibly be designated a commodity: 'credit' simply means 'belief'. Malthus, as was apparent during the bullion debates of 1810-11, understood very well that paper credit could 'command materials to work upon, tools to work with, and wherewithal to pay the wages of labour' (see pages 204-5). Basically, it is the expected demand for goods which stimulates their production, and ruin may follow if expectations are not fulfilled.

Other writers, some with practical experience of bankruptcy, were repeatedly to stress the fundamental objection to Say's Law: in certain circumstances, men would prefer to keep their money idle, and give no employment for several months, rather than risk the purchase or manufacture of commodities which they might not be able to sell quickly and profitably; those who had debts to pay were forced to dispose of stock at a loss for ready cash, and so on. It was cold comfort for such men to be told by James Mill that there could never be an excess supply of goods in relation to human wants, merely a temporarily inadequate supply of money to balance them.

With regard to the effect on prices of the quantity of money in circulation, Malthus stuck to the view which he first tentatively expressed in 1800, in his tract on *The High Price of Provisions* - that the increased amount of paper money was the result and not the cause of the high price of food; the cause of the rising prices was deficient supply, owing to bad harvests (see page 90). In the reverse situation, falling prices and insolvencies were blamed on the supposed contraction of the currency, which was alleged to have followed Peel's Act of 1819, when the Bank of England had gradually to return to the convertibility of notes to gold. This time it was Malthus's friend William Blake who in 1823 wrote a telling pamphlet - not accepted by the Ricardians - to the effect that the circulating medium had not been reduced; the cause of the falling prices was deficient demand, owing to the rapid decline in government expenditure. Malthus agreed with Blake. For him, rising or falling prices were determined by supply and demand, and were merely followed, not caused, by expansion or contraction of the quantity of money and the increased or diminished velocity of its circulation - a phrase which he himself used.

All in all, as one studies the economics literature of the period, it is puzzling at times to see why 'Mr. Ricardo's system' should have triumphed so completely as it did and, in Keynes' words, 'have constrained the subject for a full hundred years in an artificial groove'.[103]

5 The Rival Economists

It must be admitted that what Keynes called 'the almost total obliteration of Malthus's line of approach and the complete domination of Ricardo's' - 'a disaster to the progress of economics'[104] - was partly Malthus's own fault. His meaning is often difficult to follow, and not only for modern readers who stumble over 'corn wages' or 'command of labour': even the devoted contemporary disciple who reviewed the *Principles of Political Economy* in the *British Critic* concluded with the hope that Mr Malthus 'will some day favour the public with a complete system of political economy, arranged in a strictly scientific form'.[105]

It was a silly hope, but one can sympathise. Apart from anything else, Ricardo's complete and scientific system was easy to expound; this was perhaps an especially important factor between about 1815 and 1825, when political economy was high fashion, and fine ladies required their daughters' governesses to teach it.[106] Mrs Marcet followed up her *Conversations on Chemistry* with *Conversations on Political Economy* in 1816, an instant best-seller which she revised in successive editions until the seventh in 1839. For the second in 1817, and the fourth, in 1821, she sought advice from Ricardo. The conversations are between Mrs B., whose complacency and omniscience are remarkable, and Caroline, whose memory is only surpassed by her facility in summarising her lessons.

No wonder that John William Ward, an Oxonian, Canningite and bachelor MP, who became the first Earl of Dudley, praised this book highly to his old tutor Copleston, Provost of Oriel, adding 'Perhaps (though in the form of dialogues between women) you would not think it an unfit work to be placed in the hands of your under-graduates at some period of their stay in the university.'[107]

A little later the Provost could also have recommended James Mill's *Elements of Political Economy*, which appeared in the autumn of 1821. Ricardo thought this unsuitable for the school-room, because Mill used the word 'procreation' several times; other readers cannot have minded, as there was a second edition in 1824. This came out at about the same time as McCulloch's famous essay on 'Political Economy' in the *Supplement* to the *Encyclopaedia Britannica*, which he enlarged into a book the following year, and which established Ricardo's system as epitomising 'the true and correct principles of political economy'. For these principles Ricardo's followers crusaded with missionary zeal: his predominance owes much to the work of the two Mills, father and son, and even more to John Ramsay McCulloch (1789-1864). McCulloch's article on Ricardo's *Principles* in the *Edinburgh Review* is supposed to have sold out the first edition and induced Murray to hasten the second.

The Mills do not seem to have been sympathetic to Malthus; their agnosticism may have been embarrassed by his piety, and their advocacy of contraception would have been abhorrent to Malthus himself. As far as McCulloch was concerned, his dislike of Malthus amounted to hatred. Jeffrey refused to allow him to review Malthus's *Principles* in 1820, preferring to let the book pass unnoticed; it was said that McCulloch, in his turn, refused to contribute further to the *Edinburgh Review* after Empson's warm-hearted article on Malthus in 1837. At the Political Economy Club, J. L. Mallet noticed that McCulloch was 'always bitter against Malthus, the workings of an envious and mean disposition'.[108] It may have been so, but I think it is also possible that Malthus unintentionally hurt McCulloch's feelings, through his unbusinesslike way of dealing with his correspondence, and this led McCulloch to believe that the great man had slighted him.

There is a revealing sentence in a letter from Malthus to John Murray dated 16 April 1820. In this letter the author is giving his publisher directions for copies of the *Principles of Political Economy* to be sent to his father-in-law by the Bath coach and his brother-in-law Robert Taunton by the Stockbridge coach, which apparently only went on Wednesdays, and so on. Then, in a paragraph by itself: 'I shall write to Mr. McCulloch to say that I have left word for a copy to be sent to him. He once sent me a copy of a work of his with a civil note which by some strange chance was overlooked till it was too late to answer it.'

This work was the *Essay on a Reduction of the Interest of the National Debt*, of which two editions were printed in 1816. McCulloch sent a copy of the pamphlet to Ricardo in June, and received a long and courteous letter of thanks; on receipt of the amended version in November, Ricardo had replied at even more considered length.[109] It is important to remember in this context that McCulloch had not yet become the editor of the *Scotsman*. He was a poor lawyer's clerk, who had left the University of Edinburgh five years before, without taking a degree, in order to get married at the age of twenty-two; there were twelve children, of whom ten grew up and did well, the sons all going to India and the daughters all marrying.[110] Mrs McCulloch must have had a hard time of it, and it is easy to imagine how her struggling young husband in 1816 would have appreciated Ricardo's notice, so favourably contrasted with Malthus's apparent disdain.

Other extraneous factors might have contributed to Ricardo's success, one being that he was in the field three years ahead of Malthus. It is hard to believe that there could have been a market for two such long and exacting *Principles of Political Economy* in so short a time. Malthus clearly believed that such a demand existed, and Murray presumably encouraged him, for he set to work revising the book for a second edition almost as soon as the first was out. This was not conceit on Malthus's part; the controversy between the two rival economists did arouse great public interest, for after all, many people enjoy taking sides in a contest, happily regardless of what the fight is about.

Torrens noticed Malthus's *Principles* briefly in the *Traveller* on 21 April 1820. The relevant column was divided into three equal parts, and began with a report of the trial at the Old Bailey of the Cato Street conspirators, who had planned to murder the entire Cabinet; it continued with the dispute over George IV's exclusion of Queen Caroline from the Prayers for the Royal Family - and concluded with Malthus. Full-dress reviews of over a column and a half, basically hostile on account of Malthus's support of the Corn Laws, appeared in the issues of 26 April and 1 May; on the latter date most readers must have found the long account of the execution of the conspirators for high treason far more exciting than Torrens's views on Malthus's views on rent: 'The gallows had an additional erection attached to it, for the purpose of exposing the coffins to public view, and of complying with the forms of law, by severing the heads of the criminals from their bodies ... Some sawdust, for the purpose of receiving the blood, was strewed on the new scaffold.'[111]

Yet in spite of the sensations of 1820, the *Pamphleteer* for that year was dominated by Malthus. Say's *Lettres à M. Malthus* were especially translated for the periodical, under the heading 'Letters to the Rev. Mr. Malthus, on various subjects of Political Economy; particularly on the causes of the General Stagnation of Commerce'.[112] The second pamphlet in this issue was about marriage and divorce, the third on the poetical character of Pope, but the fourth was yet another letter to the Rev. T. R. Malthus, this time from Simon Gray, and 'occasioned by his attempt to maintain the division of classes into Productive and Unproductive'.[113]

Jean-Baptiste Say (1767-1832) naturally attracted more attention than the War Office clerk, but Ricardo himself did not admire the *Letters*. Say was not a pure Ricardian; indeed, he even upheld Say's Law itself less firmly than James Mill did, for Say argued that 'to create a thing, the want of which does not exist, is to create a thing without value: this would not be production' - which seems to beg the whole question of products always exchanging for products. Say managed his own cotton-mill for about eight years, after writing his first *Traité d'Économie Politique* in 1803, and this had perhaps given him a different approach to industrial production from that of Mill and Ricardo; with them any commodity produced by labour must *a priori* be endowed with 'value'.

I think Say was the first writer to state plainly and in public, 'Either the Author of the *Essay on Population* or the Author of the *Principles of Political Economy* must be wrong.'[114] And Say, like Ricardo and many others, sided with Population Malthus and against Economist Malthus. 'I cannot subscribe', he wrote to Malthus, 'to the fears which make you express on page 357 [page 320 in the 1836 edition] "That a country is always more exposed to the rapid increase of the funds destined for the support of the labouring class than of the labouring class itself". Nor am I frightened at the enormous increase of production which may result from an augmentation (so slow in its nature) of capital. I see on the contrary these new capitals and the incomes they produce distribute themselves in the most favourable manner amongst producers.'[115]

Perhaps the phrase 'distribute themselves' holds the key to Economist Malthus's failure to acquire a following. He has often been called an advocate of *laissez-faire* because he expressed the views of his day against government interference, but he was at heart a paternal interventionist. In spite of his grim statement that the children of the imprudent should be abandoned to the punishment of nature, he did not believe that population growth should be left to Providence: the government had a duty to ensure the civil liberty and the education of the poor, to give them every encouragement to delay marriage in the twin causes of comfort and respectability. Again, Malthus was a convinced free-trader, but he believed that import control might be necessary to safeguard the staple food of the people. And unlike his contemporaries, he did not assume that a free economy was self-regulating.

According to Say, people would automatically cease to save when the rate of interest sank so low as to make investment less attractive than spending; increased spending would raise prices and so make investment profitable again. Say was a good exponent of what might be called the Flowing School of economists, capital and labour flowing like water into hollows until the 'natural level' was reached. Labour, like capital, would distribute itself into the most profitable channels: if machinery made labourers redundant, they were not compelled 'to remain unemployed, but only to seek another occupation'.[116]

The comforting psychological effect of this attitude needs no comment. It runs all through Mrs Marcet's *Conversations on Political Economy*. Caroline says 'I do not exactly understand why there should be such a perfect coincidence between the wants of the public and the interest of the capitalist,' and Mrs B. is able to explain that 'The public are willing to give the highest price for things of which they stand in greatest need'; she always 'thought it one of the most beneficent ordinations of Providence that the employment of the poor should be a necessary step to the increase of the wealth of the rich', and 'their profits cannot be exorbitant, otherwise competition would in time reduce them to their natural level'. 'You will never wish', Caroline is told, 'to interfere with the natural distribution of capital.' 'The grand object to be kept in view in order to promote the general prosperity of the country is the increase of capital. But it is not in the power of the legislature to promote this end in any other way than by providing for the security of property; any attempts to interfere either with the disposal of capital or with the nature and extent of expenditure are equally discouraging to industry.'[117]

Malthus's uncomfortable belief that government interference might sometimes be necessary (and he was never quite sure of it himself) could hardly impress the public against this sort of assurance. We get a glimpse of him at Gatcomb during the Christmas vacation of 1820-1, when Ricardo wrote to McCulloch, 'I never knew a man more earnest on any subject than Mr. Malthus is on Political Economy.'[118]

Poor Malthus: it was easy to pronounce, when he was young, that 'Evil exists in the world, not to create despair, but activity.'[119] What form activity should take, to alleviate the distress of the poor, was another matter. He worked on at revising the *Principles*, writing in March 1821 that he was 'preparing a new edition and may perhaps say something on Mr. Say's letters in an Appendix'.[120] If he did, it has disappeared.

There were a number of publications in 1821 which showed how wide was public interest in the questions raised by the controversy between Malthus and Ricardo. One was by John Craig of Edinburgh, of whom little is known; in a book called *Remarks on Some Fundamental Doctrines in Political Economy* he criticised from experience and with common sense the tenets not only of Ricardo and Population Malthus, but of Economist Malthus too, on lines similar to those of Simon Gray. This lack of partisanship, which gives the modern reader a pleasant impression of maturity, seems to have infuriated McCulloch: he wrote to Ricardo on 23 April 1821 that 'A very stupid book has lately appeared here in which some parts of your great work are attacked - I would have answered it had I not thought it might perhaps have disturbed the quiet transit of the work to the pastry and the snuff shop.'[121]

McCulloch was not boasting idly, and his position as the leader of the Ricardians - and the winning side - was confirmed that year by a fellow contributor to the *Edinburgh Review*.

Macvey Napier (1776-1847) was yet another of the Scots Whig lawyers whose influence on British history was so marked at this period. From 1805 to 1837 he was Librarian to the Society of Writers to the Signet, and in 1814 he agreed to edit for his friend Archibald Constable the *Supplement* to the fourth, fifth and sixth editions of the *Encyclopaedia Britannica*; it appeared in parts, and was completed in six volumes in 1824. Napier then became Edinburgh's first Professor of Conveyancing, and in 1829 took over the editorship of the *Edinburgh Review* from Jeffrey. The *Supplement* to the *Encyclopaedia* occupied him for ten years, and he first went to London to look for suitable writers in 1814, with a letter of introduction from Dugald Stewart to Francis Horner; there he met, amongst others, his fellow Scot James Mill, who became an important contributor.

Ricardo provided an article on the Funding System, but by the time Napier had got to *P*, Ricardo was fully occupied with his parliamentary work, and it seemed appropriate that McCulloch should write - more or less on his behalf - the major essay on Political Economy; Malthus was the obvious choice for Poor Laws and Population. Thus we find Malthus writing to Macvey Napier on 27 September 1821:

314

Sir,

An absence from College has prevented my answering your obliging communication sooner. I am very far from being disengaged at present, but I think I could undertake an article on Population, though I cannot promise one on the Poor. I am not disposed to be offended at differences of opinion, particularly on such a subject as the Corn Laws, which, if justifiable, must be allowed to be an exception to the general rules of political economy; but I confess to you that I think that the general adoption of the new theories of my excellent friend Mr. Ricardo into an Encyclopaedia, while the question was yet *sub judice*, was rather premature. The more I consider the subject, the more I feel convinced that the main part of his structure will not stand.

> Your obedient servant,
> T. R. Malthus

Napier must have forwarded this note to McCulloch, who replied in a letter dated 30 September 1821:

I think the Supplement will gain credit by being among the first publications which has embodied and given circulation to the new and, notwithstanding Mr. Malthus's opinion, I will add correct, theories of political economy. Your publication was not intended merely to give a view of the science as it stood forty-five years ago ... It is, besides, a very odd error in Mr. Malthus to say that the new theories are all *sub judice*. He has himself given his complete and cordial assent to the theory of Rent, which is the most important of the whole ... It is, however, not a little surprising to hear Mr. Malthus censuring the Supplement for admitting new theories, when he has himself written a book to prove that the improvements of our machinery, and the economy of the government and of individuals, have been productive of almost all the misery we now suffer.

> Yours ever most faithfully,
> J. R. McCulloch

We do not know how Napier wrote to Malthus after receiving this, but he obviously wished to be fair as well as tactful. Malthus replied to Napier's letter as follows:

> East India College, October 8, 1821.

Dear Sir,

As I shall not be tolerably disengaged before April next, I shall certainly not have time for more than the article on 'Population', and will therefore decide at once against undertaking the article on the Poor, that I may not delay your application in some other quarter.

An article of the kind you speak of on Political Economy would, I think, be very desirable; but no one occurs to me at this moment with sufficient name and sufficient impartiality to do the subject justice. I am fully aware of the merits of Mr. McCulloch and Mr. Mill, and have a great respect for them both; but I certainly am of opinion, after much and repeated consideration, that they have adopted a theory which will not stand the test of experience. It takes a partial view of the subject, like the system of the French economists; and like that system, after having drawn into its vortex a great number of very clever men, it will be unable to support itself against the testimony of obvious facts, and the weight of those theories which, though less simple and captivating, are more just, on account of their embracing more of the causes which are in actual operation in all economical results . . .

> Your faithful humble servant,
> T. R. Malthus[122]

But the simple and captivating system was the one which triumphed during Malthus's life-time.

6. *The Measure of Value*

The *Monthly Literary Advertiser* for 10 January 1821 included in Murray's list of 'works preparing for immediate publication' the third edition of Ricardo's *Principles of Political Economy* and 'A New Edition' of Malthus's, corrected and enlarged, in two volumes. McCulloch wrote to Ricardo, 'I see Malthus is taking to his old trick of book-making - His book instead of being lengthened ought to have been curtailed one third.'[123] Ricardo's book duly appeared in May, but Malthus had written to Pierre Prévost on 26 April that his 'bookseller . . . lately advised me to defer the new edition of my last book until next Christmas'.[124]

He was probably glad of the delay. In February 1821 he had to journey up to Lincolnshire for the funeral of Henry Dalton, his cousin and the patron of his living at Walesby; the Bray and Warren letter-books show that Malthus was involved in business over this and, later, over the death on 16 March of his unmarried sister Charlotte at the Godschalls' house in Albury. On 23 March his nephew Charles (Sydenham's younger son) died at the age of fourteen, and on the 24th his widowed sister lost her eleven-year-old son Paulet Bray. On 14 June Samuel Godschall himself died, and then at the end of the year, on 26 December, Sydenham Malthus died at the age of sixty-seven; he was buried at Albury on New Year's Day 1822.

It is perhaps as well that Malthus could not have known that Sir James Mackintosh had written to Napier on 8 January 1822 to the effect that his colleague had 'undisturbed leisure and uninterrupted health'.[125] Malthus wrote to Macvey Napier on 12 February 1822 in a very different strain:

> ... Circumstances have occurred which put it quite out of my power to execute the article on Population ... Before I received your letter I had engaged to bring out a new edition of my last work on Political Economy early in this spring; and I had besides particular reasons, latterly, for wishing it to appear with as little delay as possible. When I wrote to you I thought I should be able to complete it in March or early in April, and that I should then be able to get the article on population finished by the time you mentioned: but the sickness and death of a brother whom I tenderly loved together with the subsequent business which it had occasioned, has for the last six weeks so entirely interrupted my literary pursuits that I should not be able to turn my attention to the article for the supplement till long after the time when it ought to be finished. I am therefore obliged to give up all thoughts of it; and I hope that this early notice of my inability to execute what I intended will prevent inconvenience to you, and enable you without difficulty to get the article supplied in time.[126]

Further correspondence shows that Napier must have postponed the date to August; he was certainly practised in dealing with contributors at this stage in the alphabet, for he did not receive the final part of the article on Population until January 1823.

Malthus's manuscript drafts and scraps, now in the Marshall Library at Cambridge, suggest that he worked on his *Political Economy* throughout 1822. There was serious trouble at the College in the autumn, and on 23 December he began a letter to Prévost by saying that he was 'more particularly pressed both by public and private business than I have ever been before'; he ended in the same strain:

> I am now greatly pressed for an article on Population in the Encyclopaedia Britannica, which I unwarily promised; while I am very anxious to get out as soon as I possibly can another edition of my last work in which there will be some new views on a *standard of value* which requires a good deal of care and consideration. These two engagements with others of a private nature have made me feel very much hurried of late.[127]

I think it is possible that he wanted his revised *Political Economy* to be published before McCulloch's essay in the encyclopaedia.

In any case, he carried the 'second edition' to Albemarle Street at the beginning of February 1823, just about two years after Murray had advertised it as 'preparing for immediate publication'. Then he must have arranged all his other work so that he should be free to deal with the proofs as they came through the post by instalments. On 24 February he sent Murray a letter which must go to every writer's heart:

> I am sure that you must have quite forgotten every thing about the *Principles of Political Economy* which I left with you three week ago, or I must have had a proof sheet by this time. It would be very desireable on many accounts to have it out early in May. But this will certainly not be done unless we make more haste. I shall be in Town I believe the end of the week or the beginning of next, and will then call, and shall hope to find matters in progress.

There is no record of what happened at this interview. Murray presumably decided that, in spite of all Malthus's labour on it, a second edition of the book would not be profitable; he published instead as a separate pamphlet in April 1823 *The Measure of Value Stated and Illustrated.*

In this booklet of eighty pages, Malthus went back on the view expressed in the *Principles of Political Economy*; there he had tried to work out 'a mean between corn and labour'; now he returned to the idea of labour as the only constant measure of value and the sole yardstick against which fluctuations of price might be accurately gauged. An attempt to prove such a thesis, as we have seen, can only result in confusion, and the publication was a disaster.

But we must appreciate that, for Malthus, 'a measure of value' was of great practical importance all his life. For example, when he was writing to Henry Parnell in May 1808 about an alternative to the traditional tithe, the question of the depreciated value of paper money was very much in the air: it will be remembered that some landlords were trying to insist on their rents being paid in gold, or in such an increased number of bank-notes as would purchase the quantity of gold they would have received when their leases were originally drawn up several years earlier. This sort of difficulty was obviously relevant if tithes were to be related to a proportion of rents, and Malthus wrote to Parnell on 4 May 1808 about some scheme of this kind:

> The principal objection to the third plan you have proposed is certainly the depreciation of money, and to estimate this with tolerable accuracy is most difficult, if not impossible. As it clearly depends, not on any one commodity only, but on the sum of all taken together, the difficulty of making such an estimate will readily be conceived. Adam Smith has certainly fallen into some decided errors by taking corn alone. According to his own principles he ought to have preferred labour; and though I by no means agree with

him in thinking that labour may be considered as a standard measure
of value, yet as it enters into the composition of such a vast
proportion of commodities, I should prefer taking labour to any
other one criterion that could be named. Perhaps a mean between
country labour and corn would be the best practical measure.[128]

In this context Malthus means the wages of labour and the price of corn;
at the time he was writing he thought that on many estates in England the
rents had not risen in proportion to the increase in wages and prices. It is
impossible not to speculate on how he would have regarded a modern cost
of living index. He wrote in 1820 in his *Principles of Political Economy*:

> If we are told that the wages of day-labour in a particular country
> are, at the present time, fourpence a day; or that the revenue of a
> particular sovereign, 700 to 800 years ago, was £400,000 a year; these
> statements of nominal value convey no sort of information respecting
> the condition of the lower classes of people, in the one case, or the
> resources of the sovereign, in the other. Without further knowledge
> on the subject, we should be quite at a loss to say, whether the
> labourers in the country mentioned were starving, or living in great
> plenty; whether the king in question might be considered as having a
> very inadequate revenue, or whether the sum mentioned was so great
> as to be incredible.[129]

Today what seems strange is that Malthus's 'further knowledge' should
consist of an eternally valid measure of economic value, regardless of the
narrow range of duties expected from a medieval sovereign, as compared
with government expenditure of more recent times, and of all the techno-
logical and social developments which must affect the condition of the
'lower classes of people': the prices of domestic coal, firewood and peat in
a European town only two centuries ago would not by themselves help us
to compare their comfort with that of their descendants whose homes may
be warmed with oil, gas, or electricity. We must not forget that Malthus
grew up before rapid technical progress (and Darwin) had made the idea of
continuous change a familiar concept. Samuel Bailey, whose *Critical Dissertation* exploded all his contemporaries' theories of value, did not argue along
these lines at all, but took up the debate from quite a different standpoint.
    Samuel Bailey (1791-1870) was a Sheffield man - his father was Master
Cutler in 1801 - who gave up first business and then politics for an isolated
life of study, interspersed with a little philanthropy; his *Critical Dissertation
on the Nature, Measure and Causes of Value* appeared anonymously in 1825.
It attracted the attention it deserved, including that of the young John Stuart
Mill and his friends, who met two mornings a week, before going to their
respective offices, to read and discuss the 'branches of science which we
wished to be masters of': they made political economy their first subject,

and after working through James Mill's *Elements* and Ricardo's *Principles* they turned to Bailey.[130] Later, in 1831, J. L. Mallet quoted Torrens's statement about any theory of value, 'Mr. Baillie of Leeds has settled that question' - although McCulloch still stood by his old master.[131] It is notable, however, that even in this iconoclastic book Bailey accepted as axiomatic the 'principle of population' and the differential theory of rent.

Bailey summed up Ricardo and De Quincey thus: 'Instead of regarding value as a relation between two objects, they seem to consider it as a positive result produced by a definite quantity of labour ... Even the adjunct "exchangeable" is tautological, the term value in itself implying a relation in exchange, and consequently any epithet which expresses the same idea being perfectly superfluous.' Thus it was no use Adam Smith and Mr Malthus trying to compare commodities at different periods, because they could not be exchanged across time; value could only be a relation between contemporary commodities, and labour at one period could not be compared with labour at another. Value was not measurable like length or weight: if I know the value of *A* in relation to *B*, and the value of *B* in relation to *C*, I know the value of *A* and *C* in relation to each other, but *B* is merely a medium of comparison, and cannot be likened to a foot-rule measuring two pieces of timber.[132]

With regard to Malthus's attempt in 1823 to make labour an invariable standard of value, Bailey did not mince his words: 'The very term absolute value implies the same sort of absurdity as absolute distance': distance can only be measured between two points. Food or money could not change in value relatively to labour without labour changing in value relatively to food or money, and so on.

It was easy for Bailey to be scathing about Malthus's arithmetical table - indefensible anyhow - which was an integral part of the pamphlet: 'The only commodities in question, in Mr. Malthus's table, are corn and labour; and if, as he supposes, the labour of 10 men is at one time rewarded with 120 quarters of corn, and at another time with only 80 quarters, the only condition required for an alteration of value is fulfilled, and labour, instead of being invariable, has fallen one third.'[133]

Malthus's *Measure of Value* was reviewed in over two columns of the *Morning Chronicle* on 6 September 1823. The anonymous reviewer was John Stuart Mill, and he dealt with the pamphlet seriously and fairly, though with a Ricardian bias against 'Mr. M's favourite doctrine of over-production'.[134] This review is, I think, an outstanding example of the younger Mill's powers of analysis; most of us would agree with De Quincey, who wrote in the *London Magazine*, for December 1823, that whoever takes Malthus for a guide should be able to use a compass, 'or before he has read ten pages he will find himself (as the Westmorland guides express it) "maffled" - and disposed to sit down and fall a-crying with his guide at the sad bewilderment into which they have both strayed'.[135] The obscurity of this pamphlet Samuel Bailey found especially unpardonable, because Malthus 'is master, when he chooses, of an excellent and perspicuous style'.[136]

There seems to be no reason for the lapse, and no question of the 'maffling' little book being the outcome of a period of ill-health or family bereavement. In the same year in which *Value* appeared, the *Quarterly Review* printed Malthus's review of Thomas Tooke's *High and Low Prices*, which review is as competent a piece of work as anything Malthus wrote; for the *Quarterly* of January 1824 he produced a first-rate article defending his own views (which he identified with Adam Smith's) against the 'new school', as exemplified by McCulloch's essay in the *Supplement* to the *Encyclopaedia Britannica*. Malthus's own contribution to the *Supplement*, on Population, which he was working on at the same time as *Value*, is almost as clear and forceful as the first *Essay* of 1798.

One can only say that Malthus had a kink or a crotchet, some kind of cerebral block, a patch of mental fog, with regard to standard labour as an invariable measure of value. The devoted and loyal Empson wrote that the arguments on which this proposition was grounded were 'the least satisfactory part of all Mr. Malthus's writings. This is to be attributed mostly to the subject itself, and partly to his mode of viewing it. It certainly arose by no means from want of attaching sufficient importance to it, or of taking sufficient pains about it, as all his friends, learned and unlearned, can bear witness.'[137] The friends must have suffered, but Malthus's reputation suffered more. There were many things against him: the personal antipathy of McCulloch, and perhaps also Ricardo's wealth and parliamentary standing; the whole spirit of the age of steam-engines and heavy capital investment; Malthus's own flickering torch of intuition which could throw spot-lights, but not illuminate a whole scene. There was much that could account for Malthus's failure as an economist, but with the publication of the imperspicuous and unconvincing *Measure of Value* his cause was hopeless.

CHAPTER X

The Heat of the Day (1817–25)

1 Old Pop at Haileybury

All the time Malthus was struggling with the controversial issues of the new political economy, he was carrying out considerably more than routine duties at the College: as he put it to Ricardo, he was 'completely tied by the leg in the intervals between vacations'.[1]

On 9 May 1817 *The Times* had learned 'with regret, but without surprise, that the temporary tranquility which had existed at the East India College at Haileybury had been again interrupted ... Mr. Principal is said to have been chased, with very opprobrious language, by a dog with a kettle tied to his tail.'[2] This incident is not reported in the minutes of the Committee of College, and we find the College Council actually thanking the Chairman and Deputy for their support against what seems to have been a comparatively mild outburst of window-breaking.[3] At the Visitation on 29 May the distinguished guests included Canning and the Bishop of London; they and the Directors were deeply impressed by an exhibition of some of the students' examination papers, astonished that the work was done 'without the aid of Books or any other assistance ... and that it was the duty of the Examiner to see that they had nothing with them but Pen, Ink and Paper when they answered these Questions'.[4]

The autumn of 1817 was notable for a sustained effort to get rid of Professor Christian, who must have been an intolerable colleague in every way, and whose lectures were scenes of uproar. The professors as a body sent the Committee a solemn letter praising Dr Batten's 'conciliation, forbearance and delicacy' in the face of Professor Christian's unfounded insinuations against him. Then, quite suddenly, we read in the minutes for 2 January 1818 that Christian has resigned with a pension of £200 per annum; on the 16th Sir James Mackintosh was formally appointed to succeed him.[5] Much must have gone on behind the scenes.

Sir James and Lady Mackintosh (both fifty-three in 1818) were not good managers of a modest income (they were compared unfavourably with the Sydney Smiths in this respect by Lady Macintosh's two wealthy Wedgwood sisters), nor had they a home. They therefore rejoiced in this appointment and rented a beautiful house called Mardocks, about six miles from the College, in the pretty valley of the little river Ash, a tributary of the Lea; here, according to the young Bostonian George Ticknor, who visited them in 1819, they set up 'a comfortable and somewhat ample establishment'.[6] Sir James's three daughters by his first wife had all been married in Bombay, but he and his second wife, Kitty, brought with them to Hertfordshire their two young bluestocking daughters, Fanny and Elizabeth, aged seventeen and fifteen, and twelve-year-old Robert (known as Dumfy), who was only at home from Winchester in the holidays.

Sir James only had to lecture for five hours a week, on Saturdays and Mondays, so that he could continue his duties as a member of the House of Commons; between parliamentary sessions he would work in rural retirement on his great History of England - famous and applauded, but unwritten - from the Glorious Revolution of 1688 to the French Revolution of 1789. He must have been regarded as an acquisition to local society, but from our point of view his wife and elder daughter are more important, for they kept diaries. Fanny also wrote long letters to her half-sister Mary Rich, who treasured them in Baghdad, and brought them home with her to be preserved, ultimately, in the Wedgwood archives.[7]

Thus we can see life at Haileybury with new eyes. Serious and well-read Fanny thought the College 'very fine' but most of the students were 'dandies'. An exception was John Venn, a younger son of the Evangelical rector of Clapham whom Dealtry replaced, very handsome as well as a great winner of prizes and medals, and clearly a favourite visitor at Mardocks and at the houses which the Mackintoshes rented from time to time in London; Fanny called him 'a very good specimen'.

John Venn was at Haileybury from 1818 to 1820. After two years in India he found that his health could not stand up to the climate, so he returned to England, to Cambridge and Holy Orders; he died in 1890 in Hereford, where he had been vicar of St Peter's for fifty-seven years. In his old age he reminisced about his pleasant time at the College:

> The Professors at Haileybury were a very able set of men; and amongst them was the Professor of Political Economy, the well-known Malthus. The great idea upon which Malthus was always harping was the terrible increase of our population. He was continually setting before us the fearful rate at which the population was increasing; and gravely did he urge upon us, young lads as we were, the duty and necessity of our never having more than three children when we became husbands. Indeed, he was so constantly harping upon this theme that we always called him 'old Pop'.

This is the first reference I have found to the nickname by which Malthus is still known to the descendants of his siblings; whether old Mr Venn's memory was correct about the lectures seems more than doubtful.

Venn recalled that 'Amongst the seventy or eighty students there were only two or three who seemed to have any religious feelings.'[8] This is possibly confirmed by the only noteworthy disturbance while Venn was at the College, on 7 and 8 April 1818. There is no evidence as to the cause of the 'Outrages and disorders', and the trouble was soon over, for Mr Toone wrote to the College Council 'confessing that he was the person who fired the pistol at the Windows of the Chapel'. As Mr Toone had been 'withdrawn from the College' in any case, nine of the young men who had been sent away under the 'Statute of Selection' were recalled with admonishments, and a tenth suspended until he apologised. Three students who were not rusticated also 'owned up', and the records show no interruption in the careers of any of the young men.[9]

The Times made the most of the affair, quoting a snippet from another paper on 14 April 1818 to the effect that 'about forty out of sixty' students had been sent away. The next day they amended this number to eleven, in a vituperative article which contained nothing new.[10] They must have been disappointed when the College then ceased to have any news value for four and a half years.

During this period Sanskrit Hamilton retired, and was replaced by the Assistant Professor Haughton whose appointment had triggered off the crisis of 1816-17. Haughton's place was filled by the Rev. Henry George Keene (1781-1864). Keene started his career in the Madras army, and in May 1799 led the company carrying the scaling ladders for the storming of Seringapatam. Through the influence of Lord Harris, his maternal uncle, he was transferred to the Civil Service, and left the College at Fort William in 1804 loaded with honours; he was particularly distinguished in Arabic and Persian. He resigned as a result of difficulties with the repellent Governor of Madras, Sir George Barlow, and after graduating at Cambridge in 1815 he took Orders and became a Fellow of his college, Sidney Sussex. According to the *Dictionary of National Biography* he 'had a clear and flexible style and indefatigable industry. He was much beloved by his acquaintance; but his versatility and want of worldly ambition hindered his rise.'

On 29 September 1819 there was a Secret Committee of College, which resulted in the Oriental Assistant, Mirza Maulavi Kheleel, being asked to resign, apparently as a result of a disagreement with Major Stewart.[11] He was generously pensioned and returned to India, to Fatehgarh, with his English wife, of whom one would like to know more, since in 1824 Bishop Heber referred to her as 'a singular female'.[12]

The secret cannot have been well kept, for on 21 November 1819 Malthus was writing to Arthur Young about the vacant post. The letter is, I think, worth printing in full; it shows how autocratically the Directors treated their staff and also, in the final paragraph, the way in which Malthus's theories were developing as he worked on the *Principles of Political Economy*:

Dear Sir,

I shall always be most happy to comply with a request coming from you, and only regret that in the present case I can be of little use. There can be no reason why your friend, under the circumstances in which he stands, should not apply for any employment in the Company's service which may occur at home. At the College one of our native teachers has lately retired and there has been some rumour that the vacancy would be filled up by a European Professor or assistant in the Oriental languages; but the Directors are jealous of any interference of the Professors upon these occasions, and a letter from me would do no sort of good. The only thing to be done therefore, unless you have any friends in the Direction, is to apply at once to the Chairman Mr. Majoribanks requesting to know whether there is a vacancy in the Oriental Department at the East India College, and whether it is open to your friend to become a Candidate and send in his testimonials.

I may mention as a mere report that I have heard that a brother of Sir Gore Ousely has been talked of, but the resident body are kept a good deal in the dark on the subject of appointments, and indeed we are by no means sure that any appointment will take place on the present occasion. A Director of considerable influence told the Principal not long since that he thought it would not be considered as necessary to fill up the vacancy.

Pray can you tell me in what *small* work I can obtain the best information respecting the spade husbandry which has lately been talked of. I should like also to know what you think of it; and whether you are not of opinion, that independently of the object of employing Parish Poor, our wastes are not most likely to be cultivated by saving labour on the land, rather than increasing it. The great obstacle to the cultivation of Wastes is surely that the produce does not pay the expense of procuring it; and this difficulty it appears to me is only to be overcome by skill and prices - not mere labour.

> Believe me dear Sir
> with great respect and esteem
> truly yours
> T. Rob' Malthus[13]

Mirza Maulavi Kheleel was in fact replaced by the Rev. Robert Anderson, whose appointment dated from 27 July 1820; I do not know if he was acquainted with Arthur Young. Anderson was an old student (1806-9) who went out to Madras with a plethora of medals and certificates, but had to return ten years later because of his health. He wrote a Tamil Grammar and, with Keene, urged the case for the study of the languages of southern

India as against the dominating influence of the Presidency of Bengal. These two new assistant professors put new life into the College Council; their older colleagues obviously appreciated the help they gave during the disturbances of September 1822.

This outbreak was the last of the famous Haileybury riots, although of course nobody could be aware of it at the time. According to a private letter from Keene to Le Bas, the trouble began when a youth called Taylor thought he had been ill-used in getting a *Moneo* (presumably an admonition carrying a penalty) for attending Chapel in 'a pink dressing gown'. Keene told him his manifest insolence deserved a severe punishment. Apparently a friend of Taylor's, called Clarke, blew a mail-coach horn before and after the service in Chapel on the evening of Sunday 22 September, and then sallied forth with Rowley and Lawrell Junior 'to break all the public windows of the College'.[14] Lamps were broken too. Together with other students they also blew off with gunpowder the padlock of a gate which the authorities had caused to be shut earlier than usual; they pulled down brickwork and railings; and most ingeniously, according to *The Times*, 'they contrived to insert a blacking bottle, filled with powder, into one of the pipes which act as a drain in the college square; this was also exploded, by means of a match or train, near midnight.' It caused alarm but little damage.

Fanny Mackintosh records:

Thurs. 26 Sep.	Papa was sent for to a College Council. Some bad behaviour. Gunpowder plot.
Fri. 27	Papa went again to the College.
Sat. 28	Rode to College. In great confusion there. 12 sent away. Called on Mrs. Batten & Mrs. Lebas. Emily rode home with us.
Sun. 29	I drove Emily to church & we rode out afterwards in the fields.
Mon. 30	We went to the College. Not much better. Called on Mrs. Anderson . . . A College Council . . .
Mon. 7 Oct.	Rode to the College with Papa, found all quiet.

The quiet was superficial. Also, by an unlucky coincidence, the impossible Edward Christian (who lived nearby at Hoddesdon) had been invited to dine with the new mayor of Hertford and other worthies on Monday 14 October. The guests included Lord Cranborne (1791-1868), later the second Marquess of Salisbury, then one of the MPs for the borough; at that time he was extremely unpopular for 'the introduction of potatoes and salt herrings for the food of the poor', as a measure of 'parochial economy and reform'. Cranborne was therefore greeted everywhere in Hertford with shouts of 'Red herrings!' One was actually thrust into his mouth 'or against his face'. When Christian emerged from the convivial dinner he was set upon by what he called two or three hundred men, but who were allegedly only a few boys who had been baiting Lord Cranborne; being Christian, he reacted with an absurdly detailed and pompous letter in the press, addressed to the mayor. There was, of course, no connection between the 'brutal mob' who had 'frightened Professor Christian out of his wits' and the Haileybury gunpowder plot, but the newspapers seized on both together, with the heading 'Riots at Hertford'.[15]

No one likes to be made ridiculous, and matters were too serious, I think, for anybody to enjoy the joke. Fanny Mackintosh has a sad note in her journal for 23 November, when 'poor Rowley was expelled', and the whole question of expulsion was once more taken up by the press. Was it fair that parents should be forced by Act of Parliament to send their sons to Haileybury, and then have their prospects blasted as the result of a little boyish folly, solely because the *soi-disant* professors could not maintain ordinary school discipline?

The most bitter assault on the College's monopoly, as it was called, appeared in the *Morning Chronicle* for 21 October 1822.[16] It was inspired by Dr Gilchrist, the surgeon turned Orientalist who had caused trouble at Hertford Castle in 1806, when he was giving lessons in Hindustani until Hamilton should be released by the French. In 1822 Gilchrist was sixty-three, and acting as Professor of Hindustani at the Oriental Institute in Leicester Square, in London, with a salary of £200 per annum; his pupils were mainly assistant surgeons about to sail for India in the Company's service, for whom his notorious text-books, transliterated into English spelling regardless of the appropriate script, were probably of some use. Naturally Gilchrist would have preferred the Company to devise some kind of open qualifying test for their Writers, in Eastern languages, rather than the compulsory four terms at Haileybury. What made his attack on the College very unpleasant was that he himself had twice applied for posts there in 1818, first to replace Hamilton on his retirement and then to replace Haughton on his promotion. It is impossible to follow the intrigues in detail - Gilchrist was a Proprietor of East India stock - but the anti-college party may have lost adherents through publicly enlisting an ally who was not only unpopular but even slightly disreputable.

Meanwhile, at Haileybury, young Clarke who had blown the coach-horn was only rusticated for a year, since he had been the first to confess; four others were sent away for shorter periods, but Flint, Lawrell, Rowley, Taylor and Watts were formally expelled. They all appealed to the Bishop of London. There are pathetic letters to the Bishop and to Dr Batten, from Sir Charles Flint in the Irish Office, asking why the authorities had not stopped his son from rushing to destruction. On 18 March 1823 the Bishop rejected the appeals.[17] William Flint disappears from the records, but the

327

other four all went into the Indian Army; Fanny's preference for Rowley was justified, since he was the only one who attained the rank of major.

There was an even worse crisis for Malthus and his colleagues before the Bishop made his decision. The dispute is difficult to follow, as a 'Paper' constantly referred to does not appear to be among the archives, but relations between the Committee and the College Council were so bad that there was no quarterly Visitation in the spring of 1823. It would seem that the Committee wanted a system of surveillance which would have been intolerable to staff and students alike, including the inspection of rooms without notice, and also compulsory evening lectures to prevent dissipation and idleness; these, as an anonymous memorialist pointed out, 'would only multiply demands upon a too crowded and diversified attention'.

A formal letter was sent on 3 February 1823 to 'the Revd. the Principal':

Dear Sir,

The undersigned request you to present their respectful thanks to the Hon. Chairman for his kindness in communicating to the College, at so early a stage of the proceeding, the sketch of a plan for improving the discipline of the College.

On most of the essential points, adverted to in the Chairman's notes, the Council had the honor of laying their views before the Committee.

The undersigned cannot but exceedingly regret to find the system sketched out so widely at variance with opinions which have been the result, in all of much anxious thought on these subjects, and, in some, of seventeen years experience.

Opinions, so formed, cannot be suddenly changed. They have only, therefore, respectfully to wait, till the alterations finally determined upon are put into the form of Statutes.

It will then be for them to consider in what manner these Statutes will affect the system which their experience leads them to think best suited to promote the ends of the institution;

And whether they can, consistently with their duty to themselves and to the public, undertake to carry them into effect.

We have the honor to be, Dear Sir, yours respectfully,

> E. Lewton
> T. Rob⁺ Malthus
> C. Stewart
> C. W. Le Bas
> Henry Walter
> Hen: Geo: Keene
> Robt. Anderson[18]

It is impossible to guess whether the seven signatories believed that resignation would be forced upon them. Malthus, I think, was ready for a fight. In the letter to Murray of 24 February 1823, in which he asked about the fate of the 'second edition' of his *Political Economy*, he also asked whether the unsold copies of the 1817 pamphlet about the East India College had been sent for waste paper; obviously he was planning to use it again.

Malthus's apprehensions were justified a year later. On Wednesday 25 February 1824 a special Court of Proprietors was so packed that the reporters were crammed into a gallery where, on account of 'the distance from the speakers, the want of light, and particularly the constant confusion and interruption caused by the crowd, it was impossible for them except at intervals, to hear what was said, or even see to write down the little that they heard'.

They were, however, able to report that many hours of discussion excited considerable sensation, and it is rather hard to see why: Douglas Kinnaird's speech in proposing his motion to abolish the College, supported by Joseph Hume and Randle Jackson, contained no arguments that had not been heard many times before - in fact, ever since the College was founded. The same might be said of Haileybury's defenders, even Robert Grant's excellent speech (which he caused to be printed separately) and Malthus's 1817 pamphlet, which was quoted and misquoted by both sides. There were adjournments, and *The Times* of 25 March 1824 reported Kinnaird as being so sure of victory that he asked the Chairman what ulterior steps he meant to pursue. Sir William Wigram replied 'that if that majority should unfortunately occur, it would be the duty of the Court of Directors to frame a petition to Parliament, to give effect to the decision of the Court of Proprietors'.

Then, on 1 April 1824, *The Times* had to climb down in a second leading article:

> The division on the College of Haileybury at the India House yesterday was favourable to the continuance of the institution; the numbers being - for the question, 272; against it, 400 - one hundred and twenty-eight in favour of the establishment under its present regulations. We neither regret nor are surprised at this result. We have no feeling with respect to the College, except in so far as it effects or fails of the objects for which it was formed; and if this feeble majority, upon which so important, we might say so unreasonably vast an institution depends, should tend to correct its errors and modify its extravagances, the original motion will not have been without its use.[19]

The pessimistic Malthus and his colleagues were still not sure of their future, and he wrote to Murray on 9 April 1824:

> It is thought that Mr. Hume will still bring the question of the

329

College before Parliament; and I am most strongly urged by my friends here to write something more on the subject. If I do, I should wish a small number of copies to be printed with all expedition. Can you do it? I am sorry you wasted the copies of the last. I was in hopes that I had spoken in time to save them. The question was likely to recur, and what I may write now might have been published as an Appendix to the Statements.

They need not have been anxious; Haileybury had become part of the British Establishment in less than twenty years. The College itself was to disappear with the Company, but the traditions of the Indian Civil Service (and they are not altogether to be derided) were to last much longer than the memory of Charles Grant.

2 Okewood Again

In 1818 the indefatigable William Bray published in two quarto volumes his great edition of *The Memoirs of John Evelyn*, which had hitherto existed only in manuscript and virtually unknown; he was eighty-one. His grandson Reginald Bray and his young partner Augustus Warren were obviously taking most of the firm's business off his hands, but his diary shows unusual activity for a man of his age.[20] On 12 November 1817 he had lost his 'excellent friend Lady Evelyn', but he could write on his birthday on 15 November that he had passed a year of uninterrupted health, and 'my eyesight enables me to read or write till 10 o'clock at night, tho' I think there is a little dimness. My front teeth all continue. I do not take any long rides, & am not so well disposed to long walks as I have been. On the whole I have just reason to be thankful to God.'

The following November, on Thursday 19th, 1818, he went to St George's Church in Bloomsbury at eight in the morning, when 'my grandaughter Harriet was married to Mr. Warren my partner, very much to my satisfaction, having that opinion of them both, that I think there is every prospect of happiness for them. I pray God to bless them.' In due course, in 1820, Bray recorded 'my grandau^r Warren brought to bed of a boy 16 Feb - privately Christ^d 19th by Mr. R. Malthus, named Reginald.'

William Bray must have seemed a family patriarch to the Malthus children, as well as to their Bray cousins in London - less genial than their West Country grandfather Eckersall, but a close link with the Surrey aunts, and of great importance to the adult members of the family; as one pores over his diaries, as well as the Bray and Warren letter-books and bill-books, one can hardly imagine how the Malthuses, Eckersalls, Grahams, Daltons and Symeses could have managed their affairs without him.

One of William Bray's Surrey concerns was the Okewood Chapel Trust, formed in 1743 to manage the three farms belonging to the chapel; their rents, and the sale of timber from them, paid for the maintenance of the building and the stipend of the perpetual curate. It will be remembered that the Evelyn family were the patrons. From 1811 the incumbent had been the Rev. John Hallam, but he seems to have visited Okewood rarely, and in 1820 was living in Westminster, in Park Street. He and Mr Evelyn were considering the purchase of more land for the chapel, adjoining the chapel's farm near Ockley, and with a house which might be adapted for a curate, when they were suddenly confronted by the results of the agricultural depression.

On 21 January 1821 Bray wrote to John Evelyn at Wotton: 'The Revd. Mr. Hallam has just been here respecting the Chapel Farm called Hadfold at Billinghurst. The tenant is utterly unable to go on & quits at Michaelmas next.' On 12 May he had more bad news, and wrote to Hallam: 'Mr. Clutton who has a great deal of business amongst Sussex Farms as well as others gives me such a frightful account of such as consist of poor land being left unoccupied that I know not what to say about the Chapel Farms, which I believe are very poor land.' Conditions did not improve, and in April 1822 the tenants of Steepwood Farm also gave notice to quit at Michaelmas; Mr Hallam 'had an offer of a substantial and respectable tenant, but at a very considerable reduction of rent, viz from £115 to £84 on a lease of 14 years'.

The only thing to be done was to fell some timber on Hadfold Farm, as Mr Evelyn directed, 'about £800'. This was not only valuable in itself, but enabled the tenant 'to have the use of the arable land, which it seems at present he cannot have', as the wood 'so over runs the fields that Corn cannot grow'.

It is impossible to guess exactly what happened, as so much was transacted by word of mouth. But at some stage William Bray must have appreciated that, although the chapel farms' arable land was poor, the timber made the curacy worth having; this applied especially to the underwood beneath the standard oaks; coppiced hazels could be cut periodically to provide stakes for hedges and fences, while split poles were used to make spars for thatching, hoops to bind casks or barrels, and so on. Subsequent diary entries show that the elderly John Evelyn must have given William Bray an undertaking that the latter's grandson Edward should have Okewood when old Mr Hallam died. Edward was the black sheep who 'was not disposed to settle to any business', and had been belatedly sent to Cambridge, to Peterhouse, I think at the expense of the Godschalls; he took his MA in 1822, on 2 July, when he was twenty-nine, and it must have been apparent by then that he was unsuitable for the church.

331

The eighty-six-year-old grandfather wrote in his diary for 23 February 1823:

> I went to Capt. Geo. Evelyn in Gloucester Place, & mentioned my wish that the name of my grandson William might be substituted for that of Edward for the next turn of Oakwood chapel, as Edw. did not wish to take orders. I mentioned the difference of age [William would have been about eighteen] - that I thought it right to apprize him of my wish, as he was materially interested . . .

On 1 March William Bray went to see Mr Evelyn at Wotton, and

> Mr. E very readily & at once said that if the vacancy happened in his life, & he should receive a letter from me, I might depend on it that William should have it.

But a fortnight later, on 14 March,

> Mr. Evelyn came to [Great] Russell Street & desired I would release him from his promise; that after he had made it he had received a letter from his son; I told him I did not consider him as at all bound, that I never thought of its being other than subject to the approbation of Capt. E., & that I fully released him from any promise.

Obviously somebody else had applied for Okewood at the beginning of March 1823.

John Hallam died on 20 January 1824, in his seventy-first year, and the next entries about Okewood in William Bray's journal are:

> Feb. 14 Sat. Capt. Evelyn called about chapel . . .
> Feb. 27 Fri. Mr. Evelyn sent nomination of Mr. Malthus to Okewood Chapel . . .

Bray and Warren's itemised bill to 'The Revd. T. R. Malthus - As to your Appointmt. to the Curacy of Okewood Chapel' amounted to £53. 15s. 11d. for the three years 1824-6; there are six large folio sheets, beginning on 20 February with a guinea for drawing up and ingrossing his nomination, and another £1. 12s. for stamps and parchment.

We can only guess what lies behind all this. Malthus could well have been anxious about his future early in 1823, partly because of the College crisis, partly because he was then fifty-seven and might have been expected shortly to retire; this was also the time when Murray rejected the 'second edition' of *Political Economy*. On the other hand he could simply have wanted to add to his own income, to make better provision for his widow and daughters, to have a foothold in Surrey, to be linked again with a place for which he felt a sentimental attachment - or it could have been a combination of all these things which led him to ask Captain Evelyn if he might have Okewood again on the death of John Hallam.

There were intricate accounts to be settled with Hallam's son, the Rev. William Hallam of Trinity College, Cambridge. These were chiefly concerned with the underbrush or underwood, four acres of it, of eleven years' growth and fit to be cut, about which his father had made a complicated agreement with the tenant. It need not trouble us, but a letter from Bray and Warren to William Hallam shows Malthus's characteristic attitude to such matters; it is dated 29 June 1824:

> Mr. Malthus wishes to pay Mr. Hallam's Executors the utmost they are entitled to, but he must be satisfied that in case of his own death ye next Curate can be compelled to repay what he may have advanced. If, as we apprehend, Mr. Hallam's liability to his tenant Mr. Mann arose from his permitting him to depart from the usual custom respecting ye underwood, & from his covenanting to pay him what former incumbents had not agreed to; then of course the loss should not fall on Mr. Malthus; at the same time he would not take advantage of Mr. Hallam's mistake to derive a profit from ye underwood which he would not have received on his succession to ye Curacy under different circumstances.

The other side were not so gentlemanly, and Malthus paid the fees of both barristers called upon to arbitrate in the dispute, his own and the executors'. What counsel decided was, it seems, equitably unsatisfactory to both parties, for on 31 December 1825 Bray and Warren wrote to Hallam's solicitor, Mr Domville of Lincoln's Inn:

> We enclose our account with Mr. Hallam, the balance of which we pay without prejudice both as respects Mr. Malthus and ourselves. Mr. Malthus not having let the coppices at Park Farm derives no advantage from the arrangement now contemplated except that he has not to advance the value of the underwood which he must otherwise have done.

Finding tenants was a problem. As early as 27 February 1824 Bray and Warren were advertising on Malthus's behalf in the *County Herald*, the *County Chronicle*, and the *Sussex Advertizer*. Those who looked at the farms were obviously not enthusiastic, and much time must have been spent discussing the terms of leases and the valuation of fallows and standing timber. Reminders had to be written when rents became due; one farmer promised to pay the agent 'next Market day at Dorking'. There was a complaint about damage by sheep, presumably due to rotten fences or a broken-down hedge.

There are only two indications that the long, itemised bill is primarily concerned with a place of worship. The acting curate, an unknown Mr Thornton, claimed expenses 'which we considered you ought not to be called upon for'. And on 15 November 1824, someone from the offices of Messrs Bray and Warren made three unsuccessful attempts at what was later to be called 'grant-hunting':

> Attending the Secretary of Commissioners for Building Churches to know if they had any authority to lend - found they had not - also attending the Sec^y for Enlarging Churches &c but they only gave or lent money for enlarging or rebuilding Churches & not for repairing only - procured their forms of application .... 13s. 4d.

> Attending Mr. Hodgson at Westminster (Solicitors to the Governors of Queen Anne's Bounty) but they could not lend money to repair Churches .... 6s. 8d.

There is no further evidence as to what Malthus did about fund-raising for the maintenance of the fabric, after the grant-hunting had failed.

For another aspect of Okewood one must turn from the letter-books and bill-books back to William Bray's diary. Mr Thornton did the duty as acting Curate until the summer of 1824, when Malthus appointed Alfred Parrin, a Westminster boy who went up to Cambridge as a sizar at St John's in 1809; William Bray records his calling on him in May 1826 and June 1827, and collecting a guinea on each occasion as a 'Subscription to Oakwood chapel school'. By 1829 there were between eighty and ninety boys and girls at the Okewood Sunday school, learning to read, as Otter put it, so that 'they might in due course become familiar with their Bibles and be able so to follow a service that they could make the proper responses from their own prayer books'. Otter's published sermons show that he himself was a 'strenuous and active Clergyman, for conferring the blessings of early Instruction upon the greater part of the Children of the Poor'.[21] Some of the large flock at Okewood must have been the descendants of the babies whom Malthus had christened thirty-five years before, or of their siblings, a vindication of the *Essay on Population*, since they presumably all lived within walking distance of the little chapel.

In 1829 Henry Malthus's name appears as curate of Okewood, acting for his father until he could get a living of his own. He was succeeded by his cousin William Bray; young William appears to have served for about five years, and carried on for a time with Malthus's successor, John Massey-Dawson, who held the curacy, with the rectory of Abinger, until his death in 1850.

It is tantalising not to know more about Malthus's connection with Okewood, and especially his feeling for the place. One must restrain oneself from putting into his head grateful thoughts and tender reminiscences which may not have been there; but it is impossible to believe that the activities of Messrs Bray and Warren in pursuit of tenants and timber-merchants were the most important part of the whole story.

3 'The Christian, kindred, social part'

Fanny Mackintosh's diaries are more detailed than William Bray's, although one could wish that in the earlier months she had spent more time writing about the people she met and less about her progress in Livy and Cicero. But even her lists of visitors are illuminating; they were almost all shared with the Malthuses, and thus we learn of the importance in their lives of Mr and Mrs William Busk, who must have known Malthus very well, but of whom I can find out almost nothing, except that they knew Francis Horner.[22]

They were clearly a serious couple, and lent the Mackintoshes collections of sermons for Sir James to read aloud on Sunday evenings. They also lent manuscript copies of Mrs Busk's works. Fanny read the first volume of her novel *Zeal and Experience* on 17 April 1819, and pronounced it 'just better than her Tragedies' (only the diligent student of the lady's output can appreciate this damning compliment). Yet the next day Fanny reports Papa talking with Malthus and Sismondi, first on their differences with Ricardo, then on the currency debate from Lord King's pamphlet of 1803 up to the time of the Bullion Committee, and then 'a discussion on Mrs. Busk for & against'.

This makes it slightly less surprising to find that Malthus had written a note for Murray on 13 May 1817:

> Give me leave to introduce Mr. Busk to you, a friend of mine and of Mr. Whishaw, who wishes to consult you on the publication of a Tragedy written by Mrs. Busk. It is on the same subject with Mr. Shiel's play, though treated very differently; and I believe it will bear a very advantageous comparison with it.

Mrs Busk's play was called *The Druids*, and concerned the love of the Chief Druid's daughter, Moina, for the captured Roman Paulinus; her virginal duty was to kill him with her own hands as the victim of a ritual sacrifice, both parties invoking the aid of their own gods throughout their scenes; she saved him by stabbing herself.[23] Sheil's play, called *The Apostate*, was set in the Spain of Philip II, and concerned the love of the beautiful Florinda for a Moor, who became a Christian and then returned to Islam; both end as corpses.[24] This tragedy was performed at Covent Garden in May 1817, bringing Sheil £400, and Murray gave him £300 for the copyright.

It is difficult to understand why the play should have been so successful, and Sheil's blank verse is just as uncongenial to modern readers as Mrs Busk's, but Murray obviously knew his business; Sheil's tragedies continued to make money, and Mrs Busk's works did not appear in print until they were published by subscription in 1837. The collection is today unreadable except for two sonnets. One, called 'Dotage', ends:

> But when instead of judgment ripened sage
> We hear the tongue once witty, wise, or gay,
> Drivel inanity the live-long day,
> See nature's ties forgotten, childish rage
> Or selfish nothings fill the dotard's breast,
> No longer to existence' joys we cling,
> If such debasement threaten length of years,
> Grim death, all eager hopes though he arrest
> In manhood's summer, in youth's blooming spring,
> But as a welcome remedy appears.[25]

The other sonnet is 'On the Death of the Rev. Robert Malthus'. The late Mr Robert Malthus, who read it shortly before he died in 1972, wrote that he did not think much of it as a poem, but that it gave a good picture of Old Pop according to family tradition:

> And thou art gone, son of Philosophy!
> Such as Philosophy was deemed of yore;
> Not cold disdain of all mankind adore,
> But love of wisdom, holy, deep, and high.
>
> Zeal in the search of truth, though buried lie,
> Deep, beneath mountain errors, truth's pure ore,
> Was thine, and zeal to use thy science' lore
> In the best service of humanity.
>
> Nor pride, nor thy just self-esteem could blind
> The clear perception of thy pow'rful mind;
> In thee, the rival ne'er eclipsed the friend,
> For wisdom's self could not engross thy heart;
> The patriot, Christian, kindred, social part,
> All man's best qualities, 'twas thine to blend.[26]

Of the kindred, social part Fanny Mackintosh touches the heart of the matter in one sentence. On Sunday 3 September 1820 she 'went to church at the College', as some of her family often did, accompanied by the Malthus ladies: 'Mr. M. returned after Church from his living in Lincolnshire & it was very agreeable to see Mrs. M's pleasure at seeing him.' This sympathetic observation is creditable to Fanny, because she sometimes found Mrs Malthus 'tiresome and fidgetty'; Harriet was approved, however, when she was 'ready with breakfast' for six young people who arrived from Mardocks very early one 'most lovely morning' in August, and of another visit Fanny wrote that the Malthuses were 'very hospitable and good-natured as usual'. On a single occasion she refers to Harriet as 'Malthusia'; possibly that was her nickname in Whig circles, or Fanny had picked it up from Jeffrey, a frequent visitor to Haileybury when he wanted to escape from London and hear the famous nightingales. On one occasion Jeffrey wrote to his sister-in-law in New York that he had stopped at the College on his way to Mardocks and 'took up Malthus, who is always delightful, and brought him here with me'.[27]

'Going to the College' for Fanny meant 'going to the Malthuses', and the Malthuses and their daughters came constantly to Mardocks (Hal seems to have been away at school and out of the picture). The two-hour walk through fields and lanes and Easneye Wood does not seem to have troubled either Malthus or Harriet, even on 'a snowy day'; perhaps they enjoyed the chance to be alone together. Sometimes they rode, or drove in a low gig; often some or all of one family stayed a night with the other. There were books to read aloud or exchange, Jane Austen and Sir Walter Scott, as well as Mrs Marcet and the *Reviews*, and *Frankenstein* 'by one of Mr. Godwin's daughters', 'the most *horrible* thing' Fanny had ever read; there was a joint visit to look through Mr Le Bas' microscope, 'a very good one, most wonderful machine'; there was music from harp or pianoforte, and dances or impromptu 'hops', chiefly quadrilles; and there was almost always very good talk - Fanny admits to being spoilt in this respect.

Haileybury was less satisfactory for Lady Mackintosh. She found that 'The conversation of young People of different Sexes is generally very tiresome to those who are not particularly engaged in it', and she wondered 'at the taste of Girls preferring ye conversation of Boys to Men'. According to her sister Jessie Sismondi, she 'could neither make herself nor others happy'. Madame Sismondi also wrote of Sir James's wasted life, and how 'he loved passionately and fondly only one person in the world [his wife] and she never could love him, though he was the only person in the world that truly loved her.' Catherine Mackintosh made the best of her situation, writing often to what her sister Elizabeth Wedgwood called 'her darling newspaper' - any newspaper - against slavery, or the use of little climbing boys to sweep chimneys; she attempted, 'amongst other things, to reform Smithfield Cattle Market'. She is said to have visited with money and blankets the wife of a man she had sent to prison for ill-treating his ass.[28]

It is not surprising that Lady Mackintosh should have found one evening at Mr Haughton's that 'the dance seemed to turn out very pleasant to ye young Ladies & Gentlemen & more so to me than these things generally do to me since my reign of chaperonage commenced as I had Mr. Malthus near me & had a good deal of conversation with him and Mr. Anderson.'[29]

Her references to Malthus, like Fanny's, are too many to quote, so three more must suffice. On Tuesday 13 August 1821,

> Mr. & Mrs. Malthus & their Daughters hacked over to dinner - Just before going to bed a Metaphysical argument was started which I did

not understand though Mr. M seemed to be stating it very clearly. I had not been in my Room five minutes before I saw ye matter quite clear. Conviction seemed to flow in of itself.

Unfortunately we are not told what the argument was about; but Lady Mackintosh's jottings are a reminder that, as Empson wrote, 'Mr. Malthus was a clergyman - a most conscientious one, pure and pious. We never knew one of this description so free from the vices of his caste.'[30]

Lady Mackintosh took her religion as seriously as she took everything else. Thus her journal for 1822 records that on Easter Sunday, 7 April, she went alone to the College Chapel (all the rest of the family walked to Widford church) and

> received ye Sacrament from Dr. Batten & Mr. Keene. I was much pleased to observe that not less than 12 or 15 of the young Gentlemen staid to partake of it - This would not have happened 3 or 40 years ago [sic]. Came home to tea after a pleasant early dinner with ye Malthus'.

And the following Sunday, 14 April 1822,

> John drove me in the Chair to ye College Chapel where we had the Service exceedingly well performed. The reading by Mr. Le Bas & Mr. Anderson & the Sermon by Mr. Malthus on Presumption - The text taken from . . .

Alas, she never looked it up, and the rest of the page is blank.

More significant are two undated entries in a journal used as a commonplace book; they must refer to some theological work of the period, perhaps a sermon which both Malthus and Lady Mackintosh had read. The first, although headed 'Copy', is I think a draft, as she began 'My dear Mr. Malthus', and there are two other deletions in the passage as well as two interpolations.

Copy

Dear Mr. Malthus

As according to our Bibles & common-sense the priority of creation could not have been with Man, the Optic nerve must have been adapted to the rays which the general Surface of the Earth was calculated to reflect - So that in *whatever colour* it had pleased the great Artificer to cloathe the Earth, that colour must have been the most agreeable to the organs of sight, whether it were the one we now call scarlet, crimson, or any other - from hence I infer that it is pedantic & somewhat absurd to select as a subject of *particular* Wonder & Admiration *that the Earth is clothed in Green* . . .

338

Answer

As the Earth was obviously formed before the organs of Vision, I quite agree with you in thinking that we cannot with propriety select as a subject of particular Wonder and Admiration the Circumstance of the *Earth's being clothed in Green*. But it appears to me that the Benevolence of the Deity is manifested in the same manner by his having formed the eye to suit the prevailing colour of the Earth as if he had formed ye prevailing colour of the Earth to suit the previous structure of the Eye. — —

— — Malthus

I need not add that in the Opinion contained in the last sentence of the Above I most sincerely & devoutly concur.   C.M.

For post-Darwinian generations this correspondence sounds almost medieval.

Fanny Mackintosh only notes one occasion on which Malthus went to Cambridge, on 26 November 1822, but of course there may have been others during her time at Mardocks. He would certainly have gone on 13 February 1817, had it been necessary, to vote for his 'sincere old friend E. D. Clarke', who wrote to Malthus that he would give his right hand to be University Librarian, but in the event did not need to, as his nomination was unopposed.[31]

Malthus lent Clarke the manuscripts of the journal he kept during his Norwegian tour of 1799; these were incorporated in the fifth volume of Clarke's monumental *Travels*, with his own flowery elaborations and embellishments of Malthus's words which must have made that diarist wince. Clarke had asked for this material long before, in January 1811, and clearly received some sort of rebuff, for he wrote to Otter that Malthus 'seems to swell a little about it ... I will ask for it no more'. Malthus relented later, perhaps in view of the troubles which befell the Clarke household, but requested the omission of all inverted commas in the sixth volume, so that the over-decorated 'quotations' from his Swedish journal could not be identified. As it happened, Clarke died suddenly on 9 March 1822, leaving his widow with seven children under sixteen (five others were dead) and the book was finished posthumously by his friends; in the confusion, Malthus's Swedish diaries were lost.[32]

As far as Malthus's own kin were concerned, the help they wanted from Brother, Cousin or Uncle Robert was practical rather than spiritual, academic or literary. In most families, I think, any member who achieves eminence is believed to be of supreme efficiency in every aspect of life; perhaps it is not unreasonable to expect that a political economist should be an expert in financial affairs, and competent to manage all sorts of business, but in Malthus's case nothing could be less true.

To begin with, he was clearly upset by having to fill up a form. This is shown by the mistakes he made on those in the parish registers at Albury and Walesby, and still more on the Stamp Office form in respect of the legacy duty on his sister Charlotte's estate. The descendants of baby Reginald Warren have one of these imposing documents which was never returned to the Stamp Office as it should have been (Bray and Warren must have procured a duplicate) because Malthus, as executor, had put so many of the relevant figures in the wrong places; some of them do not even appear to be correct. Charlotte's household goods and clothes were valued at £50, and Malthus also bracketed with this 'Ships and Shares of Ships', which seems unlikely.

It is also reasonable, I suppose, to assume that a celebrated author has influence with publishers, and as well as for Mrs Busk, Malthus wrote to Murray for his cousin Marianne Baillie - she who as Marianne Wathen had composed the rhyming couplets for his wedding-day. Some of her poems were privately printed by her husband, Alexander Baillie, who fell on hard times, and she was anxious to publish her journal of what may have been an enforced tour abroad; before the days of photograph and film, travel diaries were extremely popular. Malthus wrote to Murray on 14 March 1819:

> I have been disappointed not to hear from you about Mrs. Baillie's manuscript. Pray let me know the result as soon as you conveniently can; and if it should not suit you to take it, I wish you would advise me to whom I had best offer it.

Murray did take it, and on 21 September of the same year Malthus asked for an advance for Mrs Baillie, as she was 'going soon to remove from Twickenham to London, and I think that a small sum would be very convenient to her just now'.[33]

Marianne Baillie's name appears again in the Murray letters after the publication of the *Principles of Political Economy*. In a postscript on 16 April 1820 Malthus wrote, 'By the by, Mrs. Baillie talked to Mrs. Malthus as if she expected a copy, though to say the truth I did not think of her. If however you can spare one I believe she would like it.' Malthus certainly deserved his reputation for good-nature.

From 1815 until shortly before his death, Sydenham Malthus lived mainly abroad, in Switzerland and Italy, provided with introductions by his distinguished younger brother, who was given power of attorney to manage things in England. The affairs of Sydenham's step-children were the most troublesome which Malthus had to deal with, on account of the Oxford Plantation in Jamaica; indeed, poor Mrs Sydenham had buried her second husband before she received what she considered was due to her and her children from the first. The villain of the piece was Henry Swann, Tory MP for Esher, who must have been some sort of trustee for the estate of William Leigh Symes, and who had been involved in proceedings over it in the Court of Chancery; he took months to answer letters, and acted as if he thought that the Symes' step-father and uncle were intent on cheating them of their inheritance. Matters were further complicated by the husbands of two of the Symes girls, Mr Pritchard and Mr Wapshaw, who continued to press their claims to the marriage portions to which they were entitled, although Harriet Wapshaw had died within a year of her wedding.

The youngest of the Symes children, George Frederick (1794-1851), went into the Madras Artillery, and much of the correspondence concerns William Bray's attempt to get Swann to pay back from the Jamaica Estate the £200 Sydenham had advanced for his outfit. This business, again, naturally devolved upon Malthus; although Lieutenant Symes came of age in 1815, he seems not to have been expected to act on his own account, perhaps owing to the time needed to communicate with India.

All the same, Lieutenant Symes precipitated a crisis by drawing a bill for £60 on his Uncle Robert (who knew nothing about it) which was presented at Bray's office by 'the officer who brought it from India', early in November 1818. From the letter-book it is difficult to make out what happened, but it would appear that Malthus refused to accept the bill, and then had second thoughts. On 30 December 1818 Augustus Warren wrote to him when Malthus was spending Christmas with the Eckersalls in Bath:

> The Bill for £60 drawn by Lieut. Symes I suppose is returned to India as the party holding it would not incur the risk of keeping it here finding you had no advice of its being drawn on you. The Officer who brought it from India did not leave his Address but I have had an enquiry made in the City according to a direction taken down by Mr. Bray but unfortunately there is a mistake in it & I have no means of tracing the Bill - It certainly will hurt Lieut. Symes' Credit as it would any other person's to have the Bill returned, but it is perhaps better to happen with so small a sum than if it were greater. There can be no harm in asking Mr. Swann if he will pay the £60, but I suppose he will return the same Answer as before, that he has not authorised Mr. Symes to draw on him. I will not however write unless I hear from you.

There is no evidence as to what happened next in this affair. Lieutenant Symes's maternal uncle, Captain Ryves, RN, in 1819 acted for him in some business in which Malthus was told that his name had better not appear; in 1824 Symes, on leave in England, married his first cousin Katherine Ryves, and we hear of him no more.[34]

The two eldest Bray nephews, like their Uncle Sydenham, also received introductions, in their case to the literary giants of Edinburgh. Malthus killed two birds with one stone through making the young men bearers of a letter to Henry Mackenzie (1745-1831) congratulating him on the appointment of his youngest son, Holt, as secretary to the Governor General in

India. Holt Mackenzie came to the College at Hertford Castle in 1806, and won medals for political economy, classics and mathematics; a brother had already died in the Company's service in Calcutta in 1800, and another was doing well in the Indian Army. It has been suggested that Henry Mackenzie obtained posts in the East India Company for three of his six sons because of his friendship with Lord Melville; Mackenzie was a conspicuous Tory, as loyal to Pitt as the Whig group were to Fox, yet he contrived to be on visiting terms with both parties in Edinburgh, in spite of his having been made Comptroller of Taxes for Scotland in 1804.

Henry Mackenzie's popularity was due to his attractive and eccentric character and to his position as a man of letters: he had known David Hume and helped Robert Burns, and he had himself written much, including plays, which were unsuccessfully performed, and a novel written in 1771 called *The Man of Feeling*. It is heavy going now, but was so acclaimed in its day that Mackenzie was nicknamed after it by his friends as soon as his authorship became known. Henry Cockburn summed up Mackenzie's charm for a new generation of Edinburgh writers:

> Though he survived the passing away of many a literary friend, and
> many a revolution of manners, he accommodated himself to
> unavoidable change with the cheerfulness of a man of sense, above
> the weakness of supposing that the world must have been in its
> prime only when he was in his.[35]

Malthus may have met the man of feeling on some of his many visits to London, and must have regarded him - twenty-one years his senior - with considerable respect, for the letter introducing the Brays is so evenly written, without any of his usual slips and corrections, that it can only be the fair copy of a draft.

Malthus's letter to Henry Mackenzie is dated from London on 16 June 1819:

> My dear Sir,
> I am much obliged to you for your kind letter, which I assure you
> has given me the most sincere pleasure. I had always a very high
> opinion of your son Holt's understanding and talents, and it is
> particularly gratifying to me to find that they are properly
> appreciated in the country where they are now exerted with so much
> credit to himself and advantage to the government. The choice
> which has been made of him to fill so important a situation is
> certainly most highly honourable to both parties. It raises the
> government in my estimation, and would raise *him* if I had not
> before thought, that, if his health were good, there is no office in the
> Empire to which he would not be fully equal. It would give me
> great pleasure to hear from him at any time; but I am too well aware

of the full occupation of his time, and too sensible of my own deficiencies in letter writing not to find ample excuses for him. I rejoice to hear that the accounts of his health are satisfactory, and hope and trust that he will not suffer his ardour in the discharge of his duties, and in the pursuit of knowledge, to interfere with the regular exercise, and care, which I should think his constitution renders necessary.

I take the opportunity of sending this letter by my two nephews Messrs Bray. One of them the youngest (Reginald) who is in the law, has been an invalid for some months, and is in fact taking a sail to Leith for his health, but he cannot approach near to so distinguished a city as Edinburgh, without a desire to see something of it. The eldest Mr. Edward Bray accompanies his brother chiefly at the request of his mother, with the kind view of taking care of him in case he should be unwell, but actuated also by a desire of seeing Edinburgh. It is not quite certain how long they will stay in Scotland, but I should expect but a very short time. I have given them a letter to Jeffrey.

I am very sorry to hear that you suffered so much by the *influenza*. It prevailed a good deal in London, but we fortunately escaped it at Haileybury. I trust you have now quite recovered the effects of it, and are again enjoying your health.

> Believe me, my dear Sir
> with the most sincere regard,
> and wishes for your health,
> Your faithful humb^l S^{t.}
> T. Robt Malthus[36]

Malthus need not have worried about Holt Mackenzie's health, for he retired on pension after twenty-four years' service, in 1822, and died in 1876 when he was almost ninety. It is sad that I can trace no correspondence between Malthus and his pupils; evidence that he kept up with them is given in a letter to Sismondi of 12 March 1821: Malthus writes that with his best intentions towards his correspondents he is in arrear to his friends in Paris, America and the East Indies.[37]

Enough has been quoted, I think, to show that Malthus was fully concerned with the affairs of his family, friends and pupils throughout the time when he was also struggling with his own literary work and a succession of Haileybury crises. Sir James Mackintosh was hardly telling the truth when he talked about Malthus's undisturbed leisure, but he did at this period have uninterrupted health; there is no reference in the minutes of the Committee of College to his ever taking sick leave, as so many of his colleagues did for months on end, sometimes abroad, but usually on the south coast of England.

Sir James's own health was said to have been ruined by the climate of Bombay. His recurrent bouts of fever and giddiness sound like malaria, which would account for the slow progress of the History so deplored by his sisters-in-law; they attributed the dilatoriness, and his failure to make much impression in the House of Commons, to his partiality for chatting with 'old Jezebels'. Madame de Staël and the Duchess of Devonshire (formerly Lady Elizabeth Foster) are alleged to have wasted his time at the beginning of his parliamentary career. Later Lady Holland reigned supreme, and Fanny seems to have shared her aunts' disapproval: she wrote to Mary Rich from 118 Piccadilly on 4 February 1821, 'Papa is dining at the Hollands as my Lady sent her writ of summons this morning.'

Very few women visited Holland House, because the couple had eloped and had a son (in 1796) while she was still married to Sir Godfrey Webster; it was no doubt her exclusion from court and ordinary social activity which made Lady Holland eccentric and imperious. She made Malthus promise to dine at Holland House in October 1821, when he met her at Lord Cowper's Hertfordshire home, Panshanger; he went.[38]

Mackintosh is generally believed to have refused the Chair of Moral Philosophy at Edinburgh in 1820 because Lord Holland and Lord Lansdowne appealed to him to remain in the House of Commons, where he was regarded as leader of the Opposition – and actually referred to as such by Dr Chalmers when he visited Malthus in 1822.[39] The trouble was that after Whitbread's death in 1815, Horner's in 1817, and Romilly's in 1818, the principal Whigs were mainly in the House of Peers; a young exception was Lord John Russell (1792-1878), whom Fanny always found 'very agreeable' when he came to Mardocks. There was also the older William Lamb (1779-1848), who later became Queen Victoria's Lord Melbourne; his wife, Lady Caroline, in the summer of 1820 was much taken with Dumfy Mackintosh, 'talked to him all dinner and asked him to come and see her at Brocket'.

One cannot estimate what influence Malthus and Mackintosh had behind the scenes in Hertfordshire. I suspect that Mackintosh's ability as a thinker was much over-rated on account of his charm as a talker; he fascinated even his disapproving sisters-in-law, and people as different as the elderly Maria Edgeworth and the young Mr Ticknor from Boston, Massachusetts. George Ticknor wrote in April 1819 of a visit to Mardocks with the newly-married Sismondis, Lord John Russell and Malthus:

> Sir James, who delights in the stir and excitement of intellectual discussion, seemed to amuse himself by beating round on all sides, now answering Lord John with a story of the last century, now repeating poetry to Mrs. Sismondi, and now troubling the discussion of the eminent political economists with his ponderous knowledge of history, statistics, and government, in short, the subjects on which all

three were most familiar and oftenest differed. Malthus is, what anybody might anticipate, a plain man, with plain manners, apparently troubled by few prejudices, and not much by the irritability of authorship, but still talking occasionally with earnestness. In general, however, I thought he needed opposition, but he rose to the occasion, whatever it might be.[40]

Ticknor, who was twenty-seven at the time, did not mention Fanny: he might have been surprised to learn that she described him to her half-sister as 'clever and lively but rather conceited'.

In April 1823 Elizabeth Mackintosh died of tuberculosis, not unexpectedly, and was buried at Hampstead beside her infant brother Robert, who had lived for a few weeks in 1803; I have found no Mackintosh journals for 1823-5. The College Committee's minutes record on 16 June 1824 the receipt of a letter from Dr Thomson and Dr Holland stating that Sir James Mackintosh's health was 'unequal to the discharge of those laborious duties at fixed times which his Station at the East India College requires, although it does not unfit him for private study, nor for those public exertions which in a great measure leave him to the choice of his own time; and expressing a hope that the Court will permit him to retire from his Office at Midsummer with such an allowance as may be thought reasonable in the case of one who retires only because he is disabled'.[41]

Sir James was awarded a pension of £200 per annum. Although they became very fond of his successor, William Empson, the Malthuses must have regretted the departure from Mardocks; they kept their close links with the Mackintosh family, and met them frequently in London. With the College more settled, Malthus went to London more often, or so it seems from other people's memoirs. 'Even when in the busy Metropolis, at the height of the season', Malthus's old friend Smyth was remarkable for his powdered hair, 'a gay waistcoat', knee-breeches and white silk stockings, for he maintained his 'stubborn resistance to the innovation of trousers' until his death in 1849.[42] Malthus's clothes were never commented upon. Linnell shows him with his auburn hair cut short, and we can imagine him at this period wearing dark trousers with an equally dark waisted coat, and a high top hat, a figure not notably conspicuous in the West End of London until after the First World War.

4 The Public Name

It is difficult now to convey how current was the word 'Malthusian'
between, let us say, 1803 and 1835. Perhaps it could be compared with the
word 'Freudian' about a century later, which was used by people who had
little idea who Freud was, when or where he worked, or even what tenets
he held. There was a jingle:

> Professor Freud
> Would be overjoyed
> At the things I dream of you.
> And Professor Freud
> Would be most annoyed
> If you didn't dream that way too.

I have found no popular songs about Malthusianism, but allusions to Malthus
in the literature and journalism of his day are legion, quite apart from the
attacks on him by Coleridge and Southey, Cobbett, De Quincey and Hazlitt,
familiar to students of English literature, and the serious discussions of his
work familiar to students of the history of economic thought. His contemporary fame is revealed, I think, most tellingly by all the casual, passing
references to Malthus, which assume that everyone knew what he stood
for, in a range of popular works from Miss Mitford's *Our Village* to Byron's
Don Juan. Harriet Martineau (1802-76) was sick of Malthus's name before
she was fifteen, without having read a line of his work.[43]
Take Miss Mitford's Old Master Green, who was

> quite patriarchal in the number of his descendants, having had the
> Mahommedan allowance of four wives, although, after the Christian
> fashion, successively, and more children and grandchildren than he
> could conveniently count. Indeed, his computation varied a little,
> according as he happened to be drunk or sober; for he was proud of
> his long train of descendants, just as his betters may be proud of a
> long line of ancestry; and being no disciple of the Malthusian
> doctrine, thought he 'had done the state' (that is, the parish) 'some
> service', in rearing up a goodly tribe of sons and daughters, many of
> them in their turn grandfathers and grandmothers, and most of
> whom had conducted themselves passably in the world as times
> go ...[44]

Byron's Malthusian comment, in the fifteenth canto of *Don Juan*, began
with a reference to an American colony from Württemberg led by George
Rapp; according to Byron's own footnote, Rapp placed such restrictions

upon matrimony as to prevent more than a certain quantum of births in a certain number of years, which births generally arrived in a little flock, like those of a farmer's lambs, perhaps all within the same month.

XXXV

When Rapp the Harmonist embargo'd marriage
  In his harmonious settlement - (which flourishes
Strangely enough as yet without miscarriage,
  Because it breeds no more mouths that it nourishes,
Without those sad expenses which disparage
  What Nature naturally most encourages) . . .

XXXVII

But Rapp is the reverse of zealous matrons,
  Who favour, malgré Malthus, generation -
Professors of that genial art, and patrons
  Of all the modest part of propagation;
Which after all at such a desperate rate runs
  That half its produce tends to emigration,
That sad result of passions and potatoes -
Two weeds which pose our economic Catos.

XXXVIII

Had Adeline read Malthus? I can't tell;
  I wish she had: his book's the eleventh commandment,
Which says, 'Thou shalt not marry', unless *well*:
  This he (as far as I can understand) meant.
'Tis not my purpose on his views to dwell,
  Nor canvass what 'so eminent a hand' meant;
But certes it conducts to lives ascetic,
Or turning marriage into arithmetic.

This point was made earlier by Thomas Love Peacock (1785-1866) in his *Melincourt*, which appeared in 1818. It is strange that there is no reference to this satirical novel in either the Mackintosh diaries or Ricardo's correspondence, since it was mainly concerned with parliamentary reform, and Malthus is so easily identified with Mr Fax; he is made to speak in only a slightly caricatured fashion, far less ridiculous than the way in which Malthus was described by his old friend Sydney Smith.

'Bachelors and spinsters I decidedly venerate,' says Mr Fax. 'The world is overstocked with featherless bipeds. More men than corn is a fearful pre-eminence, the sole and fruitful cause of penury, disease, and war, plague, pestilence, and famine . . . The cause of all the evils of human society is single, obvious, reducible to the most exact mathematical calculation; . . . The remedy is an universal social compact, binding both sexes to equally rigid celibacy, till the prospect of maintaining the average number of six children be as clear as the arithmetic of futurity can make it.'

The hero, Mr Forester, points out that fortune is subject to rapid and sudden mutations, and in any case the present age is calculating enough to gratify the most determined votary of moral and political arithmetic: 'What is marriage but the most sordid of bargains, the most cold and slavish of all forms of commerce? ... We are in no danger of forgetting that two and two make four. There is no fear that the warm impulses of feeling will ever overpower, with us, the tangible eloquence of the pocket.'

Mr Fax agrees that this is largely correct with regard to the middle and higher classes, 'But among the lower orders the case is quite different. The baleful influence of the poor laws has utterly destroyed the principle of calculation in them.' Later on Mr Fax is made to say that 'To check the benevolence of the rich, by persuading them that all misfortune is the result of imprudence, is a great evil; but it would be a much greater evil to persuade the poor that indiscretion may have a happier result than prudence.' All the same, Mr Fax gives £5 to the unfortunate Desmond family for their arrears of rent, and deplores the villain's fashionable barouche: '"Those four horses", said Mr. Fax, as the carriage rolled away, "consume the subsistence of eight human beings for the foolish amusement of one".'[45]

I cannot agree with Richard Garnett, writing in 1891, that 'Mr. Fax appears to be an idealised portrait of Malthus';[46] still less can I share the view of J. B. Priestley, who in 1927 wrote of Mr Fax that 'his prominent part and gentle treatment are rather curious'.[47] In 1818 Population Malthus was at the height of his fame. We have seen how Ricardo had made the principle of population the corner-stone of the whole new system of political economy: in 1816 John Bird Sumner had made it theologically respectable as well.

Sumner (1780-1862) in due course became Archbishop of Canterbury. The book to which Malthus owed so much was published while he was still a Fellow of Eton, whither he had returned as a master in 1803 after taking his degree at Cambridge; it was as important to Sumner's career as it was in the consolidation of Malthus's position in what would later be called the Establishment. The work was in two volumes, with a long title: *A Treatise on the Records of the Creation, and on the Moral Attributes of the Creator; with particular reference to the Jewish History, and to the Consistency of the Principle of Population with the Wisdom and Goodness of the Deity.* It is difficult to see why it made such an impression, since Sumner only repeated what Malthus had already said about the blessing of a family as a spur to self-denial, 'severe and constant exertion', inventiveness and ingenuity, and so on. The first of the seven editions of Sumner's *Treatise* just preceded the publication of the fifth edition of *Population*, and obviously disposed many Anglicans to take a more favourable view of Malthus than they would otherwise have done; it certainly changed the attitude of the *Quarterly Review* towards him.

I cannot imagine Peacock doggedly working his way through the two volumes of Sumner's prize essay, but his sympathetic portrait of Mr Fax is probably a good picture of Malthus as seen by the educated public in the last years of George III's reign. Hazlitt continued to hate him; his cruel brilliance as an essayist is of the kind which does not date, and requires no background knowledge to enjoy; he is almost certainly responsible for much subsequent misunderstanding not only of Malthus, but of his reputation. In 1819 Hazlitt published a collection of articles written over the past twelve years, entitled *Political Essays with Sketches of Public Characters*, in which he attacked Malthus more virulently than any of his other victims:

> With respect to the article of dogs and horses, a word in Mr.
> Malthus's ear ... The pleasure and coach-horses kept in this
> kingdom consume as much of the produce of the soil as would
> maintain all the paupers in it. Let a tax be laid upon them directly, to
> defray the expense of the poor-rates, and to suspend the operation of
> Mr. Malthus's arithmetical and geometrical ratios. We see no
> physical necessity why that ingenious divine should put a stop to the
> propagation of the species, that he may keep two sleek geldings in
> his stable.

In short, Hazlitt could not be reconciled to 'Mr. Malthus's proposal of starving the children of the poor to feed the horses of the rich'.[48]

It was Peacock's Mr Fax who gave Malthus's true view of the folly of keeping superfluous horses; his colleagues may have smiled at the reference to the sleek geldings when they saw Malthus go off to Hertford in his gig, pulled by the mare whom, he boasted to Ricardo, he had driven for ten years without a fall.[49]

John Murray certainly had no doubts concerning his author's popularity at this period. With the renewed agitation about the Corn Laws, he wanted to print Malthus's pamphlets again, and a uniform edition of Collected Works must also have been discussed. One can interpret in no other way the following letter from Malthus to Murray; it is dated 26 September 1819, when the manuscript of the *Principles of Political Economy* was nearing completion:

> It would [be] a very inconvenient interruption to me now to prepare
> the pamphlets you allude to for the press; and I really think that it
> would be impolitic to connect them in any way with the present
> volume; which if left to itself will, I should hope, have an extensive
> sale. The best time to reprint them will be when you can publish a
> uniform edition of my works, which I think may be done with
> advantage in about a year or a little more from the publication of the
> present volume, when I shall certainly have more to publish on the
> same general subject. The present volume must I think be printed

closer than the last edition of the Essay, but the whole may be rendered uniform at a subsequent period.

I do not think that Malthus was being unduly optimistic or conceited about these Collected Works; but with hindsight, the letter he wrote to Murray on 30 April 1820, after the *Principles of Political Economy* had been published, is ironically pathetic:

> I have been rather expecting to hear from you how we are going on. Dr. Batten brings a very favourable account. I do not expect sudden conversions; but I have a strong persuasion that the principles which I have laid down will be found so conformable with experience that they will gradually prevail like those of the Essay on Population.

The Malthuses spent most of their summer vacation of 1820 in Paris. On their return they found a letter from the Rev. Robinson Elsdale, Second Master (and later for two years High Master) of Manchester Grammar School, a prominently Tory institution. In 1810 Elsdale had married Marianne Leeves who, like Marianne Baillie, was first cousin to Harriet Malthus. I give Malthus's reply to Elsdale in full because it illustrates so many aspects of his character; in particular, he makes no attempt to foist the *Principles of Political Economy* on to a less renowned relation; this letter shows also how Sumner had reached a public quite outside Malthus's circle, and Malthus was perhaps not unwarrantably sanguine in hoping that other writers might do the same sort of service for his principle of under-consumption:

E. I. Coll. August. 2nd. 1820

My dear Sir,
 You will probably guess that the reason of your not hearing from me is that we have been from home. We are just indeed returned from spending the greatest part of our vacation at Paris, and I only received your letter on reaching home yesterday.
 You are probably aware that the studies at the College here have no connection with a military education. At the same time it is certain that all education for India must have at least one common object, that is, some little previous knowledge of the History and State of the country.
 With this view I should recommend that your young friend should read with attention Dow's History of Hindostan, and Orme's History of the Military Transactions in Hindostan, accompanied by a good map, and Hamilton's East India Gazeteer, in order to get some notion of the situation and the state of all the places mentioned. It is much better to read a few books with attention and accuracy than many in a cursory and indolent manner. If however your young friend finds that he has time, he may add to these a History of British India not long since published by Mr. Mill. It is a large work

in three volumes quarto and contains a great mass of information both relating to the state and character of the Hindoos, and the government and transactions of the Company in India. The author however is perhaps too unfavourable to the Hindoos, and too much inclined to severity of criticism in all matters relating to government. He has however since the publication of his work been appointed to an official situation in the Company's service.

We rejoice to hear that Marianne is doing well after her lying in, and that you are settled in a more healthy and agreeable part of the Town. [Two lines have been obliterated here.] I have seen no separate Essay on Population by Mr. Sumner; but in a prize work which he published on the Records of the Creation, there is a great deal on the subject which is extremely well done; and he there states most justly that the tendency of population to increase beyond the means of subsistence is the grand stimulus to industry.

Mrs. Malthus joins me in kind love to Marianne. It would give us great pleasure to have an opportunity of seeing you in your new abode.

> Believe me truly yours
> T. R. Malthus.[50]

There is no evidence of the Malthuses visiting the Elsdales, but they may have met in family gatherings at Hollin Hall; the three young Woods, Harriet's lively nephews, went to Manchester Grammar School.

As well as an extensive correspondence, Malthus's fame brought also institutional commitments and rewards, which will be described later. For an elderly man his general health seems better than average, and his tall, slender figure was remarked upon by a number of writers, but the cleft palate probably made him more susceptible to catarrh as he grew older. When Maria Edgeworth visited Mardocks and Haileybury in January 1822 she wrote to her step-mother that 'Mr. Malthus speaks more snuffly through his nose and slower than formerly or perhaps the immediate contrast to Mackintosh's fluent eloquence ... makes it appear more striking to me and intolerable.'[51] This increasingly defective speech must have embarrassed him, and one feels he only appeared before two Select Committees of the House of Commons, in 1824 and 1827, because he considered that it was his duty to do so.

It is hard to see why Malthus was asked to give evidence before the Select Committee on Artizans and Machinery, in May 1824, unless the three leading men concerned thought that they could make use of his name. These were Joseph Hume, who was Chairman; J. R. McCulloch, who also gave evidence; and Francis Place, who regarded himself as the power behind the scenes and was responsible for coaching the working-class witnesses. The Committee could be described as part of the general campaign to do away with medieval restrictions (or attempted paternal regulation) which ham-

pered industry and commerce: these included the Usury and Navigation
Acts as well as the Corn Laws and other import duties.

The first Select Committee to which Malthus was called was appointed
'to inquire into the state of the Law of the United Kingdom, and its
consequences, respecting Artizans leaving the Kingdom, and residing
Abroad; also, into the state of the Law, and its consequences, respecting the
exportation of Tools and Machinery; and into the state of the Law, and its
effects, so far as relates to the Combination of Workmen, and others, to
raise wages, or to regulate their wages and hours of working'.

Malthus's evidence, on 10 May 1824, was extremely brief as compared
with that of most other witnesses, and in marked contrast to McCulloch's
long exposition of Ricardian economics. Malthus agreed that the current
legislation which aimed to check the export of machinery or the emigration
of skilled men was almost completely ineffective; in the latter case he stated
firmly that if the laws were efficient they would be unjust. (There was at
the time an appreciable number of English people, not artisans, who were
living abroad for the benefit of their health or their pockets.) With regard
to the export of machinery he was, like the Committee, rather more cautious
than he was about emigration, but he upheld - as always - the general
principles of free trade. Here are four successive questions and answers on
this point:

> Are you aware that there is a duty at present laid upon machinery
> exported from England to France? - I was not aware.

> If France was to lay a duty on English machinery, on importation
> into France, would not that be attempting to do what we are trying
> by the prohibitions to effect? - Certainly.

> Is it your opinion that the relaxation of the old commercial jealousy,
> and the establishment of free trade would be an advantage to this
> country? - Yes.

> Do you not conceive that the allowance of the exportation of
> English machinery, would have the effect of inducing other countries
> to establish a free trade? - I think that such would be its tendency,
> and that it is a very proper reason for relaxing those laws.

Malthus, it will be noted, talked of relaxing the laws, not repealing them.

With regard to the Combination Laws, which were Place's chief concern,
the principal conclusions of the Committee were as follows:

- 6. -

> That the laws have not only not been efficient to prevent
> Combinations, either of masters or workmen; but, on the contrary,
> have, in the opinion of many of both parties, had a tendency, to
> produce mutual irritation and distrust, and to give a violent character

to the Combinations, and to render them highly dangerous to the peace of the community.

- 7. -

That it is the opinion of this Committee, That masters and workmen should be freed from such restrictions, as regard the rate of wages and the hours of working, and be left at perfect liberty to make such agreements as they may mutually think proper.

· · · · · · · · · ·

- 11. -

That it is absolutely necessary, when repealing the Combination Laws, to enact such a law as may efficiently, and by summary process, punish either workmen or masters, who by threats, intimidation, or acts of violence, should interfere with that perfect freedom which ought to be allowed to each party, of employing his labour or capital in the manner he may deem most advantageous.[52]

Malthus agreed with all this. He had, from the time of the first *Essay*, a strong sense of the injustice of the laws under which workmen were severely punished for combining to raise wages, while their masters could unite, perhaps round a private dinner table, without punishment, to keep wages down; this was a state of affairs that violated the basic English principle of the equality of all men before the law, which was with Malthus an article of faith. But Malthus seems to have been almost alone, as we noticed earlier, in perceiving that on purely economic grounds the repeal of the Combination Laws was diametrically opposed to the principle of *laissez-faire* in a free competitive market: the repeal of the Usury Laws meant leaving the rate of interest free to find its 'natural' level, but the repeal of the Combination Laws meant that wages could be fixed - in some circumstances - at rates quite unconnected with the state of the labour market concerned, or with the demand for its products.

Thus when Malthus was asked what effect the Combination Laws had had on wages, he replied, 'They have had a partial effect; a pernicious effect, I think.'

> Tending to depress them? - They have no doubt operated against the general principle of wages finding their natural level.

> Is it your decided opinion, that masters and men, upon all occasions, should be left to make what bargains they please, both as to the mode of paying and the hours they ought to work? - I think so; but it is very important that any sort of force used on the part of the men, to prevent others taking lower wages, should be punished severely; such as acts of intimidation either towards the masters, or other men.[53]

As Professor Grampp has pointed out, these were not the sort of answers Francis Place wanted: the object of the working class was to take the determination of wages away from the market and the cruel laws of supply and demand which dictated their natural level. Professor Grampp thinks that the people were harking back to legendary good old days when the government, through the justices, was supposed to fix all wages equitably according to the current prices of bread and ale.[54] We know Malthus's views on this point, from his pamphlet on *The High Price of Provisions* in 1800 to his talks with Mallet at the close of his life, and they did not change: one cannot have what is not there; if anything in short supply is fairly divided, individual shares must be small; if a group of workers insist on wages above the market rate, some of their number will be unemployed.

This is not a popular thesis, and it is one against which there are a number of arguments; but the relevant point here is that Place and his associates, though alive to Malthus's concern for the poor, must have realised as they heard his 'crawky' voice that this was not a public name they could use for their own purposes.

5 Clubs and Societies

In spite of the hare-lip, Malthus seems to have been what Dr Johnson called 'clubbable'. The early letters to Ricardo show that his attendance at the King of Clubs dinners was regular enough for London visits to be arranged to fit in with these monthly meetings. According to Charles Marsh this club was still in existence in 1832.[55] It ceased to be important to Malthus's life, I think, with the founding of the Political Economy Club. Like other such bodies, including the Geological Society in its early days, both Malthus's dining clubs met at this period at the Freemasons' Tavern in Great Queen Street; there the similarity ended, for whereas conversation at the King of Clubs was anecdotal and witty, the Political Economy Club met seriously to discuss 'some doubt or question' proposed by two or three members in turn at each meeting, 'which may be considered by the members during the interval and form the subject of conversation at the next meeting'.

The principal founder of the Political Economy Club was Thomas Tooke (1774-1858), who drew up the London Merchants' Petition for free trade in 1820. Other prominent members (their numbers were limited to thirty) were Ricardo and Malthus, James Mill, Torrens, Mushet, the historian George Grote, Zachary Macaulay, Sir Henry Parnell, Nassau Senior, and a little later on J. R. McCulloch, when he moved to London. John Lewis Mallet (1775-1861), a colleague of Whishaw's in the Commission of Audit, was one of the first members, and his diaries provide information about the meetings; by 1836 he had grown tired of his 'dogmatical and presumptuous' fellow-members, and wrote that he hardly knew how he had stayed among them some twelve years: 'I was originally attracted by the charm of the personal characters of Malthus and Ricardo, and when they were both gone I felt I had no abiding interest there.'[56]

Malthus himself never missed a meeting, except when the family were away on holiday, from the very first on 30 April 1821 to 4 December 1834, the last before his death, apart from that of May 1831 - when there was, perhaps, a crisis over examination papers. Originally the dinners were at six o'clock on the first Monday of every month from December to June. Mallet records twenty-two as 'a large party'; there were normally fifteen or sixteen, seated round a long table, with the chairman at one end and the deputy at the other, offices which the members filled in rotation; all observations were to be addressed to whichever might be the more distant from the person speaking. Members took turns to bring guests, and Malthus's included Otter and Dealtry. But more significantly, at only the second meeting of the Club, Malthus proposed Mr Cazenove as a member.[57]

Very little is known about John Cazenove (c. 1788-1879), except that he was the son of a Genevese merchant who migrated to London. Malthus seems to have met him through Le Bas; it will be remembered that this colleague's family had connections with brewing and a draper's shop in Bond Street. In the spring of 1820 Malthus had been concerned to find some 'easy and cheap' way of sending a copy of the *Principles of Political Economy* to Pierre Prévost in Geneva: on 30 April we find him asking Murray that one might be sent 'directly' to Mr Cazenove at '42 Broad Street City'; this gentleman, having an unexpected opportunity, had been so good as to send out to Geneva 'his own copy which he had purchased'.

Cazenove became the champion of Economist Malthus's *Principles* in a pamphlet against Say, and also in reviews in the *British Critic*, but there is no evidence as to their personal relationship. In 1817 Cazenove had published *A Selection of Curious and Entertaining Games at Chess*; we know that as a young man Malthus was not 'very fond of cards', but he had beaten Count Moltke at chess (by two games to three) at a party in Trondheim.[58] Chess seems to be all that he had in common with Cazenove apart from political economy, but amateurs of that science might maintain that this was in itself a sufficient bond. Cazenove's work on economic subjects, much of it anonymous, is chiefly of interest for his contention that the weight of taxation was unjustly 'sure to be brought forward as the sole or main cause of the evil' in 'a general state of dullness or stagnation of trade'. Like Malthus's friend William Blake, he pointed out that trade had been very prosperous when taxation bore a much higher proportion to 'the increasing wealth of the community' than it did later - in 1829 in this instance.[59]

After Malthus's death, Cazenove applied for his post at Haileybury, but

remained a close friend of Richard Jones, who got it.[60] I agree with Dr
Pullen that Cazenove was certainly the anonymous editor of the posthumous
1836 version of the *Principles of Political Economy*.[61] One can only hope that
more will come to light about a man for whom Malthus and his colleagues
appear to have had a high regard.

Other characters had far more impact on the Political Economy Club. I
think it is unlikely that Malthus was distressed by McCulloch's rudeness,
or by James Mill's 'crushing criticisms' of his speeches, which survivors of
the early meetings are alleged to have remembered as late as 1882; Mill only
attended three meetings of the Club between 1826 and 1835, when he
resigned. Both Otter and Empson remark on Malthus's serenity in his latter
years: the deep interest in his subject which brought him up to London for
the meetings, his friendship with Mallet and Cazenove, with Parnell, Prévost,
Senior and Tooke himself, must have more than compensated for
McCulloch's harshness; Mallet wrote of McCulloch that his 'sallies and
exaggerations and astounding and often coarse and sarcastic expressions keep
our drowsy members alive when saturated with tavern fare'.[62] Malthus
possibly enjoyed them.

There is no evidence as to what Malthus felt about his Fellowship of the
Royal Society. To quote the Society's historian, Sir Henry Lyons: 'It was
at this time common knowledge, not only within the Society but also outside
it, and even abroad, that nearly every candidate who was proposed for the
Fellowship of the Society was admitted; and many of the Fellows realised
the extent to which its prestige had been lowered by the practice.' At this
period the 'non-scientific' Fellows outnumbered the physical scientists by
slightly more than two to one, roughly the same proportion as in 1663. To
quote Sir Henry again: 'The possession of fortune and leisure was considered
as being of more importance than a good education and wide knowledge.'[63]

The President of the Royal Society had all four. Sir Joseph Banks
(1743-1820) was a botanical enthusiast who had accompanied Captain Cook
on the voyage of the *Endeavour*; he was, incidentally, one of the first
Europeans ever to see a kangaroo, just inland from the place which the
explorers called Botany Bay. He was President of the Royal Society for
over four decades, from 1778 to 1820, and always presided at the weekly
evening meetings - which were followed by tea and conversation - in full
court dress; these were held, from 1780 onwards, in the Society's beautiful
rooms at Somerset House.

Here on 27 November 1817 Malthus's name was first proposed, as a
'Gentleman conversant with various branches of Science' desirous of becoming a Fellow of the Royal Society, and twenty-one signatories of their own
personal knowledge recommended him 'as highly deserving that honor &
likely to become an useful & valuable Member'. He was 'Ballotted for &
Elected the 5th March 1818'.[64]

It is impossible to guess how close was the 'personal knowledge' behind some of these twenty-one names. For instance, I can find no link between Malthus and Lord Hardwicke (1757-1834); nor does there seem to be any personal connection between Malthus and Sir Gilbert Blane (1749-1834), a physician famous for his work for the health of the Navy, or Thomas Harrison (1744-1829), an architect who built, amongst much else, a Benthamite panoptical prison. Sir Benjamin Hobhouse (1757-1831) is another of the older generation - his son was the more famous Lord Broughton - who appears to have no especial reason for recommending Malthus. The Rev. William Tooke (1744-1820), the father of Thomas and William the younger, might have recollected with pride that his *View of the Russian Empire* had been quoted in the *Essay on Population*. There are also two quite unknown gentlemen, S. Davis and Henry Browne.

Of the others, John Whishaw and Leonard Horner, Alexander Marcet and William Blake, Henry Holland and Peter Mark Roget, Humphry Davy and Alexander (Sanskrit) Hamilton need no introduction to the reader.

It is possible that Hamilton owed his release by the French in 1806 to Sir Joseph Banks's good offices. An earlier historian of the Royal Society, C. R. Weld, wrote in 1848 that Banks was elected in 1802 a Foreign Member of the French Institute: 'This great honour, it is said, was in some measure brought about by his having interfered successfully, on no less than ten different occasions, in restoring to France collections of natural history, which had been captured by English vessels; he even sent as far as the Cape of Good Hope to procure some chests belonging to Humboldt; and it is well known that his active exertions liberated many scientific men from foreign prisons.' An indication of the character of the Royal Society in Banks's time is given in a letter to him from Sir William Jones, written shortly before he died in Calcutta in 1794: Jones asked that his collection of Oriental manuscripts might be deposited in the Society's Library, 'so that they may be lent out without difficulty to any studious men who may apply for them'.[65] Sir Charles Wilkins (1749-1836), the East India Company's Librarian and Oriental Examiner at the College, was another FRS who signed Malthus's certificate, and a third Haileybury connection was his retired colleague Bewick Bridge.

There are two Members of Parliament on the list: William Smith, who sat for Norwich, and with whom Malthus is known to have corresponded at the time of the Corn Law agitation in 1815,[66] and the Cornishman Davies Gilbert (1767-1839), who sat for Bodmin from 1806 till 1832. Gilbert is described by Weld as 'the representative of scientific interests in the House of Commons', and was an early patron of Sir Humphry Davy; he also helped two Cornish nautical astronomers, the Rev. Malachy Hitchens and the Rev. John Hellins, as well as the two Hornblowers and Richard Trevithick, with formulae for their steam engines; Gilbert himself calculated the length of chain which Richard Telford needed for the Menai Bridge. Throughout his parliamentary career from 1807 onwards Davies Gilbert sided with Malthus over the Poor Laws and the Corn Laws (he had his windows broken), and there were personal links as well through his close friendship with Thomas Beddoes, Maria Edgeworth's brother-in-law.

Another of Malthus's signatories was also to become an MP, for Bridport, in 1826. He was Henry Warburton (1784-1858), a timber merchant's son who abandoned his father's business for science and philosophic radicalism, and was one of the early members of the Geological Society, as well as the Political Economy Club. In 1818 he made a Continental tour with William Hyde Wollaston (1766-1828), who also signed Malthus's proposal form. Dr Wollaston had retired from medical practice in 1800, and was known as a physiologist, chemist, physicist and astronomer, as well as being well versed in Greek and Hebrew. This was indeed the last golden age of universal knowledge.

Malthus's second distinction, after becoming a Fellow of the Royal Society, was to become one of the ten Royal Associates of the Royal Society of Literature, which meant that for seven years he received annually a pension of a hundred guineas from the Privy Purse. It is difficult to see why he should have been chosen, since he had, as far as I can discover, no connection with the two people most concerned - King George IV and Bishop Burgess of St Davids.

Thomas Burgess (1756-1837) was the son of a grocer of Odiham in Hampshire, and reached Corpus Christi College, Oxford, by way of the local grammar school and Winchester; he was a precocious scholar, renowned for his learned work, but as chaplain to the Bishop of Salisbury he attained a different sort of fame through writing *The Salisbury Spelling-Book*, widely used by Sunday school children throughout the country. This was 'a very useful manual, into which, in addition to the elements of spelling and reading, he introduced many pretty and edifying stories told in the simplest language'.[67] Burgess went north with Bishop Barrington when he was translated from Salisbury to Durham, and was able to keep his prebendal stall there after the Prime Minister (his old school-fellow Addington) had given him the see of St Davids in 1803. The two incomes were necessary because St Davids was a miserable diocese, long regarded merely as a stepping-stone to something better; Burgess set out to transform it. He attended Eisteddfodau, and refused to induct into Welsh-speaking parishes ministers who were ignorant of the language; he took the rite of confirmation seriously, which was unusual at the time; but most of all he was *pastor pastorum* to his poor and lonely clergy, and struggled to raise the deplorable educational standards of candidates for ordination; to this end he founded St David's College at Lampeter.

George IV gave £1,000 towards the building of St David's College in May 1822, but before this, in November 1820, the King had asked Bishop Burgess to draw up plans for a Royal Society of Literature; one therefore assumes that Burgess is responsible for the eight-page pamphlet in the

Society's archives called the *Prospectus*.[68] In the preamble it was stated that Mathematics and Natural Philosophy, however excellent and useful in other respects, could have little influence on the Character of Nations, their Manners, Morals, or Religion: 'Literature, on the contrary, is the necessary instrument of Moral and Intellectual Improvement . . . The very Life-Blood of the Body Politic.' Specifically,

> In *Political Philosophy*, incalculable Improvements may be made by wide Surveys of the various Conditions of Human Society. In this Science the Principles of Population; the natural course of Rent, Profit, and Wages; the influence of the Reformations and Revolutions, of the Inventions and Commerce of Modern Times, are fertile Fields of Discovery and Knowledge; and an attempt to reduce into Scientific Arrangement the Histories of different Governments, and by contemplating their general Classes, to investigate the Laws of their Action, is well worthy of the united efforts of sagacious and intelligent minds.

Of these minds the Bishop was President, assisted by eight Vice-Presidents, one of whom was Sir James Mackintosh, although he never seems to have played an active part in the Society's affairs. The Council of sixteen included Lords Lansdowne and Grenville, also William Empson, and the Rev. Charles Sumner, brother of the author of *Records of the Creation*.

The first full meeting of the Royal Society of Literature was held on 17 June 1823, but possibly the most eventful was that which took place on 6 May 1824 at 'the Society's Apartments, 61 Lincoln's Inn Fields', when five of the Royal Associates in attendance were each presented with a Diploma 'and with a Draught for One Hundred Guineas'. They were S. T. Coleridge, Esq; the Rev. T. R. Malthus; the Orientalist Sir William Ousely of Crickhowell (1767-1842), whose *Travels in Persia* had just been printed for him by Henry Hughes of Brecon; the Rev. Henry John Todd (1763-1845), whose list of works included editions of Milton, Spenser and Johnson's Dictionary; and Sharon Turner, Esq. (1768-1847). He was a lawyer who helped Murray on questions of copyright and libel, but his chief preoccupation was British history; he vindicated the authenticity of the 'Antient British Poems of Aneurin, Taliesin, Llywarch Hen and Merdhin'.

The other five recipients of what was derisively called the solid pudding were William Smyth's old Liverpool friend, William Roscoe; the archaeologist James Millingen; Thomas James Mathias, a satirist and Italian scholar, who must have had his pension remitted to Naples, where he lived from about 1815 until his death in 1835; the Rev. John Jamieson, a Scots antiquary and philologist; and the Rev. Edward Davies, a poor Welsh antiquary whom Burgess had also tried to help in his own diocese.

It is impossible to make out any scheme for these nominations; some, like Mathias and Davies, obviously needed their pensions, but others, like

Malthus and Todd, did not live uncomfortably. The Minutes of the Council show that the Royal Associates were proposed, seconded, and elected by ballot, but the proceedings seem to have been a formality. A story goes that the King's thousand guineas a year were the outcome of a misunderstanding with the Bishop, and that George IV had only intended to give one donation of £1,000, with an annual subscription of £100: 'As, however, his Lordship in his zeal had immediately proclaimed the King's munificence, and Fame, through the medium of the press, had almost as immediately trumpeted it with her hundred tongues throughout the country, there was no retreat, and the King not only cheerfully acquiesced, but amused himself with the incident.'[69]

Sadly we read in their Report for 1832: 'It is with pain that the Council acquaint the Meeting, that no intention, on the part of His Majesty, to continue the Payment of the Annual Royal Bounty to the Society, has hitherto been communicated.' In fact William IV fulfilled his brother's original intention, and gave the RSL a subscription of £100 a year.

No known diarist or letter-writer seems to have been present at the meeting in 1824 when the first royal largesse was distributed, so there is no account of how Coleridge behaved to the man he detested so much. Since the recipients were arranged in alphabetical order, Coleridge took precedence over Malthus as a matter of course. Each Royal Associate subscribed to a Form of Obligation, specifying 'the Branch of Literature on which it shall be his duty to communicate with the Society, once a year at least'. The Minutes continue

> The subjects selected by them are:
> Mr. Coleridge. - The relations of opposition and conjunction, in
> which the Poetry, (the Homeric and Tragic), the Religion, and the
> Mysteries, of Ancient Greece, stood to each other; with the
> differences between the sacerdotal and popular Religion; and the
> influences of Theology and Scholastic Logic, on the Language and
> Literature of Christendom, from the Eleventh Century.
> Mr. Malthus. - Political Economy and Statistics.

We have already referred to Malthus's two contributions, which were printed in the *Transactions* of the Society published by Murray. Unlike the Political Economy Club, the RSL seems to have kept no record of those present at meetings, so we cannot tell how often Malthus attended them. The Society met twice monthly from November to June, on the first and third Wednesdays; some papers took two meetings to read. It must be admitted that to a modern audience Ousely on the Koran would have been more interesting than Coleridge 'On the Prometheus of Eschylus', and that Malthus's papers were among the hardest of all to follow. Even so, one cannot but regret that the tide of specialisation has swept away from 'General and Polite Literature' so much that contributed to the mental stimulation, discipline and enrichment of the uncommitted lecture-goer.

As far as an outsider can judge, the Athenaeum Club has changed in character much less since 1824 than have both the Royal Society and the Royal Society of Literature. Malthus was one of the original members of the Athenaeum, then as now drawn solely from those 'of distinguished eminence in Science, Literature or the Arts, or for Public Services'. By 1830 the Athenaeum was housed in the building it occupies today, looking much as it does now, only without the topmost storey; indoors the Club benefits from what its historian Humphry Ward described as 'the blessed invention of electric lighting'; in Malthus's time it was lit by 'stupefying gas', chosen because oil lamps cost twice as much, and wax candles would have been eight times more expensive.[70]

The clubs of London have been so often associated with late Victorian and Edwardian extravagance that a sentence in the prospectus of 1823, before 'the Society' was called the Athenaeum, is worth quoting: 'The rules of the United Service, Union and University Clubs, which have been found to combine so much accommodation to their members with so much *economy* and good order, shall be the guide of the Committee in the formation of this new Club.' The plan was so successful that by December 1824 the original limit of 400 or 500 members was extended to 1,000. There was no false economy in the things they really cared about. Humphry Ward remarks that 'in 1830 there seemed to be little demand for accommodation for smokers and billiard players', but by 1832 the library contained 10,000 books. In the first six months of its existence the Club spent £40 on newspapers and periodicals, beginning with the *Classical Journal* and the *Zoological Journal*; before the end of 1824 the Athenaeum was taking a number of publications from the United States, including the *North American Review* and the *American Annual Register* and *National Calender*.[71] It must have been a happy resort for Malthus.

As with the return to Okewood, one should be wary of guessing at his feelings, but it is possible that these new London scenes and acquaintances to some extent compensated him for the sudden death of Ricardo on 11 September 1823. Malthus's acknowledged position among the eminent may also have counterbalanced the hurt he must surely have felt when he realised that the younger members of the Political Economy Club had met without him to discuss the Ricardo Memorial Lectures. J. L. Mallet records in his diary that on 14 October 1823 a group of them met 'at Mr. G. Grote's in the City'; they agreed

> that Political Economy was a fluctuating science, in which there were generally great differences of opinion; and that a lecturer appointed for life, or for a series of years, might have the means of disseminating erroneous opinions. Mr. Malthus was Professor of Political Economy at Hertford College, and had a considerable name

in that science; but he entertained opinions on many points, and those some of the most important, which are generally considered as unsound . . .

And in any case, a lectureship founded in Ricardo's memory 'implied a sort of pledge to adopt the principles laid down by Mr. Ricardo'.[72]

The lectures were given by McCulloch from April to June 1824. Malthus could truthfully write to Murray that his duties at the College prevented him from attending the course.

6 French and German Translations

Otter wrote in his *Memoir of Robert Malthus* that 'the high estimation in which he was held was not confined to this country . . . In truth the principle [of population] he had laid down found fewer prejudices to encounter in other countries than in this; . . . he was honoured with distinctions from several sovereigns of Europe, and elected a member of many of the most eminent literary societies, especially the French Institute and the Royal Academy at Berlin.'[73]

The Malthus family cared so little for this sort of worldly reputation that all trace of it has been lost. Ricardo's letters, on the other hand, were preserved as treasured heirlooms, first by Malthus himself, and then by Sydenham's descendants. The late Mr Robert Malthus, when travelling on the Continent as a young lad at the end of the nineteenth century, was extremely surprised to find that his name was well known in France and Germany: the remote uncle nobody had talked about at home was regarded as a great man abroad.

Dr Alexander Marcet (1770-1822) seems to have been instrumental in arranging for Malthus to see both the French and German versions of the *Essay on Population*. In spite of Napoleon's grip on most of Europe, Marcet somehow managed to keep in touch with his Genevese connections, and especially with his brother-in-law Pierre Prévost (1751-1839). Prévost had studied theology, law and medicine in his native Geneva, met Rousseau in Paris, and in Berlin added some philology and chemistry to his wide range of knowledge while lecturing on philosophy at the special request of Frederick the Great. He returned to Geneva permanently in 1784 to become Professor of Philosophy and Physics, and to translate Adam Smith, Hugh Blair, and Dugald Stewart; in 1806 he wrote a summary and review of the third edition of the *Essay on Population* for the periodical *Bibliothèque Britannique*, which later became the *Bibliothèque Universelle de Genève*.

Malthus received copies of these from Dr Marcet, whom Prévost had obviously consulted about a translation. It is interesting to find Malthus sending a note from Hummums, a Whig tavern in Covent Garden; this was fiercely scorned by Francis Place as the inn where free breakfasts were served to the unruly and venal electors of Westminster: it seems a far cry from the Athenaeum. Malthus wrote to Dr Marcet from Hummums on 2 July 1807:

> Sir,
>   I will avail myself of the kind permission you have given me to take the numbers of the Bibliotheque Brittanique [sic] into the country, and you may depend upon my returning them safe in six weeks. I have cast my eye over one or two of the extracts and see that M. Prevot [sic] has seized the spirit of the work, and that I may safely trust to his taste and judgement with regard to the abridgements which he wishes to make; but as in looking over them more at my leisure I may perhaps have a few observations to suggest, I will defer writing to M. Prevot till I have had the opportunity, and will then transmit to you a letter for him from the country.
>   I have ordered my bookseller [Johnson] to send you a copy of the new edition as soon as it is ready.
>
>   I am Sir
>   Your obed' humble S'.
>   T. Rob'. Malthus

I do not know whether Malthus made any suggestions, but Prévost's translation, *Essai sur le Principe de Population*, was published in three octavo volumes in 1809. Later there were to be more personal links through the sojourn of the Sydenham family in Geneva, and in 1828 Prévost's daughter Adèle married Lady Mackintosh's nephew Edward Drewe.

I can find no such links with the German translator, Franz Hermann Hegewisch (1783-1865), although he may possibly have met Dr Marcet. Hegewisch was also a doctor of medicine, and had attended courses in Vienna, Paris and London, after qualifying in Kiel, where his father was Professor of History. He was a propagandist as well as a translator, his maxim being that there should be no more people in a country than could enjoy daily a glass of wine and a piece of beef for their dinner. His version of the *Essay* was published in Altona in 1807. Malthus could not read German, and the following letter suggests that Hegewisch used Marcet as an intermediary in sending Malthus a complimentary copy. This time Malthus is writing to Dr Marcet from Hertford, on 29 October 1807, with a characteristic opening paragraph; the 'Mr. Prevost' here referred to is not Pierre, but his son Alexander, who worked in the same merchant banking house in London as Mrs Marcet's brother, William Haldimand.

Dear Sir,

I am ashamed to think that I have so long delayed sending to you the letter to Mr. Hegewisch, which Mr. Prevost was so good as to undertake to forward; but one or two short journeys of business from him in the early part of the time since I had the pleasure of seeing you, and some friends in the house latterly, have so engaged me, that I have hardly had a leisure hour till to day.

If Mr. Prevost thinks that a packet will go safe, I should like to send to Mr. Hegewisch a copy of the last edition of my book, with my letter to Mr. Whitbread, and his speech in the house of commons [sic], but if they are not likely to come to hand, perhaps it might be as well to send only the letter, and defer the books till the communication is restored . . .

I send Mr. Hegewisch's translation to Mr. Prevost, with my best thanks for the kind offer he has made of giving me some of its contents in a language I understand. I will only trouble him for the preface, postscript, and notes, and perhaps a part of the appendix by way of specimen; but I hope that he will on no account hurry himself, nor indeed do it at all, if it is inconvenient to him. Any expressions which he thinks he can translate more satisfactorily into French than English will do for me in the former language.

If anything should call you or Mr. Prevost out of London this way I shall be most happy to see you at Hertford, and in general shall be able to offer you a bed.

> I am dear Sir
> Yours sincerely
> T. Robt Malthus[74]

The German version of the *Essay on Population* was to have far wider repercussions than the French, although there is no evidence as to how much Malthus knew about them. He had learned himself that the Norwegians tried to prevent young men from marrying (unless they had private means to support a family) until after they had completed their military service; he did not know that there had been seventeenth- and eighteenth-century edicts prohibiting the marriage of paupers in Bavaria, Württemberg, Austria and other parts of German-speaking Europe.[75] Hegewisch's translation led to another upsurge of what Professor Glass calls 'practical Malthusianism' in Austria and the German states. This lasted into the Bismarck era and beyond, until the Weimar Constitution of 1919 fully equated Bavarian law with that of the rest of Germany; in Austria, in the Tyrol and Vorarlberg, the restrictions on marriage remained on the statute books until 1921 and 1923 respectively.

Such a form of Malthusianism was abhorrent to Malthus, who held firmly that although it was right to discourage improvident marriages, it was wrong to forbid them. The works of Weinhold, had he heard of him, would have shocked Malthus even more. Karl August Weinhold (1782-1829) was originally an army surgeon from Meissen; he travelled widely and ended his career as Professor of Medicine and Surgery at Halle. He seems to have been an excellent doctor, but was best known for his proposal to avert pauperism through the compulsory infibulation of all young men who could not prove themselves capable of supporting a family. He was derided, but other writers seriously advocated the prohibition of marriage altogether before the age of thirty, or restrictions on the marriages of the lower ranks of the army, apprentices, men out of work, and so on, Some of these restrictions became law in the 1820s and '30s, with the forseeable result that although the number of marriages fell, the number of illegitimate births soared: Professor Glass gives as an example seventy-nine parishes in Mecklenburg where, in 1851, no babies at all were born in wedlock.

It is doubtful how much Malthus was aware of these travesties of his theory which were perpetrated during his life-time; but it is as well to bear in mind that other people would have known about them (Coleridge could read German) and that they may have contributed indirectly to the blackening of his name in his last years.

In France the situation was completely different. In the small German states agriculture was still burdened by feudal charges and industry by the restrictions of medieval trade guilds; bad harvests meant desperate poverty, as in Ireland. France had emerged from the Napoleonic Wars as a united and comparatively prosperous modern nation; English travellers who disapproved of the Revolution had to admit that after it the people in general were far better off than they had been before. Thus at this time it was not Malthus's *Essay on Population* which attracted attention in Paris, but his *Principles of Political Economy*. His *Political Economy* was not translated into German until 1911.

Say published his *Lettres à M. Malthus* before *Political Economy* had been translated into French: as he said, he could not wait, although in fact the translation appeared within a few months. The French translator of Economist Malthus was yet another doctor of medicine, Francisco Solano Constancio (1777-1846), who was not French himself, but Portuguese. He was born in Lisbon, the son of the Professor of Anatomy, who was also surgeon to the King. With six other privileged companions the young Constancio was sent to study medicine abroad; he spent some time in England in 1791, where he learned the language and became an enthusiast for vaccination, which he practised on his return to Portugal. Later he settled in Paris, where he combined a diplomatic post with a spate of literary works.

International copyright did not then exist, and the first Ricardo knew of Constancio's activities was when he heard from Murray in December 1818 that his *Principles of Political Economy* had been translated into French 'with copious notes'.[76] It was later that Ricardo learned the notes were by Say, and contained as much criticism as explanation. He does not appear to have minded: Garnier's famous translation of Adam Smith had similar notes. When Malthus was in Paris in the summer of 1820 he was told by the 'bookseller' who published Ricardo's *Principes d'Économie Politique* that 900 copies had been sold. Naturally this M. Aillaud, as well as Constancio himself, must have hoped that Malthus's *Principes* would prove as profitable as Ricardo's. After he had returned to the College, Malthus wrote to Ricardo: 'My book was translating. I saw a few sheets, and fear it will not be very well done.'[77] He was right.

Meanwhile Prévost was contemplating a second French version of the *Essay on Population*, of which the enlarged fifth edition had been published in 1817; this second Genevese translation did not actually appear until 1830. On 27 March 1821 Malthus wrote to Prévost about the plan:

> I need not say how much I am flattered by your intention of giving my fifth edition to the French public; but I ought to inform you of my apprehensions that M. Constancio who has translated my last work, has thoughts of translating the last edition of the Essay on Population. M. Aillaud, a bookseller on the Quai Voltaire, when he sent me the translation of the Principles of Political Economy, asked my opinion about Mr. Constancio as a translator for this essay, and further enquired whether it were probable that there would soon be another edition. I told him in reply that I thought a translator ought in the main to agree with his author, and as it appeared from some of the notes to Mr. Constancio's translation, that he differed entirely from me on the principles of population, he was certainly not exactly the person whom I should have selected as a translator.
>
> With regard to another edition I said that Mr. Murray, my publisher, had talked of the probability of another being wanted in the course of the year ... I need not say how much I should prefer you as my translator to Mr. Constancio or indeed to anybody that I know; but I wish you to be aware of what has been intended that you may not run any risk of loss, which a knowledge of such intentions might have enabled you to avoid. If you write again, pray tell me what you think of Mr. Constancio's translation of the last work. He has certainly not always given my meaning.[78]

Fears for the translation of the *Principles of Political Economy* had not, however, spoiled the Malthuses' visit to Paris; as he wrote to Ricardo on 28 August 1820, they stayed about five weeks, 'and passed our time very agreeably. I saw most of the principal people whom I wished to see.' These included Germain Garnier (1754-1821), the translator of the *Wealth of Nations*, who attacked Ricardo violently, though it appeared to Malthus that he agreed with him in many essential points, 'perhaps without knowing it'. They also met the Duc de Broglie, who seemed inclined to adopt Ricardo's views: 'He is one of the *Doctrinaires* who are considered as very theoretical both in Politics and Political Economy.' Sraffa has discovered that Malthus lent a copy of his *Political Economy* to the widow of the physiocrat Dupont de Nemours (1739-1817), who had returned to France after her husband's death in America; she obviously liked the writer, whatever her opinion of the book: later she told Sismondi how charmed she was that he had done justice to 'notre bon Malthus' - our good Malthus - in an article against Ricardo.[79]

Also in Paris were Maria Edgeworth and her half-sisters Fanny and Harriet. Maria was suffering emotionally from having in May published the *Memoirs* of her adored father, which started with his own unfinished autobiography. Fanny Mackintosh must have read the book as soon as it came out, for she noted in her diary for 'Teusday 13th' June 1820: 'Began Miss Edgeworth's continuation which does not seem good - she is doing it against her inclinations - and I am tired of her Father's marriages and mechanicks.' Fanny's views of the book were shared by others, but Maria was able to write to her third step-mother from Paris on 24 June that 'Mr. Malthus this morning spoke most highly of it, and of its useful tendency both in a public and private light.'

From the Edgeworth ladies we can also learn that Malthus visited with them 'one of the great schools here established on the Lancaster principles'. Miss Harriet described a morning party on 29 June in which Miss Edgeworth took an Englishman to task for 'raking up all the dirt he could find in every part of a foreign country . . . instead of trying to unite in science two contending nations . . . After much warm argument against the French from Mr. Creed and Mr. Chenevix, who have been several years here, and some softening replies from Mr. Malthus, who has been here only five days, Maria was brought nearly to own that she had thought less well of the French the more she had seen of them. It was a very interesting 2 hours conversation, during which Mrs. Malthus informed me that she had known Lovell in former times before the detention in France so she cannot be very young but I dare say a long time ago she was not very ugly.' Since Lovell Edgeworth was detained in France after the collapse of the Peace of Amiens, it was presumably during her courting days that Harriet Eckersall (as she then was) had met him; in 1820 Mrs Malthus was forty-four, Miss Harriet Edgeworth only nineteen.

Thanks to a letter written by Maria Edgeworth in October 1820 we know that the Malthuses stayed at the Hotel Vauban, 366 Rue St Honoré. Here they had 'one floor of a comfortable side of the square of this hotel' completely to themselves, and 'no noise but of carriages belonging to the house that come into the yard'. The suite seems princely by modern standards, even though the sofa was 'oldish', with elegant amber silk fringed curtains in the principal bedroom, and green silk and white muslin in the 'good drawing room'; there was a small dining-room, pantry, ante-room, and closets galore, with accommodation for a man-servant as well as a maid, but alas, 'The misfortune of the house is that there are no water closets.' However, the woman of the house was 'respectable and civil', and her most distinguished tenant before Mr and Mrs Malthus was Benjamin Constant, who occupied these same apartments for two years; possibly he had moved to a grander establishment when he was elected to the Chamber of Deputies in 1819.[80]

One would like to know more. In his letter to Ricardo after his return from Paris Malthus wrote that he 'got some insight into the state of France, which is curious, but the subject is too large to enter upon now'. Fanny Mackintosh gives us a little illumination in her journal for Monday 4 September 1820: Mr and Mrs Malthus paid a kind visit to her ailing Papa, whom Fanny thought would enjoy a haunch of venison much more in their company than if he had no guests but the two elderly ladies, from a neighbouring village, who had been invited previously. So Papa was 'in good spirits, though with a headach [sic] - Talked of French News & Politicks with Mr. M - he gives but a bad account of their spirit - he very much liked the D of Broglie.' Nothing is said anywhere of the theatres which had occupied so much of Harriet Eckersall's diary in 1802, nor is there any mention of academic or other honours.

CHAPTER XI

The Population Controversies Continue

1 The Fifth Edition of the *Essay* of 1817

The main text of the three-volume fifth edition of the *Essay on Population* was essentially the same as that reprinted by the Everyman Library; the addenda of 1826 are not very important. In his preface to the fifth edition, dated 7 June 1817, Malthus wrote:

> This Essay was first published at a period of extensive warfare, combined, from peculiar circumstances, with a most prosperous foreign commerce.
>
> It came before the public, therefore, at a time when there would be an extraordinary demand for men, and very little disposition to suppose the possibility of any evil arising from the redundancy of population. Its success, under these disadvantages, was greater than could have been reasonably expected; and it may be presumed that it will not lose its interest, after a period of a different description has succeeded, which has in the most marked manner illustrated its principles and confirmed its conclusions.

With hindsight, we can say that Malthus had 'got it all wrong', but at the time, this paragraph was not regarded as boastful. To Brougham in the House of Commons as to clergymen all over the country - whose sermons were printed - 'a surplus population' seemed the obvious immediate explanation of post-war distress. The more one studies Malthus's two major works, the more creditable it appears that he should have had the courage to swim so determinedly against the tide in 1820.

The summer of 1816 was exceptionally wet and cold, so that the wretchedness everywhere apparent was at first attributed to a natural scarcity of food. Three quotations will sketch the scene: From Surrey, William Bray's diary, 3 September 1816:

> Mr. Woods begun reaping a field of wheat before his house, as had been a good deal layed by the wet, otherwise not fit to reap. In the morning a white frost lay on it, under the ears were frozen drops. He gave the reapers some liquor in memory of it.

From Somerset, James Mill to Ricardo, 25 October 1816:

> Is there much suffering about you? I do not mean of the farmers, at
> present, whose suffering is only that of comparative poverty - but of
> the people who live by the daily work of their hands; and whose
> suffering means, starvation and death.[1]

From Shropshire, the following autumn, the Rev. Reginald Heber to John
Thornton, 24 September 1817:

> The poor around us have all been sickly, with a tendency to typhus
> fever. I feel very grateful that this did not occur four or five months
> ago, when the workhouse and several of the cottages were crowded
> like slave ships.[2]

Small wonder that in these circumstances Malthus should have been preoccupied with the Corn Laws and the Poor. Joseph Townsend had died in
1816, but the *Dissertation on the Poor Laws*, which he wrote in 1785, was
reprinted in 1817 at the instigation of Lord Holland - a significant sign of
the times.

So, with regard to the fifth edition of *Population*, Malthus wrote in his
preface:

> In the third book I have given an additional chapter on the Poor-
> Laws ... and as I further wished to make some alterations in the
> chapter on Bounties upon Exportation, and add something on the
> subject of Restrictions upon Importation, I have recast and rewritten
> the chapters which stand the 8th, 9th, 10th, 11th, 12th, 13th, in the
> present edition ...
>   In the fourth book I have added a new chapter to the one entitled
> *Effects of the Knowledge of the principal Cause of Poverty on Civil
> Liberty*; and another to the chapter on the *Different Plans of
> improving the Poor*; and I have made a considerable addition to the
> Appendix, in reply to some writers on the Principles of Population,
> whose works have appeared since the last edition.
>   These are the principal additions and alterations made in the
> present edition. They consist, in a considerable degree, of the
> application of the general principles of the Essay to the present state
> of things.
>   For the accommodation of the purchasers of the former editions,
> these additions and alterations will be published in a separate volume.
> [This is sometimes mistakenly referred to as Volume IV.][3]

The whole arrangement is extremely unsatisfactory to the modern reader
unfamiliar with 'the present state of things' in Britain in 1817, particularly
as the editors of the Everyman version did not see fit to reprint the *Appendix*.
But this very patchwork is in itself indicative of how much Malthus was

writing for his own period, and how unscientific it is - or perhaps one should say unhistorical - to try to 'apply Malthus' to all times and places. Malthus himself, incidentally, took it for granted that all his readers knew he wished to abolish the Poor Law; he defends his scheme in Chapter vii of Book III, although the scheme itself is not given until Chapter viii of Book IV.*

Malthus's correspondence shows how concerned he was with the price of grain while he was working on the fifth edition, even though the public controversy over the Corn Laws had died down for a time. In his letter to Prévost of 13 October 1815, requesting friendly attention for Sydenham and his family, Malthus wrote, 'I am at present preparing a new edition of my Essay on Population . . . Pray are there accounts left at Geneva of the price of wheat in different years, and would it be possible to get such accounts for some years past? I want much to ascertain what has been the excess in the price of corn and labour in England above the average price of the rest of Europe during the last twenty years.'⁴ Three days later he made the same request to Dumont, whom he knew personally, and who therefore had a longer letter, but the question was the same: 'Pray would it be difficult to get the market price of wheat for some years back at Geneva?'⁵ Apparently no answers were forthcoming. It is possible, however, to see in the 'Corn' chapters of 1817 a half-way stage between the pamphlet of 1814 and the thesis of 1820, that it was on the monetary value of the crop that the labourers' prosperity depended. It will be remembered that in 1814 a high price of corn was considered beneficial to the labourer, not because it indicated high profits and full employment, but because it was believed that his wages must rise to meet it, and that therefore he would have more money available to spend on commodities other than bread.

In the spring of 1817 Malthus's advocacy of the Corn Laws seemed to him to be justified: 'If the present year (1816-17) had found us in a state in which our growth of corn had been habitually far short of our consumption, the distress of the country would have been dreadfully aggravated.' He repeated what he had written in 1806, when the nation was rejoicing over the battle of Trafalgar, to the effect that the object of the Navigation Acts was 'not to increase the profits of ship-owners and sailors, but the quantity of shipping and seamen'; the object of the Corn Laws was 'not to increase the profits of the farmers or the rents of the landlords, but to determine a greater quantity of the national capital to the land, and consequently to increase supply'.⁶ He let this passage stand in 1826, even though he appreciated by then that in a monetary economy barns full of grain might not mean that tables were loaded with bread in the homes of the poor.

A small sign of Malthus's change of approach may be found in Chapter vii of Book IV; this is simply headed 'Of Poor Laws - *continued*', just like

---

*See in the Everyman edn, Vol. II, p. 64 *et seq.*, and p. 200 *et seq.*

the preceding chapter, after which it was inserted – one is tempted to write 'tacked on' – in 1817. Malthus began by saying 'I told you so': the country did not, because it could not, fulfil the promise of the Poor Laws: 'the country has been wholly unable to find adequate employment for the numerous labourers and artificers who were able as well as willing to work', and 'though it may be fairly pardonable not to execute an impossibility, it is unpardonable knowingly to promise one'.

Yet although it was impossible to restore at once a brisk demand for commodities and labour, he advocated public works such as roads, bridges, railways, and canals. Thus the unemployed could work for ordinary wages and not for a dole. This would be hard on the individuals taxed to pay for them, and hard on the various other kinds of labour which the tax-payers' expenditure, in their usual channels, would have supported: 'But this is an effect which, in such cases, it is impossible to avoid; and, as a temporary measure, it is not only charitable but just to spread the evil over a larger surface in order that its violence on particular parts may be so mitigated as to be made bearable by all.'[7] The argument is similar to that used in the pamphlet of 1800 on *The High Price of Provisions*.

In short, Malthus's common sense and benevolence told him that the impossibility of employing all the poor was no reason for not trying to organise work for some of them. But he could not admit this in so many words. The Poor Law remained anathema, and in the enlarged *Appendix* of 1817 he singled out two of its defenders for individual castigation; these were John Weyland, FRS (1774–1854), and an unknown James Grahame.

Weyland was a well-to-do man whose landed possessions were extensive enough for him to be a magistrate in three counties, Oxfordshire, Berkshire and Surrey. He made a point in the Poor Law debates of 1807 which was to be taken up at the very end of the century by the campaigners for family allowances: since it was impossible to pay all labourers a wage adequate for a large family, the basic wage should be supplemented by some form of taxation or industrial levy in cases where there were many mouths to feed. 'As long as the industry of an effective man can be profitably employed', wrote Weyland, 'so long will it be in the interest of the community to go to the expence of rearing that man to perfection ... The money paid, therefore, under the operation of the Poor Laws, or of any system resembling them, may be considered in a great measure as a premium given in lieu of high wages, at once to encourage population, and enable the manufacturer to work cheap.'[8]

In 1816 Weyland followed up his pamphlets with a volume of nearly 500 pages to show why he thought population needed encouraging: *The Principles of Production and Population as they are affected by the Progress of Society with a View to Moral and Political Consequences*.

According to Malthus, 'Mr. Weyland really appears to have dictated this book with his eyes blindfolded and his ears stopped. I have a great respect for his character and intentions; but I must say that it has never been my fortune to meet with a theory so uniformly contradicted by experience.'[9] With a complete disregard for the recorded growth of population in England between 1801 and 1811, Weyland held that a society in which a third of the people lived in towns had 'arrived at its POINT OF NON-REPRODUCTION'.[10] Weyland did not think that towns need be hot-beds of vice, but he took it for granted that they must be the graves of infancy. Therefore it was essential for the state to 'keep an additional set of healthy breeders for the community; and that all unnecessary expense may be spared, it must place them in situations most favourable to child-bearing, and to the health of children, and most favourable also to their morals, that is to say, in the country villages'.[11]

It was easy for Malthus to show that in rural Sweden numbers were not increasing as rapidly as in urbanised England, and so on. But Malthus had at this time no answer to Mr Weyland's questions: 'Is it not a *fact* that . . . food is comparatively so much more plentiful, (Jan. 1816), and has increased so much more rapidly, even though produced from a soil whose most fertile spots have been long since occupied, that the actual difficulty is not now how to feed the people, but how profitably to dispose of the superfluity of the food raised for their support? Can a more convincing proof be imagined of the gratuitous nature of the fears entertained concerning the unobstructed increase of population, and the tendency which it *naturally* has in such a society to exceed the limits of the food provided for its support?'[12]

Weyland pointed out that the giving of alms to those incapable of earning would make a useful addition to effective demand, something of which Economist Malthus should have approved, but Population Malthus could be as rabid against the Poor Law in 1817 as he had been in 1798:

> Already above one-fourth of the population of England and Wales are regularly dependent upon parish relief; and if the system which Mr. Weyland recommends . . . should extend itself over the whole kingdom, there is really no saying to what height the level of pauperism may rise. While the system of making an allowance from the parish for every child above two is confined to the labourers in agriculture, whom Mr. Weyland considers as the breeders of the country, it is essentially unjust, as it lowers without compensation the wages of the manufacturer and artificer: and when it shall become just by including the whole of the working classes, what a dreadful picture does it present! what a scene of equality, indolence, rags and dependence, among one-half or three-fourths of the society![13]

Such an outburst sounds strange today, but it must be read in the context of the period. Malthus was by no means alone in his attitude towards the Poor Law. Ricardo felt the same: he generously set up a school at Minchinhampton, where Maria Edgeworth was struck at finding the rooms 'comfortably warmed - No flogging allowed'.[14] Yet Ricardo could refuse to send James Mill a subscription towards Brougham's Westminster Infant School because the children were to be given some dinner; he wrote on 12 December 1818: 'If it is part of the plan of the establishment . . . to feed as well as to take take care of and educate the children of three years of age, and upwards, belonging to the poor, I see the most serious objections to the plan, and I should be exceedingly inconsistent if I gave my countenance to it. I have invariably objected to the poor laws, and to every system which should give encouragement to excess of population.'[15]

In truth, Malthus was not nearly so dogmatic about the effect of the Poor Law in stimulating population as was Ricardo. We remarked that in a footnote to the *Appendix* to the 1807 edition Malthus admitted, after studying the census returns, that the Poor Laws 'do not encourage marriage'. In 1817 something made him change his mind again. He attached such importance to these textual changes that he wrote about them to Prévost when the second French translation was being discussed: 'I have expressed myself . . . more strongly respecting the effects of our Poor-Laws in encouraging population than I did in the Fourth edition . . . This difference I should wish to be expressed in the translation.'[16] These stronger expressions were extremely cautious: the amended footnote read that the Poor Laws 'do not *much* encourage marriage'. In the text of 1807 Malthus had written of these laws, 'I will not presume to say positively that they tend to encourage population'; in 1817 it was 'I will not presume to say positively that they greatly encourage population'.[17]

Here it is important to point out that Weyland and Grahame, who did not want the Poor Laws abolished, were just as heartless in their attitude to infant life as were Malthus and Ricardo. Malthus argued against Weyland:

> Though I have never felt any difficulty in reconciling to the goodness of the Deity the necessity of practising the virtue of moral restraint in a state allowed to be a state of discipline and trial; yet I confess that I could make no attempt to reason on the subject, if I were obliged to believe, with Mr. Weyland, that a large proportion of the human race was doomed by the inscrutable ordinations of Providence to a premature death in large towns.[18]

Weyland's was a childless marriage, and I cannot believe that James Grahame had much knowledge of pregnancy and parturition, lactation and babies. His *Inquiry into the Principle of Population*, published in Edinburgh in 1816, calmly maintains the desirability of a multitude of births, followed by many infant deaths, in order to secure the survival of the fittest: 'There is established near the threshold of life an ordeal . . . which every candidate for admission into every human community is compelled to undergo . . . naturally severer to the poor than to the rich; and it is proper that it should be so. It is, to every individual, a faithful rehearsal of his probable part in the great drama

374

of after life'[19] and so on. Malthus's optimum population, with the minimum of births and deaths, seems such an obvious desideratum to us that we are in danger of forgetting what a new idea it was in his time.

Malthus defended himself briefly against Grahame's misrepresentations, repeating that he neither approved of vice and misery nor condemned benevolence; Grahame felt that institutions such as the Poor Law were essential 'for the peaceable co-existence of wealth and poverty in the same community'.[20] But Malthus's chief reason for paying attention to Grahame in 1817 was to deny that he approved of 'the check suggested by Condorcet', which he had never adverted to 'without the most marked disapprobation':

> Indeed, I should always particularly reprobate any artificial and unnatural modes of checking population, both on account of their immorality and their tendency to remove a necessary stimulus to industry. If it were possible for each married couple to limit by a wish the number of their children, there is certainly reason to fear that the indolence of the human race would be very greatly increased; and that neither the population of individual countries, nor of the whole earth, would ever reach its natural and proper extent.[21]

Grahame was not alone in taking it for granted that Malthus meant contraceptives to be used to restrict the growth of population; that Malthus himself had only three children may have reinforced this belief. It suggests that Bentham's advocacy of the vaginal sponge had made some impact; possibly there had also been an extension of Casanova's practice of using the condom to prevent pregnancy as well as venereal disease - not that it did, in his case, but he was seventy-three when he died in 1798, and his *Memoirs* began their posthumous circulation in French.

The subject was one which could only be hinted at obliquely, and it is easy to see how Malthus's principle of population might have been misunderstood by those who had not read the *Essay*. Among them, apparently, was Ricardo's friend Hutches Trower, who wrote to him on 20 August 1816:

> I hope you are not so idle as I am, for I find I make little or no progress in my studies. I have not yet opened Weyland's Book, although I am very anxious to see his view of the subject. I intend to take that opportunity of going thoroughly into Malthus's system; for I confess, that hitherto I have felt great repugnance to the artificial checks to population he suggests. I fear the remedy would be worse than the disease - I would sooner trust to the effects of public Schools and Provident Institutions to bring about the reformation we require.[22]

What can he have meant? But it is clear that by about 1816, in certain circles, Malthusianism was already identified with something quite alien to the Rev.

Professor Malthus. At this period Malthus might well have begun to feel that Malthusianism was becoming an evil genie beyond his control.

2 Godwin Again

In his preface to the fifth edition of *Population*, Malthus did not point out that the third chapter of Book III had been completely rewritten; possibly it seemed of little practical importance compared with Corn Laws and Poor Laws.

The new chapter was simply headed 'Of Systems of Equality - *continued*', and it was principally concerned with Robert Owen. Now, in the editions of 1803, 1806 and 1807, the corresponding chapter had been called 'Observations on the Reply of Mr. Godwin': it had dealt entirely with Godwin's 1801 pamphlet in which he replied to the attacks made on him in the anonymous 1798 *Essay on Population*, Mackintosh's lectures on the *Law of Nature and Nations*, and Dr Parr's *Spital Sermon* (see pages 98-9). By 1817 Malthus clearly thought that all this was no longer of any general interest, while Robert Owen was at the height of his fame. The discussion of Godwin's *Reply* was therefore cut right out of the book, and one on Robert Owen's *New View of Society* inserted in its place. There were to be momentous consequences.

Godwin had been 'poor Godwin' for some time; his creditors knew well enough that he was not yet amongst the honourable dead. His second marriage was not especially happy, his literary work less and less successful; friends tried constantly to help him, and there was an impressive subscription list when Charles Lamb and his sister wrote their *Tales from Shakespeare* for the Godwins' Juvenile Library.

It is easy to understand how Godwin felt, at the age of sixty-one, when he found that he had been partially supplanted in the *Essay on Population* by Robert Owen. The carefully planned Owenite villages of co-operation were later derided by Cobbett as 'parallelograms of paupers' - he could hardly have been expected to appreciate even a semi-industrialised Utopia - but Malthus made the same objection to Owen's ideal societies as he did to all others, including Godwin's: the indolence engendered by equality and common property would obviate exertion and moral restraint, and the pressure of numbers on subsistence would soon reduce the whole community to misery and famine. Malthus, however, described Owen as a man of real benevolence, 'and every friend of humanity must heartily wish him success in his endeavours to procure an Act of Parliament for limiting the hours of working among the children in the cotton manufactories, and preventing them from being employed at too early an age. He is further entitled to great attention on all subjects relating to education, from an experience and knowledge he must have gained in an intercourse of many years with two thousand manufacturers.'[23]

Owen's 'manufacturers' were treated with what would today be regarded as intolerable paternalism: 'Believe me, my friends,' said their master, 'you are yet very deficient with regard to the best modes of training your children or of arranging your domestic concerns.'[24] Yet it was Owen who first, in 1815, used the term 'working classes' as distinct from 'lower orders'.[25] In spite of their literacy, his employees have unfortunately left no memorials, but presumably they appreciated their houses and allotments, their model school and working conditions, and the sight-seeing royalty, as well as nobility and gentry, who flocked from all over Europe to admire New Lanark. To poor Godwin, Robert Owen must have appeared to be endowed with every blessing - not only wealth and worldly success, but even some well-received revolutionary philosophies into the bargain.

Robert Owen (1771-1858) to a certain extent diminished his standing with the respectable, shortly after the appearance of the fifth edition of Malthus's *Essay*, by a public declaration of atheism. Nevertheless, he visited Haileybury in 1821 as the guest of Dr Batten, and Fanny Mackintosh records that he begged his host to ask her father and Mr Malthus to dine with him on Sunday 12 August: 'Mr. Owen was very full of his parallelograms - he gave Mr. Malthus 4 hours before dinner and then till ½11. Papa thought his manner mild and quiet.'

But before this Owenite ordeal took place, Godwin had published his own broadside in 1820: *Of Population. An Inquiry concerning the Power of Increase in the Numbers of Mankind; being an Answer to Mr. Malthus's Essay on that Subject.* It is painful reading, over 600 pages of repetitive bitterness, and Constancio made two volumes of it when he translated it into French at break-neck speed before being posted to Washington.

There was much facetious speculation as to why Godwin should have postponed for two decades his answer to Malthus's initial attack on *Political Justice* and *The Enquirer*. An anonymous pamphleteer (we will call him Anti-Godwin) pointed out that he had been twice as long in demolishing Mr Malthus as the Greeks were in taking Troy.[26] Malthus himself wrote, in a letter to Sismondi on 12 March 1821: 'I have lately been attacked, after a delay of twenty years, by my old antagonist Mr. Godwin.'[27] It seems strange that no one should have noticed that Godwin's interval was not in fact twenty years, but three; those familiar with recent literary history should have been well aware that Hell hath no fury like a writer scorned.

Anti-Godwin realised part of what I think is the truth. He remarked that Godwin had apparently had insufficient leisure in the last twenty years to read the book he was attacking, then went on to describe him as 'an injured and angry author; and in conformity with the maxims of the "genus irritabile", is not content to *refute* the *arguments*, but must also, if possible, *run down* and hold up to detestation the *individual* that has caused him so much uneasiness ... His insolent and bullying manner of treating his antagonist serves his cause with those readers who practise that manner themselves; it gratifies their vulgar malignity.'[28]

There is a sad contrast between Godwin's *Of Population* and his dignified *Reply* to Parr, Mackintosh and Malthus in 1801. Godwin wrote then that he approached the anonymous author of the *Essay on Population*

> with a sentiment of unfeigned approbation and respect ... He has neither laboured to excite hatred nor contempt against me or my tenets ... With the most unaffected simplicity of manner, and disdaining every parade of science, he appears to me to have made as unquestionable an addition to the theory of political economy, as any writer for a century past ... For myself, I cannot refuse to take some pride, in so far as by my writings I gave the occasion, and furnished an incentive, to the producing so valuable a treatise ... Let it be recollected, that I admit the ratios of the author in their full extent, and that I do not attempt in the slightest degree to vitiate, the great foundations of his theory. My undertaking confines itself to the task of repelling his conclusions.

Godwin's *Reply* to Malthus in 1801, in short, was based on the assertion that he entertained 'no vehement partialities for vice and misery'. He felt that the principle of population need not be an obstacle to the improvement of society if 'virtue, prudence and pride' could prevail with regard to marriage;[29] it is surprising that Malthus's detractors did not accuse him of plagiarising his doctrine of 'moral restraint' from Godwin himself.

Only one reviewer, in the *New Monthly Magazine*, seems to have looked up Godwin's 1801 pamphlet. He remarked on Godwin's unaccountable change of opinion: 'the unlicensed terms of contempt and insolent derision with which Mr. Godwin treats his departed sentiments, being the only evidence his present work contains of his having formerly harboured them. No one who simply differed from a set of opinions could entertain so virulent an animosity against the holders, as the consciousness of desertion without assignable grounds invariably inspires.'[30]

The true grounds of Godwin's virulent animosity might have been connected with jealousy of Malthus's success in the world, as well as with the rise of Robert Owen. There is no doubt that in the old days the two antagonists were friendly together at their publisher's table; for instance, there is the letter that Maria Edgeworth's father wrote to her on 17 May 1805 about a genial dinner at Johnson's with Godwin and Malthus (see page 167). Possibly Malthus and Godwin did not meet much after Joseph Johnson's death in 1809, but the fact that they had dined amicably in 1805 suggests that Godwin had been no more put out by what Malthus wrote of him in the great quarto than he had been by the first version of the *Essay*, and his position was the same in the editions of 1806 and 1807.

All this would explain why Shelley was quite happy to help Peacock with *Melincourt* during the winter of 1816-17, when he was married to Godwin's daughter. It was not until after the storm broke, with the omission of Godwin's *Reply* from the fifth edition of the *Essay on Population*, that the kindly Mr Fax became a monster. Shelley actually read *Population* for the first time in 1818, in French, and reacted with typical vehemence: in the preface to *Prometheus Unbound* he wrote that he 'had rather be damned with Plato and Lord Bacon, than go to heaven with Paley and Malthus'. It is worth remarking that the Shelleys' intensely anti-Malthusian period coincided with the death of their three-year-old son, 'Willmouse', and that their little daughter Clara had died a few months before.*

One feels that Godwin had caught something of his son-in-law's style when in 1820 he wrote that Malthus was 'a dark and terrible genius that is ever at hand to blast all the hopes of all mankind'. But 'Never certainly was there so comfortable a preacher as Mr. Malthus. No wonder that his book is always to be found in the country-seats of the court of aldermen and in the palaces of the great. Very appropriately has a retreat been provided for him by the commercial sovereigns of the regions of the East.'[31]

Yet Godwin was not altogether wrong when he wrote that 'For twenty years the heart of man in this island has been hardening through the *theories* of Mr. Malthus' (my italics). One has only to think of Ricardo refusing to contribute to Brougham's Owenite infant school. Godwin also makes a strong appeal for the children born after Malthus's plan for the gradual abolition of the Poor Laws had come into effect:

> 'Why am I thus? [asks Godwin's child] How have I deserved the series of misfortunes that incessantly pursue me? How came I into the world? I never desired it. I was compelled to come; and perhaps have never enjoyed one day of real felicity ...' However long he may exist, he shall bear about him for ever the miseries which arise from his being half-famished in the first stage of existence. And Mr. Malthus comes and tells him he 'has no right to complain' for a 'fair, distinct and precise notice' was given two years before he was born.[32]

Anti-Godwin provided the answer. According to him, this was 'the main object of Malthus's book: viz., that if there is not food for more than a certain number, it *should* operate by preventing people from being born, rather than by shortening the lives of those who are born. A most "atrocious" and "impious" object, I admit; but still we should give the devil his due and understand clearly what he *does* say.'[33]

We must also give Godwin his due and point out that his book contained

---

*To this period belongs *Swellfoot the Tyrant*, Shelley's oafish satire on the trial of Queen Caroline, where the 'Malthusian' sow-gelder also puts in an appearance.

long tables of figures as well as innumerable querulous and vindictive paragraphs. His main contentions were that populations did not increase rapidly; if they did, extra food could easily be provided; in any case, most of the earth was still uninhabited. In 1801 Godwin had accepted Benjamin Franklin's statement that the population of the United States was doubling naturally every twenty-five years; now he denied this power of increase, and attempted to prove that the population of the United States had grown more from immigration than from procreation. There was much arithmetic concerning how many thousands of emigrants could be carried by so many tons of shipping; the modern reader is reminded of the eighteenth-century disputes, in the absence of statistics, as to whether the population of England was actually rising or falling. People at the time were quick to make the point that whether an unchecked population doubled in twenty-five years or fifty was irrelevant to Malthus's general theory. Anti-Godwin had read his *Principles of Political Economy*, and explained that even if food could be increased to an unlimited extent, there would still be the problem of standing-room.

For his mathematical arguments, Godwin employed David Booth (1766-1846), a Scots schoolmaster who had migrated to London; he was not reluctant to drop in on Godwin at dinner-time and share his mutton. Booth had published *Tables of Simple Interest on a new Plan of Arrangement*, and for some years he supervised the press of the Society for the Diffusion of Useful Knowledge; he later published part of a useless *Analytical Dictionary of The English Language*. Godwin fully acknowledged Booth's distinct contribution to his book, and Booth was subsequently to call it his 'unfortunate Dissertation', in a separate pamphlet to which further reference will be made.

At first *Godwin on Population* attracted little comment. Those who glanced at the book - and not many could have done more - shared McCulloch's view as expressed in a letter to Ricardo dated 25 December 1820: 'Have you seen Godwin's work on Population? I have looked into it, and I do not think I ever saw a more miserable performance - It would be doing it far too much honour to take the least notice of it.'[34]

Then in May 1821 James Scarlett introduced a Poor Relief Bill in the House of Commons; he proposed to establish the assessments for the poor-rates of 1820 as maxima never to be exceeded, and to prohibit the giving of parochial relief to the able-bodied unemployed. Neither of these measures, as they stood, would have been satisfactory to Malthus, but the debates in both Parliament and press proceeded along 'Populationist' and 'Anti-Populationist' lines, with Godwin's 'elaborate work' being quoted in support of the former. Scarlett's Bill was withdrawn on 2 July, but it gave Francis Jeffrey an opening for which he was probably waiting. He had for some six years been unhappily placed with regard to Malthus, since he could not possibly ask him to write in the *Edinburgh Review* after the notorious Corn

Law pamphlet; all he could do for his friend was to prevent McCulloch from reviewing the *Principles of Political Economy*. Now he could with perfect propriety ask Malthus to write on Godwin's work.

The article was published (anonymously, as always) in the *Edinburgh Review* for July 1821. There was no doubt about the authorship. David Booth noted at once a mistake Malthus made over and over again in the dates of the British censuses - 1800 instead of 1801, 1810 instead of 1811 - presumably because he confused them with the decennial enumerations of the United States. Booth also noticed, because he had suffered like the present biographer, that references to Dr Price's *Reversionary Payments* were always to the fifth edition of 1792* although there had been three subsequent editions which were arranged quite differently. Booth wrote in his *Letter to the Rev. T. R. Malthus*, published in January 1823; 'Your readers, if they wish to follow you, have to grope their way through a modern copy; and if they find your quotation at all, it is sure to be at a very distant page, and often in a different volume from that to which you refer. This was sufficiently tormenting to patient perusers of your larger work, but it was rather too mischievous to cite so often from the same antiquated copy, (without even mentioning the edition), when you were writing for the more volatile readers of a modern Review.'[35] There must have been smiles.

Malthus's review was chiefly concerned with the effect of immigration on the rapid growth of numbers in the United States, and Godwin's absurd assertion that 'throughout the Union the population, as far as depends on procreation, is at a stand'. Then he returned to his own message:

> Those who, in the House of Commons, hold a language calculated to make the poor believe that there is no kind of reason for any prudential restraint on marriage, because all that are born have a mortgage upon the land, and a claim of right to be furnished with work and subsistence, certainly take upon themselves a most perilous responsibility ... We quite agree with Mr. Malthus in reprobating any positive laws against early marriages: but without any such laws, we think that something very important would be done, if the poor were fully convinced that population has a powerful tendency to increase; that the main cause of low wages is the abundance of hands, compared with the work to be done; and that the only mode of raising them effectively and permanently, is to proportion more nearly the supply of labour to the demand for it.[36]

Malthus was hard on Godwin. He was not quite as brutal as the *British Critic*, whose article began with the sentence 'Mr. Godwin is now clearly in his dotage';[37] but, in his character of an *Edinburgh* reviewer, Malthus referred to the book as 'the poorest and most old-womanish performance

---

*Booth and Malthus were both incorrect in calling this edition the fourth.

381

that has fallen from the pen of any writer of name, since we first commenced our critical career'.[38] One can assume that Godwin was hurt, and Fanny Mackintosh recorded in her diary for 6 September 1821; 'Papa wrote to Mr. Godwin about Mr. Malthus's review of him.' This letter is given in full in C. Kegan Paul's biography of Godwin: Sir James was extremely non-committal about Godwin's book, of which he had been sent a copy as a present, and he assured him that he never knew or heard anything of the *Edinburgh Review* article until he saw it in print.[39]

It is a measure of Godwin's standing as a writer of name that Malthus thought it appropriate to add a note about his lamentable work to the Appendix in the sixth edition of the *Essay*: it was such 'that I am quite sure every candid and competent inquirer after truth will agree with me in thinking that it does not require a reply'. This paragraph was dated 1825. By that time Godwin's *Population* had ceased to be important as an answer to Malthus; of far more significance was Francis Place's book, *Illustrations and Proofs of the Principle of Population*, which he in turn had written as an answer to Godwin.

3 The Birth Control Movement Begins

Francis Place, 'the radical tailor of Charing Cross', knew at first hand exactly what it felt like when population pressed hard upon subsistence. He was born in 1771, and married in 1791 when he was nineteen and his bride not quite seventeen. They had fifteen children, of whom ten grew up, and at one time, in spite of 'being only half fed on bread and water, with an occasional red herring, we were six pounds in debt to our landlord'. Place wrote, 'My temper was bad, and instead of doing everything in my power to soothe and comfort and support my wife ... of doing her homage for the exemplary manner in which she bore her sufferings ... I used at times to give way to passion, and increase her and my own misery.'[40]

By sometimes working for as much as eighteen hours a day, seven days a week, Place built up for himself a thriving business; he also became a behind-the-scenes politician of great importance. He was predominantly the adviser of men more renowned than himself, such as Robert Owen, whom he helped in drafting his early publications, and Joseph Hume. Godwin and James Mill were both indebted to Place for loans. According to his biographer, Graham Wallas, Place was badly treated by Godwin, but shook off this 'prince of spongers' in 1814, after losing something under £400.[41] Of Mill, Place became a close friend, happy to accept him as a schoolmaster, and he even strove under Mill's direction to learn some Latin, which he found a 'very, very difficult study'.

Through Mill, Place met Bentham in 1812, and he stayed with him and the Mills at Ford Abbey in 1817, having handed over the tailor's shop to his eldest son. This visit began in August, shortly after the publication of Malthus's fifth edition of *Population*, and it must surely have been discussed by the three men in their daily walk from one o'clock till two, after which they regularly separated for work again until the household dinner at six: it was more like a course than a holiday. After this visit Place became one of Bentham's inner circle of disciples, and later managed most of his small business affairs for him; he addressed him as 'My dear old Father', while Bentham started his letters to Place, 'Dear good Boy'. It is justifiable to assume that it was from Bentham that Place learned about family limitation through the use of a vaginal sponge, although in his case the information came too late.[42]

Place's earliest politico-economic activity had been over a journeymen's strike, and he learned, again at first hand, how powerless men were when the supply of labourers exceeded the demand for them. In this case the striking tailors were leather-breeches makers; it was a dying trade, as stuff breeches (which preceded trousers) were coming into fashion, to replace those made from leather. In spite of this circumstance, I do not think Place ever regarded the consumer as the ultimate employer, the real demander, for labour and everything else. He thought of population in relation to wages in simple market terms: the fewer the workmen available, the higher the price the masters would have to pay for them.

It is easy to understand why Place felt strongly the advantages of small families, but there is no record of the immediate chain of events which made Godwin's book the spring-board for his own. Place's attitude to Malthus is shown in his correspondence with the Irish political writer George Ensor (1769-1843). Ensor wrote a lengthy and solid *Refutation of Mr. Malthus's Essay on Population*, and Place replied to a letter about it, shortly before its publication, on 18 January 1818:

> As for your answer to Malthus, I shall judge of it when I see it. I do not know exactly what you mean when you say, 'I have refuted Malthus'. His propositions, assumed at random, may be easily refuted; they were assumed for the purpose of illustration, and are necessarily incorrect. Much, too, of his reasoning may be refuted. But I do not expect to see what I call the principle disproved; namely, that in all old settled countries the population presses against starvation, and is kept from increasing with the rapidity which, but for the want of produce, it would increase.[43]

Meanwhile, James Mill was working on his article, 'Colony', for the *Encyclopaedia Britannica*; it was probably finished early in 1819. In this he naturally referred to the redundant population of ancient Greece, and Greek colonisation of the surrounding territory. Then he digressed, with 'General Remarks on the Principle of Population', and concluded this section with a paragraph which was to become famous. He thought that population growth was

> the most important practical problem to which the wisdom of the
> politician and moralist can be applied. It has, till this time, been
> miserably evaded by all who have meddled with the subject ... And
> yet, if the superstitions of the nursery were discarded, and the
> principle of utility kept steadily in view, a solution might not be very
> difficult to be found; and the means of drying up one of the most
> copious sources of human evil; a source which, if all other sources of
> evil were taken away, would alone suffice to retain the great mass of
> human beings in misery, might be seen to be neither doubtful nor
> difficult to be applied.[44]

It seems strange that Mill should have thought of prejudices against contra-ception beginning in the nursery: possibly he was thinking of the midwives and gossips (Juliet's nurse, perhaps) rather than their innocent charges.

However that may be, it is clear that Bentham, Mill and Place had a completely different approach to the population question from that of Ricardo and McCulloch. Place wrote later that when he alluded to contra-ceptives in his own book on the principle of population he did so 'with the concurrence of friends who were themselves afraid to encounter the certain obloquy of such allusions'. What action Place would have taken had Godwin not produced his pitiful work when he did is open to conjecture; but Godwin indubitably provided the occasion for both the first major work on the economic problems of population and the first book to link them with family limitation for the sake of domestic happiness.

Malthus presumably knew even less than Ricardo about what was dis-cussed amongst the Benthamites. He certainly had nothing whatever to do with Place's book, apart from lending him, at Ricardo's request, his copy of the *Essay* of 1798, 'the only one which Mr. Malthus has left. He will be much obliged to Mr. Place, therefore, as soon as he has done with it, to send it to Mr. Ricardo's house in Upper Brook St., to be kept till Mr. Malthus is in town, which will be in a fortnight.' Thus far the formal note in the third person is in keeping with the manners of the time, but then Malthus broke out into an unconventional concluding sentence: 'Mr. Godwin, in his last work, has proceeded to the discussion of the principles of population with a degree of ignorance of his subject which is really quite inconceivable.'[45]

This note was dated 19 February 1821, and Place must have worked quickly, for he sent his manuscript to Ricardo on 3 September, after he had already gone through it with Mill. He did not show it to Malthus. Ricardo recommended the book to Murray, who kept it for about two and a half months, 'a shameful length of time', according to Mill, 'and at last returned it without any answer at all'.[46] Eventually Place's *Illustrations and Proofs of the Principle of Population* was published in 1822 by Longmans, who had also published Godwin.

Place's great object was to separate the harsh principle of population, which he believed in, from the harsh treatment of the poor by the rich, which he regarded as irrelevant to this principle. The poor refused to believe in the natural tendency of population to out-run capital accumulation, because, so they thought, this doctrine was preached by those who wanted them to continue in poverty and ignorance. Therefore Place attacked Godwin for his denial of the existence of superfluous children, and Malthus for his proposed remedy of late marriages.

It cannot be stressed too much that Place took the indissolubility of marriage, and marital fidelity, completely for granted; these basic assumptions of what is right and normal are implicit in all that he wrote. He thought that early marriages, with brides of eighteen or twenty, grooms about two years older, were more likely to be happy than late ones, because the young people could adapt themselves more easily to their joint life than they could if they were 'set in their ways'. Marriage was also 'the most effective mode of diminishing promiscuous intercourse': Place himself had found celibacy impossible before he was nineteen. Thus,

> If means were adopted to prevent the breeding of a larger number of children than a married couple might desire to have, and if the labouring part of the population could thus be kept below the demand for labour, wages would rise so as to afford the means of comfortable subsistence for all, and all might marry ... The benefits which might reasonably be calculated upon are very extensive and very numerous; the poors rate would soon be reduced to a minimum, and the poor laws might, with the greatest ease, be remodeled and confined to the aged and helpless, or might, if it should appear advisable, be wholly abolished.

> ... If, above all, it were once clearly understood, that it was not disreputable for married persons to avail themselves of such precautionary means as would, without being injurious to health, or destructive of female delicacy, prevent conception, a sufficient check might at once be given to the increase of population beyond the means of subsistence; vice and misery, to a prodigious extent, might be removed from society, and the object of Mr. Malthus, Mr. Godwin, and of every philanthropic person, be promoted, by the increase of comfort, of intelligence, and of moral conduct, in the mass of the population.[47]

These quotations may be said to mark the beginning of the publicity campaign for family planning, although it was not 'publicity' in the modern sense of the word. Place lived in an era of brutality quite horrible to imagine as one reads the small items of news from the magistrates' courts in such papers as the *Morning Herald*; to spend too long working on contemporary caricatures is to risk being physically sick in a famous library. Yet to most of Place's generation the use of contraceptives, in the cause of marital happiness, of healthy and well-educated children, and of national economic prosperity, was something too obscene to be openly talked about. And inevitably some of the slime – for so it was regarded – rubbed off on Malthus.

Place followed up his book with what were called the 'diabolical hand-bills'. These were three neatly printed anonymous leaflets, *To the Married of Both Sexes; To the Married of Both Sexes in Genteel Life;* and *To the Married of Both Sexes of the Working People*. Place distributed them in all sorts of ways, to people known to him, to pass on to people known to them, and also indiscriminately, wrapped around farthing candles and penny boxes of snuff. He was quite explicit over 'a piece of sponge about an inch square, being placed in the vagina previous to coition, and afterwards withdrawn by means of a double thread or bobbin attached to it'. In the leaflet for the working people, Place wrote that the sponge should be as large as a green walnut or a small apple.* He concluded, 'You cannot fail to see that this address is intended solely for your good. It is quite impossible that those who address you can receive any benefit from it, beyond the satisfaction which every benevolent person, every true Christian, must feel, at seeing you comfortable, healthy, and happy.'

In the summer of 1823, twenty-six leaflets were sent for distribution in Manchester to a Mrs Mary Fildes; Place wrote in the covering letter that 'the method recommended is getting fast into use amongst the working people in London'. Mrs Fildes was aghast. She was a parliamentary reformer, famed for her courage at 'the massacre of Peterloo' in August 1819, when a meeting at Manchester, in St Peter's Fields, was savagely dispersed by a cavalry charge. Mrs Fildes thought the parcel was a plot to get her into trouble with the authorities, and I also think she was genuinely outraged: 'I feel indignant at the insult which has been offered me; Is it possible that this infamous hand Bill has issued from the encouragers of the doctrines of the cold blooded Malthus or [his] servile supporter the detestable Lawyer Scarlett?'

Equally outraged were the maid-servants into whose basement kitchens the seventeen-year-old John Stuart Mill dropped some of the leaflets in the autumn of 1823. He had been much distressed by coming upon the body of a murdered new-born baby in a London park. Encouraged by the girls' outcry at this aspersion on their chastity, a crowd set upon him. The young

---

*It should perhaps be pointed out that these sponges were of a kind imported from the East Indies; they were much denser in texture than the large-pored Mediterranean variety which were later a feature of English bathrooms before showers became common.

Mill spent three or four days in gaol; the matter was hushed up, but everybody who was anybody knew about it. Tom Moore published a jingle containing the lines

> There are two Mr. M-lls, too, whom those that like reading
> Through all that's unreadable call very clever; -
> And, whereas M-ll Senior makes war on *good* breeding,
> M-ll Junior makes war on all *breeding* whatever![48]

Such reactions might have given way to a more sensible approach to the subject, had it not been for an anonymous publication called *Every Woman's Book, or, What is Love?* by Richard Carlile. This was a calamity. Place had tried to prevent it.

Carlile began by saying that he did not advocate 'indiscriminate intercourse', yet reported approvingly that 'An English Duchess was lately instanced to the writer, who never goes out to a dinner without being prepared with the sponge', and that 'the practice is common with the females of the more refined parts of the continent of Europe'. Worse still, 'Marriage among us is a system of degradation and slavery', and worst of all 'the cross is but the mathematical emblem of the phallus ... an emblem on which the deified principle of reason always was and always will be periodically crucified, have a temporary death and rise to life again'.[49] Carlile was more than a little mad, and later adopted a form of Christianity and called himself 'the Reverend': the damage he did to the cause of family limitation must have been incalculable.

The sponge itself was not a satisfactory method. Small pieces of natural sponge disintegrate very quickly, and portions left behind in a woman's body must frequently have had harmful or even fatal consequences. Perhaps this was the origin of the widespread belief that birth control could be more dangerous to a mother's life and health than too many babies. Contraceptive practices could not become general until the vulcanisation of rubber made possible the mass production of a variety of hygienic appliances; this process was discovered simultaneously in 1844 by Hancock in Great Britain and Goodyear in the United States. Since a collective euphemism was needed, contraceptives were advertised as 'Malthusian devices', and later the French even made up a verb, *malthusianiser*, meaning 'to practice birth control'.

This was after Malthus had died, but from 1823 onwards he was the victim of sniping innuendo. I think this is the sort of thing to which Otter was referring when he wrote of the obloquy and calumnies 'which, though they passed lightly over his family while he was alive, are calculated to aggravate their grief now they are deprived of him'.[50] For just one example we may take an embittered writer who produced two identical books (printed from the same blocks) under the names of John McIniscon in 1825 and J. C. Ross in 1827. He wrote of 'a few broad hints from some Malthusian physician, which may enable the labourers' wives to keep clear of the crime

of bearing live children'. Later, after a joke about the five thousandth edition
of the *Essay on Population* in three thousand volumes, he went on to foretell
that the *Edinburgh* and *Quarterly* reviews would 'diligently continue their
present occupation of Malthusian doctrine-pedlars, zealous missionaries of
the new faith contained in their great master's Koran, and active priests at
the altars which it directs to be raised for the peculiar and hitherto unheard-
of sacrifice of human embryos'.

It was all so easy. In 1821 there had been a debate in the Commons on
the reluctance of the East India Company to offend local religious feeling
by prohibiting suttee - the custom whereby a Hindu widow was compelled
to throw herself on to her husband's funeral pyre. Thus McIniscon could
also abuse Malthus as 'the supreme genius of political economy, whose
brilliant rays shed their zenith influence on the Hindoo women-roasters'
college'.[51] All nonsense, but the kind that can hurt an individual as well as
harm a cause.

4 Emigration

Robert Wilmot-Horton (1784-1841), handsome, clever and rich, educated
at Eton and Christ Church, became a Member of Parliament in 1818 when
he was thirty-four. In 1806 he had married the Derbyshire heiress who
inspired Byron's poem 'She walks in beauty', and she bore him four sons
and three daughters. But there is nothing romantic about his list of publications, which show him to have been in favour of Catholic Emancipation,
an earnest though not always intelligible lecturer to Mechanics' Institutes,
and - like so many men of his period - an almost pathological opponent of
the old Poor Laws.

Wilmot-Horton became obsessed with the idea of emigration as a cure
for pauperism and, in consequence, of almost all the other evils from which
the country was allegedly suffering: low wages and riotous assemblies were
both ascribed by him to the redundant population generated by parish relief.
He first put forward his views in the House of Commons in 1819, when
opposing a motion for parliamentary reform from Sir Francis Burdett, and
he was able to speak with more authority on the subject two years later,
when Lord Liverpool made him Under Secretary for War and the Colonies.
He resigned his office, with Huskisson, in 1827, but continued to speak and
write on emigration, and kept up a correspondence with Malthus until his
departure for Ceylon, as Governor and Commander-in-Chief, in 1831; there
he remained until the year of Queen Victoria's accession.

Malthus had a chapter on emigration in Book III of the *Essay*, as one of the 'Different Systems or Expedients which have been proposed, or have prevailed in society, as they affect the evils arising from the principle of population'. It followed straight after the three chapters 'Of Systems of Equality', and began with an ironical reference to them: 'Although the resource of emigration seems to be excluded from such perfect societies as the advocates of equality generally contemplate, yet in that imperfect state of improvement, which alone can rationally be expected, it may fairly enter into our consideration.'

Malthus's consideration was realistic. He had plenty of examples of attempts at colonisation which had failed, and the redundant population of paupers were inevitably people who 'must necessarily be deficient in those resources which alone could ensure success'. Characteristically he asked whether a man were to be blamed for his attachment to his native soil, his love for his parents,

> his kindred, his friends, and the companions of his early years . . . Is it no evil that he suffers, because he consents to bear it rather than snap these cords which nature has wound in close and intricate folds round the human heart? The great plan of Providence [for peopling and civilising the globe] seems to require, indeed, that these ties should sometimes be broken; but the separation does not, on that account, give less pain; and though the general good may be promoted by it, it does not cease to be an individual evil.

This was published in 1803, before Malthus became the teacher of future exiles to India. It is also important to remember that he lived before ocean-going steamships, before telegrams and cables, before the development of late Victorian imperialism. The British Empire, in his time, was England, Wales, Scotland and Ireland; the West Indies and Mauritius, the whole of Canada and the Cape of Good Hope and New South Wales (which he still called New Holland) were designated 'colonial possessions'. For those not urged by what Malthus called 'a spirit of avarice or enterprise, or of religious or political discontent', emigration often meant transportation; this punishment seemed hardly worse than the death penalty which it superseded for such crimes as petty theft or the distraught infanticide of an unmarried mother. In these circumstances it was natural that some working people should regard with terror any national or parochial schemes for the 'shovelling out of paupers' to save the rate-payers' money.

From Malthus's point of view emigration was no remedy for pauperism, since the vacuum left by the departed would be immediately filled up again, according to the principle of population, in the same way in which Süssmilch had shown that a rapid increase of marriages and births always followed the mortality caused by epidemics. In 1817, however, Malthus added a long paragraph advocating emigration as a temporary relief in peculiar circumstances. The demand for labour during the Napoleonic Wars had, according to him, given a great stimulus to population for ten or twelve years, and had then 'comparatively ceased'. Malthus wrote, 'It is clear that labour will continue flowing into the market with almost undiminished rapidity, while the means of employing and paying it have been essentially contracted ... The only real relief in such a case is emigration; and the subject at the present moment is well worthy the attention of the government, both as a matter of humanity and policy.'[52]

Wilmot-Horton sent both Malthus and Ricardo copies of his *Outline of a Plan of Emigration to Upper Canada,* which he had printed (but did not publish) in January 1823. This contained the elements of the schemes which he was to propound and defend with the zest of a crusader for the next eight years. The first basic idea was that the able-bodied unemployed should be settled in Canada with loans from the government to individual parishes on the security of their poor-rates; since a pauper cost £10 a year to maintain in England, while the whole expense of establishing him permanently in Canada was estimated at £35, this plan seemed clearly to the rate-payers' advantage.

We should bear in mind that this sort of proposal was not entirely original: for example, Robert Gourlay had published a *General Introduction* to his plan for *A Grand System of Emigration in connection with a Reform of the Poor Laws* in 1822. Poor Gourlay was a crank returned from Canada with innumerable grievances, and extremely long-winded, but his work shows how public opinion can be won over by an enthusiast:

> The vision of quickly and thickly peopling the earth with our species brightens in my imagination day after day ... The idea may be easily realized. It requires but systematic arrangement, and the judicious application of capital which we have in abundance. It will pay: it may be resorted to, not only for the performance of the first great command to multiply and replenish; but for our individual advantage and our national aggrandizement: it may be looked forward to as the peaceful means of establishing a new and a better order of things in the world ... Hope might be indulged that before the continent of America was thickly peopled to the shores of the Pacific, virtuous restraint would be quite sufficient to keep the increase of population within due bounds: that no physical means would be required to check it, as proposed by Mr. Place; and that it would no longer be a cause of vice and misery, as insisted on by Mr. Malthus ... In these ten years, were my scheme of abolishing poor laws put in execution, together with a grand system of emigration, every difficulty might be got over, every danger avoided, every evil corrected.[53]

Wilmot-Horton was not such an optimist as Gourlay, and Ricardo and Malthus were both cautious in their replies to his *Outline of a Plan.* Ricardo wrote with characteristic promptitude the day he received it, on 19 January 1823. Equally characteristically, he professed his ignorance of Parish Economy, and then explained that such parish work as was done by the able-bodied pauper would be lost to the community, so that the total saving would be less than £10 per annum, quite apart from the fact that farmers were also benefiting from 'the general saving in the wages of labour which accompany the present system'. There was also the point that 'with every emigrant we are to divest ourselves of £35 of capital'; but 'at the present moment' Ricardo preferred Wilmot-Horton's plan to 'the system actually existing . . . . What is to me by far the most important consideration, it could not fail to make the wages of labour more adequate to the support of the labourer and his family [by removing the surplus supply of labour], besides giving him that as wages which is now given to him as charity.'[54]

Malthus did not write until 21 February 1823, having been 'very particularly engaged'. He thought it extremely unjust that governments should prohibit or impede emigration, but was doubtful whether they could reasonably be expected to promote it. However, this was 'a doubt rather than an opinion', and had been 'yielding to the peculiar circumstances of the times'. Malthus's principal objection was 'that the character of the population which parishes are most inclined to get rid of would not in general make the most industrious and efficient settler . . . It is not likely that parishes should be inclined to send off their best men.' He concluded with a reminder that 'continued emigration would make room for a much larger proportion of marriages, and might in a certain time alarmingly accumulate the expenses of settling fresh families.'[55]

There is then a gap of four years in the correspondence between Malthus and Wilmot-Horton. In the interval Ricardo had died, Malthus had appeared before the Committee on the Export of Artizans and Machinery, a steam locomotive had come into use on the Stockton-Darlington Railway, and there had been a speculative financial crash in 1825. The plight of the hand-loom weavers had become so wretched that, in Scotland especially, groups of them were forming Emigration Societies of their own; there was hope that some financial help might be forthcoming from the government, and they and other workers were sending petitions to Parliament praying that 'their deep distress may be taken into favourable consideration; that they are starving and will be ejected from their dwellings in a few days'.[56] Yet the mournful condition of the Irish peasant was so much worse, with intermittent outbreaks of potato blight and typhus and no poor relief, that Irish labourers were flocking across to England and Scotland, further to increase overcrowding and depress wages.

This was the setting for the House of Commons Select Committee on Emigration from the United Kingdom, of which Wilmot-Horton was chairman. He obviously wanted Malthus's support, and on Malthus's side their new relationship began with a note from the 'E.I. Coll.' dated 18

January 1827:

> It happens unfortunately that, as our term at the College commences tomorrow, I shall be so fully engaged every day till thursday next as to make it extremely inconvenient to me to dine in Town.
>
> On monday I shall be occupied with the admission examinations nearly the whole day, but if thursday be too late, I think I could be secure of being spared for an hour or two at any time on tuesday morning, if it would suit you to call. I shall be sorry however that, with your engagements, you should have the trouble of calling, particularly as I am not aware that I can be of any use to you. My general opinions on the subject of Emigration are well known . . . but I have not attended to the details in regard to the best practical means of effecting the object . . .

As the Mackintoshes had long since left Hertfordshire, we do not have Fanny's diary to tell us whether Wilmot-Horton thought it worth while to make the journey to Haileybury.

Malthus's next letter to Wilmot-Horton is dated 8 March 1827: his main concern was with Ireland, from which a fresh influx of labour could destroy all the benefit which might be expected from the emigration plans for England and Scotland. Unhappy Ireland: 'The focus of mischief, in every point of view, is there.'

Exactly a month later, on 8 April 1827, Malthus was writing to Wilmot-Horton in some consternation:

> I received this morning the order of your Committee to attend on the first of May. As I have no facts, or results of of [sic] personal inquiries to communicate, and my opinions on the subject of Emigration are already before the public, I was in hopes, as I told Sir Henry Parnell, that I should not be called upon. If however you think it advisable that I should be summoned it would be a great convenience to me in regard to my College duties that it should be deferred till the thursday or friday following.
>
> If I am making an improper request from ignorance, you will I know have the goodness to excuse me, and I will obey the order of the Committee as it at present stands.

On 22 April he is writing again to Wilmot-Horton:

> I should have much preferred being excused giving my evidence before the Emigration Committee; and it really appeared to me that the only evidence I could give was not of the right kind for a Committee of the House of Commons. At the same time if you and Sir Henry Parnell believe that my attendance will be in any way of service to your cause, I would not, if I could, allow my inclinations to interfere.

THE POPULATION CONTROVERSIES CONTINUE

The Minutes of Evidence of the Committee show that the Rev. Thomas Robert Malthus was in fact called in and examined on *Sabbati 5° die Maii* 1827. The first question put to him was 'Have you been in Ireland?' It was with Ireland, too, that the examination concluded: on this occasion Malthus said nothing about the 'miserable hovels of Ireland' or about the 'superior prudence' of the working people in England. His detractors should note his assertion that 'One of the greatest faults in Ireland is, that the labouring classes there are not treated with proper respect by their superiors; they are treated as if they were a degraded people.' Malthus's opinion was that with education, with civil, religious and political liberty, Ireland 'might be a very rich and a very prosperous country, and that it might be richer in proportion than England, from its greater natural capabilities ... A judicious system of emigration is one of the most powerful means to accomplish that object.'[57]

Many of the questions put to Malthus were in the nature of statements to which he replied 'No doubt' or 'Certainly,' and many of his answers sound unsympathetic: cottages deserted by emigrants should be pulled down and not replaced, landlords who built new cottages on their estates should be taxed for doing so.

> 'Do you not admit', he was asked, 'that with mere reference to the wealth of the country', the demise of redundant labourers 'would not be attended with any loss?'
> 'Rather a gain, certainly,' answered Population Malthus.[58]

But it was he who reminded the Committee that 'the removal of a small part of the whole labouring population might effect a very beneficial change in the condition of the remainder', and that 'it is in fact the object of the emigration to improve the condition of the remaining labourers.'[59]

Their condition would be improved, of course, because the smaller number of labourers would be able to command higher wages. Would not these higher wages harm the country through reducing the profit of the capitalist?

> 3283. Are not the manufacturer's profits principally dependent on a low rate of wages? - I do not quite agree to that doctrine, I think that wages and profits very often rise together. When the value of the whole commodity rises from the state of the supply compared with the demand, there is a greater value to divide between the capitalist and the labourer; the labourer will have higher money wages, and the profits of stock may be higher at the same time.
>
> 3284. Is not the tendency of a redundant supply of labour ready at all times to fill up the decrease of the labouring population by want and disease, beneficial to the manufacturing and commercial interest, inasmuch as it lowers wages and raises profits, and

renders possible a successful competition with foreign capitalists? - I should think that even if it did so, no persons could possibly bring themselves to encourage such a system with that view.

3285. Compassion to the labouring poor and regard to the public peace may render the diminution of this supply of labour desirable, but a redundancy is favourable to trade and commerce, is it not? - In one respect it is, and in one respect not; it may enable the capitalist to work up his commodities cheaper, and to extend his foreign trade, but it certainly will have a tendency to diminish the home trade, and I think the home trade much more important than the foreign.[60]

Economist Malthus also gave evidence a little later on:

3304. What is your opinion of the tendency of population to increase in a greater or less ratio than the rate of capital? - There is a tendency in population to increase faster, though sometimes, no doubt, capital has increased faster than population; it is not, however, merely capital that supports labour, but capital joined with revenue.

He was not allowed to expatiate on the theme that capital is useless unless profitably employed; the next question was 'Does not the rate of increase of the population, in different countries, depend very much on the different habits existing among the people?' To this Malthus had merely to reply, 'Very much.'[61]

One point which emerges from this evidence is Malthus's changed attitude to public works, which he had recommended as a temporary measure ten years before in the fifth edition of the *Essay on Population*. He was asked

3343. What is your own opinion of the effect on the lower orders, on employing them on public works with public money? - I think it relieves them for a short time, but leaves them afterwards in a condition worse than before.

3344. Have the goodness to explain that operation. - It has a tendency to induce them to marry earlier, and it enables them at first to support their children; but when the work ceases, they are left in a more destitute condition than before. It is always an unfavourable thing for the labouring classes to have a great stimulus applied to them for a time, and then to have that stimulus withdrawn.[62]

Malthus had obviously come to the conclusion that a temporary demand for public works was no different in its results from the temporary demands of a major war.

When we turn from the Minutes of Evidence to the Third Report of the Emigration Committee, the deference shown to Malthus's opinions seems out of all proportion to the time spent in questioning him. The Report began with Ireland, and the fatal effect of the influx of 'potato-fed' immigrants upon the happiness of the 'wheat-fed' labouring classes of England. In this connection, 'The testimony which was uniformly given by the *practical witnesses* ... has been confirmed in the most absolute manner by that of Mr. Malthus; and Your Committee cannot but express their satisfaction at finding that the experience of facts is thus strengthened throughout by general reasoning and scientific principles.'[63]

As far as his own country was concerned, 'Mr. Malthus is of the opinion that parishes in England would act prudently as regards their interest, in charging their poor-rates for the purpose of raising a fund to promote Emigration, and that even a national tax would be justified for that purpose, if a bare possibility existed of the vacuum not being filled up.' His replies on this issue were given in detail: apart from pulling down the emigrants' houses, Malthus could think of no practical remedy 'except the one I myself proposed a long while ago, that those that were born after a certain time should not be allowed to have any parish assistance'. Malthus's evidence was also quoted verbatim on the subject of redundant labour generally and on the importance of high wages for the benefit of 'the home trade'.[64]

In the Concluding Observations of the Committee, 'Upon the advantages of a regulated Emigration, both to the Colonies and to the Mother Country', Malthus's evidence was summarised thus:

> If there are labourers in the country for whose labour there is no real
> demand, and who have no means of subsistence, these labourers are
> of no advantage, as far as the wealth of the country is concerned ...
> He considers labourers in this state of redundancy, as operating as a
> tax upon the community ... Mr. Malthus admits that if it can be
> shown that the expense of removing such labourers by Emigration is
> less than that of maintaining them at home, no doubt can exist as to
> the expediency of so removing them; and this, independent of any
> question of repayment ... He was of opinion that the general wealth
> of the empire would be increased by an accession of population in
> the Colonies, independently of the advantageous consequences
> resulting to this country from the abstraction of that population
> which is here in redundance; and that the introduction of English
> population into these colonies would tend to furnish a very valuable
> market for the labourers of this country, even if they were not to
> continue to belong to the British empire.[65]

It is easy to see how Malthus must have appeared hard-hearted to people who had not read, in the *Essay on Population*, his warm justification of those unwilling to leave their homes.

Wilmot-Horton did not let Malthus go, and on 8 November 1827 Malthus sent him a carefully written letter, obviously drafted first, with his doubts about the National System of Emigration [to Canada] recommended by the Select Committee. They proposed that loans should be made direct to the emigrants themselves, not to their parishes; this arrangement was essential as far as Ireland was concerned, because in that country there were no parish poor-rates. Malthus was pessimistic: there was the risk of incurring 'an amount of debt which would give rise to great complaints at home', and 'in the case of a war with the United States' the promise of an entire relief from both the debt and the interest thereon might be too tempting an offer for the Colonists to resist. He also asked whether such a burden of debt might not prove 'an obstacle in the way of a friendly and peaceable seperation of Canada from England, when the Colony had become sufficiently populous and strong to protect her own independence? Such a seperation, it appears to me, ought always to be looked forward to.'

The correspondence which Wilmot-Horton so carefully filed was obviously initiated by him rather than by Malthus; his letters are invariably in reply to one received, almost always with enclosures, and usually begin with apologies for his delay in answering. That Malthus was no great enthusiast for emigration was shown clearly in February 1830 when Wilmot-Horton asked for his views on his first pamphlet on the *Causes and Remedies of Pauperism*. The author had returned to his original scheme of loans to parishes rather than emigrants, and Malthus maintained his position that the vacuum left in England would be so quickly replenished that the expenditure might not be worth while. Yet again, on 7 June 1830, Malthus wrote of the extreme difficulty of preventing this void from being filled: he told Wilmot-Horton that if he could accomplish this, 'in an entirely unobjectionable manner, you would in my opinion be the greatest benefactor to the human race that has yet appeared'. In his next communication poor Wilmot-Horton wrote that while Malthus was employing these phrases, 'the House of Commons are finishing the Session without even condescending to allow a discussion of the subject.'

Thereafter Wilmot-Horton set out to 'demonstrate that *Pauperism never need be reproduced';* he suggested the parish loans should be paid off in ten or twelve years, because 'it is physically impossible that a population of adults and children can be reproduced in that period', and went on to develop his scheme on sixteen foolscap sheets, dated 24 July 1830. Malthus replied on 24 August with what I think was unintentional humour: 'I most fully allow that you are not required to prevent all increase of population after an emigration has taken place, but only such an increase as will occasion a return of pauperism; and you quite mistake me if you suppose I ever wish to see any other checks to population than those prudential habits and feelings to which you allude.'

Meanwhile a completely different group of enthusiasts had formed the

National Colonization Society. Edward Gibbon Wakefield (1796–1862) had been sentenced to three years' imprisonment for abducting a schoolgirl heiress; feeling that emigration was his only course, he set about studying conditions in Australia. To his surprise he found that the colonists generally were less prosperous than they should have been, owing to a shortage of labour; this was due to free grants of land for all comers, which meant that uneconomic subsistence agriculture was being carried on by widely scattered proprietors, who could not make proper use of the capital available. Wakefield therefore wrote, from Newgate Prison, his famous *Letter from Sydney*. In this he proposed, in effect, that no immigrant should be allowed to buy or rent land until he had worked for an employer for five years, and colonies were to be organised and concentrated so that advantage could be taken of the division of labour and a market economy. The cost of the emigrants' passage to Australia was to be defrayed from the sale or rental of the colonial lands, and immigration was to be strictly controlled to maintain equal numbers of both sexes.

While Wakefield was in prison, the National Colonization Society was managed by Robert Gouger, the secretary; he set up a London Committee Room at the British Coffee House in Cockspur Street, and a Provisional Committee met for the first time on 23 March 1830.[66] According to a letter which Malthus wrote to Wilmot-Horton on 17 August 1830, he had more than one interview with Gouger, and brought up many arguments against the scheme: he was therefore 'a good deal surprised at being represented as a decided approver of it'. But since it would 'cost nothing, however, to this country, I saw no harm in its being tried, if the colonists themselves were sanguine on the subject, as they were represented to be. I will further observe that though in my own opinion the plan will not succeed, I am not surprised that the Society, if they think that they have adopted it upon good grounds, and are sanguine to its success, should decline changing their views for yours.'

Later, on 25 August 1830, Malthus sent Wilmot-Horton a long, rambling letter about the new scheme:

> 10th. It is quite impossible to say that any specific plan would secure the precise degree of artificial concentration which it is desirable to introduce into a new colony. Concentration has undoubtedly its advantages; and I am quite willing to agree with the Colonization Society, that the government in fixing a price on new grants of land, ought to consult nothing but the greatest happiness of all . . .
> Anything like a persevering attempt at concentration round a single town would soon lower wages, and destroy the true principle of colonization . . . A great degree of concentration and a greater outlay of capital than can be spared in a new state, are required to make a poor soil equal to one which is naturally rich . . . At the same time it

is, as I conceive, strictly true, as I have allowed before, that it would
be advantageous to place the highest price on land which *would not
prevent the greatest possible increase of people* ... Our present
experience is not sufficient to warrant any decided change in the
system which has actually prevailed. It would be extremely rash to
affirm that the population of the United States would have increased
faster, or as fast, if they had forced a greater degree of
concentration ...

One is conscious that Malthus has become an elderly gentleman, out of his
depth in a changing world.

But there is a postscript. Two of Malthus's great-nephews were to found
in the Antipodes, in New Zealand, a family now over two hundred strong
(about half of whom bear the name of Malthus) after a little over a century.
As Dr Cecil Malthus wrote to the author from Christchurch, the colonial
Malthuses have more than vindicated Old Pop's principal theory.

5 *A Summary View*

Sometime in the autumn of 1822, when he was working on his second
translation of the *Essay*, Prévost must have asked Malthus whether he
intended to write a Reply to the works of John Barton. This John Barton
(1790-1852) was a philanthropist who promoted in Chichester a Savings
Bank, a Lancasterian School, and a Mechanics' Institution; in 1817 he
published a book on the *Condition of the Labouring Classes*, which he
followed in 1820 with one on the *Progressive Depreciation of Agricultural
Labour in Modern Times*.

In this second work Barton paid a cordial tribute to Malthus for his
concern with the poverty of individuals rather than the wealth of nations:

> Even should the progress of enquiry cast a doubt over some of Mr.
> Malthus's conclusions, the value of his labours would not be
> materially lessened. For he has done more than establish a few new
> positions; he has pointed out the path in which those who follow
> him may most successfully direct their steps. Had he merely applied
> for the first time the principles of Political Economy to an
> investigation of the sources of Poverty, he would deserve to be
> classed among the benefactors of the human race. He has added
> dignity to the pursuits of the Philanthropist by raising them to the
> rank of a science; and rendered the researches of science trebly
> interesting by shewing how they may be made immediately

subservient to the welfare of mankind. But while we do justice to his merits, we shall perhaps find that he has overrated the ill effects of our Poor Laws, in ascribing to them a tendency to create an excess of population.

According to Barton the number of paupers had not increased in proportion to the increased population, 'a very considerable' reduction has taken place in the marriages, compared with the number marriageable', and the declining death-rate alone proved that 'the condition of the lower orders is ameliorated'.[67]

Malthus wrote to Prévost about Barton's two works in the long letter of 23 December 1822 already quoted. A few sentences must suffice here, to show once more how much these able men had to argue without statistics:

> Though I have felt doubts to the degree in which our poor laws operate in increasing population, I can feel no doubt whatever that *given* the population, the effect of the poor laws is to *lower* the common wages of labour ... In many of the Southern parishes where the single man is paid much less than the married man, labourers have avowedly married for the express purpose of obtaining the allowance given for children. I quite agree with Mr. Barton however that the true way of estimating the expenditures for the poor and its pressure on the country, is, not to look at its nominal increase merely, but to consider it always with reference to the value of money and the increase of population; and in this view, which is the true one, the increase of the pressure is certainly much less than it appears. I own I should be nearly satisfied if I could once see that the proportion of the whole population in a state of dependent poverty was on an average stationary, and likely to remain so. But unless the system of allowance, in proportion to the number of children, be essentially changed, this cannot happen. Efforts however are making at present to improve the system of management; but though the nominal amount of the rates has diminished, there is reason to fear that it is owing to the cheapness of provisions, not to a diminution in the number of paupers.[68]

Malthus also pointed out to Prévost that unless he were 'regularly answering all that has of late years been said against the doctrine of population, it would hardly look well for him to single out Mr. Barton'. To reply to all his antagonists would have been impossible, there were so many of them, almost all much inferior to Barton in matter and Godwin in reputation.

In private Malthus was often extremely tolerant towards his critics, such as one who wrote under the name of Piercy Ravenstone, and declared that 'France was wretched, not because her people were too numerous, but because her gentry were too many. The destruction of the idle classes removed her misery, but whilst the number of unproductive persons has greatly diminished in France, it has greatly increased in England; it has produced the same effects.' Ravenstone also maintained that 'The growth of population is in no manner regulated by the amount of subsistence. Men give existence to food.'[69] Gently Malthus commented to Ricardo in a letter of 13 September 1821: 'I have only had an opportunity of looking a little at Mr. Ravenstone's book. It is certainly as you say full of errors, but I believe he is a well meaning man and I shall look at it again.'[70]

It is just possible that this belief was founded on some slight personal knowledge, as Ravenstone had been identified as Richard Puller, the brother of Sir Christopher (1774-1824), who had married an heiress from Hertford-shire.[71] Piercy Ravenstone was certainly merciless over Malthus's famous ratios - the increase of population in a geometrical progression, 2, 4, 8, 16, while food could only be increased arithmetically, 1, 2, 3, 4, and so on. Taking the contemporary population of the world as one thousand million, and adopting Bishop Ussher's biblical chronology, Ravenstone made some amusing calculations: for instance, assuming that Adam and Eve had only enough food for the two of them in 4004 BC, the population of the world in 1821 'must, according to this theory, be living on a quantity of food which is only sufficient for 1,328 persons'. Alternatively, if one counted backwards, one was left with the blasphemous conclusion that Adam did not have to live by the sweat of his brow, for the world in 4004 BC must have contained enough food for six million people. Not that this really helped: after the Flood in 2349 BC, the descendants of Noah would have increased to two hundred million in less than six and a half centuries (doubling every twenty-five years) while the food which was adequate for six million people at the Creation would only have increased arithmetically to a quantity sufficient for 162 million. 'Unless any country can be adduced in which men have been able to live without food, we are inevitably compelled to believe, that for the last 3,500 years the geometrical and arithmetical ratios have jogged on quietly side by side.'[72]

Anti-Godwin more charitably tried to explain away the ratios; they had been well atomised by the mathematical David Booth when he was acting as Godwin's henchman. According to Anti-Godwin,

> By 'arithmetical ratio' Malthus must be understood to mean, that in the case of food the increase has nothing to do with any *proportion* at all. It should have been properly speaking, arithmetical *progression*, and geometrical progression; the latter only having anything to do with *ratio*. One addition to a quantity of food does not make you more able to make a second addition. The first addition is no *step to*, no *material of* the second, as in population. This I believe is the substance of what is meant by the two contrasted 'ratios' in Malthus. Perhaps it might have been better, and he might have been less

misunderstood, if he had not founded his doctrine upon these two *ratios* at all.[73]

David Booth, in his pamphlet *Letter to the Rev. T. R. Malthus*, was scathing not only about the ratios, but about their originator's defence of them in the *Edinburgh Review*:

> I simply endeavoured to demonstrate that there was nothing, in the progress of Population and in the means of subsistence, that had, respectively, the most distant connexion with the Geometrical and Arithmetical Ratios which were taught me when I was a boy ... I was vain enough to imagine that I had succeeded in my undertaking, when your Review appeared and dispelled all my dreams of conquest. You there say, that my labour has been 'solemn and absurd trifling;' ... and then ask 'if he had succeeded, of what possible consequence would it be to the general argument?'
>
> ... I must agree with you, in your *New Light*, that these arrangements of figures can be of no possible consequence to the argument ... but I was gulled into the belief that you laid great stress upon their assistance ... You laid the foundation of your system on the oracular assemblage of numbers; but, having now finished the building, you seem willing to throw down the pillars on which it was raised, in the delusive confidence that your castle will remain suspended in the clouds.
>
> Well – the Ratios are abandoned. The Geometrical one has become '*irregular*', and the Arithmetical is forgotten. The necromantic lines,
>
> Population 1, 2, 4, 8, 16, 32, 64, 128, 256,
> Subsistence 1, 2, 3, 4, 5, 6, 7, 8, 9,
>
> will be left out of future editions of your work; and the ignorant, among your disciples, will be spared the trouble of talking about what they do not understand.[74]

Malthus did not in fact omit the ratios from the 1826 edition of the *Essay*, but he did from the article on Population in the *Supplement* to the *Encyclopaedia Britannica*; some two-thirds of this was reprinted separately by Murray in 1830, with the title, *A Summary View of the Principle of Population*. It is just possible that Malthus saw an advance copy of Booth's pamphlet, for in the *Encyclopaedia* article he referred to the revised seventh edition of Dr Price's *Reversionary Payments*; Booth must have been amused.

Because of the nature of the *Encyclopaedia* and the limited space, Malthus's summary of his principle of population is the most concise and well-written of all his works. He began by pointing out that a grain of wheat could sextuple itself every year, and thus wheat could 'cover the whole earthy surface of our globe in fourteen years'; sheep, who double their number every two years, would need less than seventy-six years in which to cover the whole earthy part of the world. He went on to explain that in spite of 'this prodigious *power* of increase in vegetables and animals, their actual increase is extremely slow', owing to the scarcity of fertile land and, from man's point of view, 'the decreasing proportion of produce which must necessarily be obtained from the continual additions of labour and capital applied to land already in cultivation'.*[75]

Malthus then took the United States for his example of the natural unchecked increase of men, similar to the biennial doubling of sheep, and showed that the quarter-century he allowed for the doubling of human numbers was, if anything, a slightly excessive estimate. Here one is extremely conscious of the fact that Malthus had grown up in the eighteenth century: he referred to the United States as 'formerly the North American Colonies of Great Britain'; he had been an intelligent ten-year-old when the Declaration of Independence was signed. He quoted the most up-to-date figures he could get from the American *National Calendar* and *North American Review* for October 1822, as well as lesser-known sources, and for the analysis of some statistics he gave as his authority Joshua Milne (1776-1851), whose *Treatise on the Valuation of Annuities and Assurances*, published in 1815, was the latest actuarial work available. Yet he still quoted Price's *Reversionary Payments*, first published in 1771.† Even more surprisingly, to modern readers, he again used Süssmilch's figures to prove how deaths made way for marriages; this book had first appeared in 1741.

Malthus stuck to his three checks to population of vice, misery, and moral restraint, but was more optimistic about the last than he had been: he thought that there were 'the best reasons for believing that in no other country of the same extent is there to be found so great a proportion of late marriages, or so great a proportion of persons remaining unmarried, as in Great Britain'. He also stuck to his belief that the two chief incentives to hard work were private ownership and the desire of a man to maintain or better his position in society: this sounds less like old-fashioned snobbery if we translate the phrase into 'maintain or improve his standard of living'. Where we feel Malthus is on difficult ground is when he writes:

> On a system of private property no adequate motive to the extension
> of cultivation can exist, unless the returns are sufficient not only to
> pay the wages necessary to keep up the population, which, at the
> least, must include the support of a wife and two or three children,
> but also afford a profit on the capital which has been employed. This
> necessarily excludes from cultivation a considerable portion of land,

*When the article was reprinted in 1830, Malthus struck out the reference to labour in this sentence.
†These passages were omitted in the reprint of 1830.

which might be made to bear corn.

But communal subsistence farming for all would lead to a wretched existence for all:

> And if a system of private property secures mankind from such evils, which it certainly does, in a great degree, by securing to a portion of the society the leisure necessary for the progress of the arts and sciences, it must be allowed that such a check to the increase of cultivation confers on society a most signal benefit.

Yet it was not pure gain. Malthus did not believe in Adam Smith's Invisible Hand, or Jane Marcet's Providence, ordering all things for the best:

> It is not true that the tastes and wants of the effective demanders are always, and necessarily, the most favourable to the progress of national wealth . . . The want of an adequate taste for the consumption of manufactured commodities among the possessors of surplus produce, if not fully compensated by a great desire for attendance, which it never is, would infallibly occasion a premature slackness in the demand for labour and produce, a premature fall of profits, and a premature check to cultivation.
>
> It makes little difference in the actual rate of the increase of population, or the necessary existence of checks to it, whether that state of demand and supply which occasions an insufficiency of wages to the whole of the labouring classes be produced prematurely by a bad structure of society, and an unfavourable distribution of wealth, or necessarily by the comparative exhaustion of the soil. The labourer feels the difficulty nearly in the same degree . . . And as we well know that ample wages, combined with full employment for all who choose to work, are extremely rare, and scarcely ever occur except for a certain time when the knowledge and industry of an old country is applied under favourable circumstances to a new one, it follows, that the pressure arising from the difficulty of procuring subsistence is not to be considered as a remote one, which will be felt only when the earth refuses to produce any more, but as one which not only actually exists at present over the greatest part of the globe, but, with few exceptions, has been almost constantly acting upon all countries of which we have any account.[76]

This passage provides much material for argument but it shows, I think, that Malthus had taken Say's criticism to heart; here he is trying hard to reconcile the author of the *Essay on Population* with the author of the *Principles of Political Economy*.

As regards the Poor Law, both authors were united. For Malthus this was not, fundamentally, a question either of demography or of economics, but of the basic human condition. Since without the institution of private property mankind would be even worse off than they were, it was both wrong and inconsistent to assert that all who might be born had a right to support; no one could have a right to somebody else's property, and therefore no pauper had a right to even the smallest compulsory dole from the rate-payer's purse. On this point Malthus's opponents continued to attack him until his death. Yet it is noticeable that as the years advanced towards the Victorian Age, while the little Princess was quietly doing her lessons, a more temperate and responsible tone became apparent in the controversy. Hazlitt, Coleridge, Cobbett, and some lesser writers, went on in their own old way, but their generation was passing, to be replaced by such men as Nassau Senior, Richard Whately, and William Foster Lloyd, to whom we will refer in the next chapter.

Perhaps Michael Thomas Sadler (1780-1835) may be called the last of the anti-Malthusian writers of the old school. He was a Leeds business-man who entered the House of Commons in 1829, and lived to see the first effective Factory Act, for which he had worked tirelessly. For these exertions he deserves much credit, but otherwise his virtues are lost in his prolixity. Sadler's *Law of Population*, which Murray published in 1830, was declared to be 'overcharged with matter' even by his devoted anonymous biographer: 'More than thirteen hundred closely printed pages, crowded with an hundred-and-four statistical tables, presented a task from which the great majority of readers would naturally shrink back.'[77]

Like other writers of a previous era, Sadler throughout quoted the 1803 quarto in his arguments against Malthus, and his whole style was considered too declamatory, too rhetorical and too poetical by the younger reviewers. His thesis in disproof of the superfecundity of man can be summed up in a sentence: 'The prolificness of human beings, otherwise similarly circum-stanced, varies inversely as their numbers.'[78] Small wonder that Thomas Babington Macaulay (1800-59) leaped on him in the *Edinburgh Review*, twice, for Sadler tried to defend himself in a pamphlet, which gave Macaulay the chance to go for him again.

The Tory *Blackwood's Edinburgh Magazine* supported Sadler, and it is from their issue of July 1830 that the following extracts are taken; they are typical of the spirit of Sadler's work:

> Do we not see, throughout air, earth, and water, the plain intention
> of the Deity to sustain all his creatures? . . . By diversifying the
> instinctive appetites of the different species of larger animals, [nature]
> prevents the monopoly of the means of existence by the ferocious
> and the strong; in the 'refectory of Nature' - so unlike that 'table' at
> which Malthus affirms there are no seats for millions on millions,
> who come there in hunger and in thirst, and certainly *not uninvited* -
> the separate species have all 'their separate seats and their distinct

messes,' which, though perfectly agreeable to themselves, the rest refuse to occupy or touch, and thereby the harmony and plenty which, among such various and unnumbered guests, would otherwise be constantly destroyed, is as perpetually preserved . . .

And then comes Death - and how is it that the whole earth is not sickened as with the stench of a sepulchre? 'Why, nature,' says Mr. Sadler, 'has provided numerous and diversified classes of animal undertakers,' who remove all that would otherwise taint the heavens with pollution . . . These creatures, having not to contend with their prey, are, generally speaking, the smallest and feeblest part of animated beings - but in numbers what to them are the sands of the sea! But that that number, whatever it may be, overbalances its food, would, says our author, be to imagine that, seeing the necessity, and attempting to provide for it, Nature had made so false a calculation, so bungling an attempt, as to increase the nuisance by the very means she has taken to abate it![79]

It is easy to see why there was some feeling that the *Edinburgh Review* had given Sadler's book too much prominence; Malthus called it a 'strange work', and when he asked Macvey Napier if he might print his *Encyclopaedia* article as a separate pamphlet, he wrote that he did not feel inclined to take too much trouble with such an opponent. The idea of a 'short and *cheap* account of the principle of population' had been discussed by Malthus and Murray in 1829, and if Sadler really was the spur to the publication of the *Summary View* in 1830 we have reason to be grateful to him; the original article might very likely have been lost in the bulky volumes of the *Encyclopaedia*.

Sadler's biographer, writing in 1842, took a completely different view: 'The Malthusian theory received its death-wound on the day when Mr. Sadler's work appeared; its dying struggles were decently concealed by the mantle cast over them by its friends; but the whole system has now passed away, and must be reckoned among the things that *were*.' Elsewhere he wrote,

At the moment of the appearance of Mr. Sadler's treatise, in the commencement of 1830, the writer of these lines felt it desirable to compare the two systems together; and not having a very high opinion of Mr. Malthus's work, he sought for a copy at a cheaper rate than the usual price. But the reply was, that it was never to be had even a shade below the publication-price; and that second-hand copies, in sales, brought nearly the first cost when new.

Such was the market-value of the book, in the year 1830. In the year 1835 - only five years afterwards, the publisher sold off the remainder of the edition, issued at 24*s*, - and the price he obtained for them was 5*s*. 9*d*. per copy![80]

One feels sorry for the newly-widowed Harriet, but it is possible that Sadler's biographer drew the wrong conclusion; people may have refrained from buying the two-volume *Essay* because the *Summary View* was both shorter and cheaper.

Old Cobbett certainly did not think that Sadler had settled the matter. His *Two-penny Trash* for the month of June 1831 was *Surplus Population*, a Comedy in Three Acts. The scene is the village of Nestbed, the villain is Sir Gripe Grindum, and he plans to carry off the village beauty, Betsy Birch; the hero who saves Betsy is not her affianced husband, Dick Hazle, but a visiting stranger, 'Peter Thimble, Esquire, a great Anti-Population Philosopher'. This seems inconsistent of Cobbett, but perhaps he found it impossible to be too hard on his fellow-reformer, Francis Place, and he jokes almost affectionately about Thimble's innumerable pamphlets and papers.

When Squire Thimble arrives in Nestbed, expecting to be greeted by Sir Gripe Grindum, he finds to his chagrin that his host has merely left him a letter, which he proceeds to read aloud to the audience:

'My dear Thimble, you know that our great master, Parson Malthus, lays it down that *population always treads closely upon the heels of subsistence*. Acting on this principle, and fully agreeing with you, that the country is ruined by *surplus population*, I deem it a duty to my beloved country, for the happiness and honour of which I have so long been toiling and making so many sacrifices, to suffer no subsistence to be in my house beyond a bare sufficiency to keep body and soul together. I have, therefore, told Farmer Stiles to ... provide you with bed, board, & c. and I will call on you at his house, about breakfast time.'

'Umph!' says the disappointed Thimble. 'Body and soul together! Very laudable, to be sure, to check the population in his house; but I do not very clearly see how *my* being entertained in it for a day or two could have tended to *increase* the population in it.'[81]

There is no evidence as to whether the good-natured and hospitable Malthus family enjoyed this nonsense or found it distasteful.

CHAPTER XII

Declining Sun (1825–34)

1 Family Sorrows

Lucy Malthus died on 23 May 1825, while staying with one of her maternal aunts, Lucy Taunton, at the rectory at Ashley in Hampshire. She was seventeen years old. Like so many young people of her period, she went into what was called a rapid decline: she died painlessly and quickly from tuberculosis, probably after being in bed for about three weeks. Her uncle Robert Cropp Taunton, who had married her parents, buried Lucy on Saturday 28 May. Her grave is near the hedge of the east side of the burial ground of the tiny parish church of Ashley. The church was built during the reign of Henry I, and there seems to have been little restoration after the fifteenth century; the only 'modern' addition is a small red-brick porch which was put up in 1701. In spring the whole miniature rural scene must still be very much as it was on that sad day, with the Hampshire countryside at its most beautiful, the trees in their fresh green, the scent of lilac everywhere.

Lucy's aunt Fanny Eckersall, who as a girl had exchanged verses with Richard Graves, wrote her niece's epitaph; it is still legible on the plain tombstone:

> And doth this little grassy mound
> Hold all that's left of one so dear?
> And shall her place no more be found
> Save in the Earth that moulders here?
>
> No, in affection's memory yet
> Her sweet lov'd image shall not die
> By hearts that never can forget
> Embalm'd in many a secret sigh.
>
> The promise of her youthful years
> Wastes not beneath this lowly sod.
> Immortal fruit the spirit bears;
> The pure in heart shall see their God.

All that we know of Lucy is from the 'Recollections' of her older cousin Louisa Bray: 'She was a very sweet girl, and I loved her very much. She loved me - "My Sweet Lupin" I used to call her, and the sight and smell of that flower is strongly associated with her in my mind.'

At the time of her death, Lucy's father would have been in the throes of end-of-term examinations, in order to have everything ready for Directors' Day on Friday 27 May. His absence from College on this occasion is not recorded in the Minutes, so it is possible that Malthus did not attend his daughter's funeral. The only certain fact is that on Thursday 2 June the diminished Malthus family set off for a tour of the Low Countries and the Rhine (on a route then very popular with the English) which lasted just over two months. We can learn something of Malthus's feelings from a letter which he wrote to George Tennyson on 27 February 1826; Tennyson's wife had died in the summer of 1825.

> My dear Sir,
>
> I had heard of your severe loss which I know you must have felt deeply; but judging of the feelings of others by my own on similar occasions I did not write to condole with you. Since I saw you Mrs. Malthus and I, also, have suffered a most severe loss in one of our daughters, a sweet girl of seventeen. She died in May last of a rapid decline, and it has been a cause of heart-felt grief to us. In the summer we travelled abroad, and I think it was a relief to Mrs. M's spirits.[1]

One cannot tell whether Malthus arranged this foreign tour on the spur of the moment, or whether he decided to carry out plans which had already been made. In either circumstance I think that someone like Jane Austen would have approved the scheme as a sensible one: it enabled him to avoid conventional sympathy without giving offence; it ensured the union and isolation of the family with continually changing objects of interest and entertainment, and a special inducement not to let their sorrow cloud the holiday pleasure of their fellow-travellers in every kind of vessel and public carriage.

Malthus kept a scrappy, sight-seeing tourist's diary, little more than an itinerary with comment, but there are some characteristic notes. As in Scandinavia, he was constantly observing the poor people's dress, how many women and children went bare-foot, and inquiring about the price of wheat and the common labourer's day-wages; between Antwerp and Louvain children ran after the carriage, begging, which had not happened in Holland. Emily perhaps enjoyed the Rhineland, which her father described as 'full of ruined castles, and towns and villages in picturesque situations - the villages all look extremely well at a distance, and the frequency of the old castles give a very peculiar and striking character to the scenery'.[2] After the family returned, one can imagine Malthus and Harriet going about their

duties at the College as cheerfully as they could, for other people's sake, and
Hal went back to Cambridge. Emily was perhaps the most to be pitied. It
is all a matter of guesswork, but it seems likely that Lucy's death accounted
for Malthus's making no public comment on the financial crisis of 1825, and
also perhaps for the scanty revision of the 1826 edition of *Population*. There
is a pathetic little sidelight on this in the Minutes of the Political Economy
Club for 5 December 1825. Two questions of Malthus's were considered
in the usual way:

> 1. What would be the practical effects of measuring Prices, and the
> rate of Profits, on a medium which was subject to frequent and
> considerable variations in its relation to Labour?
> 2. What do we refer to when we say a commodity is steady in its
> Value?

Then, most unusually, the Secretary added:

> Subsequent to the discussion of these questions, a great deal of
> interesting conversation occurred relative to the causes and symptoms
> of the actual state of Mercantile Distress.[3]

The Christmas vacation was probably spent at the old Eckersalls' house
in Bath, 17 Portland Place. For the summer holidays of 1826, a sociable tour
of Scotland, there is another scrappy journal. The scheme was perhaps
undertaken after a warm invitation from Jeffrey, who wrote to Malthus on
6 January 1826:

> It is long, my good friend, since we have met in quiet and comfort;
> for these little glimpses during my fevered runs to London are not
> the thing at all. Will you not bring down Mrs. Malthus, and stay a
> few weeks with us next summer at Craigcrook? I have a great deal of
> leisure after the middle of July, and I am persuaded we could find
> sufficient employment for you, both at home and on our travels. I
> was not at all surprised to learn how severely both you and she had
> suffered from the great affliction which has befallen you. I never
> look at the rosy cheeks and slender form of my own *only* child,
> without an inward shudder at the thought of how much utter
> wretchedness is suspended over me by so slight a cord. You have
> still two such holds on happiness, and may they never be
> loosened . . .
>
> God bless you, my dear Malthus. I have long been accustomed to
> quote you as the very best example I know of a wise and happy man.
> I should be sorry to be obliged to withdraw either epithet, but I
> would much rather part with the first than the last.[4]

The party travelled about too much to stay long at Craigcrook, but Malthus
must have loved the place, half castle and half country house, with rooms

small enough for warmth and social intimacy; not to be compared with Gatcomb or Panshanger, but more suitable for the climate and the company. Malthus met everyone of note, from McCulloch to Sir Walter Scott, but unfortunately he merely lists names in his diary, without any comment. There are the usual jottings on wages, prices and rents, and more evidence of his delight in landscape. He quotes Jeffrey's brother-in-law, Dr Brown, to the effect that 'the introduction of Steam boating had quite altered the habits of the people of Glasgow, and given them strong locomotive propensities. This has been assisted by the Captains not charging for children, which has encouraged parents to take pleasure jaunts with all their family.' But in spite of this apparent prosperity the aftermath of the previous year's crisis was still apparent, and Malthus also noted in Glasgow: 'The crash, and check to credit and confidence, much greater and of longer duration than was ever remembered.'[5]

Early in 1827 Malthus had a new work published, the *Definitions in Political Economy*, which must have given his friends cause for concern. The definitions themselves would have been useful to students, but they occupied only 27 of the book's 261 pages. Almost half of it was taken up with criticism of the ambiguous and contradictory use of certain words by Adam Smith, Say, Ricardo, James Mill and McCulloch. The criticisms became increasingly comprehensive and polemical, and culminated in an attack on McCulloch over the question of general gluts:

> If assertions so contrary to the most glaring facts, and remedies so
> preposterously ridiculous, in a civilized country, are said to be
> dictated by the principles of political economy, it cannot be a matter
> of wonder that many have little faith in them.[6]

The right in this instance was on Malthus's side, but it was unfortunate that he should challenge in such terms so powerful an opponent.

Even more unfortunate for Malthus's reputation was his long and bitter attack on Bailey's *Dissertation on Value*. It is painful to read, for one gets the impression that Malthus is trying to defend the whole political economy of a bygone age, in which he and Ricardo were classified together by Bailey as being alike obsessed by theories of value which were both practically useless and intellectually untenable.

Bailey did not reply, but McCulloch did, in the *Scotsman* for 10 March 1827: he afterwards printed this review of the *Definitions* as a pamphlet. He was cutting about productive and unproductive labour, but Malthus still had the better of him over the 'labour' of the wind which drove the mill and the fermenting process which matured the wine. The following year, in the first edition of his great annotated *Wealth of Nations*, McCulloch in effect yielded to Malthus and attributed the increased value of the fermented wine not to 'labour' but to the 'amount of capital wasted' before the vintner could sell his product.[7] But the review of the *Definitions* was cruel to an ageing man; it ended:

> Perhaps it may seem that we have bestowed more attention on this work than it merited. But the ancient reputation of its author, and the confidence with which he has taken upon himself to decide upon the merits of others, rendered it necessary to look a little narrowly into his qualifications for the office of Dictator in the Economical Republic: And we regret that we have not been able to report more favourably concerning them.[8]

I think that his wife and friends, possibly even Murray himself, deliberately kept this review from Malthus. In any case we find Malthus writing to his publisher on 5 October 1827:

> It is rather strange that the *Definitions* have not been anywhere reviewed, although as far as I can learn, all who have read them have approved, and thought that they would be particularly useful in introducing a greater degree of attention to the language of the science without which there is little hope of any essential progress in it. Had the book been more open to just criticism, it would have been attacked fast enough.

Perhaps only those who have themselves been famous for a quarter of a century can enter fully into Malthus's feelings. After so many years of praise and abuse, after seeing his name become part of the language, he had to learn to endure having his current ideas completely ignored. He must have known that he had had a good innings, and that he would have, posthumously, an irremovable niche in world history: but a man cannot live in either the past or the future, he must live in the present. Harriet may well have been grateful to Wilmot-Horton for giving her husband the idea that he was still a person in public affairs and not merely a 'classic' to be taken for granted in the background.

In common with many other great people, Malthus found it hard to believe that his major work was done, his literary contribution made. The letter to Murray of 5 October 1827, after the fiasco of the *Definitions*, begins with the sentence 'I have called upon you once or twice latterly without success.' It seems to me very likely that a clerk at Number 50 Albermarle Street had been told to say that Mr Murray was not at home to Mr Malthus. The letter goes on:

> I am thinking of a new edition of the Political Economy as it has been long out of print, and I understand often asked for. There will be much new matter relating to Taxation, the Level of the Precious Metals,* and other subjects. And I wished to consult you whether it would be most adviseable to publish these conjointly, or seperately.

*Could this be a revision of the undiscovered tract on Bullion? (See pp. 270-1.)

Somehow his publisher must have headed him off, for the next letter in the archives is dated 18 January 1830, and concerns Malthus's plans for the *Summary View of the Principle of Population.*

Apart from the failure of the *Definitions,* the year 1827 was an anxious one. Hal began to show signs of the tuberculosis which had killed his sister and three of his Bray cousins. He was nearly twenty-three and still an undergraduate at Trinity College, Cambridge, not having matriculated until he was almost twenty. Hal had been entered at Jesus, his father's old college, in January 1822, and the fact that he finally went to Trinity is probably due to the influence and coaching of the Rev. James Tate. Tate was a classical scholar who had made the Grammar School at Richmond, in Yorkshire, the most famous Whig educational establishment in the country; Sir Francis Burdett, Lord Lauderdale and Lord Grey had sent their sons there.[9] According to Fanny Mackintosh, Malthus had decided to send Hal to Richmond after Dr Parr's memorable visit to Mardocks in September 1821; Parr was a devoted admirer of Tate, and hoped he would be made a bishop if ever the Whigs returned to power. So Hal went off in October 1821 to 'read' with Mr Tate, in much the same way as his father had gone off to read with Gilbert Wakefield.

Hal's weak lungs may have accounted for his slow academic progress, but the little information there is suggests that he was amiable and dutiful rather than intelligent. In any case we find Malthus writing to Wilmot-Horton on 8 November 1827 - the day after he had read his second paper to the Royal Society of Literature - 'I have been much engaged lately in preparing matters to enable me to set out with my family for Bordeaux, where we are going to spend the winter, on account of the state of my son's health.' There follow two quarto sheets on Malthus's doubts about a National System of Emigration, and then he concludes, 'I am in the midst of my examinations previous to leaving the College for Bordeaux.'

As far as Hal's health was concerned, the plan was successful. He remained in Bordeaux after his parents and sister had returned to Haileybury, as is shown by a letter which Malthus wrote to Empson, who was in London, on 18 May 1828:

> You will be glad to hear that Hal returned to us yesterday afternoon looking and feeling well, and in some respects perhaps it is the more satisfactory, as I doubt whether he has been particularly cautious either as to diet or exercise. He had some very hot weather before he left Bordeaux and was a good deal on the water sailing. He staid five or six days at Paris on his way back, and crossed from Dieppe to Brighton in a Steam boat on thursday last. We were glad as you may suppose, to get him safe and well back.[10]

What Malthus did not tell anyone was that he had taken Edward Bray to Bordeaux with him, as part of his own family, to save him from being

412

arrested. This tiresome young man, known to later generations as 'wicked Uncle Edward', was thirty-four at the time, nine years older than his cousin Hal Malthus. Nothing would have been known of his uncle's good deed were it not for a shaky note in his grandfather's diary, written when William Bray was ninety-two and summing up the events of the year 1828:

> The folly and boundless extravagance of my grandson Edward so involved him, that notwithstanding the very large debts &c I had paid for him, he cd. no longer stay in Engl. but at the hazard of being arrested, & Mr. Robt Malthus intending to pass a short time in the South of France for his son's health, E.B. was persuaded to go with him, with a view to remain there when Mr. M. returned to Engld. He was to have £200 a year from me. [There is here an almost illegible scribble to the effect that Edward's brother Reginald asked for this to be increased to £250.]
>
> But the same folly and waste continued ... he spent at least £700 in about 8 months, without notice, & without any authority, & when there was no money to pay them, he drew 2 bills of £100 each which of course were refused when they became due. [Something illegible] he wrote to me a letter threatening to destroy himself if they were not pd. & he shd. be sent to a French prison. Of the wickedness of this letter to me at my time of life, and after having paid much more than £3000 for debts which he said amounted to £2600 only, & after having left debts due to honest tradesmen in Engld. of which I had no information, the demand of £200 at such a time affected me more than I can express.
>
> It wd. have been said by many of his acquaintance, my neighbours, that I had caused his death by refusing to pay the paltry sum of £200. They knew not what I had paid, nor could I have made it publicly known, especially as some of the debts [were] contracted in such a manner, that it was impossible for me to relate what I paid out - I paid the £200!

When he came into his inheritance after his grandfather's death, on 21 December 1832, Edward seems to have turned over a new leaf. He became a Justice of the Peace and Deputy Lieutenant for Surrey, dying unmarried in 1866 at the age of seventy-two. Few, if any, of those who attended his funeral would have known of the unhappiness he had caused to his widowed mother and nonagenarian grandfather, still less the additional anxiety he had been to his already deeply troubled Uncle and Aunt Malthus.

In 1829 it was the turn of their old friend Lady Mackintosh to be 'much out of health'. According to her sisters, she suffered greatly from Sir James's increasing loquacity, and in the autumn of 1829 she set out on a visit to the Sismondis with 'some vague notion of never returning'; she died at Chene on 6 May 1830.[11] There is a letter of Fanny's to her cousin Elizabeth

Wedgwood dated simply 'Wednesday evening, Clapham' - where the Mackintoshes then lived - on which someone has pencilled '1829', and which was possibly written in July: in this Fanny reports that

> Mama is gone today for a few days to the Inn at Boxhill with the Malthuses & intends to enjoy the weather and the country if it does not come to rain. She went away in a shower yesterday but as it hardly wetted the ground through, I hope it did not her - The state of the garden is very distressing & watering comes heavy . . .

Was this in the nature of a farewell from Kitty Mackintosh to Malthus? The Inn at Box Hill, on the Daltons' Manor of Thorncroft, was then called the Fox and Hounds and is mentioned by William Bray in his *History of Surrey* (1809): 'Within a few years past, a public-house at the foot of the hill at *Burford Bridge* has been fitted up with some neat rooms, walks are made, and many persons go and spend a week there.'[12] Once again, we must refrain from sentimental conjecture.

That Malthus was beginning to feel his age at this time (he was sixty-three) is shown by a letter which he sent to the Bishop of Lincoln on 7 September 1829:

> My Lord,
> I trust that your Lordship will have the goodness to excuse the liberty I take in submitting to you a question, the determination of which is of some consequence to my future views.
> I have the perpetual Curacy of the augmented free chapel of Okewood in the Parish of Wootton near Dorking in Surrey. There is no parsonage house attached to it, and it is without cure of Souls; but the customary duty is morning and evening service every sunday; it is well attended and there is a sunday school under the care of the Curate of between eighty and ninety boys and girls.
> What I am anxious to know is, whether in the case of my retiring from the East India College, a residence as near the chapel as I could conveniently place myself and family, and doing the duties of it, would either legally exempt me from residence at Walesby; or if not, would induce your Lordship, on the ground stated, to grant me a licence of non-residence in Lincolnshire. I have no immediate thoughts of leaving the College; but the determination of the question which I have taken the liberty of submitting to your Lordship would influence a decision which I may be called upon to make very soon.
> The house and the situation of Walesby would be very inconvenient to my family.

I do not know how the bishop replied. He was John Kaye (1783-1853), a celebrated scholar and strongly opposed to both pluralities and non-residence.

Malthus's Lincolnshire curate, John Cole Younge, lived in what he called Walesby Parsonage, although he also served Stainton and Tealby, the three villages 'adjoining each other and most conveniently situated as at the points of a triangle'. On 6 August 1827 this poor man, 'a widower left with four Children who are now becoming seriously chargeable', wrote to the bishop about his 'uneasiness and apprehension' over his lordship's 'reported inten- tions respecting Clergyman Serving three Churches'. The incumbents of Stainton and Tealby were 'old and infirm', and 'the Rector of this place is also old' - Malthus being then sixty-one - so that Mr Younge had a good case for his pluralism as well as for his anxiety about the future.

As far as the curate of Walesby was concerned, Bishop Kaye tempered his reforming zeal with mercy. Mr Younge retained his three pitiful curacies, with increased stipends, and on Malthus's death succeeded him as rector. Their relationship clearly had its ups and downs, for on 28 January 1829 Mr Younge wrote to the bishop: 'I beg leave to inform you that Mr. Malthus has, by a letter just received, added £10 a year to my Stipend - It is likewise due to him, to state, that the unpleasant tone of our correspondence last year, was occasioned by misconceptions, which, upon an interview, have been explained to mutual satisfaction.'[13]

The years following Lucy's death must have been trying in every way, and Malthus became ill in May 1830. Pakenham Edgeworth, Maria's half- brother, then a student at the College, wrote to his mother on the 26th, just before the term ended:

Mr. Malthus said he would have written to Maria about me but as he is unwell with a very bad cold, I am sorry to say, & has got to go to town to consult his physicians as well as other business, he cannot, & desired his best comps. to her.[14]

Maria did get her letter, however, for Malthus wrote to Wilmot-Horton on 31 May:

Your letter and 4th Series [on Pauperism] found me overwhelmed with examination papers. I have since been to Town for advice, not having been well. Mrs. Malthus has been unwell too; and we are just setting out on a Tour round by Malvern, by way of a change of air . . .

You would very much oblige me by franking the enclosed to Miss Edgeworth . . . I missed sending it by her brother who is a member of our College.

Apparently the Malthuses did not find Malvern congenial, for in his next letter to Wilmot-Horton, dated 9 June 1830 (four foolscap pages of holiday work on emigration), Malthus wrote that they were leaving the place sooner than they expected, and going on to St Catherine's Court, near Bath. This seventeenth-century house was where the Eckersalls lived during the summer from 1821 onwards, after the old house at Claverton had been pulled down. It still stands in all its beauty, and the lane up to it, along the side of a pastoral valley, must be much the same as it was then; here, too, one may worship in a church which Malthus knew, and outside it are the graves of his genial brother-in-law George, and the beloved old nurse who brought up all eleven Eckersall children without losing one of them in their infancy.

Malthus and Harriet would have returned to Haileybury in time for the beginning of the new term in August. Pakenham Edgeworth, writing home to his mother on 8 September 1830, reported that Mr Malthus, 'though he was almost quite well, is now very ill again'. Nothing is said about the nature of the complaint, but on 26 December 1830 we find Malthus writing to Wilmot-Horton from 'St Leonards, Hastings'; he does not mention his health, but this was a well-known resort for invalids and convalescents. It seems likely that Malthus was ailing for some months, possibly as the result of anxiety and overwork, and that his friends were worried about him. His old colleague Dealtry corresponded frequently with Thomas Chalmers in Scotland, and in a letter which Malthus wrote to Chalmers on 6 March 1832 he obviously felt it necessary to write explicitly, perhaps in reply to kind enquiries, 'I have been quite well for some time.'[15]

The government had fallen in November 1830, and Lord Grey became Prime Minister of a country which then seemed - to those who opposed parliamentary reform - to be on the brink of revolution. But the correspondence of the Whig ladies was more concerned with appointments and patronage. Sir James Mackintosh's friends were affronted that he got nothing better than a seat on the Indian Board of Control, while Sir James's own efforts were successfully directed towards obtaining a sinecure post for poor Godwin, which enabled that erstwhile anarchist to end his days in comfort as a pensioner of government. The appointment of the eccentric and radical Henry Brougham as Lord Chancellor gave rise to many exclamation marks, and hints that Grey had chosen this office for him because it was the one in which he could do least harm to the government. More immediately, the thought of Brougham upon the Woolsack was calculated to alarm parsons as well as lawyers, since there were many livings in the Chancellor's gift.

It was over this patronage that bitter accusations were made after Malthus's death. Otter actually wrote in the epitaph in Bath Abbey that Malthus was

RAISED BY NATIVE DIGNITY OF MIND
ABOVE THE MISREPRESENTATIONS OF THE IGNORANT
AND THE NEGLECT OF THE GREAT.

I think that Otter was hard on the great, and so was Empson in the *Edinburgh Review* for January 1837, when he implied that Lord Holland and Lord Lansdowne had both pleaded in vain for preferment in the church for the Foremost Political Economist of the Age.

Brougham wrote Macvey Napier, who then edited the *Edinburgh Review*, two hurt and angry letters. It is impossible to work out now who said what to whom, but I am convinced that Brougham did offer to do what he could and, as he wrote to Napier, 'received, through Whishaw, the warm acknowledgements of Malthus. I think the result was, his refusing something himself, and desiring it might be given to his son. What he got was, I daresay, trifling, as 99 in 100 of the Great Seal livings are: but when he got it, there was much satisfaction expressed by his father.'[16]

There was perhaps even more satisfaction felt by his mother, for Hal's living was the rectory of Poughill in Devonshire, on a healthy little hilltop, and in a county believed not only to have a favourable climate for consumptives but also to be a cheap part of the world in which to live. Hal had been ordained deacon in 1829 and priest in 1830; by the summer of 1831 his parents were visiting him in his own modest but very pretty little parsonage-house. At Poughill, as at St Catherine's, it is possible to feel close to Malthus, for externally the rectory and red sandstone church are still much as they were, and one can listen to the old Prayer Book responses in Devonshire voices and accents similar to those he must have heard. The drive to Poughill, up and down the narrow lanes, through Cheriton Fitzpaine, is in itself a delight, and Malthus came this way for the last summer holidays of his life.

In 1835, after Malthus's death, Hal was given the parish of Effingham, in Surrey. Hal married Sophia Otter in 1836, and his father-in-law, by then Bishop Otter of Chichester, gave him Donnington, in Sussex, in 1837. The Henry Malthuses lived at Effingham until Hal died in 1882, at the age of seventy-eight: his parents' care of him had not been in vain.

2 *Floreat Haileyburia*

I must confess that I found the archives of the East India College far less exciting after it had been generally accepted as part of the Company's establishment. One has a sneaking idea that Charles James Fox would have thought the new civil servants rather tame and spiritless; term after term, on Di-Day, the Chairman reported 'an almost entire absence of contumacious or puerile disorder', and 'a gratifying promise of future excellence ... no cases of misconduct had occurred to call for the exercise of extreme Severity', and so on. It is almost a relief to read in the Minutes for 12 September 1827 that the bars of the windows were to be examined, having 'been found in a recent Case (even when not loose or broken) to afford room enough for ingress or egress to Persons of small size'.[17]

More positively, the students were exhorted 'to cultivate those honourable feelings which could alone secure for them the enviable distinction of English Gentlemen'[18] - a little hard on the Scots to whom the Company owed so much. The approach of a new era is also apparent in the subjects of the prize English essays. Ancient history was not neglected, the winner in 1832 being Robert Sewell, with a 'Comparative Estimate of the Character, Views and Conquests of Alexander the Great and Tamerlaine', but in 1830 Francis Maltby had read a paper on 'The Application of Steam to Machinery, considered in reference to the probable effects on the internal condition and relative Power of Nations'.[19]

The boys still had four-poster beds with curtains, and one of Lewton's last struggles with the Committee in May 1828 (he died in 1830) was to persuade them to provide eight dozen pairs of new bed-curtains, 'the present curtains having been in use from the establishment of the College at Haileybury'.[20] The students remained behind their curtains while men-servants brought their bath-water, and female bed-makers, in winter, lit their fires; one, Mrs Draper, boasted that she could get her twelve fires going in twenty minutes. She was a motherly and religious spinster, and listened to hear the bath-water splashing, to make sure her young gentlemen would not be late for Chapel; the irreverent were pressed into piety, and saved from an imposition, with the aid of a hot cup of coffee.[21]

In 1824 the East India Company anticipated the Catholic Emancipation Bill by five years. On 19 May 1824 a Joint Committee of Correspondence and College agreed that Roman Catholics need not attend Chapel, but must have certificates of attendance at Mass from 'the Roman Catholic Minister in the neighbourhood of the College'.[22] Tolerance did not extend to colour: John Hankey Smith was rejected as a student on 23 July 1823 at a secret meeting of the Committee of College, who gave no reason for their decision. His father fought for his son's admission - he had educated him, his third boy, exclusively for the Company's service - but the Committee were adamant. John's mother was Armenian, and although there was no doubt as to his legitimacy he was finally refused admission on 7 June 1826, 'upon the ground of his complexion being dark'.[23]

On the other hand 'the learned Persian' whom Sir Gore Ouseley considered would be an acquisition for the College was appointed on 19 July 1826, and became an important member of the staff; he was treated as an equal by his colleagues and regarded with awe by the students.[24]

Changes among the professors and their assistants in his later years do not seem to have impinged upon Malthus, and I know nothing of the Captain James Michael who took over Stewart's half of Hailey House when the Major retired. Yet there was no question of Malthus withdrawing from the daily ritual of community life. According to Empson,

At the time that he was celebrated all over Europe, he continued, at an advanced age, to discharge with exemplary punctuality the most minute routine duties of the College at Haylebury [*sic*], of which he was so great an ornament. He presumed on nothing from his reputation; he sought to be excused from nothing on account of his standing and his years.

Did the younger staff sometimes wish that 'poor dear Malthus', as his successor called him, would retire into the background and let them get on with the job? According to Empson, they did not: Malthus's

discretion and urbanity, his authority and attraction, made him the most enviable colleague that the members of a public body could ever wish to act with; and his union of the severe and gentle virtues was so rare and so complete, that he was equally the object of their admiration and their love.[25]

The students' point of view was naturally a little different; but Charles Merivale's letter to his father after a week at Haileybury, which he had entered from Harrow, shows how the young men were welcomed. It is dated 3 February 1825:

I saw Empson here last Thursday and he asked me to breakfast with him tomorrow, to meet one or two of the senior term, to whom he wishes to introduce me. I don't know whether I told you that I had been asked to Dr. Batten's one evening; I met Malthus there, who is an exceedingly pleasant man, and I had a long conversation with him.

A year later, on 5 February 1826, Merivale reported his views on political economy, 'after a fortnight's attention to the study':

I have attended Mr. Malthus's lectures two or three times already. The science seems lamentably undefined, and of a nature which can never admit of any unobjectionable arrangement. It does not appear, as might be expected in so new a branch of knowledge, to go on with a progressive improvement . . .[26]

Charles Merivale (1808-93) did not go to India, and his Writership was passed on to a gangling youth who loathed the thought of serving as a civilian instead of a soldier, but who in due course became famous as Lord Lawrence. Merivale went to Cambridge, entered the church, and was later well known as a mildly reforming Dean of Ely and a writer on Roman history. Towards the end of his life he set down some autobiographical fragments which were edited by his daughter, in which he gives another picture of Malthus:

Very famous he was in those days, and his fame will never be altogether forgotten, though his book will, for his Essay on

Population, in which he inflicts such dire discouragement upon young men and maidens who marry or are intending to marry. We called him Pop; not in derision, for we had a great but rather distant respect for him. Though his theories were so cruel, his heart and manners were most kindly and courteous. His lectures indeed were very dry. They consisted in reading a bare syllabus of facts and arguments without illustration of any sort; and this syllabus the students took down from his lips and got up for examination.[27]

An equally dry picture of Malthus as a lecturer can be put together from a copy of the *Wealth of Nations*, printed in double columns and interleaved with blank pages for students' notes, which belonged to Jonathan Duncan Inverarity. He was at Haileybury from 1828 to 1830, and served in India until 1865; sometime before he died in 1882 he gave this book to Mary Paley Marshall, and it is now in the Marshall Library at Cambridge.

This volume shows that Malthus delivered a course of lectures in the form of a commentary on Adam Smith, with thirty sets of questions. These were obviously dictated to the students, who wrote them down on the blank sheets opposite to the pages on which they would find the answers: thus Question 9 of the 13th Set was 'For what express purpose was a new Bank established in Scotland & what was the result?' Inverarity duly wrote '9' alongside a paragraph of Smith's which began, 'In the midst of this clamour and distress, a new bank was established in Scotland, for the express purpose of relieving the distress of the country. The design was generous, but the execution was imprudent . . . '[28] It cannot have been either a methodical or an inspiring way of learning economics.

In justice to Malthus, however, he did give his pupils some modern illustrations:

> The Duke of Wellington [in the Peninsular War] wanted specie to pay what could only be paid in specie, such as muleteers.

There is also an echo of Malthus's first conflict with Ricardo in the note:

> It is very desirable to have the precious metals when any country does not require your commodities in exchange for its own.

And in another note Inverarity writes neatly:

> Ricardo thinks a fall of profits can take place only from the cultivation of poor land & denies the possibility of a general glut.[29]

With regard to the natural price and natural value of a commodity the student noted:

> Malthus prefers the word 'necessary' to natural – The price necessary in the actual circumstances of the society to bring the commodity regularly to market.

The natural value expresses the facility or difficulty of producing the article, which is measured by the quantity of labour it will command.[30]

As for population, Malthus used China as an example to convey his principal message:

The effects of the encouragement of marriage on the poor is to keep the reward of labour as low as possible and consequently to press them down to the most abject state of poverty.

Rather surprisingly we find:

Note - Malthus has no doubt but the now general introduction of potatoes has caused the rapid increase of population not only in England but in all Europe.

It is in this connection that Malthus's impediment in his speech seems to have led to a mistake. After noting the familiar thesis that cheap food means low wages, and that potato-eaters have no cheaper resource should the crop fail, Inverarity wrote that he styled a *Shrewd Remark*: 'They must eat the bark of trees like the Swiss in times of scarcity.'[31] Malthus must have meant 'the Swedes': it is possible that he made a slip of the tongue, or that Inverarity was not concentrating, but the error suggests that Malthus's utterance was sometimes indistinct. The late Mr Robert Malthus thought he remembered a story about the students mimicking Old Pop's diction, 'boys being what they are'.

Michael Pakenham Edgeworth (1812-81) was at the College at the same time as Inverarity, but he could not criticise Malthus in his letters home, as the professor was one of Maria's friends. Pakenham gives us the sort of information that is not found in Victorian memoirs: the well-liked Mr Walter, for instance, was known as Bobby, whereas poor Lewton was Dully. Mrs Edgeworth must have objected to 'Pop', for in his second letter to her from Haileybury, dated 1 March 1829, her son wrote: 'Malthus is called Pop because of the old story of somebody addressing him as - The pop/ular author of a pop/ular essay on pop/ulation. - But my dear Mother there is nothing vulgar in a few innocent nick names.' It was Pakenham who was innocent: 'pop' was short for 'pop-lolly', meaning a kept woman, and the appellation stuck, even when a 'brazen-faced Pop' became Countess of Darlington, as we may learn from Creevey.[32]

On this same 1 March Pakenham also wrote to his sister Lucy, with much about his pleasure in the country round the College, where he took long walks; his major interest all his life was botany, and a number of Himalayan plants are named after him. The letter ends, 'Believe me to be, with every wish that you may not marry a Haileybury professor, Your affectionate brother . . .' To his famous half-sister Maria, to whom he also wrote on that March Sunday (it must have been wet) Pakenham gave a sharp critique of one of his teachers:

> ... Mr. Malthus, well I saw him and talked to his wife and heard her jokingly attacking Le Bas (the Dean) who is a deaf, disagreeable, violent, noisy, anti-catholic man – who talks miraculous nonsense to the students when he is scolding them, talking about sins of the blackest die, & the horrible iniquity of not capping a professor, or breaking a window &c or lithobolizing (*anglice* throwing stones) &c.

It is to be hoped that Maria did not take him too seriously, for Charles Merivale remembered Le Bas as being 'considered the cleverest of all. His mathematics were a sealed book to me; but his talk was genial and his sermons were noted among the most eloquent of their day.'

Pakenham Edgeworth thought that Dr Batten, Lewton and Walter were also 'more or less Anticatholic – but you know that Malthus is not so'. A year later, in his third term, he paid an indirect tribute to Harriet as a hostess, in a jumbled letter to his mother dated 23 April 1830: 'I had after my arrival here two very nice dances one at Malthus on Wednesday the other at Dr. Battens on Friday – I counted 40 bells on one cowslip the other day – At Malthus's I danced every dance – at Principal's all but 2.' In justice to Pakenham it should be recorded that he also worked hard, and came away loaded with medals and prizes.

It is possible that neither the Edgeworth ladies nor Pakenham himself realised that the College Council were having a difficult time. Haileybury could not accommodate more than about a hundred students, which meant that at the most only fifty young men could be sent out to India each year; in 1823 this number was found insufficient to keep pace with the high death-rate and the expansion and consolidation of the Company's rule. The gap could only partially be filled by the recruitment of native and half-caste Uncovenanted Writers, and in the Presidency of Bengal it seemed that the whole administration would collapse unless two hundred more Writers could be sent from England immediately.

As the crisis was believed to be temporary, it was decided not to enlarge the East India College, but to obtain an Act of Parliament to allow Writers to proceed to India without the statutory four terms at Haileybury. The young men were required to be eighteen years old and to pass a qualifying test set by the London Board of Examiners: this consisted of four reverend gentlemen, two from Oxford and two from Cambridge. Originally the scheme was for three years, 1826-9, but it was continued for another three, and the London Board held their final examination in March 1832.[33]

The first effect of the new regulations on the College was the premature removal of many of 'its most distinguished young men, as soon as they shall have attained the age of eighteen', and an influx of youngsters. In 1829, the year Malthus was contemplating retirement, there was a peak entry of seventy-four new students. Yet the College was in such good order that the Directors could report in December 1829 that their conduct was 'remarkable for manly correctness of demeanour'. Thereafter, Haileybury's numbers fell dramatically, and the London Oriental Institution flourished. The proprietor, Thomas Wood, complained bitterly when the emergency scheme came to an end; in anticipation of a final victory for the anti-college party he had extended his premises to take boarders, and many parents had clearly found this arrangement more satisfactory than Haileybury.[34]

As far as the College was concerned, the temporary drop in numbers meant that for a time the average *per capita* cost was extremely high. The domestic staff was reduced, and in 1832 we find that seven servants were looking after twelve professors (who also had their own establishments) and thirty-four students. The old Purveyor, Matthew Campbell, protested that he was losing between £70 and £80 a term; as a contractor, he had to keep the same servants as when there were ninety students - a baker, a gardener, a cow-man and a dairy-woman.[35] Campbell died in January 1834, and was succeeded by James Coleman. This famous and well-loved character was originally one of the Malthuses' servants, and married their cook; he was toasted and cheered after 'The Professors' at a sentimental Haileybury dinner held at the Town Hall in Calcutta on 23 January 1864.[36] There seems to be no end to the list of all that Malthus did for the East India College.

The small number of students in 1832 may have meant more work for the professors. They had less written material to correct, but the same lectures to give, and possibly felt that they had to devote more attention to the young men's social life, to make up for what they were missing in the way of companionship and games, clubs and societies. Certainly these sparse years produced some remarkable men, and also gave rise to the belief that Haileybury generally only had about thirty students, an error promulgated by John Martineau in his *Life* of Sir Bartle Frere. But Martineau had plenty of evidence that the 'distinguished staff of professors' were 'on friendly and intimate terms with the students, and moreover often gathered together men and women of distinction and culture, whom the latter had the privilege of meeting at their houses'.[37] Sir Monier Monier-Williams, who became a student in 1839, wrote of Malthus that 'The tradition of his great amiability and charm of character, and of Mrs. Malthus' delightful evening parties, at which the élite of the London scientific world were often present, lingered among us at Haileybury as long as the College lasted.'[38]

3 The Old Celebrity

The reminiscences of Anna Letitia Le Breton give us a young girl's view of the ageing Malthus in London; she met him at a pretty house in Church Row, Hampstead, where she stayed with her literary aunt Lucy Aikin. When she was herself an old lady, Mrs Le Breton wrote that 'Mr. Malthus, when I knew him, was a polite, handsome, kind old man, tall and slender, with dark eyes.' Smyth and Whishaw were also visitors. Smyth 'had a fine animated countenance, and had a look, sometimes a few words, for my sister and me, at my aunt's tea-table, while Mr. Whishaw took no more notice of us than of the chairs.' Elsewhere she wrote that 'Mr. Whishaw was a short, stout man, with a cork leg, very lame, and with rather a surly manner.'[39]

They must have been a strange trio, Smyth in his eighteenth-century knee-breeches, and Malthus with his snuffly voice, yet they were much blessed in their friendship. Empson wrote of Malthus: 'By a happy use of them, he made every day the best kind of holiday. But in later years, the days which he seemed to set apart particularly to enjoy as such, were the periodical visits of Mr. Whishaw and Mr. Smyth, two of the oldest of his friends.'[40]

There is no doubt that Malthus began to feel and look like an elderly gentleman sooner than one would expect nowadays, in spite of remaining tall and slender. A letter to Wilmot-Horton of 17 August 1830, when Malthus was sixty-four, shows a state of affairs which one associates today with somebody of a rather more advanced age:

> In the first place, I wish to know how I am to send your papers back, and where I am to direct them. Secondly, I wish to say that either I never have had, or have completely mislaid, the Society's pamphlet to which you allude; and further, that I am unable to answer your second query, as I don't in the least recollect the name of Dr. McVicar ... This I have no doubt is the fault of my memory, which was always very bad and is now getting much worse, so you must excuse my requesting your assistance ...

The letter is written and signed; then,

> I have just found the pamphlet of the National Colonization Society which had strayed from the usual haunts of such productions. I suppose your Third Series, which I cannot now find, has escaped in the same way. I hope I shall have the same good fortune in recovering.
> P.S. Eureka [in Greek]. I have found the 3rd Series.

Apart from increased forgetfulness and muddled papers, Malthus showed few, if any, of the less amiable characteristics of old age; remarks on his good temper and happy demeanour are too common to be attributed to the stereotyped praise of a dead celebrity. He appears always to have worried a little about his financial position, but there is no trace of the suspiciousness which keeps some elderly people in a perpetual state of disagreeable apprehension lest they be burgled or cheated. From the Bray letter-books, it would seem that Malthus inherited some money invested in a mortgage on land in Worcestershire, and he certainly had some laid out in this way with his Lincolnshire solicitor George Tennyson. He wrote to him about it on 27 February 1826, when the country was in what would now be called a recession, following the commercial crisis of the previous year. In this situation Malthus agreed with John Stuart Mill: there was no advantage to be gained from lending money to a farmer or merchant at 5 per cent, with the risk of losing it all by his insolvency, when £100 of Government Consolidated Stock (which yielded 3 per cent) could be bought for £75 from holders desperate for ready cash.

> With regard to the mortgage [wrote Malthus to Mr Tennyson], I have only to say, that if it is particularly inconvenient to you to pay it at present, as you proposed, I would on no account insist upon it. At the same time you cannot but be aware, that with a view to laying out the money again, the delay will in all probability be as great a loss to me, as the paying it immediately could be to you, and that you are very much the richer man. When I first understood that you wished to pay off the mortgage, I mentioned, that it would be more convenient to me that it should not be discharged before the expiration of a half-year, the legal time of notice; but understanding it would be particularly convenient to you to pay it immediately, I consented to receive it then. You did not however pay it then, but proposed another period. It so happened that at that period it would have been particularly convenient to me to receive it, on account of the fall of the stocks; but for the same reason I conclude that it was inconvenient to your friend to repay your money; and I fear that the same state of things is likely to continue, that is that it will not be convenient for your friend to repay the money till the stocks rise, and I shall suffer a great loss of interest in laying the money out again. It is generally thought that things will recover themselves and the stocks be up, in May.
>
> Having said this much I leave the matter entirely to you, only reminding you that I am a poor man and you are a rich one. At all events I shall be obliged to you to pay up the interest at present of which there was half a year due on the third of Feby last. I happen to want it just now.

425

There is no evidence to show why Malthus wanted the money especially, but he got it. His next letter to George Tennyson is dated 16 March 1826:

My dear Sir,

I am utterly ashamed to think that I should have omitted to acknowledge the receipt of your draft for £43. 13. 6, which arrived quite safe. It somehow or other went out of my head in a way that I cannot account for, except that I left home the next day, which may have contributed to my forgetfulness. I really beg your pardon.

I am much obliged to your for the payment of the mortgage money, and sincerely hope that it is not inconvenient to you. I signed the Deed late last night, and sent it [to] Town by the Coach this morning. I should have answered your letter by last nights post, but was prevented by an unforseen [sic] interruption.

I hope you are well in health and free of the gout. I look forward to a chance of meeting you before the end of the summer. Mrs. Malthus is pretty well and sends kind regards.[41]

There might, one feels, have been justifiable rude comment from one of the George Tennyson's clerks; he had presumably been put to the trouble of writing a letter of inquiry concerning the whereabouts of the unacknowledged documents.

Malthus's repeated assurance that he is a poorer man than his attorney jars somewhat, but he may frequently have suffered embarrassment and annoyance from the widespread delusion that all famous people must inevitably be rich. It is impossible to find out how much money Malthus had, for in his brief will he simply left everything he possessed to his wife; it was dated 3 September 1824, and Harriet herself, and Augustus Warren, were the executors. On 24 May 1828 'Henry Malthus being now of age' was also made an executor. Malthus signed the document, but did not have it witnessed, an omission which he must have known (but had probably forgotten) had caused inconvenience after previous deaths in the family. In the event, Reginal Bray and William Empson swore to his handwriting on 9 February 1835, and the will was proved on the 12th.[42]

This will, I think, shows not only devotion to Harriet, but also faith in her good sense and competence. It is likely that she did more behind the scenes than was apparent to either Fanny Mackintosh or the Edgeworth ladies, and she seems to have been instrumental in making the arrangements for John Linnell to come to Haileybury. Linnell (1792-1882) was primarily a landscape painter, but to support his family he needed commissions for portraits, many of which he engraved himself. In 1832 he had painted William Bray shortly before his death, and his journals show that he was working on the engraving in January 1833. In February he 'began a second portrait of Lord King (the first not being quite satisfactory) in a different position and dress'. On 8 February he received a note dated simply 'E. I.

College Wednesday evening':

> Mrs. Malthus's compt[s] to Mr. Linnell and is very anxious to know if
> he is now at leisure to take Mr. Malthus's picture - and if he is so
> they will be happy to see him at the E. I. College near Hertford -
> any time after Monday next - Mr. Malthus is now in Town and will
> be obliged to Mr. Linnell to send his answer to him at A. Warren
> Esq - No 8 Charlotte St. Bloomsbury.

Linnell went to the College by the afternoon coach on 14 February, and
noted in his journal for the 15th: 'Began Mr. Malthus on panel 15 × 12. Mr.
Le Bas, Dr. Batten, Mr. Keen &c &c at Evening Party.' On the 16th he not
only proceeded with Malthus but started on a small sketch of Keene before
leaving for London. He was back again on the 20th, when he went on with
the portraits of Malthus and Keene, began what he called 'small pictures'
of Miss Malthus and Mrs Keene's mother, and also made a sketch for a
picture of Dr Batten before leaving again on the 23rd. In March he stayed
longer, and added Mrs Batten to his sitters; he noted on the 12th that he
'Began a Miniature on Ivory for Miss Malthus gratis of Miss Priscilla
Batten.' It was not all work, for the Battens asked him to an evening party,
and on the 15th he 'Dined in Hall'.

   The portrait of Mrs Malthus, a companion picture to that of her husband,
was begun on 13 March 1833. She is painted as if she were out of doors on
a cold day in summer, wearing a matronly bonnet and cloak, and standing
by one of the famous Haileybury oak-trees: this is in complete contrast to
the portraits of her husband and daughter, who are both indoors and sitting
down. There is nothing to show whether this open-air setting was Linnell's
choice or Harriet's, or even Malthus's. But it is clear from the affectionate
way he painted her that artist and sitter got on well together; there is also
the evidence of a letter which Harriet wrote to Linnell about the description
of Malthus for the Royal Academy Catalogue. It is dated 'Tuesday', but the
postmark is 27 March 1833:

> Dear Sir,
>   Mr. Malthus thinks the best way of filling up the prospectus will
> be - The Revd. T. R. Malthus M.A. F.R.S. Professor of History &
> Political Economy at the East India College - & Author of an Essay
> on the principle of Population &c: &c - the above is quite sufficient
> he says and as much as there would be room for.

This shows plainly how Malthus himself wished to be known and remembered. The letter concluded:

> I hope the originals of all the little golden haired children are well -
> and believe me to remain

> > Yours very sincerely
> > Harriet Malthus.

Two of the golden-haired children, John and James, accompained their father to the Royal Academy on 9 April, with seven portraits, including those of Malthus, Dr Batten and William Bray; the picture of Mrs Malthus was not finished until July.[43]

We know of Harriet's writing to Linnell on Malthus's behalf because he and his descendants were - and are - admirable keepers of records; but there must have been many other occasions when 'Mrs. M' made arrangements for her husband, and no doubt reminded him to reply to letters which only he could answer. She may have found this difficult, and not only because Malthus was busy and preoccupied: his modesty perhaps prevented him from understanding how much his notice, his advice or his opinion were valued by the strangers who applied to him. They wrote to him because they thought him a great man, and then felt slighted by his neglect of their unsolicited communications, or by his delay in answering them. As we have seen, Malthus probably offended McCulloch deeply through not acknow-ledging his pamphlet, and he also hurt the feelings of another Scot through inattention of a different kind.

This was the Rev. Thomas Chalmers, DD, DCL (1780-1847), a strange character of whom it would be interesting to have a modern biography. We will refer to his views on the Poor Law in a later section; they were even more extreme than those of Townsend and Malthus, for Chalmers had no objection to begging and held rigidly to the old Scots system of voluntary parochial charity for education as well as for poor relief. From 1803 until 1815 he was minister at Kilmeny, in Fife; he published a book on political economy in 1808, called *The Extent and Stability of National Resources*, which was scarcely noticed, but his fame as a popular Evangelical preacher grew rapidly, especially after he became minister of the Tron Church in Glasgow; in 1817 he preached to distinguished congregations in London. Outwardly he appeared an extremely successful man, but inwardly he must have felt a desperate need for some extraneous support other than that of his religion. This led to his binding in large volumes every scrap of correspond-ence he received, including the most trivial notes and invitation cards, amounting to about 14,000 documents in all.[44]

The first letter from Malthus in this collection is dated 23 August 1821, and contains belated thanks for a copy of Chalmers' *Christian and Civic Economy of Large Towns*. The second is almost a year later, written on 21 July 1822 from Hollin Hall. In this Malthus acknowledges another 'kind and valuable present' - more *Christian and Civic Economy* - and regrets that his family were unable to extend their northern tour from Yorkshire to Scotland. What was apparently their first meeting took place at the end of September 1822, when Dr Chalmers stayed at Haileybury in the course of an excursion to England. Malthus's former colleague the Rev. William Dealtry seems to have effected the social introduction, for we find Malthus writing to Chalmers:

We shall be at home and delighted to see you on Thursday. I know you will excuse the having your bed at Dr. Battens who will be happy to furnish that accommodation. It so happens that our two spare beds are occupied, as I told Mr. Dealtry they would be, by two invalid sisters whom I cannot remove. We dine at six o'clock and hope to see you to dinner.

Chalmers duly reported home that he had been 'very kindly and welcomely entertained', but in spite of 'much kindred and substantial converse with Mr. Malthus', his chief concern seems to have been that he missed meeting Sir James Mackintosh.[45]

In 1825 Chalmers became Professor of Moral Philosophy at St Andrews, with a course of lectures on political economy as one of his duties. This stirred a latent ambition, as is shown by the following extracts from his journal for that year:

Saturday 30 July 1825. My wish is, to deliver myself in a complete way of my political economy, and then to give all my strength to theology. O my God, let me seek first thy kingdom and thy righteousness; let not my order of study be a reversal of this holy commandment of my Saviour.

Thursday 4 August. O let the very circumstance of my being engaged with political economy make me the more watchful against the encroachments of earthliness.

Saturday 6 August: The difficulties of Ricardo engross me too much; and while I still feel called upon to prosecute political economy, I must beware of suffering it to be a thorn.[46]

Malthus kept no such journal, and the diary of his Scots tour, as we remarked, is little more than a list of places visited and people met. Thus for Thursday 29 June 1826 he notes simply: 'Breakfasted at St Andrews with Dr. Jackson. Dr. Chalmers. Cathedral. Square Tower. Dinner. Mrs. Douglas and sister.'[47]

Dr Jackson was in the habit of asking Dr Chalmers to 'do him the particular favour' of taking nine o'clock breakfast at his house, to meet distinguished travellers; but for Chalmers this was a mortifying occasion, since he was hurt that Malthus had not written to him, and perhaps suggested staying overnight. The entry for this same June day in Chalmers's journal contains the following passage:

An invitation from Dr. Jackson to breakfast with Professor Malthus. He came with the Bruces of Grangemuir, under whose guidance he was ... He made explanations to me about his not knowing that I was in St Andrews at present. This was so far well; but considering that I was his correspondent, and had been his visitor, I was not altogether pleased. The tone of our intercourse was altogether frank, natural, and easy. Yet I have to record a dependence upon man, and upon man's regard, which gives me still more convincing views of my spiritual destitution than before.[48]

There were other entries to the same effect on subsequent days. But Chalmers's reaction to the knowledge that Malthus did not much care about him was extremely generous: he gave him his own beautifully bound copy of *National Resources*, as well as the third volume of *Christian and Civic Economy*. This pathetic little book, *National Resources*, which meant so much to the giver and so little to the recipient, is now in Jesus College Library: it is inscribed, 'To Professor Malthus with the Author's best regards. St Andrews, June 29th 1826.'

Malthus responded by ordering for Chalmers a copy of his *Definitions*, and wrote saying that he had done so on 18 January 1827; there is a stiffness about his early letters to Chalmers, in spite of the fact that he is addressing a younger man:

> My dear Sir,
> I should certainly have written to you before on the subject of the two valuable presents which you were so kind as to make me, when I had the pleasure of meeting you at St Andrews last Summer, if I had not been projecting a little work which I thought would explain to you more fully than I could do it in a letter the points on which I could not help still differing from you. I have taken the liberty of sending you my publication through some correspondent of Murray in Scotland. I hope it will reach you safe and I shall be happy to hear that any part of it has met with your approbation.
> I have read with much pleasure and instruction the two works which you gave me. It is needless to say how much I agree with you on the subject of population, and how much I feel indebted to you for your most able and enlightened assistance on that question so vital to the happiness of the labouring classes of society. I feel indeed that what you have done on the subject is peculiarly and preeminently important as coming from a person with your known religious opinions; because from a strange misapprehension of the question some religious people have been strongly prejudiced against the doctrine of population.
> ... As a general question do you not rather understate the difficulty of giving effective employment to the labouring classes? Does it not appear, particularly in the Emigration Report, that a country may have the means of supporting a larger population than it can advantageously employ? Our labourers are sometimes thrown out of work at the very time that corn is cheapest. Excuse this crowded scrawl. Mrs. M joins me in kind regards to you and Mrs. Chalmers.

On the cover there is a sideways scribble: 'When shall we see you in this part of the world? I hope you will not fail to call upon us and stay awhile.'

Whether or not he was hurt by an invitation that was so obviously an afterthought, Chalmers sent Malthus a copy of his main work on political economy in the same exquisite binding as *National Resources*; it was inscribed 'with the author's profoundest admiration and esteem'. The book was entitled *On Political Economy in connexion with the Moral State and Moral Prospects of Society*; two editions were published, but it was never highly regarded by economists. One quotation will give the tenor of the whole:

> The noisy clamour of beggars on the street does not tell more significantly of an excess of population than the signs of unoccupied houses, and the flaming advertisements of commodities at prime cost, and the incessant cheapening of articles to the bankcruptcy and ruin of their owners, tell by another sort of calculation of the excess of capital. Between the two elements, in fact, there is a marvellous and multiplied accordancy. Both are subject to incessant checks from the want, each of its own proper aliment; the one from an insufficient wage, the other from an insufficient profit.[49]

Malthus agreed with this point of view; in his letter to Chalmers of January 1827 he had referred to 'the striking resemblance which exists between the laws which govern the progress of capital, and those which govern the progress of population, and ... the power of capital like the power of population to recover its losses'.

As happened so regrettably often, Malthus did not see fit to send Chalmers an interim acknowledgment of this major work before he could find the leisure to read it. Thus his letter to the unhappy author, dated 6 March 1832, began with the familiar excuses:

> I have just received your kind letter, and feel ashamed that I have let a longer time, than I intended, elapse without acknowledging your very valuable present. But I did not like to write to you till I had read your work with attention, and I have lately been a good deal interrupted - indeed I am only just returned from London at present, where I have been for some little time in the midst of too many engagements to allow me to sit down comfortably with pen and paper. I had however just finished your work before I was called away and prevented from then expressing to you with what great interest and gratification I had read it. It gave me very particular pleasure to find that you agreed with me in so many important points, and had illustrated and enforced them with your characteristic power...
>
> On a few [points] only I am compelled to differ from you. You know my views respecting the definitions of wealth and of

431

productive and unproductive labour. The term unproductive is unfortunate, and I am going to change it for *personal services*; but that some distinction is necessary between these two different means of benefitting society, I feel strongly persuaded. To use an expression of your own, 'It is for the sake of defining, not of stigmatising' that the distinction is required. I consider the services of Judges, Physicians and moral and religious instructors as vastly more important than any but the labours of agriculture and that it is paying morals a very bad compliment to put them in the same category with cottons, and estimate their value by the money which has been given for them. We have always been told, and most properly, to prefer virtue to wealth; but if morals be wealth what a confusion is at once introduced into all the language of moral and religious instruction. Besides I am strongly of opinion that the proper balance between production and consumption in regard to the progress of *wealth* (in its ordinary acceptation) depends greatly upon the proper proportion between productive labour and personal services, and if so, different terms are absolutely necessary to express such a proposition.

This is very similar to what Malthus had written to Chalmers just over five years before; but we would be wrong to dismiss him, at sixty-six, as an elderly gentleman who could only repeat his former literary and conversational gambits.

The letter to Chalmers of 6 March 1832 continues:

With respect to the doctrine of the Economists on the incidence of all taxes upon the neat rents of the Landlords, which you seem to have adopted, I should agree with you, if the taxes were direct taxes upon wages and profits all the way through, which would raise both proportionally, and leave less for the owner of the soil; but I am inclined to think that the principal operation of indirect taxation, when well applied, is to take a portion of wealth from the *individuals* in the different classes who can spare it, without altering the general wages of labour or the general profits of stock, and without therefore falling upon the landlord. A great part of the taxes derived from the excise and customs appear to me to be of this kind, and to fall *en dernier resort* upon the individual consumers. As you propose to raise the taxes required for a war within the year, would it be possible to obtain an adequate supply from this source alone? I am decidedly of opinion however that a property tax is a very good tax and might be substituted advantageously for many others.

Malthus's Whig friends would have been appalled by this last sentence. The property tax corresponded to the modern income tax: it had first been introduced by William Pitt in 1799 as a temporary war-time measure. It was duly abolished during the Peace of Amiens, and abolished permanently (as was hoped) in 1816, largely owing to the pressure of the Whigs in the Opposition; Malthus had been dead for seven years when Sir Robert Peel revived this obnoxious tax in 1841. Then, as was the case during Malthus's life-time, it was vociferously resented. The necessary 'returns' which an income tax involved were regarded as an invasion of privacy and an infringement of the liberty of the subject; the window tax, on the same principle, was considered superior to the hearth tax, since it could be assessed from outside, without the need of an inspector to go all round a house counting the fireplaces. The whole subject was beset by muddled thinking, for it was generally agreed that the wealthy should contribute more than the poor, which could hardly be arranged without a proper assessment of the wealth of individuals. Malthus's views on taxation were never published. It is possible that he envisaged a progressive property tax as an aid to the better distribution of wealth for the stimulation of demand, as well as for the expenses of government and the provision of education, but there are no revealing notes about this in Inverarity's copy of Adam Smith.

This letter to Chalmers also contains two more statements which might have surprised Malthus's contemporaries:

> I am quite of your opinion on the check to improvement in agriculture occasioned by tithes; and have stated [this] in my lectures, though not I believe in print. And I quite agree with you in regard the moral advantage of repealing the corn laws.

Later writers, who stigmatised Parson Malthus as the lackey of the landlords, might also have been astonished at the elderly economist's defence of industry and commerce against Chalmers' attacks on them. Without her export trade Great Britain would be

> less powerful, and I should certainly add less wealthy, though she might still be as strong in defensive war. It is owing to the abundance of her exports, derived from her skill, machinery and capital, that money rents and the money prices of corn and labour are high, and that with a small quantity of English labour a large quantity of the products of foreign labour is purchased. The demand for useful and beneficial personal services is limited; and after all these have been fully paid, would it not be an impoverishing and very disadvantageous exchange to substitute for the rich capitalists, and comfortable and independent traders living upon the profits of stock, a body of dependents upon the landlords?

In the last letter which Malthus wrote to Chalmers - thanking him for yet another valuable present - he returned to the same theme. The letter is dated 16 February 1833, and Malthus dashed off a postscript:

433

Do not manufactures and commerce increase the *Revenue* of a country, and *enlarge* the *returning power?* I own I cannot but think that if the taste for luxuries and superior conveniences were at an end, the cultivation of the land would be essentially deteriorated, - at least under the present division of landed property. How could the actual number of labourers have an adequate demand for the produce of the soil, if commerce and manufactures were greatly to be diminished? What numbers would be out of work! What constant calls for an extension of Poor Laws, and of all public and private charities!!

All the stiffness has gone and the kind old man is once more well away: his concern is for the labourers who are actually in existence, and the necessity of an economic demand for their produce if they are to be fully employed. It is not unnatural to feel that Malthus's attitude to the Poor Law was harsh, but it is irrational to dispute his realistic approach: the money available for wages, as well as for both public and private charity, is dependent upon the wealth of the community as a whole.

4 Changing Times

Shortly before his death, in May 1832, Sir James Mackintosh said 'that he should like to have lived in quieter times'.[50] He had been born in 1765, so that his life-span, like Malthus's, covered a period beset by every kind of dramatic innovation. It is generally considered that in British history this age of upheaval was followed by an age of reform; it is equally valid to say that the age of the individual was followed by the age of the institution. We can list the first establishment of a modern police force in 1829, the first parliamentary Reform Act in 1832, the first effective Factory Act and the first Treasury grant for education in England and Wales in 1833, the Municipal Corporations Act in 1835, the setting up of the Registrar General's Office for the proper recording of births, deaths and marriages in 1837. Apart from these developments, however, other British institutions were assuming the characteristics that were to make them influential for more than a century: Navy and Army, Church and Civil Service, public schools and universities, the great teaching hospitals, all began to have their reforms too. It is not surprising that the Industrial Revolution should render obsolete establishments which had originated in the days of the handloom and the cross-bow; they had virtually ceased to function as organisations in the modern sense, being dependent on the ability and public spirit of outstanding individuals.

So preoccupied have we been, in our history books, with tracing these reforms from one Act of Parliament to another, that we are in danger of forgetting that for people alive at the time there were other alarms and crises to contend with. Thus the years 1831-2 were marked not only by violent agitation for parliamentary reform but also by the first of the cholera epidemics which were to hit nineteenth-century Britain; as Lucy Aikin wrote to an American friend in December 1831, 'Pestilence advances, revolution threatens.' Quarantine arrangements were the responsibility of the Privy Council, who set up a Board of Health when the disease could no longer be kept out. They also tried to set up boards of health among the parish vestry councils, which were often the only form of local government in large and crowded towns; but in many cases, like one in east London, 'as they met at a public house, they all got drunk and did nothing'.[51]

The government tried other measures, and Malthus's young brother-in-law Charles Eckersall was one of the innumerable clergymen who wrote a special sermon for 21 March 1832, a day appointed for a General Fast. Charles's published sermon was called *The Wrath of God; its cause; and the means of averting it*. In this he described the visitation of cholera as God's punishment for a number of sins, from Sunday trading and swearing to gambling and body-snatching for dissection (a new one), but he did not consider at all the sin of neglecting the sanitation of the poor.[52]

Charles Greville (1794-1865), the Clerk of the Privy Council, was fully aware of the horrible conditions brought to light by attempts to control the disease: 'We, who live on the smooth and plausible surface, know little of the frightful appearance of the bowels of society.' But perhaps even more grim than the physical distress of the poor, all across Europe, was their bitter psychological plight. Greville wrote in his journal on 17 September 1831:

> The cholera, which is travelling south, is less violent than it was in the north. It is remarkable that the common people at Berlin are impressed with the same strange belief that possessed those of St Petersburg, that they have been poisoned, and Chad writes today that they believe there is no such disease, and that the deaths ascribed to that malady are produced by poison administered by the doctors, who are bribed for that purpose; that the rich, finding the poor becoming too numerous to be conveniently governed, have adopted this mode of thinning the population, which was employed with success by the English in India; that the foreign doctors are the delegates of a central committee, which is formed in London and directs the proceedings, and similar nonsense.[53]

If Malthus knew of this, he must have been very unhappy.

The illiterate leave no memoirs, so that it is impossible to discover how far such an attitude prevailed among the poor in England, but there is evidence that Malthus's name was used in this connection by someone who should have known better. When Fanny Mackintosh wrote from London to her cousin Elizabeth Wedgwood in Staffordshire, in November 1831, she told her that, since five o'clock the day before, cholera had been their only subject; like many other families, they were divided between retiring to the country to escape infection or staying on in town for the sake of better doctors. The great Dr Holland was in Brighton at the time, but he sent his distinguished patient Sir James what Fanny called a long note on Cholera 'containing nothing new, only some bad jokes about Mr. Malthus & suchlike'.

Their old friend Sydney Smith was also promulgating the 'bad jokes' that Malthus rejoiced in fatal epidemics and lamented pregnancy. The Malthuses stayed with him at Combe Florey on their way to Poughill in 1831, and in late July he wrote to Lady Holland that 'Philosopher Malthus came here last week. I got an agreeable party for him of unmarried people. There was only one Lady who had had a Child [his own married daughter], and for her I apologised ... but he is a very good natured man, and if there are no appearances of approaching fertility is civil to every lady.' In justice to Mr Smith, he did write a little later to Lord Grey: 'The honest Clergymen that I know are few. It would give great satisfaction if a Prebend were in course of time given to Malthus.'[54]

In 1832 the Malthuses again stayed at Combe Florey. Malthus used as scribbling paper, for revising the *Principles of Political Economy*, a note from Sydney Smith dated 31 July, about some garments he had left behind, and which his host had sent after him by the North Devon coach. After a reference to Joseph and Potiphar's wife (Genesis 39), in rather puerile taste, the letter concluded with an invitation to 'the philosopher' to come 'as often as parental affection leads him this Way'.[55] But the following year we find Smith writing to Lady Grey that he was forced to decline seeing Malthus because his daughter was about to have another child after a miscarriage, and 'I am convinced her last accident was entirely owing to his Visit.' Nowell Smith, who edited this letter, thought it necessary to explain in a footnote, in 1953, that Smith was only joking.[56]

Malthus was taken more seriously by three holders of the curiously endowed Drummond Chair of Political Economy at Oxford. Fortunately for us they were obliged to publish a lecture every year, and they inevitably referred to Malthus's work on population. The Rev. William Foster Lloyd (1794-1852) was the most entertaining and least important, except for one passage, which inspired Francis Place to send him a long letter. Lloyd declared, speaking of the coming generation:

> They have no feelings of anticipation of the new state into which
> they are destined to enter and, were their entrance into life to be
> delayed for a hundred or a thousand or ten thousand years they
> would not, during the interval, be rendered uneasy and miserable by

feelings of impatience and disappointment ... We must, with regard
to the period of their admittance, treat them altogether as cyphers,
which ought not to be allowed to weigh, as a feather in the scale,
against the comforts and enjoyments of the existing generation.[57]

It would have been interesting to hear Malthus's comments.

Richard Whately (1787-1863), who became Archbishop of Dublin, took
up a position against Malthus's misguided followers which was appropriate
to a man famous as an exponent of logic: according to their belief (which
he maintained was not Malthus's):

> Our own country, and almost every other in the civilized world,
> ought to possess scantier means of subsistence in proportion to the
> population, now, than some centuries ago.
>
> But we know that the reverse is the fact; and that our population,
> though so greatly increased since the time, for instance, of Henry
> VIII, is yet better off, on the average, in point of food, clothing, and
> habitations, than then.
>
> It is urged, however, that since want and misery do exist among
> the lower classes, this is a proof that their numbers have gone on
> increasing at *too great* a rate. So it is: but the *existence* of an *excess*
> does not prove that that excess is *increasing*; or that it is not
> diminishing. What would be thought of one who should reason
> thus ... There is, in February, a progress towards total darkness; for
> though each day is longer than the last, still the nights are too long
> in proportion to the days!
>
> ... I have, in the Ninth Lecture, traced the error in question to its
> origin, in the ambiguity (that common source of confusion of
> thought) in the word 'tendency'.[58]

In this note Whately was taking up a point which had been made by his
friend and pupil Nassau Senior (1790-1864); he was an able lawyer who
occupied the Drummond Chair from 1825 to 1830, when Whately briefly
succeeded him. Senior had been impressed as a child by the evils of
misdirected charity in his father's Wiltshire parish, and at the age of twenty-
five resolved to reform the English Poor Law. He did not altogether agree
with Malthus, although he reverenced him as a man. They met at the
Political Economy Club and elsewhere in London; the 'Advertisement' to
Senior's *Two Lectures on Population* is dated from Lincoln's Inn, where he
carried on his practice, which was too lucrative for him long to relinquish
for any public office.

. Although Senior's lectures on population were delivered in the spring of
1828, they were not published until 1831. Even so, this was before the
outbreak of cholera and, of course, long before the Irish famine of 1846.
Senior attacked both McCulloch (whose edition of the *Wealth of Nations*

had just been published) and James Mill, on account of their acceptance of Malthus's theory as the basis of their Ricardian system. Senior's thesis was that there exists in the human race a natural tendency to rise from barbarism to civilisation and, since the means of subsistence are proportionally more abundant in a civilised than in a savage state, 'there is a natural tendency in subsistence to increase in a greater ratio than population.'

> Now this is the case in *every* civilized country. Even Ireland, the country most likely to afford an instance of what Mr. Mill supposes to be the natural course of things, poor and populous though she is, suffers less from want with her eight millions of people, than when her only inhabitants were a few septs of hunters and fishers. In our early history, famines, and pestilence the consequences of famine, constantly recur. At present, though our numbers are trebled and quadrupled, they are unheard of.

Nevertheless,

> Although Mr. Malthus has perhaps fallen into the exaggeration which is natural to a discoverer, his error, if it be one, does not affect the practical conclusions which place him, as a benefactor to mankind, on a level with Adam Smith. Whether, in the absence of disturbing causes, it be the tendency of subsistence or of population to advance with greater rapidity, is a question of slight importance, if it be acknowledged that human happiness or misery depend principally on their relative advance, and that there are causes, and causes within human control, by which that advance can be regulated.

Here Senior, like Malthus, was thinking not of contraceptives but of 'knowledge, security of property, freedom of internal and external exchange, and equal admissibility to rank and power'. It was bad government, resulting in 'ignorance and insecurity of person or property', which diminished the productiveness of labour and led to 'that brutish state of improvidence in which the power of increase, unchecked by prudence, is always struggling to pass the limits of subsistence, and is kept down only by vice and misery'.[59]

Senior sent Malthus the text of his lectures, and the published version has as an appendix the letters which they exchanged in the spring of 1829. Senior closed the correspondence on 9 April, when he wrote that their controversy had terminated 'in mutual agreement'; this was hardly true of the principle of population, although they shared the same views on a free and liberal government. But Senior was correct when he wrote that Malthus's ideas had been caricatured by some of his followers: 'Because additional numbers *may* bring poverty, it has been supposed that they necessarily *will* do so. Because increased means of subsistence *may* be followed and neutralised by a proportionate increase in the number of persons to be subsisted, it has been supposed that such *will* necessarily be the case.' Senior was also right when he said that there were many who from 'indolence, or selfishness, or a turn to despondency', made use of this caricatured doctrine because 'It furnishes an easy escape from the trouble or expense implied by every project of improvement.'[60] In any event, Malthus and Senior became personal friends.

Another clear-sighted and admiring young friend was the Rev. William Whewell (1794-1866), who also seems to have come into Malthus's life in 1829, when he was Professor of Mineralogy at Cambridge. Whewell's fortunes were bound up with Trinity College, of which he became one of the most famous Masters, having been made a Fellow in 1817. He was the son of a master-carpenter in Lancaster, and would have been apprenticed to his father had it not been for a closed exhibition to Trinity from the Grammar School at Heversham, some twelve miles from his home. Thus began the career of a man who has been described as the last of the great 'universalists', for his work ranged from a study of the tides, which was quite important in its day, to mathematics, geology, Kantian philosophy (he spoke German like a native), theology, and ecclesiastical architecture.

Whewell's friends among his contemporaries included the astronomer John Herschel (1792-1871) and Charles Babbage (also 1792-1871), who was by now Lucasian Professor of Mathematics. Babbage must have rejoiced that he had failed to obtain Walter's post at Haileybury, since at Cambridge he was not obliged to give any lectures, and could spend most of his time at his London house, at work on his Calculating Engine, generally regarded as the forerunner of the modern computer.

But possibly Whewell's greatest friend was Richard Jones, with whom he was in the habit of discussing Malthus and Ricardo. As early as 16 August 1822, nine years before Jones's book on *Rent* was published, we find Whewell writing to him:

> What your wiseacres mean by the Metaphysics of Political Economy
> I cannot tell; for there are no peculiar principles of observation or
> deduction employed in that science - they may as well talk of the
> metaphysics of chemistry. The thing which I suppose leads them
> into error is that some abstract terms are necessarily introduced in
> your science . . . and that blockheads have thought themselves
> usefully employed in increasing the number. I have no objection to
> your calling those people metaphysical in the scurrilous meaning of
> the word . . . But never mind if other people call you so - being
> well assured that you and Malthus belong not to the *metaphysical* but
> to the *ethical* school of Political Economy.

This is certainly true, although Whewell, like Jones, belonged also to the inductive school of political economy, and he shared his friend's concern for the collection and interpretation of facts; he wrote in another letter to

Jones (in 1828) that if the political economists 'will not understand common sense because their heads are full of extravagant theory, they will be trampled down and passed over'.[61]

Thus when Whewell wrote a *Mathematical Exposition of Some Doctrines of Political Economy*, for the Cambridge Philosophical Society, he sent copies to all the economists he knew, 'by way of a challenge', as he told Jones in March 1829. Malthus replied to his on 26 May:

> I am ashamed to say that, never having been very familiar with the present algebraic notation, and for a great many years having been quite unaccustomed to it, I cannot follow you as I could wish, without more attention and application than I can give to the subject in the midst of our College examinations.
>
> I think however that you have arrived at pretty just conclusions, and am inclined to infer from what I have seen, that mathematical calculations may in some cases be introduced with advantage into the science of Political Economy ... The grand difficulty, however, with a view to practical utility, is the getting data to work upon, sufficiently near the truth, and such as can be stated distinctly in mathematical language.[62]

There is scarcely need to point out that this grand difficulty is still with us.

Malthus's letter was mainly concerned with Perronet Thompson's *True Theory of Rent*; this had reached its fifth edition by 1829, but is today of remote interest, except in so far as it was followed in 1831 by Richard Jones's *Essay on the Distribution of Wealth, and on the Sources of Taxation. Part I – Rent*. This was sent to Malthus as a joint present from Whewell and the author, but it was to Whewell that he addressed his letter of thanks. It is dated 28 February 1831; Malthus must have fallen on the book as soon as it arrived. His reactions show that although he kept up to date with both the newspapers and publications on political economy, his outlook and attitudes towards them were largely those of a decade before, when Ricardo was still alive and he himself had not begun to feel old. He wrote to Whewell:

> My dear Sir,
>   I am very much obliged to you and Mr. Jones for a valuable work on the distribution of wealth ... I am particularly gratified to find that he agrees with me on almost every point on which I differed from Mr. Ricardo. I am not sure however whether he has not gone beyond the truth in his unwillingness to admit the *tendency* of continued accumulation, and of the progress of population and cultivation, to lower the rates of profits and corn wages on the land ... If the progress of cultivation and population has no *tendency* to diminish corn wages, I do not see what cause should ever retard

the rate at which population is known to increase in the new colonies. I like much Mr. Jones' account of the different kinds of rent which prevail in different countries and at different periods; yet I certainly think that the progress of rent in new colonies not interrupted by premature monopoly and very bad government, together with the farmers' rents in the more improved states of Europe, are the most important parts of the subject, and the most practically interesting to us, particularly in this age of emigration.

. . . It is quite true as Mr. Jones observes that I have been unfortunate in my followers. I trust he is aware that the general and practical conclusions which I have myself drawn from my principles both on population and rent, have by no means the gloomy aspect given to them by many of my readers.

I am anxious to see the remaining volumes of Mr. Jones' work, and I beg you will return him my best thanks.

There were to be no more volumes from Mr Jones, but three months later Malthus was thanking Whewell for another Cambridge Philosophical Society paper: *Mathematical Exposition of some of the Leading Doctrines in Mr. Ricardo's 'Principles of Political Economy and Taxation.'* One is conscious of little gimlets of pain in this letter, dated 31 May 1831; Malthus had obviously been hurt by Torrens's referring to his anti-Ricardian stance as similar to that of Joseph Priestley's adherence to the phlogiston theory, long after everyone else had abandoned it.*[63] Malthus wrote to Whewell:

I am much gratified by the opinions of such judges as Mr. Jones and yourself as to what I may have done in Political Economy. I confess that when I felt I almost stood alone in my differences with Mr. Ricardo and was compared to Dr. Priestly amidst the new discoveries in chemistry, it would not finally be so. But I was hardly prepared to expect that in so short a time as has since elapsed, one of the questions in the political economy Club should be 'Whether any of the principles *first* advanced in Mr. Ricardo's work are now acknowledged to be correct?'[64] My apprehension at present is that the tide is setting too strong against him; and I even think that Mr. Jones is carried a little out of the right course by it. In his zeal to shew that Mr. Ricardo is quite wrong, which he certainly is, in dwelling upon the diminished returns of agricultural capital as the sole cause of increasing rents, he seems inclined to deny the undoubted truth of the natural tendency to such diminished returns in a *limited space*, unless prevented by improvements in agriculture or manufactures. Were there no such tendency, and had not such a tendency

*Priestley had died in America in 1804, but interest in his work was revived by the publication between 1817 and 1832 of his *Memoirs and Correspondence* in twenty-six volumes.

441

frequently operated, no adequate reason can be given why the accumulating capitals of a new colony should not continue to be applied to the lands first occupied, or why the inhabitants of the Eastern states of America are now emigrating in such numbers to the Western.

It seems almost as if Malthus were more hurt by Torrens's attack on Ricardo's memory at the Political Economy Club than he was by Torrens's unkind reference to his own isolated position in the *Production of Wealth* in 1821. One is reminded of his antipathy to Samuel Bailey in the *Definitions*, but in this case Malthus is not bitter, only wounded by the reaction of a new generation against the whole outlook of that vanished age when he and his contemporaries were jousting together in their intellectual prime.

As far as Whewell and Jones were concerned there was no animosity, and both of them, after his death, wrote of their real affection for Malthus. In September 1831 Whewell took Jones on a visit to Haileybury, where, he told Herschel, 'Malthus and he had divers palavers of no common length, I hope to their mutual instruction and comfort.' Whewell certainly seems to have made himself at home with the family. On 14 January 1833 he wrote to Herschel from Richard Jones's house at Brasted, in Kent, about his 'experiments with Mr. Malthus's eyes'.[65]

Hal Malthus co-operated in these, and Whewell kept a confused letter (dated simply 'Thursday') about the 'answer's' he got from his father and sister. 'I told them not to consult each other', Hal reported:

My Father says – 'The Colors in the Rainbow & in the prism have always appeared to me to divide themselves into two mainly distinguishable Halo's, blue and yellow, red heat I should call yellow.' He confuses the same colours [sic] we do, and thinks that no two people see colors exactly alike, and has read of one who could distinguish no colors but as shades of light and dark – I flatter myself that we are very far from that unfortunate predicament.[66]

From this we may conclude that Malthus, his son, and Whewell were all what is now called colour-blind. Whewell told Herschel that he would 'have gone again to Haileybury, having provided myself with a fluid prism, but the Malthi have left it for the vacation'.

An indication of the nature of this friendship is that Whewell sent Malthus a copy of a work which had nothing to do with economics: *Astronomy and General Physics considered with reference to Natural Theology.* The insane eighth Earl of Bridgewater had left £8,000 for the best work on 'The Goodness of God as manifested in the Creation', and Whewell was one of the eight winners amongst whom the Trustees divided the prize. Other notable authors of Bridgewater Treatises were Thomas Chalmers and Peter Mark Roget. Malthus's letter of thanks is dated 1 April 1833:

442

It is generally thought, and for obvious reasons, the most prudent plan to acknowledge the having received a work sent to you, immediately, and to thank the author for his *valuable* present before you have read it. You will perceive that I have not followed this course in the present instance, and my reason was that I felt a strong confidence that after reading it, I should be able to say with truth that I had received from its perusal both pleasure and profit. My anticipations in this respect have been more than realised; and I can assure you now with perfect sincerity that I have been quite delighted and much instructed by many parts of the work ... Mrs. Malthus desires me to add her testimony to the gratification which your work is calculated to afford. She admires it very much ... We hope to see you when you can come this way. Mrs. M's kind regards.

Whewell's letter to his sister telling her of Jones's appointment, six weeks after Malthus died, contains a private tribute which, had she known of it, would have gratified Harriet more than any public obituary. He wrote from Cambridge on 13 February 1835:

You will be pleased to hear that my very particular friend Jones is brought nearer me, by being made professor at the East India College ... which is about half way between this place and London. He is professor of Political Economy, succeeding Mr. Malthus, of whom you have perhaps heard, but of whom you have heard wrong if you have learnt to think any harm of him. He was a most mild and benevolent person, and I regret his death very much.[67]

This is high praise for an old celebrity from a man nearly thirty years his junior.

5 The New Age

During the last week of June 1833 the Malthuses were in Cambridge for the third meeting of the British Association for the Advancement of Science, which 'was attended by more than nine hundred members, and was honoured with the presence of several foreign philosophers'.[68]

This is not the place to detail the disturbed history of the Royal Society after the death of Sir Joseph Banks in 1820. With hindsight we can see that advancing knowledge made specialisation inevitable: the interests of the physical sciences as we now know them could not beneficially be combined with the safe-keeping and study of Sir William Jones's Asiatic manuscripts. Thus the British Association came to be founded by a group of men who were scientists in the modern sense of the word, with Charles Babbage playing a conspicuous part. The first meeting was held at York in 1831, the second at Oxford in 1832, but Cambridge hospitality the following year set a new standard.

Readers of the Tory paper *John Bull* on Sunday 7 July 1833 learned that

> There was a magnificent dinner given to upwards of five hundred persons in Trinity hall. The wines were of the first quality, and the vocal department extremely well arranged. Malibran was in high voice at the concerts, which were admirably selected. There was a ball, which was crowded to excess: the newest gallopades, and the mazurka, were introduced with great effect; and a display of fireworks, with which this most interesting assembly broke up, was pronounced to be splendid in the extreme.

According to Dr Chalmers, who replied to the toast of the Scottish Universities, there were at least 600 people at the Banquet: 'My ticket took me to Table A, near the President, where I had the good fortune to be within conversation of Mr. Malthus.'[69]

The President was the Rev. Adam Sedgwick (1785-1873), Woodwardian Professor of Geology. Whewell was one of the two secretaries for Cambridge, and also on the Committee devoted to Mathematics and General Physics. The other Committees were

II. Chemistry, Mineralogy, &c.

III. Geology and Geography.

IV. Natural History. [On the Saturday they made an excursion to the Fens]

V. Anatomy, Medicine, &c.

About a quarter of the 150 learned members of these Committees were in Holy Orders, a reminder that ordination was still required for many Oxford and Cambridge fellowships, and that it was still difficult for a married man to pursue scholarship or science without a Church of England living. But John Lindley (1799-1865), the son of a nursery-man who went bankrupt, was Professor of Botany in the newly-founded University of London, where subscription to the Anglican Thirty-nine Articles was not required; both he and his paper, on current questions in the 'Philosophy of Botany', were typical of this age of transition.

At first glance, it is hard to understand why Malthus should have been there. The reason was that at this Cambridge meeting the British Association established a sixth Committee, for Statistics. Professor Babbage was the Chairman; the Secretary was John Elliott Drinkwater, later Bethune, (1801-51), a barrister who was Counsel to the Home Office and was of great service in drafting legislation for the reforming ministries of Lord Grey and Lord Melbourne. Malthus, Empson and Richard Jones were three of the fourteen ordinary members.

Apart from Malthus, the most distinguished man in the Statistical Section was one of the 'foreign philosophers', M. Quetelet from Brussels. Adolphe Quetelet (1796-1874) was a notable mathematician and astronomer - he also painted a little and wrote verses - who came to statistics and demography by way of some research to help life insurance societies. In 1828 he was appointed director of an observatory which was not yet built, and the Belgian Revolution involved further delay; Quetelet used his enforced leisure to continue working on social statistics, of which he may be said to be the originator, and the father of *l'homme moyen*; criminal statistics were among the most readily available, and he was shocked to find how constant the figures were. Queen Victoria's Uncle Leopold, King of the Belgians, had a high regard for Quetelet, and in due course he became one of the most influential of Prince Albert's tutors during the time he spent in Brussels.

On Thursday 27 June 1833 Malthus took the chair at a meeting of eight 'Gentlemen desirous of forming a Statistical Section of the British Association'. Drinkwater made pencil notes in a little book. The remarks of Dr Somerville, Richard Jones and the Rev. D'Oyley - Otter's brother-in-law - are not recorded; but Quetelet talked about 'some of the results of his inquiries into the proportion of crime at different ages & in different parts of France and Belgium'. (He had also sent in papers to the Association about falling stars and the inequality of magnetic intensity at the top and the base of mountains.) Colonel Sykes (1790-1872) 'offered for us his analysis of the Population Returns of the four Collectorates of the Deccan under the Bombay Government - incl. no. of ploughs, draught- pack- and domestic cattle, land under cultivation & waste-land, number of schools, etc, etc.' Babbage exhibited 'a set of curves drawn with a view to show the effect of averages in producing a perceptible law in phenomena apparently of the most arbitrary character when considered separately' - such as persons committed for drunkenness in the Metropolis.[70]

Malthus must have been very happy. On the evening of the same day he chaired another meeting, when Drinkwater was able to list twenty-five 'noblemen and gentlemen' who had intimated their desire of attaching themselves to the Statistical Section; there was in fact only one nobleman, Earl Fitzwilliam. The following day, Friday, Richard Jones took the chair in the morning and Lord Fitzwilliam in the evening, but there was a contretemps: Professor Sedgwick objected 'to the manner of the formation of the Section. He considered that even the consent of the General Meeting to its establishment was insufficient without the previous sanction of the

General Committee & all recognition of the Section was postponed accordingly.' But on Saturday Messrs Babbage and Drinkwater attended the General Committee on behalf of the Statistical Section, and the position was regularised.

Sedgwick was obviously on difficult ground, and felt it necessary to say in his concluding address that some members might feel that the study of statistics was 'ill-fitted to a Society formed only for the promotion of natural science'. But he decided that statistical inquiries could be compatible with the objects of the British Association and 'taken into the bosom of our Society'. By science, he said, he understood 'the consideration of all subjects, whether of a pure or mixed nature, capable of being reduced to measurement and calculation. All things comprehended under the categories of space, time and number properly belong to our investigations; and all phenomena capable of being brought under the semblance of a law are legitimate objects of our inquiries.'[71]

Apparently Malthus went up to London almost immediately after the meeting, for he sent a letter to Adolphe Quetelet dated Tuesday 2 July 1833 from the Athenaeum:

Dear Sir,

I have put down in a hurry a few questions for your consideration. Perhaps I shall have the pleasure of seeing you at Mr. Babbage's tomorrow. A note will find me either at the Athenaeum, or at the St Albans Hotel, Charles Street St James Square, where I sleep. I leave Town friday morning early for the neighbourhood of Bath.

truly Yours
T. R. Malthus

The questions are headed *Desiderata*:

The number of births to each marriage in the course of its duration.

The proportion of the born which lives to marry.

The number of living children to each marriage.

The money wages of labour manufacturing and agricultural in the different provinces, particularly the wages of common *day labour* in agricultural employment.

The quantity of wheat which the wages of such day labour will purchase [Malthus first wrote 'command' and then crossed it out] in ordinary times.

The ordinary prices of different kinds of grain.

The ordinary food of the common day-labourer.

Proportion of barren marriages.
Proportion of marriages with five or more living children.[72]

A similar letter to a very different correspondent shows how much Malthus's mind was running on population statistics. It was addressed to 'Monsr. Czörnig, Milan'. This was Karl Friedrich Czörnig von Czernhausen (1804–89), a civil servant of imperial Austria. He had read law at the universities of Prague and Vienna, and after two years in Trieste was posted to Milan in 1831. Here he became involved in statistical surveys of Lombardy and Venetia; later, in Vienna, he became Director of the Statistical Bureau, and later still his name was mainly associated with his work for the development of the Austria-Hungarian railways. We do not know whether Malthus received from this young man the information he was seeking. His letter is dated from the East India College on 11 November 1833:

Sir,
    I am much flattered by what you say of my work on Population, and am very happy to hear that it has been of use to you in your Statistical studies and inquiries.
    It is quite true as you observe that the vast provinces belonging to the Austrian Empire have come very little under my notice. One reason was, that which you state, namely that the Statistical information relating to them was not very easily accessible; and another was, that the information which I could collect without much difficulty appeared to me to embrace a sufficient number of instances to establish the principle which I had in view.
    I still however feel a great interest in further details from new countries and in more complete registers from old ones; and shall therefore be very much obliged to you for the information which you are so good as to offer me relating to the Provinces of the Austrian Empire. I have seen occasionally in periodical papers statistical accounts of some of these countries, but I did not know how far I could rely on them, and they were often defective on very essential points. What I am most interested about is to obtain in many different countries correct lists of births, deaths and marriages, with their proportions to the whole population; and to get data from which may be deduced with more accuracy than has hitherto been done the proportion of the born which lives to marry, and the proportion of births to each marriage. The latter proportion you are probably aware is not represented correctly, in an increasing population by the proportion of contemporary births to marriages. An interesting account of the Statistics of Belgium has lately been published by M. Quetelet under the title of 'Recherches sur la Reproduction et la Mortalité de L'Homme &c: et sur la Population de la Belgique.' Among other tables, it contains one which gives the

447

proportions of Celibataires, hommes et femmes, to the mariés, and the veufs et veuves. Another table contains the ages at which marriages have taken place from which is deduced the average age of marriage. Any information of this kind is interesting, as it tends to show the degree in which what I have called the preventive check or prudential restraint prevails.

Perhaps in the registers of some of the countries with which you are acquainted, there may be the means of tracing for a considerable period the proportion of persons dying married, to those dying unmarried above the age of puberty. This information would be curious; but I should not expect that the proportion of the unmarried would be so great in your more Southern countries as with us ...

I shall be very happy to receive from you any information on these subjects which it may suit your convenience to communicate, and feel much obliged to you for your letter and kind offers.

I am, dear Sir,
with great respect,
Your obed' humb' S'
T. Rob' Malthus.

I should like much to know the ordinary money price of common agricultural labour in Lombardy, Austria, Hungary, Bohemia, Trieste &c: And in regard to Registers of births deaths and marriages, to have your opinion as to their correctness. I much fear that our own registers are not correct in the births and deaths.[73]

Malthus would have known that work was going forward to organise the accurate registration of all English births and deaths as distinct from Anglican baptisms and burials; Harcourt's Act of 1752 to prevent clandestine weddings meant that from the middle of the eighteenth century it was possible - very laboriously, from parish registers - to collect uniform information about the age and status of all who were legally married.

One can understand how concerned Malthus must have been over the foundation of the 'Statistical Society of London' (Manchester had one already) as distinct from the Statistical Section of the British Association. The first steps seem to have been taken very early in 1834, and Malthus sent a hurried note to Babbage dated 12 February:

As I am only just returned to the College from an absence of four or five days, I cannot conscienciously [sic] leave it so soon again, particularly as you wish me to be present at the general meeting. I shall be very much obliged to you to let me know, as soon as it is settled, when the public meeting will be, that I may make arrangements accordingly. I hope it may be on a friday saturday or monday. On any other day of the week I could hardly attend. I

448

should have had great pleasure in meeting you on friday next, if my College duties had allowed me.[74]

Malthus's request was granted, for Babbage asked Drinkwater to summon to his house 'all whose addresses he was then acquainted with' on Friday 21 February. Probably some of them were given an opportunity to look at the calculating machine.

A resolution was carried, proposed by Malthus and Richard Jones, 'That it is advisable to take immediate steps to establish a Statistical Society in London, *the object of which shall be the collection and classification of all facts illustrative of the present condition and prospects of society.*' The words which Drinkwater underlined were added to the original resolution 'on the suggestion of Mr. Malthus'.

The first General Meeting was held on 15 March, at the rooms of the Horticultural Society in Regent Street; thereafter the Society arranged to meet on the first Friday of every month, from 1 November to 1 July, except Good Friday, at the house of the Royal Society of Literature, 4 St Martin's Place, Trafalgar Square.

Had Malthus died in the spring of 1834 the founding of the Statistical Society, later the Royal Statistical Society, would have been his most appropriate happy ending. There could have been no better moment for the curtain to fall on the life of a man who had consistently tried to seek truth through the interpretation of ascertained fact. But he was destined to live a few months longer, and on 17 April Lord Althorp introduced in the House of Commons the Poor Law Amendment Bill; the repercussions of this were to cause much suffering to Malthus, and even more to his family.

6 Final Storm

His correspondence with Chalmers shows that Malthus had many doubts about his 'plan for the gradual abolition of the poor laws'. In a letter dated 23 August 1821 he wrote:

> Your personal experience of the practicality of throwing the poor almost entirely on their own resources, with little risk of extreme distress, even in such a town as Glasgow and at so unfavourable a period, is of the highest importance. I confess I had almost despaired on the subject, and almost begun to think that in a highly manufacturing state where so large a portion of the population must be subject to the fluctuations of trade, and the consequent sudden variations of wages, it might not be possible entirely to give up a

compulsory provision without the sacrifice of too many individuals to the good of the whole.

Almost a year later, on 21 July 1822, Malthus was writing to Chalmers again:

> I see little prospect at present of the opinion against the system of the Poor Laws becoming sufficiently general to warrant the adoption of measures for their abolition. The subject of population is no doubt very much more generally understood than it was; but the actual situation of England *with* her poor laws, and her comparative exemption from famines and excessive poverty, together with a great fear of the increase of mendicity, operate very powerfully on the public mind, and it certainly would not do to attempt a fundamental change, without a pretty general conviction of the importance of it, among the higher and middle classes of society, and the best informed among the labouring classes. Practically therefore I am inclined to look forward to the first improvement as likely to come from an improved administration of our actual laws, together with a more general system of education and moral superintendance.
>
> I really think, now that the principle of population is more generally understood, that something considerable may be done in this way, if while we administer relief more judiciously, we take great care not to remove or weaken the indirect effects of the poor laws in checking population. The obligation on each parish to support its own poor has certainly had a great effect in checking the building of numerous and wretched hovels; and though it would be most desirable on other accounts to have the freest possible circulation of labour, yet I think that anything like an abolition of the present laws of settlement would be accompanied with more evil than good.

It was well that Chalmers, as far as I know, never talked about this letter, and that Ricardo and McCulloch never heard of it. After Malthus had promulgated the belief that the Poor Law encouraged improvident marriages and superfluous population, it was indeed a *volte-face* to suggest that some aspects of it might in fact check population growth, however indirectly.

By 9 November 1822 Malthus seems to have changed his mind again, for he wrote to Chalmers that he had latterly felt compelled to restrain his hopes of anything like a complete abolition of the Poor Laws, 'but your ardour and energy, together with your experience, have renewed my hopes; and I wait with anxiety to see what may be the result'. Chalmers's fanatical antagonism to compulsory poor-rates was in fact derived from very limited experience, and his bound volumes of correspondence are full of letters from 'vexed and disappointed' ministers describing the failure of voluntary charitable schemes 'for the reformation of pauperism'. Malthus's doubts and changes of mind, and consideration for public opinion, seem more psychologically wholesome as well as more sensible than Chalmers's blinkered dogmatism. But nothing could change the popular view of Malthus as the man who wanted to abolish the Poor Law and starve the labouring classes into miserable and vicious sterility.

Otter wrote feelingly that Malthus's reputation had 'in many instances suffered more from the headlong zeal of his followers and imitators than from the mistakes and even malice of his enemies'. Yet I think Otter's own injudicious friendship did Malthus's posthumous fame as much harm as any, for Otter wrote that 'The Essay on Population and the Poor Laws Amendment Bill will stand or fall together.'[75] Nothing could be further from the truth, as Francis Place had tried to explain in an earlier context. But even worse for the popular image of Malthus were the moral tales of Harriet Martineau, surely one of the most unlovable of all neurotic literary ladies, whose *Illustrations of Political Economy* enjoyed a reputation, and sales, incomprehensible to modern readers.

Lucy Aikin wrote to her American friend Dr Channing on 13 June 1833:

> I dined yesterday in the company of Mr. Malthus and Miss
> Martineau who are great friends and allies. Perhaps you may, and
> perhaps you may not, have taken the trouble to read the pro. and
> con. articles respecting Miss M. in the 'Quarterly' and 'Edinburgh'
> Reviews, of which the first is full of malice, and the second, I think,
> very empty of sound critical matter.[76]

Today we sympathise with 'Christopher North' (John Wilson) in the *Quarterly*; Empson's favourable review in the *Edinburgh* is hard to credit, so absurdly unrealistic are Miss Martineau's stories, so unnatural her characters, so uncongenial her conclusions. She held that Poor Laws were degrading and self-defeating, maternity hospitals a bounty on improvidence, and almshouses a temptation to idleness, since people should save from their wages for their old age; provision for the elderly also encouraged numbers of young people to 'marry under the expectation of getting their helpless parents maintained by the public'. Education, however, since it was not essential to existence, might fairly be offered gratis to the poor, until they had learned to consider it indispensable.[77]

Brougham was so impressed by Harriet Martineau that he persuaded her to write four 'Poor-law Tales' for the Society for the Diffusion of Useful Knowledge. She must have helped to diffuse detestation of Malthus as well as of the workhouse.

The only man in Malthus's circle who resisted the blandishments of her ivory ear-trumpet appears to have been William Smyth, for Miss Martineau went out of her way to attack him posthumously in 1863, when she was writing an obituary of the Marquess of Lansdowne, formerly Lord Henry

451

Petty, in the *Daily News*. Referring to Lord Henry's giving his old friend the Chair of Modern History at Cambridge, she remarked: 'There is no saying what benefit might have accrued to British statesmanship if a man of more vigour, philosophy and comprehensiveness of mind than Professor Smyth had been appointed to so important a chair.'[78]

Miss Martineau stayed some time with the Malthuses in August 1833, writing during the day, and exploring the neighbourhood on horse-back, 'a pleasant riding-party of five or six', in the cool of the evening.[79] It would be interesting to know what her hostesses thought of her, for women were more critical than men of the 'deaf girl from Norwich'. Anna Letitia Le Breton was even sceptical about the deafness, for 'she could hear perfectly in a carriage',[80] and the Wedgwood ladies found her 'happy, good-humoured and conceited'.[81]

Maria Edgeworth gave Pakenham her views of Harriet Martineau in the spring of 1834; she was writing him a long account of a tour she had made in Connemara, with Sir Culling and Lady Smith, née Isabella Carr. There had been a diversion at a subterranean passage called the Pigeon-hole, and one Madgy Bourke had lit bundles of straw for them, which illuminated the rocks as they floated away on an underground stream:

> Well [wrote Maria], Madgy got her sixpence extraordinary from me at any rate, and I believe from Isabella, but Sir Culling held out and slipped into the boat with the consciousness of being worthy, no doubt, of all Miss Martineau's political economy admiration. And may be, Mr. Pakenham, you don't know who Miss Martineau is - though all London has been ringing many months with her fame and her political economy stories exemplifying the mischief of charity, etc. I have not time to explain. But in time the waft of the perfume of her fame will reach Indy and you, no doubt, at Amballah, perhaps by the time that there is no whiff of it left in these countries.[82]

The unpleasant whiff was never to be so strong again, although Harriet Martineau had a successful career. She left for two years in America on 4 August 1834, and the Poor Law Amendment Bill received the Royal Assent on the 14th.

It is unnecessary here to add to all that has already been written about this controversial Act, although it is worth bearing in mind what Sidney and Beatrice Webb were among the first to point out: the complete absence of statistics, particularly with regard to the numbers of young and healthy unemployed, who might rapidly reproduce themselves, as compared with the old, the sick and disabled, and the little children, who could not, and who were soon found to constitute the majority of those seeking assistance. There was no real basis for the widespread belief that the typical pauper was the eighteen-year-old lad who, putting 'the parish hat gaily on one side ... marched off to seek the lady of his choice, singing at the top of his voice that song which echoes in the summer time through all the green lanes and all the dusty roads in the southern counties . . .

> Hang sorrow and cast away care,
> The parish is bound to maintain us.'[83]

As the Webbs wrote, the Assistant Commissioners who were sent round the country to collect information did not return with facts and figures, but with opinions and picturesque anecdotes.[84] Nassau Senior was mainly responsible for writing the Report of the Royal Commission which led up to the Act. In brief, it provided for the appointment of three permanent Commissioners in London, to make regulations and supervise the building of workhouses all over the country; locally relief was to be organised not by Unions of parishes, but by Boards of Guardians of the Poor, who were to be elected by the rate-payers specifically for that purpose. Outdoor relief was to be curtailed, and denied altogether to the able-bodied; the declared principle was that the lot of the pauper was to be made 'less eligible' than that of the very poorest of the independent poor. Three years later Charles Dickens was to express the popular view of the new system in *Oliver Twist*; it was his first serious novel.

Malthus was in touch with Senior while he was writing his Report, as the following letter shows; it is dated 30 January 1834, from the East India College.

> My dear Senior,
> I have been routing about my books, and looking all over my pamphlets, but cannot find M. Aravabenè's account of his visit to the Dutch Colonies, though I am pretty sure I must have had it. I have found his 'Considerations sur les principaux moyens d'améliorer le sort des Classes Ouvrieres,' but I suppose you do not want that. I conclude I must have lent the other.

'M. Aravabenè' was in fact Count Giovanni Arrivabene (1787-1881). He came of a noble family in Mantua, and was a refugee from Austrian imperial tyranny who had been condemned to death in his absence. The Lancasterian school which he founded was closed, and he himself imprisoned for a time; he escaped to Switzerland and then to England (with the help of the Sismondis, amongst others) where he stayed from the autumn of 1822 until the spring of 1827, when he went to live in Belgium. His 'account of his visit to the Dutch Colonies' was actually a description of small-holdings established in Belgium as pauper settlements, *Lettre sur les Colonies Agricoles de la Belgique*, published in January 1833 in Brussels. According to the *Dizionario Biografico degli Italiani* he established 'una viva e durata amicizia col Senior', and among his miscellaneous economic writings are translations into French of Senior's Oxford lectures. Malthus's letter to Senior continued:

I am glad to hear that you are so near the period of parturition. I hope and trust that you will have no after pains. I fear that you have been by no means exempt from them during gestation. When once children are born I always wish them to *live*, and I sincerely hope and expect that that will be the case in this instance.

Are we to meet [at the Political Economy Club] this day week? I have had no notice on the subject yet. I wish the notices were earlier, so as to allow more time for the country gentlemen to make their arrangements.

Most truly Yours

T. Rob' Malthus.[85]

Senior's Report certainly lived. The Bill based upon it went through all its stages quickly, and it was the press, especially *The Times*, rather than the members of either House, who thundered against the 'Prussian' idea of a Central Board: it was a 'new-fangled institution', with no minister responsible to Parliament; this 'pinch-pauper triumvirate' and their satellites would draw enormous salaries themselves and be empowered to regulate the way in which the poor-rates were spent all over the country, regardless of the wishes of the actual rate-payers. On Friday 23 May *The Times* pontificated: 'Our firm conviction, therefore, is that Parliament will never pass this Poor Law Amendment Bill, nor any other bill that bears the remotest semblance to it.'

It was not until a fortnight later that the campaign against 'the Poor Law Revolution Bill' switched from constitutional to humanitarian issues, over the harsh treatment of unmarried mothers and the splitting-up of families in 'classified' workhouses. Cobbett fulminated against 'the Poor Man Robbery Bill', but the speech which would have hurt Malthus most was made by an inconspicuous MP called John Benett on 16 June:

> Mr. Benett would not concede that there was any surplus population. The dreadful distress which pervaded the country was attributable to nothing of the sort. The whole and sole cause of that distress consisted in the overwhelming embargo which was laid upon the industry and capital of the country connected with land, in the shape of enormous taxation. Human labour was the wealth of the country, and the more we sent abroad, the more we must really impoverish the country. The meanest beast we had - an ass for instance - was worth 15*s*; but a child was considered a nuisance, and, according to some of our political economists, it would be a good thing if, without any violation of all the laws of humanity, we could put a thousand children to death at a time.[86]

Other people took up the point, and *The Times* quoted at length from Jonathan Swift's *Modest Proposal for preventing the Children of Poor People from being a Burden to their Parents or the Country.* The idea was to fatten the Irish babies until they were a year old, to make food for the rich; culinary suggestions (at least for some readers) were the culminating horror of the satire.

When the Bill reached the House of Lords, Brougham thought fit to pronounce what was called 'a flaming eulogy on Mr. Malthus'. After referring to the imprudent marriages encouraged by the Poor Law, Brougham said:

> As he was on the subject of population, [he would] step aside for a moment to do justice to a most learned, able, and virtuous individual, whose name had been pursued by the deepest, and he was sorry to say in many instances by the most wilful misrepresentation, that any man of science had ever been subjected to ... That individual was distinguished for his amiable feelings and virtues in private life. Not only was he the ornament of the scientific society in which he moved, but he was the delight and the ornament of every private social circle in which he mingled. It was scarcely necessary for him to say that the individual to whom he was alluding was one than whom the Church of England did not possess a brighter character – the Rev. Mr. Malthus ...

There was no reason why Brougham should have stepped aside in this way; one can only conclude that he inserted this unfortunate passage to indicate to his Whig critics that he was still keeping Malthus in mind for preferment in the church.

The Times reported Brougham's oration on Tuesday 22 July,[87] and on Wednesday they printed a long letter from 'Invitus'. He wrote that he did not despair of hearing Brougham 'panegyrize the "preventive check" of Mr. Carlile as well as that of Mr. Malthus'.[88] It must have been a wretched day for the family, but on Thursday 24 July a leading article may have hurt even more. The Editor expressed alarm that the Lord Chancellor should 'revive and laud with profuse flattery the cold-blooded and cruel code of Malthus'. After a reference to Swift's proposal that the children of the poor should be *eaten*, he went on:

> The savages have an equally efficient mode of getting rid of the aged and infirm of their tribes. They *kill* them; which is, at least, more humane than the plan of Mr. Malthus; for starvation must be a painful and lingering death, whereas the tomahawk is as speedy as it is certain in its operation. Why not bring in a short bill combining these two plans – that of Dean Swift and that of the savages?[89]

The next day there appeared a letter from 'A Working Man', describing the 'miserable objects' seeking admission to a hospital:

> Will our philosophers say to these unfortunates, in the language of

455

Mr. Malthus, 'Nature has provided no cover at her table for you; the hand of charity ought not to be stretched out to save you'.[90]

Malthus was never to escape from those beggars at Nature's table whom he had expunged from the *Essay* nearly thirty years before.

But 1834 was not all unhappiness for the Malthi, and one of their sources of pleasure was the distribution of Linnell's engraving of Malthus's portrait to all their friends and relations; it is easy to understand the importance of such prints before photography was invented. Harriet wrote to Linnell,

> I hardly know whether to prefer the dark or light - some think the light best for the likeness - however I have myself selected a dark one as a present from me to Mr. George Batten in India ... Dr. Dealtry's direction is - Clapham - Professor Smythe [*sic*] Peter house Cambridge ... Mr. Malthus will take the first opportunity of sending the one intended for Jesus College to its destination - My Brother Mr. Charles Eckersall would be obliged if you let him have a good impression on the same terms ...

and so on. Harriet concluded, 'The prints are very much approved by all who have seen them.'

Otter was now Principal of King's College, London, but the family seem to have kept on a house in Shropshire, at Kinlet, which perhaps explains why they had two copies of the engraving. Harriet gave the one destined for their father 'as a present to the young ladies', and he in due course ordered a second print for himself, 'framed in the same manner in wood as the copy Mrs. Bray has'.

James Coleman, the College Purveyor, also acquired one or more of the framed prints which he appears to have ordered through his old master; presumably he had no bank account, for on 22 August 1834 Malthus sent Linnell a cheque with a brief note:[91]

> I have just received from Colman the sum of eleven pounds ten shillings which he requests me to remit to you by draft. I enclose you therefore a check on my bankers Mess[rs] Hoare 37 Fleet for the amount, the receipt of which I shall be obliged to you to acknowledge.
>
> I hope you have been quite well. Mrs. Malthus and my daughter send their compliments. My son is in Devonshire.

The last known letter in Malthus's hand was written some three weeks later, addressed to Mrs Otter at Kinlet and dated 15 September 1834.[92] By that time Grey had resigned, Melbourne was Prime Minister, and Parliament dispersed for the summer. Brougham's conduct was justifying *The Times*'s aspersions on his sanity: he travelled north in a sort of royal progress, not only making rash and inconsistent speeches on the way, but getting drunk at country house parties and even, it was alleged, losing the Great Seal during a game of blind man's buff; he should not have had the Seal with him in any case. On that 15 September, Brougham was in fact in Edinburgh, making one of his most indiscreet speeches at a dinner in honour of Lord Grey; his irresponsible conduct was one of the reasons why the King dismissed the ministry in November. Malthus wrote:

> My dear Mrs. Otter,
>
> I am much obliged to you for your letter, and your kind care of my interests in regard to the wine, about to be bottled. I find I was quite right in applying to you, and giving up his Reverence the Principal, who in spite of his misdoings I am rejoiced to hear is particularly well. But I am much concerned to hear of my dear friend Emily's illness. I hope I have been wrong in understanding you to say that you have been unwell too; you have mentioned yourself in the third person, and there may perhaps be some mistake. It would be very unfortunate if you were to have a second unfavourable summer at Kinlet.
>
> As to the wine, I doubt whether I can say with perfect accuracy how much I am entitled to. The case is this. Otter had four dozen of my cask, after it had been bottled, and I calculated that it came to a little above 2£ a dozen. I was to have an equivalent from his cask, which was higher priced, but I do not now recollect in what proportion exactly. If I have 3 dozen of yours I shall be amply repaid; but I may not be entitled to so much. You know the price of yours and can calculate an equivalent to 8£. The hamper may be sent by any waggon going from your neighbourhood to London to be forwarded by Fishers Hertford Waggon Bishopsgate Street to the East India College. Be so good as to let me have a line to say when and by what conveyance it is sent to London, that I may apprize Fisher of it. I hope to hear a much improved account of Emily and yourself.
>
> It is difficult to know what to say of Lord Brougham. He is no doubt rash and uncertain; but I still think he has been treated by the Times Examiner &c: much worse than he deserves. I am sorry that Lord Grey has retired, but am still inclined to look on the fair side of things in regard to Lord Melbourne.
>
> Most truly Yours
> T. R. Malthus.

This letter occupied two quarto sheets. The third side was taken up with a note to Jacqueline: this was not the baptismal name of any of Otter's daughters, but it may have been a pet-name; alternatively she may have been a young relative who lived with the family.[93] Mrs Otter must have described

457

some occasion on which this girl had spoken up for their old friend. Malthus wrote to her:

> My dear Jacqueline,
>
> I am very proud of you as my defender, and beg you will continue with equal skill and ability to execute that office (to which I hereby regularly appoint you) whenever you are in a company where I am attacked. I shall feel myself quite safe in your hands and that you will not only vindicate me against the accusation of massacring children, but say that I have specifically proposed as the best criterion of the happiness and good government of a country the number of the children born who arrive at the age of puberty.
>
> It is astonishing how many express a horror of my book who have never read it.
>
> The post man waits.
>
> > Yours affectionate friend
> > T. R. Malthus.
>
> Emily is expecting a letter from Sophia. All well and send love.

Dear Jacqueline, intelligent and loyal. Was she also pretty? Did she become a Victorian grandmother? Malthus must have written other letters in the three and a half months that were left to him, but none later have been found. It is certainly possible that the unknown Jacqueline was the recipient of Malthus's last word on the subject of population.

Two months after this letter was written, the Government went out of office; the Duke of Wellington held the fort for the Tories until Sir Robert Peel could be summoned back from Italy to become Prime Minister. On 21 November 1834 Samuel Rogers wrote to Richard Sharp:

> What a strange hubbub there is just now! The ex-Ministers come in shoals to Brooks's, and are hand and glove with everybody, all but Brougham, who has gone nowhere, not even to Holland House . . . His last gift was of a Canonry of Norwich to Sedgwick. He filled up twelve livings the last day. Nothing to Malthus. A very pretty living near Hertford fell to Lord Holland in October, and he offered it to M, but he must have given up the college and he declined it.[94]

As so often in Malthus's life story, one longs to know more: whether he and Harriet lay awake night after night discussing the arguments for and against leaving Hailey House, or whether he had long ago decided that he was too old to bear transplanting.

458

Epilogue

On 31 December 1834 Bray and Warren arranged for the insertion in four newspapers of what they called 'Advertizements of Mr. Malthus death'. Those in the *Courier* and the *Globe* appeared the same evening; those in the *Morning Chronicle* and *The Times* on Thursday 1 January 1835: 'On the 29th ult., at Bath, after a few days' illness, the Rev. Thomas Robert Malthus.'

Otter elaborated a little in the *Memoir*: 'He left London a few days before his death, on a visit to his father-in-law at Bath, in good spirits, and apparently in strong health, anticipating a cheerful Christmas with his children and other members of his family who were invited to meet him; but Providence had ordained otherwise – the meeting took place but the joy was not there; Mr. Malthus was taken ill soon after his arrival, of a disorder of the heart, of which it is believed he was never conscious.'[1]

The obituary notices in *The Times* and the *Morning Post* were mere snippets, based on a paragraph in the *Globe*: Malthus was 'a man whose private virtues were not and could not be disputed by those who were most hostile to his views of social economy'. In the next line *The Times* reported that Lord Auckland, the First Lord of the Admiralty, had removed to his former residence in Grosvenor Street. The *Morning Post*, even more incongruously, announced Malthus's death, 'with very sincere concern', in the 'Fashionable World' column, which concluded with the news that the East Sussex Foxhounds 'had a splendid run on Monday'.

The *Morning Chronicle* gave Malthus a long article which would nowadays be regarded as distastefully critical for an obituary:

> The work on Population took a strong hold on the public, and ever since its appearance the doctrines he advanced have more or less entered into all speculations with regard to the condition and future prospects of mankind. He is also the author of various tracts on the Corn Laws, &c, and a work on Political Economy; but these publications did not add much to his reputation. He committed the capital blunder of supposing that a glut could exist in all commodities at the same time, which amounts to a positive contradiction in terms.
>
> . . . Mr. Malthus has neither correctly expounded the doctrine of population, not done justice to the many able modern writers who, long before the appearance of his work, advanced opinions on the

subject similar to his own. He has uniformly placed the tendency of
our species to increase beyond their means of subsistence under a
somewhat gloomy aspect. It is, however, to this tendency that we are
indebted for all our advancement in civilization ... The fear of
sinking stimulates to invention, and every addition thereby made to
the enjoyments of mankind, enlarges their notions of what they
ought to obtain, and becomes then a point from which further
advances are made.

At this juncture, Malthus's friends must have thrown up their hands in
exasperated despair. The article concluded, 'Mr. Malthus was beloved by
all who had the advantage of knowing him. He was, in truth, a most amiable
and accomplished gentleman.'[2]

Otter naturally said the same - it was indubitable - in the *Memoir* prefixed
to Cazenove's posthumous edition of the *Principles of Political Economy*.
Henry Malthus sent Brougham a copy, with a brief note, on 12 February
1837; Otter was by that time Bishop of Chichester and Hal's father-in-law,
and Hal described him to Brougham as Malthus's 'most intimate friend'.[3]
Apart from this memoir, and Empson's *Edinburgh Review* article, Malthus's
death attracted surprisingly little attention among the literary: they were far
more concerned with Coleridge's death on 25 July (1834), and then with
Charles Lamb's on 27 December, just two days before Malthus.

On 6 January 1835 Malthus was buried in what was then the north
aisle of Bath Abbey. When, in 1863, this was covered by pews, the memorial
tablet was placed in its present position in the north porch at the west end
of the church. The long epitaph is believed to have been written by Otter,
and seems rather pompous now:

> ... HE LIVED A SERENE AND HAPPY LIFE
> DEVOTED TO THE PURSUIT AND COMMUNICATION
> OF TRUTH
> SUPPORTED BY A CALM BUT FIRM CONVICTION OF THE
> USEFULNESS OF HIS LABORS
> CONTENT WITH THE APPROBATION OF THE WISE AND
> GOOD ...

More congenial to us are the jottings which Richard Jones set down in a
note-book. They were not published until 1859, when John Cazenove edited
posthumously Jones's *Literary Remains*, with a 'Prefatory Notice' from
Whewell. At some time, for the notes are given all in a jumble, Jones was
inspired to write thus of Malthus on Population:[4]

Columbus saw but little of the new world, his discovery of which
was to exercise such wide dominion over the fortunes and habits of
the old. Yet his name is stamped in the annals of mankind, fixing
upon it an interest which no subsequent discoverers share, however

accurately they have surveyed its unknown coasts, or corrected our imperfect notions of its form and bearing.

It is just so with that new and vast branch of knowledge which Malthus has revealed to us. Its influence on the habits and happiness of nations has fastened itself upon us, and all subsequent progress in enlarging or correcting his views, will only throw more light on the name and services of him who first effectually dispelled our ignorance of its influence.

There is much to be supplied and something to be amended in Malthus's views and language; but as the founder, not the finisher, of an important branch of knowledge, we owe him thanks and reverence.

Notes and References

I have not given the sources of information from standard works of reference such as *Burke's Landed Gentry*, the Oxford 'Companions', the *Dictionary of National Biography*, and the Austrian, Belgian, Danish, French, German and Italian equivalents. Nor have I thought it necessary explicitly to state obvious references to Venn's *Alumni Cantabrigienses*, Foster's *Alumni Oxonienses*, and so on.

Where papers were privately owned or uncatalogued at the time I was working on them, I have tried to be particularly careful to give the relevant dates in the text, so that the passages should be fairly easy to find.

With regard to printed books, reference is made wherever possible to the latest editions, or to those most likely to be accessible to the ordinary student or general reader. It will be appreciated that much work by Malthus and his contemporaries can only be read in a few libraries in large towns or universities.

ABBREVIATIONS

IOR: India Office Records.
PRO: Public Record Office.
Sraffa's *Ricardo: The Works and Correspondence of David Ricardo*, edited in eleven volumes by Piero Sraffa (Cambridge University Press 1951–73).

PROLOGUE

1 Parish register of Wotton, Surrey, and Burial Register of Bath Abbey.
2 Everyman reprints of 1958 and 1967 (2 vols), Vol. I, p. vi.
3 John Man, *History and Antiquities of the Borough of Reading* (Reading, 1816), p. 150.
4 J. M. Guilding, ed., *The Diary of the Corporation of Reading* (3 vols, London, 1895), Vol. II, pp. 61, 67, 140, 202; Vol. III, pp. 197, 329–30, 351.
5 Quitclaims, Bonds and Releases in the Berkshire Record Office. See also John Orlebar Payne, *Collections for a History of the Family of Malthus* (privately printed, 1890), especially pp. 25, 34, 77. Payne is not reliable, and bowdlerises the contents of wills in the interests of respectability. He does, however, give a useful preliminary guide to the sources of some of the Malthus family archives.
6 Berkshire Record Office, ref. D/EX 265 L2.

7 Charles Coates, *History and Antiquities of Reading* (London, 1802), p. 391.
8 Berkshire Record Office, ref. D/EB 6 Q2.
9 W. E. M. Blandy, *A History of the Reading Municipal Charities* (Reading, 1962), p. 2.
10 The correct name of Reading Blue Coat School is Aldworth's Hospital; it was founded in 1646.
11 Payne, *Family of Malthus*, p. 80.
12 I am indebted for this information to the kindness of Mr W. R. Le Fanu, Librarian of the Royal College of Surgeons.
13 James Bonar, *Malthus and his Work* (2nd edn, Allen & Unwin, London, 1924), p. 409.
14 Lady Theresa Lewis, ed., *Extracts of the Journals and Correspondence of Miss Berry* (3 vols, London, 1865), Vol. II, p. 475.
15 Harriet Martineau, *Autobiography* (2nd edn, 3 vols, London, 1877), Vol. I, pp. 327-8.
16 Henry Holland, *Recollections of Past Life* (London, 1872), p. 241.
17 Christina Colvin, ed., *Maria Edgeworth: Letters from England 1813-1844* (Oxford University Press, 1971), pp. 331, 423-4.

Chapter I BACKGROUND

1 Leslie G. Matthews, *The Royal Apothecaries* (Wellcome, London, 1967), pp. 138-59.
2 Information kindly supplied by Mr Richard Jeffree.
3 Philip Morant, *The History and Antiquities of the County of Essex* (2 vols, folio 1760, 1768), Vol. II, p. 543.
4 PRO, L.C.3.53 (21).
5 Historical Manuscripts Commission, Report on the MSS of the Marquess of Downshire by Sir William Trumbull, Vol. I, pt II, p. 902.
6 PRO, L.S.13.35 (52); L.S.13.36 (17).
7 PRO, L.S.13.40 (8).
8 A notebook lent by Mr Noel Vicars-Harris.
9 PRO, L.S.13.46 *passim.*
10 Jonathan Swift, *Journal to Stella*, ed. Harold Williams (2 vols, Oxford University Press, 1948), Vol. I, p. 202.
11 John Gay, *Poetry and Prose*, ed. V. A. Dearing and C. E. Beckwith (2 vols, Oxford University Press, 1974), Vol. I, p. 259; Commentary, Vol. II, p. 598.
12 George Sherburn, ed., *Correspondence of Alexander Pope* (5 vols, Oxford University Press, 1956), Vol. II, pp. 33-4. The date is 21 February 1719/20.
13 Notebooks lent by Mr Noel Vicars-Harris.
14 *Ibid.*
15 A bound folio lent by the late Mr George Nixon-Eckersall, ff. 28, 62-3.
16 A notebook lent by the late Mr George Nixon-Eckersall.
17 A notebook lent by Mr Noel Vicars-Harris.
18 A notebook lent by the late Mr George Nixon-Eckersall.
19 PRO, L.C.5.53 (24a); L.C.5.168 (30).
20 Parish registers of Harrow-on-the-Hill.

21 I am indebted to Mr Anthony Boynton Wood of Hollin Hall for drawing my attention to this picture of his cousins.
22 This picture is now in the Birmingham City Museum and Art Gallery.
23 Owen Manning (d. 1801) and William Bray, History of Surrey (3 vols, London, 1804, 1809, 1814), Vol. I, p. 578.
24 John Timbs, A Picturesque Promenade round Dorking (2nd edn, London, 1823), pp. 201-2.
25 Manning and Bray, op. cit., Vol. I, p. 578n.
26 Louis-Jean Courtois, Le Séjour de Jean-Jacques Rousseau en Angleterre 1766-1767 (Geneva, 1911), passim, especially pp. 204-22.
27 Wotton parish register.
28 The original manuscript of Louisa Bray's 'Recollections' is lost, but there is a typescript copy in Guildford Muniment Room (ref. 85/23), which I have been able to check with a transcription made in 1882 by Col. Sydenham Malthus (1831-1916).
29 [William Otter], Memoir of Robert Malthus, pp. xxi-xxii. This was published with the posthumous 2nd edn of Malthus's Principles of Political Economy (London, 1836). It has been reprinted by Augustus M. Kelley of New York, in 1951 and 1964, with the original pagination.
30 Richard Graves, Senilities (London, 1801), pp. 224-7.
31 Richard Graves, The Triflers (London, 1806), p. 13.
32 Quoted by Charles Jarvis Hill in Richard Graves (Smith College Studies in Modern Languages, Northampton, Mass., 1932), p. 8.
33 Richard Graves, Euphrosyne (2 vols, London, 1783), Vol. I, pp. 36-40.
34 City of Bath Archives, and The History of the Parish of Claverton, compiled by members of the Claverton Down Women's Institute (Bath, 1962).
35 John Britton, Autobiography (London, 1850), p. 185.
36 There are innumerable collections of prints of Bath, of which perhaps Britton's Views (London, 1829) is the best.
37 James Bonar, Malthus and his Work, (2nd edn, Allen & Unwin, London, 1924), p. 405, dates this letter 10 August 1780, when Don Roberto would have been fourteen.
38 Otter's Memoir, pp. xxix-xxxi.
39 Richard Graves, Euphrosyne, Vol. II, pp. 135-6.
40 Otter's Memoir, p. xxiv.
41 John Aikin, MD, A Description of the Country from thirty to forty Miles round Manchester (London, 1795), pp. 300-4. Malthus quoted this work in the Essay on Population, Everyman edn, Vol. II, pp. 131-2. For the Aikins' background see Betsy Rodgers' Georgian Chronicle: Mrs. Barbauld and her Family (Methuen, London, 1958).
42 Gilbert Wakefield, Memoirs, written by himself: edited and continued by J. T. Rutt and A. Wainewright (2 vols, London, 1804), Vol. I, p. 216.
43 Ibid., Vol. I, pp. 247, 249.
44 Ibid., Vol. II, pp. 307-8n, 309n.
45 [William Empson], 'Life, Writings and Character of Mr. Malthus', Edinburgh Review, January 1837, Vol. LXIV, p. 505.
46 Mrs Le Breton [Anna Letitia Aikin], Memories of Seventy Years (London, 1884), p. 195.

47 Bonar, *Malthus and his Work*, pp. 406-7.
48 *Ibid.*, p. 404.
49 Wakefield's *Memoirs*, Vol. I, p. 507.
50 *Poems by the late George Monck Berkeley, Esq.* (London, 1797), preface, pp. xliv, li, cxxxi, clxxxix-xxx; poems, pp. 63, 71.
51 G. M. Berkeley, *An Elegy on the Death of Miss M - s* (London, 1786), see especially pp. vii, 18.
52 Louisa Bray's 'Recollections'. The epitaph was adapted for her sister Mary in 1819.
53 [Empson] *Edinburgh Review*, January 1837, Vol. LXIV, p. 477.
54 MS letter to William Otter from E. D. Clarke, 15 April 1798, in the Archives of Jesus College, Cambridge.
55 Bonar, *op. cit.*, pp. 407-8.
56 William Otter, *Life and Remains of Edward Daniel Clarke* (2nd edn, 2 vols, London, 1825), Vol. I, p. 73.
57 Henry Gunning, *Reminiscences of the University, Town and County of Cambridge from the year 1780* (2nd edn, 2 vols, London, 1855), Vol. I, p. 188.
58 George Pryme, *Autobiographic Recollections* ed. by his daughter Alicia Bayne (Cambridge, 1870), p. 44.
59 Otter's *Memoir*, pp. xxxii-xxxiii.
60 *Ibid.*, p. xxxv.
61 Bonar, *op cit.*, p. 410.
62 Otter's *Memoir*, pp. xxxvi-xxxviii.
63 Bonar, *op cit.*, pp. 409-10.
64 Otter's *Memoir*, p. xxv.
65 William Frend, *Thoughts on Subscription to Religious Tests* (Cambridge, 1787), preface to 1st edn, p. x.
66 G. W. Meadley, *Memoirs of William Paley D.D.* (Sunderland, 1809), pp. 42-3.
67 Gunning, *op cit.*, Vol. I, pp. 86-7.
68 Bonar, *op cit.*, p. 412.
69 Louisa Bray's 'Recollections'.
70 It is to three of these descendants of Daniel Malthus, the late Miss Helen Lloyd of Albury and the Misses Warren of Shere, that I owe most of the information about the Surrey background of their 'Uncle Robert'.
71 Through the good offices of the Leger Galleries, Ltd., I learned that this picture is now in a private collection in Rome.
72 The picture belongs to one of her descendants. Mrs Brenda McCleary kindly supplied the dates from Reynolds's sitter-books.
73 The Guildford Muniment Room references for William Bray's diary are 85/1/1-76.
74 Quoted by E. M. Forster in *Marianne Thornton* (Arnold, London, 1956), p. 35.
75 Otter's *Memoir*, p. xxv.
76 PRO, Prob. 11. Piece no. 1646, f. 415.
77 This picture belongs to one of her descendants.
78 PRO, Prob. 11. Piece no. 1652, f. 32.

79 Information from the MS book of family notes compiled by Col. Sydenham Malthus and kindly lent by Miss Jane Catchpole.

Chapter II THE PRINCIPLE OF POPULATION

Wherever possible, I give a reference to the Everyman edition of Malthus's second version of the *Essay on the Principle of Population*: this is based on the sixth edition of 1826; the latest printing of 1973 is bound in one volume, but the pagination of the earlier two-volume versions is retained. In 1966 Macmillan reproduced the anonymous 'First Essay' of 1798 with the original pagination, and this I quote where appropriate. The editions of 1803, 1806, 1807 and 1817 are hard to find, and I refer to them only when it is essential to do so, to show how Malthus changed his mind in the course of twenty years of war, riot and economic depression.

1 Otter's *Memoir* (see Chap. I, n. 29), pp. xxviii-xxix.
2 The diaries of William Man Godschall are in Guildford Muniment Room, ref. 52/1/2.
3 Surrey Record Society, No. XXV (London, 1927), pp. vii-ix.
4 [Malthus] *An Essay on the Principle of Population* (hereinafter cited as *Population*) (London, 1798), p. 73.
5 Sir Frederick Morton Eden, *The State of the Poor* (3 vols, quarto, London, 1797), Vol. I, p. 553.
6 *Drawings of Gainsborough*, Introd. by Lord Ronald Sutherland Gower (London, 1906), Plate XIV.
7 Okewood Chapel Register, Guildford Muniment Room, ref. PSH/OK/1/1.
8 Owen Manning and William Bray, *History of Surrey* (3 vols, London), Vol. II, 1809, p. 159.
9 Henry Cockburn, *Memorials of his Time* (2 vols, Edinburgh, 1856), Vol. I, p. 80.
10 William Godwin, *Thoughts Occasioned by the Perusal of Dr. Parr's Spital Sermon* (London, 1801), p. 56.
11 Arthur Gray and Frederick Brittain, *A History of Jesus College Cambridge* (Heinemann, London, 1960), pp. 123-30.
12 Edith Morley, 'Some Contemporary Allusions to Coleridge's Death', in Edmund Blunden and Earl Leslie Griggs, eds, *Coleridge: Studies by Several Hands on the Hundredth Anniversary of his Death* (Constable, London, 1934), p. 93.
13 Frida Knight, *University Rebel: The Life of William Frend* (Gollancz, London, 1971), *passim*.
14 William Frend, *Peace and Union* (St Ives, 1793), p. 36.
15 *Ibid.*, pp. 31-2.
16 *Ibid.*, p. 43.
17 A. J. Eagleston, 'Wordsworth, Coleridge and the Spy' in Blunden and Griggs, *op. cit.*, pp. 73-87.
18 [Empson] *Edinburgh Review*, January 1837, Vol. LXIV, pp. 479, 481-3.
19 Otter's *Memoir*, p. xxxvin.

20 James Bonar, *Malthus and his Work* (2nd edn, Allen & Unwin, London, 1924), pp. 413-14.

21 Earl of Ilchester, ed., *Journal of Lady Holland* (2nd edn, 2 vols, London, 1908), Vol. I, p. 258.

22 *Sir James Mackintosh* by his son (2nd edn, 2 vols, London, 1836), Vol. I, p. 246.

23 Gilbert Wakefield, *A Reply to some parts of the Bishop of Llandaff's Address to the People of Great Britain* (2nd edn, London, 1798), pp. 30, 35.

24 [Malthus] *Population*, 1798, p. 356 and n.

25 Samuel Johnson, *Lives of the English Poets* (Everyman edn, 2 vols, London, 1925), 'Milton', Vol. I, pp. 62-3.

26 William Wales, *An Inquiry into the Present State of the Population in England and Wales; and the Proportion which the present Number of Inhabitants bears to the Number at former Periods* (London, 1781), p. 7.

27 *Ibid.*, p. 77.

28 John Howlett, *An Examination of Dr. Price's Essay on the Population of England and Wales, and the Doctrine of an Increased Population in this Kingdom established by Facts* (Maidstone, 1781), p. ix.

29 Sir F. M. Eden, *An Estimate of the Number of Inhabitants in Great Britain and Ireland* (London, 1800), p. 48.

30 *Ibid.*, p. 3.

31 Robert Wallace, *Various Prospects of Mankind, Nature, and Providence* (Edinburgh, 1761), p. iv.

32 *Ibid.*, pp. 114-15.

33 *Ibid.*, pp. 119, 120, 121.

34 William Godwin, *An Enquiry into Political Justice* (3rd edn, 2 vols octavo, London, 1798), Vol. II, p. 504.

35 *Ibid.*, Vol. II, p. 528.

36 [Malthus] *Population*, 1798, p. 173.

37 Amelia Heber, *The Life of Reginald Heber* (2 vols, London, 1830), Vol. I, p. 13.

38 William Godwin, *An Enquiry into Political Justice* (1st edn, 2 vols quarto, London, 1793), Vol. II, pp. 867-8.

39 Marie-Jean-Antoine-Nicolas Caritat, Marquis de Condorcet (1743-94), *Esquisse d'un Tableau Historique des Progrès de l'Esprit Humain* (2nd edn, Paris, 1795), p. 358:

'Si on suppose ... le progrès de la raison ayent marché de pair avec ceux des sciences et des arts, que les ridicules préjugés de la superstition, ayent cessé de répandre sur la morale, une austérité qui la corrompt et la dégrade au lieu de l'épurer et de l'élever; les hommes sauront alors que, s'ils ont des obligations à l'égard des êtres qui ne sont pas encore, elles ne consistent pas à leur donner l'existence, mais le bonheur; elles ont pour objet le bien-être général de l'espèce humaine ou de la société dans laquelle ils vivent; de la famille à laquelle ils sont attachés; et non la puérile idée de charger la terre d'êtres inutiles et malheureux. Il pourroit donc y avoir une limite à la masse possible des subsistances, et par consequent à la plus grande population possible, sans qu'il en résultât cette destruction prématurée ... d'une partie des êtres qui ont reçu la vie.'

40 [Malthus] *Population*, 1798, Preface, p. i.

41 Otter's *Memoir*, pp. xxxviii-xxxix.
42 George Pryme, *Autobiographic Recollections* (Cambridge, 1870), p. 66.
43 [Malthus] *Population*, 1798, pp. 37-8.
44 *Ibid.*, pp. 21, 23, 25-6.
45 *Ibid.*, p. 23.
46 *Ibid.*, p. iv.
47 *Ibid.*, p. 201.
48 *Ibid.*, pp. 72-3.
49 *Ibid.*, pp. 223-7.
50 Mary Berry, *Journals* (see Prologue, n. 14), Vol. II, pp. 72-4.
51 Knight, *op. cit.*, p. 303.
52 Mary Russell Mitford, *Our Village* (4th edn, London, 1828), Vol. I, p. 104.
53 [Malthus] *Population*, 1798, pp. 75-6.
54 *Ibid.*, pp. 134-5.
55 *The Analytical Review*, published by Joseph Johnson, was 'the first British literary and scientific monthly aimed at the general educated public and consisting almost entirely of book reviews'. It lasted from May 1788 to June 1799. (See Claire Tomalin's *The Life and Death of Mary Wollstonecraft*, Weidenfeld & Nicolson, London, 1974, p. 70n.) The anonymous *Essay on Population* was reviewed in the *Analytical Review* for August 1798, pp. 119-25.
56 [Malthus] *Population*, 1798, pp. 312-13 and p. 307.
57 *Ibid.*, p. 307.
58 *Ibid.*, pp. 335-6.
59 *New Annual Register*, Issue of 1799 (Robinson, London), p. 229. The *Essay on Population* received just under two columns, after twenty-seven columns of reviews of theological works, including a choice 'from the mass of single sermons published during the year'.
60 [Malthus] *Population*, 1798, p. 390.
61 *Ibid.*, p. 376.
62 *Ibid.*, p. 373.
63 *Ibid.*, p. 395.
64 *Ibid.*, p. 358.
65 *Ibid.*, pp. 370-1.
66 *Ibid.*, pp. 211-12.
67 *Ibid.*, pp. 63-5.
68 This letter is given in full in Charles Kegan Paul's *William Godwin: His Friends and Contemporaries* (2 vols, London, 1876), Vol. I, pp. 321-5; also in James Bonar's *Notes* on the 1798 *Essay* reprinted by Macmillan in 1966, pp. iii-viii.
69 Anon. ['The Remarker'] *Remarks on Mr. Malthus's Essay on the Principle of Population* (London, 1803), p. 1.
70 Malthus, *Population*, Everyman edn, Vol. I, p. 1.
71 Bonar, *op cit.*, pp. 414-15. For a note on Süssmilch see below, p. 471.
72 MS letter to Otter from Clarke in the Archives of Jesus College, Cambridge.
73 William Otter, *Life and Remains of Edward Daniel Clarke* (2nd edn, 2 vols, London, 1825), Vol. I, pp. 64, 38.
74 *Ibid.*, Vol. I, p. 437.

75 *Ibid.*, Vol. I, pp. 440-3.
76 Patricia James, ed., *The Travel Diaries of T. R. Malthus* (Cambridge University Press, 1966), *passim* pp. 28-219.
77 PRO, Prob. 11. Piece no. 1335, f. 46.
78 *Gentleman's Magazine*, January-June 1800, Vol. LXX; Obituary, p. 177; 'Additions and Corrections' p. 281.
79 In the Dalton Hill Library at Jesus College, Cambridge.
80 For a note on John Murray see below, p. 483.
81 PRO, Prob. 11. Piece no. 1588, f. 14.

Chapter III   THE GREAT QUARTO OF 1803

1 Sraffa's *Ricardo*, Vol. VI, p. 346.
2 Mary Berry, *Journals* (see Prologue, n. 14), Vol. II, p. 466.
3 Robert Southey, *Letters from England* by Don Manuel Alvarez Espriella (3 vols, London, 1807), Vol. I, p. 142. Or see p. 77 of the edition ed. Jack Simmons, published by the Cresset Press in 1951.
4 William Smyth, *Memoir of Mr. Sheridan* (Leeds, 1840), p. 36.
5 *Ibid.*, p. 11.
6 Robert Donald Thornton, *James Currie* (Oliver & Boyd, Edinburgh and London, 1963), pp. 164-5, 194-5.
7 Mrs Le Breton [Anne Letitia Aikin], *Memories of Seventy Years* (London, 1884), p. 139.
8 P. W. Clayden, *The Early Life of Samuel Rogers* (London, 1887), p. 449.
9 Thomas Pinney, ed., *The Letters of Thomas Babington Macaulay* (Cambridge University Press), Vol. II (1974), p. 313.
10 *Sir James Mackintosh* by his son (2nd edn, 2 vols, London, 1836), Vol. I, p. 46.
11 *Ibid.*, Vol. I, p. 87.
12 Josiah C. Wedgwood, *A History of the Wedgwood Family* (London, 1908), p. 183 n. 3.
13 Lady Seymour, ed., *The 'Pope' of Holland House:* Selections from the Correspondence of John Whishaw and his Friends, with a *Memoir* and an account of the King of Clubs by W. P. Courtney (London, 1906), *passim*.
14 William Beattie, ed., *Life and Letters of Thomas Campbell* (3 vols, London, 1849), Vol. I, p. 450.
15 Christina Colvin, ed., *Maria Edgeworth: Letters from England 1813-1844* (Oxford University Press, 1971), p. 61.
16 *Memoirs of the Life of Sir Samuel Romilly* written by himself, with a selection from his correspondence edited by his sons (2nd edn, 3 vols, London, 1840), Vol. II, p. 207.
17 *Ibid.*, Vol. II, p. 224.
18 *Ibid.*, Vol. III, p. 144.
19 Amelia Heber, *The Life of Reginald Heber* (2 vols, London, 1830), Vol. I, p. 19.
20 Arthur Young, *The Question of Scarcity Plainly Stated* (London, 1800), pp. 83-6.

21 This letter was printed in the *Economic Journal* in 1897, Vol. VII, pp. 270-1. The MS may be seen in the Paleography Room of the University of London Library.

22 [Malthus] *An Investigation of the Cause of the Present High Price of Provisions* by the Author of the Essay on the Principle of Population (2nd edn, London, 1800), p. 4n.

23 Romilly, *Memoirs*, Vol. II, pp. 74-5.

24 [Malthus] *High Price of Provisions*, pp. 5-7.

25 *Ibid.*, pp. 19-20.

26 *Ibid.*, p. 10.

27 *Ibid.*, p. 21.

28 *Ibid.*, pp. 23-5.

29 *Ibid.*, pp. 26-8.

30 Edward Gardner, of Frampton-upon-Severn, *Reflections upon the Evil Effects of an Increasing Population upon the Present High Price of Provisions* (R. Raikes, Gloucester, 1800), p. 5.

31 William Otter, *Life and Remains of Edward Daniel Clarke* (2nd edn, 2 vols, London, 1825), Vol. II, p. 203n.

32 Malthus, *Population*, Everyman edn, Vol. I, p. 38.

33 *Ibid.*, Vol. I, p. 143 n. 2.

34 François Le Vaillant (1753-1824), *Voyage dans l'Intérieure de l'Afrique* (2 vols, Paris, 1790). Le Vaillant was a wealthy gentleman who travelled in South Africa in 1780-5, being impelled to go there because 'c'étoit la terre encore vierge'. In fact he was scarcely ever very far from the Dutch at the Cape of Good Hope.

35 Jean Baptiste Duhalde (1674-1743). Malthus used a four-volume edition translated by R. Brookes, published in London in 1736 under the title: *The General History of China containing a Geographical, Historical, Chronological, Political and Physical Description of the Empire of China, Chinese-Tartary, Corea and Tibet, including an Exact and Particular Account of their Customs, Manners, Ceremonies, Religion, Arts and Sciences*.

36 Franciscus Creuxius (François de Creux 1596-1666), *Historiae Canadiensis seu Novae Franciae* (Quarto, Paris, 1664). At page 480 there is a sort of pull-out engraving of Jesuits and their converts being heroically martyred in every conceivable way; they are being burned on bonfires, stabbed with daggers, shot at with both bows and arrows and muskets, hacked with tomahawks; only some spears about the place are apparently not in use.

37 *Lettres Édifiantes et Curieuses, écrites des Missions Étrangères*. Malthus possessed all twenty-four volumes of an edition published piecemeal in Paris in the 1780s.

38 William Robertson (1721-93), *History of America*. Malthus used the 5th edn, 3 vols octavo, London, 1788.

39 Antonio Ulloa (1716-95). The French translation Malthus used was published by Arkstée & Merkus, Amsterdam and Leipzig, 1752, under the title *Voyage Historique de l'Amérique Méridionale*. According to Professor Anthony Flew, an English version had in fact been published in 1758, translated by J. Adams as *A Voyage to South America* (Penguin Books, Malthus's 1798 *Essay* and *Summary View*, Harmondsworth, 1970, p. 275).

NOTES TO PAGES 95-104

Don Antonio Ulloa, captured and released by the British, was made a Fellow of the Royal Society.

40 Johann Peter Süssmilch (1707-67), *Die göttliche Ordnung in den Veränderungen des menschlichen Geschlechts, aus der Geburt, dem Tode und der Fortplantzung desselben erwiesen*, 1st edn, Berlin, 1741, subsequent versions 1761, 1765, posthumous 1775. Süssmilch is regarded in Germany as the founder of social biology; Malthus may only have known of his work through Price's *Reversionary Payments*.

41 August Friedrich Wilhelm Crome (1753-1833), *Uber die Grösse und Bevölkerung der sämtlichen europäischen Staaten*, Leipzig, 1785, revised 1792. There are French, Dutch and English translations of this work, but I have not been able to find a copy of one which Malthus might have used.

42 Frederik Thaarup (1766-1845), *Statistik der danischen Monarchie*, 2 vols, Copenhagen, 1795, 1796. See Malthus's *Travel Diaries*, pp. 208-10.

43 Peter Simon Pallas (1741-1811), a native of Berlin, where he died. The four volumes of his *Découvertes russes* were published in Berne and Lausanne in 1781 and 1784, according to Malthus (Everyman edn, Vol. I, p. 83n). He was able to obtain Pallas' *Voyages ... en différentes Provinces de l'Empire de Russie*, published in Paris in 5 vols in 1788 (Everyman edn, Vol. I, pp. 102-8).

44 Letter of 16 March 1802 from Constantinople, printed in Otter's *Life of Clarke*, Vol. II, p. 175.

45 James Bruce (1730-94), *Travels to Discover the Source of the Nile* (5 vols, London, 1790). Otter's *Life of Clarke*, Vol. II, p. 175.

46 Guildford Muniment Room, ref. 52/1/2.

47 Harriet's MS diary is now, with Malthus's MS travel diaries, in the Cambridge University Library.

48 Warren Derry, *Dr. Parr* (Oxford University Press, 1966), pp. 210-18.

49 William Godwin, *Thoughts Occasioned by the Perusal of Dr. Parr's Spital Sermon* (London, 1801), pp. 46-7, 37, 43.

50 In Dr Williams's Library, London; Letter no. 34.

51 *Edinburgh Review*, No. 1, October 1802, p. 89.

52 [Malthus] *Population*, 1798, p. 382n.

53 Malthus, *Population*, Everyman edn, Vol. II, p. 203.

54 Malthus, *Population*, 1803, pp. 531-2.

55 Malthus, *Population*, 1806, Vol. I, p. xii.

56 Malthus, *Population*, 1803, pp. 549-50.

57 The Lincoln Diocesan and County Archives are housed in the Castle at Lincoln, where the old Walesby registers are also deposited.

58 The Bray and Warren letter-books are now in the Greater London Record Office, ref. Ac.71.38.

59 Kenneth Curry, ed., *New Letters of Robert Southey* (2 vols, Columbia University Press, New York and London, 1965), Vol. I, pp. 326-7.

60 Malthus, *Population*, Everyman edn, Vol. I, p. 1.

61 Sir James Steuart, *An Inquiry into the Principles of Political Oeconomy*, ed. with an Introduction by Andrew S. Skinner (2 vols, Oliver & Boyd, Edinburgh and London, 1966), Vol. I, p. 137.

62 *Ibid.*, pp. 36-7.
63 *Ibid.*, p. 88.
64 *Ibid.*, p. 39.
65 *Ibid.*, p. 44.
66 *Ibid.*, p. 40.
67 *Ibid.*, p. 119.
68 *Ibid.*, pp. 121, 122, 124.
69 *Ibid.*, p. 98.
70 *Ibid.*, p. 32.
71 Benjamin Franklin, *Political, Miscellaneous and Philosophical Pieces, now first collected* ... (London, 1799), p. 8. Or see *The Writings of Benjamin Franklin*, ed. Albert Henry Smyth (10 vols, New York, 1907), Vol. III, p. 64.
72 Franklin, *op. cit.*, pp. 9-11; Smyth edn, pp. 70-2.
73 Malthus, *Population*, Everyman edn, Vol. I, pp. 225-6.
74 Joseph Townsend, *A Journey through Spain in the Years 1786 and 1787; with particular attention to the Agriculture, Manufactures, Commerce, Population, Taxes and Revenue* ... (3 vols, London, 1791), Vol. III, p. 107.
75 *Ibid.*, Vol. II, pp. 389-91.
76 Jeremy Bentham, 'The Situation and Relief of the Poor', *Annals of Agriculture*, 1797, Vol. XXIX, pp. 393-426. The 'spunge' is mentioned on p. 423.
77 John Stuart Mill, *Collected Works* (University of Toronto Press), Vol. IV, 1967, 'The Claims of Labour', p. 366.
78 *Monthly Review*, January 1804, Vol. XLIII, pp. 68, 70.
79 *British Critic*, March 1804, Vol. XXIII, p. 245.
80 Curry, ed., *New Letters of Robert Southey*, Vol, I, p. 357.
81 Anon. ['The Remarker'] *Remarks on a Late Publication entitled An Essay on the Principle of Population* (London, 1803), pp. 4-5.
82 Letter in Dr Williams's Library from Thomas Robinson (postmark Bury St Edmunds, 27 December 1803) to his brother Henry Crabb Robinson in Jena.
83 William Currie, ed., *Memoir of the Life, Writings and Correspondence of James Currie M.D., F.R.S. of Liverpool* (2 vols, London, 1831), Vol. II, pp. 249-52, 248.
84 Henry Cockburn, *Life of Lord Jeffrey* (2 vols, Edinburgh, 1852), Vol. II, pp. 83, 89.
85 Leonard Horner, ed., *Memoirs and Correspondence of Francis Horner M.P.* (2 vols, London, 1843), Vol. I, p. 256.
86 Cockburn's *Jeffrey*, Vol. II, p. 93.
87 *Ibid.*, Vol. II, p. 95.
88 Horner, *Memoirs*, Vol. I, pp. 122-3.
89 *Ibid.*, p. 129.
90 William Petersen, *Malthus for Moderns* (Harvard University Press, 1979).
91 *Monthly Magazine*, Vol. XVIII, No. 119, pp. 93-6; No. 120, pp. 186-90; No. 121, p. 288; No. 122, pp. 404-5; Vol. XIX, No. 125, pp. 116-18.
92 [Southey] *Annual Review*, 1804, Vol. II, p. 301.
93 Horner, *Memoirs*, Vol. I, pp. 438-9, 457.

Chapter IV THE POPULATION CONTROVERSIES BEGIN

1 Malthus's *Reply* of 1806, quarto version, pp. 1-2.
2 Thomas Jarrold, MD, *Dissertations on Man, Philosophical, Physiological and Political, in Answer to Mr. Malthus's Essay* (London, 1806), p. 363.
3 Robert Acklom Ingram, *Disquisitions on Population in which the Principles of the Essay on Population by the Rev. T. R. Malthus are Examined and Refuted* (London, 1808), p. 5.
4 Anon. ['The Awakener'] *A Summons of Wakening or the Evil Tendency and Danger of Speculative Philosophy* (Hawick, 1807), p. 123.
5 'Simplex', *An Inquiry into the Constitution, Government and Practices of the Church of Christ ... with Strictures on ... Mr. Malthus on Population* (Edinburgh, 1808), p. 225.
6 Ingram, *op. cit.*, pp. 24, 22.
7 'Awakener', *op. cit.*, p. 89.
8 Jarrold, *op. cit.*, p. 328.
9 Ingram, *op. cit.*, p. 9-10.
10 Alexander Dyce, ed., *Recollections of the Table Talk of Samuel Rogers* (London, 1887), p. 197.
11 *Christian Observer*, September 1805, Vol. IV, p. 539.
12 Malthus, *Population*, 1803, p. v.
13 *Christian Observer*, Vol. IV, pp. 540-1.
14 Malthus, *Population*, Everyman edn, Vol. II, p. 217.
15 Otter's *Memoir* (see Chap. I, n. 29) pp. lii-liii.
16 'Simplex', *op. cit.*, p. 211.
17 *Ibid.*, pp. 223, 212.
18 [Southey] *Annual Review*, 1804, Vol. II, p. 296.
19 William Hazlitt, *Complete Works*, ed. P. P. Howe (21 vols, London, 1930), Vol. I, p. 236.
20 [Southey] *Annual Review*, Vol. II, p. 301.
21 *Ibid.*, pp. 298-9.
22 'Remarker', *op. cit.*, pp. 40-2.
23 Ingram, *op. cit.*, pp. 77-80.
24 'Remarker', *op. cit.*, p. 35.
25 Malthus's *Reply*, 1806 quarto version, p. 23n.
26 Malthus, *Population*, Everyman edn, Vol. II, pp. 175-7.
27 *Analytical Review*, Vol. XXVIII, p. 124.
28 *Monthly Review*, Vol. XLII, p. 351.
29 *Ibid.*, Vol. XLIII, p. 111.
30 Malthus's *Reply*, 1806 quarto version, pp. 4-5.
31 *Ibid.*, pp. 34-6.
32 Cobbett's *Weekly Political Register*, 16 February 1805, cols. 230-1.

33 *Ibid.*, 18 January 1806, cols. 73-6.
34 MS letter in the Library of King's College, Cambridge.
35 [Empson] *Edinburgh Review*, January 1837, Vol. LXIV, pp. 504 and 496.
36 Joseph Townsend, *Journey Through Spain* (3 vols, London, 1791), Vol. II, p. 337.
37 *Ibid.*, Vol. I, pp. 378-9.
38 [Joseph Townsend] *A Dissertation on the Poor Laws* by a Well-Wisher to Mankind (London, 1786), pp. 13, 14, 20-1, 34-5, 36, 37.
39 *Ibid.*, pp. 70, 71, 73.
40 *Ibid.*, pp. 88-90.
41 *Ibid.*, p. 91.
42 *Ibid.*, p. 94.
43 Quoted by Tom Girtin in *Doctor with Two Aunts* (Hutchinson, London, 1959), pp. 169-70.
44 Malthus, *Population*, Everyman edn, Vol. II, p. 49.
45 *Ibid.*, Vol. II, p. 47.
46 *Ibid.*, Vol. II, p. 46.
47 *Ibid.*, Vol. II, p. 54.
48 *Ibid.*, Vol. II, p. 201.
49 Malthus's *Reply*, 1806 quarto version, p. 18.
50 Malthus, *Population*, 1803, p. 538; Everyman edn, Vol. II, pp. 201-2.
51 Malthus, *Population*, Everyman edn, Vol. II, pp. 202-3.
52 Ingram, *op. cit.*, p. 69.
53 'Simplex', *op. cit.*, pp. 216-17.
54 Malthus, *Population*: quarto 1803, p. 408; third edn, 1806, Vol. II, pp. 168-9; Everyman edn, Vol. II, p. 47.
55 Malthus, *Population*, Everyman edn, Vol. II, p. 203.
56 *Imperial Review or London and Dublin Literary Journal*, January 1804, Vol. I, p. 122.
57 *Monthly Magazine*, December 1804, Vol. XVIII, pp. 381-2.
58 'Remarker', *op. cit.*, pp. 53, 50, 52.
59 *Ibid.*, p. 61.
60 Malthus, *Population*, Everyman edn, Vol. II, p. 132.
61 F. A. von Hayek, Introduction to his edn of Henry Thornton's *Paper Credit* (Allen & Unwin, London, 1939), p. 38.
62 B. R. Mitchell and Phyllis Deane, *Abstract of British Historical Statistics* (Cambridge University Press, 1962), p. 392.
63 George Rose, *Observations on the Poor Laws and on the Management of the Poor in Great Britain* (London, 1805), p. 11.
64 *Ibid.*, p. 27n.
65 Samuel Whitbread, *Substance of a Speech on the Poor Laws* (2nd edn, London, 1807), p. 10.
66 Malthus, *A Letter to Samuel Whitbread Esq. M.P. on his proposed Bill for the Amendment of the Poor Laws* (2nd edn, London, 1807), p. 13.

67 Whitbread, *Poor Laws*, p. 14.
68 *Ibid.*, p. 16.
69 *Ibid.*, pp. 19-20.
70 *Ibid.*, p. 81.
71 Malthus, *Letter to Whitbread*, p. 16.
72 Malthus, *Reply*, 1807. This will be found as an *Appendix* to the fourth edn of *Population*, Vol. II, p. 473n.
73 Malthus, *Letter to Whitbread*, pp. 16-17.
74 *Ibid.*, pp. 12-13.
75 *Ibid.*, p. 30.
76 *Ibid.*, p. 25.
77 *Ibid.*, pp. 14, 35, 34.
78 Cobbett's *Weekly Political Register*, 21 March 1807, col. 440.
79 'Pope' of Holland House (see Chap. 3, n. 13), W. P. Courtney's *Memoir*, pp. 37, 24.
80 2nd Lord Teignmouth, *Reminiscences of Many Years* (2 vols, Edinburgh, 1878), Vol. I, p. 66.
81 William Smyth, *A List of Books recommended and referred to in the Lectures on Modern History* (Cambridge, 1817), *passim*.
82 [Mary Ann Kelty] *Visiting my Relations* (London, 1851), p. 332.
83 Henry Cockburn, *Life of Lord Jeffrey* (2 vols, Edinburgh, 1852), Vol. II, p. 92.
84 Leonard Horner, ed., *Memoirs and Correspondence of Francis Horner, M.P.* (2 vols, London, 1843), Vol. II, p. 385.
85 [William Parnell] *An Inquiry into the Causes of Popular Discontents in Ireland* by an Irish Country Gentleman (London, 1804), p. 42.
86 [John Wilson Croker] *Sketch of the State of Ireland Past and Present* (London and Dublin, 1808), p. 13.
87 [W. Parnell] *Inquiry into Discontents*, p. 29.
88 [Croker] *Sketch of Ireland*, pp. 18-20.
89 William Parnell, *An Historical Apology for the Irish Catholics* (2nd edn, Dublin, 1807), p. 94.
90 [W. Parnell] *Inquiry into Discontents*, p. 29.
91 [Croker] *Sketch of Ireland*, p. 47.
92 W. Parnell, *Apology for Catholics*, pp. 139-40.
93 [W. Parnell] *Inquiry into Discontents*, p. 12.
94 W. Parnell, *Apology for Catholics*, p. 135.
95 Thomas Newenham, *A View of the Natural, Political and Commercial Circumstances of Ireland* (quarto, London 1808), p. 179.
96 Henry Parnell, *A Corrected Report of the Speech ... in the House of Commons on Friday 13 April 1810 on a Motion for a Select Committee to inquire into the Collection of Tythes in Ireland* (London, 1810), p. 13.
97 [W. Parnell] *Inquiry into Discontents*, p. 27.
98 Malthus, *Population*, Everyman edn, Vol. I, pp. 277-8.

99 *Ibid.*, Vol. II, p. 207.
100 William Richardson, *Simple Measures by which the Recurrence of Famines may be Prevented* . . . Printed in the *Pamphleteer*, 1816, Vol. VIII, p. 160.
101 *Ibid.*, p. 205.
102 *Ibid.*, p. 208.
103 *Annals of Agriculture*, 1801, Vol. XXXVII, p. 525.
104 *Annals of Agriculture*, 1804, Vol. XLI, pp. 219-20.
105 Malthus's *Reply*, 1806 quarto version, pp. 19, 27.
106 Horner, *Memoirs*, Vol. I, pp. 406, 301.
107 *Ibid.*, Vol. I, p. 419.
108 Cockburn's *Life of Jeffrey*, Vol. II, p. 125.
109 Horner, *Memoirs*, Vol. I, p. 437.
110 Bernard Semmel, ed. with an Introductory Essay, *Occasional Papers of T. R. Malthus* . . . from Contemporary Journals, written anonymously and hitherto uncollected (New York, 1963).
111 [Malthus] *Edinburgh Review*, July 1808, Vol. XII, p. 336.
112 Cockburn's *Life of Jeffrey*, Vol. I, p. 194.
113 [Malthus] *Edinburgh Review*, Vol. XII pp. 338-9.
114 *Ibid.*, p. 342.
115 Thomas Newenham, *A Statistical and Historical Inquiry into the Progress and Magnitude of the Population of Ireland* (London, 1805), pp. 132-3.
116 [Malthus] *Edinburgh Review*, Vol. XII, p. 343.
117 *Ibid.*, pp. 346-7.
118 *Ibid.*, p. 348.
119 *Ibid.*, p. 352.
120 *Ibid.*, pp. 353, 354.
121 *Ibid.*, p. 349.
122 [Malthus] *Edinburgh Review*, April 1809, Vol. XIV, p. 153.
123 *Ibid.*, pp. 157-9.
124 *London Review*, May 1809, No. II, p. 322.
125 [Malthus] *Edinburgh Review*, Vol. XIV, p. 154.
126 *Ibid.*, p. 167.
127 *Ibid.*, pp. 168-9.
128 Horner, *Memoirs*, Vol. II, p. 57.
129 MS Letter in the Horner Collection, British Library of Political and Economic Science.
130 These MS letters belong to Lord Congleton. I am grateful to him for allowing me to use them and to Professor F. W. Fetter for obtaining photocopies of them for me to work from.

Chapter V A MARRIED PROFESSOR (1804—10)

1 MS letter in the Library of King's College, Cambridge.
2 William Otter, *Life and Remains of Edward Daniel Clarke* (2nd edn, 2 vols, London, 1825), Vol. II, pp. 230-1.
3 *Ibid.*, Vol. II, p. 224.
4 *Ibid.*, Vol. II, p. 211.
5 Lincoln Archives, Tennyson d'Eyncourt Papers.
6 William Leeves, *In Memoriam* (privately printed by Mrs. A. M. Moon, 1873), pp. 74-6. Harriet Eckersall and Marianne Wathen were both nieces of the Rev. W. Leeves, which accounts for Marianne's juvenile verse being included in this collection.
7 Mary Russell Mitford, *Our Village* (Vol. IV, London, 1830), 'Little Miss Wren', p. 91.
8 *The Tauntons of Oxford* by One of Them (London, 1902), p. 63.
9 *A Selection of Views in the County of Lincoln* engraved by Bartholomew Howlett (William Miller, London, 1801).
10 The Walesby registers are deposited in the Lincoln Record Office.
11 R. W. Chapman, ed., *Jane Austen's Letters* (Oxford University Press, 2nd edn, 1952), p. 132.
12 MS letter in the City of Bath Municipal Library.
13 MS letter in the Library of the University of Illinois at Urbana-Champaign.
14 Samuel Jackson Pratt, *Harvest Home* (3 vols, London, 1805), Vol. III, p. 491. In an account of Graves's death Pratt wrote: 'Mr. [Prince] Hoare was seldom out of his presence for the last three or four days. One of his scholars likewise, Mr. Matthias (Author of the Essay on Population) was then on a visit to his father-in-law, Mr. Eckersall, at Claverton "Great House". He attended his kind old master, and administered the sacrament to him.' This reference was kindly supplied by Dr Clarence Tracy.
15 *Memoir of James Currie* (see Chap. III, n. 83), Vol. I, p. 381.
16 Claverton parish registers.
17 I am indebted for this quotation to Mrs Christina Colvin.
18 Henry Morris, *Life of Charles Grant* (London, 1904), *passim*. See also A. T. Embree, *Charles Grant and British Rule in India* (Allen & Unwin, London, 1962).
19 John William Kaye, *The Administration of the East India Company* (2nd edn, London, 1853), pp. 632-3.
20 See (1) B. B. Misra, *The Central Administration of the East India Company 1773-1834* (Manchester University Press, 1959);
(2) C. H. Philips, *The East India Company 1784-1834* (Manchester University Press, 1961).
21 Walter F. C. Chichele Plowden, *Records of the Chichele Plowdens A.D. 1590-1913* (privately printed 1914), pp. 160-1.
22 *Memorials of Old Haileybury College* (London, 1894), *passim*. This is mainly the work of Sir Monier Monier-Williams (1819-99).
23 Morris, *Charles Grant*, pp. 250-8.

24 IOR, J/2/1 ff. 1-17.
25 *Memoir of the Life and Correspondence of John [Shore] Lord Teignmouth* by his son, the 2nd Lord Teignmouth (2 vols, London, 1843), Vol. I, p. 10.
26 *The Times*, 1805: 8 January, p. 2, col. d; 26 February, p. 3, col. b; 2 March, p. 3, col. a.
27 IOR, J/2/1 f. 33.
28 *Ibid.*, J/1/19 ff. 468-9.
29 *Ibid.*, J/2/1 f. 18.
30 *Ibid.*, J/1/19 ff. 506-7.
31 Guy Chapman, *Beckford* (Jonathan Cape, London, 1937), pp. 153-82.
32 IOR, J/1/19 ff. 510-11, 466-7, 517-18.
33 IOR, J/2/1 ff. 37-9, 41, 49-50. See also C. M. Matthews, *Haileybury since Roman Times* (privately printed 1959), pp. 142-8.
34 IOR, J/2/1 ff. 67-9.
35 IOR, J/1/19 ff. 466-7.
36 *Ibid.*, ff. 500-1.
37 IOR, J/2/1 ff. 30-1.
38 *Ibid.*, ff. 58-9.
39 Pryme, *Autobiographic Recollections* (see Chap. I, n. 58), p. 51.
40 IOR, J/2/1 ff. 75-87. The Prospectus was called 'A Preliminary View of the Establishment of the Honourable East India Company in Hertfordshire for the Education of Young Persons appointed to the Civil Service in India'. It was printed by Watts of Broxbourne in 1806.
41 'Preliminary View', pp. 8-10.
42 *Ibid.*, pp. 14-15.
43 Morris, *Charles Grant*, p. 245.
44 IOR, J/2/1 ff. 107-8.
45 Gunning, *Reminiscences* (see Chap. I, n. 57), Vol. I, p. 200.
46 IOR, J/2/1 f. 498.
47 Henry Cockburn, *Life of Lord Jeffrey* (2 vols, Edinburgh, 1852), Vol. I, pp. 141, 105-15.
48 IOR, J/2/1 ff. 347-8.
49 Henry Angelo, *Reminiscences* (2 vols, London, 1904, but first pub. 1828), Vol. II, p. 3; Vol. I, pp. 117-18.
50 IOR, J/2/1 ff. 269-94. See also J/1/23 ff. 430-1.
51 IOR, J/1/23 f. 416.
52 Matthews, *Haileybury since Roman Times*, p. 155.
53 IOR, J/1/24 ff. 495-6, 503-11.
54 *Ibid.*, f. 493.
55 IOR, J/2/1 ff. 433, 457-62.
56 IOR, J/1/38 ff. 218-21.
57 Augustus Henry Bosanquet, *India Seventy Years Ago* (London, 1881), p. 9.
58 *Ibid.*, p. 7.
59 IOR, J/2/1 f. 407.
60 *The Times*, 7 July 1809, p. 3, col. c.
61 IOR, J/2/1 f. 409.
62 Matthews, *Haileybury since Roman Times*, p. 143.
63 IOR, J/2/1 ff. 316, 338-9, 500.

64 Cockburn, *Life of Jeffrey*, Vol. II, p. 339.
65 IOR, J/2/2 ff. 253-4.
66 IOR, J/2/1 f. 39.
67 IOR, J/2/2 f. 177.
68 IOR, J/2/7 ff. 54, 203.
69 IOR, J/2/4 f. 306.
70 IOR, J/1/32 ff. 251-3.
71 [Malthus] *Population*, 1798, Macmillan reprint, 1966, Bonar's Notes, p.v.
72 Otter's *Memoir* (see Chapt. I, n. 29), pp. xl-xli, li.
73 Sraffa's *Ricardo*, Vol. VIII, p. 107.
74 Colvin's *Maria Edgeworth from England* (see Prologue, n. 17), p. 64.
75 Extracts from unpublished correspondence made available by Mrs Colvin.
76 This sketch is with the archives of Mr A. H. Boynton Wood at Hollin Hall.
77 *Life of Robert Owen* by Himself (London, 1857), p. 103.
78 IOR, J/2/1 f. 107.
79 MS letter in the Special Collections (801 Butler Library) of Columbia University Libraries, New York.

Chapter VI PAPER MONEY

Material for this chapter is taken largely from:

Clapham, Sir John. *The Bank of England* (2 vols, Cambridge University Press, 1944).

Fetter, Frank Whitson. *The Development of British Monetary Orthodoxy* (Harvard University Press, 1965).

1 *Memorials of Old Haileybury* (see Chapt. V, n. 22), pp. 121-2.
2 F. A. von Hayek, Introduction to his edn of Henry Thornton's *Paper Credit* (Allen & Unwin, London, 1939), p. 17.
3 Sraffa's *Ricardo*, Vol. III, p. 188.
4 Hayek, Introduction to *Paper Credit*, p. 47.
5 Malthus, *Population*, Everyman edn, Vol. II, p. 43.
6 *Ibid.*, Vol. II, pp. 44-5.
7 Sraffa's *Ricardo*, Vol. VI, p. 231.
8 Lord King, *Thoughts on the Effects of the Bank Restrictions*; Second Edition, enlarged, including some Remarks on the Coinage. (London, 1804), pp. 46-7.
9 *Ibid.*, p. 64n.
10 Robert Mushet, *An Enquiry into . . . the Bank Restriction Bill* (2nd edn, London, 1809), pp. 31-2.
11 W. H. B. Court, *A Concise Economic History of Britain* (Cambridge University Press Paperback, 1967), pp. 99-100.
12 F. W. Fetter, *Development of British Monetary Orthodoxy*, p. 62.
13 Quoted in Sraffa's *Ricardo*, Vol. III, p. 10.
14 Malthus's *Travel Diaries* (see Chap. II, n. 76), p. 222.

15 MS letters in the Horner Collection, British Library of Political and Economic Science.
16 [Malthus] *Edinburgh Review,*.February 1811, Vol. XVII, p. 341.
17 *Ibid.*, p. 342.
18 *Ibid.*, p. 343.
19 *Ibid.*, p. 344.
20 *Ibid.*, p. 345.
21 *Ibid.*, p. 349.
22 *Ibid.*, p. 352.
23 *Ibid.*, p. 356.
24 *Ibid.*, p. 358.
25 *Ibid.*, p. 359.
26 MS letter in the Horner Collection, British Library of Political and Economic Science.
27 Adam, Smith, *Wealth of Nations*, ed. Edwin Cannan (Methuen University Paperbacks, London, 2 vols, 1961), Vol. I, p. 359.
28 *Ibid.*, Vol. I, p. 352.
29 [Malthus] *Edinburgh Review*, Vol. XVIII, pp. 363-4, 366.
30 *Ibid.*, p. 352.
31 Sraffa's *Ricardo*, Vol. III, p. 108.
32 Quoted in Sraffa's *Ricardo*, Vol. III, p. 12.
33 MS letter in the Horner Collection, British Library of Political and Economic Science.
34 MS letter in the Department of Manuscripts, National Library of Scotland, ref. MS. Acc. 6230.
35 Sraffa's *Ricardo*, Vol. VI, pp. 21-8.
36 *Ibid.*, Vol. VI, p. 29.
37 The biographical information is from Sraffa's *Ricardo*, Vol. X.
38 Horace B. Woodward, *The History of the Geological Society of London* (London, 1907), Appendix, pp. 268-75.
39 [Empson] *Edinburgh Review*, Vol. LXIV, p. 499.
40 Colvin's *Maria Edgeworth from England* (see Prologue, n. 17), p. 260.
41 Sraffa's *Ricardo*, Vol. X, p. 45.
42 *Ibid.*, Vol. X, p. 344.
43 Sraffa's *Ricardo*, Vol. VI, p. 47.
44 [Malthus] *Edinburgh Review*, August 1811, Vol. XVIII, p. 459.
45 *Ibid.*, p. 453.
46 *Ibid.*, p. 463.
47 *Ibid.*, p. 470.

Chapter VII THE HAILEYBURY CHAMPION (1811-17)

1 Boynton Wood family archives at Hollin Hall.
2 Amelia Heber, *The Life of Reginald Heber* (2 vols, London, 1830), Vol. I, p. 370.
3 William Smyth, *English Lyricks* (5th edn, 1850), p. 129.
4 A Civilian [Benjamin Guy Babington] *A Letter to the ... Court of Directors of the East India Company on the Subject of the College at Haileybury* (London, 1823), p. 20.
5 IOR, J/2/2C f. 5.
6 IOR, J/2/1 ff. 163-4.
7 *The Times*, 1811: 28 November p. 2, cols. c, d.
8 *Ibid.*, 13 December, p. 3, cols. d, e.
9 *Ibid.*, 20 December, p. 2, cols. a, b.
10 IOR, J/2/1B f. 193.
11 IOR, J/3/1. Proceedings of the Court of Directors.
12 IOR, B/238 ff. 1169, 1175. Appendix to the Minutes of the Court of Directors; Copies of Dissents.
13 A.T. Embree, *Charles Grant and British Rule in India* (Allen & Unwin, London, 1962), p. 163n (his speech in the House of Commons on 14 June 1813).
14 Henry Morris, *Life of Charles Grant* (London, 1904), p. 237.
15 *Sir James Mackintosh* by his son (2nd edn, 2 vols, London, 1836), Vol. I, pp. 388, 226.
16 *Ibid.*, Vol. II, p. 261.
17 Malthus, *Letter to Lord Grenville* (London, 1813), pp. 2-3.
18 *Ibid.*, p. 31.
19 *Ibid.*, pp. 36-7.
20 *Ibid.*, p. 19.
21 *Ibid.*, pp. 27-8.
22 *Ibid.*, p. 24.
23 *Ibid.*, p. 30.
24 *Ibid.*, p. 34.
25 *Ibid.*, pp. 13-14.
26 *Ibid.*, p. 15.
27 *Ibid.*, p. 35.
28 MS letter in the Horner Collection, British Library of Political and Economic Science.
29 Joseph Hume, *An Account of the Provident Institution for Savings ... with Observations upon different Publications relating to such Establishments and some Suggestions for rendering them General by the Assistance of Government* (London, 1816), p. 8.
30 *Ibid.*, p. 49.
31 *Ibid.*, p. 9.
32 Otter, *Life of Clarke* (See Chap. I, n. 56), Vol. II, p. 258.
33 Gunning, *Reminiscences* (See Chap I, n. 57), Vol. II, p. 259.

34 2nd Lord Teignmouth, *Reminiscences of Many Years* (2 vols, Edinburgh, 1878), Vol. I, p. 44.
35 Malthus's *Travel Diaries* (see Chap. II, n. 76), pp. 18-19.
36 Otter, *Life of Clarke*, Vol. I, p. 263.
37 MS letter of 15 March 1812 from Clarke to Mrs Otter, in the Archives of Jesus College, Cambridge.
38 Leonard Horner, ed., *Memoirs and Correspondence of Francis Horner, M.P.* (2 vols, London, 1843), Vol. II, pp. 97-8.
39 MS letter in the Horner Collection, British Library of Political and Economic Science.
40 *Sir James Mackintosh* by his son, Vol. II, p. 262.
41 Henry Holland, *Recollections of Past Life* (London, 1872), p. 241.
42 Colvin's *Maria Edgeworth from England* (see Prologue, n. 17), pp. 51, 63-4.
43 Romilly, *Memoirs* (see Chap. III, n. 16) (2nd edn, 1840), Vol. III, p. 149.
44 MS letter in the Brougham Collection of the D.M.S. Watson Library of University College, London.
45 Horner, *Memoirs*, Vol. II, pp. 243, 247.
46 Romilly, *Memoirs*, Vol. III, p. 167.
47 Sraffa's *Ricardo*, Vol. VI, p. 235.
48 *Ibid.*, p. 231.
49 MS letter in the Library of the University of Illinois at Urbana-Champaign.
50 IOR, J/2/2 ff. 57, 58-9.
51 IOR, J/2/2B ff. 235-8. Charles Babbage in his reminiscences gives a different story; see *Passages from the Life of a Philosopher* (London, 1864), p. 473.
52 Sir William Wilson Hunter, *Life of Brian Houghton Hodgson (1800–1894)* (London, 1896), p. 15.
53 IOR, J/2/2B f. 43.
54 Great Amwell parish registers, now in the Hertfordshire County Record Office.
55 IOR, J/2/4 ff. 330-1.
56 IOR, J/2/2 ff. 292-8.
57 IOR, J/2/2B ff. 96-7.
58 *Ibid.*, f. 119.
59 *Ibid.*, ff. 129-30.
60 MS letter in the Horner Collection, British Library of Political and Economic Science.
61 MS letter in the Archives of the present Haileybury College founded in 1862.
62 *Memorials of Old Haileybury* (see Chap. V, n. 22), p. 83.
63 IOR, J/2/2B ff. 258-9.
64 Sraffa's *Ricardo*, Vol. VI, p. 341.
65 *Ibid.*, pp. 346-7.
66 *Ibid.*, p. 289.
67 IOR, J/2/2B ff. 295, 299, 301, 303.
68 IOR, J/2/2C ff. 5-8, 17-18, 29-30, 33-4.
69 Sraffa's *Ricardo*, Vol. VII, p. 21.
70 *Ibid.*, p. 51.

71 IOR, J/2/2C f. 117.
72 *The Times*, 19 December 1816, p. 3, cols b, c, d.
73 IOR, J/2/3 ff. 133, 150.
74 *The Times*, 20 December 1816, p. 2, col. e; p. 3, col. a.
75 *Ibid.*, 25 December 1816, p. 2, cols d, e; p. 3, cols c, d.
76 MS letter in the Murray Archives, the repository of all the letters quoted in this book from Malthus to John Murray II (1778-1843). It was he who in 1812 moved his father's publishing firm from Fleet Street to the house in Albemarle Street where it still flourishes; Murray became the foremost publisher of his time, perhaps remembered more for his connection with Byron than with Malthus or Ricardo.
77 *The Times*, 27 December 1816, p. 2, cols c, d.
78 *Ibid.*, 28 December 1816, p. 3, col. b.
79 *Morning Chronicle*, 6 January 1817, p. 3, cols c, d.
80 Malthus, *Statements Respecting the East India College* (London, 1817), pp. 65, 66, 74.
81 *Ibid.*, pp. 83, 86.
82 *Ibid.*, pp. 87, 89.
83 *Ibid.*, pp. 87, 88.
84 *Ibid.*, pp. 98, 102.
85 *Ibid.*, p. 105.
86 *The Times*, 9 January 1817, p. 3, cols a, b, c.
87 *Morning Chronicle*, 7 February 1817, p. 3, cols c, d.
88 *The Times*, 7 February 1817, p. 3, cols c, d.
89 Sraffa's *Ricardo*, Vol. VII, pp. 135-6.
90 MS letter in the Murray Archives, dated 20 February 1817.
91 *The Times* 21 February 1817, p. 3, cols d, e.
92 *Ibid.*, 26 February 1817, p. 3, col. e.
93 *Ibid.*, 5 March 1817, p. 3, cols b, c, d.
94 Sraffa's *Ricardo*, Vol. VII, pp. 135-6.
95 Malthus, *Statements Respecting the East India College*, p. 103n.
96 Sraffa's *Ricardo*, Vol. VII, pp. 137-8.
97 Sir W. W. Hunter, *Life of Brian Houghton Hodgson*, pp. 6-7.
98 *Ibid.*, pp. 15-16.
99 *Ibid.*, p. 23.
100 Malthus, *Statements Respecting the East India College*, p. 100.
101 P. H. Le Breton, ed., *Memories, Miscellanies and Letters of Lucy Aikin* (London, 1864), pp. 152-3. The letter, written on 2 January 1835, is to J. L. Mallet; I think Miss Aikin hoped that he would undertake Malthus's biography, 'with all his regret and affection full upon him'.

Chapter VIII LITERARY MISFORTUNES (1812-15)

1 MS letter in the Houghton Library, Harvard University.
2 Theodore Besterman, ed., *The Publishing Firm of Cadell & Davies*, Select Correspondence and Accounts 1793-1836. (Oxford University Press, 1938), pp. 163-4.

3 *Ibid.*, p. xv.
4 Sraffa's *Ricardo*, Vol. VI, p. 159n.
5 *Ibid.*, pp. 159, 169, 159n.
6 Sraffa's *Ricardo*, Vol. II, p. 105.
7 David Buchanan, ed., *Wealth of Nations* (4 vols, Edinburgh and London, 1814), Vol. IV, p. xi.
8 Adam Smith, *Wealth of Nations* (Methuen University Paperback of Cannan's edn, 2 vols, London, 1961), Vol. I, p. 182.
9 [Malthus] *Population*, 1798, pp. 335-6.
10 Malthus, *Population*, quarto 2nd edn, 1803, pp. 449-51.
11 Malthus, *Population*, 3rd edn, 2 vols, 1806, Vol. II, pp. 237-8.
12 Buchanan's *Wealth of Nations* (1814), Vol. II, p. 195.
13 Lord Holland, *Further Memoirs of the Whig Party 1807-1821* (London, 1905), p. 215.
14 Earl of Lauderdale, *A Letter on the Corn Laws* (London, 1814), p. 71.
15 Malthus, *Observations on the Effects of the Corn Laws* (London, 1814), p. 24. and pp. 30-31.
16 *Ibid.*, pp. 30-1.
17 Buchanan's *Wealth of Nations* (1814), Vol. IV, pp. 59-60.
18 Malthus, *Observations on the Effects of the Corn Laws*, pp. 5-6.
19 *Ibid.*, p. 42 and n.
20 Sir Edward West, *The Price of Corn and Wages of Labour* (London, 1826), pp. 8-9.
21 Cockburn's *Life of Jeffrey* (see Chap. III, n. 84), Vol. II pp. 145-6.
22 Sraffa's *Ricardo*, Vol. VI, pp. 107, 109-10.
23 *Ibid.*, p. 130.
24 Colvin's *Maria Edgeworth from England* (see Prologue, n. 17), pp. 268-9.
25 Sraffa's *Ricardo*. Vol. VII, p. 29.
26 *The Correspondence of the Rt. Hon. Sir John Sinclair, Bart.* ed. by Himself (2 vols, London, 1831), Vol. I, p. 391.
27 Lord David Cecil, *Melbourne* (Constable, London 1965), p. 19.
28 Malthus, *Grounds of an Opinion on the Policy of Restricting the Importation of Foreign Corn* (London, 1815), pp. 6-7, 7n.
29 *Ibid.*, pp. 9-10.
30 *Ibid.*, pp. 11-12, 15.
31 *Ibid.*, pp. 16, 18.
32 Horner, *Memoirs* (see Chap. III, n. 85), Vol. II, pp. 229-30.
33 Malthus, *Grounds for Restriction*, pp. 21-2.
34 *Ibid.*, pp. 23, 24, 25.
35 *Ibid.*, pp. 29-30, 33-4.
36 *Ibid.*, p. 35.
37 *Ibid.*, p. 36n.
38 *Ibid.*, pp. 38-42.
39 *Ibid.*, pp. 46-8.
40 Horner, *Memoirs*, Vol. II, pp. 227-8.
41 Seymour's *'Pope' of Holland House* (see Chap. III, n. 13), p. 93.
42 *Edinburgh Review*, February 1815, Vol. XXIV, p. 499.
43 *Ibid.*, p. 501.

44 *Ibid.*, pp. 404-5. This article was perhaps written by David Buchanan.
45 Lord Sheffield, *Letter on the Corn Laws* (2nd edn, London, 1815), pp. 61-2.
46 Robert Torrens, *Essay on the External Corn Trade* (London, 1815), pp. viii-ix, xi-xii.
47 Mary Berry, *Journals* (see Prologue, n. 14), Vol. II, p. 43.
48 Romilly *Memoirs* (see Chap. III, n. 16), Vol. III, p. 157.
49 Sraffa's *Ricardo*, Vol. VI, p. 183n.
50 *Ibid.*, p. 183.
51 *Ibid.*, p. 188.
52 *Ibid.*, pp. 185, 188.
53 *Ibid.*, pp. 201-2.
54 *Ibid.*, pp. 205-6.
55 *Ibid.*, p. 211.
56 [Empson] *Edinburgh Review*, January 1835, Vol. LXIV, pp. 496-7.
57 MS letter from the Halsted Vander Poel Collection in the Manuscript Division of the Reference Department of the Library of Congress, Washington, DC.
58 Derek Hudson, *Martin Tupper: His Rise and Fall* (Constable, London, 1949), p. 138.
59 MS letter in the Brougham Collection of the D.M.S. Watson Library of University College, London.

Chapter IX THE PRINCIPLES OF POLITICAL ECONOMY

In writing this chapter I have been helped by the following works, although no specific reference is made to them:

Barucci, Piero, *Introduzione* to his translation of Malthus's *Principles of Political Economy* into Italian (Istituto Editoriale Internazionale, Milan, 1972).
Blaug, Mark, *Ricardian Economics. A Historical Study* (Yale University Press, 1958).
Blaug, Mark, *Economic Theory in Retrospect* (Heinemann, London, 1964).
Cannan, Edwin, *A History of the Theories of Production and Distribution in English Political Economy from 1776 to 1848* (2nd edn, London, 1903).
Corry, Bernard A., *Money, Saving and Investment in English Economics 1800-1850* (Macmillan, London, 1962).
Derry, T. K., *A Short Economic History of Britain* (Oxford University Press, 1965).
Dobb, Maurice, *Political Economy and Capitalism* (Routledge, London, 1946).
Meek, R. L., *The Economics of Physiocracy* (Allen & Unwin, London, 1962).
Paglin, Morton, *Malthus and Lauderdale. The Anti-Ricardian Tradition* (New York, 1961).
Robbins, Lionel, *The Theory of Economic Policy in English Classical Political Economy* (Macmillan, London, 1952).
Robbins, Lionel, *Robert Torrens and the Evolution of Classical Economics* (Macmillan, London, 1958).
Roll, Eric, *A History of Economic Thought* (Faber & Faber, London, 1966).
Smith, V. E., 'The Classicists' Use of Demand', *Journal of Political Economy*,

June 1951, Vol. LIX, No. 3, pp. 242-57.

Smith, V. E., 'Malthus's Theory of Demand and Its Influence on Value Theory', *Scottish Journal of Political Economy*, October 1956, Vol. III, pp. 205-20.

Tucker, G. S. L., *Progress and Profits in British Economic Thought* (Cambridge University Press, 1960).

Wherever possible, references to Malthus's *Principles of Political Economy*, 1820, are to Sraffa's reproduction in Vol. II of his *Works of David Ricardo*; with Ricardo's 'Notes on Malthus' are printed over two-thirds of Malthus's own book. There is a reprint of the posthumous 1836 version of Malthus's *Political Economy* (by Augustus M. Kelley of New York), but the original 1820 edition is very rare.

1 [Henry Brougham] *Edinburgh Review*, July 1804, Vol. IV, p. 344, a review of Lord Lauderdale's *Public Wealth*.

2 [Thomas De Quincey] X.Y.Z. in the *London Magazine*, December 1823, Vol. VIII, pp. 586-7. Or see De Quincey's *Collected Writings*, ed. David Masson (14 vols, Edinburgh, 1889-90), Vol. IX, pp. 32-3, 34.

3 Phyllis Deane and W. A. Cole, *British Economic Growth 1688-1959* (Cambridge University Press, 1962), p. 271, table 70.

4 Malthus, *Population*, quarto 2nd edn, 1803, p. 444.

5 *Ibid.*, p. 460.

6 Malthus, *Population*, 3rd edn, 2 vols, 1806, Vol. II, p. 266.

7 Malthus, *Population*, quarto 2nd edn, 1803, p. 433.

8 David Buchanan, ed., *Wealth of Nations* (2 vols, Edinburgh and London, 1814), Vol. II, p. 55.

9 Adam Smith, *Wealth of Nations* (Methuen University Paperback of Cannan's edn, 2 vols, London, 1961), Vol. I, pp. 56-7.

10 Buchanan's *Wealth of Nations* (1814), Vol. I, p. 80.

11 Malthus, *Nature and Progress of Rent* (1815), pp. 5-6; Sraffa's *Ricardo*, Vol. II (1820), p. 105; Malthus's 1836 *Political Economy*, pp. 138-9.

12 Malthus, *Rent* (1815), pp. 8-9.

13 Sraffa's *Ricardo*, Vol. II [1820], p. 107; Malthus's 1836 *Political Economy*, p. 140.

14 Malthus *Rent* (1815), p. 17; Sraffa's *Ricardo*, Vol. II [1820], p. 120. Malthus's 1836 *Political Economy*, p. 149.

15 Malthus *Rent* (1815), pp. 57-8; Sraffa's *Ricardo*, Vol. II [1820], pp. 183-4; Malthus's 1836 *Political Economy*, p. 192, where 'gentlemen' is altered to 'landlords'.

16 Malthus *Rent* (1815), p. 20; Sraffa's *Ricardo*, Vol. II [1820], pp. 126-8; Malthus's 1836 *Political Economy*, p. 153.

17 Malthus *Rent* (1815), p. 32; Sraffa's *Ricardo*, Vol. II [1820], p. 160, slightly amended; Malthus's 1836 *Political Economy*, p. 173, altered again.

18 Sraffa's *Ricardo*, Vol. I, p. 77.

19 Malthus *Rent* (1815), pp. 47, 48, 49. These passages were omitted in 1820, as was the footnote on pp. 48-9.

20 Malthus, *Rent* (1815), pp. 54-5; Sraffa's *Ricardo*, Vol. II [1820], p. 182; Malthus's 1836 *Political Economy*, p. 190, where Malthus (or Cazenove) has

changed the paragraph considerably.

21 Malthus *Rent* (1815), p. 57; Sraffa's *Ricardo*, Vol. II [1820], p. 183; Malthus's 1836 *Political Economy*, p. 191.

22 Sraffa's *Ricardo*, Vol. VI, pp. 237, 279.

23 MS letters kindly lent by Mrs Christina Colvin.

24 Malthus, *Principles of Political Economy*, Considered with a View to their Practical Application (London, 1820), pp. 253-4; 2nd edn, 1836, pp. 228-9, slightly different.

25 Malthus, *The Measure of Value Stated and Illustrated* (London, 1823), p. 27.

26 Richard Jones, *An Essay on the Distribution of Wealth and on the Sources of Taxation, Part I, Rent* (London, 1831), pp. 199, 208. A bushel is a measure of capacity, but in general a bushel of wheat weighed about 60 lb.

27 *Ibid.*, p. ix.

28 Sraffa's *Ricardo*, Vol. II [1820], pp. 67-8, 69.

29 *Ibid.*, p. 75.

30 *Quarterly Review*, January 1824, Vol. XXX, No. 60 [Malthus] Article I, p. 309. This was a review of McCulloch's contribution on 'Political Economy' to the *Supplement* to the *Encyclopaedia Britannica*. It gives an excellent and readable résumé of Malthus's own position as an economist; according to Empson (*Edinburgh Review*, Vol. LXIV, p. 496) Malthus himself considered this article 'one of the best things which he had ever done in Political Economy'. It is reproduced in Bernard Semmel's *Occasional Papers of T. R. Malthus* (New York, 1963).

31 F. Dawtrey Drewitt, *Bombay in the Days of George IV* (2nd edn, London, 1935), p. 17.

32 Richard Jones, *Rent*, p. vii.

33 Sraffa's *Ricardo*, Vol. I, 'The Principles of Political Economy', pp. 205, 143.

34 *Ibid.*, Vol. II, 'Notes on Malthus', p. 165.

35 Buchanan's *Wealth of Nations* (1814), Vol. I, pp. 109-10.

36 Sraffa's *Ricardo*, Vol. IV, pamphlet 'On Protection to Agriculture' (1822) p. 215.

37 British Sessional Papers, House of Commons 5:44,45, Report of the Select Committee on Artizans and Machinery, 1824, p. 46.

38 Sraffa's *Ricardo*, Vol. IV, 'On Protection to Agriculture', p. 234.

39 *Ibid.*, Vol. II, 'Notes on Malthus', p. 198.

40 [Malthus] *Population*, 1798, p. 312 *et seq.*

41 Malthus, *Population*, quarto 2nd edn, 1803, p. 421.

42 Sraffa's *Ricardo*, Vol. II [1820], p. 234.

43 *Ibid.*, Vol. I, 'The Principles of Political Economy', p. 393.

44 *Ibid.*, Vol. II [1820], pp. 411-12; Malthus's 1836 *Political Economy*, pp. 393-4.

45 *British Critic*, August 1820, Vol. XIV, New Series, 'Malthus on Political Economy', pp. 118-19.

46 Malthus, *Principles of Political Economy*, 1836 edn, p. 261.

47 *Quarterly Review*, January 1824, Vol. XXX, No. 60, p. 315.

48 William Blake, FRS, *Observations on the Effects Produced by the Expenditure of Government during the Restriction of Cash Payments* (London, 1823).

Blake's main thesis was that prices had risen during the war because of increased demand for all commodities, including gold; the depreciation of paper money was the result of this rapid rise in government expenditure and not of an excessive note issue.

49 Sraffa's *Ricardo*, Vol. II [1820], pp. 189-91; Malthus's 1836 *Political Economy*, pp. 200-1.

50 Malthus, *Principles of Political Economy*, 1820 edn, p. 211; 1836 edn, p. 199.

51 *Ibid.*, 1820 edn, p. 400; 1836 edn, p. 350.

52 Robert Torrens, *Essay on the Production of Wealth* (London, 1821), p. v.

53 Sraffa's *Ricardo*, Vol. II, p.209; Malthus's 1836 *Political Economy*, p. 208.

54 Sraffa's *Ricardo*, Vol. VI, p. 162.

55 J. Overbeek, *History of Population Theories* (Rotterdam University Press, 1974), p. 46.

56 Malthus, *Principles of Political Economy*, 1836 edn, p. 267.

57 Sraffa's *Ricardo*, Vol. II [1820], p. 284; Malthus's 1836 *Political Economy*, p. 289, which is an improvement.

58 Sraffa's *Ricardo*, Vol. I, p. 11.

59 Adam Smith, *Wealth of Nations* (Methuen University Paperback, 1961), Vol. I, p. 53.

60 Samuel Read, *An Inquiry into the Natural Grounds of Right to Vendible Property or Wealth* (Edinburgh, 1829), p. xxix.

61 Sraffa's *Ricardo*, Vol. IX, pp. 330-1.

62 [Samuel Bailey] *A Letter to a Political Economist occasioned by an article in the Westminster Review on the Subject of Value* by the Author of the *Critical Dissertation* therein reviewed (London, 1826), p. 20.

63 Seymour's *'Pope' of Holland House* (see Chap. III, n. 13), p. 176. Whishaw's letter is dated 14 March 1817.

64 'Six Letters from Malthus to Pierre Prévost' ed. George William Zinke, *Journal of Economic History*, 1942, Vol. II, p. 180. Malthus's letter is dated 27 March 1821.

65 Malthus, *Principles of Political Economy*, 1836 edn, p. 116.

66 I am grateful for being allowed to see specimens of these at Nuffield College, Oxford.

67 G. D. H. Cole, *Life of Robert Owen* (Macmillan, London, 1930), pp. 263-6.

68 *Political Economy Club Centenary Volume* (VI, London, 1921), p. 21. The question was put up for discussion by John Cazenove.

69 *Ibid.*, pp. 246-7.

70 Sraffa's *Ricardo*, Vol. IX, pp. 20, 25.

71 These were published (by John Murray) in the *Transactions of the Royal Society of Literature*, the first in Vol. I, pp. 171-8; the second in Vol. II, pp. 74-81.

72 *Ibid.*, Vol. I, p. 171n.

73 *Ibid.*, Vol. II, p. 74.

74 Sraffa's *Ricardo*, Vol. II [1820], pp. 45-6; Malthus's 1836 *Political Economy*, p. 71, where 'principle' is changed to 'law'.

75 Malthus, *Principles of Political Economy*, 1836 edn, p. 405n.

76 Malthus, *Definitions in Political Economy* (London, 1827), p. 234.

77 Horner, *Memoirs* (see Chap. III, n. 85), pp. 146-7.

78 *Edinburgh Review*, July 1804, Vol. IV, pp. 354-62.
79 Hansard, Vol. 814, 1392-8, Anthony Barber's Budget Speech, 30 March 1971.
80 See page 428 for Malthus's unpublished letters to Dr Chalmers.
81 'John McIniscon, A Fisherman', *Principles of Political Economy and of Population* including an Examination of Mr. Malthus's Essay on those Subjects (2 vols, London, 1825), Vol. II, p. 383n.
82 Simon Gray, *All Classes Productive of National Wealth* (2nd edn, London, 1840), p. iii. First publ. 1817 under the pseudonym of 'George Purves'.
83 Sraffa's *Ricardo*, Vol. VIII, p. 40.
84 Alexander H. Everett, *New Ideas on Population* (London, 1823), pp. vi, viii-ix.
85 'Dr Purves', *All Classes Productive of National Wealth* (London, 1817), p. 28.
86 *Ibid.*, pp. 227-8.
87 *Ibid.*, p. 7.
88 *Ibid.*, pp. 127-8.
89 *Ibid.*, p. 162.
90 *Ibid.*, pp. 95-8.
91 Malthus, *Principles of Political Economy*, 1836 edn, p. 408.
92 'Dr Purves', *All Classes Productive of National Wealth*, pp. 43, 45-6.
93 *Political Economy Club Centenary Volume* (VI, 1921), p. 27.
94 Malthus, *Principles of Political Economy*, 1836 edn, p. 408.
95 Deane and Cole, *op. cit.*, p. 142, Table 30.
96 Sraffa's *Ricardo*, Vol. II, pp. 421, 425.
97 *Ibid.*, pp. 427-8.
98 *British Critic*, September 1820, Vol. XIV, p. 286.
99 Sraffa's *Ricardo*, Vol. II, p. 446, Malthus's own 1820 Summary. Compare with the expanded version in the 1836 *Political Economy*, pp. 403-4.
100 Sraffa's *Ricardo*, Vol. II [1820], pp. 428-9; Malthus's 1836 *Political Economy*, pp. 403-4.
101 Sraffa's *Ricardo*, Vol. II [1820], pp. 9-10; Malthus's 1836 *Political Economy*, p. 7.
102 James Mill, *Elements of Political Economy* (2nd edn, London, 1824), p. 231. Or see p. 332 of James Mill's *Selected Economic Writings*, ed. Donald Winch (Oliver & Boyd, Edinburgh and London, 1966).
103 John Maynard Keynes, *Essays in Biography* (2nd edn, Rupert Hart-Davis, London, 1951), p. 103.
104 *Ibid.*, p. 117.
105 *British Critic*, Vol. IV, p. 293.
106 Colvin's *Maria Edgeworth from England* (see Prologue, n. 17), p. 364.
107 *Letters of the Earl of Dudley to the Bishop of Llandaff* (London, 1841), p. 161. The bishop was Edward Copleston (1776-1849).
108 *Political Economy Club Centenary Volume* (VI, 1921), p. 265.
109 Sraffa's *Ricardo*, Vol. VII, pp. 37-8, 102-6.
110 D. P. O'Brien, *J. R. McCulloch. A Study in Classical Economics* (Allen & Unwin, London, 1970), pp. 17-19.
111 *Traveller*, 1820: 21 April, p. 3, col. a; 26 April, p. 2, cols a, b; 1 May, p.

2, cols a, b, d.

112 *Pamphleteer*, 1820, Vol. XVII, nos 33 and 34, pp. 289-347.

113 *Ibid.*, pp. 385-417.

114 *Ibid.*, p. 311.

115 *Ibid.*, p. 315. For a modern printing of this translation of Say's *Letters* see that published by Wheeler in 1936 with an Introduction by Harold Laski, pp. 28, 34, 62.

116 *Pamphleteer*, 1820, Vol. XVII, nos 33 and 34, p. 336.

117 [Jane Marcet] *Conversations on Political Economy* (6th edn, London, 1827), pp. 193, 98, 381, 200, 477.

118 Sraffa's *Ricardo*, Vol. VIII, p. 336.

119 [Malthus] *Population*, 1798, p. 395.

120 'Six Letters from Malthus to Pierre Prévost' ed. G. W. Zinke, *Journal of Economic History*, 1942, Vol. II, p. 181.

121 Sraffa's *Ricardo*, Vol. VIII, p. 378.

122 *Selections from the Correspondence of the late Macvey Napier* ed. by his son (London, 1879), pp. 29, 31-2.

123 Sraffa's *Ricardo*, Vol. VIII, p. 341 and n.

124 *Journal of Economic History*, 1942, Vol. II, p. 181.

125 *Correspondence of Macvey Napier*, p. 33.

126 'Letters of Malthus to Macvey Napier' supplied by J. H. Hollander, *Economic Journal*, 1897, Vol. VII, pp. 265-6.

127 *Journal of Economic History*, 1942, Vol. II, p. 182.

128 MS letter kindly supplied by Lord Congleton; see pp. 157-9 and 476.

129 Sraffa's *Ricardo*, Vol. II [1820], p. 27. Compare with the completely different version in the 1836 *Political Economy*, p. 56.

130 John Stuart Mill, *Autobiography* (Columbia University Press, New York, 1924), p. 84.

131 *Political Economy Club Centenary Volume* (VI, 1921), pp. 223-4.

132 [Samuel Bailey] *A Critical Dissertation on the Nature, Measure and Causes of Value*; chiefly in reference to the Writings of Mr. Ricardo and his Followers (London, 1825), pp. 30, 39, 71-2, 96-7.

133 *Ibid.*, pp. 24, 25, 146.

134 *Morning Chronicle*, 6 September 1823, p. 2, cols b, c, d.

135 *London Magazine*, December 1823, Vol. VIII p. 587; or De Quincey's *Collected Writings* (Edinburgh, 1889-90), Vol. IX, pp. 32-3, 34.

136 [Samuel Bailey] *Dissertation on Value*, p. 22n.

137 [Empson] *Edinburgh Review*, January 1837, Vol. LXIV, p. 469.

Chapter X   THE HEAT OF THE DAY (1817-25)

1 Sraffa's *Ricardo*, Vol. VIII, p. 259.

2 *The Times*, 9 May 1817, p. 3, col. c.

3 IOR, J/2/2C ff. 224-9, 238.

4 *Ibid.*, ff. 242, 250.

5 IOR, J/2/3 ff. 55-7, 60-1, 85-6, 238.

6 George Ticknor, *Life, Letters and Journals* (2nd edn, 2 vols, London, 1876), Vol. I, p. 240.

7 These diaries and letters are with the Mosley Papers in the Wedgwood Archives at the University of Keele.

8 John Venn, *Annals of a Clerical Family* (London, 1904), pp. 179, 180.

9 IOR, J/2/3 ff. 122-3.

10 *The Times*, 1818: 14 April, p. 3, col. e; 15 April, p. 3, col. c.

11 IOR, J/2/3 ff. 252-3.

12 Reginald Heber, *Travels and Letters*, ed. Amelia Heber (3 vols, London, 1828), Vol. II, p. 80.

13 British Library Add. MSS 35, 133 ff. 456-7.

14 IOR, J/4/4 ff. 141, 159.

15 *The Times*, 19 October 1822, p. 3, cols a, b.

16 *Morning Chronicle*, 21 October 1822, p. 3, cols c, d.

17 IOR, J/1/38 ff. 230-47, 254, 276-7.

18 *Ibid.*, J/1/38 f. 208.

19 *The Times*, 1824: 26 February, p. 3, col. c; 25 March, p. 3, col. a; 1 April, p. 2, col. b.

20 The material for Section 2 comes from William Bray's diary and the Okewood Chapel archives in Guildford Muniment Room, and the Bray and Warren letter-books and bill-books which are now in the Greater London Record Office.

21 The quotations from William Otter are from his sermon *Upon the Influence of the Clergy in Improving the Condition of the Poor*; this was preached at Ludlow on 26 May 1818 and published at Shrewsbury ('at the Salopian Journal Office') in the same year.

22 MS letter in the Horner Collection, British Library of Political and Economic Science.

23 Mrs William Busk, *Plays and Poems* (2 vols, London, 1837), Vol. I, *The Druids* is the first of three plays.

24 Richard Lalor Sheil, (1791-1851), *The Apostate* (London, 1817).

25 Busk, *op. cit.*, Vol. II, p. 285.

26 *Ibid.*, p. 276.

27 Cockburn, *Life of Jeffrey* (see Chap. III, n. 84), Vol. II, p. 207.

28 Henrietta Litchfield, ed., *Emma Darwin: A Century of Family Letters* (2 vols, London, 1915), Vol. I, pp. 230, 249, 184, 206.

29 Lady Mackintosh's MS journal for 7 November 1821.

30 [Empson] *Edinburgh Review*, January 1837, Vol. LXIV, p. 481.

31 MS letter in the Archives of Jesus College, Cambridge.

32 Patricia James, ed., *Travel Diaries of T. R. Malthus* (Cambridge University Press, 1966), pp. 18-22.

33 Murray published in 1819 Marianne Baillie's *First Impressions of a Tour upon the Continent in the Summer of 1818*. A two-volume work, *Lisbon in the Years 1821, '22, and '23*, went into two editions, so Murray presumably did not lose by his kindness.

34 Information from the Bray and Warren letter-books and the MS notes of Col. Sydenham Malthus.

35 Henry Cockburn, *Memorials of His Time* (2 vols, Edinburgh, 1856), Vol.

I, p. 265.

36 MS letter in the Library of the University of Illinois at Urbana-Champaign.

37 Sraffa's *Ricardo*, Vol. VIII, p. 375.

38 *Ibid.*, Vol. IX, pp. 94, 101.

39 *Memoirs of Thomas Chalmers*, ed. Wm. Hanna (2 vols, Edinburgh, 1854), Vol. I, p. 624.

40 George Ticknor, *Life, Letters and Journals*, Vol. I, p. 241.

41 IOR, J/2/4 ff. 285-6.

42 A. L. Le Breton, *Memories of Seventy Years* (London, 1884), p. 162; 2nd Lord Teignmouth, *Reminiscences of Many Years* (2 vols, Edinburgh, 1878), Vol. I, p. 66.

43 Harriet Martineau, *Autobiography* (2nd edn, 3 vols, London, 1877), Vol. I, p. 71.

44 Mary Russell Mitford, *Our Village* (4th edn, London, 1832), Vol. V, pp. 191-2.

45 Thomas Love Peacock, *Works*, ed. F. H. Brett-Smith and C. E. Jones (10 vols, Constable, London), Vol. II, 1924, pp. 75-9, 126, 150.

46 Peacock, *Melincourt*, ed. Richard Garnett (2 vols, London, 1891), Vol. I, p. 72n. The passages quoted here will be found in this edition in Vol. I, pp. 74-8, 117, 139.

47 J. B. Priestley, *Thomas Love Peacock* (2nd edn, Macmillan, 1966), p. 36.

48 William Hazlitt, second article on 'The Distressed State of the Agriculture of the Country' in *Complete Works*, ed. P. P. Howe (London, 1930), Vol. VII, p. 113.

49 Sraffa's *Ricardo*, Vol. VI, p. 131.

50 MS letter in the Library of the University of Illinois at Urbana-Champaign.

51 Colvin's *Maria Edgeworth from England* (see Prologue, n. 17), p. 331.

52 British Sessional Papers, House of Commons 5:44,45, pp. 589, 600, 590.

53 *Ibid.*, p. 601.

54 William Grampp, 'The Economists and the Combination Laws', a paper read at the annual meeting of the Western Economic Association at Vancouver in August 1971.

55 [Charles Marsh] *The Clubs of London* (2 vols, London, 1832), Vol. II, pp. 159-69.

56 *Political Economy Club Centenary Volume* (VI, London, 1921), p. 273.

57 *Minutes of the Proceedings of the Political Economy Club 1821-1882* (Vol. IV, London, 1882), *passim*, esp. p. 41.

58 Malthus, *Travel Diaries*, p. 159.

59 John Cazenove, *Questions respecting the National Debt and Taxation stated and answered* (London, 1829), pp. 3-4, 11.

60 IOR, L/F/1/2 f. 306 (Minutes of the East India Company's Finance and Home Committee, 11 February 1835).

61 Dr John Pullen, of the University of New England, Australia, has written a thesis comparing the 1820 and 1836 versions of Malthus's *Principles of Political Economy*.

62 *Political Economy Club Centenary Volume*, VI, p. 268.

63 Sir Henry Lyons, *The Royal Society 1660-1940* (Cambridge University Press, 1944), pp. 244, 205.

64 Malthus's Certificate of Election in the Library of the Royal Society.
65 C. R. Weld, *History of the Royal Society* (2 vols, London, 1848), Vol. II, pp. 113, 203, 422-3.
66 I have not seen this letter, which was advertised in Miss Winifred Myers's Catalogue for 1960.
67 John S. Harford, *The Life of Thomas Burgess* (London, 1840), p. 104.
68 Archives of the Royal Society of Literature.
69 Harford, *Thomas Burgess*, pp. 344-5.
70 Humphry Ward, *History of the Athenaeum 1824-1925* (London, 1926), p. 50.
71 *Ibid.*, pp. 11, 39, 98-101.
72 From a photocopy of J. L. Mallet's Political Diaries in the Bodleian Library, MS Facs. d 146 f. 74.
73 Otter's *Memoir* (see Chap. I, n. 29), p. xli.
74 Both Malthus's letters to Dr Marcet are in New York, in the Special Collections (801 Butler Library) of the Columbia University Libraries.
75 For much of this information I am indebted to *Introduction to Malthus* ed. D. V. Glass (Watts & Co, London, 1953). See especially Professor Glass on 'Malthus and the Limitation of Population Growth', pp. 39-46.
76 Sraffa's *Ricardo*, Vol. VII, p. 361, letter to James Mill.
77 *Ibid.*, Vol. VIII, p. 225.
78 'Six Letters from Malthus to Pierre Prévost' ed. George William Zinke, *Journal of Economic History*, 1942, Vol. II, pp. 179-80.
79 Sraffa's *Ricardo*, Vol. VIII, pp. 224-5, p. 224 n. 2.
80 MS letters kindly supplied by Mrs Christina Colvin.

Chapter XI   THE POPULATION CONTROVERSIES CONTINUE

1 Sraffa's *Ricardo*, Vol. VII, p. 87.
2 Amelia Heber, *The Life of Reginald Heber* (2 vols, London, 1830), Vol. I, p. 484.
3 Malthus, *Essay on the Principle of Population* (3 vols, London, 1817), Vol. I, pp. xi-xiii. This Preface is not reprinted in the Everyman edition.
4 *Journal of Economic History*, 1942, Vol. II, p. 176.
5 Professor Zinke kindly provided me with a photocopy of this letter, which is in the Bibliothèque Publique et Universitaire at Geneva.
6 Malthus, *Population*, Everyman edn, Vol. II, pp. 101, 105.
7 *Ibid.*, Vol. II, pp. 57, 61.
8 [John Weyland] *A Short Inquiry into the Policy, Humanity and Past Effects of the Poor Laws* by one of His Majesty's Justices of the Peace for Three Inland Counties (London, 1807), pp. 42, 49. In the same year Weyland published under his own name his *Observations on Mr. Whitbread's Poor Bill and on the Population of England*.
9 Malthus, *Appendix* to the Fifth Edition of *Population*, 1817, Vol. III, p. 412.
10 John Weyland, *The Principles of Population and Production* (London, 1816), p. 109.
11 *Ibid.*, p. 172.

12 *Ibid.*, p. 129.
13 Malthus, *Appendix* to *Population*, 1817, Vol. III, pp. 416-17.
14 Colvin's *Maria Edgeworth from England* (see Prologue, n. 17), p. 260.
15 Sraffa's *Ricardo*, Vol. VII, pp. 359-60.
16 *Journal of Economic History*, 1942, Vol. II, p. 179. Malthus's letter to Prévost is dated 27 March 1821.
17 Malthus, *Population, Appendix*, 1807, Vol. II, pp. 472, 473n; *Appendix*, 1817, Vol. III, p. 373 and n.
18 Malthus, *Appendix* to *Population*, 1817, Vol. III, pp. 423-4.
19 James Grahame, *An Inquiry into the Principle of Population including an Exposition of the Cause and the Advantages of a Tendency to Exuberance of Numbers in Society, a Defence of Poor Laws, etc.* (Edinburgh, 1816), pp. 167-8.
20 *Ibid.*, p. 208.
21 Malthus, *Appendix* to *Population*, 1817, Vol. III, p. 393.
22 Sraffa's *Ricardo*, Vol. VII, p. 63.
23 Malthus, *Population*, Everyman edn, Vol. II, p. 24.
24 Robert Owen, *An Address to the Inhabitants of New Lanark* ... at the opening of the Institution established for the Formation of Character (London, 1816), p. 16.
25 Robert Owen, *A New View of Society* (3rd edn, London, 1817), p. 15.
26 Anon. ['Anti-Godwin'] *Remarks on Mr. Godwin's Enquiry concerning Population* (London, 1821), p. 3.
27 Sraffa's *Ricardo*, Vol. VIII, p. 376.
28 'Anti-Godwin', *op. cit.*, p. 37.
29 William Godwin, *Thoughts Occasioned by the Perusal of Dr. Parr's Spital Sermon* ... *being a Reply to the attacks of Dr. Parr, Mr. Mackintosh, the Author of an Essay on Population and Others* (London,1801), pp. 55, 56, 61, 76.
30 *New Monthly Magazine*, 1822, Vol. IV, p. 541 (a review of Francis Place's *Illustrations and Proofs of the Principle of Population*).
31 William Godwin, *Of Population. An Enquiry concerning the Power of Increase in the Numbers of Mankind*, being an Answer to Mr. Malthus's Essay on that Subject (London, 1820), pp. 310, 565.
32 *Ibid.*, pp. 110, 551-2.
33 'Anti-Godwin', *op. cit.*, p. 63.
34 Sraffa's *Ricardo*, Vol. VIII, p. 326.
35 David Booth, *A Letter to the Rev. T. R. Malthus, M.A., F.R.S.*; being an Answer to the Criticism on Mr. Godwin's Work on Population which was inserted in the LXXth number of the Edinburgh Review: to which is added An Examination of the Censuses of Great Britain and Ireland. (London, 1823), pp. 68-70.
36 [Malthus] *Edinburgh Review*, July, 1821, Vol. XXXV, pp. 376-7, article headed 'Godwin on Malthus'.
37 *British Critic*, March 1821, Vol. XV, New Series, p. 247.
38 [Malthus] *Edinburgh Review*, Vol. XXXV, p. 362.
39 C. Kegan Paul, *William Godwin: His Friends and Contemporaries* (2 vols, London, 1876), Vol. II, pp. 274-5.
40 Graham Wallas, *Life of Francis Place* (London, 1898), pp. 10-12.

41 *Ibid.*, pp. 58-60.
42 *Ibid.*, pp. 72-8, 81-2, 82 n.
43 *Ibid.*, p. 166.
44 *Supplement to the Encyclopaedia Britannica* (Edinburgh, 1824), Vol. III, p. 261.
45 Quoted by James Bonar, *Letters of Ricardo to Malthus* (Oxford, 1887), p. 207.
46 Sraffa's *Ricardo*, Vol. IX, p. 116.
47 Francis Place, *Illustrations and Proofs of the Principle of Population* including an Examination of the proposed Remedies of Mr. Malthus, and a Reply to the Objections of Mr. Godwin and Others (London, 1822), pp. 176-7, 165.
48 Peter Fryer, *The Birth Controllers* (Secker & Warburg, London, 1965), pp. 43-7. Tom Moore printed this verse under his own name in his *Collected Works* which he brought out in 1841 in ten volumes. See Vol. VIII, p. 156. In this volume Moore made two facetious references to Malthus:

> p. 144 (1826): Propagation in reason - a small child or two -
> Even Reverend Malthus himself is a friend to.

> p. 263 (1827): Said Malthus, one day, to a clown
> Lying stretch'd on the beach, in the sun, -
> 'What's the number of souls in this town?' -
> 'The number? Lord bless you, there's none.

> We have nothing but *dabs* in this place,
> Of *them* a great plenty there are; -
> But the *soles*, please your rev'rence and grace,
> Are all t'other side of the bar'.

49 Richard Carlile, *Every Woman's Book, or What is Love?* (4th edn, London, 1826), pp. 16-17, 38, 27, 43.
50 Otter's *Memoir* (see Chap. I, n. 29), p. xv.
51 'John McIniscon, A Fisherman', *Principles of Political Economy and of Population* including an Examination of Mr. Malthus's Essay on those Subjects (2 vols, London, 1825), Vol. II, pp. 57, 60, 418.
52 Malthus, *Population*, Everyman edn, Vol. II, pp. 30, 33, 34, 36-7.
53 Robert Gourlay, *General Introduction to a Statistical Account of Upper Canada compiled with a View to a Grand System of Emigration in connection with a Reform of the Poor Laws* (London, 1822), pp. cccxxxviii, ccclxii, ccclxiii.
54 Sraffa's *Ricardo*, Vol. XI, p. xv.
55 Malthus's correspondence with Wilmot-Horton is in the Catton Collection in the Central Library of the City of Derby.
56 Irish University Press Series of British Parliamentary Papers. Emigration 2. First, Second and Third Reports from the Select Committee on Emigration from the United Kingdom with Minutes of Evidence, Appendix and Index. Petition of Glasgow Tradesmen, p. 507.
57 *Ibid.*, pp. 311, 326 (Question 3417), 327 (Questions 3433-4).
58 *Ibid.*, p. 314 (Question 3245).
59 *Ibid.*, pp. 315 (Question 3259), 316 (Question 3274).

60 *Ibid.*, p. 317.
61 *Ibid.*, pp. 318-19.
62 *Ibid.*, p. 321.
63 *Ibid.*, p. 9.
64 *Ibid.*, pp. 11, 12.
65 *Ibid.*, pp. 38-9.
66 [Robert Gouger, ? Wakefield, Edward Gibbon] *A Statement of the Principles and Objects of a proposed National Society for the Cure and Prevention of Pauperism by means of Systematic Colonization* (London, 1830).
67 John Barton, *An Inquiry into the Causes of the Progressive Depreciation of Agricultural Labour in modern times*, with Suggestions for it's [*sic*] Remedy (London, 1820), pp. 21-2, 42-3.
68 *Journal of Economic History*, 1942, Vol. II, pp. 184-5.
69 'Piercy Ravenstone', *A Few Doubts as to the Correctness of some Opinions generally entertained on the Subjects of Population and Political Economy* (London, 1821), pp. 285-6, 429.
70 Sraffa's *Ricardo*, Vol. IX, p. 64.
71 *Ibid.*, Vol. XI, p. xxviii.
72 'Ravenstone', *op. cit.*, pp. 157, 161-3.
73 Anon. ['Anti-Godwin'] *Remarks on Mr. Godwin's Enquiry concerning Population* (London, 1821), p. 61.
74 David Booth, *A Letter to the Rev. T. R. Malthus* (London, 1823), pp. 3-5.
75 There are a number of reprints of Malthus's *Summary View of the Principle of Population*. References here are to that edited by Antony Flew (Penguin Books, Harmondsworth, 1970), pp. 224-5.
76 *Ibid.*, pp. 237, 245-7.
77 Anon., *Memoirs of the Life and Writings of Michael Thomas Sadler, Esq., M.P., F.R.S.* (London, 1842), p. 188.
78 Michael Thomas Sadler, *The Law of Population*: A treatise, in six books, in disproof of the superfecundity of human beings, and developing the real principle of their increase (2 vols, London, 1830), Vol. II, p. 352.
79 *Blackwood's Magazine*, July 1830, Vol. XXVIII, pp. 116-17.
80 *Memoirs of Sadler*, pp. 193, 199.
81 William Cobbett, *Two-penny Trash*, June 1831, No. XII, pp. 267-8.

Chapter XII   DECLINING SUN (1825-34)

1 Lincoln Archives, Tennyson d'Eyncourt Papers H/15/1.
2 Patricia James, ed., *The Travel Diaries of T. R. Malthus* (Cambridge University Press, 1966), pp. 228-43.
3 *Minutes of the Proceedings of the Political Economy Club*, Vol. IV, p. 75.
4 Cockburn's *Life of Jeffrey* (see Chap. III, n. 84), Vol. II, pp. 220-1. I am grateful to Messrs Alison & Hutchinson & Partners, Architects, Engineers and Planning Consultants, for their hospitality at Craigcrook Castle.
5 Malthus's *Travel Diaries*, pp. 258-67.
6 Malthus, *Definitions in Political Economy* preceded by an Inquiry into the Rules which ought to guide Political Economists in the Definition and Use

of their Terms: with Remarks on the Deviation from these Rules in their Writings (London, 1827), p. 123.

7 D. P. O'Brien, *J. R. McCulloch. A Study in Classical Economics* (Allen & Unwin, London, 1970), p. 140.

8 [J. R. McCulloch] *A Review of Definitions in Political Economy by the Rev. T. R. Malthus* (London, 1827), p. 10.

9 Leslie P. Wenham, *The History of Richmond School, Yorkshire* (The Herald Press, Arbroath, 1958), pp. 62-77. See also the same author's edition of the *Letters of James Tate* published in 1966 by the Yorkshire Archeological Society.

10 MS letter in the Library of the University of Illinois at Urbana-Champaign.

11 H. Litchfield, *A Century of Family Letters* (see Chap. X, n. 28), pp. 222, 229-30.

12 Manning and Bray, *History of Surrey* (see Chap. I, n. 23), Vol. II, p. 649.

13 Lincoln Archives, COR.B.4/61/7.

14 For these MS 'letters home' of Pakenham Edgeworth, from which further quotation will be made, I am indebted to Mrs Christina Colvin.

15 Malthus's MS letters to Thomas Chalmers are in the New College Library (Faculty of Divinity) of the University of Edinburgh.

16 *Selections from the Correspondence of the late Macvey Napier* ed. by his son (London, 1879), pp. 187-8.

17 IOR, J/2/6 f. 105; J/2/10 f. 31.

18 IOR, J/2/8 f. 58 (28 May 1829. The speaker was William Astell).

19 IOR, J/2/11 f. 47; J/2/9 f. 98.

20 IOR, J/2/7 f. 223.

21 [Mary Draper] *Mary Roper's Story* or What she told her Girls over the Classroom Fire (S.P.C.K., 1885), pp. 129, 133, 137. See *Memorials of Old Haileybury* (London, 1894), p. 62 and n.

22 IOR, J/2/4 f. 273.

23 IOR, J/2/4 ff. 215-16, 462.

24 IOR, J/2/4 ff. 458, 475.

25 [Empson] *Edinburgh Review*, Vol. LXIV, p. 505.

26 Judith Anne Merivale, ed., *Autobiography and Letters of Dean Merivale* (Oxford, 1895, for private circulation), pp. 123, 126. The published version (London, 1899) does not contain the young Merivale's letters from Harrow and Haileybury.

27 *Autobiography of Dean Merivale* (London, 1899), p. 43.

28 Adam Smith, *Wealth of Nations* (Edinburgh University Press, 1829). Annotated copy in the Marshall Library, p. 128.

29 *Ibid.*, pp. 179, 224, 145.

30 *Ibid.*, p. 23.

31 *Ibid.*, pp. 30, 68.

32 Sir Herbert Maxwell, ed., *The Creevey Papers* (London, 1923), pp. 428-9.

33 IOR, J/2/4 f. 510; J/2/6 ff. 30-1, 50; J/2/8 ff. 85, 102; J/2/11 f. 53; J/2/12 f. 19.

34 IOR, J/2/7 f. 56; J/2/8 f. 119; J/2/11 ff. 109-11.

35 IOR, J/2/11 ff. 182, 157.

36 *Memorials of Old Haileybury*, pp. 79, 95.

37 John Martineau, *Sir Bartle Frere* (2 vols, London, 1895), Vol. I, pp. 8-9.
38 *Memorials of Old Haileybury*, pp. 198-9.
39 A. L. Le Breton, *Memories of Seventy Years* (London, 1884), pp. 159, 162-3.
40 [Empson] *Edinburgh Review*, Vol. LXIV, p. 505.
41 Lincoln Archives, Tennyson d'Eyncourt Papers H/15/1.
42 PRO, Prov. 11. Piece no. 1843, f. 109.
43 I am indebted to Mrs Linnell Burton for all the material from her family archives.
44 I must point out that although I spent a happy week in the New College Library at Edinburgh, and searched diligently, it is quite possible that I missed something of importance in this overwhelming store of MS material.
45 Rev. William Hanna, ed., *Memoirs of Thomas Chalmers* (2 vols, Edinburgh, 1854), Vol. I, pp. 623-4.
46 *Ibid.*, Vol. II, pp. 74-6.
47 Malthus's *Travel Diaries*, p. 260.
48 *Memoirs of Thomas Chalmers*, ed. Wm. Hanna (2 vols, Edinburgh, 1854), Vol. II, pp. 82-3.
49 Dr Thomas Chalmers, *On Political Economy in connexion with the Moral State and Moral Prospects of Society* (2nd edn, Glasgow, 1832), p. 136.
50 *Sir James Mackintosh* by his son (2nd edn, 2 vols, London, 1836), Vol. II, p. 483.
51 Henry Reeve, ed., *The Greville Memoirs* (2 vols, London, 1888), Vol. II, p. 262.
52 Rev. Charles Eckersall, Sermon on *The Wrath of God; its cause; and the means of averting it*, preached at the church of St Philip, Birmingham, where he was a curate, on 21 March 1832, 'being the day appointed by proclamation for a general fast and humiliation before God' (London, 1832).
53 *Greville Memoirs*, Vol. II, pp. 319, 197.
54 Nowell C. Smith, ed., *The Letters of Sydney Smith* (2 vols, Oxford, 1953), Vol. II, pp. 536, 545.
55 This MS note is with the Malthus papers in the Marshall Library at Cambridge.
56 *Letters of Sydney Smith* (ed. N. C. Smith), Vol. II, p. 575.
57 William Foster Lloyd, *Lectures on Population* Michaelmas Term 1832 (Oxford, 1833), p. 44.
58 Richard Whately, *Introductory Lectures on Political Economy* Easter Term 1831 (2nd edn, London 1832), pp. 185-6n.
59 Nassau William Senior, *Two Lectures on Population* delivered before the University of Oxford in Easter Term 1828 ... to which is added a Correspondence between the Author and the Rev. T. R. Malthus (London, 1831), pp. 48, 51.
60 Almost the entire text of this correspondence is given in *The Malthusian Population Theory* by G. F. McCleary (Faber & Faber, London, 1953), pp. 114-27.
61 I. Todhunter, *William Whewell, An Account of his Writings, with Selections from his Literary and Scientific Correspondence* (2 vols, London, 1876), Vol. II, pp. 48, 94.
62 Malthus's letters to Whewell are published in *Economica*, November 1973,

pp. 379-93, ed. by N. B. de Marchi and R. P. Sturges.
63 Robert Torrens, *Essay on the Production of Wealth* (London, 1821), p. xiii: 'A few years ago, when the brilliant discoveries in chymistry began to supersede the ancient doctrine of phlogiston, controversies analogous to those which now exist amongst Political Economists, divided the professors of natural knowledge; and Dr. Priestley, like Mr. Malthus, appeared as the pertinacious champion of the theories which the facts established by himself had so largely contributed to overthrow.... With respect to Political Economy the period of controversy is passing away, and that of unanimity rapidly approaching. Twenty years hence there will scarcely exist a doubt respecting any of its fundamental principles.'
64 See *Political Economy Club Centenary Volume* (VI, 1921), pp. 220-5 for J. L. Mallet's account of the meetings at which Torrens's question was discussed, 13 January and 14 April 1831.
65 Todhunter's *Whewell*, Vol. II, pp. 134, 152-3.
66 MS letter in the Library of Trinity College, Cambridge.
67 Mrs Stair Douglas, *Life and Selections from the Correspondence of William Whewell* (2nd edn, London, 1882), p. 171.
68 *Report of the Third Meeting of the British Association for the Advancement of Science* held at Cambridge in 1833 (London, 1834), p. ix.
69 Hanna, *Memoirs of Thomas Chalmers*, Vol. II, p. 299.
70 Archives of the Royal Statistical Society.
71 *Report of the British Association's Third Meeting*, p. xxviii.
72 These papers are the property of the Academie Royale de Belgique, at present deposited in the Bibliothèque Royale Albert Ier, ref. 1697. I am greatly indebted for a photocopy to Madame Wellens-De Donder of the Centre National d'Histoire des Sciences in Brussels. She ran the documents to earth for me after a chase which involved Monsieur Wyfells, Archiviste Général du Royaume, and Monsieur Philips of the Bibliothèque Fonds Quetelet, Ministère des Affaires Économiques, to both of whom I should like to express my thanks.
73 MS letter in the Library of the University of Illinois at Urbana-Champaign.
74 British Library Add MSS 37188 ff. 201-2.
75 Otter's *Memoir* (see Chap. I, n. 29), pp. xlviii, xix.
76 Lucy Aikin's *Memoirs, Miscellanies and Letters* (London, 1864), p. 285.
77 Harriet Martineau produced nine volumes of *Illustrations of Political Economy*, each little duodecimo book containing three tales. 'Cousin Marshall' (the second story in Vol. III) gives the gist of her most extreme views; see especially pp. 37-50, 73.
78 Harriet Martineau, *Biographical Sketches 1852-1875* (London, 1885), pp. 94-5.
79 Harriet Martineau, *Autobiography* (2nd edn, 3 vols, London, 1877), Vol. I, pp. 328-9.
80 A. L. Le Breton, *Memories of Seventy Years* (London, 1884), p. 158.
81 H. Litchfield, ed., *Emma Darwin: A Century of Family Letters* (2 vols, London, 1915), Vol. I, p. 257.
82 Maria Edgeworth, *Tour in Connemara and the Martins of Ballinahinch*, ed. H. E. Butler (Constable, London, 1950), pp. 24-5.

83 Parliamentary Debates, 2nd Series, Vol. XVII, col. 1533. From the speech of Robert Slaney, MP for Shrewsbury, 17 April 1828, on his motion for an Inquiry into the State of the Poor Laws.

84 Sidney and Beatrice Webb, English Poor Law History: Part II: The Last Hundred Years (2 vols, London, 1929), Chapter I, esp. pp. 88-9.

85 MS letter in the Baker Library of the Graduate School of Business Administration at Harvard University.

86 Parliamentary Debates, 3rd Series, Vol. XXIV, col. 473.

87 The Times 1834: 22 July, p. 3, cols d, e.

88 Ibid., 23 July, p. 8 col. b.

89 Ibid., 24 July, p. 5, cols b, c.

90 Ibid., 25 July, p. 5, col. d.

91 A photocopy of this letter was generously sent by Goodspeed's Book Shop, Inc., of Boston, Mass., through the kind offices of Miss Winifred Myers.

92 MS letter in the Library of the University of Illinois at Urbana-Champaign.

93 I am grateful to the Bedford County Record Office, the Rev. L. B. Impson, Rector of Wilden with Colmworth, and the Rev. J. C. Hill, Rector of Newport with Chetwynd, for their help in a determined search for Jacqueline.

94 P. W. Clayden, Rogers and his Contemporaries (2 vols, London, 1889), Vol. II, p. 104.

EPILOGUE

1 Otter's Memoir (see Chap. I, n. 29), p. xlii.

2 Morning Chronicle, 1 January 1835, p. 2, cols b, c.

3 MS letter in the Brougham Collection of the D.M.S. Watson Library at University College, London.

4 Literary Remains ... of the Late Rev. Richard Jones (London, 1859), pp. 592-3.

Index

The index has been expanded to provide information which, it is hoped, will be of use to readers unfamiliar with British history and institutions.

Where men have more than one name or title, they are entered under that by which Malthus was most likely to have known them. Married women are given their husbands' names, according to the custom of the period.

Grenville, William Wyndham, Lord
(1759-1834) Whig statesman, 136-7,
141, 143-4, 169, 253, 329; M's *Letter* to
(1813), 218-21
Greville, Charles Cavendish Fulke
(1794-1865) political diarist, 435
Grey, Charles, 2nd Earl (1764-1845)
Whig statesman, 227, 253, 266; Prime
Minister (1830-4), 416, 436, 456-7
Grote, George (1794-1871) liberal
reformer and historian of Greece,
354, 361
growth, economic, *see* wealth,
progress of
Gunning, Henry (1768-1854) Senior
Esquire Bedell of the University of
Cambridge: *Reminiscences*, 26-7, 33,
178-9, 223

Hackshaw, Mrs Humphrey, née Anne
Malthus, paternal aunt of M, 9, 76
Haileybury, Herts, 174-5, 180-2, 184-5,
241; *see mainly* East India College
Hailey House, M's home at E. I. Coll.
1809-34, 185-7, 229, 258, 418, 458
hairdressing, 26-7, 141, 179-80, 302, 345
Hallam, Henry (1777-1859) Whig
historian, esp. of Middle Ages, father
of Tennyson's friend Arthur Henry
H., 206
Hallam, Rev. John, curate of Okewood,
331-3
Hamilton, Capt. Alexander (1762-1824)
Prof. of Hindu Literature at E. I.
Coll. 1806-18, 175, 179, 182, 231, 324,
357
happiness (as Utilitarian goal), 20,
109-10, 119-20, 123, 254, 261, 262,
263, 397
Harrow-on-the-Hill, Middx, 9, 24
Hastings, Sussex, 87, 416
Haughton, Sir Graves Champney
(1788-1849) Oriental Prof. at E. I.
Coll. 1818-27, knighted 1833, 234-5,
237, 241, 324, 337
Hayek, F. A.: Introd. to Thornton's
Paper Credit, 135
Hazlitt, William (1778-1830) prolific
essayist: attacks M, 121, 152, 161, 346,
349, 404; *Edinburgh Review* on, 115,
117

Heber, Rev. Reginald (1783-1826) misc.
writer, incl. hymns, 2nd Anglican
Bishop of Calcutta, 60, 86, 213, 324,
370
Hegewisch, Franz Hermann, MD
(1783-1865) German translator of M's
Population, 363-4
Henley, Rev. Samuel, DD (1740-1815)
1st Principal of E. I. Coll. 1805-15,
173-6, 182-3, 186, 216, 222, 229, 237
Herschel, Sir John Frederick William
(1792-1871) astronomer, friend of
Babbage and Whewell, 229, 439, 442
Hertford Castle, 1st domicile of E. I.
Coll., 172, 174, 180
High Price of Provisions, see Cause of the . . .
Hodgson, Brian Houghton (1800-94) E.
I. Coll. student (1817), 243-4
Hogarth, William (1697-1764) painter
and engraver, famous for *The Rake's
Progress*, etc., 9
Holland, Elizabeth Vassall Fox, Lady
(1770-1845), 54, 344
Holland, Henry Richard Vassall Fox,
Lord (1773-1840) reforming Whig
politician, nephew of Charles James
Fox, 83, 253, 344, 370, 416, 458
Holland, Sir Henry, MD (1788-1873)
fashionable physician, 3, 226, 345, 357,
436
Hollin Hall, Ripon, N. Yorks, seat of
Wood family, 213, 351, 428
Horner, Francis (1778-1817) Pl. 8 (a):
account of, 112-13; views on
Bourbons, 227; on bullion
controversy, 197, 198-9, 203, 206-7;
on corn question, 253, 260-1, 264, 266;
on country banks, 199; on E. I. Coll.,
222, 231-2; on education, 224-5; on
Ireland, 145, 156; on M, 148-9, 150,
199; on music bottled, 302; on
sinecures, 142; *other refs*, 137, 208, 248,
314

Horner, Leonard (1785-1864) bro. of
Francis, geologist and educational
pioneer, 208, 225, 357
horses: agricultural use of, 129, 261;
extravagant to keep, 129, 134, 348, 349
housing, M against for poor, 139, 140,
393, 395
Howlett, Rev. John (1731-1804) writer
on population, 56-8

Melbourne, Lady—*cont.*
Wm Lamb, later 2nd Viscount
Melbourne, 259
Melbourne, William Lamb, 2nd
Viscount (1779-1848) Whig
statesman, Prime Minister 1834,
1835-41, 344, 456
Merivale, Rev. Charles (1808-93) student
at E. I. Coll. 1825, later Dean of Ely,
419-20, 422
middle classes, M's views on, 51, 254
Militia, a home defence force reorganised
in counties in 1757, succeeded by the
Territorial Army in 1908, 71, 182-3
Mill, James (1773-1836): *Commerce
Defended* (1808), 277; *History of British
India* (1817), 350-1; *Elements of
Political Economy* (1821), 310, 320; on
contraception, 384; distress of 1816,
370; and M, 310-11, 316, 356, 410; and
Francis Place, 382-4; at Political
Economy Club, 354, 356; and Ricardo,
208, 248, 277; on Say's Law, 308-9; on
'theoretical labour', 297; *other refs*,
374, 437-8
Mill, John Stuart (1806-73) Utilitarian
liberal writer, son of James: on M,
109, 310-11, 320; *other refs*, 319, 386-7,
425
Milne, Joshua (1776-1851) actuary of Sun
Life Assurance Society, 402
Mitford, Mary Russell (1787-1855)
popular writer, esp. essays on *Our
Village* (1824-32), 64, 163, 346
money: as capital, 191, 204-5;
depreciation of, 90, 195-7, 200-2,
204-6, 210-11; the best 'equivalent',
105, 191, 205; gold standard, 191-3,
195-6, 202, 211-12; medium of
exchange, 88, 90, 191, 202, 204;
prosperity measured in, 289-92, 295
Monier-Williams, Sir Monier (1819-99)
E. I. Coll. student 1839, 423
Montagu, Basil (1770-1851) barrister and
man of letters, 188-9
Montesquieu, Charles Louis de Secondat,
Baron de (1689-1755) French
philosophical historian, in England
1729-32: *De l'Esprit des Lois* (1748),
47, 103, 105
Monthly Literary Advertiser, 316
Monthly Magazine, 66, 77, 110, 111,
114-15, 133-4, 161

Monthly Review, 110
Moore, Thomas (1779-1852) Irish poet
and song writer, 387, 495
Morning Chronicle, London Whig daily
newspaper (1746-1862): bullion
correspondence, 196-7; E. I. Coll.,
239, 241, 327; *Measure of Value*
reviewed, 320; M's obituary, 459-60
Morning Herald, 386
Morning Post, 459
Murray, John, II (1778-1843) Pl. 5(*c*):
account of, 483; becomes M's
publisher, 270-2; Corn Laws and
Rent, 259, 266-9, 282; E. I. Coll.
pamphlet (1817), 237-9, 329-30; 5th
edn *Population* (1817), 233, 237-9;
'Collected Works' mooted 1819,
349-50; *Political Economy* (1820),
311-12, 316-18, 350; 6th edn
Population mooted 1821, 366;
Definitions in Political Economy (1827),
410-11, 430; letters from M, re Mrs
Baillie, 340, re Mrs Busk, 335, re other
subjects, 241, 259, 355, 362; *other refs*,
248, 311, 365, 384-5, 401, 411-12, 430
Mushet, Robert (1782-1828) of the Royal
Mint, 196, 200, 354

Napier, Macvey (1776-1847) ed.
*Supplement to Encyclopaedia
Britannica, passim* 314-16
Napoleon, *see* Bonaparte
National Calendar (US), 361, 402
National Colonization Society (founded
1830), 396-7
Navigation Acts (Laws which confined
almost all British trade to British
shipping, dating from 1381, the most
important Act being that of 1651;
modified 1825, repealed 1849), 352, 371
Newenham, Thomas (1762-1831)
member of Irish Parliament, opposed
Union with England, 144, 149-52,
154-6
New Monthly Magazine, 378
Newton, Sir Isaac (1642-1727), 25, 28-9,
191
Nonconformists, *see* Dissenters
Norfolk, Charles Howard, 11th Duke of
(1746-1815), 85
North American Review (US), 361, 402
Norway, 72, 76, 138-40 and n

Read, Samuel: *Natural Grounds of Right to Vendible Property or Wealth* (1829), 297

Reading, 1-2

religion, *see* Malthus, T. R., II, as clergyman

religious tests, 19, 31-3, 51, **444**

'Remarker', pamphleteer opponent of M on population (1803), 69, 111, 122-3, 134-5

Rennell, Rev. Thomas (1754-1840) Dean of Winchester: *Sermons* (1801), 99

rent, theory of: *passim* 276-85, 320; Jones on, 283-4, 440-2; M on, 276-85, 293, 315, 440-2

rents: M on, 152-3, 157-8, 280-1, 293; at Okewood, 45, 331, 333; at Walesby, 102, 162

Repton, Humphry (1752-1818) famous landscape gardener, 185

revenue: national, 135-6; proportion to capital, 204, 307-8; those paid from, 302-6

Reynolds, Sir Joshua (1772-1823) painter, 1st President of Royal Academy, 35

Ricardo, David (1772-1823) Pl. 5(*b*): accounts of, 208-9, 258; and bullion controversy, *passim* 196-212; on combinations and employment, 299; corresp. with M on personal matters, 79, 187, 233, 322, 368, on political economy, 248-9, 252, 258, 268 (*see also under subjects*); and E. I Coll. debates, 241-2; on emigration, 390-1; on general gluts, 205-6, 306-7, 420; and labour cost theory of value, 296-7, 306; and Political Economy Club, 354-5, 361-2; on Poor Law, 373-4; on productive and unproductive labour, 306-7; on profits, 282, 286-8, 291-2; on rent, 282-3, 286; on wages, 282, 286-8, 291-2; and 'Waterloo stock', 227-8; *other refs*, 222, 304, 314, 380, 384

Ricardo, Mrs David, née Priscilla Wilkinson (1768-1849), 209, 258

Richardson, Rev. William, DD (1740-1820) Irish writer on geology and agriculture, 146-7

Rickman, John (1771-1840) responsible for British censuses 1801-31, 103, 110

riots, 49, 87-8, 266-7

Robinson, [Frederick] John (1782-1859) later Viscount Goderich, moderate Tory MP, Prime Minister 1827-8, *passim* 266-7

Robinson, Thomas, bro. of Henry Crabb R. (1775-1867), man of letters and *Times* correspondent, 99, 111

Rogers, Samuel (1763-1855) Whig banker and poet, 82-3, 118-19, **458**

Roget, Peter Mark, MD (1779-1869) compiled *Thesaurus*, 85, 357, **442**

Romilly, Sir Samuel (1757-1818) Whig MP: account of, 85-6; on corn riots, 87-8, 266; on France, 47, 227; *other refs*, 113, 136, 145, 225, 226

Rookery, the, Surrey birthplace of M, 10, 13, 76

Roscoe, William (1753-1831) Liverpool banker and art collector, 81-2, 167, 359

Rose, George (1744-1818) MP, supporter of Pitt: on Poor Laws, 136

Rousseau, Jean-Jacques (1712-78), 10-13, 76, 78, 98

Rowlandson, Thomas (1756-1827) artist known ch. for caricatures, Pl. 7(*a*) (*b*)

Rowley, Maj. George, 2nd Bombay Light Cavalry, E. I. Coll. student (1822), *passim* 326-8

Royal Household, 5-9

Royal Society (founded 1660), 356-8, 443-4

Royal Society of Literature (founded 1823), 300, 358-61, 449

Russell, Lord John (1792-1878) Whig statesman, Prime Minister 1846-52 and 1865-6, 344

Ryves, Marianna Georgina, *see* Malthus, Mrs Sydenham, II

Ryves, Mrs Thomas, née Anna Maria Graham, M's maternal aunt, 9, 39

Sadler, Michael Thomas (1780-1835) philanthropist and reforming Tory MP: *Law of Population* (1830), 404-6

St Catherine's Court nr Bath, summer home of Eckersalls from 1821, 415-16

St Davids, Bishop of, *see* Burgess, Thomas

St-Pierre, J. H. B. de (1737-1814) French Romantic writer: Eng. trans. of *Paul et Virginie*, 77-8